KIBBLE AND TIDBITS FROM

Doin' The Northwest With Your Pooch

WHERE TO STAY
Choose a place to snooze for you and furface from more than 1,500 hotels in Oregon and Washington. You'll find accommodations in every price range to suit every taste; historic inns, 5-star resorts, motels and B&Bs.

- Fluff Fido's pillow and say sweet dreams at the Marriott Hotel in Portland or the Westin Hotel in Seattle (pages 216 & 448).

- Cozy up with the furball on San Juan Island or Orcas Island at the Westwinds B&B or the Northshore Cottages (pages 442 & 405).

- Whisk the sniffmeister away for a hiking adventure at the Mt. Hood Inn in Government Camp, Oregon (page 133).

- Put on the dog at the historic Lake Quinault or Kalaloch Lodges on the Olympic Peninsula (pages 374 & 366).

- Walk the beach and ogle Haystack Rock when you and your beach bum Bowser stay at Cannon Beach's Tolovana Inn (page 71).

- Start your day with the world famous 7-course breakfast when you and the wagging machine stay at Hood River's Columbia Gorge Hotel (page 142).

KIBBLE AND TIDBITS FROM

Doin' The Northwest With Your Pooch

WHAT TO DO
Impress your dog with more than a thousand hikes, parks, lakes, forests and other dog-friendly recreation.

- Get wet and wild with your wagger on a white-water rafting trip in Merlin, Oregon (page 178).

- Set your woofer's tail in motion with a trip to one of Seattle's leash-free dog parks (page 448).

- Give your hound his ticket to ride on the Sumpter Valley Rail Ride in Baker City, Oregon (page 51).

- Mellow out with the pupster when you make tracks through the stunning rain forest in Quinault, Washington (page 427).

- Sniff out the tide pools all along the Oregon coast as the barkmeister talks to the sea lions (page 608).

- Explore hundreds of miles of hiking trails with your hound in pristine national forests, state parks and historical sites (see Oregon and Washington Hiking Indexes, pages 631 & 645).

KIBBLE AND TIDBITS FROM

Doin' The Northwest With Your Pooch

HOW TO DO IT

See the extensive training section for some traveling tips.

- How To Pack For Your Pooch (page 549).
- Traveling By Plane (page 560).
- Travel Training (page 539).

Old dogs can learn new tricks.

- Crate Training Is Great Training (page 545).
- 10 Ways To Prevent Aggression (page 547).
- Training Do's And Don'ts (page 544).

Make a night of it with the pooch.

- Lodging Guidelines (page 25).
- Canine Camper (page 604).

Enhance your travel knowledge.

- 100 Ways To Be A Better Hiker (page 584).
- 37 Ways To Have A Better Vacation (page 564).
- First-Aid Emergency Tips (page 599).

Directories by Eileen Barish

DOIN' ARIZONA WITH YOUR POOCH

DOIN' CALIFORNIA WITH YOUR POOCH

DOIN' NEW YORK WITH YOUR POOCH

DOIN' THE NORTHWEST WITH YOUR POOCH

DOIN' TEXAS WITH YOUR POOCH

VACATIONING WITH YOUR PET

Novels by Eileen Barish

ARIZONA TERRITORY

Eileen's Directory of Dog-Friendly Lodging & Outdoor Recreation in Oregon & Washington

Pet-Friendly Publications
P.O. Box 8459, Scottsdale, AZ 85252
Tel: (800) 638-3637

DOIN' THE NORTHWEST WITH YOUR POOCH
by Eileen Barish

Pet-Friendly Publications
P.O. Box 8459, Scottsdale, AZ 85252
Tel: (800) 638-3637

ISBN #1-884465-06-4
Library of Congress Catalog Card Number: 96-070501
Printed and bound in the United States of America.
Second printing

While due care has been exercised in the compilation
of this directory, we are not responsible for errors or omis-
sions. We are sorry for any inconvenience. Inclusion in this
guide does not constitute endorsement or recommendation by
the author or publisher. It is intended as a guide to assist in
providing information to the public and the listings are
offered as an aid to travelers.

Eileen's directories are available at special discounts when purchased in
bulk for premiums and special sales promotions as well as for fund-
raising or educational use. Special editions or book excerpts can also be
created to specification. For details, call 1-800-638-3637.

CREDITS

Author & Managing Editor — Eileen Barish

Associate Editor — Harvey Barish

Lodging & Research Editor — Phyllis Holmes

Senior Writer/Research — Tiffany Geoghegan

Research/Writing Staff— Amy Campbell
Courtney Mechling

Illustrator — Gregg Myers

Book Layout — Harvey Barish

Photographer — Ken Friedman

ACKNOWLEDGEMENTS

Doin' the northwest with my smooch Harvey
has been the best.

Special thanks to a doggone great staff.

And for Sam, the "best friend"
who is always with us.

SPECIAL ACKNOWLEDGEMENTS

I would like to thank the management of the following lodging establishments for the gracious hospitality extended to me during the research phase of this book.

OREGON

CANNON BEACH
Haystack Resort
Kim Christiansen, GM

Tolovana Inn
Doug Neileagh, GM

DIAMOND LAKE
Diamond Lake Resort
Steve Koch, GM

EUGENE
Valley River Inn
Ron Gladney, GM

HOOD RIVER
Columbia Gorge Hotel
Boyd Graves, Owner

KLAMATH FALLS
Best Western Klamath Inn
Donna Bocklemann, GM

NEWPORT
Hallmark Resort
Steve Cockrell, GM

Holiday Inn at Agate Beach
Thomas Deats, GM

PORTLAND
Portland Marriott Hotel
John Jenkins, GM

REEDSPORT
Salbasgeon Inn of the Umpqua
David Edel, Owner

WASHINGTON

PORT ANGELES
Doubletree Bayshore Inn
Sarah Kidder, GM

PORT TOWNSEND
The Historic Palace Hotel
Spring Thomas, GM

QUINAULT
Lake Quinault Lodge
Russell Steele, GM

SAN JUAN ISLANDS
Northshore Cottages
Elizabeth Rennie, Owner
(Eastsound on Orcas Is.)

Westwinds Bed & Breakfast
Chris Durbin, GM
(Friday Harbor on San Juan Is.)

SEATTLE
The Alexis Hotel
Michael DeFrino, GM

The Westin Hotel
David Zenske, GM

VANCOUVER
Shilo Inn Downtown
Kevin Foreman, GM

WHIDBEY ISLAND
House by the Sea Cottages
Linda Walsh, Innkeeper
(Clinton on Whidbey Is.)

EUREKA, CALIFORNIA
Eureka Inn Historic Hotel
Stephanie Lakin, GM

TABLE OF CONTENTS

OREGON DIRECTORY OF DOG-FRIENDLY LODGING AND OUTDOOR RECREATION

WASHINGTON DIRECTORY OF DOG-FRIENDLY LODGING AND OUTDOOR RECREATION

GET READY TO TRAVEL

HOW TO USE THIS DIRECTORY

Pooch comes along

If you're planning to travel in the northwest with your pooch or if you live in the northwest and would like to enjoy more of your home states with your canine buddy beside you, *Doin' The Northwest With Your Pooch* is the only reference source you'll need. Included are over fifteen hundred dog-friendly accommodations and outdoor adventures as well as chapters covering everything from travel training to travel etiquette.

Simplify vacation planning

The user-friendly format of *Doin' The Northwest With Your Pooch* combines lodging and recreation under individual city headings. Pick a city, decide on lodging and then reference the outdoor activities listed under that city. Or if you've always wanted to hike a certain trail or visit a particular park, just reverse the process. Using the index, locate the activity of choice, find the closest lodging and go from there. It's that easy to plan a vacation you and your pooch will enjoy.

No more sneaking Snoopy

Choose lodging from hotels, B&Bs (aka Bed & Biscuits), motels, resorts, inns and ranches that welcome you and your dog, *through the front door*. From big cities to tiny hamlets, *Doin' The Northwest With Your Pooch* provides the names, addresses, phone numbers and room rates of dog-friendly accommodations. Arranged in an easy-to-use alphabetical format, this directory covers the northwest from Agness, Oregon to Zillah, Washington.

Just do it

No matter what your budget or outdoor preference, with this directory you'll be able to put together the perfect day, weekend or month-long odyssey. Okay, now you've got your pooch packed and you're ready for the fun to begin. How will you make the most of your travel or vacation time?

If you're into hiking, you'll find information on hundreds of trails. The descriptions will tell you what to expect - from the trail rating (beginner, intermediate, expert) to the trail's terrain, restrictions, best times to hike, etc. If laid-back pastimes are more to your liking, you'll find green grassy areas ideal for picnics or plain chilling out. For parks, monuments and other attractions, expect anything from a quickie overview to a lengthy description. Written in a conversational tone, it'll be easy for you to visualize each area. Directions from the nearest city are included.

Increase your options

Many of the recreational opportunities listed in **Doin' The Northwest With Your Pooch** can be accessed from more than one city. To expand your options, check out the activities located in cities adjacent to your lodging choice.

How to do it

Numerous chapters are devoted to making your travel times safer and more pleasurable. Training do's and don'ts, crate use and selection, driving and packing tips, wilderness survival, doggie massage, pet etiquette, travel manners, what and how to pack for your pooch, first-aid advice, hiking tips and a pet identification form are just a sampling of the topics covered.

A "must-have" reference for every Northwesterner who owns a dog

Owning a copy of **Doin' The Northwest With Your Pooch** means you won't have to leave your trusted companion at home while you explore the beautiful states of Oregon and Washington. Remember that exercise and outdoor stimulation are as good for your dog's health as they are for yours. So include old brown eyes when you decide to take a walk, picnic in a forest glade, hike a mountain trail or rent a boat for the day. Armed with this guide, Northwesterners who love their hounds can travel with their pooches and discover all that Oregon and Washington have to offer. No matter where you hang your dog collar, you'll find dozens of places in your own backyard just perfect for a day's outing. *Doin' The Northwest With Your Pooch* answers the question of what to do with the pooch when you travel, take him along.

Do hotel and motel policies differ regarding pets?

Yes, but all the accommodations in *Doin' The Northwest With Your Pooch* allow dogs. Policies can vary on charges and sometimes on dog size. Some might require a damage deposit and some combine their deposit with a daily and/or one-time charge. Others may restrict pets to specific rooms, perhaps cabins or cottages. Residence-type inns which cater to long-term guests may charge a long-term fee. Some also require advance notice. But most accommodations do not charge fees or place restrictions in any manner. As with all travel arrangements, it is recommended that you call in advance to confirm policies and room availability.

Prior to publication, all of the accommodations in this book received a copy of their listing information for verification.

Be aware, hotel policies may change. At the time your reservations are made, confirm the policies of your lodging choice.

Traveling With Your Pet Can Be A Rewarding Experience

You never have to leave your best friend home or kenneled in a small cage while you vacation. Bring your four-legged buddy along. Double your enjoyment and increase your safety. If your dog is a great companion at home, he can be just as companionable when you travel.

INTRODUCTION

Doing the northwest with your pooch can be a fun-filled adventure. It doesn't require special training or expertise. Just a little planning and a little patience. The rewards are worth the effort. This directory is filled with information to make traveling with your dog more pleasurable. From training tips to what to take along, to the do's and don'ts of travel, virtually all of your questions will be addressed.

Vacationing with dogs

Not something I thought I'd ever do. But as the adage goes, necessity is the mother of invention. What began as a necessity turned into a lifestyle. A lifestyle that has improved every aspect of my vacation and travel time.

Although my family had dogs on and off during my childhood, it wasn't until my early thirties that I decided it was time to bring another dog into my life. And the lives of my young children. I wanted them to grow up with a dog; to know what it was like to have a canine companion, a playmate, a friend who would always be there, to love you, no questions asked. A four-legged pal who would be the first to lick your teary face or your bloody knee. Enter Samson, our family's first Golden Retriever.

Samson

For nearly fifteen years, Sammy was everything a family could want from their dog. Loyal, forgiving, sweet, funny, neurotic, playful, sensitive, smart, too smart, puddle loving, fearless, strong and cuddly. He could melt your heart with a woebegone expression or make your hair stand on end with one of his pranks. Like the time he methodically opened the seam on a bean bag chair and then cheerfully spread the beans everywhere. Or when he followed a jogger and ended up in a shelter more than 20 miles from home.

As the years passed, Sam's face turned white and one by one our kids headed off to college. Preparing for the inevitable, my husband Harvey and I decided that when Sam died, no other dog would take his place. We wanted our freedom, not the responsibility of another dog.

Sammy left us one sunny June morning with so little fanfare that we couldn't believe he was actually gone. Little did we realize the void that would remain when our white-faced Golden Boy was no longer with us.

Life goes on...Rosie and Maxwell

After planning a two-week vacation through California, with an ultimate destination of Lake Tahoe, Harvey and I had our hearts stolen by two Golden Retriever puppies, Rosie and Maxwell. Two little balls of fur that would help to fill the emptiness Sam's death had created. The puppies were ready to leave their mom and come home with us only weeks before our scheduled departure. What to do? Kennel them? Hire a caretaker? Neither felt right.

Sooo...we took them along

Oh, the fun we had. And the friends we made. Both the two-legged and four-legged variety. Having dogs on our trip made us more a part of the places we visited. We learned that dogs are natural conversation starters. Rosie and Maxwell were the prime movers in some lasting friendships we made during that first trip together. Now when we revisit Lake Tahoe, we have old friends to see as well as new ones to make. The locals we met made us feel at home, offering insider information on little known hikes, wonderful restaurants and quiet neighborhood parks. This knowledge enhanced our trip and filled every day with wonder.

Since that first trip, our travels have taken us to many places. We've visited national forests, mountain resorts, seaside villages, island retreats, big cities and tiny hamlets. We've shared everything from luxury hotel rooms to rustic cabin getaways. I can't imagine going anywhere without our dogs.

Only one regret remained. Why hadn't it occurred to me to take Sammy along on our travels? He would have loved the adventure. That regret led to the writing of this book. I wanted others to know how easy it could be to vacation with their dogs.

When I watch Rosie and Maxwell frolic in a lake or when they accompany us on a hike, I think of Sammy and remember the legacy of love and friendship he left behind. So for those of you who regularly take your dog along and those who would if you knew how, come share my travel knowledge. And happy trails and tails to you and yours.

Is my pooch vacation-friendly

Most dogs can be excellent traveling companions. Naturally, the younger they are when you accustom them to traveling, the more quickly they will adapt. But that doesn't mean that an older dog won't love vacationing with you. And it doesn't mean that the transition has to be a difficult one.

Even if your dog hasn't traveled with you in the past, chances are he'll make a wonderful companion. You'll find yourself enjoying pensive moments watching him in new surroundings, laughing with others at his antics. But most of all, you'll find that spending quality time with your dog enhances your vacations. So get ready for a unique and rewarding experience, filled with memories to last a lifetime.

A socialized pooch is a sophisticated traveler

Of course, every pooch is different. And you know yours better than anyone. To be sure that he will travel like a pro, accustom him to different situations. Take him for long walks around your neighborhood. Let him accompany you while you do errands. If your chores include stair climbing or using an elevator, take him along. The more exposure to people, places and things, the better. Make your wagger worldly. The sophistication will pay off in a better behaved, less frightened pet. It won't be long until he will happily share travel and vacation times with you.

Just ordinary dogs

Rosie and Maxwell, my traveling companions, are not exceptional dogs to anyone but me. Their training was neither intensive nor professionally rendered. They were trained with kindness, praise, consistency and love. And not all of their training came about when they were puppies. I too had a lot to learn. And as I learned what I wanted of them, their training continued. It was a sharing and growing experience. Old dogs (and humans too) can learn new tricks. Rosie and Maxwell never fail to surprise me. Their ability to adapt to new situations has never stopped. So don't think you have to start with a puppy. Every dog, young and old, can be taught to be travel friendly.

Rosie and Maxwell know when I begin putting their things together that another holiday is about to begin. Their excitement mounts with every phase of preparation. They stick like glue - remaining at my side as I organize their belongings. By the time I've finished, they can barely contain their joy. Rosie grabs her leash and prances about the kitchen holding it in her mouth while Max sits on his haunches and howls. If they could talk, they'd tell you how much they enjoy traveling. But since they can't, trust this directory to lead you to a different kind of experience. One that's filled with lots of love and an opportunity for shared adventure. So with an open mind and an open heart, pack your bags and pack your pooch. Slip this handy book into your suitcase or the glove compartment of your car and let the fun begin.

Lodging Guidelines For You and Your Pooch

Conduct yourself in a courteous manner and you'll continue to be welcome anywhere you travel. Never do anything on vacation with your pooch that you wouldn't do at home. Some quick tips that can make traveling with your canine more enjoyable.

1. Don't allow your dog to sleep on the bed with you. If that's what your dog is accustomed to doing, take along a sheet or favorite blanket and put that on top of the bedding provided by your lodging.

2. Bring a towel or small mat to use under your dog's food and water dishes. Feed your dog in the bathroom where cleanup is easier should an accident occur.

3. Try to keep your dog off the furniture. Take along a lint and hair remover to eliminate unwanted hairs.

4. When you walk your dog, carry plastic bags and/or paper towels for cleanup.

5. Always keep your dog on a leash on the hotel and motel grounds.

Be aware, hotel policies may change.
At the time your reservations are made,
confirm the policies of your lodging choice.

Can my pooch be left alone in the room?

Only you know the answer to that. If your dog is not destructive, if he doesn't bark incessantly and the hotel allows unattended dogs, you might consider leaving him in the room for short periods of time — say when you dine out. In any case, hang the "Do Not Disturb" sign on your door to alert the chambermaid or anyone else that your room shouldn't be entered.

Consider doing the following when you plan to leave your dog unattended:

1. Walk or otherwise exercise your pooch. An exercised dog will fall asleep more easily.

2. Provide a favorite toy.

3. Turn on the TV or radio for audio/ visual companionship.

4. Make sure there is an ample amount of fresh water available.

5. Calm your dog with a reassuring goodbye and a stroke of your hand.

Go Take A Hike

Hundreds of the best day hikes in Oregon and Washington are detailed in *Doin' The Northwest With Your Pooch.* Each hike indicates degree of difficulty, approximate time to complete the hike and round-trip distances. Unless otherwise indicated, trailhead access is free and parking is available, although it is sometimes limited. To assist you in your travel plans, phone numbers are included for most recreation sites.

When leashes are mandatory, notice is provided.

Please obey local ordinances so dogs continue to be welcome

Hike ratings

The majority of the hikes included in this book are rated beginner or intermediate. As a rule of thumb, beginner hikes are generally easy, flat trails suited to every member of the family. Intermediate hikes require more exertion and a little more preparation, but can usually be accomplished by anyone accustomed to some physical exercise, such as fast-paced walking, biking, skiing, swimming, etc. Some expert trails have also been included. Many times, their inclusion signals some outstanding feature. Expert hikes should only be considered if you feel certain of your own and your dog's abilities. But whatever your ability, remember, if the hike you've undertaken is too difficult you can always turn around and retrace your steps. You're there to have a good time, not to prove anything.

Seasons change, so do conditions

Seasonal changes may effect ratings. If you're hiking during rainy season, you might encounter slippery going. Or if you've decided to hike during the winter and there's mud or snow underfoot, that can up the difficulty rating. In the spring, small creeks can become rushing, perhaps impassable rivers. Whenever you're outdoors, particularly in wilderness areas, exercise caution. Know yourself and know your dog.

Hike time

Times indicated are for general reference. If you're short on time or energy, hike as long as you like. Never push yourself or your canine beyond either's endurance. Never begin a hike too late in the day, particularly in canyon areas where the sun can disappear quickly.

Directions

Directions are generally provided from the closest city. Odometer accuracy can vary so be alert to road signs. Unless specifically noted, roads and trailheads are accessible by all types of vehicles. In winter, some areas experience inclement weather conditions where 4WD or chains are required. Remember too that forest roads can be narrow and twisting and are often used by logging trucks. Exercise caution. Slow down around blind corners.

Permits/Fees

Proof of rabies vaccination is required for all pets entering state parks and forests. In addition, most state parks and forests charge a nominal entrance fee.

Common sense, don't hike without it

Consider potential hazards. Know your limitations. The overview descriptions included with hikes and other activities are provided for general information. They are not meant to represent that a particular hike or excursion will be safe for you or your dog. Only you can make that determination.

Weather, terrain, wildlife and trail conditions should always be considered. It is up to you to assume responsibility for yourself and your canine. Apply common sense to your outings and they'll prove safe and enjoyable.

Leashes

Some hikes and other recreation areas do not require that dogs be leashed, but wildlife exists in all outdoor areas so always use caution and good sense. When a leash is not mandatory, notations will be made. Restrictions, if any, are also noted. In any case, keep a leash accessible. You never know when the need might suddenly arise.

Pooch Rules & Regulations

BE A RESPONSIBLE DOG OWNER AND OBEY THE RULES.

- Clean up after your dog even if no one has seen him do his business.
- Leash your dog in areas that require leashing.
- Train your dog to be well behaved.
- Control your dog in public places so that he's not a nuisance to others.

Note: When leashes are required, they must be six feet or less in length. Leashes should be carried at all times. They are prudent safety measures.

FIDO FACT:

- *Problems with dogs in many recreation areas have increased in recent years. The few rules that apply to dogs are meant to assure that you and other visitors have enjoyable outdoor experiences.*

OREGON'S REGIONS

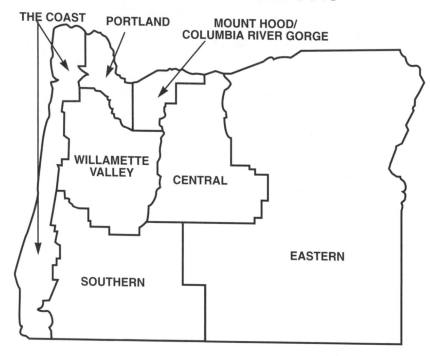

THE COAST   PORTLAND   MOUNT HOOD/
COLUMBIA RIVER GORGE

WILLAMETTE
VALLEY

CENTRAL

EASTERN

SOUTHERN

Population:
3,132,000

Capital:
Salem

Highest Point:
Mt. Hood - 11,235'

Lowest Point:
Sea level - the Pacific Ocean

Nickname:
The Beaver State

State Flower:
Oregon Grape

State Tree:
Douglas Fir

State Bird:
Western Meadowlark

State Animal:
Beaver

State Fish:
Chinook Salmon

State Gem:
Sunstone

State Rock:
The Thunder Egg

OREGON CITIES BY REGION

CENTRAL
Bend, Camp Sherman, Crooked River Ranch, Dufur, LaPine, Madras, Maupin, Odell Lake, Paulina, Powell Butte, Prineville, Redmond, Sisters, Sunriver, Warm Springs

Forests: Deschutes, Ochoco

COAST
Agness, Astoria, Bandon, Brookings, Cannon Beach, Charleston, Coos Bay, Coquille, Depoe Bay, Florence, Garibaldi, Gearhart, Gleneden Beach, Gold Beach, Harbor, Lakeside, Lincoln City, Manzanita, Myrtle Point, Necanicum Junction, Neskia Beach, Neskowin, Netarts, Newport, North Bend, Otter Rock, Pacific City, Pistol River, Port Orford, Powers, Reedsport, Rockaway Beach, Seaside, South Beach, Tillamook, Waldport, Warrenton, Westport, Wheeler, Winchester Bay, Yachats

Forests: Suislaw, Siskiyou

EASTERN
Arlington, Baker City, Boardman, Burns, Dale, Dayville, Echo, Elgin, Enterprise, Fossil, Halfway, Heppner, Hermiston, John Day, Jordan Valley, Joseph, La Grande, Lakeview, Long Creek, Milton-Freewater, Mitchell, North Powder, Nyssa, Ontario, Pendleton, Pilot Rock, Prairie City, Summer Lake, Sumpter, Troy, Ukiah, Umatilla, Union, Unity, Vale, Wallowa, Weston

Forests: Fremont, Malheur, Umatilla, Wallowa-Whitman

MT HOOD/COLUMBIA GORGE
Cascade Locks, Detroit, Estacada, Government Camp, Gresham, Hood River, Mosier, Mount Hood, Rufus, The Dalles, Troutdale, Welches, Zigzag

Forest: Mt. Hood

PORTLAND

Beaverton, Clatskanie, Forest Grove, Gladstone, Hillsboro, Lake Oswego, Milwaukie, Oregon City, Portland, Rainier, St. Helens, Sandy, Scappoose, Silverton, Tigard, Tualatin, Veronia, Wilsonville

SOUTHERN

Ashland, Beatty, Canyonville, Cave Junction, Chemult, Chiloquin, Crater Lake, Crescent, Crescent Lake Jct., Curtin, Diamond Lake, Fort Klamath, Glide, Grants Pass, Idleyld Park, Jacksonville, Keno, Kerby, Klamath Falls, Lowell, Medford, Merlin, Merrill, Oakland, Prospect, Rogue River, Roseburg, Sunny Valley, Sutherlin, Union Creek

Forests: Rogue River, Siskiyou, Umpqua, Winema

WILLAMETTE VALLEY

Albany, Blue River, Clackamas, Corvallis, Cottage Grove, Creswell, Dallas, Eugene, Halsey, Junction City, Lebanon, Mapleton, McKenzie Bridge, McMinnville, Molalla, Monmouth, Newburg, Oakridge, Philomath, Salem, Springfield, Stayton, Sublimity, Sweet Home, Vida, Waterloo, Westfir, Westlake, Woodburn, Yamhill

Forest: Willamette

WASHINGTON'S REGIONS

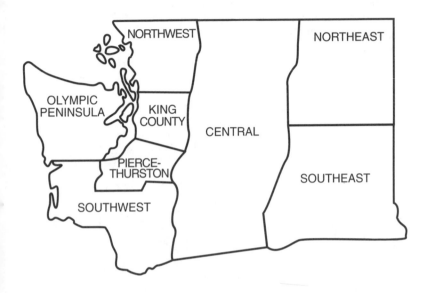

Population:
5.3 million

Capital:
Olympia

Highest Point:
Mt. Rainier - 14,411'

Lowest Point:
Ebey Island - 5' below
sea level

Nickname:
The Evergreen State

State Flower:
Coast Rhodedendron

State Tree:
Western Hemlock

State Bird:
Willow Goldfinch

State Animal:
Roosevelt Elk

State Gem:
Petrified Wood

State Motto:
Alki
(From the Chinook, means
"by-and-by")

WASHINGTON CITIES BY REGION

Southeast
Asotin, Clarkston, Connell, Kennewick, Othello, Pasco, Pomeroy, Prosser, Pullman, Richland, Ritzville, Starbuck, Walla Walla.

Forests: Umatilla

Northeast
Airway Heights, Cheney, Chewelah, Colville, Curlew, Cusick, Deer Park, Elk, Green Acres, Inchelium, Ione, Kettle Falls, Metaline Falls, Newport, Odessa, Republic, Spokane, Sprague, Usk, Valley, Veradale, Wilbur.

Forests: Colville, Okanagan

Central
Bingen, Brewster, Bridgeport, Cashmere, Chelan, Cle Elum, Conconully, Coulee City, Coulee Dam, East Wenatchee, Ellensburg, Ephrata, Glenwood, Goldendale, Grand Coulee, Grandview, Leavenworth, Mattawa, Mazama, Moses Lake, Naches, Okanogan, Omak, Orondo, Oroville, Pateros, Peshastin, Quincy, Roslyn, Soap Lake, Sunnyside, Thorp, Tonasket, Toppenish, Trout Lake, Twisp, Union Gap, Warden, Wenatchee, White Pass, White Salmon, Winthrop, Yakima, Zillah.

Forests: Mt. Baker/Snoqualmie, Okanagan, Wenatchee

Northwest
Anacortes, Bellingham, Birch Bay, Blaine, Burlington, Deming, Eastsound, Ferndale, Fir Island, Friday Harbor, Glacier, La Conner, Lopez Island, Lynden, Maple Falls, Mount Vernon, Orcas Island, Point Roberts, Rockport, San Juan Island, San Juan Islands, Sedro-Woolley, Shaw Island, Sumas.

King County

Arlington, Auburn, Bainbridge Island, Bellevue, Black Diamond, Bothell, Bremerton, Buckley, Camano Island, Carnation, Clinton, Coupeville, Darrington, Des Moines, Edmonds, Enumclaw, Everett, Federal Way, Freeland, Gig Harbor, Granite Falls, Greenwater, Hansville, Index, Issaquah, Kent, Kingston, Kirkland, Lakewood, Langley, Mercer Island, Monroe, Oak Harbor, Olalla, Port Orchard, Poulsbo, Puyallup, Redmond, Renton, Seabeck, SeaTac, Seattle, Shoreline, Silverdale, Skykomish, Snohomish, Snoqualmie, Snoqualmie Pass, Sultan, Tukwila, Vashon Island, Whidbey Island.

Pierce-Thurston

Ashford, Belfair, Centralia, Chehalis, Eatonville, Elbe, Fife, Lacey, Lake Bay, Morton, Mossyroc, Olympia, Packwood, Rainier, Randle, Tacoma, Tenino, Toldeo, Tumwater, Winlock, Yelm.

Southwest

Battle Ground, Camas, Carson, Castle Rock, Cathlamet, Grayland, Home Valley, Ilwaco, Kalama, Kelso, Long Beach Peninsula, Longview, Lynnwood, Marysville, Montesano, Nahcotta, Naselle, Ocean Park, Ocean Shores, Oysterville, Raymond, Seaview, Silver Creek, Silver Lake, South Bend, Stevenson, Tokeland, Vancouver, Washougal, Westport, Woodland, Yacolt.

Forests: Gifford Pinchot

Olympic Peninsula

Aberdeen, Amanda Park, Beaver, Brinnon, Clallam Bay, Copalis Beach, Dayton, Forks, Hoodsport, Hoquiam, Kalaloch, Kitsap, Lake Crescent, Lilliwaup, Moclips, Neah Bay, Ocean City, Olympic National Park, Pacific Beach, Port Angeles, Port Hadlock, Port Ludlow, Port Townsend, Quilcene, Quinault, Sekiu, Sequim, Shelton, Union.

Forests: Olympic

OREGON DIRECTORY OF DOG-FRIENDLY LODGING & OUTDOOR ACTIVITIES

Hotel Policies May Be Subject To Change

AGNESS

LODGING

LUCAS PIONEER RANCH & LODGE
03904 Cougar Ln (97406)
Rates: $30-$60
Tel: (541) 247-7443

SINGING SPRINGS RESORT
34501 Agness Illahe Rd (97406)
Rates: $30-$50
Tel: (541) 247-6162

RECREATION

LOWER ROGUE RIVER TRAIL HIKE

Intermediate/1.0-24.0 miles/0.5-14.0 hours

Info: Plan an all-day excursion or an afternoon delight but don't miss this pristine and picturesque trail through one of Oregon's majestic rain forests. Other than a few moderate slopes, this trail is easy on the paws and pleasing to the senses. No bones about it, this locale will certainly give the dawgus something to bark home about.

Inhabited by Bambi look-alikes, there's a good chance you'll encounter one of these doe-eyed beauties. Getting your feet wet is part of the fun too, so come prepared. You'll cross a series of little creeks before reaching a stunning waterfall at Auberry Creek. The enchanting spot beckons you and the gleeful biscuitmesiter to break some bread. Your route will include the site of an old homestead and school. In spring, a profusion of wildflowers decorate the already pretty prairieland. The shade is compliments of the stately Douglas firs. Between the woodlands, riparian habitats and the simple splendor of the landscape, you'll wish the day would never end. But when it does, turn the hound around, you're homeward bound. For more information: (800) 525-2334.

Directions: The trailhead is located at the community building just past the old Agness Post Office.

Note: A shuttle system is possible by leaving one car at the east trailhead (directions above) and another at the west trailhead located 10 miles east off Jerry's Flat Road to the Lobster Creek Bridge. Take the first right after the bridge onto FS 340 and follow signs. This shortens the trip to 12 miles one-way.

ALBANY

LODGING

BEST WESTERN PONY SOLDIER INN
315 Airport Rd SE (97321)
Rates: $69-$88
Tel: (541) 928-6322
(800) 634-7669

BUDGET INN
2727 Pacific Blvd SE (97321)
Rates: $36-$44
Tel: (541) 926-4246
(800) 527-0700

CITY CENTER MOTEL
1730 Pacific Blvd SE (97321)
Rates: $27-$45
Tel: (541) 926-8442

COMFORT INN
251 Airport Way SE (97321)
Rates: $59-$149
Tel: (541) 928-0921
(800) 228-5150

HOLIDAY INN EXPRESS
1100 Price Rd SE (97321)
Rates: $40-$80
Tel: (541) 928-5050
(800) 928-5657

MARCO POLO MOTEL
2410 Pacific Blvd SE (97321)
Rates: $22-$40
Tel: (541) 926-4401

MOTEL ORLEANS
1212 Price Rd SE (97321)
Rates: $38-$44
Tel: (541) 926-0170
(800) 626-1900

STARDUST MOTEL
2735 E Pacific Blvd (97321)
Rates: $38-$68
Tel: (541) 926-4233

VAL-U-INN MOTEL
3125 Santiam Hwy SE (97321)
Rates: $40-$80
Tel: (541) 926-1538
(800) 547-0106

ARLINGTON

LODGING

VILLAGE INN MOTEL
131 Beech St (97812)
Rates: $42+
Tel: (541) 454-2646

ASHLAND

LODGING

ASHLAND MOTEL
1145 Siskiyou Blvd (97520)
Rates: $30-$43
Tel: (541) 482-2561
(800) 460-8858

ASHLAND PATTERSON HOUSE B&B
639 N Main St (97520)
Rates: $70-$105
Tel: (541) 482-9171
(888) 482-9171

Locate Other Dog-Friendly Activities...Check Nearby Cities

BEST WESTERN BARD'S INN
132 N Main St (97520)
Rates: $52-$125
Tel: (541) 482-0049
(800) 528-1234

BEST WESTERN HERITAGE INN
434 Valley View Rd (97520)
Rates: $46-$150
Tel: (541) 482-6932
(800) 528-1234

CEDARWOOD INN
1801 Siskiyou Blvd (97520)
Rates: $68+
Tel: (541) 488-2000
(800) 547-4141

GREEN SPRINGS INN
11470 Hwy 66 (97520)
Rates: $40-$99
Tel: (541) 482-0614

GREEN SPRINGS BOX R RANCH
16799 Hwy 66 (97520)
Rates: $110-$150
Tel: (541) 482-1873

JACKSONVILLE INN
175 E California St (97520)
Rates: $95-$235
Tel: (541) 899-1900
(800) 321-9344

KNIGHTS INN MOTEL
2359 Ashland St (97520)
Rates: $32-$58
Tel: (541) 482-5111
(800) 547-4566

MARK ANTONY HOTEL
212 E Main St (97520)
Rates: n/a
Tel: (541) 482-1721

PHOENIX MOTEL
510 N Main St (97520)
Rates: n/a
Tel: (541) 535-1555

QUALITY INN FLAGSHIP
2520 Ashland St (97520)
Rates: $44-$113
Tel: (541) 488-2330
(800) 334-2330

RODEWAY INN
1193 Siskiyou Blvd (97520)
Rates: $38-$82
Tel: (541) 482-2641
(800) 547-6414

WINDMILL'S ASHLAND HILLS INN
2525 Ashland St (97520)
Rates: $67-$250
Tel: (541) 482-8310
(800) 547-4747

RECREATION

BEAVER DAM TRAIL HIKE

Beginner/4.2 miles/2.0 hours

Info: Come and explore a slice of Mother Nature along this beautiful trail and while you're at it, you and furface can experience two different habitats, riparian streamside and forest. The three small creeks that meander through grassy banks and beaver ponds equate to puppy nirvana. Every so often, the sun will peek through the cool canopy of Douglas fir and white pine to create playful patterns on the forest floor. Visit in springtime when bleeding heart, calypso orchid and trillium throw a wildflower party and paint the meadows and marshes in vivid colors. Birders with binocs might espy a red-breasted nuthatch, belted kingfisher or a woodpecker hanging out in

Hotel Policies May Be Subject To Change

the dead tree snags. Lucky dogs have also been known to spot a beaver scampering off to work on their namesake trail. For more information: (541) 482-3333.

Directions: From Ashland, travel east on Route 66 for one mile to Dead Indian Highway. Turn left for 22 miles to FS 37. Make another left and continue 1.5 miles to the trailhead at Daley Creek Campground.

Note: Trail is recommended for use May-October.

BROWN MOUNTAIN TRAIL HIKE

Intermediate/10.6 miles/6.0 hours

Info: Strap on the pawdometer and plan to go the distance on this one. You and the dogster will have it made in the shade as you hustle your butts through western hemlock, Englemann spruce, Pacific yew, western white pine, chinquipin, dogwood and white, red and Douglas fir, a mere sampling of the trees that canopy the trail. Add a touch of aqua fria in the form of Little Butte Creek and you'll definitely keep your cool on those hot diggety dog days. The occasional break in the trees provides a glimpse of Brown Mountain and the lava flows. The trail forks at just over 5 miles. Follow the right fork a short distance to the end of the trail at FS 3640. Sniffmeisters, plan a springtime excursion and witness the dogwoods and wild-flowers doing their pretty thing. If you're long on yearning but short on time, leave a car at each end of the trail and shorten your adventure. For more information: (541) 382-3333.

Directions: From Ashland, travel east on Route 66 for one mile to Dead Indian Highway. Turn left for 22 miles to FS 37. Head north on FS 37 for 6 miles to FS 3705. Go east on FS 3705 approximately 3.5 miles to the first trailhead. To access the other trailhead at FS 3640, continue on FS 3705 for one mile to FS 3720. Head east on FS 3720 for 1.5 miles to FS 700. Follow FS 700 northeast about 3 miles to FS 3640. Go north on FS 3640 for 1.5 miles to the trailhead.

BULL GAP TRAIL HIKE

Intermediate/5.0 miles/3.0 hours

Info: You and your wagalong will make tracks on an old road that was once the only route from town to Mt. Ashland. You'll wind your way up the mountainside through stunning hardwood stands, gaining over 1,000' in elevation as you do. But every huff and puff will be rewarded with an ooh and aah once you reach Mt. Ashland Ski Lodge, your turnaround point. Not only is the air fresh and crisp, but the panoramas will knock your socks off. Pack plenty of film, you'll definitely want to take home some memories. For more information: (541) 482-3333.

Directions: From the Ashland Ranger Station (645 Washington), drive west on Highway 66 (Ashland Street) for one block to Tolman Creek Road. Turn left and drive 16.6 miles to the trailhead at Bull Gap. (Tolman Creek Road becomes FS 2080 once you enter the national forest).

Note: Trail is open June-October.

DOG PARK

Info: Impress your pooch with a jaunt to this fur-friendly bark park. Two fenced acres create a puppy paradise ideal for leashless abandon. Lots of locals visit so be prepared for some socializing. FYI: Water and pooper scoopers are provided.

Directions: Off Nevada Street behind the Ashland Greenhouses.

DUNLOP TRAIL HIKE

Intermediate/3.0 miles/1.5 hours

Info: Hikers with a penchant for fishing, this trail has your name on it. You'll shake a leg through beautiful meadowlands (once an old homestead site) and if your timing's right, you'll encounter dazzling wildflower displays. If you find yourself awestruck by the ponderosa pines, you're in good company. This particular stand is one of the most beautiful in the United States. Breathe deeply of the vanilla-scented air as you continue to the canyon of the South Fork of Butte Creek, your fishing hole bonus where cutthroat and rainbow trout abound.

Chances are you'll get lucky and go home with din-din. When you've bagged your limit, turn the snout about and head on out. For more information: (541) 482-3333.

Directions: From Ashland, travel east on Route 66 for one mile to Dead Indian Highway. Turn left and drive 18 miles to Shell Peak Road and turn left. Stay to your right at the first fork and you'll reach the national forest boundary. Continue on Shell Peak Road (FS 2500/100) for 5 miles to the trailhead on the right.

Note: Trail is open May-October.

FISH LAKE TRAIL HIKE

Beginner/10.0 miles/5.0 hours

Info: This scenic sojourn saunters beside the North Fork of Little Butte Creek. Take note of the small riparian meadows which are seasonally dotted with colorful flowers. Listen to the birdsong that drifts your way through the pine-scented woodlands. If lunch alfresco sounds appealing, stock up with goodies at the Fish Lake Resort and then find yourself a pretty picnic nook along the shores of Fish Lake.

Après lunch, travel east from the lakeside terrain into the sun-dappled woodlands. Geologist wannabes, don't miss the chunky basalt that edges the forest. At 4.6 miles, a fascinating site awaits. In the early 1900s, the Cascade Canal was built to carry water from Four Mile Lake to Fish Lake and Medford. The canal disappears into a lava tube and doesn't reappear until it enters Fish Lake, a mile away. At the junction with the Pacific Crest Trail, do a 180° and head for home. For more information: (541) 482-3333.

Directions: From Ashland, travel east on Route 66 for one mile to Dead Indian Highway. Turn left for 22 miles to FS 37. Turn left on FS 37 and drive 7 miles to the North Fork campground. Parking for the trailhead is on the right, opposite the campground.

Note: Trail is open May-October

LAMB MINE TRAIL HIKE

Beginner/1.0 miles/0.5 hours

Info: Tranquility and ease go hand-in-hand on this trail less traveled. Find serenity as you and the dawgus romp through songbird-filled woodlands on your journey to the Reeder Reservoir overlook. This spot is hot! The panoramas of the reservoir and the Ashland watershed are definitely photoworthy. Springtime heralds the awesome beauty of trillium, tiger lily, aster and scarlet gilia. The views of Ashland Creek and Wagner Butte aren't too shabby either. Heads up history sniffers - relics from the old mining days dot the landscape. Two paws up for this interesting trail. For more information: (541) 482-3333.

Directions: From the Ashland Ranger Station (645 Washington), drive west on Highway 66 for 0.1 miles to Tolman Creek Road and turn left. Follow for 7.7 miles to FS 2080/600 and continue on this road, staying to the right for 1.1 miles to Four Corners. Turn right onto FS 2060 and drive 1.7 miles to the trailhead parking on left.

Note: Trail is open March-November.

WHITE RABBIT TRAIL HIKE - Leashes

Intermediate/4.6 miles/3.0 hours

Info: You may not see the namesake thumper but you're sure to feel like you've entered the magical world of Alice in Wonderland as you journey through this diverse terrain where spur options like the Queen of Hearts, Mad Hatter, March Hare and Cheshire Cat add to the allure. Each little loop-de-loop leads to a unique scenic surprise. But if you choose to stay on track, you'll walk in shaded splendor through a wonderland of nature all the way to the national forest boundary. Listen for the free concert compliments of nature's musicians. Pack power snacks and H_2O for you and your faithful furball. When you reach trail's end at FS 2060, retrace your steps. Don't be tempted to eat any of the mushrooms. For more information: (541) 482-3333.

Directions: The trailhead is located at the top of Park Street, at the green gate entry point to Siskiyou Mountain Park.

Note: Trail may be closed during heavy rains. Parking is limited on Park Street.

ASTORIA

LODGING

BAYSHORE MOTOR INN
555 Hamburg (97103)
Rates: $65-$80
Tel: (503) 325-2205
(800) 621-0641

CREST MOTEL
5366 Leif Erickson Dr (97103)
Rates: $53-$83
Tel: (503) 325-3141
(800) 421-3141

LAMPLIGHTER MOTEL
131 W Marine Dr (97103)
Rates: $34-$68
Tel: (503) 325-4051

RED LION INN
400 Industry St (97103)
Rates: $50-$115
Tel: (503) 325-7373
(800) 547-8010

RECREATION

FORT ASTORIA PARK - Leashes

Info: This small city park packs a hefty punch of history. Originally founded in 1811 by the Pacific Fur Company, Fort Astoria remains a partial replica of the original. Take the time to read the interpretive signs and acquire some insight into the olden days. For more information: (503) 325-2203.

Directions: At the corner of 15th and Exchange Streets.

FORT CLATSOP NATIONAL MEMORIAL - Leashes

Info: Do some time traveling with your doggistorian and visit the last pit stop on Lewis and Clark's famous expedition. The fort is named for the Clatsops, an American Indian tribe that befriended the members of Lewis and Clark's party. The explorers wintered at this very spot from December 1805 to March 1806 before returning home. When they heard the thundering roar of the Pacific, they knew their mission had been accomplished. In summer, dramatic reenactments of this historic period are performed by volunteers. If hiking's more to your liking, you and furface can make tracks to the canoe landing along the banks of the Lewis and Clark River. For more information: (503) 861-2471.

Directions: From Astoria, travel Highway 101 southwest about 6 miles to the signed exit for Fort Clatsop.

Note: $4 entrance fee/car. Dogs are not permitted in buildings.

Locate Other Dog-Friendly Activities...Check Nearby Cities

BAKER CITY

LODGING

BAKER CITY MOTEL
880 Elm St (97814)
Rates: $25-$33
Tel: (541) 523-6391
(800) 931-9229

EL DORADO MOTEL
695 Campbell (97814)
Rates: $36-$44
Tel: (541) 523-6494
(800) 537-5756

GEISER GRAND HOTEL
1996 Main St (97814)
Rates: $65-$125
Tel: (541) 523-1889

GREEN GABLES MOTEL
2533 10th St (97814)
Rates: $30+
Tel: (541) 523-5588

OREGON TRAIL MOTEL & RESORT
211 Bridge St (97814)
Rates: $32-$38
Tel: (541) 523-5844
(800) 628-3982

POWDER RIVER B&B
HCR 87, Box 500 (97814)
Rates: $60-$65
Tel: (541) 523-7143
(800) 600-7143

QUALITY INN
810 Campbell (97814)
Rates: $40-$61
Tel: (541) 523-2242
(800) 221-2222

THE WESTERN MOTEL
3055 10th St (97814)
Rates: $28-$36
Tel: (541) 523-3700
(800) 481-3701

TRAIL MOTEL
2815 10th St (97814)
Rates: n/a
Tel: (541) 523-4646

WARNERS SLOUGH HOUSE B&B
Rt 2, Box 135 (97814)
Rates: n/a
Tel: (541) 523-6196

RECREATION

ANTHONY LAKE SHORELINE TRAIL HIKE

Beginner/1.0 miles/0.5 hours

Info: A little pain and a lot of gain could be the motto of this trail. You and the pupster will amble lakeside on a gravel pathway while you enjoy a smidgen of nature. Birders, pack your binocs. Several species of songbirds fill the airways with their music. Kodak moments also await. Gunsight Mountain creates a picturesque backdrop perfect for some camera clicking. For more information: (541) 523-4476.

Directions: From Baker City, take Highway 30 north about 10 miles to Haines and turn west on CR 1146 following the Elkhorn Drive Scenic Byway (FS 73) signs to Anthony Lake (about 32 miles from Baker City). The trailhead is located at the Anthony Lake Guard Station.

Note: Permit may be required.

Hotel Policies May Be Subject To Change

BLACK LAKE TRAIL HIKE

Intermediate/2.0 miles/1.0 hours

Info: From the get-go, you'll know you're in for one helluva scenic hike. Lovely Lilypad Lake is dotted with yellow lilypad blossoms all summer long. You and the dogster will skirt this tranquil scene and skedaddle across a wet meadow or two before hooking up with the Elkhorn Crest Trail where you'll continue a few hundred feet, take a turnoff and arrive at Black Lake. This is just the place for afishionados to make their dreams come true. And aqua pups can partake of some cool water dunks. When you and the dirty dog can tear yourselves away, backtrack to the trailhead. For more information: (541) 523-4476.

Directions: From Baker City, take Highway 30 north about 10 miles to Haines and turn west on CR 1146 following the Elkhorn Drive Scenic Byway (FS 73) signs to Anthony Lake (about 32 miles from Baker City). Continue on FS 73 to the Anthony Lake Campground and drive on Campground Road (FS 170) to the trailhead.

Note: Permit may be required.

CRAWFISH BASIN TRAIL HIKE

Intermediate/4.0 miles/2.0 hours

Info: This lofty jaunt escorts you and furface 400' above colorful Crawfish Meadow where you'll have a bird's-eye view of the rock and spruce islands as well as serpentine Crawfish Creek. Zoom on to the junction with the Elkhorn Crest Trail and take in the outstanding views of Lakes Lookout, Lee Peak and Angels Peak. At trail's end, munch on lunch before retracing your steps. If you're up for more, hop on the Elkhorn Crest Trail and make tracks to some serious scenery. For more information: (541) 523-4476.

Directions: From Baker City, take Highway 30 north about 10 miles to Haines and turn west on CR 1146 following the Elkhorn Drive Scenic Byway (FS 73) signs to Anthony Lake (about 32 miles from Baker City). Continue on FS 73 past the Elkhorn Summit to FS 210 (about 38 miles from Baker City). Follow FS 210 to FS 187 and turn south to the trailhead.

Note: Permit may be required.

Locate Other Dog-Friendly Activities...Check Nearby Cities

CRAWFISH LAKE TRAIL HIKE

Intermediate/4.0 miles/2.0 hours

Info: For a taste of the North Fork John Day Wilderness and a hike on the northwest side of the Elkhorn Mountains, set your sights on this trail. You and the barkmeister will kick up some dust on an old dirt road and after a mile you'll ascend through some thick stands of young fir, spruce and lodgepole pine. Picturesque Crawfish Meadow leads to sun-drenched Crawfish Lake where pooch shenanigans with a wet slant are de rigueur. When splish-splashing time is over, continue lakeside to an abrupt half-mile descent and then a vigorous climb amidst an eerie stand of blackened trees, remnants of the fire of '86. Take some time to relish in the quietude of your surroundings. The Upper Crawfish Lake Trailhead signals about-face time. For more information: (541) 523-4476.

Directions: From Baker City, take Highway 30 north about 10 miles to Haines and turn west on CR 1146 following the Elkhorn Drive Scenic Byway (FS 73) signs to Anthony Lake (about 32 miles from Baker City). Continue on FS 73 past the Elkhorn Summit to FS 320. Take FS 320 to the trailhead.

Note: Permit may be required.

FLAGSTAFF HILL INTERPRETIVE TRAIL SYSTEM - Leashes

Beginner-Intermediate/0.5-4.2 miles/0.25-2.5 hours

Info: Return to the days of yesteryear with a visit to this region. History buffs can experience the sights, sounds and smells encountered by the emigrants on the great sagebrush steppe between the Rockies and the Cascades on this numero uno hike. Built to interpret and preserve the Oregon Trail heritage, this trail system loops around Flagstaff Hill and leads you and your Curious George on a time travel adventure encompassing interesting viewpoints and sites. Follow the footsteps of pioneers along one or two short trails or do it all, see it all. While some routes are tougher than others, all are rich with historical significance and worth the effort. The site contains fifteen miles of wagon ruts left by the emigrants' wagons. As you journey through this region, picture how the land looked to the settlers

Hotel Policies May Be Subject To Change

and imagine the hardships they endured almost a century ago. For more information: (541) 523-1843.

Directions: From Baker City, travel Highway 84 north. Take the first exit (304), turn right. Continue about 4 miles to the next left. The Oregon Trail Center is located on the hill. Pick up a trail guide at the center.

Note: Dogs are prohibited in the building and indoor theater.

LAKES LOOKOUT TRAIL HIKE

Intermediate/1.4 miles/1.0 hours

Info: Don't let the short length of this trail fool you, this hike is bound to test your perseverance. You'll boogie with Bowser through a jumble of massive boulders and rock faces to the summit at 8,522'. Break out the Fuji - you'll definitely want to take home some memories. Eight sparkling alpine lakes blue-dot the sweeping landscape. Everywhere you turn, the peaks of the Elkhorns loom tall and majestic, their presence almost humbling. When day is done, turn the hound around, you're homeward bound. For more information: (541) 523-4476.

Directions: From Baker City, take Highway 30 north about 10 miles to Haines and turn west on CR 1146 following the Elkhorn Drive Scenic Byway (FS 73) signs to Anthony Lake past the Elkhorn Summit to FS 210 (approximately 38 miles from Baker City). Follow FS 210 to FS 187 and turn south to reach the trailhead just before the end of the road.

Note: Permit may be required.

NORTH SHORE TRAIL HIKE

Beginner/7.8 miles/4.0 hours

Info: Birdwatchers, look sharp. Countless coves and hidden inlets translate to incredible birding ops including a variety of waterfowl and shorebirds. Perky pups might even catch sight of a Bambi or two. All along this pretty pathway, you'll encounter outstanding views. Savor your surroundings as you wiggle this way and that through a woodland of young ponderosa. Aah, smell the sweet vanilla fragrance of the pines.

Locate Other Dog-Friendly Activities...Check Nearby Cities

Take five and frolic with your Fido in the grasslands beside the reservoir. Visit in spring and summer when the wildflower party is in full swing and ogle the vivid red and violet splotches that paint the landscape. The Social Security Point signals turnaround time. For more information: (541) 523-4476.

Directions: From Baker City, travel south on Highway 7 approximately 16.5 miles to the Mason Dam Viewpoint and the entrance to the Mason Dam Boat Launch. The trailhead is at the Mason Dam Boat Ramp.

Note: Permit may be required.

SUMPTER VALLEY RAIL RIDE - Leashes

Info: Choo-choose this ride for a fun-filled summer adventure. Well behaved owners can accompany their leashed pooches on a rail ride through historic Sumpter Valley. Thanks to the dogged determination of a group of volunteers, a portion of the original Sumpter Valley Railroad (1890-1947) has been restored and is once again accessible to the public. Pack your binocs, claim a seat on the viewing car and then get ready, get set for the show to begin. You'll chug by dense woodlands where beaver, muskrat, elk and deer abound. Look skyward for sandhill cranes, hawks, geese, ducks and bluebirds. Include a biscuit basket and munch on lunch at the pretty picnicking area near the depot. For more information: (541) 894-2268.

Directions: From Baker City, travel Highway 7 southwest about 7 miles to the fork, veer right (staying on Highway 7) and drive about 9 miles to the McEwen Station, just past Phillips Lake. Or continue to the Sumpter Station, located off Highway 7 at the Sumpter Valley Dredge State Heritage Area.

Note: Operates on weekends and holidays from Memorial Day to the last weekend in September. Fees: Adult $9.50, children $6.50.

VAN PATTEN LAKE TRAIL HIKE

Expert/3.0 miles/2.0 hours

Info: In traileze, this one's a buttkicker. But every huff and puff will be rewarded with an ooh and aah. So stretch out and get psyched to endure. The first section you'll tackle is a switchbacking forest road (#131) which will deposit you and

Hotel Policies May Be Subject To Change

the dawgus at the former Little Alps Ski Area. Another half-mile sojourn leads through a pretty lodgepole pine forest. In springtime, the landscape is blanketed with bouncy, colorful wildflowers. When you reach Van Patten Lake, you'll barely have time to catch your breath before the sweeping panoramas of the North Powder Valley and Wallowa Mountains take it away. If you've backpacked a picnic lunch, this is the place to break some bread and biscuits. Hot diggety dogs can chill out in the frosty lake before doing the descent thing. Carpe diem Duke. For more information: (503) 523-4476.

Directions: From Baker City, take Highway 30 north about 10 miles to Haines and turn west on CR 1146. Continue on CR 1146, following the Elkhorn Drive Scenic Byway signs to Anthony Lake. Drive on FS 73 to Van Patten Lake trailhead sign (about 29.5 miles from Baker City). Turn onto FS 130 to the lower trailhead. Parking is available near the maintenance shed at the base of the hill.

Note: Permit may be required. High-clearance vehicles can drive on FS 131 to the upper trailhead (Trail 1634). From this point, the trail is 0.5 miles long.

BANDON

Lodging

BANDON BEACH MOTEL
1110 11th St SW (97411)
Rates: $45-$85
Tel: (541) 347-4430
(800) 822-8765

CAPRICE MOTEL
Rt 1, Box 530 (97411)
Rates: $38-$60
Tel: (541) 347-4494

DRIFTWOOD MOTEL
460 Hwy 101 (97411)
Rates: $35-$70
Tel: (541) 347-9022
(888) 374-3893

THE INN AT FACE ROCK MOTEL
3225 Beach Loop Rd (97411)
Rates: $49-$129
Tel: (541) 347-9441
(800) 638-3092

LA KRIS MOTEL
Hwy 101 S at 9th St (97411)
Rates: $32-$65
Tel: (541) 347-3610

PACIFIC HOUSE B&B
2165 Beach Loop Dr (97411)
Rates: $75-$90
Tel: (541) 347-9526

SUNSET OCEANFRONT ACCOMMODATIONS
Box 373 (97411)
Rates: $53-$175
Tel: (541) 347-2453
(800) 842-2407

TABLE ROCK MOTEL
840 Beach Loop Rd (97411)
Rates: $30-$80
Tel: (541) 347-2700

<u>RECREATION</u>

BULLARDS BEACH STATE PARK - Leashes

Info: Outdoor enthusiasts rate this locale two paws up. Situated beside the banks of the lovely Coquille River and the shoreline of the Pacific, Bullards Beach is a picturesque tableau where the river meets the sea. You and your furball will discover plenty of scenery and funnery in the 120+ acres of beach, dune and forest terrain. Fishy tales can come true if you try your luck in the ocean or river. Crabbing and clamming are also popular pastimes during low tides. BYOB (bring your own biscuits), find a secluded spot and dine with your canine while cool ocean breezes blow your cares away. Hikers, you and the dawgus can leave your prints in the sand as you travel on the trail to the Coquille River Lighthouse. An historic landmark, it was built in 1896, decommissioned in 1936, restored in 1976 and relit in 1991. So when you're looking for a day with a little bit of this and a little bit of that, set your sights on this pretty little spot. FYI: In December and from March through May, migrating whales can often be seen from Face Rock Wayside. The best orca ogling is in the early morning hours. For more information: (541) 347-2209.

Directions: From Bandon, travel north on Highway 101 for 2 miles to park entrance.

Note: Day use fee may be required.

COQUILLE RIVER SANCTUARY
OREGON ISLANDS NATIONAL WILDLIFE PRESERVE - Leashes

Info: A paved trail wiggles this way and that amid a blufftop region of grasses and coastal shrubs to lookout points where dramatic rock formations jut out from the thunderous Pacific. The Coquille River Sanctuary, seen to the north, is aptly named the "24-Hour Supermarket." As an estuary, this partially enclosed body of water is a mingling of fresh and sea water that creates a rich habitat. Harbor seals, diving ducks, dabbling ducks, shorebirds and sea birds have an all-you-can-eat buffet every day, feasting on flounder, sole, underwater clams, worms, invertebrates, eelgrass, tubers of marsh plants, smelt and herring.

Hotel Policies May Be Subject To Change

The islands themselves are closed to public use, but if you're toting binocs, you might experience a close encounter of the sea life kind. From the blufftop, you can view the breeding and resting areas set aside for seabirds and marine mammals. Even without sightings, the dramatic rock formations, unusual birdlife and the crashing Pacific are reward enough. If your timing's right, you can give tide pooling a try. But remember, do not disturb anything in this very natural area.

To make your visit more enjoyable, consider the following: thirty-eight species of marine mammals inhabit the Pacific, six of which occur nowhere else in the world. These adaptable creatures live in a variety of habitats from frigid, icebound shores to warm subtropical shoals. Some migrate while others stay put.

The male Stellar sea lion can grow to more than ten feet in length and weigh over a ton. Capable of diving more than 800', these mammals feed at night. They have front flippers much larger than their hind ones. The hind flippers rotate so they're able to use all four on land. Much noisier than seals, sea lions bark or roar and pup on land.

The harbor seal is a homebody who does not migrate on a regular basis and prefers to forage in shallow waters. Diving 300', they can remain submerged up to ten minutes. Talk about holding your breath! When they dive, breathing stops, their heart slows and to help them see in the dark, murky waters, their pupils dilate. They have small hind flippers which do not rotate. On land, they inch along, they are usually quiet and they pup in the water or at its edge.

The terrain of the northern elephant seals extends from the Gulf of Alaska to Baja. They breed and pup on the islands in the southern part of this region. At sea for seven months, they spend 85% of their lives underwater, diving as deep as 4,000' (gadzooks, that's 400 stories underwater). The relatively small amount of time they spend on land is for critical R&R.

Orcas are nicknamed killer whales because they are capable of killing and consuming almost any sea creature. Some pods (whale families) reside in this water year-round. Along this section of coastline, orcas feed on seals and sea lions. For more information: (541) 867-4550.

Locate Other Dog-Friendly Activities...Check Nearby Cities

Directions: On the western edge of Bandon, off Highway 101 on Beach Loop Drive. Turn west at the light at Milepost 270.8 (11th Street). The parking lot for the refuge is located at the end of 11th Street SW.

FACE ROCK WAYSIDE - Leashes

Info: At this overlook of the Oregon Islands marine and bird-life sanctuaries, you'll discover a wild and primitive setting. A paved trail and wooden stairs lead to the beach where you and the woofer can hoof it to some excellent tide pooling. You're bound to earn some puppy points with this excursion. The air is salt-tinged, the scenery breathtaking and the wildflowers plentiful. Yellow, pink, purple and white clusters brighten the coastal shrubbery that clings to the bluffsides. FYI: This extremely rugged stretch of coastline may be perilous at high tide and during stormy weather. Be aware of the hazards. For more information: (800) 551-6949

Directions: On the western edge of Bandon, off Highway 101 at milepost 270.8 on Beach Loop Drive. Turn west at the light at Milepost 270.8 (11th Street). The parking lot for the refuge is located at the end of 11th Street SW.

BEATTY

LODGING

BEATTY MOTEL
Hwy 140, P.O.
Box 335 (97621)
Rates: n/a
Tel: (541) 533-2689

BEAVERTON

LODGING

GREENWOOD INN
10700 SW Allen Blvd (97005)
Rates: $97-$133
Tel: (503) 643-7444
(800) 289-1300

PEPPERTREE MOTEL
10720 SW Allen Blvd (97005)
Rates: $52-$69
Tel: (503) 641-7477
(800) 453-6219

SHILO INNS
9900 SW Canyon Rd (97225)
Rates: $76-$105
Tel: (503) 297-2551
(800) 222-2244

VAL-U-INN MOTEL
12255 SW Canyon Rd (97005)
Rates: $36-$51
Tel: (503) 643-6621
(800) 443-7777

BEND

LODGING

**ARLINE McDONALD'S
VACATION HOMES**
1530 NW Jacksonville (97701)
Rates: $150-$250
Tel: (541) 382-4534

BEND RIVERSIDE MOTEL & CONDO
1565 NW Hill St (97702)
Rates: $49-$110
Tel: (541) 389-2363
(800) 284-2363

BEST WESTERN ENTRADA LODGE
19221 Century Dr (97702)
Rates: $49-$89
Tel: (541) 382-4080
(800) 528-1234

BEST WESTERN INN & SUITES
721 NE 3rd (97701)
Rates: $49-$99
Tel: (541) 382-1515
(800) 528-1234

CASCADE MOTEL LODGE
420 SE 3rd St (97702)
Rates: $85
Tel: (541) 382-2612
(800) 852-6031

CASCADE VIEW RANCH GUEST HOUSE
60435 Tekampe Rd (97702)
Rates: $150-$285
Tel: (541) 388-5658

CHALET MOTEL
510 SE 3rd St (97702)
Rates: $29-$40
Tel: (541) 382-6124

CIMARRON MOTOR INN
201 NE 3rd St (97701)
Rates: $44-$59
Tel: (541) 382-8282
(800) 304-4050

CIMARRON NORTH
437 NE 3rd St (97701)
Rates: $39-$54
Tel: (541) 382-7711
(800) 304-4050

COMFORT INN
61200 S Hwy 97 (97702)
Rates: $40-$145
Tel: (541) 388-2227
(800) 228-5150

CULTUS LAKE RESORT
P.O. Box 262 (97709)
Rates: $52-$89
Tel: (541) 389-3230

DESCHUTES RIVER RANCH
20210 Swalley Rd (97701)
Rates: $150-$160
Tel: (541) 382-7240

Locate Other Dog-Friendly Activities...Check Nearby Cities

GUEST HOUSE B&B
20020 Glen Vista Rd (97702)
Rates: n/a
Tel: (541) 382-8565

HAMPTON INN
15 NE Butler Market Rd (97701)
Rates: $58-$77
Tel: (541) 388-4114
(800) 426-7866

HOLIDAY MOTEL
880 SE 3rd St (97702)
Rates: $34-$38
Tel: (541) 382-4620
(800) 252-0121

MOTEL WEST
228 NE Irving (97701)
Rates: $36-$50
Tel: (541) 389-5577
(800) 282-5577

PALMER'S MOTEL
645 NE Greenwood Ave (97701)
Rates: $30-$55
Tel: (541) 382-1197

PLAZA MOTEL
1430 NW Hill St (97702)
Rates: $28-$60
Tel: (541) 389-0235

RED LION-SOUTH
849 NE 3rd St (97701)
Rates: $74-$99
Tel: (541) 382-8384
(800) 733-5466

THE RIVERHOUSE RESORT
3075 N Hwy 97 (97701)
Rates: $65-$175
Tel: (541) 389-3111
(800) 547-3928

RODEWAY INN
3705 N Hwy 97 (97701)
Rates: $30-$50
Tel: (541) 382-2211
(800) 507-2211

SCANDIA PINES LODGE
61405 S Hwy 97 (97702)
Rates: $39-$89
Tel: (541) 389-5910
(800) 500-5910

SHILO INNS SUITES HOTEL
3105 O B Riley Rd (97701)
Rates: $75-$120
Tel: (541) 389-9600
(800) 222-2244

SLEEP INN
600 NE Bellevue (97701)
Rates: $49-$69
Tel: (541) 330-0050
(800) 62-SLEEP

SONOMA LODGE
450 SE 3rd St (97702)
Rates: $35-$49
Tel: (541) 382-4891

SUPER 8 MOTEL
1275 S Hwy 97 (97702)
Rates: $52-$62
Tel: (541) 388-6888
(800) 800-8000

SWALLOW RIDGE B&B
65711 Twin Bridges Rd (97701)
Rates: $45-$55
Tel: (541) 389-1913

WESTWARD HO MOTEL
904 SE 3rd St (97702)
Rates: $34-$75
Tel: (541) 382-2111
(800) 999-8143

<u>RECREATION</u>

BENHAM FALLS TRAIL HIKE - Leashes

Beginner/1.5 miles/0.75 hours

Info: In doggiedom, this short but sweet hike rates two paws up. The wagging machine will be full speed ahead once you hit the pathway to the white waters of the Deschutes River. A former logging site, the pupular trail leads to the misty blues

Hotel Policies May Be Subject To Change

of Benham Falls. Tote lunch and watch the cascading waters as they mix and swirl with the raging river. If you're feeling ambitious, this trail connects with several others in the Lava Butte Area. For more information: (541) 593-2421.

Directions: From Bend, travel Highway 97 south about 7 miles to the Lava Lands Visitor Center. Turn right onto Road 9702 and continue 3 miles to the trailhead at the end of the road.

GREEN LAKES TRAIL HIKE - Leashes

Expert/10.0 miles/6.0 hours

Info: An arduous wilderness hike, this tour of the Green Lakes area is one of the most enchanting journeys you'll ever experience. The unusual color of the lakes is caused by the very fine silt ground by adjacent Lewis Glacier. You and Mighty Dog won't know where to look first, the forests, mountain vistas or lakes. The trail initially skirts roaring Fall Creek, a rambunctious waterway that's brimming with gorgeous cascades and a bounty of petite plungers. Before you know it though, you and the one with the ear-to-ear grin will be zooming through a fragrant fir forest of canopied shade where keeping your cool comes easy. About halfway into the trek, you'll say adieu to the creek, pass a junction with Moraine Lake Trail and then hightail it to a wondrous wall of black obsidian glass, the hardened lava that flowed from South Sister eons ago. Your turnaround point will be the Green Lakes region, spectacular dollops of water ensconced between Broken Top and South Sister Mountain. If you can, visit in early autumn when the weather's still lovely, the landscape's emblazoned with sprays of golden hues and the trail is less traveled. Carpe diem Duke. For more information: (541) 388-5664.

Directions: From Bend, take US 97 about 27 miles following signs to Mt. Bachelor. Continue another 4.5 miles (south) on Highway 46 (Cascade Lakes Highway) to the Green Lakes Trailhead on the north side of the highway.

LAVA BUTTE CRATER RIM TRAIL HIKE - Leashes

Beginner/0.25 miles/0.25 hours

Info: Amateur geologists will get a quick kick out of this pupsqueak hike. The path traverses the top of the 500' Lava Butte cinder cone. Interpretive signs explain this amazing natural phenomenon. Chill out topside before retracing your steps. A dog-friendly shuttle provides the transportation to the trailhead. Bone voyage. For more information: (541) 593-2421.

Directions: From Bend, travel Highway 97 south about 7 miles to the Lava Lands Visitor Center. Take the shuttle to the trailhead.

LAVA CAST FOREST TRAIL HIKE - Leashes

Beginner/1.0 miles/0.5 hours

Info: This trail is a must-see, must-do for budding botanists and rock hounds alike. The paved loop escorts you amidst the eerie world of pine tree molds in the Lava Cast Forest. These molds were formed over 6,000 years ago by molten lava that engulfed the pine trees. Broaden your knowledge of these natural wonders by picking up a brochure at the trailhead. For more information: (541) 593-2421.

Directions: From Bend, travel Highway 97 south about 10 miles to Road 9720 and turn left. Continue 2 miles to the trailhead on the left side of the Lava Cast Forest.

PAULINA FALLS TRAIL HIKE - Leashes

Beginner/0.50 miles/0.25 hours

Info: If you like your nature fix on the wet and bosky side, knock wood, you're gonna love this easy does it stroll to the cascading waters of Paulina Falls. Traipsing through a forest of towering trees, some as tall as 80', the short path leads to the bottom of Paulina Falls where wet shenanigans are part of the package. If the mood strikes, clock a few more miles with a climb to Paulina Peak for a look-see at the lay of the land. For more information: (541) 593-2421.

Directions: From Bend, travel Highway 97 south about 22 miles to FS 21 . Turn left and travel to the fork. Take the right side of the fork, continuing on FS 21 to the marked trailhead-opposite the Paulina Falls Trailhead.

Hotel Policies May Be Subject To Change

PAULINA LAKESHORE LOOP TRAIL HIKE - Leashes

Intermediate/7.5 miles/4.0 hours

Info: Spend the afternoon in lakeside splendor with an excursion along this charming trail. Forget your cares as you amble through thick, shady forests where chatty birds provide the entertainment. In summer, if you check out the black sand beaches, watch Rover's paws, the sand can get very hot. In springtime, you've got a standing invitation to a meadowland wildflower party. But without a doubt, the highlight of your day will be the water. Deep, cool and ultra refreshing, it's the best way to turn your hot dog into a chilly dog. For more information: (541) 388-5664..

Directions: From Bend, travel Highway 97 south for 22 miles to FS 21. Turn left and park at the Paulina Lake Lodge to find the trailhead.

PAULINA PEAK TRAIL HIKE - Leashes

Beginner/0.50 miles/0.25 hours

Info: When you want to get away from it all on a hot summer day, this trail provides the escape route. You won't regret a moment spent in this area of watering holes and interesting scenery. Zooming off from a paved road, you and your canine climber will be deposited peak top, above the rim of an old volcano. Sweeping views of Paulina and East Lakes will greet you from your 8,000' perch. An opulent mix of water, lava and diverse terrain, the first thing you'll want to do is jump in a lake. Nestled side by side in the volcanic cone of Newberry Volcano, these two lakes were once a single body of water separated eons ago by a mammoth lava flow. As with many calderas, the clear waters are deep and icy cold and fringed by meadows, forests and black sand beaches. There are lots of trails around the rim if you and your hiking noodnick are up for the workout. Pick up a trail map and learn more about this unusual area. For more information: (541) 593-2421.

Directions: From Bend, travel Highway 97 south for 22 miles to FS 21. Turn left and travel to the fork. Take the right side of the fork, continuing on FS 21 to the marked trailhead on the right side of the road.

Locate Other Dog-Friendly Activities...Check Nearby Cities

TRAIL OF THE MOLTEN LANDS HIKE- Leashes

Beginner/0.75 miles/0.5 hours

Info: For an up-close gander at a natural wonder, hop on this paved pathway. You and your geomutt will find yourselves out on the lava flow to the breach in Lava Butte. Even if you're not into rocks, the sheer natural beauty of the place is worth a slot in your plans. For more information: (541) 593-2421.

Directions: From Bend, travel Highway 97 south about 7 miles to the Lava Lands Visitor Center. The trailhead is located at the Lava Lands Patio.

TRAIL OF THE WHISPERING PINES HIKE- Leashes

Beginner/0.75 miles/0.5 hours

Info: This paw-pleasing trail meanders amidst shady whispering pines - hence the name - skirting the edge of the lava flow. You'll have it made in the shade while you admire the astounding beauty of the butte. For optimal viewing pleasure, combine this path with the Trail of the Molten Lands and get two different perspective of the Lava Butte. For more information: (541) 593-2421.

Directions: From Bend, travel Highway 97 south about 7 miles to the Lava Lands Visitor Center. The trailhead is located at the Lava Lands Patio.

BLUE RIVER

LODGING

McKENZIE RIVER B&B
55482 Delta Rd (97413)
Rates: $70-$85
Tel: (541) 822-8232
(888) 355-2583

RECREATION

CARPENTER MOUNTAIN TRAIL HIKE

Intermediate/2.0 miles/1.0 hours

Info: For a mini workout and gorgeous views mixed with a slice of history, you can't go wrong on this somewhat challenging hike to the summit of Carpenter Mountain. Bring your camera to take home glossy memories and a biscuit basket for a lunch time treat. Check out the historical lookout tower before retracing your steps. For more information: (541) 822-3317.

Directions: From Blue River, head east on Highway 126 for 3 miles to FS 15. Turn left on FS 15 and drive for 3.5 miles to FS 1506. Make a right on FS 1506 to Spur Road 350 and the trailhead at the end of the road.

CHUCKSNEY MOUNTAIN LOOP TRAIL HIKE

Intermediate/10.5 miles/6.0 hours

Info: Make this outing an all day affair and include some high energy munchies and lots of H$_2$O. Your journey actually begins with the two-mile Grasshopper Trail that hooks up with the Chucksney Loop. Once on the loop, you'll traipse through a medley of forestlands and pretty wildflower-strewn meadows, topping out at 5,760' Chucksney Mountain. Do lunch, frolic with the pup and enjoy the terrific views before finishing the loop-de-loop. For more information: (541) 822-3317.

Directions: From Blue River, head east on Highway 126 for 4.6 miles to FS 19 (Aufderheide Drive). Turn right on FS 19 and drive 26 miles to Box Canyon Horse Camp and turn right to the Grasshopper Trailhead. Hike the Grasshopper Trail for 2 miles to access the Chucksney Mountain Loop Trail.

DELTA OLD-GROWTH GROVE NATURE TRAIL HIKE

Beginner/0.5 miles/0.25 hours

Info: Nature and education go hand-in-paw on this peanut-sized looping trail through an old-growth forest. Numbered posts and a corresponding trail guide identify and describe the unique features of this interesting habitat. Take note of the spectacular Douglas fir and western red cedar trees. These 500 year old specimens have attained heights of 200' and weights of 10-12 tons. Wowser Bowser. For more information: (541) 822-3317.

Directions: From Blue River, head east on Highway 126 for 4.6 miles to FS 19 (Aufderheide Drive), turn right and continue to Delta Campground, just past the bridge. The trailhead is located beyond the first few campsites.

FRISSELL TRAIL HIKE

Expert/5.0 miles/3.0 hours

Info: This trail spells TOUGH from the get-go. But if you and old brown eyes have the experience and stamina, Frissell Ridge has the views. Pack plenty of water and power snacks, you'll need them. For more information: (541) 822-3317.

Directions: From Blue River, head east on Highway 126 for 7 miles to the "dump road" (refuse disposal site). Turn on the "dump road" and stay right on FS 2633-705. After about one mile, the road forks - keep right on FS 3633-700. Follow FS 3633-700 to FS 2633-704 and turn left. Continue on FS 2633-704 for about .5 miles to the trailhead at road's end.

UPPER CASTLE ROCK TRAIL HIKE

Intermediate/3.6 miles/2.0 hours

Info: You and your hot dog are gonna love the cool shade of this forested trail to the top of Castle Rock. At the trailhead, follow the right fork or you'll miss the spectacular vistas from the old fire lookout. Way to go Fido. For more information: (541) 822-3317.

Directions: From Blue River, head east on Highway 126 for 4.6 miles to FS 19 (Aufderheide Drive), turn right. Continue on FS 19 for a half-mile to the stop sign. Stay left for approximately .4 miles to gravel road FS 2639 (King Road). Make a right on FS 2639 for .5 miles to Spur Road 480. Go right on Spur Road 480 to the trailhead at road's end.

Hotel Policies May Be Subject To Change

BOARDMAN

Lodging

DODGE CITY INN
1st & Front Sts (97818)
Rates: $38-$42
Tel: (541) 481-2451
(800) 233-2368

NUGGET INN
105 Front St SW (97818)
Rates: $40-$43
Tel: (541) 481-2375
(800) 336-4485

RIVERVIEW MOTEL
200 Front St NE (97818)
Rates: $32-$42
Tel: (541) 481-2775

BROOKINGS

Lodging

BEAVER STATE MOTEL
437 Chetco Ave (97415)
Rates: $42-$55
Tel: (541) 469-5361

BONN MOTEL
1216 Chetco Ave (97415)
Rates: $38-$48
Tel: (541) 469-2161

CHART HOUSE OUTFITTERS
15833 Pedrioli Rd (97415)
Rates: $38-$75
Tel: (541) 469-3867
(800) 290-6208

HARBOR INN MOTEL
15991 Hwy 101 S (97415)
Rates: $48-$70
Tel: (541) 469-3194
(800) 469-8884

LOWDEN'S BEACHFRONT B&B
14626 Wollam Rd (97415)
Rates: $59-$160
Tel: (541) 469-7045
(800) 453-4768

PACIFIC SUNSET INN
1144 Chetco Ave (97415)
Rates: $28-$53
Tel: (541) 469-2141
(800) 469-2141

SEA DREAMER INN B&B
15167 McVay Ln (97415)
Rates: $38-$75
Tel: (541) 469-6629
(800) 408-4367

Recreation

ALFRED A. LOEB STATE PARK - Leashes

Info: Located on what is called "The Banana Belt," this 320-acre park is known for its warm, tropical-like weather. With the Chetco River flowing like a blue ribbon beside the rolling greens, this spacious scene is the ideal getaway. The fishing's

Locate Other Dog-Friendly Activities...Check Nearby Cities

fine so drop a line. Who knows, you might dine on salmon, rock fish or trout. Two splendid hiking trails slice deeply into the woodlands, where river tributaries, a mix of flora and fauna and a slew of botanical rarities set the stage for a memorable afternoon. So simply relax with Max or pick a trail. For more information: (541) 469-2021.

Directions: From Brookings, travel Highway 101 south to North Bank Chetco River Road (located on the ouskirts of Brookings), turn left. Follow North Bank Chetco River Road about 8 miles to the park entrance.

Note: Day use fee may be charged. Be aware of poison oak.

The numbered hikes that follow are within Alfred A. Loeb State Park:

1) REDWOOD NATURE TRAIL HIKE - Leashes

Intermediate/1.0 miles/0.5 hours

Info: When you're in the mood for a hike amidst a grabbag of woodlands, you can't miss on this nature walk. The looping path traverses old-growth redwood, mixed conifer and hardwood forests interlaced with a splash of streams. Budding botanists, you'll get a quickie education on the region's trees. The stand of majestic redwoods (redwoods grow taller than any other tree), will impress you with their lofty heights and tree circumferences (some stand as tall as 300' and measure 15-20 feet in diameter). Notice too the life beneath the redwoods - broad leafed evergreens comprise the understory. The tanoak tree is one specimen that commonly grows among the redwoods and Douglas firs. There's also the huckleberry shrub, a specimen that adds color to the forest setting with its vibrant green leaves and dark blue berries. Go and see the forest for the trees and put a spin on the dog's tail. For more information: (541) 469-2021.

Directions: From Brookings, travel Highway 101 south to North Bank Chetco River Road (located on the ouskirts of Brookings), turn left. Follow North Bank Chetco River Road about 8 miles to the park entrance. Continue another half mile past the park entrance to the marked trail.

2) RIVERVIEW NATURE TRAIL HIKE - Leashes

Beginner/1.5 miles/0.75 hours

Info: If you're as much of a tree enthusiast as your canine cohort, this trail is the way to go. Following the north bank of the Chetco River through a mixed woodland, you and the pooch will feel a little like Lewis and Clark exploring the unknown wilderness. Interpretive signs can broaden your knowledge of the diversified flora and fauna of the area which includes a stand of western hemlocks with drooping, feathery foliage. The Oregon myrtlewood trees all about you have such deep root systems that they can survive even after falling. As you penetrate the bosky terrain, you'll encounter Douglas fir and red alder. FYI: The large holes in the ground are made by mountain beavers who look more like gophers than beavers. These burrows are actually entrances to underground tunnels for the thriving beaver community. For more information: (541) 469-2021.

Directions: From Brookings, travel Highway 101 south to North Bank Chetco River Road (located on the ouskirts of Brookings), turn left. Follow North Bank Chetco River Road about 8 miles to the park entrance. The trailhead is located in the picnic area on the left side of the road as you drive into the park.

AZALEA CITY PARK - Leashes

Info: Every year this charming parkland of 26 acres comes alive with color when over 1,000 wild azaleas do their springtime thing. Musically inclined mutts will take a shine to the summer series of outdoor concerts held in this popular setting.

Directions: Located in downtown Brookings about 3 miles off of Highway 101 on North Bank Road.

BOMBSITE TRAIL HIKE - Leashes

Beginner/1.0 miles/0.5 hours

Info: This cinchy hike is perfect for sofa loafers. The trail follows a simple course to the historic site which marks the only spot in the continental United States where the Japanese dropped a bomb during WWII. For more information: (541) 469-2196.

Locate Other Dog-Friendly Activities...Check Nearby Cities

Directions: From Brookings, travel south on Highway 101 about one mile to CR 808 (South Bank Road). Turn left and drive about 6 miles to FS 1205 (Mt. Emily Road), turn right. Continue on FS 1205 about 5 miles to the trailhead located just past Spur Road 260.

HARRIS BEACH STATE PARK - Leashes

Info: Like its cousin to the east, this 220-acre park is also in the warm "Banana Belt," which translates to year-round mild weather. Resting on the shores of the Pacific Ocean, the park has miles of beachfront property for you and your seadog to explore. Play tagalong with your wagalong on the sandy beaches as the water laps at and cools your tootsies. Or do some tide pooling and study the ocean's inhabitants. Bring along the red checks, find a cozy inlet and cloudgaze the day away. This park spells relax with a capital R. For more information: (541) 469-0224.

Directions: From Brookings, travel north on Highway 101 about 2 miles to the park located on the right side.

Note: Day use fee may be charged.

LITTLE VULCAN LAKE TRAIL HIKE - Leashes

Intermediate/3.0 miles/1.5 hours

Info: An afternoon of water sports awaits you and the dawgus at this delightful little lake. Simply hike the Vulcan Lake Trail for 1.3 miles and then take the short .2-mile spur to Little Vulcan Lake. Do the doggie paddle or the lunch thing before following your paw prints back to the trailhead. For more information: (541) 469-2196.

Directions: From the junction of Highway 101 and CR 784 (North Bank Road) in Brookings, travel northeast on CR 784 about 7 miles until it becomes FS 1376. Continue east on FS 1376 about 8 miles to FS 1917 and turn right. Follow FS 1917 about 6 miles to its junction with FS 1909 and take the left fork to the Vulcan Lake Trailhead on Spur Road 260. Hike approximately 1.3 miles of the Vulcan Lake Trail to the Little Vulcan Lake Trail.

SAMUEL H. BOARDMAN STATE SCENIC CORRIDOR

Info: Naturalist alert. When you're doing the coast trip, stop puppyfooting around and plan a stop at this paw-pleasing patch. You'll get an up-close peek at the beauty you've been admiring from afar. There are pull-outs for Arch Rock Point, Natural Bridges Cove and Thomas Creek Bridge. Explore a tableau of woodsy cliffs, grassy headlands, steep canyons and rock islands. For solitude, views of windswept beaches and a taste of Oregon at its best, you can't beat this quick, easy to access package.

Directions: From Brookings, travel north on Highway 101. The "Corridor" starts at milepost 343 and runs to milepost 353.

*The numbered hikes that follow are within the
Samuel H. Boardman State Scenic Corridor:*

1) COAST TRAIL HIKE

Beginner/0.25 miles/0.5 hours

Info: This beauty of a peanut-sized jaunt slices a narrow path amidst a dense woodland of towering spruce and plops you and your peanut on the wind-tossed, often fog-enshrouded but always spectacular Oregon coast.

Directions: From Brookings, go north on Highway 101 to milepost 347.5 and the North Island Trail trailhead to the Coast Trail.

2) OREGON COAST TRAIL HIKE to INDIAN SANDS

Intermediate/6.0 miles/4.0 hours

Info: Probably one of the prettiest stretches of the much-loved Oregon Coast Trail, you and the gleeful one will march across blufftops on your way to House Rock Viewpoint before making like Hansel and Gretel through woods of spruce and meadows of green. Your beach bum Bowser will grin when you hit the sandy shores leading to Indian Sands, extraordinary pine-fringed dunes. After you absorb the postcardian beauty, repeat the beat on your retreat and consider yourselves a couple of lucky dogs.

Directions: From Brookings, travel north on Highway 101 to Lone Ranch picnic area and trailhead, at milepost 352.6.

SNOW CAMP LOOKOUT TRAIL HIKE - Leashes

Intermediate/9.2 miles/5.0 hours

Info: You'll want to include plenty of water and Scooby snacks before setting out on this long day hike to the top of Snow Camp Mountain. You'll boogie with Bowser to the 4,223' peak where magnificent vistas are your reward. Listen up aquapups, along the way you'll cross Windy Valley Creek. You know what that means - wet paws! For more information: (541) 469-2196.

Directions: From the junction of Highway 101 and CR 784 (North Bank Road) in Brookings, travel northeast on CR 784 about 7 miles until it becomes FS 1376. Continue east on FS 1376 approximately 15 miles to the trailhead.

VULCAN LAKE TRAIL HIKE - Leashes

Intermediate/2.8 miles/1.5 hours

Info: Pack the biscuit basket and a fun attitude and then kick up some dust on this trail to pretty Vulcan Lake. This outing gives you and the pooch a one-two punch. A mini workout and chill out lakeside fun. The lake is a cool oasis, especially during the dog days of summer. For more information: (541) 469-2196.

Directions: From the junction of Highway 101 and CR 784 (North Bank Road) in Brookings, travel northeast on CR 784 about 7 miles until it becomes FS 1376. Continue east on FS 1376 about 8 miles to FS 1917, turn right. Follow FS 1917 about 6 miles to its junction with FS 1909 and take the left fork to the trailhead on Spur Road 260.

BURNS

LODGING

BEST WESTERN PONDEROSA
577 W Monroe (97720)
Rates: $53-$73
Tel: (541) 573-2047
(800) 303-2047

ROYAL INN
999 Oregon Ave (97720)
Rates: $38-$72
Tel: (541) 573-1700

SILVER SPUR MOTEL
789 N Broadway (97720)
Rates: $33-$38
Tel: (541) 573-2077
(800) 400-2077

Hotel Policies May Be Subject To Change

RECREATION

MALHEUR NATIONAL WILDLIFE REFUGE

Info: When nothing but the best of Mother Nature will do, plan an odyssey to this special locale. The 185,000-acre refuge is comprised of marshes, ponds, lakes, meadows and desert terrain. With more than 300 species of birds and 50 species of mammals, this region is a primo spot for you and Spot to do some wildlife viewing. Tote your binocs and pack plenty of Fuji as you watch for sandhill cranes, one of the oldest living species of birds. Thanks to management efforts, this rare bird is making a comeback and more than 250 nesting pairs reside at the refuge from February to October. These majestic birds are a wondrous sight to behold. The species is eight million years old and when they call to one another, the prehistoric sound is chilling to hear.

Birders will go bonkers at Malheur Lake, a major feeding and nesting stop along the Pacific flyway. Flocks of snow and Ross' geese often stop on their migrations. Watch for raptors as well, from August to December, a variety of hawks, eagles and falcons call this place home. Remember, this is the epitome of natural; leave only footprints, take only memories. For more information: (541) 493-2612.

Directions: From Burns, travel east on Highway 78 for 2 miles to Highway 205. Follow Highway 205 south for 25 miles to the signed County Road leading to Princeton. Turn east and drive 5 miles to the entrance.

Note: Leashes or voice control obedience mandatory. Be prepared to encounter temperature extremes and long, gravel roads. Make sure your vehicle is in good condition and your gas tank is full.

WEST MYRTLE CREEK TRAIL HIKE - Leashes

Intermediate/4.0 miles/2.0 hours

Info: Jumpstart your day on this popular hike through a lush forest beside Myrtle Creek. This riparian oasis is perfect for lunch alfresco and a cooling bit of splish-splashing fun. You and the wet wagger will be treated to astounding views of the river basin and surrounding valley. When day is done, retrace your steps. For more information: (541) 573-7292.

Locate Other Dog-Friendly Activities...Check Nearby Cities

Directions: From Burns, take Highway 395 north for 19 miles to FS 31. Turn left on FS 31 and continue 19 miles to FS 37. Turn left on FS 37 and drive 4 miles to FS 440. Take a left on FS 440 and drive to the trailhead at the end of the road.

CAMP SHERMAN

LODGING

BLACK BUTTE RESORT MOTEL
35 Suttle-Sherman Rd (97730)
Rates: $55-$65
Tel: (541) 595-6514

COLD SPRINGS RESORT & RV PARK
25615 Cold Springs Resort Ln (97730)
Rates: $93-$103
Tel: (541) 595-6271

METOLIUS RIVER LODGES
12390 SW FS Rd 1419-700 (97730)
Rates: $57-$105
Tel: (541) 595-6290
(800) 595-6290

TWIN VIEW RESORT
13860 SW FS Rd 1419 (97730)
Rates: $54-$98
Tel: (541) 595-6125

CANNON BEACH

LODGING

CANNON BEACH ECOLA CREEK LODGE
208 5th St (97110)
Rates: $60-$99
Tel: (503) 436-2776
(800) 873-2749

CANNON VILLAGE MOTEL
3163 S Hemlock St (97110)
Rates: $65-$120
Tel: (503) 436-2317

HALLMARK RESORT
1400 S Hemlock St (97110)
Rates: $69-$189
Tel: (503) 436-1566
(800) 345-5675

HAYSTACK RESORT
3339 S Hemlock St (97110)
Rates: $89-$159
Tel: (503) 436-1577
(800) 499-2220

McBEE MOTEL COTTAGES
888 S Hemlock St (97110)
Rates: $39-$99
Tel: (503) 436-2569

QUIET CANNON LODGINGS
372 N Spruce St (97110)
Rates: $85-$95
Tel: (503) 436-1405

SURFSAND RESORT
Oceanfront & Gower Sts (97110)
Rates: $109-$299
Tel: (503) 436-2274
(800) 546-6100

TOLOVANA INN
3400 S Hemlock St (97110)
Rates: $68-$239
Tel: (503) 436-2211
(800) 333-8890

VIKING MOTEL
Matanuska & S Pacific (97110)
Rates: $139-$159
Tel: (503) 436-2274
(800) 547-6100

Hotel Policies May Be Subject To Change

RECREATION

ECOLA STATE PARK - Leashes

Info: A 1300-acre park, this seaside oasis serves up miles of shoreline scenery for you and the pupster to explore. Fabulous views of Cannon Beach, Haystack Rock, the Coast Range, Tillamook Rock Lighthouse and the Pacific Ocean are part of the lure. In 1806, Captain William Clark of the Lewis and Clark Expedition named a creek in this area Ecola Creek from the Chinook Indian word "Ekoli" meaning whale.

The mixture of basalt and sedimentary rock which comprises the cliffs provides an interesting contrast of colors and textures, while splendid examples of old-growth Sitka spruce enhance the setting. Don't be surprised if an elegant elk or black-tailed deer crosses your path. Tote a camera and snap to your heart's content. Birders, don't forget the binocs, the diversity of songbirds and shorebirds is outstanding. If you're in the mood for a little Rexercise, hightail it to the cliff trail that spans the distance of the park. FYI: The 100' high basalt sea stack standing a mile offshore is Tillamook Rock. For more information: (503) 436-2844.

Directions: From Cannon Beach, travel north on Highway 101 for 2 miles to the signed park entrance.

Note: Entrance fee may be charged.

HAYSTACK ROCK - Leashes

Info: The most photographed haystack, this basalt monolith rises 235' above the beach. Like sentinels of old, the haystacks seem to guard the waters. You and your beach hound can walk for miles on the hard-packed shoreline watching the pretty Pacific, the unending rolling waves capped in foamy white. Between April and June, observe colorful tufted puffins, adorable little critters that favor this spot at nesting time. These squat, black birds have large, bright orange bills, white facial features and tufts of white feathers above their eyes. They can be seen on the grassy north slope of Haystack Rock where they burrow tunnels into the soil to protect their eggs and chicks from predators.

On the south facing cliffs of the rock, Pelagic cormorants build nests of seaweed on the narrow ledges high above the surf. This species is also easy to identify. They're lanky, greenish-black birds who, after crash diving for din-din, hold their wings outstretched to dry in the breeze. A designated "Marine Garden," this territory is home to a wide array of bird and marine life. At low tide, you and the wagger can sample some interesting tide pooling which might include multicolored starfish, crabs and chitons. For more information: (503) 436-2623.

Directions: Located off Highway 101 at milepost 30.5.

HUG POINT STATE PARK - Leashes

Info: The name of this park is derived from the fact that the old road leading past this section of beach was so treacherous that travelers literally had to hug the rock to pass around the point. Get a jumpstart on your morning and walk this often misty, moody beach. Not only will you be treated to an expansive beach setting but you're bound to make some friends. Although the sign indicates leashes, during the off season, you'll meet plenty of local canines running free. Rosie and Max met some and they'd like to bark their hellos to Charlie Bear, Annie Oakley, Butch Cassidy and Calamity Jane, four lucky dogs and their people, Barbara, Kandy and Nancy. As dog owners know, one dog leads to another and another and some of the best friendships you'll ever have. For more information: (800) 551-6949.

Directions: Located several miles south of Cannon Beach off Highway 101 at milepost 33.7.

KLOOTCHIE CREEK PARK - Leashes

Info: Tree hounds, you'll want to make a stop at this pretty little park and check out the largest Sitka spruce in the U.S. The 400-year old tree stands by a popular fishing area.

Directions: From Cannon Beach Junction, take Highway 26 east for five miles to the park.

OSWALD WEST STATE PARK - Leashes

Info: It's hard to imagine the thunderous Pacific on one side and a verdant songbird-filled rain forest on the other, but that's exactly what you and your gleeful goofball will unearth if you plan an afternoon delight at this charming park of nearly 2,500 acres. A combination of dirt and gravel pathways slice through a landscape of plush greenery. Wooden bridges, clear running streams, dew-dappled vegetation like sword fern, moss and lichen, grassy expanses (think picnic), majestic towering trees and huge nurse logs come together to form a postcardian setting. Park on the east side of the parking lot, walk towards the restrooms, cross the wooden bridge to the picnic area and find yourself in a forested haven. Après lunch, try some tootsie dipping or take a hike and consider yourself one lucky dog. For more information: (800) 551-6949.

Directions: From Cannon Beach, travel south on Highway 101 for 10 miles to milepost 39 and the parking area.

The numbered hike that follows is within Oswald West State Park:

1) COAST TRAIL HIKE - Leashes

Beginner/0.75 miles/0.50 hours

Info: Although you can hear the sounds of the highway at the onset, that distraction will soon be forgotten, replaced by the pleasant gurgling of the fast-running stream and the quietude of the rain forest ambience. Tree huggers, you're gonna love the amazing collection of trees and other flora that envelop you like a warm green cocoon. Hundreds of species survive side by side in this lush environment, each finding their own niche. The boardwalk bridge signals the nearness of the sand. FYI: The towering trees that provide the shade are Sitka spruce, giant sentinels that guard the moody, often fog-enshrouded coastline. The rugged, pristine beach is a favorite with the surfing set. And who can blame them. The setting is idyllic. Tall cliffs backdrop the sandy shores which are riddled with driftwood and inhabited by pelicans and other sea birds. Beachcomb for sand dollars or agate. If it's low tide, try tide pooling. Wowser Bowser, what an adventure. Just heed the warnings about the unpredictability of the Pacific.

Directions: From Cannon Beach, travel south on Highway 101 for 10 miles to milepost 39 and parking area.

TOLOVANA BEACH STATE WAYSIDE - Leashes

Info: Here you'll find beach access, picnic tables, benches, a water fountain and lots of parking. The walkable beach stretches for miles in either direction, offering grand views of the haystacks. Take the pupster for an early morning jaunt when the beach is nearly deserted and enjoy the solitude and serenity of the setting. For more information: (800) 551-6949

Directions: From Cannon Beach, travel south on Highway 101 to milepost 30.8 and signs.

CANYONVILLE

LODGING

LEISURE INN
554 SW Pine St (97417)
Rates: $31-$50
Tel: (541) 839-4278

RECREATION

BEAVER SWAMP TRAIL to FISH LAKE HIKE

Intermediate/3.5 miles/2.0 hours

Info: When you'd like to combine a road trip with a hiking excursion, pencil in this adventure in your filofax and put a twinkle in the hikemeister's eyes. Although it may not seem that way after the lengthy drive, this is the shortest route to pretty Fish Lake. Once you've arrived, you and the pup will zigzag through a variety of hardwoods and evergreenery while you're serenaded by songbirds. An interesting perspective of forest fire damage can be yours on this trail which leads amidst an area burned by a lightning fire in 1987. Look for signs of rejuvenation and pioneer plantlife in this region. When you junction with Fish Lake Trail, it's less than half a mile to your final destination, shimmering Fish Lake. Chill out with some doggie paddling. If you've planned ahead, break some bread and biscuits with your best bud and just enjoy the solitude. Do an about-face at day's end. For more information: (541) 825-3201.

Hotel Policies May Be Subject To Change

Directions: From Canyonville, travel east on Route 1 for 23 miles to the Tiller Ranger Station. From the Ranger Station, take CR 46 which becomes South Umpqua Road (#28). Travel FS 28 to FS 2823 and drive to the junction with FS 2830. Follow FS 2830 to FS 2840. Take FS 2840 past Fish Lake Trailhead to FS 2840-400 and the Beaver Swamp Trailhead.

Note: The trail is approximately 55 miles from Canyonville and 32 miles from the Tiller Ranger Station. Proceed with caution on forest roads. Trail is not recommended for hiking in winter.

PUP PRAIRIE TRAIL HIKE

Beginner/4.0 miles/2.0 hours

Info: This trek along the Rogue-Umpqua divide is nothing short of spectacular. From the get-go, you'll know you're about to experience one howl of a great hike. At the intersection with the Asker Divide Trail, take a quick 200' jaunt to your left for an encounter with a near record-setting Douglas fir that has a diameter measuring 10' 6". Talk about thick waisted. Backtrack to the trail and get set to enter an enchanted world of fragrant firs and incense cedars. You're sure to get tails wagging in the breeze as you skedaddle across three mountain meadows that, in summer, are emblazoned with vibrant wildflowers. Pack plenty of Kodak, this place eats film. At Trail #1470, turn the hound around, you're homeward bound. For more information: (541) 825-3201.

Directions: From Canyonville, travel east on Route 1 for 23 miles to Tiller Ranger Station. From the Ranger Station, travel CR 46 to Jackson Creek Road (#29). Follow Road #29 to FS 2947. Take 2947 to 2947-400 and veer right at the fork to the Cripple Camp Trailhead.

Note: Trail is approximately 51 miles from Canyonville and 28 miles from the Tiller Ranger Station. Proceed with caution on forest roads. Trail is not recommended for hiking in winter or early spring.

CASCADE LOCKS

LODGING

BEST WESTERN COLUMBIA RIVER INN
735 Wanapa St (97014)
Rates: $54-$119
Tel: (541) 374-8777
(800) 595-7108

SCANDIAN MOTOR LODGE
25 Oneonta St (97014)
Rates: $32-$48
Tel: (541) 374-8417

BRIDGE OF THE GODS MOTEL
630 Wanapa St (97014)
Rates: $46-$65
Tel: (541) 374-8628

RECREATION

CASCADE LOCKS MARINE PARK - Leashes

Info: Doggistorians give this national historic site in the heart of Cascade Locks the high five. Built in 1896, the locks allowed travelers to traverse the often treacherous Columbia. Submerged in 1938, only the upper portion of Marine Park remains as a testament to the craftsmanship of a time gone by. The chilly and often rough waters of the Columbia River ripple beside the 20-acre parkland where you and your canine companion can pull up a shady spot and do nothing for a change. Another slice of the past is Oregon's first locomotive, "The Oregon Pony," preserved in the park. And if hiking's to your liking, a two-mile section of the Pacific Crest Trail bisects the park. Go ahead, make your mutt's day. For more information: (541) 374-8619.

Directions: Off Wa-Na-Pa Street on Marine Park Drive.

Note: Dogs are prohibited from the museums but permitted in the visitor's center.

HERMAN CREEK TRAIL HIKE

Intermediate/2.0 miles/1.0 hours

Info: You and your soon-to-be-dirty dog will skirt the namesake creek in Herman Canyon where water hijinks come with the territory. Portions of the trail hook up with the Pacific Crest National Scenic Trail, a clue to the prettiness that awaits. You can expand your options on the spur to Nick Eaton Ridge and postcardian vistas. If you'd like to make a day of it, pack your sack with snacks, a good read, a tough chew and go for it. For more information: (503) 668-1400.

Hotel Policies May Be Subject To Change

Directions: From Cascade Locks, take Forest Lane east to the trailhead at the forest service work center on Forest Lane.

COLUMBIA RIVER GORGE

Info: See Hood River, Portland, The Dalles and Troutdale for additional lodging and recreation.

CAVE JUNCTION

LODGING

COUNTRY HILLS RESORT
7901 Caves Hwy (97523)
Rates: $40-$50
Tel: (541) 592-3406
(800) 997-8464

RUSK RANCH COUNTRY COTTAGE
27742 Redwood Hwy
Box 270 (97523)
Rates: $48-$75
Tel: (541) 592-4658

RECREATION

BABYFOOT LAKE TRAIL HIKE - Leashes

Beginner/5.2 miles/3.0 hours

Info: Set in a region of wineries, this pretty trail makes for a delightful afternoon of fun with Fido. The icy cold waters of the alpine lake are a sure cure for those lazy, hazy days of summer. Fishing fiends, pack your gear, who knows, you might dine on eastern brook trout. If flowers power the sniffmeister's tail, come in springtime for a bonus of kaleidoscopic wild ones. The trail ends at the Chetco Trail junction. For more information: (541) 592-2166.

Directions: From Cave Junction, head north on Highway 199 approximately 4 miles to C R 5240 and turn left (west). Follow C R 5240 to FS 4201. Continue west on FS 4201 about 11 miles to a left on FS 140 to the trailhead.

BOLAN LAKE TRAIL HIKE - Leashes

Beginner/Intermediate/3.6 miles/2.0 hours

Info: Lovely Bolan Lake and panoramic Bolan Lookout are just two bonafido good reasons to hike this trail. Taking off from the lake, the trail climbs a ridge through an open timber stand and shimmies through high mountain meadows before topping out at the lookout. After your workout, try your line, the fishing's fine. For more information: (541) 592-2166.

Directions: From Cave Junction, head south on Highway 199 for one mile to a left at Rockydale Road. Go approximately 8 miles to road's end, making a left on Happy Camp Road (#5828). Follow Happy Camp Road about 15 miles to Bolan Lake Road (#4812) and turn left. Continue on Bolan Lake Road for 6 miles to a signed junction. Make a left onto FS 040 to the trailhead at the lake.

CAVE CREEK TRAIL HIKE - Leashes

Beginner/Intermediate/4.0 miles/2.0 hours

Info: If your pooch is a water dog at heart, he'll cover your face with puppy kisses when he sees what's in store along this delightful trail. Cave Creek can't be beat on those hot diggety dog diggety days of summer. Once you reach the Oregon Caves National Monument boundary, turn the hound around, you're homeward bound. Nope, dogs aren't permitted in the caves. For more information: (541) 592-2166.

Directions: From Cave Junction, head east on Highway 46 for 17 miles to the trailhead at the Cave Creek Campground.

ELK CREEK TRAIL HIKE - Leashes

Intermediate/4.0 miles/2.0 hours

Info: You and Snoopy can work out the kinks with some water hijinks on this cool hike that skirts creekside through dense woodlands before ending at a scenic ridgetop. Partake of the views and do some tootsie dipping in the refreshing creek before calling it a day. For more information: (541) 592-2166.

Directions: From Cave Junction, head east on Highway 46 about 9 miles to FS 4611. Follow FS 4611 southeast about 4 miles to FS 079. Turn right and follow FS 079 to the trailhead.

FEHLEY GULCH TRAIL HIKE - Leashes

Intermediate/5.2 miles/3.0 hours

Info: Dollars to dog biscuits, you and your gung-ho hiker are bound to burn some kibble on this steep hike through the Red Buttes Wilderness. Once you access the trail, you're in for a 1.6-mile trek that covers a 1,300' ascent. Take your time to make for a fun-filled day of mini explorations. Along the way, stop every so often for a few well deserved dips in the "brrr" waters of Fehley Gulch. For more information: (541) 592-2166.

Directions: From Cave Junction, head east on Highway 46 about 9 miles to FS 4612. Turn right on FS 4612 and continue about 6 miles to FS 098. Follow FS 098 to the Sucker Creek Trailhead. Hike this trail about one mile to the Fehley Gulch Trail junction.

KALMIOPSIS RIM TRAIL HIKE - Leashes

Intermediate/9.0 miles/5.0 hours

Info: In order to make the most of your outing, plan to spend the day on this trail. The spectacular views, wildflower-strewn ridges and rugged scenery will leave you breathless and glad you made the effort. Load up on Fuji, power snacks and H_2O. You're about to experience an unforgettable afternoon of hiking pleasure. For more information: (541) 592-2166.

Directions: From Cave Junction, head north on Highway 199 approximately 4 miles to C R 5240 and turn left (west). Follow C R 5240 to FS 4201. Continue west on FS 4201 about 11 miles to FS 141. Make a right on FS 141 to the trailhead at the end of the road.

KINGS SADDLE TRAIL HIKE - Leashes

Beginner/1.2 miles/0.75 hours

Info: Short, sweet and scenic, the trail meanders atop a ridge passing through old-growth forests and beautiful mountain meadows, a pretty avenue to both Bolan Lake and Bolan Lookout. If flowers power Bowser's tail, plan a spring sojourn when the wildflowers strut their fabulous stuff. For more information: (541) 592-2166.

Directions: From Cave Junction, head south on Highway 199 for one mile to a left at Rockydale Road. Go approximately 8 miles to road's end, making a left on Happy Camp Road (#5828). Follow Happy Camp Road about 15 miles to Bolan Lake Road (#4812) and turn left. Continue on Bolan Lake Road for 6 miles to a signed junction. Make a right onto FS 041 to the trailhead.

MEADOW MOUNTAIN TRAIL HIKE - Leashes

Intermediate/2.2 miles/1.5 hours

Info: Filled with lakes, this mountain-based trek offers incredible scenery along with sun-splashed alpine watering holes. Triple your pleasure in springtime when the wild ones throw their annual party. This hike rates two paws up in the color department. Tote a panoramic camera and take home some wide and wonderful glossies. For more information: (541) 592-2166.

Directions: From Cave Junction, head east on Highway 46 about 9 miles to FS 4613. Turn left on FS 4613 and continue about 2 miles to FS 070 and make a right to reach the trailhead.

SANGER CREEK TRAIL HIKE - Leashes

Intermediate/3.6 miles/2.5 hours

Info: When quietude and solitude top your list, this hike's got your name on it. Hop on and find yourself in a high elevation woodland in the Suzuki Wilderness, where nature and serenity reign supreme. Cool your tootsies in the Illinois River and spend some quality time with your numero uno pal. Retrace the pawprints on the return trip. For more information: (541) 592-2166.

Directions: From Cave Junction, head south on Highway 199 about 5 miles to Waldo Road. Turn left on Waldo Road and continue south about 2 miles to FS 4803. Turn right and follow FS 4803 to FS 130. Turn left on FS 130, following it past Whiskey Lake to the trailhead.

Hotel Policies May Be Subject To Change

SANGER PEAK LOOKOUT TRAIL HIKE - Leashes

Intermediate/1.2 miles/1.0 hours

Info: Short on distance but long on effort, you and the furball are in for a steep, rocky climb to Sanger Peak Lookout. But if you're up for the challenge, this peekaboo point has a slew of rugged vistas for your memory banks. On a clear day, you'll feel like you can see forever. For more information: (541) 592-2166.

Directions: From Cave Junction, head south on Highway 199 about 5 miles to Waldo Road. Turn left on Waldo Road and continue south about 2 miles to FS 4803. Turn right and follow FS 4803 to the trailhead.

SUCKER CREEK TRAIL HIKE - Leashes

Beginner/Intermediate/5.0 miles/3.0 hours

Info: When you're seeking a fairly easy way to experience a wilderness adventure, don't miss this beaut. Complete with wildflower-splashed meadows and refreshing Sucker Creek, you and the dawgus will get your money's worth out of this one. For more information: (541) 592-2166.

Directions: From Cave Junction, head east on Highway 46 about 9 miles to FS 4612. Turn right on FS 4612 and continue about 6 miles to FS 098. Follow FS 098 to the trailhead.

TANNEN LAKES TRAIL HIKE - Leashes

Beginner/Intermediate/8.0 miles/5.0 hours

Info: Covering the gamut of dense forests, verdant meadows, beautiful alpine lakes and spectacular wildflower displays, this ruggedly scenic hike has something for every outdoor breed. Able anglers, bring your gear and try your luck in one of the trail's namesakes. BYOB (bring your own biscuits) and do lunch beside the lake or in a bosky grove. Pack plenty of water, this is a long haul and you're gonna need it. For more information: (541) 592-2166.

Directions: From Cave Junction, head south on Highway 199 for one mile to Rocky Dale Road. Turn left on Rocky Dale

Road approximately 8 miles to road's end, making a left on Happy Camp Road (#5828). Follow Happy Camp Road about 15 miles to Bolan Lake Road (#4812) and turn left. Continue on Bolan Lake Road for 6 miles to a signed junction. Make a right onto FS 041 to the trailhead.

CHARLESTON

LODGING

CAPTAIN JOHN'S MOTEL
8061 Kingfisher Dr (97420)
Rates: $40-$70
Tel: (541) 888-4041

RECREATION

SOUTH SLOUGH NATIONAL ESTUARINE RESERVE - Leashes

Info: Hightail it to the place where the rivers meet the sea and see the unique environment that's created when freshwater mixes with saltwater. You and the wagger will have a bounty of plant, animal and bird life to observe in one of the world's most productive natural resources. South Slough's 4,400 acres provide a rare opportunity to visit an estuary left in a virtually wild and pristine state. Make tracks along one of the trails and come away with a sense of what nature is all about. For more information: (541) 888-5558.

Directions: From Charleston, take Seven Devils Road south for 4 miles to the reserve.

The numbered hikes that follow are within
South Slough National Estuarine Reserve:

1) ESTUARY STUDY TRAIL HIKE - Leashes

Intermediate/3.0 miles/1.5 hours

Info: You and old brown eyes will begin your trek in the uplands where flyboys flutter through the treetops and raccoons, bobcats and bald eagles find refuge in the forestlands. Follow the Hidden Creek drainage down the valley to the slough and while you traverse the terrain, take note of the dra-

Hotel Policies May Be Subject To Change

matic change of scenery. As you descend to the lower elevations, the woodlands give way to open channels and salt marshes. Expect wet paws and tootsies and a grin from ear-to-ear when you crisscross the creek a couple times before reaching the boardwalk which guides you amidst the fresh and saltwater marshes. Binocs give you the opportunity for up-close observations of the interesting shorebirds. You'll eventually arrive at an overlook where views of the mudflats and open water channel complete the picture. Once you make it to the edge, finish your loop-de-loop or lead your Curious George along the shoreline trail back to the starting gate.

Directions: From Charleston, take Seven Devils Road south for 4 miles to the reserve. To the trailhead, follow the sign at the interpretive center to a parking lot located a short distance down the gravel road. The trailhead begins at this parking lot.

2) TEN MINUTE LOOP TRAIL HIKE - Leashes

Beginner/0.25 miles/0.25 hours

Info: Put on your thinking caps, pick up a pamphlet at the interpretive center and get set to learn as you sojourn along this lovely little pathway. At the onset, on the uphill side, you'll notice unique needle-like plants that resemble a sword. These plants are indicative of common wetland flora that flourishes where the soil is waterlogged for long periods of time. Keep a keen snout out for salal, evergreen, huckleberry and Pacific wax myrtle. If you feel the leaves of these plants, you'll notice a leathery texture which allows water to drip off the leaf, nature's way of discouraging molds. These leaves also discourage insects and other plant eaters from foraging. Make note of the soil and rocks and the way the plants are dispersed. This pupsqueak trail packs a hefty punch of nature and puts you smack dab in the center of a fascinating world of beauty and discovery.

Directions: From Charleston, take Seven Devils Road south for 4 miles to the reserve. The trail begins at the interpretive center.

3) WASSON CREEK TRAIL HIKE - Leashes

Beginner/0.75 miles/0.5 hours

Info: Compact in length but bursting with diversity, you and the pupster will wander and gadabout a wonderful variety of habitats on this minute-sized trail. Beginning at a freshwater wetland where birds are abundant and wildflowers make their presence known, you'll quickly cross the valley and zoom through a soothing upland forest. Listen for nature's musicians as they serenade. Watch for birds of prey and elk and deer as you zigzag through the woodlands. Take your time on this one, it'll be over in a blink.

Directions: From Charleston, take Seven Devils Road south for 4 miles to the reserve. From the interpretive center, turn left onto Seven Devils Road and drive to Hinch Road. Make a left and drive one mile to a small "binocular" sign and the trailhead.

CHEMULT

LODGING

CHEMULT MOTEL
Hwy 97, Box 117 (97731)
Rates: $38-$44
Tel: (541) 365-2228

CRATER LAKE MOTEL & RV PARK
Hwy 97,
P.O. Box 190 (97731)
Rates: $27-$80
Tel: (541) 365-2241

DAWSON HOUSE LODGE
Hwy 97 & 1st St (97731)
Rates: $38-$55
Tel: (541) 365-2232

FEATHERBED INN
P.O. Box 128 (97731)
Rates: $27-$48
Tel: (541) 365-2235

HOLIDAY VILLAGE MOTEL & RV PARK
Hwy 97, Milepost 209 (97731)
Rates: $34-$36
Tel: (541) 365-2394

SINGING PINES RANCH MOTEL
Hwy 97, Box 117 (97731)
Rates: n/a
Tel: (541) 365-9909

Hotel Policies May Be Subject To Change

CHILOQUIN

LODGING

AGENCY LAKE RESORT
37000 Modoc Rd (97624)
Rates: $30-$45
Tel: (541) 783-2489

MELITA's MOTEL & RV PARK
39500 Hwy 97 N (97624)
Rates: $26-$53
Tel: (541) 783-2401

SPRING CREEK RANCH MOTEL
47600 Hwy 97 N (97624)
Rates: $22-$40
Tel: (541) 783-2775
(800) 626-1292

WILLIAMSON RIVER RESORT
31900 Modoc Rd (97624)
Rates: $25-$50
Tel: (541) 783-2071

RECREATION

UPPER KLAMATH MARSH NATIONAL WILDLIFE REFUGE - Leashes

Info: This sanctuary is a slice of an enormous refuge system that spans more than 180,000 acres in southern Oregon and northern California. A diverse habitat comprised of over 14,000 acres, this region represents the ultimate in escapism for nature and animal lovers. You and your gleeful pup will find a little bit of everything you adore in one very special place. This lush land is a combination of freshwater marsh and open water including Upper Klamath Lake, Pelican Bay and Agency Lake. In birdspeak, this site is perfect for the nesting and brood-rearing of waterfowl and colonial nesting birds like the American white pelican (the county mascot, this bird is a familiar sight on the local rivers and lakes) and a multitude of heron. Even the elusive and reclusive bald eagle is happy in the timberlands surrounding the lake. Lucky ducky dogs may spot one of these regal raptors soaring over the lake in search of food for its brood. The eagle, which mates for life, begins scouting for a good nesting spot in February with the young hatching around April. Tote your binocs or a scope for an up-close encounter of the eagle kind. Other bird sightings include pacific loon, western screech, spotted owl and a few wood-pecker species. Camera buffs, plan accordingly, this wonder-land eats Fuji. For more information: (916) 667-2231.

Directions: From Chiloquin, travel Route 97 north about 20 miles to Silver Lake Road, turn right. Follow Silver Lake Road to the refuge bordered by Highway 140, Route 97 and Highway 62.

Locate Other Dog-Friendly Activities...Check Nearby Cities

CLACKAMAS

LODGING

CLACKAMAS INN
16010 SE 82nd Dr (97266)
Rates: $110
Tel: (503) 650-5340
(800) 874-6560

CLATSKANIE

LODGING

NORTHWOODS INN
945 E Columbia River Hwy (97016)
Rates: n/a
Tel: (503) 728-4311

COLUMBIA RIVER GORGE

See Cascade Locks, Hood River, The Dalles, Portland and Troutdale for additional lodging and recreation.

RECREATION

Info: Starting just east of Portland and continuing to The Dalles, the Columbia River Gorge is America's largest and oldest national scenic area. The ancestral Columbia River canyon was formed 12,000 years ago when receding glaciers in northern Idaho and Montana created a series of floods which swept down the Columbia River Valley. I-84 and the scenic Historic Columbia Highway run parallel to the river.

Your travels will be bordered by steep cliffs, misty mountains and woodsy trails that are meant to tempt you to have a look-see. You can hike waterfall trails, explore gorges, picnic in green oases or park yourself under a tree and become one with nature. Wildflower devotees, you'll think the flora is heavenscent. The Gorge's wide ranges of elevation and precipitation equate to a profusion of bloomers. Many of the species are found only in the Gorge, their glorious pink, yellow, fuschia and white colors grace the rocky areas, moist slopes, basalt cliffs, shaded banks and open woods of this pristine region. For more information: (503) 668-1400.

Hotel Policies May Be Subject To Change

COOS BAY

LODGING

BEST WESTERN HOLIDAY MOTEL
411 N Bayshore Dr (97420)
Rates: $55-$115
Tel: (541) 269-5111
(800) 228-8655

COOS BAY MANOR B&B
955 S 5th St (97420)
Rates: $65-$100
Tel: (541) 269-1224
(800) 269-1224

EDGEWATER INN
275 E Johnson St (97420)
Rates: $67-$72
Tel: (541) 267-0423
(800) 233-0423

LAZY J MOTEL
1143 Hill St (97420)
Rates: n/a
Tel: (541) 269-9666

MOTEL 6 PREMIER
1445 N Bayshore Dr (97420)
Rates: $32-$42
Tel: (541) 267-7171
(800) 440-6000

PLAINVIEW MOTEL & RV PARK
2760 Cape Arago Hwy (97420)
Rates: $29-$50
Tel: (541) 888-5166
(800) 962-2815

RED LION INN
1313 N Bayshore Dr (97420)
Rates: $69-$104
Tel: (541) 267-4141
(800) 547-8010

SEA PSALM MOTEL
1250 Cape Arago Hwy (97420)
Rates: $30-$35
Tel: (541) 888-9053

TIMBER LODGE MOTEL
1001 N Bayshore Dr (97420)
Rates: n/a
Tel: (541) 267-7066
(800) 782-7592

RECREATION

BASTENDORFF BEACH COUNTY PARK - Leashes

Info: Maximize your pleasure at this beachside park with a visit in early evening when you can witness the drama and beauty of the setting sun. As streaks of orange and purple slowly become one with the blueness of the bay, you'll be mesmerized by the loveliness of it all. For a feel good stroll, nothing can top a beachside saunter with your numero uno Bruno at sunset.

Directions: From Coos Bay, travel Cape Arago Highway south to the hamlet of Charleston. Pass through Charleston, heading east to the exit for the park.

Note: Dogs are not permitted in picnic area, viewing platform or playground. Keep your dog off the grass.

Locate Other Dog-Friendly Activities...Check Nearby Cities

BAY FRONT WALK - Leashes

Info: Nautical noodnicks and old sea dogs won't want to miss this short tour through downtown Coos Bay. The paved path wanders past a flag display and busy shipping port where you're likely to see cargoes of wood chips (a major export) being loaded aboard the seabound vessels. Bring your binocs, seabirds on the fly and marine mammals sunning on the rocks are part of the diorama.

Directions: Off Anderson Street in downtown Coos Bay.

EMPIRE LAKES PARK - Leashes

Info: When you're looking for a slice of primitive nature, take the pup to this relatively untouched parcel of land. Get your Rexercise along a hiking/biking trail that laces the parkland and get an eyeful of scenic views as you do. Lots of flyboys cover the treetops so tote your binocs and do some birding as well.

Directions: Located off Newmark Avenue.

MINGUS PARK - Leashes

Info: This park is guaranteed to tantalize the senses. For canine connoisseurs, the elegant Japanese and rhododendron gardens are enhanced by a gazebo and a charming duck pond. The Mingus Park Pond Walk is a quickie half-mile jaunt to the garden and pond, where bobbing ducks provide the entertainment. This neighborhood green scene comes complete with picnic tables, scenic and photo viewpoints, softball fields and tennis courts. The mutt will definitely want to strut his stuff at this busy setting.

Directions: Located on 10th and Commercial.

SIMPSON REEF OVERLOOK - Leashes

Info: Salty sea dogs might be hard pressed to leave this great overlook, the perfect place for some whale watching during migrating seasons (November through May). But no matter what season, the antics of the resident sea lions and seals can always be counted upon to amuse.

Directions: From Coos Bay, travel Cape Arago Highway south about 13.5 miles to the overlook.

Hotel Policies May Be Subject To Change

SUNSET BAY STATE PARK - Leashes

Info: For a combo plate of green and blue, this oceanside tableau fills the bill. A 400-acre park, there's enough to do to warrant an all-day excursion. The small bay is set inside deep sandstone bluffs with a narrow passage to the Pacific. Stroll the rocky intertidal pathway where a variety of sea life thrives, like sea stars, purple sea urchins, chitons, snails, mussels, crabs, sponges and shrimp. Between the deep blue sea and the trickling waters of Big Creek which winds through the grassy plains, you'll find lots of pupportunities for wet and wild adventures. Leave your paw prints behind as you amble along the sandy beach. Pack a beach blanket, a good read for yourself and a tough chew for your barking buddy and enjoy a dog's life. For more information: (541) 888-4902.

Directions: From Coos Bay, travel 12 miles south on the Cape Arago Highway and follow signs to the park.

COQUILLE

LODGING

MYRTLE LANE MOTEL
787 N Central (97423)
Rates: $35-$37
Tel: (541) 396-2102

RECREATION

LAVERNE COUNTY PARK - Leashes

Info: Situated on the north fork of the Coquille River, this 300-acre oasis offers fine fishing and lots of playful pupportunities, particularly in summer. Fishy dreams can come true if you try your fly on cutthroat trout, Chinook salmon and winter steelhead. Pull up a green square and cloudgaze the day away. Or burn some kibble with a bit of exploring. For more information: (541) 396-2344.

Directions: From Coquille, travel 15 miles north on the Coquille-Fairview Road to the park entrance.

CORVALLIS

LODGING

ASHWOOD B&B
2940 NW Ashwood Dr (97330)
Rates: $60-$70
Tel: (541) 757-9772
(800) 306-5136

BUDGET INN
1480 SW 3rd St (97330)
Rates: $38-$65
Tel: (541) 752-8756

ECONO LODGE
345 NW 2nd St (97330)
Rates: $36-$50
Tel: (541) 752-9601
(800) 553-2666

HARRISON HOUSE B&B
2310 NW Harrison (97330)
Rates: $45-$65
Tel: (541) 752-6248
(800) 233-6248

JASON INN
800 NW 9th St (97330)
Rates: $36-$48
Tel: (541) 753-7326
(800) 346-3291

MOTEL ORLEANS
935 NW Garfield (97330)
Rates: $36-$50
Tel: (541) 758-9125
(800) 626-1900

SHANICO INN
1113 NW 9th St (97330)
Rates: $48-$64
Tel: (541) 754-7474
(800) 432-1233

SUPER 8 MOTEL
407 NW 2nd St (97330)
Rates: $47-$65
Tel: (541) 758-8088
(800) 800-8000

TOWNE HOUSE MOTOR INN
350 SW 4th St (97330)
Rates: $45-$50
Tel: (541) 753-4496
(800) 898-4496

RECREATION

E.E. WILSON WILDLIFE AREA - Leashes

Info: Established in 1950, this former WWII training facility encompasses more than 1,600 acres, providing a vast wildlife refuge for conservation and education. The region includes an array of habitat communities and supports a bounty of animal life including sensitive species like the western pond turtle, trumpeter swan and bald eagle. A gamut of flyboys, swimmers and four-legged critters reside in a diversified environment of Oregon white oak woodlands, ash swales and remnants of native prairies. If you're into photography, you'll be impressed by the number of photo ops you'll encounter. Broaden your knowledge and explore the interpretive nature trail where you'll come away with insight into these fascinat-

Hotel Policies May Be Subject To Change

ing habitats. Anyway you slice it, this refuge is a doggone nice way to spend the day. For more information: (541) 745-5334.

Directions: From Corvallis, travel Highway 99W north about 9 miles to the E. E. Wilson Wildlife Area on the east side of Highway 99W.

Note: Use extreme caution during hunting season. Open daily during daylight hours.

The numbered hike that follows is within the E. E. Wilson Wildlife Area:

1) INTERPRETIVE TRAIL HIKE - Leashes

Beginner/1.0 miles/0.5 hours

Info: Get a major dose of flora and fauna on this interesting and educational pathway. Interpretive signs guide you and your tagalong through a myriad of habitats including forests and wetlands and a stand of Oregon white oak. Watch for the squirrel-like dusky footed wood rat, beaver, wood duck and black-tailed deer. And learn what you can about the flora which combines an extraordinary mix of trees with a lush understory. Quiet canines will be treated to the soulful sounds of songbirds as they drift through the oak trees. No bones about it, this is one delightful jaunt. For more information: (541) 745-5334.

Directions: From Corvallis, travel Highway 99W north about 9 miles to the E. E. Wilson Wildlife Area on the east side of Highway 99W. The trailhead is behind the holding pens.

Note: Use extreme caution during hunting season. Open daily during daylight hours.

McDONALD RESEARCH FOREST - Leashes

Info: If you're as much a tree enthusiast as your sniffmeister, you won't want to miss this 7,000-acre research forest. The lush land is primarily used as a living laboratory for research and education but serves up plenty of recreation for you and your inquisitive canine. Investigate the interesting landscape while you and furball peruse the 70 research projects in the works. Over 10 miles of interpretive trails honeycomb the woodlands and highlight numerous aspects of forest ecology and management. Just point your nose in any direction and the let the sniff fest begin. For more information: (541) 737-4452.

Locate Other Dog-Friendly Activities...Check Nearby Cities

Directions: From Corvallis, head west on Harrison Boulevard about 2 miles until it becomes Oak Creek Drive, leading to the forest entrance. You can also access the forest off Lester Avenue, Lewisburg Avenue, Soap Creek Road, Highway 99W and through the Peavy Arboretum off Arboretum Road.

Note: Leave research projects undisturbed. Closed from 10 p.m. to 5 a.m.

The numbered activity that follows is within the McDonald Research Forest:

1) PEAVY ARBORETUM - Leashes

Info: Located within the McDonald Research Forest, this 40-acre woodland is the perfect place for the whiffing woofer. The fragrant thicket is a small chunk of the 7,000-acre research forest where over seventy research projects are underway. Test your tree knowledge and see how many of the 200 native and non-native trees and shrubs you can identify. Several pathways await you and your carousing canine at this tree-fest where an up-close encounter with the natural and historical richness of the region awaits. And while you're indulging yourself in a botany lesson, you'll be soothed by the coolness and quietude of your surroundings. For more information: (541) 737-4452.

Directions: From Corvallis, travel Highway 99W to Arboretum Road. Take Arboretum Road to the entrance.

Note: Leave research projects undisturbed. Closed from 10 p.m. to 5 a.m.

MEADOW EDGE TRAIL HIKE

Beginner/1.6 miles/1.0 hours

Info: On a clear day, you'll be able to see forever, or so it will seem, when you hop on the trail and traverse the 4,097' summit of Mary's Peak. From your lofty perch, staggering views of western Oregon, Mount Jefferson, Mount Hood, Mount Bachelor, The Sisters, Mount Rainier, Mount Adams and Mount St. Helens will greet you at every turn, inviting you to click your Kodak and perhaps capture the scenic wonder of it all. Springtime doubles your pleasure with a kaleidoscopic bounty of wildflowers. Complete the perfect afternoon interlude with a biscuit basket for two. For more information: (541) 487-5811.

Hotel Policies May Be Subject To Change

Directions: From Corvallis, travel west on Highway 20 about 4 miles to the junction with Highway 34. Take Highway 34 south to Mary's Peak and turn right. Proceed to Mary's Peak Campground and the trailhead, located about 6 miles west of Highway 34.

Note: Day use permit required.

COTTAGE GROVE

LODGING

BEST WESTERN VILLAGE GREEN
725 Row River Rd (97424)
Rates: $59-$89
Tel: (541) 942-2491
(800) 528-1234

CITY CENTER MOTEL
737 Hwy 99 S (97424)
Rates: $30-$35
Tel: (541) 942-8322

COMFORT INN
845 Gateway Blvd (97424)
Rates: $60-$100
Tel: (541) 942-9747
(800) 944-0287

HOLIDAY INN EXPRESS
1601 Gateway Blvd (97424)
Rates: $40-$125
Tel: (541) 941-1000
(800) 465-4329

RAINBOW MOTEL
1030 Pacific Hwy 99 N (97424)
Rates: $25-$30
Tel: (541) 942-5132

RIVER COUNTRY INN
71864 London Rd (97424)
Rates: $65
Tel: (541) 942-9334

RECREATION

BOHEMIA MOUNTAIN TRAIL HIKE - Leashes

Intermediate/1.6 miles/1.0 hours

Info: A perfect trail for some Rexercise and exploring, you'll step lively up the side of Bohemia Mountain, the highest point in the Cottage Grove District. On a crisp autumn day when wispy clouds float by, you'll feel like you can see forever from your airy aerie. The peaks of the evergreen Cascades quickly come into view, stretching from Mt. Hood to Mt. Shasta. As you traverse the mountainside, look below and you'll see Music Mine and Bohemia City. Sharp eyes will uncover evidence of past gold mining activity. In springtime, your voyage will include a polka dot showing of wildflowers along the rocky meadows and bluffs. Way to go Fido. For more information: (541) 942-5591.

Locate Other Dog-Friendly Activities...Check Nearby Cities

Directions: From Cottage Grove, travel Row River Road (FS 2400) east for 19 miles to Brice Creek Road (FS 2470). Turn right onto FS 2470 and drive 12 miles to Noonday Road (FS 2212). Make a right and continue on FS 2212 for 8.8 miles to the Champion Saddle junction with Sharps Creek Road (FS 2460). Turn left on FS 2460 and drive 1.1 miles to Bohemia Saddle. Turn left on the road leading to Bohemia Saddle County Park and look for the trailhead 200' on the right.

Note: Many of the forest roads are gravel, drive with care. The trail is recommended for use summer-fall.

SWORDFERN TRAIL HIKE

Beginner / 1.5 miles / 0.75 hours

Info: A doggone terrific exploration beckons to you and poochface beside Layng Creek where a stunning stand of second-growth Douglas fir creates a cooling, serene canopy and lush sword fern tells the understory. In summer, this is one cool loop-de-loop hike for hot dogs. When you leave Layng Creek behind, you'll be up, up and on your way to an old logging road where evidence of early 20th century logging activity is still visible to keen eyes. If you choose to visit in fall, you'll find an enchanting mix of autumnal colors splashed over the landscape. For more information: (541) 952-5591.

Directions: From Cottage Grove, travel Row River Road (FS 2400) east 17 miles to Layng Creek Road (FS 17) and turn left. Drive 2 miles to the Rujada Campground on the left-hand side. The trail begins at the Rujada Picnic Area.

CRATER LAKE

LODGING

WHISPERING PINES MOTEL
Hwy 138 & 97
Diamond Lake Jct (97604)
Rates: $30-$35
Tel: (541) 365-2259

Hotel Policies May Be Subject To Change

CRESCENT

LODGING

WOODSMAN COUNTRY LODGE
Hwy 97, P.O. Box 54 (97733)
Rates: $35-$47
Tel: (541) 433-2710

RECREATION

MAIDEN LAKE TRAIL HIKE - Leashes

Intermediate/12.0 miles/7.0 hours

Info: When you truly want to get away from it all on a day-long excursion, strap on the pawdometer, pack a hearty biscuit basket and just do it. You and your canine companion will find yourselves in a dramatic stand of mountain hemlock and fir. You'll also encounter aromatic lodgepole pines and plenty of scenic resting spots, aka picnic nooks. If you do the distance on this one, you and old brown eyes will be rewarded with Rosary Lakes at the end of your journey, the ideal locale for pooch shenanigans with a wet slant. Chill out and take it all in before backtracking to the trailhead. For more information: (541) 433-2234.

Directions: From Crescent, take CR 61 to Cascade Lakes Highway (FS 46) and turn right for 3.5 miles to FS 4660, turn left. Drive 4 miles to the fork, go straight onto FS 4664 for one mile to #4660-100 and turn left. Travel 0.8 miles to the trailhead.

Note: Trail is recommended for use in spring, summer and fall.

CRESCENT LAKE JUNCTION

LODGING

CRESCENT CREEK COTTAGES
Hwy 58, Milepost 71 (97425)
Rates: $30-$50
Tel: (541) 433-2324

CRESCENT LAKE LODGE & RESORT
P.O. Box 73 (97425)
Rates: $45-$120
Tel: (541) 433-2505

ODELL LAKE LODGE & RESORT
Hwy 58, Milepost 67 (97425)
Rates: $45-$75
Tel: (541) 433-2540

SHELTER COVE RESORT
W Odell Lake Rd, Hwy 58 (97425)
Rates: $65-$85
Tel: (541) 433-2548

WILLAMETTE PASS INN
Hwy 58, Milepost 69 (97425)
Rates: $58-$88
Tel: (541) 433-2211

Locate Other Dog-Friendly Activities...Check Nearby Cities

RECREATION

BIG MARSH NATURE TRAIL HIKE - Leashes

Beginner/2.6 miles/1.5 hours

Info: This simple trail leads you and the wagging machine through a wonderland of nature. An avian haven, listen for the birds and watch for wildlife as you zig and zag in this semi-wet marshland. There's a barely noticeable uphill trek where panoramic views of Big Marsh and the surrounding buttes are waiting to be captured on film. A little known sweet spot, don't be surprised if the only things you encounter are solitude and serenity. For more information: (541) 433-2234.

Directions: From Crescent Lake Junction, travel south on Highway 58 for 7 miles to FS 5825. Turn right and drive approximately 5 miles to FS 5825-540. Turn right and follow FS 5825-540 directly to trailhead.

Note: Trail is recommended for use in summer and fall.

WINDY LAKES TRAIL HIKE - Leashes

Intermediate/11.4 miles/7.0 hours

Info: We're talking all-day excursion here so travel prepared. From the get-go, you'll know you've picked a beaut. You and your die-hard hiking hound will skedaddle through a mature stand of lodgepole pine before beginning a moderate ascent through open woodlands of cool mountain hemlock. Take the time to absorb the serenery around you as you kick up the dust to aptly named Windy Lakes. Hey, how about some paw-dipping and chill-out time with your numero uno pal? Now that's a thought. When it's time to call it a day, do an about-face. For more information: (541) 433-2234.

Directions: From Crescent Lake Junction, head west on Crescent Lake Highway about 2 miles. Turn right on the first paved road after the railroad tracks (FS 60). Take FS 60 about 6 miles to the trailhead on your left.

Note: Trail is recommended for use in spring, summer and fall.

Hotel Policies May Be Subject To Change

CRESWELL

LODGING

MOTEL ORLEANS
345 E Oregon Ave (97426)
Rates: $32-$66
Tel: (541) 895-3341
(800) 626-1900

CROOKED RIVER RANCH

LODGING

OLALLIE LAKE RESORT CABINS
13445 Golden Mantle Rd (97760)
Rates: $25-$75
Tel: (541) 504-1010

CURTIN

LODGING

STARDUST MOTEL
455 Bear Creek Rd,
P.O. Box 80 (97428)
Rates: $25-$30
Tel: (541) 942-5706

DALE

RECREATION

LAKE CREEK TRAIL HIKE

Intermediate/9.8 miles/5.5 hours

Info: If you and your furry sidekick are looking to burn some kibble, don't miss this wilderness hike. In just under 5 miles, the trail drops 2,200' to Snowshoe Springs. The Granite Creek Trail junction marks the end of the descent portion of your trek. Enjoy the refreshing springs and restore your energy - for as every hiker knows, what goes down, must come up. Be prepared for a huff and puff ascent. For more information: (503) 427-3231.

Directions: From Dale, head east on FS 10 about 4 miles to FS 1010. Turn left on FS 1010 and continue for 15 miles to the trailhead on the north side of the road.

Locate Other Dog-Friendly Activities...Check Nearby Cities

DALLAS

LODGING

RIVERSIDE INN
517 Main St (97338)
Rates: $45-$75
Tel: (541) 623-8163

DAYVILLE

LODGING

FISH HOUSE INN B&B & RV PARK
110 Franklin
Hwy 26 (97825)
Rates: $40-$65
Tel: (541) 987-2124

RECREATION

JOHN DAY FOSSIL BEDS NATIONAL MONUMENT - Leashes

Info: Geologist wannabes and rock hounds, this natural phenomenon is a must-see, must-do expedition. Heavy erosion of volcanic deposits has revealed a myriad of plant and animal fossils in the John Day River Basin. The extraordinary fossils span more than 40 of the 65 million years of the Cenozoic Era, commonly referred to as the Age of Mammals. The 14,000-acre park is divided into three units, each laced with a network of trails, where you can witness some of the richest fossil beds in the world. These beds contain vestiges of the actual soils, ponds, rivers, ashfalls, middens, prairies and forests of a time long forgotten but well-preserved. The rocks, rich with the remnants of the ancient inhabitants, are a tableau of the changing environment of the area's landscape, climate, flora and fauna. For optimal satisfaction and a bundle of interesting facts to take home, try to tour more than one unit of this incredible monument. For more information: (541) 987-2333.

Directions: From Dayville, travel Highway 26 about 7 miles to the junction with Route 19. Continue north on Route 19 about one mile to the monument.

Note: Open during daylight hours. No admission costs. Donations accepted.

Hotel Policies May Be Subject To Change

*The numbered hikes that follow are located within the
John Day Fossil Beds National Monument:*

1) BLUE BASIN OVERLOOK TRAIL HIKE - Leashes

Intermediate/3.0 miles/2.0 hours

Info: The longest trail in the Sheep Rock area, this hike is somewhat strenuous but well worth the effort. The loop takes you and your rockhound to a spectacular vista overlooking the breadth of the John Day River Valley. The huffing and puffing will become oohing and aahing as you peruse the gorgeous scenery. For an interesting experience you won't soon forget, do some time traveling and see if you can imagine the valley as it must have looked 20 million years ago. For more information: (541) 987-2333.

Directions: From Dayville, travel Highway 26 about 7 miles to the junction with Route 19. Continue north on Route 19 about one mile to the monument. The trailhead is located off Highway 19 on the right side.

Note: Off-trail use of the Blue Basin is prohibited.

2) FLOOD OF FIRE TRAIL HIKE - Leashes

Beginner/0.25 miles/0.25 hours

Info: This peanut-sized trail still packs a big punch. Introduce your pupsqueak to the mysteries of this majestic land with a quickie jaunt. The gentle path crosses a ridge to a viewpoint which provides sweeping views of the John Day River Valley backdropped by breathtaking basalt cliffs. Pack extra Fuji, this place eats film. After the teasing glimpse of the valley below, you might be inclined to tackle another trail for a closer looksee. For more information: (541) 987-2333.

Directions: From Dayville, travel Highway 26 about 7 miles to the junction with Route 19. Continue north on Route 19 about one mile to the monument. The trailhead is located off Highway 19 on the right side.

3) ISLAND IN TIME TRAIL HIKE - Leashes

Beginner/1.0 miles/0.5 hours

Info: One of the most popular trails in the monument, this path leads to an amphitheater carved out of the blue-green claystone of the John Day Formation. Eons ago, multiple volcanic activity led to the deposition of the area by producing an abundance of volcanic ash. Over the years, the ash turned into claystone and preserved a rich variety of vertebrate fossils. You and your waga-long will see fossil replicas marked by interpretive signs and come away with a pocketful of knowledge as well as an after-noon of adventure. For more information: (541) 987-2333.

Directions: From Dayville, travel Highway 26 about 7 miles to the junction with Route 19. Continue north on Route 19 about one mile to the monument. The trailhead is located off Highway 19 on the right side.

4) STORY IN STONE TRAIL HIKE - Leashes

Beginner/0.25 miles/0.25 hours

Info: Pick up some geological tidbits on this trail which offers an intimate look at the John Day Formation which was carved 25 to 30 million years ago, but who's counting? Skirting the basin of blue-green claystone, this cinchy stroll features hands-on exhibits that provide a memorable tactile experience. Long ago, subtropical forests were replaced with deciduous forests, leaving behind a vast number of fossilized plants and species. The fossilized remains of more than 100 groups of mammals, including dogs, cats, swine, horses, camels and rodents have been unearthed in this intriguing formation. Wowser Bowser! For more information: (541) 987-2333.

Directions: From Dayville, travel Highway 26 about 7 miles to the junction with Route 19. Continue north on Route 19 about one mile to the monument. The trailhead is located off Highway 19 on the right side.

Note: Off-trail use of the Blue Basin is prohibited.

DEPOE BAY

LODGING

HOLIDAY SURF LODGE & RV PARK
939 NW Hwy 101 (97341)
Rates: $39-$335
Tel: (541) 765-2133
(800) 451-2108

INN AT ARCH ROCK
70 NW Sunset St (97341)
Rates: $45-$140
Tel: (541) 765-2560
(800) 765-8655

TROLLERS LODGE
355 SW Hwy 101 (97341)
Rates: $52-$89
Tel: (541) 765-2287
(800) 472-9335

WHALE INN AT DEPOE BAY
416 Hwy 101 N (97341)
Rates: $60-$90
Tel: (541) 765-2789

RECREATION

OTTER ROCK/
DEVILS PUNCHBOWL STATE NATURAL AREA - Leashes

Info: Your salty sea dog will feel right at home in this rich tidal habitat where ochre stars, sea grass, gumboot chitons, purple urchins, hermit crabs, seaweed, barnacles, green anemones and turban snails are permanent residents. The Marine Gardens you'll espy from the cliff are special intertidal areas set aside and protected so that visitors can learn about marine ecosystems. Consider the following:

- Expect to get wet, it comes with the territory.
- Cameras equate to memories.
- Bring binocs - migrating gray whales, seals and nesting seabirds are often seen.
- Patience definitely has its rewards, study a tide pool for a full minute, you'll see movement.
- Don't touch.
- Wear shoes with good traction and walk with care, rocks and algae are very slippery.
- View the gardens at tides of zero feet and lower.
- Allow at least an hour visit.

The punchbowl is located in the center of the viewing area and is best viewed during high tide and stormy weather but use caution, too stormy and you'll be putting yourself and your Curious George in danger.

Locate Other Dog-Friendly Activities...Check Nearby Cities

The punchbowl was formed when the roof over two sea caves collapsed. Notice how the waves crash in from every direction, churning up the sea with unimaginable force, forcing water through openings in the sandstone resulting in a continuous sculpting of this extraordinary formation.

Hop on the paved path that circles the park area. Listen to the cacophony of the thunderous Pacific and watch the sun-glinted spray exploding against the unusually shaped cliffs. BYOB (bring your own biscuits), you'll find a pleasant grassy area, picnic benches and a constant breeze, the perfect combo for some coastline ponderings.

To access the beach trail, park in the day use area just before the viewpoint. A very steep path leads to the beach. FYI: The whale watching in Depoe Bay is reputed to be among the finest on the coast.

Directions: From Depoe Bay take Highway 101 south to milepost 132.5 and signs to Otter Rock-Devils Punchbowl State Natural Area.

DETROIT

LODGING

ALL SEASONS MOTEL
130 Breitenbush Rd (97342)
Rates: $40-$80
Tel: (503) 854-3421

RECREATION

DETROIT LAKE STATE RECREATION AREA - Leashes

Info: If yours is an aqua pup, then this place dishes up some waterful fun. Tote a boat and float across the shimmering surface of Detroit Lake. If terra firma is more to your liking, find a cozy lakeside spot and dine à la blanket with your best buddy. Fishing fiends, how does rainbow trout or landlocked chinook sound for din-din? For more information: (503) 854-3406.

Directions: About 2.5 miles west of Detroit off Highway 22.

Note: Day use fee charged.

Hotel Policies May Be Subject To Change

HUMBUG FLATS TRAIL HIKE

Beginner/2.0 miles/1.0 hours

Info: Three words describe this hike - piece of cake. The trail skirts the Breitenbush River and includes travel amidst an old-growth forest. Maybe you can find a quiet spot and indulge in some splish-splashing fun. The river's a great way to cool those tootsies. Fishing hounds, pack your gear and see if you can make your fishy dreams come true. Sniffmeisters, don't miss this hike in late spring when wildflowers splatter the landscape in technicolor hues. For more information: (503) 854-3366.

Directions: From Detroit, head northeast on Breitenbush Road FS 46) for 3.5 miles to Humbug Campground and turn right. The trailhead is located behind sites 9 and 10.

LEONE LAKE TRAIL HIKE

Intermediate/1.2 miles/1.0 hours

Info: You and the dogster are just a hop, skip and a jump away from hours of wet and wild fun at Leone Lake. Simply hike the short trail through an old-growth forest and let the water hijinks begin. Able anglers, try to catch some sup for you and the pup. For more information: (503) 854-3366.

Directions: From Detroit, follow FS 46 north for 6.5 miles to Cleator Bend and turn right across the bridge. After the bridge, keep left on FS 2231 to the trailhead on the right at the top of the grade.

DIAMOND LAKE

LODGING

DIAMOND LAKE RESORT
Diamond Lake (97601)
Rates: $56-$135
Tel: (541) 793-3333
(800) 733-7593

LEMOLO FALLS TRAIL HIKE - Leashes

Beginner/3.0 miles/1.5 hours

Info: The setting of this trail has an almost picture book quality. Babbling brooks nestled in a lush green setting honeycomb the forest floor and twinkle in the afternoon sunshine. Birdsong drifts from the towering treetops. Enchanting cascades entice you and the wet one to shimmy on over. If this sounds like your kind of place, pack a biscuit basket and put a grin on the wagger's face. For more information: (541) 498-2531.

Directions: From Diamond Lake, travel west on Highway 138 for six miles to FS 2610 (Birds Point Road) and turn right. Continue six miles and take the left fork in the road, just across the Lemolo Lake Dam onto FS 2610-680. Continue .6 miles to the wooden bridge and turn left across it into the trailhead parking lot.

MT. THIELSEN TRAIL HIKE - Leashes

Intermediate/2.0 miles/1.0 hour

Info: Known as the "Lightning Rod of the Cascades," the needle-like spire of Mt. Thielsen is often struck by its namesake, creating carrot-shaped tubes and glass rock formations at the summit. You and your trailblazer will meet your exercise quotient for the afternoon with a jaunt on this pleasant trail. A steady ascent, you'll travel through sun-dappled forested terrain where the air is sweetly scented by ponderosa pine. Stop and listen, cranes can often be heard in the distance. After about a mile, pretty Diamond Lake will play peek-a-boo through the trees and signal turnaround time. If you rank in the expert class of hikers, the trail continues upward on a much steeper grade. For more information: (541) 498-2531.

Directions: From Diamond Lake, travel south on Route 138 for 3.5 miles to the cutoff for the trail.

Hotel Policies May Be Subject To Change

WATSON FALLS TRAIL HIKE - Leashes

Intermediate/1.2 miles/1.0 hours

Info: If you love your waterfalls tall and plummeting, you won't want to miss this one. The third tallest waterfall in Oregon, you'll have to earn your view points along a somewhat difficult trail which leads to a wooden bridge at the base of the falls. Do an about-face when you've had your fill and then break some bread and biscuits with Bowser at the picnic area before heading out. Bone voyage. For more information: (541) 498-2531.

Directions: From Diamond Lake, travel west on Highway 138 for 19 miles to FS 37 and turn left to the trailhead parking lot.

WHITEHORSE FALLS - Leashes

Info: Waterfall devotees, this plunger cascades over a forty foot drop into a glistening pool. A brown bagger with the wagger at one of the picnic tables will round out the day. For more information: (541) 498-2531.

Directions: From Diamond Lake, travel west on Highway 138 for 13.3 miles (3.8 miles past Clearwater Falls) and turn right at the USFS sign and the parking area.

WINDIGO PASS TRAIL HIKE - Leashes

Beginner/2.0 miles/1.0 hours

Info: This doggone delightful trail leads to a lovely interlude in a charming bosky setting. A thick canopy of pine shades you and the dawgus as you merrily roll along a pine-cushioned pathway. Pretty as can be sunlight streams through the treetops and paints zigzag patterns on the forest floor. Easy on the paws and easy on the eyes, you won't regret a moment spent. FYI: Much of the lush understory is Oregon grape. For more information: (541) 498-2531.

Directions: From Diamond Lake, travel Highway 138 north to FS 60 (Windigo Pass Road) and continue north to the trailhead.

DUFUR

RECREATION

BONNY MEADOWS LOOP TRAIL HIKE - Leashes

Beginner/7.5 miles/4.0 hours

Info: A bonafido hiking adventure, this delightfully scenic trail lets you and the pupster enjoy a slice of nature's best. The mostly level path wiggles and waggles through a lush grassy meadow. Spring and summer months are the most colorful, it's the time when the wildflowers do their showy thing among the rolling greens. Not to be outdone, splendid views of Boulder and Little Boulder Lakes round out the pretty picture. Show your buddy who's number one and plan an excursion to this charming milieu. For more information: (541) 467-2291.

Directions: From Dufur, travel Highway 44 west about 12 miles to the junction with Highway 35, turn south onto Highway 35. Continue about 4 miles to Bennet Pass and FS 3550, turn left. Travel about 4 miles to FS #4891, turn right and travel to Bonney Meadows Campground. Follow trail #473 east out of the campground and then follow #472 to complete the loop.

Note: Open July through November.

GUMJUWAC-BADGER LOOP TRAIL HIKE - Leashes

Beginner/6.5 miles/3.5 hours

Info: City slickers can join their country cousins on a journey to this delightful region for a day of fun in Mother Nature. On your way to Badger Lake, you and your wagging machine will climb through an old-growth forest sprinkled with a lush understory. A visit in springtime will tickle your senses as wildflowers dot the trail, creek and lake, adding perky colors to the landscape. Along the route, you'll collect great views of Mt. Hood looming in the distance. When you reach the cooling waters of Badger Lake, throw a line, the fishing's fine. Or lay down with dogs in a shady nook. To complete your loop du jour, follow the Gumjuwac Saddle Trail. For more information: (541) 467-2291.

Directions: From Dufur, travel Highway 44 west about 12 miles to the junction with Highway 35, turn south onto Highway 35. Continue about 4 miles to Bennet Pass and FS 3550, turn left. Travel FS 3550 to Gumjuwac Saddle. The trail begins at the saddle. Follow Trail #480 east about 2 miles, turn right on Trail #479 and go upstream about 2 miles to Badger Lake. To complete the loop, turn right on Trail #458.

Note: Open July through November.

ECHO

RECREATION
ECHO MEADOWS OREGON TRAIL SITE - Leashes

Beginner/3.0 miles/1.5 hours

Info: Even sofa loafers will take to this easy stretch of the Oregon Trail. The gentle path traverses a petite piece of land where wagon ruts from pioneer times are still visible. The seldom used trail escorts you and your history sniffing mutt through a sagebrush area and a pond rich in wildlife to an excellent lookout on a sandy knoll. Do some time traveling in your mind and consider the difficulties the settlers must have endured. For more information: (541) 376-8411.

Directions: From Echo, go west on Route 320 for 5.5 miles to a gravel road on the right. Turn right onto the gravel road and continue about a half-mile to the entrance and parking area.

FORT HENRIETTA RIVER PARK - Leashes

Info: Doggistorians will definitely want to put this little park at the top of their agendas. A tiny half-acre, the park is the former camping locale of the emigrants of the 1850s and 60s. The blockhouse, built in 1985, is a replica of past times. Peruse the interpretive panels and come away much smarter. The park overlooks the Umatilla River. Go ahead, make your dog's day, break out the red checks beside the tranquil waterway and munch on lunch.

Directions: Located along Highway 320 (Main Street).

ELGIN

LODGING

CITY CENTRE MOTEL
51 South 7th Ave (97827)
Rates: $38-$46
Tel: (541) 437-2441

MINAM MOTEL
72601 Hwy 82 (97827)
Rates: $27-$48
Tel: (541) 437-4475

ENTERPRISE

LODGING

BOUCHER GUEST COTTAGE
83162 W Dorrance Ln (97828)
Rates: $55+
Tel: (541) 426-3209

PONDEROSA MOTEL
102 SE Greenwood (97828)
Rates: $33-$46
Tel: (541) 426-3186

SHILO INNS-WILDERNESS RETREAT
84570 Bartlett Rd (97828)
Rates: $39-$79
Tel: (541) 828-7741
(800) 222-2244

WILDERNESS INN
301 W North St (97828)
Rates: $39-$115
Tel: (541) 965-1205

RECREATION

BOWMAN TRAIL to CHIMNEY LAKE HIKE - Leashes

Intermediate/10.0 miles/6.0 hours

Info: Get a sampling of Mother Nature's handiwork on this invigorating hike through the pristine Eagle Cap Wilderness. Plan accordingly and be prepared for wet going, you and your soon-to-be-dirty dog will encounter several stream crossings on this lake-bound journey. Your tree hound will have a grin from ear to ear as you step lively through the bosky, bird-filled terrain. Lucky dogs might catch a fleeting glimpse of an elk or a Bambi look-alike bounding across the forest floor. Splish-splashing fun and chill-out pupportunities are yours for the taking at Chimney Lake. If you've brought a good read and a tough chew, there are R&R places galore. No bones about it, this is the stuff of good times. For more information: (541) 426-5546.

Directions: From Enterprise, travel Highway 82 west about 8 miles to Lostine then go south 14 miles on the Lostine River Road (FS #8210) to the trailhead.

Note: Permit may be required. Day-use permits cost $3 and are for sale at all Wallowa-Whitman National Forest offices. Rd #8210 is gravel for the last 8 miles.

Hotel Policies May Be Subject To Change

ESTACADA

<u>RECREATION</u>

CLACKAMAS RIVER TRAIL HIKE - Leashes

Intermediate/7.0 miles/4.0 hours

Info: Take your river Rover for a day of fun and adventure with a wet and wild slant. This low elevation trail borders the southwest side of the Clackamas River and happily serves up plenty of pooch shenanigans. Along the trail, you and your aqua pup will be entranced by a number of watery delights including the sparkling cascades of Pup Creek Falls. On this path less traveled, you'll honeycomb through an old-growth forest, hopscotch over rocky outcroppings, play tagalong with your wagalong beside the river bank, bound across a wide flat section of the Roaring River and (whew), come to a junction. The junction marks the 700' side trail to breathtaking Pup Creek Falls, which tumbles from 100' above. Find a cozy nook, pat yourself on the back for planning such a terrific day and then do lunch with your favorite biscuitmesiter. For more information: (503) 630-6861.

Directions: From Estacada, travel south on Highway 224 about 16 miles to FS 54, turn right and cross a bridge. Take the first right into the Fish Creek trailhead parking lot. The trail-head is located across the road from the parking lot past the end of the bridge.

Note: Leashes strongly recommended for your dog's safety and protection. Recommended season April through November. The parking lot serves as a barrier-free fishing pier for the Clackamas River.

FANTON TRAIL HIKE - Leashes

Beginner/8.8 miles/5.0 hours

Info: For a paw-loose and fancy free kind of day, you won't regret a moment spent in this delightfully rustic getaway. The mostly level pathway guides you and the dawgus deep into the forest where several trickling streams add to the outdoor ambiance. When the woods thin out and the canopy opens up, postcardian pictures of the surrounding wilderness come into view, including the summits of Squaw and Old Baldy

Mountains. If you're visiting in early autumn and your pooch goes crazy for piles of fallen leaves, expect a manic moment. Pack plenty of power snacks and H_2O, you're gonna want to spend the day. For more information: (503) 630-6861.

Directions: From Estacada, travel Highway 224 south about 3 miles to Fall Creek Road, turn left and continue about 1.5 miles to the end at Divers Road, turn left and continue about 0.2 miles, then turn right onto Squaw Mountain Road. Continue on Squaw Mountain Road, which becomes FS 4614, about 9.5 miles to a junction on the right with FS 4613, turn right about 0.3 miles to the beginning of the Fanton Trail #505 on the left.

Note: Leashes strongly recommended for your dog's safety and protection. Recommended season June through November.

PANSY LAKE TRAIL HIKE - Leashes

Beginner/3.0 miles/1.5 hours

Info: This feel good hike is an easy way to experience the natural prettiness of the region without breaking a sweat. You and your mellow fellow will journey about a mile to Pansy Basin before the trail circles a meadow, heading toward a rock slide. Look around as you do the stroll, you're smack dab in the middle of a lovely little setting. It's another half-mile to the shimmering waters of Pansy Lake. You and old brown eyes can simply relax away the hours or if fishing fuels you, tempt the local trout to take a bite. For more ambitious breeds, numerous side trails to other lakes and viewpoints await. For more information: (503) 630-6861.

Directions: From Estacada, travel Highway 224 south about 20 miles to FS 46, turn right. Continue on FS 46 to the fork and go onto FS 63. Travel FS 63 to the fork with FS 6340 and go right. Continue on FS 6340 about 1.5 miles to where it becomes FS 6341. The trailhead is located on the south side of FS 634.

Note: Leashes strongly recommended for your dog's safety and protection. Recommended season April through November.

Hotel Policies May Be Subject To Change

SERENE LAKE TRAIL HIKE - Leashes

Intermediate/6.0 miles/4.0 hours

Info: On your way to the aptly named waters of Serene Lake, you and the pupster can kick up your heels in a myriad of environs including old-growth forests, sub-alpine woodlands and lush open meadows. Springtime heralds the arrival of color when the wildflowers make their grand entrance. If your licker's a lake lover, take the itsy bitsy .5 mile side trail to Middle Rock and Upper Rock Lakes and triple your lake quotient. The route to Serene Lake travels below an ancient rock slide before the switchbacking ascent to the lake. FYI: This watering hole is a favorite hangout for swimmers and afishionados alike. For more information: (503) 630-6861.

Directions: From Estacada, travel Highway 224 south about 25 miles to FS 57, just past the bridge over Oak Grove Fork of the Clackamas River, turn left. Continue on FS 57 about 8 miles to FS 58, turn left. Continue on FS 58 6 miles to FS 4610, turn left. Continue on FS 4610 about 1.2 miles until you reach 4610-240. Follow FS 4610-240 about 4.4 miles to Frazier Turnaround and the trailhead.

Note: Leashes strongly recommended for your dog's safety and protection. Recommended season June through November.

EUGENE

Lodging

ANGUS INN MOTEL
2121 Franklin Blvd (97403)
Rates: $36-$70
Tel: (541) 342-1243
(800) 456-6487

BARRON'S MOTOR INN
1859 Franklin Blvd (97403)
Rates: $47-$61
Tel: (541) 342-6383
(800) 444-6383

BEST WESTERN NEW OREGON MOTEL
1655 Franklin Blvd (97403)
Rates: $58-$78
Tel: (541) 683-3669
(800) 528-1234

CAMILLE'S B&B
3277 Onyx Pl (97405)
Rates: $55-$70
Tel: (541) 344-9576

CAMPUS INN
390 East Broadway (97401)
Rates: $54-$70
Tel: (541) 343-3376
(800) 888-6313

CLASSIC RESIDENCE INN
1140 W 6th Ave (97402)
Rates: $30-$40
Tel: (541) 343-0730

COUNTRY SQUIRE INN
33100 Van Duyn Rd (97401)
Rates: $39-$100
Tel: (541) 484-2000

COURTESY INN
345 W 6th Ave (97401)
Rates: $40-$50
Tel: (541) 345-3391
(800) 459-3000

EUGENE MOTOR LODGE
476 E Broadway (97401)
Rates: $28-$60
Tel: (541) 344-5233

EUGENE TRAVELERS INN
540 E Broadway (97401)
Rates: $33-$49
Tel: (541) 342-1109
(800) 432-5999

HILTON HOTEL-EUGENE
66 E 6th & Oak Sts (97401)
Rates: $89-$155
Tel: (541) 342-2000
(800) 445-8667

PINE KNOT MOTEL
1410 W 6th Ave (97402)
Rates: $25-$55
Tel: (541) 485-0742

RAMADA INN
225 Coburg Rd (97401)
Rates: $58-$78
Tel: (541) 342-5181
(800) 272-6232

RED LION INN
205 Coburg Rd (97401)
Rates: $66-$97
Tel: (541) 342-5201
(800) 547-8010

SIXTY-SIX MOTEL
755 E Broadway (97401)
Rates: $24-$34
Tel: (541) 342-5041

TIMBERS MOTEL
1015 Pearl St (97401)
Rates: $32-$68
Tel: (541) 343-3345
(800) 643-4167

THE VALLEY RIVER INN
1000 Valley River Way (97440)
Rates: $110-$300
Tel: (541) 687-0123
(800) 543-8266

Hotel Policies May Be Subject To Change

<u>RECREATION</u>
ALTON BAKER PARK DOG RUN

Info: Almost anytime you stop by this dog-friendly park, you're bound to enjoy some canine communing. You and your mutt will find plenty of room for running, playing and fetching so tote a Frisbee or a fuzzy tennie. And hey, a biscuit or two will only make the day better.

Directions: Located on the south side of Day Road, about 0.25 miles into the park off Club Road.

AMAZON PARK DOG RUN

Info: Nestled within an 80-acre park, you'll find an enclosed dog run that's bound to wag some tails. The dawgus will have a howl of a good time carousing with his canine cousins and you might end up making some new friends as well. No bones about it, visit this park and happy tails will be wagging in the breeze.

Directions: Located east of 29th and Amazon Parkway. Park at 29th and Amazon or park west of 28th and Hilyard Streets.

ASCOT PARK - Leashes

Info: When you're in the neighborhood and an afternoon interlude with your canine companion sounds like a plan, this parkland fits the bill. You'll find a walking path and plenty of open ballfields. So tote a tennie. Who knows, a quick catch 'n fetch might be in the cards.

Directions: Located at 170 Bailey Lane.

BLANTON RIDGE - Leashes

Info: City weary waggers will appreciate this easy getaway. The natural area and hiking trail are a scenic bonus. Pack plenty of water, some Scooby snacks and take a biscuit break somewhere pretty along the trail.

Directions: Located at Ridgewood Drive and Blanton Road.

Locate Other Dog-Friendly Activities...Check Nearby Cities

BLOOMBERG PARK - Leashes

Info: BYOB (bring your own biscuits) and make some time to enjoy the great outdoors with your wagalong. Savor the undeveloped open space in this 20-acre scene of green.

Directions: Located at the west end of Bloomberg Road.

CANDLELIGHT PARK - Leashes

Info: Twelve acres are perfect for some Rexercise and relaxing moments for you and furface. Pack your own Perrier, there are no amenities.

Directions: Located at Royal Avenue and Candlelight.

DELTA PONDS - Leashes

Info: Yippee, Skippy. Eighty-five acres of greenery and scenery beckon to you and your pooch. Bring your trusty rod and reel, the stocked ponds might just make your fishy dreams come true. Don't forget a rawhide chew for your patient pal.

Directions: Located on Goodpasture Island at Valley River.

DILLARD/SKYLINE PARK - Leashes

Info: This primo natural area is a great place for hiking hounds. The pathways are well-shaded and beautiful, affording magnificent views and the airwaves are filled with the melodic tunes of Mother Nature's flyboys. The next sunny afternoon that comes your way, just go for it and make your dog's day.

Directions: Located east of Dillard Road.

EAST SPENCER BUTTE - Leashes

Info: Leash up your little sofa surfer and get set for a kibble-burning adventure at the Butte. Hiking trails lace the lovely landscape, providing pawfect pupportunities for close encounters of the natural kind.

Directions: Located at Spencer Butte and Fox Hollow Road.

Hotel Policies May Be Subject To Change

ELIJAH BRISTOW STATE PARK - Leashes

Info: The Willamette River runs through this 800-acre region and creates a stunning riparian habitat for you and your Curious George to explore. Pick a pathway and zoom into the rich, cool forestland where chatty songbirds provide the music. Or find a streamside spot where you can be a lazybones and let sleeping dogs lie. If you'd rather burn some kibble, set your sights on the Soggy Trail and scope out the marsh. Lucky dogs might catch a glimpse of a regal blue heron strutting on the shoreline. Bullfrogs are always croaking about this beautiful place, so check it out yourself. One thing's certain, no matter how you spend your day, you won't regret a moment spent in this delightful parkland. For more information: (541) 686-7592.

Directions: From Eugene, travel southeast on Highway 58 (Willamette Highway) 15 miles to the park entrance on the north side of the highway.

Note: Day use fee may be required.

GOLDEN GARDENS PARK - Leashes

Info: Treat your Golden to an afternoon at Golden Gardens. This 36-acre park, complete with shade trees and dewy grass, is bound to please your pooch. Hey fishing fiends, pack your pole and hope for dinner. There's a stocked lake waiting to make your dreams come true.

Directions: Located north of Golden Garden Avenue.

HENDRICKS PARK - Leashes

Info: A smell fest extraordinaire, the floral display in this stunning 80-acre park is not to be missed. During mid to late May, more than 6,000 rhododendrons and azaleas come into bloom and cover the landscape in dramatic color. When your senses have had their fill, do something special for your body. Although dogs are excluded from the Rhododendron Garden, there's a walking path for Sunday strollers and a woodsy hiking route for more energetic breeds. No matter how you slice this green piece of pie, you're gonna like the taste it leaves behind.

Directions: Located at Summit and Skyline.

Locate Other Dog-Friendly Activities...Check Nearby Cities

HILEMAN LANDING PARK - Leashes

Info: Ahoy, mate - this place is perfect for aqua pups. Tote a boat and do a float, or just kick back with the biscuitmeister and enjoy the waterful scene.

Directions: Located north of East Beacon Drive.

MAURIE JACOBS PARK - Leashes

Info: Tails will be spinning with joy at the snifforama contained within this lovely community garden. Après flower power, take a turn on the paved walkway or put some bounce in Bowser's step along the unimproved jogging path. For a getaway kind of afternoon, plan an escape to this 23-acre urban oasis.

Directions: Located at the River House to Greenway Bridge.

MELVIN MILLER PARK - Leashes

Info: Pack a fun attitude and get set for a howl of a good time. Whether you simply kick back and watch your canine carouse with his paisanos in the fenced area or do some social communing yourself, this place has the makings of a good time.

Directions: Located on West 25th Avenue off Hawkins Lane.

MORSE RANCH DOG RUN

Info: Paw-loose and fancy free, tails will go into high gear mode at this park. The fur-friendly fenced area could become a habit for you and your best pal.

Directions: Located at Crest Drive and Lincoln Street. Park in the main parking area at 595 Crest Drive.

NORTH WESTMORELAND PARK - Leashes

Info: Dotted with softball and soccer fields, this neighborhood park caters to the recreational crowd. Pull up a square and cheer for the home team. If you'd rather make your own fun and games, hightail it on the paved walkway and get some Rexercise.

Directions: Located on West 15th/18th & Chambers/Taylor.

Hotel Policies May Be Subject To Change

SHELDON PARK - Leashes

Info: You can't beat this 11-acre number for your AM constitutional. If time is on your side, pack a good read and a tough chew and see where the day leads.

Directions: Located at 2445 Willakenzie Road.

SKINNER'S BUTTE - Leashes

Info: Smack dab in the midst of beautiful scenery, Skinner's Butte is a wonderful place to relax with the lickmeister. Find a cozy cranny and take a biscuit break with your best bud. Tote your binocs, Skinner's Butte is popular with rock climbers, so people watching is an option too.

Directions: Located off Cheshire Street, from Ferry to Lincoln.

SPENCER BUTTE - Leashes

Info: One of the prettiest parks in a city noted for its green scenes, you'll uncover more than 300 spectacular acres to explore. Get your daily dose of exercise in a beautiful environment. Make tracks on the South Hills Ridgeline Trail where you'll find yourself in a coniferous forest, the canopied path a delight year round. Savor the aromatic scents while you listen to the local flyboys. And don't miss the park's namesake, 2,065′ Spencer Butte, the highest point in the area. Lots of flora and fauna can be seen wherever your travels take you. Bone voyage.

Directions: Located at the ridgeline from Fox Hollow to Willamette Streets.

TUGMAN PARK - Leashes

Info: Set out early with Curly and do a turn or two on the paved walking path that winds around this pleasant parkland.

Directions: Located off Hilyard Street from 36th - 38th Avenues.

Locate Other Dog-Friendly Activities...Check Nearby Cities

WASHINGTON/JEFFERSON PARK - Leashes

Info: If it's a lovely day and you're in the neighborhood, treat your dog to this 21-acre park. A favorite Frisbee will only add to the pleasure of your outing.

Directions: Located from 1st to 7th Avenues.

WEST BANK PARK - Leashes

Info: A relaxing riverside pathway crooks a little finger at you and the wagger in this lovely parkland. Afishionados, try your luck on the trout - who knows, you might end up with a tasty treat.

Directions: Located at the Greenway Bridge - Owosso.

WEST SPENCER BUTTE - Leashes

Info: Lace up those hiking boots and head out with your snout to this breathtaking expanse. Hike as little or as long as you'd like, find that perfect resting spot and share a biscuit basket with the barkmeister.

Directions: Located between Butte, 52nd and Willamette.

WESTMORELAND PARK - Leashes

Info: You and your disc doggie can have a little fun at the Frisbee golf course in this 33-acre expanse. Or discover a shaded glen and do lunch alfresco. Bone appétit.

Directions: Located at 18th/24th Avenues, Polk/Fillmore Streets.

OTHER PARKS IN EUGENE - Leashes

- ACORN PARK, east of Buck Street
- AWBREY PARK, off River Road, N of Spring Creek Dr
- BERKELEY PARK, 3629 W 14th Ave
- BOND LANE PARK, 355 Bond Lane
- BREWER PARK, 1820 Brewer Lane
- CHARNEL MULLIGAN PARK, 17th Ave & Charnelton St
- COUNTRY LANE PARK, 2975 Country Lane
- CRESCENT PARK, Coburg Rd & Hillview
- CREST HEIGHTS PARK, end of Hionda & Mesa
- EAST BANK PARK, Goodpasture Island Rd

- ECHO HOLLOW PARK, 1655 Echo Hollow Road
- EDGEWOOD PARK, 4600 Hilyard St
- FAIRMOUNT PARK, E 15th Ave & Fairmount Blvd
- 52ND & WILLAMETTE PARK, 52nd & Willamette Streets
- FRANKLIN PARK, Franklin Blvd at Judkins Pt
- FRIENDLY PARK, 27th Ave & Monroe St
- GARFIELD PARK, 16th Ave & Garfield St
- GILBERT PARK, Gilbert & Elmira
- GLEN OAK PARK, 36th Ave & Glen Oak Dr
- HAWKINS HEIGHTS PARK, Hawkins Hts & Highland Oaks
- IRWIN PARK, Barger Dr & W Irwin Way
- JEFFERSON PARK, W 16th Ave & Jefferson St
- KINCAID PARK, E 39th Ave & Kincaid St
- KINNEY PARK, W Amazon & Martin St
- LAFFERTY PARK, Mary Ln at Arden Way
- LAUREL HILL PARK, E 26th & Augusta St
- MANGAN STREET PARK, Mangan & Wagner Sts
- MARCHE CHASE PARK, Centennial Blvd
- MARTIN LUTHER KING PARK, 10th Ave & Grant St
- MILTON PARK, 3300 University St
- MISSION PARK, end of Mission
- MONROE PARK, 10th Ave & Monroe St
- OAKMONT PARK, Oakmont Way near Oakmont Rd
- PETERSEN PARK, 870 Berntzen Rd
- RIVER HOUSE PARK, 301 N Adams St
- SCOBERT PARK, 1180 W 4th Ave
- SHADOW WOOD PARK, South of 43rd Ave
- SLADDEN PARK, N Adams St & Cheshire St
- SORREL WAY PARK, SW off Sorrel Way & Rustic Pl
- STATE STREET PARK, Dakota & Burnett Sts
- TANDY TURN PARK, Tandy Turn & Sharon Way
- TRAINSONG PARK, end of Edison off Bethel Dr
- UNIVERSITY PARK, E 24th Ave & University St
- WASHBURN PARK, E 21st Ave & Agate St
- WASHINGTON PARK, off Washington St, 19th - 21st Aves
- WEST UNIVERSITY PARK, 14th Ave & Hilyard St
- WHITLEY LANDING PARK, E River Loop 1 & Chapman Ln
- WILLIS PARK, 36th Ave, E of Knob Hill
- WILLOW CREEK PARK, 18th Ave, W of Bailey Hill Rd

Locate Other Dog-Friendly Activities...Check Nearby Cities

FLORENCE

LODGING

MERCER LAKE RESORT
88875 Bay Berry Ln (97439)
Rates: $53-$65
Tel: (541) 997-3633
(800) 355-3633

MONEY SAVER MOTEL
170 Hwy 101 (97439)
Rates: $46-$64
Tel: (541) 997-7131

PARK MOTEL
85034 Hwy 101 S (97439)
Rates: $34-$79
Tel: (541) 997-2634
(800) 392-0441

SILVER SANDS MOTEL
1449 Hwy 101 N (97439)
Rates: $34-$68
Tel: (541) 997-3459

VILLA WEST MOTEL
901 Hwy 101 (97439)
Rates: $35-$55
Tel: (541) 997-3457

RECREATION

CARTER DUNES TRAIL HIKE - Leashes

Beginner/3.0 miles/1.5 hours

Info: For a wonderful, windswept jaunt with your beach bum buddy, devote an afternoon to this incredible trail. You'll dig your feet into the thick white sand and kick up your heels in joy as you frolic over the duney areas on your journey to the often desolate beach. Visit winter through early summer for the best wildlife watching. Pack your binocs and keep your furry one still, you're bound to encounter a critter or two in the deflation plain. When the trail forks, continue straight ahead (west) to reach the beach. Follow the leader on this trail amidst a medley of trees where cool salty sea breezes rustle the evergreens and bring a sense of serenity to your spirit. For more information: (541) 271-3611.

Directions: From Florence, travel 7.5 miles south on Highway 101 to the Carter Lake Campground and the trailhead on the west side of the Highway 101.

CHIEF TSILTCOOS TRAIL HIKE - Leashes

Beginner/1.25 miles/1.0 hours

Info: For a quick burst of evergreenery, this trail can't be beat. You'll meander on a gentle grade through a coastal forest of huckleberry and rhododendron (imagine the gorgeous colors in spring) on your way over hill and dale. Gung-ho hounds, there's a second trail that loops around the hilltop and offers a bonus of striking panoramas. Take your time on this one and take some treats - nothing can be finer than to dine as you recline. Bone appétit. For more information: (541) 271-3611.

Directions: From Florence, travel 7 miles south on Highway 101 to Siltcoos Beach Road. Turn right (west) on Siltcoos Beach Road and drive 1.25 miles to the trailhead located across the road from the Stagecoach Trailhead.

JESSIE M. HONEYMAN STATE PARK - Leashes

Info: Named after an early proponent of the Oregon state park system, you and the aqua pup will uncover three lakes at this 522-acre park. There's Woahink, Cleawox and Lily. At Lily Lake, you and your canine cohort can rent a boat and do a bit of exploring. For a day of simple pleasures, there are a number of trails that fit the bill, including a loop-de-loop around Cleawox Lake.

Directions: From Florence, travel south on Highway 101 to signs for the park at milepost 193.4.

LAGOON TRAIL HIKE - Leashes

Beginner/1.0 miles/0.5 hours

Info: If you're short on time but long on yearning, then this hike's got your name on it. You and furface will skedaddle atop wooden boardwalks as you wiggle and waggle through a maze of flora including many beautiful flowering species. Keep your binocs handy - beaver, nutria, duck, heron and bittern are commonly sighted. The trail follows an arm of the Siltcoos River that was cut off when the road was built and earned the nickname, "The River of No Return Nature Trail." For more information: (541) 271-3611.

Directions: From Florence, travel 7 miles south on Highway 101 to Siltcoos Beach Road. Turn right (west) on Siltcoos Beach Road and drive one mile to the Lagoon Campground and trailhead.

PAWN OLD-GROWTH TRAIL HIKE - Leashes

Beginner/0.75 miles/0.75 hours

Info: For a quickie nature excursion, have a go at this simple trail. You'll find yourself in a cool old-growth forest where tweet-tweet music accompanies your every step. Pick up a pamphlet from the Mapleton Ranger District Station and broaden your knowledge of the local flora. FYI: Pawn is an acronym for the four families in the early 1900s who fought to establish a post office on the upper portion of the North Fork Siuslaw River above Minerva. For more information: (541) 268-4473.

Directions: From Florence, drive east on Highway 126 for one mile to North Fork Siuslaw River Road and follow for 17 miles and bear right to cross the bridge to the trailhead parking lot.

SILTCOOS LAKE TRAIL HIKE - Leashes

Intermediate/4.5 miles/3.0 hours

Info: You'll walk in shaded splendor beneath a dense canopy of trees which were planted in the 1930s. You and the furball can take a gander at the massive cedar snags, stumps and valley floor marshes along this enchanting pathway. At the midway point, the trail forks. Follow either one to the lake and then loop back to the halfway point. Anglers, you'll want to tote your gear. Stocked with rainbow trout, the lake has an outstanding natural supply of yellow perch, bullhead catfish, crappie, largemouth bass and bluegill. When you've bagged your limit, do an about-face or for a change of scenery, follow the path less traveled on your return trek. For more information: (541) 271-3611.

Directions: From Florence, travel 7 miles south on Highway 101 to Siltcoos Beach Road. The trailhead is located on the east side of Highway 101, across from Siltcoos Beach Road.

SUTTON TRAIL HIKE - Leashes

Beginner/6.0 miles/3.0 hours

Info: This duney hike will fill your eyes with wondrous beauty and soothe your senses with its serene aura. Plan an alfresco repast at Holman Vista, the pawfect place to watch the sunset or ogle the orcas. Pack your binoculars, birders go bonkers in this avian havian. More than 200 species have been spotted.

Come early in the morning, nearly 50 species of wildlife, from chipmunk to deer inhabit these piney woods. All along your journey, the air will be sweetened with refreshing ocean breezes and the scent of shore pine. Take note of the twists and bends of the pines, their unusual forms have been created by eons of windy weather. If you're berry lucky, you might be visiting when a fruity bunch is in bloom, like blueberry, huckleberry, salal, salmonberry, blackberry and thimbleberry. Happy blue tongue to you. For more information: (541) 268-4473.

Directions: From the junction of Highways 126 and 101 in Florence, head north on Highway 101 for 6 miles to the Sutton Campground and the trailhead.

Note: If you can't tell edible berries from inedible berries, don't experiment.

TAYLOR DUNES TRAIL HIKE - Leashes

Beginner/1.0 miles/0.5 hours

Info: This beautiful, barrier-free trail escorts you and your Sandy to an incredible platform of endless vistas. Some of the oldest conifers in the Oregon Dunes share the surf's turf with rhododendrons and gnarled spruce trees. When you reach the platform, you'll be glad you packed your Kodak. The marshy deflation plains and turbulent Pacific are sights you'll want to capture on film. When it's time to head back, do a 180° and retrace your steps. For more information: (541) 271-3611.

Directions: From Florence, travel 7.5 miles south on Highway 101 to the Carter Lake Campground and the trailhead on the west side of the Highway 101.

WAXMYRTLE TRAIL HIKE - Leashes

Beginner/3.0 miles/1.5 hours

Info: Give the biscuitmeister something to bark home about and include this voyage on your itinerary. And then hi ho, hi ho, it's off to the beach you'll go. The views of the powerful Pacific and the lower estuary are definitely photo worthy, so pack plenty of Fuji. Be sure to keep your furry little wanderer leashed at all times, the surrounding region is a nesting ground for the endangered snowy plover. Lucky dogs might catch sight of one of these rare feathered fellows. The beach signals turnaround time. For more information: (541) 271-3611.

Directions: From Florence, travel 7 miles south on Highway 101 to Siltcoos Beach Road. Turn right (west) on Siltcoos Beach Road and drive to the Waxmyrtle Campground and the trailhead.

Note: Signs are posted in fragile nesting areas. Please heed the warnings and respect the habitat of the snowy plover.

FOREST GROVE

LODGING

HOLIDAY MOTEL
3224 Pacific Ave (97116)
Rates: $33-$48
Tel: (541) 357-7411

FORT KLAMATH

LODGING

CRATER LAKE RESORT & CABINS
50711 Hwy 62, Milepost 92 (97626)
Rates: $32-$53
Tel: (541) 381-2349

WILSON'S COTTAGES
57997 Hwy 62 (97626)
Rates: $40-$75
Tel: (541) 381-2209

SUN PASS RANCH B&B
52125 Hwy 62 (97626)
Rates: n/a
Tel: (541) 381-2259

FOSSIL

RECREATION

JOHN DAY FOSSIL BEDS NATIONAL MONUMENT - Leashes

Info: See DAYVILLE for description of John Day Fossil Beds National Monument.

Directions: From Fossil, travel Highway 218 southwest about 18 miles. The Clarno Unit is located off Highway 218 on the right side.

Note: Open during daylight hours. No admission costs. Donations accepted.

The numbered hikes that follow are located within the John Day Fossil Beds National Monument:

1) CLARNO ARCH TRAIL HIKE - Leashes

Beginner/0.5 hours/0.5 miles

Info: Although this trail is rated beginner, there are steep sections and it is frequently slippery. Sure-footed explorers will be rewarded with a look-see at the petrified logs and limbcasts. The trail's namesake at the end is Clarno Arch, an unusual erosional feature. Make the most of your visit and combine this short walk with the self-guided Trail of the Fossils which follows. Plan ahead and end your morning on a high note with a little lunch alfresco in the picnic area. For more information: (541) 987-2333.

Directions: From Fossil, travel Highway 218 southwest about 18 miles. The Clarno Unit is located off Highway 218 on the right side. The trailhead is located about one-quarter mile west of the Clarno picnic area on Highway 28. A spur trail from the picnic area leads to other trailheads.

2) TRAIL OF THE FOSSILS HIKE - Leashes

Beginner/0.5 hours/0.5 miles

Info: Another quickie traipse, this self-guided loop shows how mudflows inundated a subtropical forest and created the Clarno Formation 45 million years ago. Over the course of time, the mudflows turned to their present rock state. Erosion has added a special touch by exposing evidence of the former environments all along your route. Add the Clarno Arch Trail to your day's pursuits and you'll come away with a richer understanding of this unusual region. For more information: (541) 987-2333.

Directions: From Fossil, travel Highway 218 southwest about 18 miles. The Clarno Unit is located off Highway 218 on the right side. The trailhead is located about one-quarter mile west of the Clarno picnic area on Highway 28. A spur trail from the picnic area leads to other trailheads.

Locate Other Dog-Friendly Activities...Check Nearby Cities

GARIBALDI

LODGING

BAY SHORE INN
227 Garibaldi Ave (97118)
Rates: $69-$110
Tel: (541) 322-2552

HARBOR VIEW INN & RV PARK
302 S 7th St (97118)
Rates: $30-$55
Tel: (541) 322-3251

TILLA-BAY MOTEL
805 Garibaldi Ave (97118)
Rates: $39+
Tel: (541) 322-3405

RECREATION

MIAMI RIVER - Leashes

Info: Set up shop beside the river and see how many trout you can bag for the day. Tote a rawhide and reward the barkmeister for his companionable presence.

Directions: From Garibaldi, travel south on Highway 101 to milepost 56.9 and signs for the river.

GEARHART

LODGING

GEARHART BY THE SEA
1157 N Marion (97138)
Rates: $119-$184
Tel: (503) 738-8331
(800) 547-0115

SURFSIDE CONDOS ON THE BEACH
P.O. Box 2591 (97138)
Rates: $69-$145
Tel: (503) 738-6384

WINDJAMMER MOTEL
4253 Hwy 101 N (97138)
Rates: $48-$117
Tel: (503) 738-3250
(800) 479-5191

GLADSTONE

LODGING

BUDGET INN
19240 SE McLaughlin Blvd (97027)
Rates: $35-$85
Tel: (503) 656-1955
(800) 655-9368

Hotel Policies May Be Subject To Change

GLENEDEN BEACH

LODGING

SALISHAN LODGE
7760 Hwy 101 N (98388)
Rates: $110-$250
Tel: (541) 764-3600
(800) 452-2300

GLIDE

LODGING

STEELHEAD RUN B&B
23049 N Umpqua Hwy,
Box 639 (97443)
Rates: $70-$95
Tel: (541) 496-0563
(800) 348-0563

RECREATION

BIG SQUAW TRAIL HIKE

Intermediate/3.0 miles/1.5 hours

Info: From the onset, you'll be able to see your lofty destination, Big Squaw Mountain. The trail traverses an open meadow (spring heralds the sprinkling of polka dot colors) before depositing you in an old-growth Douglas fir forest. Teaser views at the clearings in the timberline add to the picture perfect setting. The switchbacks signal you're up, up and away to the top. From your catbird seat, you and your mighty mutt will have the Little River and South Umpqua drainage beneath you as well as the towering Black and Foster Buttes. Take five and break some bread and biscuits before you play follow the leader back to the starting point. For more information: (541) 496-3532.

Directions: From Glide, travel Highway 138 west for 0.25 miles to Little River Road (FS 17). Take FS 17 southeast for 16.5 miles to the Coolwater Campground. FS 17 becomes FS 27. Travel FS 27 about 3 miles to the end of the pavement and FS 2719. Turn right and drive 10 miles to FS 2719-617 and turn left. Continue 1.5 miles to FS 2719-650. Turn right and drive one mile to the trailhead.

Note: Trail is not recommended for winter hiking.

Locate Other Dog-Friendly Activities...Check Nearby Cities

CANTON CREEK FALLS TRAIL HIKE

Beginner/3.0 miles/1.5 hours

Info: Wet paws are the name of the game when you maneuver along this trail during high water times so come prepared. Pack extra socks and a fun attitude and let the good times roll. Beginning at Canton Creek, you'll cross the rushing water several times. This moist locale accounts for the lush environment which is highlighted by thick mosses and tall red huckleberry bushes. Your happy, albeit dirty dog will run with glee all the way to the 100′ cascades nestled between steep canyon walls. Surrounding the falls, massive Douglas fir and western red cedar provide the coolness and the color. Pack some munchies and plan to hang out with your snout in this pristine neck of the woods. When you can tear the wet one away, backtrack to the trailhead. For more information: (541) 496-3532.

Directions: From Glide, travel Highway 138 east for 28 miles to Steamboat Creek Road then follow to Canton Creek Road and turn left. Drive to the junction with Upper Canton Creek Road (FS 26) and proceed to Saddle Camp Road (2300-600). Turn right and travel about a half-mile to the trailhead.

Note: Trail is not recommended for winter hiking.

FULLER LAKE TRAIL HIKE

Intermediate/1.0 miles/0.5 hours

Info: If fishing is your passion, this relatively simple jaunt will bring you within striking distance of brook and rainbow trout. Include a tough chew in your tackle box to keep old faithful busy while you try your luck. A visit in late summer rounds out the food plan with an abundance of fresh huckleberries. When you've bagged your limit, retrace the paw prints while you plan the fish fry. For more information: (541) 496-3532.

Directions: From Glide, travel 23 miles east on Highway 138 to Steamboat Creek Road (FS 38) and follow about 9 miles to FS 3817. Take FS 3817 3.5 miles to FS 3850. Take FS 3850 10 miles to FS 3810. Then, veer left on FS 3810 and drive for 0.25 miles to FS 380. Turn left and drive approximately one mile to the trailhead.

Note: Trail is recommended for use summer-fall. If you are unsure of what edible berries look like, don't experiment.

GROTTO FALLS TRAIL HIKE - Leashes

Beginner/0.6 miles/0.5 hours

Info: A great little sojourn on a hot summer day, you'll start off with a section of switchbacks through an open area where pretty little wildflowers enhance the setting. Frolic through an old-growth forest and voilà, you'll be at the marvelous cascades. Find a chill out spot and contemplate the beauty of nature. If you've brought the makings for a picnic, check out the Grotto Falls Dispersed Area at the trailhead and end your day on a fun note. For more information: (541) 496-3532.

Directions: From Glide, travel Highway 138 west 0.25 miles to Little River Road (FS 17). Follow FS 17 for 16.5 miles to Coolwater Campground Road (FS 2703). Turn left on 2703 and drive 3 miles to FS 2703-150. Continue about 2 miles to the trailhead just beyond Emile Creek Bridge.

HEMLOCK FALLS TRAIL HIKE

Intermediate/1.0 miles/0.5 hours

Info: Naturalists, you'll give this hike the high five. Short but steep, the rewards are worth the huffing and puffing. Take the time to study the majesty of the old-growth forest as you and the tree hound skedaddle through its bosky beauty. If you're lucky enough be to visiting in spring, wildflowers will double your pleasure with an extravagant colorama. But don't forget the name of the game, Hemlock Falls. The cascades plummet more than eighty feet before splashing into Hemlock Creek. Sit a spell and enjoy the beauty of the setting before doing a 180° and heading back. For more information: (541) 496-3532.

Directions: From Glide, travel Highway 138 west for 0.25 miles to Little River Road (FS 17). Follow FS 17 for 20 miles to where it becomes FS 27 and the surface becomes gravel. Continue on FS 27 to the Lake in the Woods Campground on the right-hand side of the road.

Note: The trail is not recommended for winter hiking.

GOLD BEACH

LODGING

**BEST WESTERN INN
OF THE BEACHCOMBER**
29266 Ellensburg Ave (97444)
Rates: $53-$97
Tel: (541) 247-6691
(800) 528-1234

CITY CENTER MOTEL
94200 Harlow St (97444)
Rates: $40-$80
Tel: (541) 247-6675

DRIFT IN MOTEL
94250 Port Dr (97444)
Rates: $50-$64
Tel: (541) 247-4547
(800) 424-3833

INN AT GOLD BEACH
1435 S Ellensburg Ave (97444)
Rates: $35-$125
Tel: (541) 247-6606
(800) 503-0833

IRELAND'S RUSTIC LODGES
29330 S Ellensburg Ave (97444)
Rates: $47-$80
Tel: (541) 247-7718

JOT'S RESORT & CONDOS
94360 Wedderburn Loop Rd (97444)
Rates: $50-$115
Tel: (541) 247-6676
(800) 367-5687

KIMBALL CREEK BEND RESORT
97136 N Bank Rogue (97444)
Rates: $41-$70
Tel: (541) 247-7580

MOTEL 6
94433 Jerry's Flat Rd (97444)
Rates: $45-$79
Tel: (541) 247-4533
(800) 759-4533

NESIKA BEACH VACATION RENTAL
33026 Nesika Rd (97444)
Rates: $75-$80
Tel: (541) 247-6434

OREGON TRAIL LODGE
29855 N Ellensburg Ave (97444)
Rates: $38-$65
Tel: (541) 247-6030

ROGUE LANDING
94749 Jerry's Flat Rd (97444)
Rates: $20-$50
Tel: (541) 247-6105

SAND 'N SEA MOTEL
29362 S Ellensburg Ave (97444)
Rates: $41-$90
Tel: (541) 247-6658
(800) 808-7263

WESTERN VILLAGE MOTEL
29399 S Ellensburg Ave (97444)
Rates: $40-$60
Tel: (541) 247-6611

**THE WHIMSEY HOUSE
VACATION RENTAL**
94249 Third St (97444)
Rates: $85
Tel: (541) 247-2661

RECREATION

PUPP'S CAMP TRAIL HIKE

Intermediate/12.0 miles/7.0 hours

Info: When you're looking to get away from it all in a pristine slice of Mother Nature, make a slot in your touring plans for this one. You and furface will trek through the Kalmiopsis Wilderness along this serene trail. Be prepared for a bonafido

workout, much of the going is steep and rocky and surefooted-
ness is a prerequisite. But if you and your rugged Rover are up
for the challenge, this hike packs a scenic punch. The views of
Collier Creek and the Illinois River drainages are nothing short
of outstanding and the pupportunities for tranquility along
(aptly named) Pupp's Camp are almost guaranteed. Get a
jumpstart on your day so you can do it all, see it all. Wildlife in
many forms will be evident throughout your journey. Your trip
will be akin to roaming a museum outdoor-style. But remember, this is a designated wilderness, so leave only footprints,
take only memories. For more information: (541) 247-6651.

Directions: From Gold Beach, travel south on Highway 101
about 1.5 miles to CR 635 (Hunter Creek Road) and turn left.
Take CR 635 about 4 miles to FS 3680 and turn left. Take 3680
approximately 20 miles to FS 400, veer right and continue 8
miles to the trailhead at Game Lake.

SHRADER OLD-GROWTH TRAIL HIKE - Leashes

Beginner/1.0 miles/0 5 hours

Info: This trail dishes up an excellent outdoor learning experience for you and the wagster. You're about to enter an ancient
forest that has evolved over hundreds of years into a world of
enchantment of virgin forests that are still dense, lush and
evergreen. The wistful sounds of flyboys may be the only
sounds you'll hear. In this serene woodland, you'll get an up-
close glimpse of the giants of the Northwest - Douglas fir and
Port Orford cedars tower 200 to 250 feet above you. These
unusual trees are set apart from the others by their large, irreg-
ularly shaped tops as opposed to the pyramidal tops of the
younger trees that comprise the understory. Make note of the
nurse logs (fallen trees). These logs, perhaps the most important characteristic of an old-growth forest, serve as a nesting
place for young plants and often live for more than 250 years.
Plan a visit to this neck of the woods in spring and treat yourself to a blaze of pink glory when the wild rhodies strut their
showy stuff. You'll find countless secluded niches just perfect
for R&R or a picnic repast, so pack a biscuit basket and do
lunch. This all gain, no pain journey will definitely win your
heart. For more information: (800) 525-2334.

Locate Other Dog-Friendly Activities...Check Nearby Cities

Directions: From Gold Beach, take Jerry's Flat Road (FS 3300) east about 10 miles to Lobster Creek. Turn right on FS 090 and follow signs to the trailhead. Parking is available on the left-hand side of the road near the trailhead.

GOVERNMENT CAMP

LODGING

MT. HOOD INN
87450 E Govt Camp Loop (97028)
Rates: $125-$155
Tel: (503) 272-3205
(800) 443-7777

SUMMIT MEADOW CABINS
P.O. Box 235 (97028)
Rates: $90-$170
Tel: (503) 272-3494

RECREATION

HIDDEN LAKE TRAIL HIKE - Leashes

Beginner/4.0 miles/2.0 hours

Info: Make the most of this trail's assets and plan a visit in June when the wild rhododendrons bloom, splashing their glorious pink color over the lush green backdrop. A gentle path ascends to the crystal clear waters of Hidden Lake where you can spread the red checks and break some bread and biscuits with your number one furface. If you're feeling energetic, take to one of the side trails and explore to your heart's content. A favorite with the locals, expect company in the summer season. For more information: (503) 666-0704.

Directions: From Government Camp, travel Highway 26 west about 6 miles to Kiwanis Club Road (Road 2639) and turn north. Continue on Kiwanis Club Road about 2 miles to the marked trailhead on the left just after the Kiwanis Camp entrance.

Note: Open June through October.

MIRROR LAKE TRAIL HIKE - Leashes

Beginner/4.0 miles/2.0 hours

Info: A popular trail with the locals, you and your canine crony can try a weekday jaunt and avoid the crowded weekends. On your journey to Mirror Lake, you'll be treated to bird's-eye views of the lush Zigzag Valley and moody Mt. Hood. The still waters of Mirror Lake beckon you to explore. Maybe you and the barker will uncover the perfect picnic spot. There's also a short side trail which zooms off from the west shore of the lake and deposits you at another lake with a nice view of Tom, Dick and Harry Mountains. Peregrine falcons are often seen soaring over the ridges that backdrop the lake. Maybe you'll be a lucky dog and see one yourself. For more information: (503) 666-0704.

Directions: From Government Camp, travel Highway 26 west to the Yocum Falls Sno-Park near the footbridge over Camp Creek and park. The trailhead is located at the footbridge.

Note: Open June through October except from July 30 to September 10 for peregrine falcon release.

MOUNTAINEER TRAIL HIKE - Leashes

Beginner/2.0 miles/1.0 hours

Info: No bones about it, this easy hike packs a panoramic zinger. You'll collect excellent views as you and your hiking guru experience a gentle ascent through gnarled timber to the historic Silcox Hut, a 1939 Civilian Conservation Corps structure that has been renovated and reopened. At the top, be prepared to see forever. The majestic peaks of Mt. Jefferson, Three Sisters and Broken Top rise dramatically in the distance and what seems like all of eastern Oregon can be viewed from your lofty perch. On a clear day, the beautiful Coast Range is also within sighting distance. If you and the hikemeister are still raring to go, extend your trek with a side trip along the Pacific Crest Trail a little farther west from the top. For more information: (503) 666-0704.

Directions: From Government Camp, turn north onto Timberline Road (Forest Service Road 50). Follow the signs about 5 miles to Timberline Lodge and parking area. The trailhead is on the east side of Timberline Lodge.

Note: Open August through October.

TIMBERLINE TRAIL HIKE - Leashes

Intermediate-Expert/2.0-40 miles/1.0 hours-5 days

Info: When you want to have an unparalleled look at Mount Hood, this one's for you. The trail circles the 11,000'+ volcanic peak and travels close to the timberline most of the way. You'll collect extraordinary views in every direction and witness the many faces and incredible profiles of Mount Hood. If flowers power your wagging machine, the wildflower meadows on the north side begin at Cairn Basin. Play follow the sniffmeister to Eden Park, Wy'East Basin and Elk Grove, each a technicolor vision. Depending on how far you travel, you'll pass canyons, waterfalls, glaciers and meadows, hopscotch rocks on stream crossings and scramble up hillsides. The epitome of outdoor Oregon, be prepared for the challenge this trail represents. It drops in elevation as low as 3,200' and climbs to over 7,300'. And no matter what side excursions might tempt you, take the time to smell the flowers by hooking up with the spur trail to Paradise Park. Aah, this is the stuff of doggie dreams. FYI: Snowstorms start as early as October and it is not uncommon for the trail to be snow covered until July. Plan accordingly. For more information: (503) 666-0704.

Directions: From Government Camp, turn north onto Timberline Road (Forest Service Road 50). Follow the signs about 5 miles to Timberline Lodge and parking area. The trailhead is located 200 yards north of Timberline Lodge.

GRANTS PASS

LODGING

**BEST WESTERN INN
AT THE ROGUE**
8959 Rogue River Hwy (97527)
Rates: $45-$75
Tel: (541) 582-2200
(800) 238-0700

BUDGET INN
1253 NE 6th St (97526)
Rates: $35-$45
Tel: (541) 479-2952

CITY CENTER MOTEL
741 NE 6th St (97526)
Rates: n/a
Tel: (541) 476-6134

FLAMINGO INN
728 NW 6th St (97526)
Rates: $30-$42
Tel: (541) 476-6601

Hotel Policies May Be Subject To Change

GOLDEN INN MOTEL
1950 NW Vine St (97526)
Rates: $40-$48
Tel: (541) 479-6611

HOLIDAY INN EXPRESS
105 NE Agness (97526)
Rates: $59-$84
Tel: (541) 471-6144
(800) 465-4329

KNIGHTS INN
104 SE 7th St (97526)
Rates: $38-$44
Tel: (541) 479-5595
(800) 826-6835

MOTEL ORLEANS
1889 NE 6th St (97526)
Rates: $45-$63
Tel: (541) 479-8301
(800) 626-1900

MOTEL 6
1800 NE 7th St (97526)
Rates: $30-$36
Tel: (541) 474-1331
(800) 440-6000

REDWOOD MOTEL
815 NE 6th St (97526)
Rates: $46-$50
Tel: (541) 476-0878

RIVERSIDE INN RESORT & CONF CTR
971 SE 6th St (97526)
Rates: $62-$275
Tel: (541) 476-6873
(800) 334-4567

ROD & REEL MOTEL
7875 Rogue River Hwy (97527)
Rates: $40-$75
Tel: (541) 582-1516
(800) 516-5557

ROGUE RIVER INN
6285 Rogue River Hwy (97527)
Rates: $43-$79
Tel: (541) 582-1120
(800) 822-2895

ROGUE VALLEY MOTEL
7799 Rogue River Hwy (97527)
Rates: $42-$72
Tel: (541) 582-3762

SHILO INNS
1880 NW 6th St (97526)
Rates: $62-$75
Tel: (541) 479-8391
(800) 222-2244

SUPER 8 MOTEL
1949 NE 7th St (97526)
Rates: $47-$53
Tel: (541) 474-0888
(800) 800-8000

THRIFTLODGE
748 SE 7th St (97526)
Rates: $30-$45
Tel: (541) 476-7793
(800) 525-9055

WEASKU INN
5560 Rogue River Hwy (97527)
Rates: $125-$275
Tel: (541) 476-4190
(800) 493-2758

RECREATION

BIG PINE TRAIL HIKE - Leashes

Beginner/0.2-1.75 miles/0.25-1.0 hours

Info: A virtual snifforama, your hound will be in tree heaven in these Hansel and Gretel-like piney woods. Comprised of four interconnecting looping trails, the Big Pine Trail has a little something for every breed. Lazybones can check out the pupsqueak .2-mile Creek Loop Trail, while go-go Fidos can kick up some dust on the .75-mile Challenge Loop Trail. Tree buffs won't want to miss the .3-mile Big Pine Loop and the .5-mile

Sunshine Loop, where one of the world's tallest ponderosa pines, the 250′ Big Pine, awaits your inspection. Go ahead, make your dog's day and do all four loop-de-loops. For more information: (541) 476-3830.

Directions: From Grants Pass, head north on Interstate 5 to the Merlin exit (#61). At the light, make a left on Merlin-Galice Road and proceed 10 miles to FS 25. Turn left on FS 25 and drive 12 miles to the Big Pine Campground and the trailhead.

CHINA CREEK TRAIL HIKE - Leashes

Intermediate/Expert/9.8 miles/6.0 hours

Info: If water equates to paradise for you and ol′ twinkle paws, then you've found nirvana. But nothing great comes easy. Expect to encounter miles of steep switchbacks and creek crossings. The beauty of your surroundings and the chance for wet and wild pooch shenanigans is your payback. Pack plenty of H_2O and high energy snacks and biscuits, you'll both need the boost. For more information: (541) 476-3830.

Directions: From Grants Pass, head north on Interstate 5 to the Merlin exit (#61). At the light, make a left on Merlin-Galice Road and proceed 10 miles to FS 25. Turn left on FS 25 and drive approximately 7 miles to the trailhead at China Creek.

RED DOG TRAIL HIKE - Leashes

Beginner/5.0 miles/2.5 hours

Info: Water-loving gadabouts will be grinning from ear to ear when they get a load of the splish-splashing fun that awaits on this creekside odyssey. The scenic trail skirts Red Dog Creek to its end at the Briggs Creek Trail intersection and Briggs Creek, aka puppy paradise. Go ahead, be a kid again. A brown bagger to share with the wagger will make your afternoon complete. For more information: (541) 476-3830.

Directions: From Grants Pass, head north on Interstate 5 to the Merlin exit (#61). At the light, make a left on Merlin-Galice Road and proceed 10 miles to FS 25. Turn left on FS 25 and drive approximately 12 miles to FS 2512 make a right and travel 8 miles to FS 068. Follow FS 068 to the trailhead.

SHAN CREEK TRAIL HIKE - Leashes

Intermediate/4.2 miles/2.5 hours

Info: For some Rexercise in a pretty locale far from the maddening crowds, treat your furbanite to this outdoor excursion brimming with great views. You'll hike beside Shan Creek and then boogie to a ridgetop with beautiful panoramas of the Shan Creek drainage. The creek and a swimming hole provide cool off spots on those dog days of summer. Hey, don't forget a fuzzy tennie and a fun attitude, both will make the day even more memorable. For more information: (541) 476-3830.

Directions: From Grants Pass, head west on Highway 199 about 10 miles to the Applegate River, turning north on Riverbanks Road. Continue to FS 2706 (Shan Creek Road) and go west approximately 1.2 miles to the trailhead.

GRESHAM

LODGING

HOLIDAY INN EXPRESS
2323 NE 181st St (97230)
Rates: $55-$79
Tel: (503) 492-4000
(800) 465-4329

HALFWAY

LODGING

CLEAR CREEK FARM B&B
Rt 1, Box 138 (97834)
Rates: $55-$60
Tel: (541) 742-2238
(800) 742-4992

PINE VALLEY LODGE
163 N Main St (97834)
Rates: $65-$140
Tel: (541) 742-2027

HALSEY

LODGING

PIONEER VILLA TRUCK PLAZA
33180 Hwy 228 (97348)
Rates: $45
Tel: (541) 369-2801

Locate Other Dog-Friendly Activities...Check Nearby Cities

HARBOR

LODGING

BEST WESTERN BEACHFRONT INN
16008 Boat Basin Rd (97415)
Rates: $65-$172
Tel: (541) 469-7779
(800) 528-1234

HEPPNER

RECREATION

ALDER CREEK TRAIL HIKE

Intermediate/6.0 miles/4.0 hours

Info: If wet paws and water hijinks equate to pupster joy, this is your kinda trail. You and the soon-to-be-wet one will follow a shaded course along Alder Creek where tootsie dipping pupportunities come free of charge. When you can successfully convince your aqua pup to leave this cool oasis, there's more fun ahead. From the creek, you'll ascend a hillside to its end at the Copple Butte Trail junction. Muscular mutts can continue west on the Copple Butte Trail for a 2 miler to the top of Madison Butte and plenty of eye popping scenery. Then just skedaddle back to the Skookum Trail junction to create a return loop to the trailhead or retrace your steps for another dose of waterful fun. For more information: (541) 676-9187.

Directions: From Heppner, head south on Highway 207 approximately 26 miles to Anson Wright County Park. Make a left on County Road 670, which turns into FS 22 after about 3 miles. Drive to FS 2119, turn left and continue 3 miles to FS 21. Make another left on FS 21 for 3 miles to FS 21-140, turn left and follow to the trailhead located near the tank trap.

ANSON WRIGHT COUNTY PARK - Leashes

Info: For a peaceful afternoon away from it all, come and explore the 18 acres of this pretty parkland. Check out the nifty fishing pond just 100' wide by 200' long and only six' deep in the deepest spot. Petite? Perhaps, but stocked with rainbow trout that might just grace your dinner table that night. Lazybones will want to include a blanket, a good read and a tough chew. There are plenty of chill-out ops. For more information: (541) 676-5536.

Directions: From Heppner, head south on Highway 207 approximately 26 miles to Anson Wright County Park.

BULL PRAIRIE LAKE TRAIL HIKE

Beginner/0.5 miles/0.25 hours

Info: Simple and simply pretty, this hike gets the high five from die-hard sofa loafers. The quickie loop around sun-drenched Bull Prairie Lake uncovers a multitude of picnicking possibilities. Able anglers, don't forget to pack your gear. The lake is annually stocked with rainbow trout, making it a primo fishing spot. For more information: (541) 676-9187.

Directions: From Heppner, head south on Highway 207 for 45 miles to FS 2039. Turn left on FS 2039 and follow to the Bull Prairie Recreation Area. The trailheads is accessible anywhere you want along the lake.

CUTSFORTH PARK - Leashes

Info: Pondamania is the name of the game at this charming green scene. The largest pond measures 120 by 250 feet and is teeming with yummy rainbow trout. If your fishy dreams don't come true in the big pond, give the smaller one a go. No matter how your luck goes, there's always the streamside serenity to make your day worthwhile. For more information: (541) 676-5536.

Directions: From Heppner, travel 20 miles southeast on CR 678 (FS 53) to the park entrance.

Note: FS 53 is part of the Blue Mountain National Scenic Byway and is open from May 15 - November 15. Fall closures vary due to weather conditions.

MADISON BUTTE TRAIL HIKE

Intermediate/6.0 miles/4.0 hours

Info: A combo plate worth pursuing, Rexercise and scenery go hand in hand on this trail. The uphill course provides an aerobic workout for the body and marvelous views for the soul. Mt. Hood, Mt. Adams and Madison Butte vie for your attention along the route. At trail's end, do the descent thing or if you've got the stamina for more, hightail it along the one miler to Madison Butte Lookout. From your lofty perch, the spectacular views are to die for. Bone voyage. For more information: (541) 676-9187.

Directions: From Heppner, head south on Highway 207 approximately 26 miles to Anson Wright County Park. Make a left on County Road 670, which turns into FS 22 and continue to FS 2119. Turn left on FS 2119 for 3 miles to FS 21. Make another left on FS 21, travel past the cattle guard to the trailhead on the left just before Tupper Work Center.

SKOOKUM TRAIL HIKE

Intermediate/3.5 miles/2.0 hours

Info: For an invigorating workout in a postcardian setting, ink this hike in your filofax. Climbing nearly 1,000' in less than 2 miles, you're sure to burn some kibble. As you and Hercules hightail it through the scattered pinelands, the views will make you glad you came. For a change of scenery on your outbound voyage, head east on the Copple Butte Trail to the Alder Creek Trail and loop back to the trailhead. For more information: (541) 676-9187.

Directions: From Heppner, head south on Highway 207 approximately 26 miles to Anson Wright County Park. Make a left on County Road 670, which turns into FS 22 and continue to FS 2119. Turn left on FS 2119 for 3 miles to FS 21. Make another left on FS 21 for 3 miles to FS 21-140. Turn left on FS 21-140 for a half-mile to FS 21-146. Make a left and follow FS 21-146 to the trailhead located on the right, just past the FS 142 junction.

HERMISTON

LODGING

SANDS MOTEL
835 N 1st St (97838)
Rates: $35-$65
Tel: (541) 567-5516
(888) 567-9521

THE WAY INN
635 S Hwy 395 (97838)
Rates: $32-$34
Tel: (541) 567-5561
(888) 564-8767

HILLSBORO

LODGING

BEST WESTERN HALLMARK INN
3500 NE Cornell Rd (97124)
Rates: $55-$60
Tel: (503) 648-3500
(800) 528-1234

RESIDENCE INN PORTLAND WEST
18855 NW Tanasbourne Dr (97124)
Rates: $89-$145
Tel: (503) 531-3200
(800) 331-3131

HOOD RIVER

LODGING

BERYL HOUSE B&B
4079 Barrett Dr (97031)
Rates: $60-$70
Tel: (541) 386-5567

BEST WESTERN HOOD RIVER INN
1108 E Marina Way (97031)
Rates: $49-$165
Tel: (541) 386-2200
(800) 828-7873

COLUMBIA GORGE HOTEL
4000 Westcliff Dr (97031)
Rates: $150-$270
Tel: (541) 386-5566
(800) 345-1921

HACKETT HOUSE B&B
922 State St (97031)
Rates: $45-$75
Tel: (541) 386-1014

HOOD RIVER HOTEL
102 Oak St (97031)
Rates: $49-$145
Tel: (541) 386-1900
(800) 386-1859

HOOD RIVER VACATION RENTALS
823 Cascade Ave (97031)
Rates: n/a
Tel: (541) 387-3113

LOST LAKE RESORT & CAMPGROUND
P.O. Box 90, Lost Lake Rd (97031)
Rates: $45-$95
Tel: (541) 386-6366

MEREDITH GORGE MOTEL
4300 Westcliff Dr (97031)
Rates: $34-$54
Tel: (541) 386-1515

VAGABOND LODGE
4070 Westcliff Dr (97031)
Rates: $33-$62
Tel: (541) 386-2992

Locate Other Dog-Friendly Activities...Check Nearby Cities

<u>RECREATION</u>

COLUMBIA RIVER GORGE

Info: See Cascade Locks, Portland, The Dalles and Troutdale for additional lodging and recreation.

LOST LAKE BUTTE TRAIL HIKE

Intermediate/4.0 miles/2.5 hours

Info: When you want to sample Mother Nature at her best and get a workout to boot, set your sights on this somewhat challenging hike to a lofty summit. In spring, the vibrancy of the blooming rhodies will add a bounce to your step. Take your camera and lots of film, this place eats Fuji. The last 0.75 miles are the toughest. You'll switchback to the summit but know this, evey huff and puff will be rewarded with an ooh and aah. On a clear day you might not see forever, but you'll see Mounts Hood, Jefferson, Rainier, St. Helens and Adams. If that's not enough, get an eyeful of Mount Defiance, Indian and Larch Mountains, Lost Lake and the Upper Hood River Valley. Phew! With the vistas, the colors and the snowcaps, you'll find it hard to leave. When the time comes to do the descent thing, turn the hound around, you're homeward bound. For more information: (541) 352-6002.

Directions: From Hood River, travel south on Highway 35 approximately 14 miles to Woodworth Road. Turn west and drive 3 miles to Dee Highway (#281), turn north. Continue about 5 miles to the Dee Hardboard Plant. Make a sharp left and stay to your left after the bridge crossing, following the signs to Lost Lake. The trail begins in the campground near the first road junction, but the forest service recommends parking where the trail crosses FS 1340.

Note: The trail is snow free from June-September.

OAK RIDGE TRAIL HIKE

Intermediate/4.6 miles/3.0 hours

Info: This one's a bit of a buttkicker but the payback equals the effort. You'll begin with a switchback journey through open

Hotel Policies May Be Subject To Change

grassy slopes (read spring wildflower extravaganza). If you're a fall guy for autumn colors and your pooch goes crazy for a roll in crunchy leaves, expect a manic moment when the Golden Retriever-hued colors create a blazing contrast to the evergreen hillsides. When you begrudgingly leave the leafers behind, heads up, you'll be entering a heavenscent world of pine and fir. At the top, let yourself be awed by the stunning, unobstructed views of Mounts Hood, Adams, St. Helens and Rainier. The Hood River Valley will compete for your attention as well. Take the time to enjoy the eye feast before retracing your steps to the trailhead. For more information: (541) 352-6002.

Directions: From Hood River, travel Highway 35 south about 16 miles to Smullin Road. Turn left and travel to the fork. Stay left on a dirt road and look for the trailhead 0.75 miles up the road.

Note: Trail is free of snow from April-October. The dirt road may be impassable after a heavy rain.

PANORAMA POINT - Leashes

Info: Make a pit stop here and take a lunch break while you and the dawgus enjoy spectacular views of the Hood River.

Directions: Located on Eastside Road, north of Old Dalles Road junction.

RUTHTON POINT - Leashes

Info: Plan a picnic lunch to feed the body while you feast your eyes on the memorable gorge views this sweet spot has to offer.

Directions: Located on Westcliff Drive off Interstate 84, west of The Fruit Tree.

IDLEYLD PARK

<u>LODGING</u>

NORTH UMPQUA RESORT
23885 N Umpqua Hwy (97447)
Rates: $29-$55
Tel: (541) 496-0149

CLEARWATER RIVER TRAIL HIKE - Leashes

Beginner/3.4 miles/2.0 hours

Info: When spring is in the air, toss off the winter doldrums and head out for some fun in the sun. You and your numero uno pal will skirt the Clearwater River along this pleasant path. Look around as your journey unfolds and admire Mother Nature's handiwork. The riverway abounds with clear blue pools, rushing whitewater riffles and petite waterfalls that catch the golden sunlight. A dense canopy of old-growth Douglas fir and refreshingly scented cedar provide the cooling shade while flowering dogwoods, rhododendrons and wildflowers provide the pizazz and contrast for a joyous warm weather journey. For more information: (541) 498-2531.

Directions: From Idleyld Park, travel Highway 138 east approximately 44 miles to FS 4776 and turn left. Drive about 0.25 miles to the trailhead on the left, just past the Clearwater River Bridge.

TOKETEE LAKE TRAIL HIKE

Beginner/0.8 miles/0.5 hours

Info: This lovely lakeside jaunt offers mucho pupportunities for wildlife watching. Otter, beaver and duck often take to the waters of the lake. Afishionados, you'll be happy to know that brown and rainbow trout are abundant in these parts. Who knows, maybe a couple have your name on them. On a hot diggety dog diggety day, this easy hike and the lake environs make for a charming escape. For more information: (541) 498-2531.

Directions: From Idleyld Park, travel Highway 138 east approximately 40 miles to Milepost 59 and turn left onto FS 34. Follow FS 34 to the bottom of the hill and turn left to cross two concrete bridges. There are three access points located near the northwest side of the lake. Park in the gravel turnouts for the trailhead.

JACKSONVILLE

LODGING

THE STAGE LODGE
830 N 5th St (97530)
Rates: $53-$74
Tel: (541) 899-3953
(800) 253-8254

RECREATION

APPLEGATE LAKE

Info: If lakeside recreation gets the wagging machine in high gear, this place will equate to overdrive. Popular for good reason, the forested slopes and towering peaks of the Siskiyou Mountains are dramatically reflected in the crystal clear waters of this dreamy locale.

Directions: From Jacksonville, travel Route 238 south about 8 miles to Applegate Road, turn left. Follow Applegate Road about 15 miles to Applegate Lake.

JOHN DAY

LODGING

BEST WESTERN INN
315 W Main St (97845)
Rates: $52-$105
Tel: (541) 575-1700
(800) 528-1234

BUDGET 8 MOTEL
711 W Main St (97845)
Rates: $38-$54
Tel: (541) 575-2155

BUDGET INN
250 E Main S t (97845)
Rates: $38-$43
Tel: (541) 575-2100
(800) 854-4442

DREAMERS LODGE
144 N Canyon Blvd (97845)
Rates: $46-$50
Tel: (541) 575-0526
(800) 654-2849

SUNSET INN
390 W Main St (97845)
Rates: $44-$56
Tel: (541) 575-1462
(800) 452-4899

TRAVELLER'S MOTEL
755 S Canyon Blvd (97845)
Rates: $30+
Tel: (541) 575-2076

<u>RECREATION</u>

ARCH ROCK TRAIL HIKE - Leashes

Beginner/0.8 miles/0.5 hours

Info: Short and scenic best describe this trail. A hop, skip and a jump and you're on the way to Arch Rock, a unique geologic structure formed by volcanic activity. FYI: The small cavelike openings set into the arch are a direct result of wind erosion. When you feel the refreshing breeze in your hair, think about the power of Mother Nature and how much time it took to erode the rock. When you're ready to leave, retrace those paw-prints. For more information: (541) 575-2110.

Directions: From John Day, take Highway 26 east for 9 miles to Bear Creek Road. Turn right (north) onto Bear Creek Road (CR 18) and drive approximately 10 miles to FS 36. Travel northeast on FS 36 about 10 miles to FS 3650. Take a right on FS 3650 and drive 0.75 miles to the trailhead on the right.

BLACKEYE TRAIL HIKE - Leashes

Intermediate/5.2 miles/3.0 hours

Info: A sure cure for the dog days of summer, this odyssey dishes up miles of shaded terrain and plenty of special paw-dipping oases. Expect company of the wildlife kind, deer, elk and big spruce grouse inhabit the dense thickets. If you're packing a camera, give it a workout and see if you can capture these bounders on film. Geology buffs, this could be your lucky day. Small quartz geodes have been discovered in the creek valleys along your route. You'll definitely want to include some trail mix and H_2O. And don't forget Bowser's biscuits. For more information: (541) 575-2110.

Directions: From John Day, travel east on Highway 26 for 28 miles to Route 7. Turn left on Route 7 and drive 2 miles to CR 20. Take CR 20 west 7 miles to FS 4550. Turn right and travel to 4559. Make a right and drive to the trailhead at the end of the road.

Note: Leash your dog and use extreme caution during hunting season.

Hotel Policies May Be Subject To Change

CEDAR GROVE TRAIL HIKE - Leashes

Beginner/2.0 miles/1.0 hours

Info: The fresh scent of cedar perfumes the air, so breathe deeply and get your fill. You'll wind this way and that through the Cedar Botanical Area, a region surrounded by spectacular steep-walled canyons. You'll have it made in the shade of stately (you guessed it) cedars in this virtual snifforama. No bones about it, you can beat the heat while you explore a pretty piece of the country on this refreshingly cool trail. For more information: (541) 575-2110.

Directions: From John Day, travel 18 miles west on US 26 to FS 21 (Fields Creek Road). Turn south (left) on FS 21 and drive 9 miles to FS 2150. Turn west (right) onto FS 2150 and continue 5 miles to the trailhead.

CLYDE HOLLIDAY STATE RECREATION SITE - Leashes

Info: With 20 acres of grasslands bordering the rippling waters of the John Day River, you and your river rover can loll the hours away soaking up the scenery at this lovely locale. Tote the red checks along with a biscuit basket, there's a shaded picnic niche where you and your best bud can munch on lunch. Pull up a square of green you can call your own and settle in for an R&R kind of day. During the summer months, there are scheduled programs at the amphitheater. Call ahead and see what's on tap. For more information: (541) 575-2773.

Directions: From John Day, travel west on Route 26 for 6 miles to the park entrance.

Note: Day use fee may be charged.

FIELDS PEAK TRAIL HIKE - Leashes

Intermediate/8.0 miles/5.0 hours

Info: For a fun-filled, somewhat challenging journey through forested mountainsides, highlight this trek on your agenda. You'll start at an elevation of 6,600' and end at a lofty 7,400', the highest point in the Malheur National Forest. Your bird's-eye view will encompass picturesque John Day Valley and

Locate Other Dog-Friendly Activities...Check Nearby Cities

majestic McClellan Mountain. As you shimmy up the mountainside, you and your hiking hound will walk in the cool shade of fragrant spruce and pine. If you can tear your eyes away from the fabulous views that greet you at every turn, watch for the local flyboys as they whiz through the treetops. For more information: (541) 575-2110.

Directions: From John Day, take Highway 26 west for 18 miles to Fields Creek Road (FS 21). Turn left on Fields Creek Road and travel 4.5 miles south to FS 115. Turn left on FS 115 and continue 1.5 miles east on FS 115 to the trailhead.

MAGONE LAKE LOOP TRAIL HIKE - Leashes

Beginner/1.5 miles/0.75 hours

Info: The lure of a level trail with mucho scenery and wildlife makes this a popular one with locals and visitors alike, so adopt a social attitude and be prepared to meet and greet. You'll circle shimmering, sun-dappled Magone Lake where cozy nooks await. At the first sign of spring and long into summer, the lakeside meadows put on quite a wildflower show, so stow some extra film. An avian havian, chatty songbirds are everywhere. Not to mention the fishy tales waiting to come true for able anglers. One visit and you'll understand why you're not alone on this easy-does-it trail. For more information: (541) 575-2110.

Directions: From John Day, take Highway 26 east for 9 miles to CR 18. Turn left on CR 18 and drive 12 miles to FS 3620. Turn left on 3620 and drive 1.5 miles to FS 3618. Turn right on FS 3618 and drive to the Magone Lake day-use area and the trailhead.

MAGONE SLIDE TRAIL HIKE - Leashes

Intermediate/1.0 miles/1.0 hours

Info: A bit more challenging than the lake loop, this trail offers a chance for solitude and serenity in another pretty milieu. From the get-go, you'll know you're in for one howl of a good time. After a moderate 300' ascent through a pine-scented stand of ponderosa, you'll be rewarded by sweeping vistas of the surrounding valleys and interesting rock faces. Look closely for evidence of an enormous landslide that flattened the region in the 1860s. When the ogling is over, do an about-face. For more information: (541) 575-2110.

Directions: From John Day, take Highway 26 east for 9 miles to CR 18. Turn left on CR 18 and drive 12 miles to FS 3620. Turn left on 3620 and drive 1.5 miles to FS 3618. Turn right on FS 3618 and drive to the Magone Lake day-use area and the trailhead.

NIPPLE BUTTE TRAIL HIKE

Intermediate/6.2 miles/4.0 hours

Info: Go west, young pup, about 400 yards to the trailhead at the fenceline off FS 296. Then you're off on a secluded journey in a pristine landscape. Jagged peaks and steep-walled rock faces are part of the pretty picture. The vistas are nothing short of breathtaking. You and the one with the ear-to-ear grin will gain a modest 500' in elevation as you skedaddle atop the ridge to Nipple Butte. Save some film for the outstanding panoramas of the East Fork Beech and John Day Valleys, Nipple Creek Canyon and the far reaching Malheur National Forest. Break some bread and biscuits at the summit before turning the hound around and heading back down. For more information: (541) 575-2110.

Directions: From John Day, take Highway 26 east for 9 miles to CR 18. Turn left on CR 18 and drive 14 miles to FS 279. Turn left on FS 279 and drive 0.75 miles to FS 296. Park here and walk to the trailhead.

RILEY CREEK TRAIL HIKE

Beginner/4.5 miles/2.5 hours

Info: For a bonafido walk in the woods, set your sights on this hike. The thick canopy of lodgepole pine and alder creates a cool, aromatic environment for you and the one with his nose to the ground. Tote your binoculars and espy what's a-fly. Check out the way the sun slips through the treetops to form interesting patterns on the forest floor. The McClellan Trail signals your turnaround point. For more information: (541) 575-2110.

Directions: From John Day, take Highway 395 south approximately 15 miles to CR 63. Turn right on CR 63 and travel 6 miles to FS 21. Take FS 21 for 7 miles to FS 2190. Turn right on FS 2190 and drive to the trailhead at the end of the road.

TAMARACK CREEK TRAIL HIKE

Intermediate/8.0 miles/5.0 hours

Info: Fall hikers are in for a treat when the colors of the leafy tamaracks (aka western larch) do their presto chango routine. The landscape shimmers in Golden Retriever hues, a postcardian pretty site backdropped by the forest's rich evergreenery. But almost any time of year promises and delivers all that you and the pooch crave in an outdoor adventure. At the onset, you'll wander atop a lofty ridge before the pathway dips into Tamarack Basin, a riparian oasis for water lovers and birdwatchers alike. Lucky dogs might experience a bighorn sheep sighting. These reclusive, elusive mammals are a sight to behold, so walk softly and carry a loaded camera. For more information: (541) 575-2110.

Directions: From John Day, travel south on Highway 395 approximately 9 miles to CR 65. Turn left on CR 65 and drive 4 miles to FS 6510. Head north on FS 6510 to the trailhead at the end of the road.

Note: Leash your dog when approaching wildlife. Do not allow your dog to chase or harass wildlife.

TEMPEST MINE TRAIL HIKE - Leashes

Intermediate/7.0 miles/4.0 hours

Info: Doggistorians will have something to bark home about after a visit to this historic locale. Quite a few relics of the old west mining days can be seen along this trail. The path consists mostly of old wagon roads, but in spring and early summer, rainbowesque wildflowers edge these history-rich routes and turn a muted landscape into a picture pretty setting. Keep a keen snout out for a Bambi or two bounding through the woodsy sections and listen closely for the sweet tweets of songbirds. When you reach Tempest Mine, throw the old dog a bone and enjoy a bit of R&R before retracing your steps to the trailhead. For more information: (541) 575-2110.

Hotel Policies May Be Subject To Change

Directions: From John Day, travel east on Highway 26 for 28 miles to Route 7. Turn left on Route 7 and drive 2 miles to CR 20. Take CR 20 west 7 miles to FS 4550. Turn right and travel to 4559. Make a right and drive to the trailhead at the end of the road.

Note: Leash your dog and use extreme caution when approaching mining areas.

JORDAN VALLEY

LODGING

SAHARA MOTEL
607 Main, Hwy 95 (97910)
Rates: $36-$38
Tel: (541) 586-2810
(800) 828-4432

JOSEPH

LODGING

DRAGON MEADOWS B&B
504 N Lake St (97846)
Rates: $65+
Tel: (541) 432-1027

INDIAN LODGE MOTEL
201 S Main St (97846)
Rates: $36-$57
Tel: (541) 432-2651

FLYING ARROW RESORT
59782 Wallowa Lake Hwy (97846)
Rates: $63-$170
Tel: (541) 432-2951

STEIN'S CABINS
84681 Ponderosa Ln (97846)
Rates: $55-$85
Tel: (541) 432-2391

RECREATION

WALLOWA LAKE STATE RECREATION AREA - Leashes

Info: Set in the heart of the Wallowa Mountains (aka The Switzerland of America), this serene green scene is a pretty way to spend the day. Stake a claim to a cozy spot beside the shores of picturesque Wallowa Lake and make your fishy dreams come true. Rainbow trout or kokanee could come home as dinner. If you'd like to exercise more than your fishing prerogative, there's a lovely nature trail waiting to be explored. Lazy dogs can kick back in the grassy area and do nothing but cloudgaze. For more information: (541) 432-8855.

Directions: From Joseph, travel south on Route 82 for 6 miles to park entrance.

Note: Day use fee may be charged.

JUNCTION CITY

LODGING

GUEST HOUSE MOTEL
1335 Ivy St (97448)
Rates: $41-$67
Tel: (541) 998-6524
(800) 835-5170

KENO

LODGING

GREEN SPRINGS BOX R RANCH
16799 Hwy 66 (97627)
Rates: $110-$150
Tel: (541) 482-1873

KERBY

LODGING

HOLIDAY MOTEL
24810 Redwood Hwy (97531)
Rates: $44-$48
Tel: (503) 592-3003

KLAMATH FALLS

LODGING

A-1 BUDGET MOTEL
3844 Hwy 97 N (97601)
Rates: $38-$50
Tel: (541) 884-8104

BEST WESTERN KLAMATH INN
4061 S 6th St (97603)
Rates: $59-$85
Tel: (541) 882-1200
(800) 528-1234

CIMARRON MOTOR INN
3060 S 6th St (97603)
Rates: $43-$63
Tel: (541) 882-4601
(800) 742-2648

HARRIMAN SPRINGS RESORT
26661 Rocky Point Rd (97601)
Rates: n/a
Tel: (541) 356-2331

HIGH CHAPARRAL MOTEL
5440 Hwy 97 N (97601)
Rates: $22-$90
Tel: (541) 882-4675

HILL VIEW MOTEL
5543 S 6th St (97601)
Rates: $45-$70
Tel: (541) 883-7771

Hotel Policies May Be Subject To Change

LA VISTA MOTOR LODGE
Hwy 97 N (97601)
Rates: $36-$46
Tel: (541) 882-8844

LAKE OF THE WOODS RESORT
950 Harriman Rd (97601)
Rates: $55-$80
Tel: (541) 949-8300

MAVERICK MOTEL
1220 Main St (97601)
Rates: $31-$39
Tel: (541) 882-6688
(800) 404-6690

OLYMPIC LODGE
3006 Green Springs Dr (97601)
Rates: $30-$57
Tel: (541) 883-8800

OREGON MOTEL 8
5225 Hwy 97 N (97601)
Rates: $36-$39
Tel: (541) 883-3431

QUALITY INN
100 Main St (97601)
Rates: $59-$72
Tel: (541) 882-4666
(800) 732-4666

RED LION INN
3612 S 6th St (97603)
Rates: $56-$84
Tel: (541) 882-8864
(800) 547-8010

ROCK-WOOD MOTEL
2005 Biehn St (97601)
Rates: n/a
Tel: (541) 882-9992

ROCKY POINT RESORT
28121 Rocky Point Rd (97601)
Rates: $48-$89
Tel: (541) 356-2287

SHILO INNS
2500 Almond St (97601)
Rates: $89-$129
Tel: (541) 885-7980
(800) 222-2244

SOUTH ENTRANCE MOTEL
9339 Hwy 97 S (97601)
Rates: n/a
Tel: (541) 883-1994

SUPER 8 MOTEL
3805 Hwy 97 N (97601)
Rates: $46-$52
Tel: (541) 884-8880
(800) 800-8000

RECREATION

BADGER LAKE TRAIL HIKE

Beginner/Intermediate/10.4 miles/6.0 hours

Info: Okay, so your pooch loves nothing more than wet and wild shenanigans. And you're looking for a great getaway hike. Eureka, you've found both. This lake-hopping adventure (aka puppy paradise) is an outing to remember. The trail zigzags among forested slopes that are blue-dotted with pretty lakes. Eeny, meeny, miney, moe, take your pick and go, go, go. You'll find lakes and grassy knolls all along the way. On this journey, you're the maker of your own destiny. In addition to the enchanting landscape and great watering holes, the views are spectacular, so tote your Kodak and lots of film. Carpe diem old wet one. For more information: (541) 885-3400.

Locate Other Dog-Friendly Activities...Check Nearby Cities

Directions: From Klamath Falls, head northwest on Highway 140 for 32 miles to FS 3661, just north of Lake of the Woods. Turn right on FS 3661 approximately 5.6 miles to the Fourmile Campground at road's end. Make a left on the campground road to the trailhead at the east end of the campground.

CLOVER CREEK TRAIL HIKE

Intermediate/8.0 miles/5.0 hours

Info: An easy start but a tough finish is what you and the dogster can expect on this pleasant trail to Clover Creek. Play tagalong with your wagalong amid dense groves of spruce, pine, hemlock and Douglas fir. Once you reach the creek though, you'll trade the gentle terrain for a steep climb along the meadows and ridges of the creek drainage until Clover Lake. Aah, the pain will definitely be worth the gain. You'll literally be in clover, this lake is considered one of the area's most beautiful alpine watering holes. Take five, take a dive and enjoy. For more information: (541) 885-3400.

Directions: From Klamath Falls, head south on Highway 97 to Highway 66 west. Follow Highway 66 approximately 9 miles to Clover Creek Road and turn right. Continue on Clover Creek Road for 15.5 miles to FS 3852. Make a right on FS 3852 for 3.3 miles to the trailhead at road's end.

COLD SPRINGS TRAIL HIKE

Beginner/5.4 miles/3.0 hours

Info: A simple trail, plan ahead and make a day of it. You'll find lots of shade and pretty resting spots that beckon you and the biscuitmeister to partake of lunch alfresco. When you want to combine a bit of exercise with a heavy dose of nature, look no further. The Sky Lakes Trail junction marks trail's end and the start of your return journey. For more information: (541) 885-3400.

Directions: From Klamath Falls, head northwest on Highway 140 for 22 miles to FS 3651. Turn right on FS 3651 for 10.2 miles to the trailhead at road's end.

COLLIER MEMORIAL STATE PARK - Leashes

Info: Spend some time pawrusing the outdoor exhibits at this interesting park and you'll come away with some insight into the logging industry. The pooch won't chase the "Cats" here, they're old crawler tractors. The nickname stems from the brand name Caterpillar. The displays are presented in a progressive format, beginning with the earliest logging tools and finishing with the enormous engine near the parking lot. This engine produced enough power to run an entire sawmill. There's also a quaint nature trail that concentrates on the regrowth of trees. A quickie half miler, it takes you from one picnic area to another. Pick your favorite and do lunch alfresco. For more information: (541) 783-2471.

Directions: From Klamath Falls, travel Highway 97 north 30 miles to the park entrance.

LOST CREEK TRAIL HIKE

Beginner/3.0 miles/1.5 hours

Info: Paw-dipping opportunities coupled with gentle terrain create a popular hike for aqua pups and sofa loafers alike. The trail follows an easy course through dense pine and fir woodlands on the slopes of Lost Peak. En route, you'll have to play hopscotch across Lost Creek, so pack your water sandals. The junction with the Pacific Crest Trail signals the end of your journey. If you're still raring to go, another .5 miles west will bring you to splish-splashing fun at Island Lake or .3 miles east and you'll arrive at Bert Lake. For more information: (541) 885-3400.

Directions: From Klamath Falls, head northwest on Highway 140 for 22 miles to FS 3651. Turn right on FS 3651 approximately 8 miles to FS 3659. Make a left on FS 3659 for one mile to the trailhead.

MOUNTAIN LAKES TRAIL HIKE

Intermediate/10.2 miles/7.0 hours

Info: You and your hiking guru will experience a 2,200' elevation change as you scramble up the Seldom Creek drainage through a varied terrain of verdant meadows and volcanic outcroppings on this all day excursion. The Mountain Lakes Loop Trail junction is your turnaround point. For more information: (541) 885-3400.

Directions: From Klamath Falls, travel Highway 97 south about 2 miles to Highway 140. Head northwest on Highway 140 approximately 25 miles to the Dead Indian Highway and turn left. Follow Dead Indian Highway for 0.1 miles to FS 3610. Make a left on FS 3610 for .08 miles to FS 3660. The trailhead is located about 0.8 miles up FS 3660.

SEVENMILE TRAIL HIKE

Beginner/3.8 miles/2.0 hours

Info: Hikers with a penchant for waterful adventures give the creek crossing of this trail two thumbs up. On the other paw, sniffmeisters will flip over the section through wildflower-splashed meadows and dense forests. Birders can have a field day too at this popular avian havian. The trail ends at the Pacific Crest Trail junction. For more information: (541) 885-3400.

Directions: From Klamath Falls, travel Highway 97 south about 2 miles to Highway 140. Take 140 north about 23 miles to West Side Highway. Stay to your right and continue north on the West Side Highway for 11 miles to its end at Sevenmile Road and the junction with FS 33. Continue traveling north on FS 33 (which turns into FS 3334) to the trailhead at the end of the road.

SOUTH ROCK CREEK TRAIL HIKE

Beginner/4.6 miles/2.5 hours

Info: Once you access this simple trail, it's a short 1.6-mile scenic journey to beautiful Heavenly Twins Lakes and chill-out spots galore. The trail slices through a bosque of pine, hemlock and spruce and then follows the headwaters of Rock Creek before ending at the lakes and the Sky Lakes Trail junction. The crystalline waters are icy cold and unbelievably refreshing on a doggone hot day. Enjoy some R&R in the peacefulness of the setting before doing a 180° and returning to earth. Bone voyage. For more information: (541) 885-3400.

Directions: From Klamath Falls, travel Highway 97 south about 2 miles to Highway 140. Head northwest on 140 for 22 miles to FS 3651. Turn right on FS 3651 for 10.2 miles to the Cold Springs Trailhead at road's end. Hike the Cold Springs Trail for .7 miles to access the South Rock Creek Trail.

TWIN PONDS LAKE TRAIL

Beginner/5.0 miles/2.5 hours

Info: Spend some quality time with old brown eyes on this no-sweat hike. You'll meander through pine thickets on the old 1864 Fort Klamath-Jacksonville Military Wagon Road which ends at the Pacific Crest Trail junction. For more information: (541) 885-3400.

Directions: From Klamath Falls, travel Highway 97 south about 2 miles to Highway 140. Head northwest on 140 for 32 miles to FS 3661, just north of Lake of the Woods. Turn right on FS 3661 approximately 5.6 miles to the Fourmile Campground at road's end. Make a left on the campground road to the trailhead at the west end of the campground.

VARNEY CREEK TRAIL HIKE

Intermediate/8.8 miles/5.0 hours

Info: A bounty of nature can be unearthed by you and the loyal one on this terrific hike. Mother Nature has outdone herself in this divine hunk of heaven. From wildflower-strewn slopes to dense pine forests, sun-splashed streams to towering peaks, you'll encounter beauty at every turn. Talk about Kodak moments. Wowser Bowser. For more information: (541) 885-3400.

Directions: From Klamath Falls, travel Highway 97 south for 2 miles to Highway 140. Head northwest on 140 for 20 miles to FS 3637. Turn left on FS 3637 for 1.8 miles to FS 3664. Make a left on FS 3664 for 2 miles to the trailhead at road's end.

LA GRANDE

LODGING

BEST WESTERN PONY SOLDIER INN
2612 Island Ave (97850)
Rates: $64-$85
Tel: (541) 963-7195
(800) 528-1234

BUDGET INN
2215 Adams Ave (97850)
Rates: $32-$49
Tel: (541) 963-7116

GREENWELL MOTEL
305 Adams Ave (97850)
Rates: $25-$30
Tel: (541) 963-4134
(800) 772-0991

MOON MOTEL
2116 Adams Ave (97850)
Rates: n/a
Tel: (541) 963-2724

ORCHARD MOTEL
2206 Adams Ave (97850)
Rates: $30-$39
Tel: (541) 963-6160

QUAIL RUN MOTOR INN
2400 Adams Ave (97850)
Rates: $28-$30
Tel: (541) 963-3400

STARDUST LODGE
402 Adams Ave (97850)
Rates: $25-$45
Tel: (541) 963-4166

WENDELL'S CORNER
2309 Adams Ave (97850)
Rates: n/a
Tel: (541) 963-4424

RECREATION - (NOTE: THIS PARK NO LONGER ACCEPTS PETS)
BLUE MOUNTAIN CROSSING INTERPRETIVE PARK - Leashes

Info: Doggistorians and their people won't want to pass up this one. Set aside by the forest service to preserve the heritage of the emigrants who settled the Oregon Territory, this pristine parkland offers insight into pioneer life along the Oregon Trail. Pick an interpretive pathway and get a quickie education as you stroll through a sylvan environment. For more information: (541) 963-7186.

Directions: From La Grande, travel Interstate 84 approximately 13 miles to exit 248. Follow signs for 3 miles to Blue Mountain Crossing and the park entrance.

The numbered hikes that follow are within Blue Mountain Interpretive Park:

1) INDEPENDENCE LOOP TRAIL HIKE - Leashes

Beginner/0.75 miles/0.5 hours

Info: See if the sniffmeister can snout out the barely visible wheel tracks marking the passage of the pioneers so many years ago.

Hotel Policies May Be Subject To Change

The interpretive signs will broaden your knowledge of this historic era in American life. Use your imagination as you follow the footsteps of those settlers and perhaps come away with a new-found appreciation for the hardships they endured. Pick up a pamphlet from the forest service and get yourself a history lesson.

Directions: From La Grande, travel Interstate 84 approximately 13 miles to exit 248. Follow signs for 3 miles to Blue Mountain Crossing and the park entrance.

2) OREGON CITY LOOP TRAIL HIKE - Leashes

Beginner/0.25 miles/0.25 hours

Info: Listen for the echoes of the past as you and your sidekick stroll this pupsqueak-sized pathway. The numbered posts correspond with a pamphlet, so pick up one before starting out. Do some time traveling and imagine yourself journeying along the Oregon Trail more than 150 years ago.

Directions: From La Grande, travel Interstate 84 approximately 13 miles to exit 248. Follow signs for 3 miles to Blue Mountain Crossing and the park entrance.

LAKE OSWEGO

LODGING

BEST WESTERN SHERWOOD INN
15700 SW Upper
Boones Ferry Rd (97034)
Rates: $50-$85
Tel: (503) 620-2980
(800) 528-1234

CROWNE PLAZA
14811 Kruse Oaks Blvd (97035)
Rates: $95-$135
Tel: (503) 624-8400
(800) 227-6963

RESIDENCE INN PORTLAND SOUTH
15200 SW Bangy Rd (97035)
Rates: $108-$142
Tel: (503) 684-2603
(800) 331-3131

LAKESIDE

LODGING

LAKESHORE LODGE
290 S 8th St (97449)
Rates: $34-$49
Tel: (541) 759-3161
(800) 759-3951

SEADRIFT MOTEL & CAMPGROUND
11022 Coast Hwy 101 (97449)
Rates: $36-$44
Tel: (541) 759-3102

RECREATION

TENMILE LAKE PARK - Leashes

Info: Here's a chance to do nothing but enjoy the prettiness of Oregon's fourth largest lake. Watch sailboats tack into the wind as they swiftly and expertly ply the clear blue waters. A bonafido fun day is in the making as you lollygag lakeside. If you have a penchant for finding the perfect fishing hole, this could be the place. Throw your poor dog a bone and partake of some reel-time pleasures. A generous bounty of Coho salmon, steelhead, rainbow trout, cutthroat, largemouth bass, catfish, bluegill, yellow perch and brown bullhead could make your fishing fantasies come true. For more information: (541) 396-3121 ext. 354.

Directions: At the south end of 11th Street and Park Avenue.

LAKEVIEW

LODGING

BUDGET INN
411 North F St (97630)
Rates: $28+
Tel: (541) 947-2201

LAKEVIEW LODGE MOTEL
301 North G St (97630)
Rates: $40-$64
Tel: (541) 947-2181

HUNTER'S HOT SPRINGS RESORT
Hwy 395 N (97630)
Rates: $45-$55
Tel: (541) 947-4800

RIM ROCK MOTEL
727 South F St (97630)
Rates: $30-$34
Tel: (541) 947-2185

INTERSTATE 8 MOTEL
354 North K St (97630)
Rates: $34-$40
Tel: (541) 947-3341

Hotel Policies May Be Subject To Change

RECREATION

COTTONWOOD CREEK TRAIL HIKE

Beginner/5.0 miles/2.5 hours

Info: Make the most of a sunny day and hustle your buttsky on this delightful trail. A natural pathway skirts Cottonwood Creek to the Cottonwood Reservoir, where you can cool your jets and do the doggie paddle with an expert. There's something fishy going on in this waterway so drop a line, the fishing's fine. The balmy days of summer bring showy wildflowers that sprinkle the landscape with vibrant colors while adding a fragrant scent to the woodsy air. This hike is so rewarding, you'll be planning your return trip before you're back at your car. For more information: (541) 947-6359.

Directions: From Lakeview, travel Highway 140 west about 11 miles to CR 2-20, turn right. Continue on CR 2-20 about 6 miles. CR 2-20 becomes FS 3870. Follow FS 3870 about 3 miles to FS 014, turn right. The marked trailhead is located about a mile off FS 014.

Note: Recommended season June through October.

HART MOUNTAIN NATIONAL ANTELOPE REFUGE - Leashes

Info: Come to where the deer and the antelope play. Established in 1936 to provide a spring, summer and fall range for antelope herds, this 275,000-acre region is a safe harbor for an abundance of wildlife including mule deer, bighorn sheep and several other mammals. An Eden in the desert, the landscape is blue-dotted with springs and quaint lakes. Antelope are commonly seen in the morning near refuge headquarters or from the lookout point. If you're more of a lazybones, late afternoon is a good time too. Birders will see more than two in the bush in this slice of avian havian. From countless songbirds to birds of prey, you'll get a chance to check off quite a few sightings. If what's underwater is more your specialty, give the trout a run for their money. This stunning high desert oasis is definitely worth a slot in your vacation plans. For more information: (541) 947-3315.

Directions: From Lakeview, travel Highway 395 north to Highway 140. Turn east and drive about 15 miles to the Plush-Hart Mountain NWR turnoff and follow signs to the Plush cutoff Road. Continue through the town of Plush and drive 23 miles to refuge headquarters. The road will become a dirt road before you reach headquarters, so drive with care.

Note: The refuge is 65 miles northeast of Lakeview and is located in a very remote area. Use extreme caution and heed all signs during hunting season.

LaPINE

LODGING

**DIAMOND STONE
GUEST LODGE B&B**
16693 Sprague Loop (97739)
Rates: $75-$120
Tel: (541) 536-6263
(800) 600-6263

EAST LAKE RESORT & RV PARK
22430 East Lake Rd (97739)
Rates: $35-$100
Tel: (541) 536-2230

HIGHLANDER MOTEL & RV PARK
51511 Hwy 97 S (97739)
Rates: $32-$43
Tel: (541) 536-2131

LAMPLITER MOTEL & RV PARK
51526 Hwy 97 S (97739)
Rates: $32-$36
Tel: (541) 536-2931

NEWBERRY STATION MOTEL
16515 Reed Rd & Hwy 97 (97739)
Rates: $55-$150
Tel: (541) 536-5130
(800) 210-8616

PAULINA LAKE RESORT
P.O. Box 7 (97739)
Rates: $65-$135
Tel: (541) 536-2240

TIMBERCREST INN
52560 Hwy 97 S (97739)
Rates: $35-$45
Tel: (541) 536-1737

WEST VIEW MOTEL
51371 Hwy 97 S (97739)
Rates: $36-$44
Tel: (541) 536-2115
(800) 440-2115

RECREATION

HAGER MOUNTAIN TRAIL HIKE

Intermediate/1.0-16.2 miles/0.5-10.0 hours

Info: Hop on this pristine slice of the National Recreation Trail which traverses 95 miles of the Fremont National Forest and experience the beauty and serenity of the region. You'll encounter a somewhat steep grade as you ascend to the peak of Hager Mountain where outstanding views of the valley beckon your perusal. Along the well-maintained trail, rock outcroppings invite you to spread the red checks and do lunch in a gorgeous setting. A scattering of wildflowers dot the landscape, their vibrancy an interesting contrast to the rich greens and muted browns of the landscape. Whether you go the distance or tackle only a portion of the trail, you and your hound will come away feeling like champs. For more information: (541) 947-3334.

Directions: From LaPine, travel Highway 97 south for 2 miles to the junction with Highway 31. Take Highway 31 south 44 miles to the city of Silver Lake. From Silver Lake, travel about a half mile west on Highway 31 to CR 4-11, turn left. CR 4-11 becomes FS 27. Continue on FS 27 about 12 miles. The marked trailhead is on the left side of FS 27.

Note: Recommended season June through October.

LaPINE STATE PARK - Leashes

Info: A sun-dappled horseshoe bend in the Deschutes River is the setting for this charming park. Pack a snack and munch on lunch with your furball while you enjoy some old-fashioned R&R on a cushy carpet of pine needles. Songbirds will serenade as you watch the clouds drift by. If your woofer's a hoofer, make tracks to Big Tree. With a circumference of 326" and standing at 191', this impressive ponderosa is the largest in Oregon and is tied for first place as the biggest in the nation. The sniffmeister will probably have to navigate the base of the tree several times to satisfy his curiosity. The aroma that fills the air is the sweet vanilla tinged scent of ponderosa. For more information: (541) 382-3586.

Directions: From LaPine, travel Highway 97 north about 9 miles to Highway 21. Head west about 2 miles to the entrance to LaPine State Park on the left-hand side.

Note: Day use fee may be charged.

LEBANON

<u>LODGING</u>

CASCADE CITY CENTER MOTEL
1296 Main St (97355)
Rates: $32-$45
Tel: (541) 258-8154

SHANICO INN
1840 Main St (97355)
Rates: $40-$46
Tel: (541) 259-2601

Locate Other Dog-Friendly Activities...Check Nearby Cities

LINCOLN CITY

LODGING

ANCHOR MOTEL AND LODGE
4417 SW Hwy 101 (97367)
Rates: $40-$60
Tel: (541) 996-3810
(800) 582-8611

BEL-AIRE MOTEL
2945 NW Hwy 101 (97367)
Rates: n/a
Tel: (541) 994-2984

BLUE HERON LANDING MOTEL
4006 W Devils Lake Rd (97367)
Rates: $59-$64
Tel: (541) 994-4708

CAPTAIN COOK INN
2626 NE Hwy 101 (97367)
Rates: $39-$59
Tel: (541) 994-2522
(800) 994-2522

CITY CENTER MOTEL
1014 NE Hwy 101 (97367)
Rates: $28-$32
Tel: (541) 994-2612

COHO INN
1635 NW Harbor (97367)
Rates: $79-$96
Tel: (541) 994-3684
(800) 848-7006

DOCK OF THE BAY MOTEL
1116 SW 51st St (97367)
Rates: $89-$149
Tel: (541) 996-3549
(800) 362-5229

DOLPHIN MOTEL
1018 SE Hwy 101 (97367)
Rates: $35-$75
Tel: (541) 996-2124

EDGECLIFF MOTEL
3733 SW Hwy 101 (97367)
Rates: $50-$95
Tel: (541) 996-2055

ENCHANTED COTTAGE B&B
4507 SW Coast (97367)
Rates: n/a
Tel: (541) 996-4101

ESTER LEE MOTEL
3803 SW Hwy 101 (97367)
Rates: $45-$125
Tel: (541) 996-3606
(888) 996-3606

HIDEAWAY OCEANFRONT MOTEL
810 SW 10th St (97367)
Rates: n/a
Tel: (541) 994-8874

HOLIDAY INN EXPRESS
1091 SE 1st St (97367)
Rates: n/a
Tel: (541) 996-4400
(800) 465-4329

OVERLOOK MOTEL
3521 SW Anchor (97367)
Rates: $52-$115
Tel: (541) 996-3300

PACIFIC REST B&B
1611 NE 11th St (97367)
Rates: n/a
Tel: (541) 994-2337

RODEWAY INN ON THE BAY
861 SW 51st St (97367)
Rates: $45-$155
Tel: (541) 996-3996
(800) 228-2000

SAILOR JACK'S HIDDEN COVE
1035 NW Harbor Ave (97367)
Rates: $59-$138
Tel: (541) 994-3696
(888) 432-8346

SEA ECHO MOTEL
3510 NE Hwy 101 (97367)
Rates: $38-$59
Tel: (541) 994-2575

SEA HORSE OCEANFRONT LODGING
2039 N Harbor Dr (97367)
Rates: $50-$150
Tel: (541) 994-2101
(800) 622-2101

SEA REST MOTEL
1249 NW 15th St (97367)
Rates: n/a
Tel: (541) 994-3053

SEAGULL BEACHFRONT MOTEL
1511 NW Harbor Ave (97367)
Rates: $50-$180
Tel: (541) 994-2948
(800) 422-0219

SHILO INNS-OCEANFRONT RESORT
1501 NW 40th St (97367)
Rates: $79-$179
Tel: (541) 994-3655
(800) 222-2244

SURFTIDES BEACH RESORT
2945 NW Jetty Ave (97367)
Rates: $52-$95
Tel: (541) 994-2191
(800) 452-2159

WESTSHORE OCEANFRONT MOTEL
3127 SW Anchor Ave (97367)
Rates: $69-$79
Tel: (541) 996-2091
(800) 621-3187

WHISTLING WINDS
3264 NW Jetty Ave (97367)
Rates: n/a
Tel: (541) 994-6155

RECREATION

CASCADE HEAD TRAIL HIKE

Intermediate/6.0 miles/3.0 hours

Info: Without a doubt, you'll be bragging to anyone who'll listen about the charms of this wonderland. Massive rocky outcrops tower above the Pacific and set the stage for the countless streams that cascade into the powerful Pacific from picturesque gorges. If your timing's right, find an elevated perch and watch for whales on their centuries old migratory route. Or lose yourself in the bosky beauty of the woodlands where wildlife sightings are common. You'll reach your turnaround point on Falls Creek much too soon. Stretch your experience to the max with a biscuit break creekside as you contemplate the serenity. But know this, your outbound trek will be just as marvelous and surprisingly different as your inbound journey. Wowser Bowser and then some! For more information: (503) 392-3161.

Directions: From the intersection of Highways 18 and 101 in Lincoln City, travel Highway 101 north for one mile to Three Rocks Road. The trail is well signed and located adjacent to the highway off Falls Creek Road.

Note: Voice control obedience or leashes are mandatory.

D RIVER STATE WAYSIDE AREA- Leashes

Info: This river which connects Devils Lake with the Pacific has achieved a certain amount of recognition. It appears in

"The Guinness Book of World Records" as the world's shortest river, measuring a mere 440'. You and your river rover can check it out from the wayside area and then skedaddle to the coast for some beach bum activity. And hey, if you're into kite flying or kite watching, this windy beach can't be beat.

Directions: From Lincoln City, travel south on Highway 101 to milepost 115 and signs for parking.

DEVILS LAKE STATE PARK - Leashes

Info: A visit to this region means water with a capital W. Tote a boat and do a floating lunch atop the brilliant surface of Devil's Lake. If you're angling for some dinner, yellow perch, largemouth bass, rainbow trout, black crappie and brown bullhead might be on the colorful menu. If terra firma is more to your liking, find a cozy spot and break out the binocs. A couple of species of cormorants, rafts of Western grebes and eight species of duck are common to the area. Or step lively to the eastern side of Devil's Lake and hope to be a lucky dog. There's an active nest of bald eagles in residence. FYI: Indian legend has it that if a boat crosses the moon's reflection in the center of the lake, a strange chill of fear will leave your fur standing on end. For more information: (541) 994-2002.

Directions: Located just south of Lincoln City off Highway 101. Use East or West Devils Lake Road for access.

Note: If you catch a Chinese grass carp (white amur), you must release it immediately. Possession of the fish is strictly prohibited.

DRIFT CREEK COVERED BRIDGE

Info: History buffs might like to take a gander at the oldest covered bridge in the state. Tote the Kodak, this picturesque locale might make your album.

Directions: From Lincoln City, travel south on Highway 101 to Drift Creek Road (milepost 119.2). Continue east for 2.5 miles to the bridge.

SILETZ BAY PARK - Leashes

Info: Do a leg stretch and a thirst quench at this pretty grassy scene where bay views are part of the package. Have a peek at the driftwood-strewn beach and rocky, treed outcrops as you relax under the covered ramada. Or make yourself comfortable at one of the picnic tables where interpretive signs offer a smidgen of education along with the views. Learn a tidbit or two about local marine life, birdlife and tides.

Directions: Just south of Lincoln City off Highway 101.

LONG CREEK

LODGING

LONG CREEK LODGE
171 W Main St (97856)
Rates: $40-$48
Tel: (541) 421-9212

LOWELL

RECREATION

CLARK BUTTE TRAIL HIKE

Expert/4.4 miles/3.0 hours

Info: For a workout that's bound to challenge even experienced hikers, hustle your buttsky over to this trail. Don't let the first half-mile fool you, this easy section is part of the Clark Creek Nature Trail. But once you hook up with the Butte, it's definitely a beaut. Let the calories burn. For more information: (541) 937-2129.

Directions: From Lowell, head north on Jasper Lowell Road about 3 miles to Unity Bridge. Turn right, following FS 18 up Fall Creek approximately 13 miles to Clark Creek Organizational Camp. Make a left and park in the Clark Creek Nature Trail parking area. Take the Clark Creek Nature Trail for .5 miles to access the Clark Butte Trail. Stay straight ahead when the nature trail veers left.

FALL CREEK NATIONAL RECREATION TRAIL HIKE

Intermediate/1.0-28.0 miles/0.5 hours-2 days

Info: No matter what your hiking preference, this diverse trail has something to please the most finicky of breeds. You can simply get the lead out with an hour's stroll, hike the entire day or plan an overnighter on this national gem. The call of the wild can be heard throughout the dense woodlands and the call for fun can be answered at Fall Creek where wet and wild hijinks are the name of the game. If you like your hiking journeys to include some reel-time pleasures, hone your skills on the resident trout. A springtime sojourn packs a wallop of wildflowers at their showiest best so pack your Kodak. Utilize a shuttle system and add to your exploration time. For more information: (541) 937-2129.

Directions: From Lowell, head north on Jasper Lowell Road about 3 miles to Unity Bridge. Turn right, following FS 18 up Fall Creek approximately 10 miles to Dolly Varden Campground. The trailhead is located just south of the campground, across Fall Creek. Other trailhead access points are located on FS 1821 at Bedrock Campground and on FS 1828.

GOLD POINT TRAIL HIKE

Expert/8.6 miles/5.0 hours

Info: If you're in fine physical fettle and you've accumulated your share of serious hiking points, strap on the pawdometer and take the challenge. This buttkicker is one sure way to separate the dogs from the pups. Switchbacks begin at the get-go, ascending from Logan Creek Valley to postcardian Gold Point. Pack plenty of Perrier and power munchies, you and your canine cohort will need them. For more information: (541) 937-2129.

Directions: From Lowell, head north on Jasper Lowell Road about 3 miles to Unity Bridge. Turn right, following FS 18 up Fall Creek approximately 17 miles to FS 1825. Make a right on FS 1825 for 2 miles to FS 1835. Go left on FS 1835 for a half-mile to Spur Road 220. Turn left on Spur Road 220 for .5 miles to the trailhead.

JOHNNY CREEK NATURE TRAIL HIKE

Beginner/1.4 miles/1.0 hours

Info: This instructive nature trail has a two-fold benefit, a pleasant outdoor interlude combined with a learning experience. You'll walk in the cool shade of Douglas fir with frequent stops to peruse the interpretive signs. Après hiking, dine alfresco at the small picnic area. For more information: (541) 937-2129.

Directions: From Lowell, head north on Jasper Lowell Road about 3 miles to Unity Bridge. Turn right, following FS 18 up Fall Creek approximately 15 miles to FS 1821 and make a right. Follow FS 1821 to the trailhead.

LONE WOLF/PATTERSON MOUNTAIN TRAIL HIKE

Beginner/Intermediate/5.0 miles/3.0 hours

Info: When push comes to shove and good times prevail, treat your rugged Rover to an afternoon of romping, stomping fun. This trail lets you savor woodsy scents and panoramic vistas while you burn some kibble. You'll skedaddle in the cool quietude of dense old-growth forests and lush green meadows before topping out at Patterson Mountain. Get a load of the quiet lushness of the Willamette Valley that stretches out below you. For more information: (541) 937-2129.

Directions: From Lowell, head southeast on Highway 58 for 16 miles to FS 5847. Turn right on FS 5847 for 8 miles to Spur Road 555. Go right on Spur Road 555 for a quarter-mile to the trailhead.

MADRAS

LODGING

BEST WESTERN RAMA INN
12 SW 4th (97741)
Rates: $52-$90
Tel (541) 475-6141
(800) 528-1234

BUDGET INN
133 NE 5th St (97741)
Rates: $35-$60
Tel: (541) 475-3831

HOFFY'S MOTEL
600 N Hwy 26 (97741)
Rates: $32-$125
Tel: (541) 475-4633
(800) 227-6865

JUNIPER MOTEL
414 N Hwy 26 (97741)
Rates: $28-$65
Tel: (541) 475-6186
(800) 244-1399

Locate Other Dog-Friendly Activities...Check Nearby Cities

ROYAL DUTCH MOTEL
1101 SW Hwy 97 (97741)
Rates: $28-$44
Tel: (541) 475-2281

SONNY'S MOTEL
1539 SW Hwy 97 (97741)
Rates: $44-$75
Tel: (541) 475-7217
(800) 624-6137

<u>RECREATION</u>

COVE PALISADES STATE PARK - Leashes

Info: Aqua pups, listen up. This lovely parkland offers boating on Lake Billy Chinook, so get your person to tote the float of choice and paddle, row or skim across the shimmering blue surface. Drop a line at any time and see what's biting. Landlubbers, there's a great fishing pier and lots of cozy crannies for a picnic with your noodnick. FYI: Three geologically distinctive canyons have been carved by the Deschutes, the Metolius and the Crooked Rivers which converge in the park. For more information: (541) 546-3412.

Directions: From the intersection of Highways 97 and 361 (Old Culver Highway) in Madras, veer right onto Highway 361 and drive about 12 miles to Gem Lane. Turn right and follow signs to the park entrance.

MANZANITA

<u>LODGING</u>

SUNSET SURF MOTEL
248 Ocean Rd (97130)
Rates: $55-$119
Tel: (541) 368-5224
(800) 243-8035

MAPLETON

<u>RECREATION</u>

KENTUCKY FALLS TRAIL HIKE - Leashes

Intermediate/4.0 miles/2.0 hours

Info: After you hike this one, you'll understand why people get the blues for their ol' Kentucky home. This incredible trail dishes up a wondrous, waterful journey through songbird-filled thickets.

Hotel Policies May Be Subject To Change

You'll encounter not one but three waterfalls on your wilderness journey. Each waterfall is more than 80' high and all are equally beautiful. This primo getaway comes complete with a dollop of solitude as well as a much needed change of pace from the often crowded coastal tracks. Don't be surprised if you experience an encounter of the elk kind, the abundant woodlands are favorite foraging grounds. For more information: (541) 268-4473.

Directions: From Mapleton, travel Highway 126 east for 12.5 miles to the signed turnoff for the Whittaker Creek Recreation Area. Turn south and travel 1.5 miles to an unsigned road on the right-hand side. Travel 1.5 miles to Dunn Ridge Road, veer left and drive 6.9 miles. Take another left at the signs for Reedsport. Drive 2.7 miles to FS 23 and turn right. Proceed 1.6 miles to FS 2300-919 and take a right. Travel another 2.7 miles to the trailhead on the left-hand side of the road.

SWEET CREEK TRAIL HIKE - Leashes

Intermediate/6.0 miles/3.0 hours

Info: Named after a courageous family of pioneers from Pennsylvania, Sweet Creek is a gorgeous waterway with a significant historic slant. The creek provided fish as a food source, water for crops and livestock as well as a lovely recreation site for homesteaders. Play tagalong with your wagalong and be treated to eleven waterfalls, many ensconced in a region of rich green mosses and ferns and all qualifying as photo worthy. The grade is relatively flat and the river is overflowing with pupportunities for R&R and reel-time pleasures. Pack a biscuit basket and make a day of it. Bone appétit. For more information: (541) 268-4473.

Directions: From the Siuslaw Bridge in Mapleton, head south on Sweet Creek Road. Drive 11 miles to the trailhead.

MAUPIN

LODGING

DESCHUTES MOTEL
616 Mill St (97037)
Rates: $35-$75
Tel: (541) 395-2626

THE OASIS RESORT
609 Hwy 197 (97037)
Rates: $35-$55
Tel: (541) 395-2611

<u>RECREATION</u>
WHITE RIVER STATE PARK - Leashes

Info: A little-known beauty, this park is one of the crown jewels in Wasco County. Striking waterfalls, picnic areas and scenery to die for are among the assets of this delightful retreat. The ruins of an historic hydroelectric plant which supplied power to turn millstones at the turn of the century makes for an adventuresome hiking excursion. And the dramatic waterfalls will take your breath away. So pack up a brown bagger to share with the wagger and make tracks to this charming locale.

Directions: From Maupin, travel Highway 197 north 7 miles to the junction with Oregon 216 in Tygh Valley. Turn east onto Oregon 216 and continue about 4 miles to the park.

Note: Closed in winter.

McKENZIE BRIDGE

<u>LODGING</u>

THE COUNTRY PLACE
56245 Delta Dr (97413)
Rates: $63-$220
Tel: (541) 822-6008

McMINNVILLE

<u>LODGING</u>

PARAGON MOTEL
2065 Hwy 99 West (97128)
Rates: $39-$91
Tel: (503) 472-9493
(800) 525-5469

MEDFORD

Lodging

BEST WESTERN MEDFORD INN
1015 S Riverside Ave (97501)
Rates: $45-$92
Tel: (541) 773-8266
(800) 528-1234

BEST WESTERN PONY SOLDIER INN
2340 Crater Lake Hwy (97504)
Rates: $69-$86
Tel: (541) 779-2011
(800) 528-1234

CAPRI MOTEL
250 Barnett Rd (97501)
Rates: $29-$38
Tel: (541) 773-7796

CEDAR LODGE MOTOR INN
518 N Riverside Ave (97501)
Rates: $32-$45
Tel: (541) 773-7361
(800) 282-3419

DAYS INN
850 Alba Dr (97504)
Rates: $45-$70
Tel: (541) 779-6730
(800) 329-7466

FISH LAKE RESORT
P.O. Box 40 (97501)
Rates: n/a
Tel: (541) 949-8500

HORIZON MOTOR INN
1150 E Barnett Rd (97501)
Rates: $55-$64
Tel: (541) 779-5085
(800) 452-2255

PEAR TREE MOTEL
3730 Fern Valley Rd (97504)
Rates: $55-$58
Tel: (541) 535-4445

RED LION INN
200 N Riverside Ave (97501)
Rates: $82-$164
Tel: (541) 779-5811
(800) 547-8010

RESTON HOTEL
2300 Crater Lake Hwy (97504)
Rates: $52-$72
Tel: (541) 779-3141
(800) 779-7829

SHILO INNS
2111 Biddle Rd (97504)
Rates: $49-$80
Tel: (541) 770-5151
(800) 222-2244

WINDMILL INN OF MEDFORD
1950 Biddle Rd (97504)
Rates: $59-$78
Tel: (541) 779-0050
(800) 547-4747

Recreation

BEAR CREEK PARK - Leashes

Info: This expansive district park offers plenty of playtime ops for you and furface. Lollygag along the banks of the river and be dazzled by the sunlight bouncing off the windy ripples of the water. If a picnic repast makes your day special, you'll uncover idyllic green scenes everywhere you turn.

Directions: Located at the river between Barnett Road and Siskiyou Boulevard.

EARHART PARK - Leashes

Info: Don't let the day get away from you without at least one fun break. Make the time for a quick romp outdoors with the pupster beside you.

Directions: Located at Siskiyou Boulevard and Eastwood.

FICHTNER-MAINWARING PARK - Leashes

Info: You'll find some fun in the sun at this urban scene. Lots of locals meet and greet so go ahead, make your dog's day.

Directions: Located at Stewart Avenue and Holly Street.

HAWTHORNE PARK - Leashes

Info: Take your bark for a lark in the park and punch up your day with puppy playtime.

Directions: Located at Jackson Street and I-5, across from the Medford Center.

HOLMES PARK - Leashes

Info: Let the good times roll as you and the barkmeister sniff your way through this enticing park. A brown bagger with the wagger will double your pleasure.

Directions: Located at Modoc Avenue and White Oaks Road.

HOOVER PARK - Leashes

Info: For a terrific time of presidential proportions, city weary waggers vote for Hoover Park. Beat the summer doldrums and do the stroll beneath the shade of majestic trees.

Directions: Located at Piccadilly and Amber.

HOWARD PARK - Leashes

Info: Dollars to dog biscuits, you're gonna love a traipse through this charming parkland. For a smidgen of solitude, visit in the early morning hours and watch the mist as it rises off the lovely landscape.

Directions: Located at Merriman and Midway Roads.

Hotel Policies May Be Subject To Change

JACKSON PARK - Leashes

Info: Find a little slice of doggie nirvana with a trip to this locale. The city licker will cover your face with wet kisses after one look at the paw-pleasing pupportunities that await.

Directions: Located at Jackson Street and Summit.

JEFFERSON PARK - Leashes

Info: Sunshine and good times go hand-in-hand at this pleasant neighborhood parkland.

Directions: Located at Holly and Garfield Streets.

KENNEDY PARK - Leashes

Info: The dawgus will think he's found Camelot when he gets a whiff and a sniff of Kennedy Park.

Directions: Off Springbrook just south of Delta Waters Road.

LONE PINE PARK - Leashes

Info: Perfect for your daily dose of Rexercise, visit during the off hours and you and the parkmeister might have Lone Pine to your lonesomes.

Directions: Located at Lone Pine Road and Brookdale Avenue.

RUHL PARK - Leashes

Info: Every dog should have his day. Make yours moist and soothing underfoot with a perusal of this petite parkland.

Directions: Located off Ruhl Avenue, just past the intersection of Jackson and Main Streets.

SODA SPRINGS TRAIL HIKE

Expert/5.0 miles/3.0 hours

Info: The interpretive leg at the start of this trail explains the remnants of an intricate rock fountain. When your education is over, your workout begins with a steep ascent. At the first fork, stay right and keep trekking. You'll reach a stand of stunning Oregon white oak and a good place to refuel. Continue on your journey and trade Oregon oaks for a thick stand of California black oak (imagine the magnificent colors in autumn). As the forest opens up, views of Mt. McLoughlin and Brown Mountain come into view. When the trail once again enters the forest, you won't be far from the junction with FS 2500185, your about-face point. For more information: (541) 482-3333.

Directions: From Medford, travel Highway 62 east for 6 miles to Highway 140. Turn right and drive 12.6 miles to Lake Creek Road and turn right. Follow Lake Creek Road 11.5 miles to the cattle-guard at the forest boundary. Continue 2.5 miles to FS 3730800. Turn right, cross the bridge and travel 0.6 miles to the trailhead.

UNION PARK - Leashes

Info: Make lickety split to this little oasis and put a twinkle in the parkmeister's eyes.

Directions: Located at Union and 13th Streets.

WILSON PARK - Leashes

Info: Looking for a nature fix? You'll find it at this attractive parkland.

Directions: Located at Corona and Johnson.

OTHER PARKS IN MEDFORD - Leashes

•NORTH HIGH PARK, between Keene Way and Springbrook
•ROOSEVELT PARK, between Academy and Lindley
•WASHINGTON PARK, Peach and Dakota Avenue

MERLIN

LODGING

DOUBLETREE RANCH
6000 Abegg Rd (97523)
Rates: $65-$75
Tel: (541) 476-1686

RECREATION
FERRON'S FUN TRIPS

Info: Wet and wild waggers, buckle up. You're in for one dog-gone great time when you choose this adventure. Learn a little about the surrounding riparian vegetation from your knowledgeable guide as you careen atop the whitewater on this exciting rafting tour. Your heart will pound as the craft flies and bounces over the rapids and whitecaps of the exhilarating Rogue River. Thrillseekers - you'll think you've struck gold. Bow wow! For more information: (800) 404-2201; (541) 474-2201.

Directions: The outfitters are located at 585 Rogue Rim Drive.

Note: Hours and fees vary. Call to reserve a trip.

MERRILL

LODGING
MERRILL MOTEL
P.O. Box 323 (97633)
Rates: n/a
Tel: (541) 798-5598

MILTON-FREEWATER

LODGING

MORGAN INN
104 N Columbia (97862)
Rates: $45-$105
Tel: (541) 938-5547
(800) 443-3487

OUT WEST MOTEL
Rt 1, Box 210-F (97862)
Rates: $33-$40
Tel: (541) 938-6647
(800) 881-6647

RECREATION
HARRIS PARK - Leashes

Info: Fun and games can be high on the agenda at this charming 90-acre green scene. The shaded banks of the Walla Walla River make for pleasant picnicking while the open grassy area is a great place to play with poochface. Anglers, try your fly and see what's tugging at your line. If hiking's more to your liking, pretty pathways honeycomb the acreage, so lace up those boots and check it out.

Directions: At the end of South Fork Walla Walla River Road.

MILWAUKIE

LODGING

MILWAUKIE INN
14015 SE McLoughlin Blvd (97267)
Rates: $35-$65
Tel: (503) 659-2125
(800) 255-1553

OCEANVIEW VACATION RENTALS
9981 SE 32nd Ave (97222)
Rates: $60-$70
Tel: (503) 653-8378

MITCHELL

RECREATION

JOHN DAY FOSSIL BEDS NATIONAL MONUMENT - Leashes

Info: See DAYVILLE for description of John Day Fossil Beds National Monument.

Directions: From Mitchell, travel Route 26 west about 3.5 miles to Burnt Ranch Road, turn right. Continue on Burnt Ranch Road about 6 miles to Painted Hills-Bear Creek Road, turn left into the Painted Hills Unit.

Note: Open during daylight hours. No admission costs. Donations accepted.

The numbered hikes that follow are located within the John Day Fossil Beds National Monument:

1) CARROLL RIM TRAIL HIKE - Leashes

Intermediate/1.5 miles/1.0 hours

Info: Let your spirits soar as you and your mighty mutt ascend this interesting rim trail. The rocks forming the cliffs are ignimbrite, a layer of welded volcanic ash. When you and furface reach the top of Carroll Rim, sit a spell and peruse the panoramic views of the Painted Hills and nearby Sutton Mountain. For more information: (541) 987-2333.

Directions: From Mitchell, travel Route 26 west about 3.5 miles to Burnt Ranch Road, turn right. Continue on Burnt Ranch Road about 6 miles to Painted Hills-Bear Creek Road, turn left into the Painted Hills Unit. The trailhead is near the road junction to the Painted Hills Outlook.

2) LEAF HILL TRAIL HIKE - Leashes

Beginner/0.25 miles/0.25 hours

Info: It takes only minutes to see what took nature millions of years to create. Remains from a 30 million-year-old hardwood forest are well preserved along this itsy-bitsy but intriguing trail. You and your rockhound will circle the hill which encompasses the forest. A mini-education can be yours by reading the fossil leaf exhibits. Since your journey will be over lickety split, check out the other trails in the Painted Hills area and get your money's worth. For more information: (541) 987-2333.

Directions: From Mitchell, travel Route 26 west about 3.5 miles to Burnt Ranch Road, turn right. Continue on Burnt Ranch Road about 6 miles to Painted Hills-Bear Creek Road, turn left into the Painted Hills Unit. The marked trail is the last of the four trails in the Painted Hills Unit.

3) PAINTED COVE TRAIL HIKE - Leashes

Beginner/0.25 miles/0.25 hours

Info: This self-guided quickie loop zooms right off to what makes this area so pretty - the rich, colorful Painted Hills terrain. Pick up a guide at the trailhead and see what facts you can unearth. For more information: (541) 987-2333.

Directions: From Mitchell, travel Route 26 west about 3.5 miles to Burnt Ranch Road, turn right. Continue on Burnt Ranch Road about 6 miles to Painted Hills-Bear Creek Road, turn left into the Painted Hills Unit. The trailhead is located just after the Painted Hills Overlook Trail Hike.

4) PAINTED HILLS OVERLOOK TRAIL HIKE - Leashes

Beginner/0.50 miles/0.50 hours

Info: This simple path gives you an express ticket to sweeping views of the Painted Hills. Softly colored layers of claystone have been exposed and sculpted by years of water erosion in this handsome land. Ponder for a moment the factors that went into the creation of this spectacular slice of nature. If you're craving more goodies, hop on the Painted Cove Trail for an up-close gander of the striking Painted Hills soil. For more information: (541) 987-2333.

Directions: From Mitchell, travel Route 26 west about 3.5 miles to Burnt Ranch Road, turn right. Continue on Burnt Ranch Road about 6 miles to Painted Hills-Bear Creek Road, turn left into the Painted Hills Unit. The trailhead is located near the junction with the Carroll Rim Trail Hike.

MOLALLA

LODGING

STAGE COACH INN MOTEL
415 Grange St (97038)
Rates: $42-$65
Tel: (503) 829-4382

MONMOUTH

LODGING

COLLEGE INN MOTEL
235 S Pacific Ave (97361)
Rates: $35-$58
Tel: (503) 838-1711

COURTESY INN
270 N Pacific Hwy (97361)
Rates: $45-$60
Tel: (503) 838-4438

MOSIER

LODGING

HEWETT'S B&B
501 Third St (97040)
Rates: $45-$75
Tel: (541) 478-3455

MOUNT HOOD

LODGING

MT. HOOD INN
87450 E Govt Camp Loop (97028)
Rates: $125-$135
Tel: (503) 272-3205
(800) 443-7777

SHAMROCK FOREST INN
59550 E Hwy 26 (97028)
Rates: $38-$69
Tel: (503) 622-4003

Hotel Policies May Be Subject To Change

<u>RECREATION</u>

COOPER SPUR LOOP TRAIL HIKE - Leashes

Expert/8.0 miles/5.0 hours

Info: No bones about it, this is one helluva tough trek. But if you like your hikes straight up, this could be the trail of your dreams. Starting at an elevation of almost 6,000', you and your Herculean hound will ascend another 2,500' before reaching the remains of the stone Cooper Spur Shelter. Considering the demands this journey entails, don't be surprised if you and the panter have this primitive route all to yourselves. Travel with clothing you can layer, the alpine air has a nip to it even in summer. If the climb doesn't leave you breathless, the scenery will. The north side of Mt. Hood and the Elliott Glacier loom majestically in the distance. Do the descent thing via the Tilly Jane Trail to complete the loop. For more information: (541) 352-6002.

Directions: From Mount Hood, travel Highway 35 south to the signs for the Cooper Spur Ski Area, between mileposts 73 and 74. Turn west onto Cooper Spur Road (FS 3510). Continue on Cooper Spur Road about 3 miles to the junction with FS 3512, turn left. Drive about 10 miles to Cloud Cap Campground and park. Follow the Timberline Trail #600 south to the junction with Tilly Jane Trail #600A, turn right and follow the rough trail (Cooper Spur Trail).

Note: Open June through October.

DOG RIVER TRAIL HIKE

Intermediate/12.0 miles/7.0 hours

Info: This aptly named trail takes cuteness one step further when it crosses Puppy Creek. Yup, dogs and puppies will feel very special traversing the wooden bridge and then meandering along the hillside above the river. The bosky beauties include cedar, fir, hemlock and spruce.

At two miles, another bridge crosses Dog River and then forget the easy part, you'll be up, up and away to a scenic saddle above the river and Highway 35 and a switchbacking climb to some spectacular views of 11,235' snow-capped Mt. Hood, the

Locate Other Dog-Friendly Activities...Check Nearby Cities

state's highest point. When you reach the rocky outcrops at the top of the ridge, find a flat spot and break out the bread and biscuits. Make the most of the day while you enjoy a lofty, picturesque lunch in a setting of splendid isolation.

The second half of your journey is more like a walk in the park. You'll boogie with Bowser through contrasting north- and south-facing vegetation zones to your turnaround point at the junction with the Surveyors Ridge Trail. If you'd like to see Mt. Hood from a different perspective, travel a few hundred feet straight ahead from the junction to a primo vista point. For more information: (541) 352-6002.

Directions: From Mount Hood, travel south on Highway 35 for 5 miles, then turn left (east) on a gravel road located 100 yards before the East Fork of the Hood River crossing. Park before the road forks to the left and begins to climb. The trailhead is located at this point.

EAST FORK TRAIL HIKE - Leashes

Intermediate/12.0 miles/7.0 hours

Info: Strap on the pawdometer and get ready to clock some major miles on this lengthy undertaking. The elevation change is a mere 250', making this straight, level path a little easier than many in the area. You and the dogster will follow the clear waters of the East Fork Hood River through dense thickets where birdsong is sure to be playing on the airwaves. If your Retriever's nose is twitching, he's probably picked up the scent of wood duck or mallard, both are common to the region. For more information: (541) 352-6002.

Directions: From Mount Hood, travel Highway 35 south about 15 miles to the signed entrance for the Robinhood Campground. The trailhead (#650) begins at the north end of the campground.

Note: Open June through October.

TAMANAWAS FALLS LOOP TRAIL HIKE - Leashes

Beginner/5.0 miles/3.0 hours

Info: You'll need some basic navigational skills for this one so make sure your pal's snoot is up to snuff. Right off the bat, you'll traverse a log bridge across the East Fork of the Hood River and go right (north) on the East Fork Trail (#650). Continue traveling riverside along the west bank for a half-mile to the junction with the Tamanawas Falls Trail (#650A). Follow Snoopy straight ahead to the Cold Spring Creek crossing, then turn left. The river will be your guide post, it's with you all the way. The water will soothe you while Douglas fir and fragrant cedar provide the shade and sweetly scent the air. If you're a lucky dog, you might get to share your afternoon with a few busy little beavers who regularly look for work about a half-mile from the bridge.

After a quick hop, skip and jump through the woodlands, you'll come to the Tamanawas Tie Trail (#650B). Turn left and do another stream crossing on the log bridge. You're now traversing the south bank of the river which leads to a series of log steps. Keep the faith, you and the loyal furball are only a short distance from the thundering falls at this point. Can you hear them? One quick climb up Talus Slope and you're practically there. The falls will make your effort worthwhile. The mesmerizing cascades are 100' high and 40' wide.

Make the most of this splendid spot and seek out a perfect alfresco site. When you've chilled out and filled up, say adieu and follow the Tamanawas Tie Trail on its gentle climb out of the canyon where it hooks up with the Elk Meadows Trail (#645). A right turn and an easy quarter-mile downhill walk will deposit you at the Polallie Parking Area. Make another right and follow the trail to the Tamanawas Parking Area, your starting point. Hey, there's more. Don't miss the quickie sidetrip to an overlook of Polallie Creek where evidence of an avalanche of mud and debris (the consistency of wet cement) flattened the vegetation in 1980. Check out the signs of regrowth and rejuvenation as you trace the path of the avalanche. For more information: (541) 352-6002.

Directions: From Mt. Hood, travel approximately 10 miles south on Highway 35 to the Tamanawas Falls Trailhead Parking Area. The trailhead is one mile north of the Sherwood Campground.

TILLY JANE/POLALLIE RIDGE LOOP TRAIL HIKE- Leashes

Expert/5.0 miles/3.0 hours

Info: This challenging hike which covers a 1,400' rise in elevation provides all the workout you and old brown eyes will need for the day. Polallie Ridge and the Tilly Jane Trails lead to the same destination. While you're building upper and lower body strength, you'll witness eye-candy views all along the way. Conquering this rugged chunk of mountain will make you and the wonder woofer feel like champs. When day is done, do the descent thing. For more information: (541) 352-6002.

Directions: From Mount Hood, travel Highway 35 south to the signs for the Cooper Spur Ski Area, between mileposts 73 and 74. Turn west onto Cooper Spur Road (FS 3510). Continue on Cooper Spur Road about 3 miles to the junction with FS 3512, turn left and drive to the end of the paved road and the Tilly Jane Ski Trail parking area. Follow the Tilly Jane Ski Trail #643 to the junction with Polallie Ridge Trail #643A. Follow #643A to Tilly Jane Campground. Return via Tilly Jane Ski Trail to complete the loop.

Note: Open June through October.

MYRTLE POINT

<u>LODGING</u>

MYRTLE TREES MOTEL
1010 8th St (97458)
Rates: $38-$44
Tel: (541) 572-5811

NECANICUM JUNCTION

<u>RECREATION</u>

SADDLE MOUNTAIN STATE PARK - Leashes

Info: A mountain retreat, Saddle Mountain State Park is the perfect escape route for city weary pooches and their people to commune with nature and their country cousins. At this deer and elk refuge, coyote and squirrel often provide the unexpected entertainment. Birdwatchers, you'll get a chance to check off great-horned owl, nuthatch and rufous hummingbird on your sighting list. Pack a biscuit basket and plan a mountainside repast under a leafy green canopy. If you've got a penchant for hiking and you've got the experience to handle an expert rating, don't let any grass grow under your feet. Make tracks instead to Saddle Mountain Trail and just do it. For more information: (503) 861-1671.

Directions: From Highway 26 in Necanicum Junction, travel north on Saddle Mountain Road for 8 miles to the park entrance.

Note: Day use fee may be charged.

The numbered hike that follows is within Saddle Mountain State Park:

1) SADDLE MOUNTAIN TRAIL HIKE - Leashes

Expert/5.0 miles/3.0 hours

Info: Physical stamina combined with endurance is what you and your rugged Rover will need to qualify for this beauty of a hike to the summit of Saddle Mountain. The first mile is an easy switchback amidst a songbird-filled forest. Soon after your ascent begins, you'll enter a meadowland where rainbow-colored wildflowers grace the springtime scene. Through the leas to rock ledges and steep terrain you'll go, go, go. Put your best sure-footedness forward, the ledges are difficult to navigate. Continue onward and you'll find yourself at 3,283', the highest summit in northwest Oregon. This lofty aerie dishes up some of the best panoramas to be had. Scope out Nehalem Bay and the Pacific to the west, the Columbia River to the north and the snow-capped peaks of the Cascades to the east.

When you've had your Fuji fix, repeat the beat on your retreat. As you'll see, the downhill vistas offer quite a different perspective as special views of the northern and southern horn, Onion Peak and Humbug Mountain come into view. There's a good chance you and your canine connoisseur will have this place all to yourselves so enjoy the quietude and solitude to its fullest before everyday life catches up with you once again.

Directions: From Highway 26 in Necanicum Junction, travel north on Saddle Mountain for 8 miles to the park entrance. The trailhead is located at the parking area for the campground.

Note: The last half-mile of the trail can be extremely hazardous.

NESIKA BEACH

LODGING

BREAKER HOUSE AT NESIKA BEACH
32864 Nesika Beach Rd (97444)
Rates: $80-$145
Tel: (541) 247-6670

NESKOWIN

LODGING

THE BREAKERS CONDOMINUMS
48060 Breakers Blvd (97149)
Rates: $80-$200
Tel: (503) 392-3417

NETARTS

LODGING

EDGEWATER MOTEL
First St (97143)
Rates: $72-$82
Tel: (503) 842-1300

SAMS VACATION RENTALS
1035 5th St Loop (97143)
Rates: $55
Tel: (503) 842-5814

TERIMORE LODGING BY THE SEA
5105 Crab Ave (97143)
Rates: $45-$87
Tel: (503) 842-4623
(800) 635-1821

THREE CAPES INN
4800 Netarts Hwy W (97143)
Rates: $45-$60
Tel: (503) 842-4003

Hotel Policies May Be Subject To Change

NEWBERG

<u>LODGING</u>

SHILO INNS
501 Sitka Ave (97132)
Rates: $59-$75
Tel: (503) 537-0303
(800) 222-2244

<u>RECREATION</u>

CHAMPOEG STATE PARK - Leashes

Info: History buffs and doggistorians will come away a little smarter after an expedition to this diverse parkland. Champoeg was the site of the 1843 vote to form the provisional government for the first American Commonwealth in the Pacific Northwest.

The prairie is at its peak in springtime when wildflowers polka dot the landscape. A maze of pathways leads you to songbird-filled woodlands, riparian streamside vegetation and open meadows. You can pretty much close your eyes and pick a cozy spot where you can reflect on your delightful experience. There are also two canine exercise areas where leashless abandon comes with the territory. For more information: (503) 678-1251.

Directions: From the junction of Highways 99W and 219 in Newburgh, travel south on 219 approximately 3 miles, then follow signs for Champoeg Road and the park to the east.

Note: Day use fee may be charged.

NEWPORT

<u>LODGING</u>

AGATE BEACH OCEAN FRONT MOTEL
175 NW Gilbert Way (97365)
Rates: $90-$100
Tel: (541) 265-8746
(800) 755-5674

THE ANCHORAGE
7743 N Coast Hwy (97365)
Rates: $60-$66
Tel: (541) 265-5463

BEST WESTERN HALLMARK RESORT
744 SW Elizabeth St (97365)
Rates: $79-$239
Tel: (541) 265-2600
(800) 528-1234
(888) 448-4449 (OR)

CITY CENTER MOTEL
538 SW Coast Hwy (97365)
Rates: $38-$65
Tel: (541) 265-7381
(800) 628-9665

DRIFTWOOD VILLAGE MOTEL
7947 N Coast Hwy (97365)
Rates: $55-$125
Tel: (541) 265-5738

HOTEL NEWPORT AT AGATE BEACH
3019 N Coast Hwy (97365)
Rates: $104-$155
Tel: (541) 265-9411
(800) 547-3310

MONEY SAVER MOTEL
861 SW Coast Hwy 101 (97365)
Rates: $30-$65
Tel: (541) 265-2277

NEWPORT MOTOR INN
1311 N Hwy 101 (97365)
Rates: $32-$50
Tel: (541) 265-8516

PENNY SAVER MOTEL
710 N Hwy 101 (97365)
Rates: $38-$65
Tel: (541) 265-6631
(800) 477-3669

SANDS MOTOR LODGE
206 N Coast Hwy (97365)
Rates: $36-$48
Tel: (541) 265-5321

SHILO INNS OCEANFRONT
536 SW Elizabeth St (97365)
Rates: $76-$164
Tel: (541) 265-7701
(800) 222-2244

STARFISH POINT CONDOS
140 NW 48th St (97365)
Rates: $115-$175
Tel: (541) 265-3751

SURF 'N SAND MOTEL
8143 N Hwy 101 (97365)
Rates: $58-$89
Tel: (541) 265-2215

TIDES INN MOTEL
715 SW Bay St (97365)
Rates: $38-$55
Tel: (541) 265-7202

TRAVELERS INN
606 SW Coast Hwy (97365)
Rates: $35-$75
Tel: (541) 265-7723
(800) 615-2627

VAL-U-INN MOTEL
531 SW Fall St (97365)
Rates: $65-$125
Tel: (541) 265-6203
(800) 443-7777

THE VIKINGS COTTAGES
729 NW Coast St (97365)
Rates: $50-$95
Tel: (541) 265-2477
(800) 480-2477

WAVES MOTEL
820 NW Coast St (97365)
Rates: $58-$150
Tel: (541) 265-4661
(800) 282-6993

WEST WIND MOTEL
747 SW Coast Hwy (97365)
Rates: $40-$55
Tel: (541) 265-5388
(800) 305-5388

WHALER MOTEL
155 SW Elizabeth St (97365)
Rates: $91-$125
Tel: (541) 265-9261
(800) 443-9444

WILLER'S MOTEL
754 SW Coast Hwy (97365)
Rates: $38-$80
Tel: (541) 265-2241
(800) 945-5377

RECREATION

BEVERLY BEACH STATE PARK - Leashes

Info: From vast, open beachy terrain to thick forests of alder and spruce, this diverse region offers a cornucopia of nature for you and furface to explore. Watch the waves for whale tails

Hotel Policies May Be Subject To Change

or look to the sky and see what's a-fly. Shake a leg on the nature trail or leave pawprints on a seaside pathway. Able anglers might get lucky in the ocean, while basket toters can find that perfect lunching spot. This park packs quite a scenic punch. It will have the hounddog howling all the way home. For more information: (541) 265-9278.

Directions: From Newport, travel Highway 101 north seven miles to park entrance on the east side of the highway.

Note: Day use fee may be required.

MIKE MILLER PARK EDUCATIONAL TRAIL - Leashes

Beginner/1.0 miles/.45 hours

Info: You'll boogie with Bowser past remnants of thick forests, beaches, logging sites and rail tracks on this educational walking loop.

Directions: From Newport, travel Highway 101 south 5 miles to milepost 144 and the trail on the east side of the highway.

ONA BEACH STATE PARK - Leashes

Info: Grassy fields dotted with wildflowers greet you from the get-go. Trees, picnic benches and a lake combine to round out the picture. Stroll the pretty grounds while chatty birds entertain. The driftwood-scattered landscape is filled with coast rhododendron, western azaleas and box blueberry so if you're around in the spring, expect a color extravaganza. For a dollop of exercise, take a pipsqueak jaunt on the paved trail that traverses the bosky terrain. Cross a gray, weathered wooden bridge which spans a placid body of water (the antithesis of the ferocious Pacific you'll hear in the distance) and then lickety-split, you'll sink your feet into a soft sand pathway that leads to the beach. Don't be surprised to see a wild goose or two during your visit, they consider this their territory. For more information: (800) 551-6949

Directions: From Newport, take Highway 101 south about 10 miles to signs for the park at milepost 149.

SOUTH BEACH STATE PARK - Leashes

Info: The rhythmic sounds of crashing waves and the distinct call of shorebirds drift through the cool salty air filling you and your mellow fellow with a sense of serenity. Ocean scenery, sandy terrain and waterside vegetation are a feast for the eyes. This enchanting coastal retreat is the place to forget your cares and do whatever pleases you. For a close encounter of the natural kind, romping breeds can kick up some sand on the trail. Rock hounds can sniff till their whiffer quits or until they unearth agate, jasper, petrified wood or any of the other pretty stones near the North Yaquina Jetty. If you've a penchant for fishing, try your luck on ling cod, sea bass, perch and salmon and take home the fixings for a neighborhood fish fry. For more information: (541) 867-7451.

Directions: From Newport, travel Highway 101 south 2 miles to park entrance.

Note: Day use fee charged.

The numbered hike that follows is within South Beach State Park:

1) COOPER RIDGE NATURE TRAIL HIKE - Leashes

Beginner/3.5 miles/2.0 hours

Info: Take your time and be alert for wildlife, birdlife and beauty as you walk softly through this sensitive ecosystem. You'll be surprised at what might make an unexpected appearance. Birders will want to include binocs - plenty of interesting flyboys cover the air waves. You'll skirt the eastern edge of the campground all the way to your turnaround point, the junction with South Jetty Trail.

Directions: From Newport, travel Highway 101 south 2 miles to park entrance. The trailhead is located just beyond the camper registration booth.

YAQUINA HEAD OUTSTANDING NATURAL AREA - Leashes

Info: Considered outstanding for good reason, you and your Curious George will gain insight into the history and marine life of the Oregon Coast while you're treated to some interesting hiking and walking options.

Hotel Policies May Be Subject To Change

Yaquina Head is a coastal headland that stretches deep into the thunderous Pacific. Since 1873, mariners have counted upon the Yaquina Head Lighthouse to guide them safely into port. Considered one of the most beautiful lighthouses in America, the light is visible nineteen miles out to sea.

For good, good, good, good migrations, you and the pupster won't find a better place to whale watch. From March through May, gray whales pass Yaquina Head on their journey to the Arctic. From December to early February, most reverse direction and head south to birthing grounds in Baja, California, but some stay put year round. Whales won't be the only sightings to set the wagster's tail in motion. Harbor seals are permanent residents and when the sun shines, you'll often see them basking on the nearby rocky outcrops. An avian havian, this unusual area is home to thousands of seabirds and shorebirds including cormorants, black oystercatchers with long red bills, western gulls and seasonal birds like the common murres, brown pelicans who love to divebomb for dinner, adorably decked out tufted puffins and rhinoceros auklets. For more information: (541) 574-3100.

Directions: From Newport, travel Highway 101 north for three miles and follow the signs.

Note: Dogs are not permitted in the Interpretive Center.

The numbered hikes and recreation areas that follow are within the Yaquina Head Outstanding Natural Area

1) COBBLE BEACH TRAIL HIKE - Leashes

Beginner/0.25 miles/0.25 hours

Info: Sounds, quite different than anything you've heard before await you and the maestro at this unusual beach scene. If the conditions are right and the water is rushing onto shore, the tossing and jumbling of the cobble stones create a singular sound. Please don't be tempted to collect even one cobble. It took 14 million years to create this extraordinary beach from boiling hot lava to eroded fragments. Not for the soft of paw, the beach's surface is far from smooth and difficult to navigate.

Directions: From Newport, travel Highway 101 north for three miles and follow the signs.

Locate Other Dog-Friendly Activities...Check Nearby Cities

2) COMMUNICATIONS HILL TRAIL HIKE - Leashes

Intermediate/1.0 miles/0.5 hours

Info: Shore pine and Sitka spruce dominate the landscape along this trail. Heads up naturalists, you might be treated to a surprise appearance of a chickadee, chipmunk or wren, so keep your binocs and Kodak at the ready. The name of this trail says it all, the Coast Guard maintains navigation communications equipment on top of the hill.

Directions: From Newport, travel Highway 101 north for three miles and follow the signs.

3) QUARRY COVE TIDE POOLS - Leashes

Info: A reclaimed rock quarry that was allowed to evolve naturally, this locale supports a range of marine organisms, from seaweeds to shore crabs. Pick your path and pick your tidal pool. Depending on the tidal zone, you might see acorn barnacle, black turban snail, hermit crab, green anemone, red sea cucumber, purple sea urchin, sunflower sea star and dozens of other examples representative of the teeming marine life. The local flyboys include peregrine falcon, western gull and black oystercatcher.

Directions: From Newport, travel Highway 101 north for three miles and follow the signs.

Note: Fragile ecosystem, look but do not touch.

4) QUARRY COVE TRAIL HIKE - Leashes

Intermediate/0.75 mile/1.0 hours

Info: If you and the pupster want to combine a walk with some interesting tidal pool observations, come at low tide. The innovative rocky intertidal area was built from a former rock quarry. You'll be surprised by the number of plants and animals that now inhabit this rich coastal area. This connector trail between the Ocean Bluff Observation Area and Quarry Cove follows the crest of Yaquina Head's southern edge. Carry your Kodak for this one, the views to Agate and Nye Beaches are photo worthy.

Directions: From Newport, travel Highway 101 north for three miles and follow the signs.

Note: Fragile ecosystem, look but do not touch.

Hotel Policies May Be Subject To Change

5) SALAL HILL TRAIL HIKE - Leashes

Intermediate/1.0 mile/0.5 hours

Info: Short but steep, you and your hearty hound will earn your kibble on your zigzag to the top. Be prepared to be wowed by the vistas which include panoramas of the Pacific, Newport and the evergreenery to the east. In springtime, the landscape is postcard pretty with smatterings of salmonberry, angelica, common horsetail, salal and false lily-of-the-valley.

Directions: From Newport, travel Highway 101 north for three miles and follow the signs.

NORTH BEND

LODGING

BAY BRIDGE MOTEL
33 US 101 (97459)
Rates: $42-$55
Tel: (541) 756-3151
(800) 557-3156

CITY CENTER MOTEL
750 Connecticut at 101 (97459)
Rates: $28-$40
Tel: (541) 756-5118

ITTY BITTY INN B&B MOTEL
1504 Sherman Ave (97459)
Rates: $40-$45
Tel: (541) 756-6398
(888) 2ITYBTY

PARKSIDE INN
1480 Sherman Ave (97459)
Rates: n/a
Tel: (541) 756-4124

PONY VILLAGE MOTOR LODGE
Virginia Ave (97459)
Rates: $45-$60
Tel: (541) 756-3191

RECREATION

BLUEBILL TRAIL HIKE - Leashes

Beginner/1.0 miles/0.5 hours

Info: From the get-go, you'll know you've picked a marvelous trail for you and furface. Zigzagging amidst enchanting stands of western hemlock and evergreen huckleberry, you'll be deposited at a boardwalk. The planks cross Bluebill Lake, a dry lake bed that becomes an impassable marsh during rainy periods. Once you reach the western part of the trail, you'll have two options. Follow the edge of Bluebird Lake and you and the sniffmeister will get a close look at shoreline vegetation and animal tracks. Or hop on the parallel trail where sunlight pokes through the needle-rich branches of shore pine to create enchanting patterns on the forest floor. Birders, you can't go wrong either way. Birds sing and trill, zoom and thrill wherever you wander. Both trails return to the starting point. For more information: (541) 271-3611.

Directions: From North Bend, travel 4 miles north on Highway 101 to Horsefall Dune and Beach Road. Turn west and drive 2.5 miles to the trailhead parking area on the left-hand side.

PONY POINT PARK - Leashes

Info: Clamming reigns supreme along the coastline at this beachside park. Mussels, softshell, empire, cockle and littleneck clams line the beaches. If you're more interested in what's atop the water, scope out the ships on their voyage through the channel or watch and admire the skill and agility of the windsurfers as they gracefully skim the bay waters.

Directions: From the intersection of Virginia Avenue and Pony Point Road head north on Pony Point Road to its end.

SIMPSON PARK - Leashes

Info: Start your day off on the right paw and take your bark for a lark in this lovely park on the bay, where briny breezes caress and tingle your senses. Consider breakfast à la beachside while you watch the tide come in.

Directions: Adjacent to North Bend Visitor's Center and Coos County Historical Society Museum.

NORTH POWDER

LODGING

POWDER RIVER MOTEL
850 2nd St (97867)
Rates: $25-$38
Tel: (541) 898-2829

Hotel Policies May Be Subject To Change

NYSSA

RECREATION

LESLIE GULCH

Info: Say ta ta to the summertime blues and hello to fun times at this spectacular wilderness region. Naturalists will rave about this pristine slice of heaven to anyone who'll listen. The Leslie Gulch Tuff, created over 15 million years ago, is a rhyolite air-fall tuff that erupted from a volcano in a series of violent explosions. Most of the tuff fell back into the volcano's caldera as a gaseous deposit of fine ash and rock fragments to create a stunning geological setting of colorful steep slopes, vertical towers and sheer cliffs. Several trails honeycomb the terrain and lead you and your lucky dog to the native flora and fauna. Bighorn sheep (a California transplant), mule deer or elk might startle you with an unexpected appearance. Bird-dogs might spy a chukar, raptor, California quail or white-throated swift riding the air currents. An occasional songbird will reveal its presence with a sweet melody that the wind captures and then calls its own. Although a rare sight, an elusive bobcat or coyote could arrive on the scene. The rich soils nourish some exclusive plant species including Packard's blazing star and Etter's grounsel. These rare plants exist only in the Leslie Gulch drainage. A few more rarities in case you're counting, grimy ivesia, sterile milk-vetch and Owyhee Clover can be found here and there in isolated spots. With a dash of spice and everything nice, this unique land of 11,000 acres definitely qualifies as the perfect getaway with your favorite fur-ball. For more information: (541) 473-3144.

Directions: From Nyssa, travel south on Route 201 past the hamlet of Adrian to Succor Creek Road, turn right. Follow Succor Creek Road through Succor Creek State Recreation Area to Leslie Gulch Road, turn right. Follow the Bureau of Land Management (BLM) signs to the Leslie Gulch area.

Note: Dogs must be under control at all times.

Locate Other Dog-Friendly Activities...Check Nearby Cities

LOWER OWYHEE CANYON WATCHABLE WILDLIFE AREA

Info: Travel through this area in slo-mo and increase your wildlife sighting odds. Cars are excellent viewing blinds, so clean off the lick and sniff marks from the windows and then just "sit." Patience will have its rewards - in the form of mule deer, coyote, bobcat, mink, porcupine and a bounty of other woodland inhabitants. Birders flock to this region hoping for an opportunity to witness a great blue heron standing stock still, poised to strike at mealtime. Golden eagle, turkey vulture, great-horned owl and countless songbirds also inhabit this gorgeous refuge. If you're tackling this place on foot and paw, there are plenty of pathways to suit your exploration style. Or find an Edenesque spot in the canyon's cool, riparian environment and simply take it all in. There's a pamphlet available which offers a mini-education on this fascinating region. For more information: (541) 473-3144.

Directions: From Nyssa, travel south on Route 201 just past the hamlet of Adrian and continue to Snively Gulch Road. Turn right on Snively Gulch Road and follow to its end at Lake Owyhee Road. Turn left and follow Lake Owyhee Road and signs to the Wildlife Area.

Note: Voice control obedience is mandatory and leashes are strongly recommended. Early morning or evening are best wildlife viewing times. Wear dark-colored or camouflage clothing to blend with the environment.

OAKLAND

LODGING

RANCH MOTEL
581 John Long Rd (97462)
Rates: $27-$75
Tel: (541) 849-2126

Hotel Policies May Be Subject To Change

OAKRIDGE

LODGING

ARBOR INN
48229 Hwy 58 (97463)
Rates: $27-$34
Tel: (541) 782-2611
(800) 505-9047

BEST WESTERN OAKRIDGE INN
47433 Hwy 58 (97463)
Rates: $45-$62
Tel: (541) 782-2212
(800) 528-1234

CASCADE MOTEL
47487 Hwy 58 (97463)
Rates: n/a
Tel: (541) 782-2602

OAKRIDGE MOTEL
48197 Hwy 58 E (97463)
Rates: $26-$30
Tel: (541) 782-2432

RECREATION

BEARBONES MOUNTAIN TRAIL HIKE

Intermediate/2.2 miles/1.5 hours

Info: This trail has you covered with interesting flora from top to bottom. You and furface will hightail it beneath a canopy of old-growth Douglas fir, while a picturesque medley of ferns, mosses and Oregon grape creates a combo plate understory. The site of the old fire tower lookout signals Kodak moments are about to happen. The 360° views are among the best in the entire forest and include Dome Rock, Diamond Peak, Moon Point, Hills Creek Reservoir and the distant, sprawling woodlands of the Umpqua National Forest. For more information: (541) 782-2266.

Directions: From Oakridge, take Highway 58 east for 2 miles to Kiston Springs Road and turn right for a half-mile to FS 21. Follow FS 21 for 16.5 miles to the junction with FS 2127 and turn right for 4 miles to FS 5850. Continue west on FS 5850 about 3 miles to the trailhead on the right.

Note: Trail is recommended for use June-October.

BETTY LAKE TRAIL HIKE

Beginner/3.5 miles/2.0 hours

Info: Sun-splashed Betty Lake (aka puppy paradise) is only a hop, skip and a jump from the trailhead, a quarter-mile to be exact. From the lake, you and your deliriously happy aqua pup will continue 1.5 miles to the end at Waldo Lake Trail

Locate Other Dog-Friendly Activities...Check Nearby Cities

junction. FYI: The early angler gets the tastiest trout. For more information: (541) 782-2291.

Directions: From Oakridge, head east on Highway 58 for 27 miles to Waldo Lake Road (FS 5897). Turn left and follow Waldo Lake Road for 5.5 miles to the trailhead on the left.

BIG SWAMP GROVE via MIDDLE FORK TRAIL HIKE

Beginner/4.0 miles/2.0 hours

Info: Your tree hound will sniff till his whiffer quits on this trail edged by an old-growth forest, nature's time capsules. Canopied by towering Douglas fir, western red cedar, graceful Englemann spruce and western hemlock, you'll have it made in the shade, the only way to go on those dog days of summer. Don't call it quits until you check out Big Swamp. This large marshy meadow is a popular hangout with the local wildlife. For more information: (541) 782-2291.

Directions: From Oakridge, head east on Highway 58 for 2 miles to Kitson Springs Road. Turn right on Kitson Springs Road for a half-mile to FS 21. Make a right on FS 21 and continue for 32 miles to FS 2153. Follow FS 2153 approximately 3.5 miles to the trailhead.

BOBBY LAKE TRAIL HIKE

Beginner/4.0 miles/2.0 hours

Info: Like snakes and snails and puppy dog tails - a little bit of this and a little bit of that is what this trail is made of. You'll begin with a cool saunter through dense mountain hemlocks to sun-drenched Bobby Lake. Doggie paddling, grassy picnicking and Frisbee fetching could be the main activities of the day. Way to go Fido. For more information: (541) 782-2291.

Directions: From Oakridge, head east on Highway 58 for 27 miles to Waldo Lake Road (FS 5897). Turn left and follow Waldo Lake Road for 5.5 miles to the trailhead on the right.

DIAMOND CREEK FALLS TRAIL HIKE

Intermediate/2.5 miles/1.5 hours

Info: A perfect ten on the scenery scale, even blasé Bowsers give this trail two paws up. And you know what that means - Kodak moments. As you and the dawgus loop around the canyon rims of Salt Creek and Diamond Creek, photo ops are everywhere. Let's not overlook beautiful Diamond Creek Falls, upper Diamond Creek Falls and plummeting Salt Creek Falls either. The quarter-mile trek is steep and demanding, but make it to the falls and you'll pat yourself on the back, we're talking gorgeous. For more information: (541) 782-2291.

Directions: From Oakridge, head east on Highway 58 for 22 miles to the Salt Creek Falls turnoff (Road 5893). The observation site and parking area are approximately one mile from the Highway 58 junction. Make a right on FS Road 5893-010 just before the Salt Creek Bridge to the trailhead.

FUJI MOUNTAIN TRAIL HIKE

Intermediate/12.2 miles/7.0 hours

Info: If you've missed the gym or avoided the Stairmaster, this toughie will assuage your guilt. A heart pumping aerobic workout awaits you and your rugged Rover (know your dog's limitations) on this long, arduous and steep ascent to the summit of 7,144' Fuji Mountain. From the lake, climb past the South Waldo Trail junction (#3585) for .7 miles to a second junction and stay right to reach the peak. If the effort is within your capabilities, you won't regret the sweat, the 360° mountaintop vistas are the best in town and include Waldo Lake, Diamond Peak and the Three Sisters. Bring plenty of Fuji and snap up some photo worthy memories. At the second trail junction, keep right to stay on track. For more information: (541) 782-2291.

Directions: From Oakridge, head east on Highway 58 for 27 miles to Waldo Lake Road (FS 5897). Turn left and follow Waldo Lake Road for 2 miles to the trailhead.

HEMLOCK BUTTE TRAIL HIKE

Intermediate/1.4 miles/1.0 hours

Info: This hike dishes up a combo plate that lets you taste and sample nature's goodies without a big commitment of time or energy. There's plenty of greenery, scenery and serenery to go around. And the views from atop Hemlock Butte are outstanding. Actually there's nothing standing in the way of you and the dawgus having a great little interlude. For more information: (541) 782-2291.

Directions: From Oakridge, head east on Highway 58 for 2 miles to the Hills Creek Reservoir sign (FS Road 23). Turn right on FS Road 23 for 18 miles to the trailhead.

INDIGO LAKE TRAIL HIKE

Beginner/3.8 miles/2.0 hours

Info: Send your water woofer's tail into overdrive with this cinchy hike to spectacular Indigo Lake. The trail beebops through dense woodlands and verdant alpine meadows before reaching your destination point. Named for its deep blue color, Indigo Lake guarantees an unforgettable afternoon. If you've got a penchant for fishing, this lake is aiming to please with its bounty of rainbow and cutthroat trout. Yum! For more information: (541) 782-2291.

Directions: From Oakridge, head east on Highway 58 for 2 miles to Kitson Springs Road. Turn right on Kitson Springs Road and continue a half-mile to FS 21 and go right. Follow FS 21 for 32 miles to FS 2154. Go left on FS 2154 for 12 miles to the trailhead at Timpanogas Campground.

LARISON ROCK TRAIL HIKE

Intermediate/8.6 miles/5.0 hours

Info: This journey to the tippy top of Larison Rock is bound to get the juices flowing and the kibble burning. You and the biscuitmeister will follow a challenging course in a grabbag forest of Douglas fir, dogwood, cedar, madrone and hemlock before reaching a dramatic panoramic end. Spectacular views are spread out before you like an offering from the mountain gods. **Caution: There is a 70-foot vertical drop on the west side of the rock.** For more information: (541) 782-2291.

Directions: From Oakridge, head east on Highway 58 for 2 miles to Kitson Springs Road. Turn right on Kitson Springs Road for a half-mile to FS 21. Make a right on FS 21 for .5 miles to FS 5852. Go right on FS 5852 for 2 miles to the trailhead.

MIDDLE FORK TRAIL HIKE

Beginner/5.0 miles/2.5 hours

Info: This is the perfect easy-does-it, wet paws, smiley face kind of hike every summer vacation deserves. There's nothing that's particularly outstanding, just a lot of little pleasantries rolled into one day. The riverside trail beside the Willamette is soft underfoot and cooled by a lush canopy. Pretty shade trees, lots of evergreenery and tweet-tweet music are part of the picture. There's fishing too if you're so inclined. And wildlife enthusiasts won't go home empty-eyed. Deer, elk, heron, beaver and mallard finish off nature's offering. Carpe diem Duke. For more information: (541) 782-2291.

Directions: From Oakridge, head east on Highway 58 for 2 miles to Kitson Springs Road. Turn right for a half-mile to FS 21. Make a right on FS 21 for 12 miles to the trailhead.

MIDDLE FORK TRAIL to INDIGO SPRINGS HIKE

Beginner/3.0 miles/1.5 hours

Info: You and your hiking guru will have it made in the shade on this no-sweat hike. The shade is compliments of cottonwoods, big leaf maples and mixed conifers. As you play tagalong with your wagalong from Chuckle Springs to Indigo Springs, your wet wagger, aka Lucky, will have a grin from ear to ear. Go ahead, make your dog's day. For more information: (541) 782-2291.

Directions: From Oakridge, head east on Highway 58 for 2 miles to Kitson Springs Road. Turn right for a half-mile to FS 21. Make a right on FS 21 for 30 miles to the Chuckle Springs sign. Turn right on FS 21-404 for .5 miles to the trailhead.

Locate Other Dog-Friendly Activities...Check Nearby Cities

MOON POINT TRAIL HIKE

Beginner/2.2 miles/1.0 hours

Info: Diversity is the name of the game on this simple trail that wanders from wet meadows to dry meadows and from rocky cliffs to groves of high elevation conifers. Don't forget your camera, the views from Moon Point are pawsitively worth a click. For more information: (541) 782-2291.

Directions: From Oakridge, head east on Highway 58 for 2 miles to Kitson Springs Road. Turn right for a half-mile to FS 21. Make a right on FS 21 for 18 miles to FS 2129. Go left on FS 2129 for 9 miles to the trailhead.

SALT CREEK FALLS - Leashes

Info: The second highest falls in the state, a layer of basalt more than 300' deep forms the backdrop to this remarkable feat of Mother Nature. The sunburst pattern behind the falls resulted from contracting and shrinking of the basalt during the volcanic cooling process. You and the wagster will have several viewing options. There's the easy to reach viewpoint trail which is no work and all play. One gander and you'll become a die-hard waterfall devotee. There's a one-mile butt-kicker which leads to a lower, more dramatic vista of the falls, but you'll earn every eye catching moment. And then there's the middle ground approach where you and the dawgus can enjoy this pristine slice of nature without too much effort.

After taking a peek at the falls from the viewpoint, turn tail and head for doggiedom at its finest hour. A riparian oasis of cushioned paths beneath a thick canopy of trees beckons you and Bowser to browser and make the most of the cool breezes and sweet pine-scented air. Picnic sites, Huck Finn creekside fishing and charming nooks and crannies are everywhere. Your soon-to-be-dirty dog will be grinning from ear to ear, wet tootsies happily sloshing around in the cold babbling creeks, the tail factor a surefire #10. If you're a super duper lucky dog and visiting in spring, expect to be tickled pink by the wild rhododendrons that do their thing in May.

Hotel Policies May Be Subject To Change

Directions: From Oakridge, head east on Highway 58 for 22 miles to the Salt Creek Falls turnoff (Road 5893). The observation site and parking area are approximately one mile from the Highway 58 junction. Make a right on FS 5893-010 just before the Salt Creek Bridge to the trailhead.

SPIRIT LAKE TRAIL HIKE - Leashes

Beginner/1.0 miles/0.5 hours

Info: Solitude is free of charge on this trail. You'll stroll through a delightful forestland where the wind whistles through the treetops, harmonizing with nature's musicians. Visit in springtime when the lakeside meadows dress up in their prettiest wildflowers. Or beat the summer doldrums with some paw-dipping in the aqua fria. For a bonafido good time that's easy as pie, look no further than this excursion. For more information: (541) 782-2291.

Directions: From downtown Oakridge, travel east on Salmon Creek Road for 13 miles to FS 2422. Turn left and drive 9 miles to the trailhead on the right-hand side.

SWAN LAKE TRAIL HIKE

Beginner/1.6 miles/1.0 hours

Info: The birds might not have the music down pat, but as you trip the light fantastic on this pristine trail to soulful Swan Lake, you'll definitely enjoy the serenade of the local flyboys and the pretty backdrop of your surroundings. Pack a biscuit basket and take an intermission lakeside with your little maestro while you watch the sunlight dance on the blueness of the water. When the curtain comes down on your lovely day, backtrack through the bosky woods to the trailhead, humming Tchaikovsky all the way. Ta-ta tutu. For more information: (541) 782-2291.

Directions: From downtown Oakridge, head east on Salmon Creek Road 11 miles to FS 2417. Turn left and follow FS 2417 12 miles to the trailhead at the end of the road.

TWIN PEAKS TRAIL HIKE

Expert/6.6 miles/4.0 hours

Info: If you're an experienced A-1 hiker and your mutt's as muscular as Mighty Dog, then go for it. You'll be exhilarated by the challenge of this trail to the summit of Twin Peaks. Steep and steeper, you'll experience a rubber legs workout. If you need a reward, other than feeling like champs, the views are expansive and memorable. Wowser Bowser. For more information: (541) 782-2291.

Directions: From Oakridge, head east on Highway 58 for 27 miles to Waldo Lake Road (FS 5897). Turn left and follow Waldo Lake Road for 6 miles to the trailhead.

WALDO LAKE TRAIL HIKE

Intermediate/1.0-22.0 miles/0.5 hours-2 days

Info: Hike a mile or overnight, you won't soon forget this outstanding journey. Circling beautiful Waldo Lake, the postcardian pretty trail follows a relatively level course through forested hills and lush meadows (in spring, read riot of color). Exercise gurus don't fret, several steep sections are part of the package, certainly enough to keep you on your toes. Bring your Nikon and make like Ansel Adams and see if you can capture the glory of this deep blue crystal clear lake, one of the world's purest. Take a biscuit break at a trailside bench and lose yourself in the idyllic setting. Aah, let this day last forever (or maybe overnight). For more information: (541) 782-2291.

Directions: From Oakridge, head east on Highway 58 for 27 miles to Waldo Lake Road (FS 5897). Turn left and follow FS 5897 north approximately 13 miles to North Waldo Campground. The trailhead is located on the north side of the boat launch parking area.

YORAN LAKE TRAIL HIKE - Leashes

Intermediate/10.6 miles/6.0 hours

Info: This sloping trail guides you and your hiking noodnick through impressive stands of thick graceful Engelmann spruce,

Hotel Policies May Be Subject To Change

silver and noble fir. After a mile of pine-scented skedaddling, you'll find yourself in a moist meadow, the ideal setting for a spring wildflower gala. Before you know it - ZAP - you're doing the stroll into a mountain hemlock and white fir forest on your way to stunning Yoran Lake. Chill out with the cold nose before leading the snout out by turning about. Dollars to dog biscuits, you're gonna like this breezy, shade-dappled trail. Happy tails. For more information: (541) 433-2234.

Directions: From Oakridge, drive east on Highway 58 about 27 miles to FS 5810. Turn south onto FS 5810 and travel 1.5 miles to trailhead parking on the right-hand side of the road. The trailhead is located about 0.25 miles before the Trapper Creek Campground.

Note: Trail is recommended for use in spring, summer and fall.

ODELL LAKE

LODGING

SHELTER COVE RESORT
Hwy 58, W Odell Lake Rd
Rates: $60-$85
Tel: (541) 433-2548

ONTARIO

LODGING

BEST WESTERN INN
251 Goodfellow St (97914)
Rates: n/a
Tel: (541) 889-2600
(800) 528-1234

BUDGET COLONIAL INN
1395 Tapadera Ave (97914)
Rates: $27-$55
Tel: (541) 889-9615

BUDGET INN
1737 N Oregon St (97914)
Rates: $35-$80
Tel: (541) 889-3101
(800) 905-0024

CARLILE MOTEL
589 N Oregon St (97914)
Rates: $36-$64
Tel: (541) 889-8658
(800) 640-8658

HOLIDAY INN
1249 Tapadera Ave (97914)
Rates: $68+
Tel: (541) 889-8621
(800) 465-4329

HOLIDAY MOTOR INN
615 E Idaho (97914)
Rates: $27-$50
Tel: (541) 889-9188

Locate Other Dog-Friendly Activities...Check Nearby Cities

OREGON TRAIL MOTEL
92 E Idaho Ave (97914)
Rates: $20-$70
Tel: (541) 889-8633
(800) 895-7945

PLAZA MOTEL
1144 SW 4th Ave (97914)
Rates: $25-$95
Tel: (541) 889-9641

STOCKMAN'S MOTEL
81 SW 1st St (97914)
Rates: $32-$45
Tel: (541) 889-4446

RECREATION

FAREWELL BEND STATE PARK - Leashes

Info: Stop puppyfooting around and plan a lark in the park with your bark. Smack dab in the middle of this desert region you'll unearth a beautiful shade-studded oasis, so hustle your buttsky on over. There's a large tree-lined day use area beside the shore of scenic Snake River where R&R pupportunities await. Do lunch alfresco and fill your tummy while you fill your eyes with the rolling hillsides and charming riparian scenery. Afishionados, have it your way with the bass and catfish. Geologist wannabes, this is rockhounding utopia. Wildlife watchers, tote your binocs and keep the pooch quiet, this is also where the deer and the antelope play (as well as geese, eagle, chukar and Hungarian partridge). Springtime, as you might have guessed, brings rainbow-colored wildflowers everywhere you turn. For more information: (541) 869-2365.

Directions: From Ontario, travel Highway 84 northwest 25 miles to exit 353 and the park.

Note: Day use fee may be charged.

OREGON CITY

LODGING

VAL-U-INN MOTEL
1900 Clackamette Dr (97045)
Rates: $61-$71
Tel: (503) 655-7141
(800) 443-7777

OTTER ROCK

LODGING

ALPINE CHALETS
7045 Otter Crest Loop (97369)
Rates: $75-$90
Tel: (541) 765-2572
(800) 825-5768

PACIFIC CITY

LODGING

ANCHORAGE MOTEL
6585 Pacific Ave (97135)
Rates: $37-$59
Tel: (503) 965-6773
(800) 941-6250

SEA VIEW VACATION RENTALS
P.O. Box 1049 (97135)
Rates: $75-$235
Tel: (503) 965-7888

INN AT PACIFIC CITY
35215 Brooten Rd (97135)
Rates: $49-$89
Tel: (503) 965-6366
(888) 722-2489

RECREATION

MUNSON CREEK FALLS TRAIL HIKE

Beginner/0.5 miles/1.0 hours

Info: If you and your canine companion are doing the Oregon coast, this pristine waterfall setting is definitely worth the short detour. The change of scenery begins the moment you turn off Highway 101. You'll find yourself in a pastoral and heavily wooded terrain of leafstrewn, moss-laden limbs, trunks and droopy trees. The lower portion of the trail follows creekside amidst a landscape of thick greenery. Your first glimpse of the pretty tumbler will pop out unexpectedly, offering a preview of the natural beauty to unfold. Lucky dogs will be treated to the dramatic sight of water careening over rocks, plunging down the cliffside. The highest waterfall on the coast, Munson Creek Falls measures 266'. You'll be hard pressed to see the tippy top. You and the grinning wet-tailed wonder might just have this enchanting place to yourselves. Aah, what a wondrous slice of heaven. Two paws up for scenery, serenity and coolness. There's even a

Locate Other Dog-Friendly Activities...Check Nearby Cities

picnic table and benches in a cozy cranny where you can break bread with Bowser while you admire the cascades.

Towards the end of the trail, you'll have to pick and choose your way, the flood of '96 left behind some damage. Be prepared for wet going almost any time of the year. Don't be tempted by the trail that leads to the top of the falls. It's rated expert and was severely eroded by the same flood. For more information: (541) 750-7000.

Directions: From Pacific City, travel Highway 101 to milepost 72.9 and the turnoff. You'll travel 1.5 miles over a paved and unpaved road to the parking area and the trailhead.

PAULINA

RECREATION

COTTONWOOD TRAIL HIKE

Intermediate/8.0 miles/5.0 hours

Info: You'll wind your way through a dense forest of mixed conifers on your climb to the top. Plush, wildflower-dotted meadows create a stark contrast to the green blanketed woodlands, so take it all in. If it's solitude you and the loyal one are craving, you've found utopia. This less-traveled path roams through remote regions where the views of Cottonwood Valley are excellent and the panoramas are nothing short of stunning. At the 4-mile mark, turn the snout about and head on out. For more information: (541) 416-6645.

Directions: From Paulina, travel Beaver Creek Road north 8 miles to FS 42. Take FS 42 for 1.5 miles to FS 3810 and turn right. Drive 6.5 miles to the fork, veer left (staying on FS 3810) and continue to FS 38. Follow FS 38 for 18 miles to the trailhead.

SUGAR CREEK TRAIL HIKE - Leashes

Beginner/1.4 miles/1.0 hours

Info: For a simple, easy getaway that puts you in touch with nature and with yourself, you can't miss with this picturesque riverside jaunt. Stop, look and listen. Let the sound of rushing water soothe you, the sweet music of songbirds lift your spirits and the scent of the fresh air clear your mind as you explore the ponderosa filled hillsides or fish the river. For more information: (541) 416-6645.

Directions: From Paulina, travel Beaver Creek Road north 8 miles to FS 58 and turn right. Drive 10 miles to the Sugar Creek Campground and the trailhead on the right.

Note: Trail is recommended for summertime hiking.

PENDLETON

LODGING

CHAPARRAL MOTEL
620 SW Tutuilla (97801)
Rates: $45
Tel: (541) 276-8654

LET 'ER BUCK MOTEL
205 SE Dorion Ave (97801)
Rates: $28-$34
Tel: (541) 276-3293

LONG HORN MOTEL
411 SW Dorion Ave (97801)
Rates: $28-$50
Tel: (541) 276-7531

RED LION HOTEL
304 SE Nye Ave (97801)
Rates: $63-$80
Tel: (541) 276-6141
(800) 733-5466

7 INN
I-84 exit 202 (97801)
Rates: $31-$84
Tel: (541) 276-4711

SUPER 8 MOTEL
601 SE Nye Ave (97801)
Rates: $43-$59
Tel: (541) 276-8881
(800) 800-8000

TAPADERA MOTOR INN
105 SE Court (97801)
Rates: $34-$58
Tel: (541) 276-3231
(800) 722-8277

TRAVELER'S INN
310 SE Dorion Ave (97801)
Rates: n/a
Tel: (541) 276-6231

VAGABOND INN
210 SW Court Ave (97801)
Rates: $28-$57
Tel: (541) 276-5252
(800) 522-1555

WILDHORSE RESORT MOTEL
72779 Hwy 331 (97801)
Rates: $45-$65
Tel: (541) 278-2274
(800) 654-WILD

RECREATION

BEAVER MARSH TRAIL HIKE

Beginner/0.5 miles/0.5 hours

Info: Spend your morning hours in the company of beavers on this cinchy hike where nature is the name of the game. This quick but interesting little jaunt will start your day off on the right paw. For more information: (509) 522-6290.

Locate Other Dog-Friendly Activities...Check Nearby Cities

Directions: From Pendleton, take Umatilla River Road (CR 900) east approximately 40 miles to where it becomes FS 32. Continue on FS 32 past the Umatilla Forks Campground to the FS 32-030 junction. Turn left on FS 32-030 to the trailhead at road's end.

EMIGRANT SPRINGS STATE HERITAGE AREA - Leashes

Info: If your hound's a history sniffer at heart, you've come to the right place. Dedicated to the brave men and women who traveled west via the Oregon Trail, Emigrant Springs is alive with the past. Keep noses to the ground on the self-guided nature trail near the registration booth and pick up a bit of knowledge about the local flora. Hightail it to the campground and inspect the replicas of the covered wagons used in days of old. Or find a cozy cranny, dine à la blanket and catch forty winks. For more information: (541) 983-2277.

Directions: From Pendleton, travel Highway 84 south 24 miles to exit 234E and the park entrance.

NORTH FORK MEACHAM TRAIL HIKE

Expert/4.2 miles/3.0 hours

Info: Tough and tougher best describe this mucho difficult hike which is bound and determined to get the juices flowing. You and your muscular mutt will shake a leg through Bear Creek Valley to trail's end at the confluence of North Fork Meacham Creek and Pot Creek. If hiking's not your only passion, indulge in some reel-time pleasures. The resident rainbow trout are particularly tasty. Whenever the time is right, retrace your steps. For more information: (509) 522-6290.

Directions: From Pendleton, take Highway 84 east for 33 miles to the Mt. Emily exit (Summit Forest Road 31). Head east on Summit Forest Road 31 for 12.5 miles to the FS 3113 junction. Turn left on FS 3113 and drive one mile to the trailhead across from the Summit Guard Station.

Hotel Policies May Be Subject To Change

SOUTH FORK UMATILLA TRAIL HIKE

Intermediate/4.4 miles/3.0 hours

Info: If wet paws equate to happiness, your pooch will think he's found heaven. Following a relatively level course, the trail crisscrosses the river several times. No matter what your mindset, water hijinks can't be avoided or denied. So just say yes. Milepost 2.2 off Goodman Ridge marks the end of the trail. For more information: (509) 522-6290.

Directions: From Pendleton, take Umatilla River Road (CR 900) east approximately 40 miles to where it becomes FS 32. Continue on FS 32 past the Umatilla Forks Campground to the trailhead at the South Fork Bridge.

PHILOMATH

<u>RECREATION</u>

STARKER FORESTRY TOUR - Leashes

Beginner/0.25 miles/0.25 hours

Info: Minute-sized but very sweet, this walk along a graveled pathway is like a stepping stone to knowledge. You and your tree hound will learn about the practice of good forestry. And while you're at it, there's a good chance one of the local beavers will be doing an earth moving routine. Lucky lick-meisters might even catch a fleeting glimpse of deer or elk in the more heavily forested sections. The nine-stop journey explains forest ecology, beginning with seedlings and ending with towering trees grown for harvesting. If you're in this neck of the woods, stop by for a shaded stroll and a songbird serenade. For more information: (541) 929-2477.

Directions: From Philomath, drive Highway 20 west 8 miles to the hamlet of Blodgett. Cross over the railroad tracks and look for the Blodgett School signpost. Turn left onto a paved road, then veer left at the "Y" onto Tum Tum Road. Follow Tum Tum Road for 2 miles to Lasky Creek Road and the signed entrance on the right. Parking is off Lasky Creek Road on the left-hand side.

Locate Other Dog-Friendly Activities...Check Nearby Cities

PILOT ROCK

LODGING

PILOT ROCK MOTEL
362 NE 4th St (97868)
Rates: $30-$53
Tel: (541) 443-2851

PISTOL RIVER

LODGING

**ARCADIA ON THE OREGON COAST
VACATION HOME**
23154 Hwy 101 (97444)
Rates: n/a
Tel: (888) 227-1963

PORT ORFORD

LODGING

CASTAWAY-BY-THE-SEA MOTEL
545 W 5th St (97465)
Rates: $45-$75
Tel: (541) 332-4502

SHORELINE MOTEL
206 6th St (97465)
Rates: $36-$46
Tel: (541) 332-2903

SEA CREST MOTEL
Hwy 101, P.O. Box C (97465)
Rates: $38-$60
Tel: (541) 332-3040

RECREATION

CAPE BLANCO STATE PARK - Leashes

Info: Cape Blanco was named by Spanish explorers for its chalky appearance which is attributed to a concentration of fossilized shells. Originally a privately owned ranch, Cape Blanco has been preserved for its historical value and for the fascinating lighthouse that is part of the property. Eenie, meeny, miney, moe, pick a pathway and off you'll go. There are scenic surprises wherever you wander. Make tracks to the lighthouse, holder of at least four Oregon records, including the oldest continuously operating light (in use since 1870), the most westerly, the highest above sea and the home to the first

Hotel Policies May Be Subject To Change

female lighthouse keeper in Oregon, not to mention its picturesque locale on the craggy coastline. Hustle your butt to the Eastlake Victorian-style historic Hughes Ranch House, circa 1898, where your imagination will be your guide to the past and to life as a rancher in the 1800s. Before it was turned over to the state, the Hughes family occupied the house for 111 years. If you're seeking some of Mother Nature's handiwork, check out the Sixes River and its stunning environs. Or be a lazybones for the day and kick back cliffside. Consider a brown bagger with the wagger while you watch for migrating whales. For more information: (541) 332-6774.

Directions: From Port Orford, travel Highway 101 north for 9 miles to the park.

Note: Day use fee may be charged. Dogs are not permitted buildings.

GRASSY KNOB TRAIL HIKE - Leashes

Intermediate/1.6 miles/1.0 hours

Info: As you and the lickmeister make lickety split along this trail to the summit of Grassy Knob, teasing glimpses of the Grassy Knob Wilderness and Pacific Ocean hint at what's in store. The serenery you'll encounter is so beautiful, you might want to make like Ansel Adams and take home some glossy memories. For more information: (541) 439-3011.

Directions: From Port Orford, head north on Highway 101 to CR 196 (Grassy Knob Road). Turn right (east) on CR 196 to FS 5105. Follow FS 5105 to the trailhead.

HUMBUG MOUNTAIN STATE PARK

Info: Getting to this park is just about as breathtaking as being in the park. The scenic drive includes spectacular vistas of the coastline and dramatic passage through a lush rain forest along your zigzag journey through tree-covered canyons. If you're visiting in autumn, the setting is made even more dramatic by the rich fall colors. Pretty even on foggy days, the mistiness adds a surrealistic quality to the landscape. An 1800-acre green scene, the park includes 1,750' Humbug Mountain, home to a dreamy old-growth forest. As you and the sniffmeister wiggle this way and that through a grabbag forest of pine and deciduous trees, the hound's nose will be glued to the moist ground, the wagging tool in permanent overdrive. If you're feeling like Hercules, play follow the leader on the three miler to the summit.

Directions: From Port Orford, travel south on Highway 101 for six miles to milepost 305.5 and the parking lot for the summit trail.

PORTLAND

LODGING

ALADDIN MOTOR INN
8905 SW 30th Ave (97219)
Rates: $39-$69
Tel: (503) 246-8241
(800) 292-4466

THE BENSON HOTEL
309 SW Broadway at Oak (97205)
Rates: $190-$600
Tel: (503) 228-2000
(800) 426-0670

BEST VALUE INN
3310 SE 82nd Ave (97266)
Rates: $33-$50
Tel: (503) 777-4786
(800) 358-5066

BEST WESTERN HERITAGE INN
4319 NW Yeon (97210)
Rates: $54-$115
Tel: (503) 497-9044
(800) 528-1234

BEST WESTERN INN CONV CENTER
420 NE Holladay St (97232)
Rates: $60-$85
Tel: (503) 233-6331
(800) 528-1234

**BEST WESTERN INN
AT THE MEADOWS**
1215 N Hayden Meadows Dr (97217)
Rates: $80-$150
Tel: (503) 286-9600
(800) 528-1234

BUDGET VALUE VIKING MOTEL
6701 N Interstate Ave (97217)
Rates: $38-$48
Tel: (503) 285-6687
(800) 308-5097

COMFORT INN-LLOYD CENTER
431 NE Multnomah St (97232)
Rates: $56-$99
Tel: (503) 233-7933
(800) 228-5150

CYPRESS INN-DOWNTOWN
809 SW King St (97205)
Rates: $45-$80
Tel: (503) 226-6288
(800) 532-9543

DAYS INN AIRPORT
3828 NE 82nd Ave (97220)
Rates: $55-$85
Tel: (503) 256-2550
(800) 329-7466

DELTA INN
9930 N Whitaker (97217)
Rates: $60-$80
Tel: (503) 289-1800
(800) 833-1800

DOUBLETREE HOTEL JANTZEN BEACH
909 N Hayden Island Dr (97217)
Rates: $98-$130
Tel: (503) 283-4466
(800) 222-8733

Hotel Policies May Be Subject To Change

FIFTH AVENUE SUITES
521 SW 5th Ave (97204)
Rates: $150-$195
Tel: (503) 222-0001
(800) 711-2971

4TH AVENUE MOTEL
1889 SW 4th Ave (97201)
Rates: $40-$45
Tel: (503) 226-7646

HISTORIC HOTEL VINTAGE PLAZA
422 SW Broadway (97205)
Rates: $165-$300
Tel: (503) 228-1212
(800) 243-0555

HOLIDAY MOTEL
8050 NE Martin Luther King (97211)
Rates: $35-$45
Tel: (503) 285-3661

HOWARD JOHNSON AIRPORT
7101 NE 82nd Ave (97220)
Rates: $65-$88
Tel: (503) 255-6722
(800) 345-3896

IMPERIAL HOTEL
400 SW Broadway
& Stark St (97205)
Rates: $87-$109
Tel: (503) 228-7221
(800) 452-2323

MADISON SUITES
3620 NE 82nd Ave (97220)
Rates: $40-$50
Tel: (503) 257-4981
(800) 945-4425

MALLORY HOTEL
729 SW 15th (97205)
Rates: $75-$120
Tel: (503) 223-6311
(800) 228-8657

THE MARK SPENCER HOTEL
409 SW 11th Ave (97205)
Rates: $75-$120
Tel: (503) 224-3293
(800) 548-3934

MARRIOTT PORTLAND
1401 SW Front Ave (97201)
Rates: $137-$500
Tel: (503) 226-7600
(800) 228-9290

MEL'S MOTOR INN
5205 N Interstate Ave (97217)
Rates: $40-$55
Tel: (503) 285-2556

OLALLIE LAKE RESORT CABINS
21222 NW Cannes Dr (97229)
Rates: $70
Tel: (503) 557-1010

OXFORD SUITES
12226 N Jantzen Dr (97217)
Rates: $66-$105
Tel: (503) 283-3030
(800) 548-7848

PORTLAND CENTER APARTMENTS
200 SW Harrison St (97201)
Rates: n/a
Tel: (503) 224-3030

QUALITY INN AIRPORT
8247 NE Sandy Blvd (97220)
Rates: $70-$125
Tel: (503) 256-4111
(800) 221-2222

RANCH INN MOTEL
10138 SW Barbur Blvd (97219)
Rates: $33-$40
Tel: (503) 246-3375

RED LION HOTEL COLUMBIA RIVER
1401 N Hayden
Island Dr (97217)
Rates: $103-$145
Tel: (503) 283-2111
(800) 547-8010

RED LION HOTEL DOWNTOWN
310 SW Lincoln (97201)
Rates: $125-$160
Tel: (503) 221-0450
(800) 547-8010

RED LION INN COLISEUM
1224 N Thunderbird Way (97227)
Rates: $64-$84
Tel: (503) 235-8311
(800) 547-8010

RESIDENCE INN LLOYD CENTER
1710 NE Multnomah St (97232)
Rates: $130-$185
Tel: (503) 288-1400
(800) 331-3131

Locate Other Dog-Friendly Activities...Check Nearby Cities

RIVER PLACE HOTEL
1510 SW Harbor Way (97201)
Rates: $195-$700
Tel: (503) 228-3233
(800) 227-1333

THE RIVERSIDE INN
50 SW Morrison St (97204)
Rates: $79-$129
Tel: (503) 221-0711
(800) 899-0247

RODEWAY INN CITY CENTER
3800 NE Sandy Blvd (97232)
Rates: $49-$74
Tel: (503) 460-9000
(800) 228-2000

RODEWAY INN LLOYD CENTER
1506 NE 2nd Ave (97232)
Rates: $55-$75
Tel: (503) 231-7665
(800) 228-2000

ROSE MANOR INN
4546 SE McLoughlin Blvd (97202)
Rates: $30-$51
Tel: (503) 236-4175
(800) 252-8222

ROSE MOTEL
8920 SW Barbur (97219)
Rates: n/a
Tel: (503) 244-0107

SILVER CLOUD INN OF PORTLAND
2426 NW Vaughn St (97210)
Rates: $75-$83
Tel: (503) 242-2400
(800) 205-6939

**SIXTH AVENUE
AMERICAN HOSPITALITY INN**
2221 SW 6th Ave (97201)
Rates: $45-$55
Tel: (503) 226-2979

SULLIVAN'S GULCH B&B
1744 NE Clackamas St (97232)
Rates: $70-$85
Tel: (503) 331-1104

TRAVELODGE PORTLAND AIRPORT
9727 NE Sandy Blvd (97220)
Rates: $49-$55
Tel: (503) 255-1400
(800) 556-0006

TRAVELODGE SUITES
7740 SE Powell Blvd (97206)
Rates: $70-$75
Tel: (503) 788-9394
(800) 578-7878

VALUE INN DOWNTOWN
415 SW Montgomery St (97201)
Rates: $35-$60
Tel: (503) 226-4751

RECREATION

CATHEDRAL PARK - Leashes

Info: Spend a pleasant afternoon with your pooch at this neighborhood favorite where paw-friendly pathways provide the opportunity for your daily dose of Rexercise.

Directions: Located on Edison and Pittsburgh.

CHIMNEY PARK - Leashes

Info: If hiking's to your liking, mix it with a splash of green and enjoy a fun-filled excursion to this 16-acre park. Kick up some dust on the trails and then settle down for some R&R with your one and only mutt.

Directions: Located at 9360 N. Columbia.

Hotel Policies May Be Subject To Change

CITY HALL/DOWNTOWN DISTRICT PARKS - Leashes

Info: If you're staying at one of the hotels in the southwest part of town, the following green scenes are just the place for your morning constitutional. Or at lunchtime, brown bag it with the wag it and treat yourself to a slice of country in the city. You'll find plush grass, pretty trees, park benches and lots of interesting people watching opportunities.

The numbered parks that follow are within the downtown district:

1) CHAPMAN & LOWNSDALE SQUARES - Leashes

Info: These blocks were dedicated as public squares in 1852. Because a bull elk was rumored to have grazed here in the early 19th century, Mayor David P. Thompson donated a Roland Perry elk statue in its honor. The statue stands in the middle of the street between the two blocks.

Directions: Located on Southwest Fourth Avenue, between Madison and Salmon Streets.

2) IRA KELLER MEMORIAL FOUNTAIN - Leashes

Info: There's something about the sound of water and the softness of a misty spray that soothes the psyche and calms the pupster. Located across from the Portland Civic Auditorium, you and your companion will find such a fountain. Divided into two levels, the upper features babbling brooks that flow through a tree-shaded plaza and end their journey in the form of an elegant waterfall and a sparkling pool at the lower level. Aah, imagine the cooling mist on your face one sunny afternoon.

Directions: Located on Southwest Fourth Avenue, between Market and Clay Streets.

3) PIONEER COURTHOUSE SQUARE - Leashes

Info: Home to Portland's first real schoolhouse (built in 1858), it then housed the beloved Portland Hotel. In the 1970s, the land was donated to the city, destined to become a public square. More than 64,000 citizens funded the construction by buying the "named" bricks that pave the square.

Directions: Located on Broadway, between Yamhill and Morrison Streets.

Locate Other Dog-Friendly Activities...Check Nearby Cities

COLUMBIA PARK - Leashes

Info: Hey sport, this fine community park is just the place to root for the home team. Pack a fun attitude and your hot diggety dog because however you like your good times, this 33-acre park spells fun with a capital F.

Directions: Located on N. Lombard and Woolsey.

COLUMBIA RIVER GORGE

See Cascade Locks, Hood River, The Dalles and Troutdale for additional lodging and recreation.

Info: Starting just east of Portland and continuing to The Dalles, the Columbia River Gorge is America's largest and oldest national scenic area. The ancestral Columbia River canyon was formed 12,000 years ago when receding glaciers in northern Idaho and Montana created a series of floods which swept down the Columbia River Valley. I-84 and the scenic Historic Columbia Highway run parallel to the river.

Your travels will be bordered by steep cliffs, misty mountains and woodsy trails that are meant to tempt you to have a look-see. You can hike waterfall trails, explore gorges, picnic in green oases or park yourself under a tree and become one with nature. Wildflower devotees, you'll think the flora is heavenscent. The Gorge's wide ranges of elevation and precipitation equate to a profusion of bloomers. Many of the species are found only in the Gorge, their glorious pink, yellow, fuschia and white colors grace the rocky areas, basalt cliffs, shaded banks, open woods and moist slopes of this pristine region. For more information: (503) 668-1400.

The numbered hikes and activities that follow are located within the scenic and historic Columbia River Gorge. They are listed in order as you drive east from Portland on Route 84.

1) LARCH MOUNTAIN TRAIL to MULTNOMAH CREEK WAY HIKE

Intermediate/4.0 miles/3.0 hours

Info: If waterful playtime and unforgettable beauty get two paws up from the pupster, you're gonna love the high drama of this region, a place where visions of tiptoeing through the toad flax, a sunny, yellow blossom, will fill your mind while steep, forested cliffs will leave you wanting more. But the best part of the trail is the rainbow at the end, wet and wild Multnomah Creek, a delightfully cool and refreshing oasis. The trail traverses steep cliffs so you'll want to keep the pooch leashed. And get an early start since evening shadows fall quickly on the north face of the Gorge. Make the most of your outing and pack some goodies for a creekside repast and a memorable day. Way to go Fido. FYI: If you're visiting during huckleberry season, fill up a basket or two with this small, succulent cousin of the blueberry and color your tongue purple. For more information: (503) 668-1400.

Directions: From I-84, take the Corbett exit 22. Continue on Corbett Hill and turn left on U.S. Highway 30. Drive 3 miles to the Larch Mountain Road turnoff on the right. Travel fourteen miles to the Larch Mountain upper trailhead sign.

Note: Closed in winter. Be sure you know what huckleberries look like before eating them.

2) BRIDAL VEIL FALLS OVERLOOK LOOP TRAIL HIKE - Leashes

Beginner/1.0 miles/0.5 hours

Info: Put a sparkle in the sniffmeister's eyes and hop on this loop trail in spring or summer when the riotous wildflower party is in full swing. You and the gleeful pup will witness some blooms that are found only in these parts, like the delicate white Oregon Sullivantia, the bright yellow Long Beard Hawkweed or Howell's Daisy, a white-petaled lovely, not to forget the other garden varieties that fill the landscape in glorious colors. Bridal Veil Falls is classified as a tier fall since it falls, then falls and then falls again. This mesmerizing charmer has separate falls that can all be viewed at once. From the overlook, you'll also get to see one of the last remaining fields of camus. Wowser Bowser. For more information: (503) 668-1400.

Directions: From Portland, travel Highway 84 east for 28 miles to the Bridal Veil exit (#28) and go right (west) on Highway 30 for one mile to the parking lot. The trailhead is at the far end of the parking lot.

3) ANGEL'S REST LOOKOUT TRAIL HIKE - Leashes

Intermediate/4.4 miles/3.0 hours

Info: Expect a workout as you and the hound head up, up and away to Angel's Rest. When the climb's over, you'll rest with the Angels atop a lofty perch that offers some of the best views around. Panoramas of the gorge as well as sweeping views to the east and west are part of the package. You'll barely have time to catch your breath before the stunning surroundings will steal it away. Do an about-face when day is done and consider yourselves two lucky dogs. For more information: (503) 668-1400.

Directions: From Portland, travel east on Highway 84 for 28 miles to the Bridal Veil exit (#28). Follow the off-ramp to the intersection with the Historic Columbia River Highway and park in the dirt lot on the right-hand side. Walk across the highway to reach the trailhead.

4) LATOURELL FALLS TRAIL HIKE- Leashes

Beginner/1.2 miles/0.5 hours

Info: Located in woodsy, cool and fragrant Talbot State Park, this easy jaunt escorts you and old brown eyes to a pretty cascade. A plunger type falls, Latourell drops vertically from the cliffside without making contact with bedrock. On a bright summer day, the cooling spray catches the rays of the sun and brightens the landscape in sparkling brilliance. For more information: (503) 668-1400.

Directions: From Portland, travel Highway 84 east for 28 miles to the Bridal Veil exit (#28) and turn right (west) on Highway 30. Drive 3 miles to the parking lot on the south side of the road.

5) PONYTAIL FALLS TRAIL HIKE - Leashes

Beginner/2.0 miles/1.0 hours

Info: Get set to do a bit of switchbacking at the onset of this trail. You'll zigzag around Horsetail Falls to a trail junction. Stay to the right for your odyssey to Ponytail where you and the wide-eyed one will find yourselves behind the rushing water. Experience an awestruck moment as you gaze at the

Hotel Policies May Be Subject To Change

water crashing around you, the sheer cliffs zooming skyward. Leaving the falls behind, the scenic descent into Oneonta Gorge comes next. At the trail junction (about 1.1 miles) bear right and play follow the leader on the path that parallels the Historic Columbia River Highway. It's another half-mile to the finish line. For more information: (503) 668-1400.

Directions: From Portland, travel Highway 84 east for 28 miles to the Bridal Veil exit and turn left (east) on Highway 30. Drive 5.5 miles to the parking lot on the north side of the road. Walk across the highway to the Horsetail Falls Trailhead.

6) MULTNOMAH FALLS TRAIL HIKE - Leashes

Intermediate/2.2 miles/2.0 hours

Info: If anything serves as the official postcard of Oregon's waterfalls, it's this ribbon of cascading water, the fourth highest falls in the United States. A classic example of a plunge type waterfall, it drops vertically and away from the cliffside and loses contact with bedrock. Expect company on your trek, this is the most popular waterfall in the Gorge. Cascading hundreds of feet, it's bound to astound you and the hound. You'll travel uphill on a paved pathway to the Art Deco concrete bridge arch that serves as a viewpoint over the upper falls. Located on the north face of the southern cliffs, this moody site is one of the most dramatic and definitely the most photographed, so don't forget your camera, you'll want to flick the Fuji and document the beauty of it all. From the falls, scan the river and the mountain range as you're spritzed with the wind-tossed spray. Actually two falls in one, the upper falls drop from the cliff to a pool 560' below. The second section ends near the historic Multnomah Lodge. If flowers are your passion, see if you can spot some of the endemic species that thrive on the wet cliffs and rocky slopes. For more information: (503) 668-1400.

Directions: From Portland, travel Highway 84 east for 31 miles to exit 31. The trailhead is located just west of Multnomah Falls Lodge.

7) ELOWAH FALLS TRAIL HIKE - Leashes

Beginner/1.6 miles/1.0 hours

Info: Another popular waterfall hike, be prepared to meet and greet people and their pooches. Follow the left forks for Elowah Falls, a 290' cascade, the perfect spot to turn your hot dog into a chilly dog. The cooling mist from the falls will refresh and delight you and the dawgus but be careful on the boardwalk, the moisture can make for slippery going. If wildflowers equate to wondrous joy, expect a manic moment from the trillium that blooms like crazy in spring. When you've had your fill of the falls (can that be possible?), turn the snout about and head on out. For more information: (503) 668-1400.

Directions: From Portland, travel Highway 84 for 35 miles to exit 35. Turn left and follow the Historic Columbia River Highway for 2.5 miles to the parking lot on the right. The trailhead is located at the west end of the parking lot.

8) WAHCLELLA FALLS TRAIL HIKE - Leashes

Beginner/1.8 miles/1.0 hours

Info: If you like your hikes cinchy but postcard pretty, pencil this charmer in your travel agenda. Summer's a great time to do this cool gorge trail which leads to a water oasis in picturesque Tanner Creek. The crisp scent of cedar will accompany you and the sniffmeister all the way to the cascades where the soothing sound of the water is guaranteed to chase your cares away. Any which way you turn at the fork will take you where you want to go on this loop-de-loop. Bone voyage. For more information: (503) 668-1400.

Directions: From Portland, travel 40 miles on Highway 84 to exit 40. Then make two quick rights to reach the Wahclella Falls Trailhead at the far end of the looping road.

9) EAGLE CREEK TRAIL HIKE to PUNCHBOWL FALLS- Leashes

Beginner/4.2 miles/2.0 hours

Info: This geologic wonder will set the pupster's tail in the wagging mode and keep it there. From the parking area, the first burst of water hijinks will call to you in the form of a rushing creek. Let the gleeful one do his wet and wild thing before you begin your journey through this slender slice of magnificence. You'll climb through the gorge, the water beneath you, breathtaking scenery wherever you turn. Birdsong will drift your way from the treetops as you climb up, up and away into a cool world of mossy woodlands and cliffs. If you're visiting in spring, expect to be awed by the fabulous wildflowers. Look for the thin, white petals of the Columbia Gorge Daisy. You'll find a profusion beneath overhanging basalt cliffs in the west end of the Gorge. If you find yourself at the Gorge on a hot summer day, do like the locals, wade upstream or along the banks of Eagle Creek and fall in love with the hanging gardens that flourish in this unbelievably Gorge-ous region.

This popular trek through some of Mother Nature's handiwork is not without peril. On the cliffside journey, you'll encounter a couple of hairy spots where the drops are quite steep. Watch your footing, keep a leash on the pup and stay on track, the trail takes you to not one, but two wonderful falls. At 1.5 miles, look for a trail on your right for the sidetrip to Metlako Falls, a charmer you won't want to miss, but don't stop there. At 1.8 miles, the trail zooms to the Punchbowl Overlook. This sweet spot, where water from the falls collides with the deep pool far below, is guaranteed to bowl you over. Gung-ho hikers, continue for as little or as long as you'd like, but Punchbowl marks the turnaround point for the 4-mile trek. For more information: (503) 668-1400.

Directions: From Portland, travel 41 miles east on Highway 84 to exit 41, Eagle Creek Road. **There is no westbound exit to Eagle Creek Road.** Turn right and continue south for 0.3 miles to the Eagle Creek Trailhead.

10) WAUNA VIEWPOINT TRAIL HIKE - Leashes

Intermediate/3.6 miles/2.0 hours

Info: This adventurous journey guides you through a cornucopia of nature. First stop, Eagle Creek, aka puppy playland with a wet slant. Have a bit of splish-splashing fun beside the banks of Eagle Creek before veering left and heading south up the hill. When you reach the tip of the trail, you'll find yourself in a nearly treeless terrain with gaga views in every direction. From this lofty, albeit bare perch, you and the wagging wonder will have an eyeful of Table Mountain and the often snow-capped peaks of the Washington Cascades. Sit a spell and let sleeping dogs lie until it's time to call it a doggone great day. For more information: (503) 668-1400.

Directions: From Portland, travel 41 miles east on Highway 84 to exit 41. Turn right and head south for about 0.1 miles to the parking area on the left-hand side by the picnic area. The trail begins at the other side of the suspension bridge.

COUNCIL CREST PARK - Leashes

Info: Give your pooch something to bark home about when you set your sights on this lovely green scene. You'll have a bonafido country experience in this charming 42-acre setting. A little bit of exploring will unearth a natural area and a one miler that honeycombs the park. Break some bread with your favorite furface beside the sparkling, sun-speckled waters of the fountain.

Directions: Located on SW Council Crest Drive.

CRYSTAL SPRINGS RHODODENDRON GARDEN - Leashes

Info: From February through June, flower power takes center stage and the garden becomes a land of multi-hued enchantment. This petite Eden contains an enticing array of rare species and hybrid rhododendrons, azaleas and mucho bloomers. Companion plants and unusual trees complete the picture. In birdspeak, this locale rates two tweets. A spring-fed lake surrounds most of the gardens and lures countless species of waterfowl and songbirds. Aqua pups will undoubtedly sniff out the pretty waterfall before you do. Don't miss the interesting arched bridge as you travel lickety-split on the shaded paths to the lake. For more information: (503) 771-8386.

Directions: Off SE 28th Avenue, one block north of Woodstock.
Note: Open all year. Admission fee charged. You must pick up after your pet.

DELTA PARK EAST - Leashes

Info: A little smaller than its western counterpart, you'll still find lots of romping room for you and your romper. Over 85 acres, including a natural area, equate to pupportunities galore.

Directions: Located on N. Denver and MLK.

DELTA PARK WEST - Leashes

Info: Almost seven times the size of its sister, this 600-acre park is the ultimate getaway. Picnic ops abound so BYOB (bring your own biscuits) and partake of lunch alfrisky. Looking for a way to work out the kinks? There's a one miler that loops through the lush landscape. If you'd rather be a lazybones, no problem. Just find a cozy nook and spend some down time with your canine cohort.

Directions: Located on N. Denver and Victory.

ELK ROCK ISLAND - Leashes

Info: If the sound of rushing water stills the savage beast in you, this riparian oasis should get the nod. The natural 15-acre domain is situated beside the flowing waters of the Willamette River. For a quickie outdoor interlude, you and the pupster can leave your prints on the riverside hiking trail.

Directions: Located near SE 19th and Sparrow.

FERNHILL PARK - Leashes

Info: If you and your Hair Jordan like the hustle and bustle of ball games, you're gonna love this neighborhood arena of 25 acres. Catch a game of hoops or tote a bouncy Spalding, find an empty field and create your own action.

Directions: Located on NE 37th and Ainsworth.

FOREST PARK - Leashes

Info: You and the dawgus can't get much closer to nature à la Lewis and Clark than this sprawling region. Stretching for miles in every direction, this 4,800-acre park is a sure cure for the summertime blahs. Hiking hounds in particular rate this place two paws up for its numero uno 27-mile Wildwood Trail. The Wildwood begins at the Vietnam Memorial, winds through Forest Park, Washington Park and the Hoyt Arboretum and traverses the local byways before ending at BPA Road. A myriad of side trails emanate from the main route raising the distance covered to more than 50 miles. Whether you're looking for a place to strut the mutt or a hiking trial that tops them all, this green scene deserves a slot in your plans. FYI: A number of side trails are dedicated to bikers and equestrian riders only.

Directions: Location is West Hills - NW Skyline to St. Helens. The main trailhead begins at the Vietnam Memorial off Knights Boulevard.

GABRIEL PARK - Leashes

Info: There's a mass of green for you and your parkhound to peruse and use in at this 90-acre park. Pack a fuzzie tennie or a flying disk and go for it.

Directions: Located on SW 45th and Vermont.

GEORGE HIMES PARK - Leashes

Info: Take your city slicker out for a day of fun in the sun at this natural habitat and tails will be wagging in the breeze. Or put a grin on the barkmeister's mug with a jaunt on the hiking trail that slices and dices through this 35-acre grassy realm.

Directions: Located on SW Terwilliger and Slavin

GOVERNOR TOM McCALL WATERFRONT PARK - Leashes

Info: A dollop of plush greenery awaits you and your old tar at this park that fringes the Willamette River. Do the stroll from beginning to end and then walk up Burnside Street into Chinatown where you can check out an ethnic slice of the city. Walk south from the park and you'll discover a bevy of charming shops and restaurants where people watching is the name of the game. If waterplay is more your thing, cool off under 100 jets of shooting water at the Salmon Street Springs.

Directions: On SW Front Avenue from Clay to Gleason.

Hotel Policies May Be Subject To Change

GRANT PARK - Leashes

Info: Every dog should have his day. Make yours a fun one with a visit to this 20-acre parkland where you can scamper across the huge football and softball fields. Or tote a biscuit basket and relax in the shade.

Directions: Located on NE 33rd and U.S. Grant Place.

KELLY BUTTE PARK - Leashes

Info: Grab the gadabout and do a roundabout in this 18-acre grassland. You'll uncover a short hiking trail, just perfect for your AM constitutional.

Directions: Located on SE 103rd and Clinton.

KELLEY POINT PARK - Leashes

Info: Hit the trails at this 96-acre park and give the dawgus something to bark home about. A delightful trail zigzags through the area providing the perfect pupportunity for some Rexercise.

Directions: On N. Kelley Point Park Road and Marine Drive.

LAURELHURST PARK - Leashes

Info: Fun and games can be yours in the grass of this 34-acre developed park. Tote a biscuit basket and do lunch pondside while a flock of chatty birds provide the entertainment. Or work out the kinks on one of the trails that lace the park.

Directions: Located on SE 39th and Stark.

LENTS PARK - Leashes

Info: Root, root, root for the home team or tote a ball of your own and do the catch thing with your wild thing.

Directions: Located on SE 92nd and Holgate.

LOVEJOY FOUNTAIN PARK - Leashes

Info: The highlight of this charming park is the namesake fountain which spurts water from a concrete mountaintop to a canyon and wading pool below.

Directions: At the Portland Center Building, SW Hall Street.

Locate Other Dog-Friendly Activities...Check Nearby Cities

MARQUAM NATURE PARK - Leashes

Info: As the name implies, this lovely parkland is nature with a capitol N. Cruise the one-mile hiking path and get a first-hand peek at the park's 76 acres. Or bring the red checks along and picnic with the pooch. For more information: (503) 823-2223.

Directions: Located on SW Marquam and Sam Jackson.

The numbered hike that follows is within Marquam Nature Park:

1) BROADWAY TRAIL HIKE

Intermediate/0.6 miles/0.5 hours

Info: Short on distance but long on effort, it's an uphill trek all the way to the turnaround point at the stairway which junctions with Broadway Drive. Naturalists, you'll be enthralled by the extraordinary flora while you're entertained by tweet, tweet music drifting from nearly every treetop. Ivy and moss climb the tall pines that reach as if on tippytoes to grab their share of sunshine in this shaded oasis. The heady scent that fills the air comes from the fragrant vanilla leaf that carpets the forest floor.

A narrow pathway slices through a thick understory and deposits you and the pantmeister at a lofty bench. Botanist wannabes, in this one very special locale, you'll find five species of fern, fifty-seven of herbs, five of conifers and five of deciduous trees including fir, western red cedar, western hemlock and Pacific yew. No matter when you visit, there's bound to be a passel of flowers to admire like yellow wood violets, inside out flowers, fairy bells, trillium, honeysuckle, columbine, miner's lettuce, starflower and pearly everlasting. So close to the city beat, this retreat is a refreshing change of pace just about any time of the year. When you've filled your senses with the beauty around you, let the dogster get his fill of freshwater from the doggie fountain at the trailhead.

Directions: Located on SW Marquam and Sam Jackson.

MARSHALL PARK - Leashes

Info: A great way to break up your day, just take five in a shady nook of this 23-acre park or burn some kibble on the one miler.

Directions: Located on SW 18th Place.

Hotel Policies May Be Subject To Change

MT. TABOR PARK - Leashes

Info: For a doggone great outdoor excursion, pack a sack of snacks and make tracks to this 195-acre developed park. Actually an extinct volcanic cinder cone, this area serves up great views of Mt. Hood and downtown Portland. When you find that perfect resting spot, kick back and do a little cloud-gazing with your tail wagger.

Directions: Located on SE 60th and Salmon.

NOB HILL NEIGHBORHOOD- Leashes

Info: When you've exercised your body at one of the nearby park trails, give your credit cards a workout in this trendy neighborhood of boutiques and restaurants. Do the stroll along NW 21st and NW 23rd Avenues between Burnside and Division Streets. You'll find plenty of dog-friendly shopkeepers and lots of whimsical canine merchandise in addition to upscale clothing and handsome home furnishings. In the fair weather months, you'll have your pick of restaurants and coffee houses where you can dine with your canine at an outdoor table while you pass the time of day.

Directions: NW 21st Avenue and NW 23rd Avenue from Burnside to Division Streets.

PIER PARK - Leashes

Info: Dollars to dog biscuits, you won't have any trouble finding some fun in the sun at this 77-acre green expanse. Tote a good read and a tough chew and double your pleasure.

Directions: Located on N Seneca and St. Johns.

SALMON STREET SPRINGS - Leashes

Info: This is a pupular place with the wet set. The fountain, designed by Robert Perron, celebrates urban life, the water patterns changing to match the city's mood. One hundred jets do their best to cool down hot summer days. If a little mist with a twist works for you, highlight this park on your agenda.

Directions: Located at the intersection of Front Avenue and SW Salmon Street.

SKIDMORE FOUNTAIN - Leashes

Info: Finally, a fountain with thirsty dogs in mind. The four lower troughs, filled by spillover from the bottom pool, were designed to water pooches and horses. The flowing waters empty into an upper bowl supported by four female figures before spilling into the bottom pool. FYI: The brass rings once held copper cups for residents to quench their thirst. Waggers give this fountain two slurps up.

Directions: Located on SW First Avenue and Ankeny Street at Ankeny Plaza.

SMITH AND BYBEE LAKES - Leashes

Info: Furbanites can sample the life of their country cousins with an excursion to this very natural region. You and your hiking hound can hit the trails that lace the parkland or just do the stroll atop the green. Shaded nooks and hidden crannies beckon you to savor the tranquility of this special locale. You and your bow wow will go wow wow over this pristine slice of Mother Nature.

Directions: Located on N Columbia and Simmons.

SOUTH PARK BLOCKS -Leashes

Info: Situated in the Cultural District, you and your canine connoisseur can frolic amidst the lovely grounds of this citi-fied green scene. The pretty landscape and impressive statuary are reminiscent of many of the parks found in European capitals. Stretching for several blocks, you and the parkmeister can watch the traffic whiz by from one of the benches or people watch from a grassy square. Filled with sweet smelling roses and a mélange of magnificent trees, it's the perfect place for an afternoon interlude. Think brown bagger and delight the wagger with a tasty chew and a touch of Mother Nature smack dab in the middle of the city. Museums, history centers, the performing arts and other interesting structures flank the boulevards. If you have a penchant for trompe l'oiell, take a gander at the face of the Oregon History Center building. Incredible doesn't do justice to describing this artistic achievement. A depiction of the Lewis and Clark Expedition, your own little explorer will be delighted to see that Seaman, the loyal Newfy who accompanied Lewis and Clark, is grandly portrayed. Settle in at one of the benches in the building's courtyard and study the interesting tour d'art.

Directions: Located on Southwest 9th Avenue, between Market and Salmon Streets.

TRYON CREEK STATE PARK - Leashes

Info: For a change of scenery and a guaranteed good time, head out to this neck of the woods. This oasis was set aside for people and pooches who want nothing more than to walk in natural splendor. So pack your sack and leave your city cares behind. You and the old brown eyes are about to experience one howl of a great day. For more information: (503) 636-9886.

Directions: From Portland, travel south on Highway 5 to exit 297 (Terwilliger Boulevard). Continue south on Terwilliger Boulevard for 2.5 miles to the signed entrance to the park.

Note: Day use fee may be required.

The numbered hikes that follow are within Tryon Creek State Park:

1) TRILLIUM NATURE TRAIL HIKE - Leashes

Beginner/0.3 miles/0.25 hours

Info: This pupsqueak-sized, barrier-free trail is a wonderful introduction to all this stunning green scene has to offer. Complete with benches, paved pathways, drinking fountains and viewing decks, you'll dawdle this way and that amidst a charming, flower-bedecked milieu. The sniffmeister can check out the fragrant trilliums while you check out the interpretive signs and come away with a mini education.

Directions: From Portland, travel south on Highway 5 to exit 297 (Terwilliger Boulevard). Continue south on Terwilliger Boulevard for 2.5 miles to the signed entrance to the park. The trail is located at the Nature Center.

Locate Other Dog-Friendly Activities...Check Nearby Cities

2) TRYON CREEK TRAIL SYSTEM - Leashes

Beginner/8.0 miles/4.0 hours

Info: Wowser Bowser. And hooray for the environmental comeback of this area. Heavily logged in the 1880s by the Oregon Iron Company to provide fuel for the iron smelter in nearby Lake Oswego, red alder, Douglas fir, big-leaf maple and western red cedar now blanket the land and create a fabulous forest canopy. You won't believe how gorgeous the colors can be in autumn unless you see them first hand. There's more than one pathway for your hiking pleasure. A maze of trails lace the woodlands, each encompassing a scenic surprise. Naturalists, you're gonna love everything about this place, from the flyboys singing overhead to the busy beavers running to and fro. When the wildflower party begins in spring, pockets of joyous color brighten the bosky terrain. But perhaps fall is the most beautiful of all. The fiery contrast of the maples against the lush green backdrop is guaranteed to enchant. Pick up a trail map at the Nature Center to make sure you and the pupster don't miss a trick.

Directions: From Portland, travel south on Highway 5 to exit 297 (Terwilliger Boulevard). Continue south on Terwilliger Boulevard for 2.5 miles to the signed entrance to the park. The main trailhead is located at the Nature Center.

TWIN LAKES/PALMATEER POINT LOOP TRAIL HIKE - Leashes

Intermediate/8.0 miles/5.0 hours

Info: This trail is a favorite with the locals. It'll lead you and your aqua pup to two backcountry lakes as well as an excellent vista at Palmateer Point. After gaining a little ground, you'll reach the still waters of the first lake where you can boogie with Bowser around the lake to the upper lake. Another couple of miles will bring you to Palmateer Point and incredible views of the valley and Devil's Half Acre, an old camp on Barlow Road and an early wagon-train route. You have two choices for your return trip. Go back the way you came or hike the Pacific Crest Trail, located about a mile west of the main trail. For more information: (503) 352-6002.

Hotel Policies May Be Subject To Change

Directions: From Portland, travel east on Highway 26 to the Frog Lake Sno-Park which is about 8 miles east of Government Camp and 4.5 miles south of the Highway 35 junction. The trailhead is the Pacific Crest Trail marker on the left side of the parking lot. Follow the Pacific Crest Trail Hike about 1.25 miles to a junction. Continue to the right to reach Twin Lakes.

Note: Open June through October.

WASHINGTON PARK - Leashes

Info: Stop puppyfooting around and wipe that hangdog expression off the city licker's mug. You and your gadabout will be mad about the hills and dales of this 145-acre oasis. The tranquil atmosphere will transport you to a different era, a time of old-fashioned leisure, of ladies twirling parasols and gentlemen in waistcoats. Surprises unfold at every turn in this extraordinary storybook milieu. Meandering pathways lead to grassy knolls (AKA perfect playtime spots for Spot) and stone stairways covered with moss lead to multi-levels of park terrain. Unexpected statuary, secluded picnic benches and lone wildflowers that poke through the thick understory contribute to the scenery of the park. Ferns and ivy decorate the gentle slopes while pine trees and hundred-foot redwoods loom overhead. Berry trees with clusters of red and white fruit thrive beside a solitary mimosa. Fir, red maples and more tree species and flora than you can possibly identify mingle together like old friends. But what you'll find most in the quietude of this singular setting is enchantment. Enchantment beneath a cool misty canopy, the perfect venue for daydreaming and good times.

Let your mood be your guide. Hike to your heart's content on the paw-pleasing Wildwood Trail or the quickie M.A.C. Trail. Be a lazybones and just grab some R&R while sleeping dogs lie. Stash a fuzzy tennie and add to your pup's pleasure. Go ahead and make your dog's day while you make some great memories. Without a doubt, don't do without a visit (or two) to this special green scene. Your pooch will cover you with licks and love you forever. For more information: (503) 823-2223.

Directions: Located at the head of SW Park Place.

The numbered activities that follow are within Washington Park:

1) HOYT ARBORETUM - Leashes

Info: For a diorama à la nature, this scenic locale of wood-lands and meadows is the stuff of doggie dreams. More than 800 species of trees and shrubs from around the globe make this bosky beauty a must-see destination. A treehound's delight, you'll find excellent examples of Brewer's weeping spruce, Himalayan spruce, dawn redwood, Chinese lacebark pine, the largest collection of conifers in the country and a maturing grove of coast and giant redwoods. Whew! One hundred year old native firs and cedars do their share by cre-ating a canopy of shade guaranteed to cool. Ten miles of trails interlace this 75-acre region. Come in the spring and bask in the wonder of flower-bedecked meadows, the sensuous beau-ty and sweet fragrance of the dogwoods and magnolias. This treasure trove enchants in autumn as well. The time when Mother Nature takes a broad paintbrush to the landscape and colors your world in a rush of bronzy, russet hues. No matter when you're visiting, don't overlook this sweet spot. Bone voyage. For more information: (503) 228-8733.

Directions: Take the "Zoo-OMSI" exit off Highway 26 and fol-low the signs to the Hoyt Arboretum at 4000 SW Fairview Blvd.

2) INTERNATIONAL ROSE TEST GARDENS - Leashes

Info: A snifforama extraordinaire can happen to you at this scentsational gardenscape. Rose devotees rejoice, this is the place of your dreams. Before you even begin your tour de nose, look around. Founded in 1917, this is the oldest public rose test garden in the United States. An idyllic setting, the site was carefully selected to include panoramas of Portland. Rows upon rows of fragrant, exquisite roses are backdropped and framed by a skyline of skyscrapers nestled against the imposing Cascade mountain range. Together they create an alluring juxtaposition of man-made and nature-made.

Stone stairways escort you to a multi-leveled rose arboretum. You won't know where to look or smell first. Take your time, this place is worth the exploration. It's hard to assimilate the enormous array of roses that bedeck the landscape. Stop for a moment and examine the charming amphitheater of grass-divided rows. Make note of the wall of rhododendrons that fringe the garden. Come springtime, this bank of color adds yet another element of beauty to this Edenesque realm.

Divided by distinct areas, you can wander through the All American Rose Test Garden, Miniature Rose Garden, Queens Walk and Gold Award Gardens to name a few. Just about any variety you and the Rose Girl want to sniff can be sampled here. Just check the main index near the entrance and then twitch noses in that direction. Within this fragrant wonderland, you'll also discover brushed stainless steel structures which invite you to linger longer. Don't miss the Shakespearean Garden where you and your Hamlet hound will be transported to another time and place. You won't need the sign to tell you when you've arrived. The feeling of English drama permeates the air. Whether you like your roses long stemmed, sweet or spicy, one thing is certain, you and your garden variety mutt will carry the scents and the beauty of this gem with you long after you leave. A rose by any other name would and does smell as sweet.

Directions: Entrance is located at 400 SW Kingston Boulevard.

WESTMORELAND PARK - Leashes

Info: When walk time calls, answer it with a stroll in 27 acres of grassland. For canine connoisseurs, this creative capped park has a scattering of art.

Directions: Located on SE McLouglin and Bybee.

WILLAMETTE GREENWAY TRAIL HIKE - Leashes

Beginner/1.0 miles/0.5 hours

Info: Stroll beside the Willamette with your Willie and enjoy the harborside sights. Shop till you drop or pull up a park bench and be a lazybones. A popular walkway with pooches and their people, expect to meet and greet.

Directions: Along the waterfront, one block east of SW Front Avenue on Harbor Way.

Locate Other Dog-Friendly Activities...Check Nearby Cities

WILLAMETTE PARK - Leashes

Info: When nothing but a riverside roam will do, this park should be your destination point. You and the wagger will find 30 acres beside the Willamette where you'll have it made in the shade while you watch the skiffs skim the cool blues. Now that's relaxing.

Directions: Located on SW Macadam and Nebraska.

WOODS MEMORIAL PARK - Leashes

Info: Go munch on lunch with the furry one at this 13-acre getaway. The park is only semi-developed so you and your Portland trailblazer can make your own good times.

Directions: Located on SW 45th and Woods.

OTHER PARKS IN PORTLAND - Leashes

- ALBERT KELLY PARK, SW Dosch & Mitchell
- APRIL HILL PARK, SW 58th & Miles
- ARBOR LODGE PARK, N Bryant & Delaware
- ARGAY PARK, NE 141st & Failing
- BERKELEY PARK, SE 39th & Bybee
- BERRYDALE PARK, SE 92nd & Taylor
- BLOOMINGTON PARK, SE 100th & Steele
- BRENTWOOD PARK, SE 60th & Duke
- BURLINGAME (FALCON) PARK, SW 12th & Falcon
- CHERRY PARK, SE 110th & Stephens
- CLINTON PARK, SE 55th & Woodward
- COLONEL SUMMERS PARK, SE 17th & Taylor
- COUCH PARK, NW 19th & Glisan
- CRESTON PARK, SE 44th & Powell
- CLUSTER PARK, SW 21st & Capitol Hill
- DAWSON PARK, N Stanton & Williams
- DICKINSON PARK, SW Alfred & Dickinson
- DUNWAY PARK, SW 6th & Sheridan
- EAST LYNCHWOOD PARK, SE 170th & Haig
- EASTRIDGE PARK, SE 141st & Crystal Springs Street
- ED BENEDICT (MT. HOOD) PARK, SE 100th & Powell
- ESSEX PARK, SE 79th & Center

Hotel Policies May Be Subject To Change

- FARRAGUT PARK, N Kerby & Farragut
- FLAVEL PARK, SE 75th & Flavel
- FOREST HEIGHTS PARK, Access from NW Miller Road
- FRAZER PARK, NE 52nd & Hassalo
- FULTON PARK, SW 2nd & Miles, off Barbur
- GAMMANS PARK, N. Buffalo & Burrage
- GEORGE PARK, 10000 N Burr at Fessenden
- GILBERT HEIGHTS PARK, SE 130th & Boise
- GILBERT PRIMARY PARK, SE 134th & Foster
- GLENFAIR PARK, NE 154th & Davis
- GLENHAVEN PARK, NE 82nd & Siskiyou
- GLENWOOD PARK, SE 87th & Claybourne
- GOVERNORS PARK, SW 13th & Davenport
- HAMILTON PARK, SW 45th & Hamilton
- HANCOCK PARK, NE 90th & Tilamook
- HARBOR VIEW PARK, N Willamette & Macrum
- HARNEY PARK, SE 67th & Harney
- HARRISON PARK, SE 84th & Harrison
- HEALY HEIGHTS PARK, SW Patrick Place & Council Crest
- HILLSDALE PARK, NW Culpepper Terrace
- HOLLADAY PARK EAST, NE 128th & Holladay
- HOLLADAY PARK WEST, NE 11th & Holladay
- IRVING PARK, NE 7th & Fremont
- JOHN LUBY PARK, NE 128th & Brazee
- JOHNSON CREEK PARK, SE 21st & Clatsop
- JOHNSON LAKE PARK, easterly portion of Johnson Lake
- JOHNSWOOD PARK, N Oswego & Swift
- JOSEPH WOOD HILL PARK, NE Rocky Butte Road
- KENILWORTH PARK, SE 34th & Holgate
- KENTON PARK, N Delaware & Kilpatrick
- KERN PARK, SE 67th & Center
- KNOTT PARK, NE 117th & Knott
- LAIR HILL PARK, SW 2nd & Woods
- LESSER PARK, SW 57th & Haines
- LILLIS-ALBINA PARK, N Flint & Russell
- LYNCHVIEW PARK, SE 165th & Market
- MADRONA PARK, N Greeley & Going Court
- McKENNA PARK, N Wall & Princeton
- MERRIEFIELD PARK, NE 117th & Eugene
- MIDLAND PARK, SE 122nd & Morrison
- MILL PARK, SE 117th & Eugene

Locate Other Dog-Friendly Activities...Check Nearby Cities

- MONTAVILLA PARK, NE 82nd & Glisan
- MT SCOTT PARK, SE 72nd & Harold
- NORMANDALE PARK, NE 57th & Halsey
- NORTH PARK BLOCKS, NW Park, from Ankeny to Glisan
- NORTH POWELLHURST PARK, SE 135th & Main
- NORTHGATE PARK, N Geneva & Fessenden
- OREGON PARK, NE 30th & Oregon
- OVERLOOK PARK, N Fremont & Interstate
- PARKLANE PARK, SE 155th & Main
- PENDLETON PARK, SW 55th & Iowa
- PETTYGROVE PARK, SW 1st & Harrison
- PICCOLO PARK, SE 28th & Clinton
- PORTLAND CENTER PARK, 300 SW Lincoln
- PORTLAND HEIGHTS PARK, SW Patton & Old Orchard Rd
- PORTSMOUTH PARK, N Stanford & Depauw
- POWELL BUTTE NATURE PARK, SE 162nd & Powell
- POWELL PARK, SE 26th & Powell
- POWERS MARINE PARK, SW Macadam, Sellwood Bridge S
- RAYMOND PARK, SE 118th & Raymond
- ROSE CITY PARK, NE 62nd & Tilamook
- ROSEMONT BLUFF, NE 68th & Halsey
- SACAJAWEA PARK, NE 75th & Alberta
- SCOTTSRIDGE (ELASSER) PARK, SE 108th & Henderson
- ST JOHNS PARK, N John & Central
- SELLWOOD PARK, SE 7th & Miller
- SELLWOOD RIVERFRONT PARK, SE Spokane & Oaks Pkwy
- SEWALLCREST PARK, SE 31st & Market
- THOMPSON PARK , NE 138th & Thompson
- TIDEMAN JOHNSON PARK, SE 37th & Tenino
- TRENTON PARK, N Hamlin & Trenton
- UNIVERSITY PARK, 9009 N Foss
- VENTURA PARK, SE 115th & Stark
- WALLACE PARK, NW 25th & Raleigh
- WELLINGTON PARK, NE 66th & Mason
- WEST PORTLAND PARK, SW 39th & Pamona
- WEST POWELLHURST PARK, SE 115th & Division
- WILLAMETTE MOORAGE, SW Macadam, N Sellwood Bridge
- WILSHIRE PARK, NE 33rd & Skidmore
- WOODLAWN PARK, NE 13th & Dekum
- WOODSTOCK PARK, SE 47th & Steele

POWERS

AZALEA LAKE TRAIL HIKE - Leashes

Intermediate/Expert/2.4 miles/2.0 hours

Info: Replace your Stairmaster routine with this demanding hike to Azalea Lake and get the benefits of exercise along with a great time with your numero uno canine cohort. The trail follows an old logging road to the lake and involves two steep sections meant to test your endurance. For more information: (541) 439-3011.

Directions: From Powers, take CR 219 south to FS 33. Continue south on FS 33 about 15 miles to FS 3347. Turn right and follow FS 3347 to the signed trailhead.

COQUILLE RIVER FALLS TRAIL HIKE - Leashes

Intermediate/Expert/1.0 miles/1.0 hours

Info: Short but steep, this trail ascends over 500' as it zigzags through a fir, hemlock and cedar forest to spectacular Coquille Falls. The going may be tough but the scenic views are a definite payback. For more information: (541) 439-3011.

Directions: From Powers, take CR 219 south to FS 33. Continue south on FS 33 about 16 miles to FS 3348. Turn right and follow FS 3348 to the signed trailhead.

ELK CREEK FALLS TRAIL HIKE - Leashes

Intermediate/Expert/2.0 miles/1.5 hours

Info: When packing for this hike, include a coin so that you and your furry sidekick can flip a coin at the fork. Left is a creekside jaunt to a scenic overlook of Elk Creek Falls. Right, a switchbacking climb through woodlands to Big Tree Park, the aptly named location of the world's largest Port Orford cedar tree. No matter which fork you follow, picnic spots prevail so stow some munchies for a time out treat. For more information: (541) 439-3011.

Directions: From Powers, take CR 219 south to FS 33. Continue south on FS 33 about 10 miles to the trailhead.

JOHNSON CREEK TRAIL HIKE - Leashes

Intermediate/4.8 miles/3.0 hours

Info: Wanna wipe that hangdog expression off the pooch's face, whisper wet tootsies in his ear. This trail descends to Sucker Creek and a smattering of other creeks and springs where water hijinks can't be denied. You and the one with the ear to ear grin will have to ford the creek to access the remainder of the trail which skirts the waterway, ending near Johnson Creek at FS 5591, yet another arena for splish-splashing fun. Retrace the pawprints on your return. For more information: (541) 439-3011.

Directions: From Powers, take CR 219 south to FS 33. Continue south on FS 33 about 8 miles to FS 3353. Veer right on FS 3353 to Spur Road 260 and follow to the trailhead.

Note: Don't cross the creeks after periods of heavy rain.

MT. BOLIVAR TRAIL HIKE - Leashes

Intermediate/2.8 miles/1.5 hours

Info: If spectacular views fuel the furry one, then this one will fill his tank. The trail climbs through the pristine Wild Rogue Wilderness, topping out at the summit of Mt. Bolivar, where, you guessed, vistas await. For more information: (541) 439-3011.

Directions: From Powers, take CR 219 south to FS 33. Continue south on FS 33 about 16 miles to FS 3348. Turn right on FS 3348 and continue to BLM Road 32-9-3. Follow BLM Road 32-9-3 to the trailhead.

PRAIRIE CITY

LODGING

STRAWBERRY MOUNTAIN INN
HCR 77, 940 Hwy 26 E (97869)
Rates: $55-$85
Tel: (541) 820-4522
(800) 545-6913

Hotel Policies May Be Subject To Change

<u>RECREATION</u>

MEADOW FORK TRAIL HIKE

Intermediate/9.0 miles/5.0 hours

Info: The sweet scent of spruce and fir are the extra perks of this trek. A river runs through it so the wet and wild one will have mucho pupporunities to do the doggie paddle and get down and dirty. Leaving the water antics behind, you'll climb out of the valley to meadowlands that reach their glory in springtime. While you won't find any vistas at the end of your journey, you will find yourself ensconced in a tranquil forest where quietude is everywhere. Continue your ascent to the Big River Basin and be dazzled by views of Slide Mountain and the verdant valleys. When day is done, turn the snout about and head on out. For more information: (541) 820-3311.

Directions: From Prairie City, travel CR 62 south for 22 miles to FS 16. Turn right onto FS 16 and drive 8.5 miles to FS 924. Turn right on FS 924 and travel 1.5 miles to FS 039. Turn right and continue to the trailhead at the end of the road.

REYNOLDS CREEK TRAIL HIKE

Beginner/3.0 miles/1.5 hours

Info: Wet waggers rate this streamside hike two paws up. You'll skirt Reynolds Creek and frolic through a charming woodland where nature's musicians do their best to entertain. For a technicolor treat, visit in spring when the wildflowers sprinkle the landscape with splashy hues. For more information: (541) 820-3311.

Directions: From Prairie City, travel south on CR 62 for 6 miles to FS 2635. Turn left and drive 4 miles to the trailhead.

SNOWSHOE TRAIL to SKYLINE HIKE

Intermediate/5.6 miles/3.0 hours

Info: Get back to basics on this down to earth hike that serves up a healthy dose of solitude and tranquility. Imagine the quiet you'll find in thickets of spruce and fir on your journey through the Big Creek and Snowshoe Valleys, where the deer and the antelope truly do play. When the warmth of spring is in the air, there are always flowers fluttering in a sea of green grasses. You can't ask for a prettier way to get away from it all. When you top out at the Skyline Trail, take five before repeating the beat. For more information: (541) 820-3311.

Directions: From Prairie City, take CR 62 south for 22 miles to FS 16 and turn right. Drive approximately 8.5 miles to FS 924-021. Turn right and continue 2.5 miles to the trailhead.

PRINEVILLE

Lodging

CAROLINA MOTEL
1050 E 3rd St (97754)
Rates: $26-$59
Tel: (541) 447-4152

CITY CENTER MOTEL
509 E 3rd St (97754)
Rates: $28-$45
Tel: (541) 447-5522

OCHOCO INN & MOTEL
123 E 3rd St (97754)
Rates: $38-$54
Tel: (541) 447-6231

RUSTLERS ROOST MOTEL
960 W 3rd St (97754)
Rates: $40-$60
Tel: (541) 447-4185

Recreation

INDEPENDENT MINE TRAIL HIKE

Intermediate/8.0 miles/5.0 hours

Info: You and your botany buff will have a good time skedaddling through looming stands of old-growth fir and pine on this 8-mile loop. As you slowly gain elevation, you'll climb out of the thickets into stunning mountain meadows. Imagine springtime when the lushness is emblazoned with rich Crayola-colored wildflowers. At the catbird seat atop Lookout Mountain, crack out the camera and make like a pro, the mountain and valley views are memorable. For your return, sniff your way on the old road about .3 miles and turn left. From this halfway point, it's four miles to the finish line. For more information: (541) 416-6645.

Directions: From Prineville, travel 15 miles east on Highway 26. Turn right onto CR 123 and drive 8 miles to the Ochoco Ranger Station. Just past the ranger station, make a right on FS 42 and drive 6.5 miles to the trailhead.

Note: Trail is not recommended for hiking in winter.

Hotel Policies May Be Subject To Change

OCHOCO LAKE STATE RECREATION SITE - Leashes

Info: Ochoco Lake's rippling waters bluedot the green landscape at this 10-acre lakeside park. A favorite fishing hole with the local set, tote your pole and give it a go. Of course, there's always a simple stroll to be had alongside the lake. For more information: (541) 447-4363.

Directions: From Prineville, travel Highway 26 east about 7 miles to the signed park entrance.

Note: Day use fee may be charged.

PONDEROSA LOOP TRAIL HIKE - Leashes

Beginner/1.4 miles/1.0 hours

Info: If you're anywhere in the vicinity and you've got an hour to spare, this charming walk could make your day. You and the pupster will saunter through a fragrant forest of handsome ponderosa pine which tower majestically over the rolling hills. Wildflowers flourish in the sunny months of spring and add a blush of color to the greens. Dollars to dog biscuits, this is one of those tranquil hikes you won't want to end. Bone voyage. For more information: (541) 416-6645.

Directions: From Prineville, travel Highway 26 east about 22 miles to the Bandit Springs Rest Area and turn left. The trailhead is located in the rest area.

PRINEVILLE RESERVOIR STATE PARK - Leashes

Info: A memorable day is in the making when you plan an excursion to this combo plate of terra firma and aqua fria. Nestled beside the Prineville Reservoir, you'll find 400 acres of interesting terrain to explore. The color and texture of the sagebrush/juniper hillsides and basalt rock outcroppings form a vivid contrast to the clear blue waters and create a serene oasis. Fishy dreams can come true for anglers who try their luck on the trout, bass and brown bullheads. In the frosty months of winter, you might catch a glimpse of a mule deer or bald eagle. Birders prefer the warmer months when a myriad of flyboys can be sighted along the shores of the reservoir. For more information: (541) 447-4363.

Locate Other Dog-Friendly Activities...Check Nearby Cities

Directions: From Prineville, travel the Paulina Highway south about 1 mile to Juniper Canyon Road. Exit right on Juniper Canyon Road and continue 14 miles to the park entrance.

Note: Day use fee may be charged.

RIMROCK SPRINGS TRAIL HIKE - Leashes

Beginner/1.5 miles/1.0 hours

Info: Skirting the edges of the Rimrock Springs Wildlife Area, this sweet retreat is ideal for naturalists. You and the woofer will hoof it through a high desert environment of juniper and sage. One mile into your journey, you'll be rewarded big time with a wildlife viewing platform. Patient pooches will get a chance to observe the local residents scampering through the brush or soaring through the skies. Continuing on the loop, you'll arrive at a second viewing area where additional wildlife ops await. For more information: (541) 416-6645.

Directions: From Prineville, travel northwest on Highway 26 about 18 miles. The Rimrock Springs Wildlife Refuge and trailhead are located just off Highway 26 on the east side.

STEIN'S PILLAR TRAIL HIKE - Leashes

Intermediate/5.0 miles/3.0 hours

Info: Treehounds give this wonderful trail the high five for its forestlands of old-growth pine and fir. The bonus of this trek is Stein's Pillar, an elongated rock pillar, 350' tall, 120' in diameter. The last 1.4 miles before the trail's namesake, you'll encounter some steep sections that require a sure-footed approach. And hey, check out the panoramas of Mill Creek along the way. When pillar ogling is over, do an about-face. For more information: (541) 416-6645.

Directions: From Prineville, travel Highway 26 east for 9 miles to Mill Creek Road (FS 33). Turn left on Mill Creek Road for 6.5 miles to FS 3300-500. Turn right and drive a short distance to the trailhead.

Note: Trail is not recommended for hiking in winter.

PROSPECT

LODGING

PROSPECT HISTORICAL HOTEL
391 Mill Creek Dr (97536)
Rates: $50-$85
Tel: (541) 560-3664
(800) 994-6490

RECREATION

AVENUE OF THE BOULDERS WATERFALL SITE - Leashes

Info: Waterfall devotees, you and your canine cohort won't want to miss a stop at this scenic slice of nature. Mill Creek Falls and Barr Creek Falls have lured photographers and oglers alike to come and take a peek. These extraordinary cascades are made even more beautiful by a backdrop of lush forest greenery and unusual volcanic rock formations.

Directions: From Prospect, travel southwest on Highway 62 to Mill Creek Drive and turn left.

JOSEPH H. STEWART STATE PARK - Leashes

Info: Stock up on trout for your next fish fry at Lost Creek Reservoir. Tote a boat or try your luck from the terra firma. You and Old Brown Eyes can also check out the grounds. Dotted with pear, apple and English walnut trees, the day use area provides plenty of romping room for you and furface. Depending on the season, you might witness a cascading waterfall on your exploration. For more information: (541) 560-3334.

Directions: From Prospect, travel southwest on Highway 62 about 10 miles to the park entrance.

Note: Day use fee may be charged.

RAINIER

LODGING

BUDGET INN
120 "A" St W (97048)
Rates: $35-$85
Tel: (503) 556-4231

Locate Other Dog-Friendly Activities...Check Nearby Cities

REDMOND

LODGING

THE HUB MOTEL
1128 Hwy 97 N (97756)
Rates: $38-$45
Tel: (541) 548-2101
(800) 7-THE-HUB

REDMOND INN
1545 Hwy 97 N (97756)
Rates: $44-$58
Tel: (541) 548-1091
(800) 833-3259

SUPER 8 MOTEL
3629 21st Place (97756)
Rates: $49-$65
Tel: (541) 548-8881
(800) 800-8000

RECREATION

PETERSEN ROCK GARDENS - Leashes

Info: In 1935, Danish immigrant Rasmus Petersen began an extraordinary undertaking on his 4-acre property. He built castles, bridges, terraces and replicas of historic structures using petrified wood, agate, jasper, thundereggs, malachite and obsidian glass for his creations. You and your rockhound can inspect the miniature churches, the United States flag and an incredible replica of the Statue of Liberty. After your rocky start, take the time to smell the flowers and admire the lovely flora that dot this parkland. Expect colorful company if you plan to picnic. The free-roaming peacocks aren't too proud to take a handout. Not to mention the chickens and ducks who'll also be clucking and quacking for a morsel or two. For more information: (541) 382-5574.

Directions: Located 7 miles southwest of Redmond off Highway 97 at 7930 SW 77th Street (2.5 miles west of Highway 97).

Note: $2 entrance fee suggested to help with maintenance and operation. Do not allow your dog to chase the resident birds or cats.

REEDSPORT

LODGING

ANCHOR BAY INN
1821 Winchester Ave (97467)
Rates: $33-$53
Tel: (541) 271-2149
(800) 767-1821

BEST BUDGET INN
1894 Winchester Ave (97467)
Rates: $34-$36
Tel: (541) 271-3686

Hotel Policies May Be Subject To Change

BEST WESTERN SALBASGEON INN
1400 Hwy Ave 101 (97467)
Rates: $56-$86
Tel: (541) 271-4831
(800) 528-1234

FIR GROVE MOTEL
2178 Winchester Ave (97467)
Rates: $34-$45
Tel: (541) 271-4848

SALBASGEON INN OF THE UMPQUA
45209 Hwy 38 (97467)
Rates: $65-$85
Tel: (541) 271-2025

SALTY SEAGULL MOTEL
1806 Winchester Ave (97467)
Rates: $29-$44
Tel: (541) 271-3729
(800) 476-8336

TROPICANA MOTEL
1593 Highway Ave (97467)
Rates: $29-$60
Tel: (541) 271-3671
(800) 799-9970

RECREATION

DEAN CREEK ELK VIEWING AREA - Leashes

Info: A naturalist's delight, this preserve was established in 1987 to protect elk and other wildlife that inhabit the area. Encompassing over 1,000 acres of pasture and timberland, this is the place to see the awe-inspiring Roosevelt elk, Oregon's largest land mammal. Weighing up to 1,100 pounds and standing as tall as 5' at the shoulder, the antlers can reach spreads of nearly 3'. Numbering as many as 120, these splendid animals roam freely, their whereabouts changing with the seasons. Dollars to dog biscuits, you'll experience a sighting if you plan a visit in early morning or at dusk when the elk come out to play.

If you're visiting in autumn, you might see the "bugling," the time when harems are disputed and breeding cycles begin. There's one particular setting which is as camera worthy as it gets. A couple of miles from Reedsport on Highway 38, you'll come to a field near a campground where dinner à la grass is served at dusk. The elk, backdropped by the greenery and the old red building will stay with you long after you've headed on to another adventure. Wildlife devotees will be happy to learn that elk aren't the only creatures to be observed in this riparian region. Canada geese, osprey, bald eagle, great blue heron, black-tailed deer, beaver, nutria and muskrat have all staked a claim to part of the territory. For more info: (541) 888-5515.

Directions: From Reedsport, travel three miles east on Highway 38 to the Elk Viewing Area signs. Within a 3-mile stretch, there are two viewing areas and several observation pull-outs.

Note: Pull completely off the road to view wildlife. Don't let your dog run loose.

Locate Other Dog-Friendly Activities...Check Nearby Cities

EEL DUNES TRAIL HIKE - Leashes

Beginner/1.5 miles/1.0 hours

Info: A combination of woodlands and dunes, this intriguing jaunt gives you a taste of two environments as well as insight into the low-growing coastal plants. Watch for lichen and flowers as you and the wagster skedaddle through the terrain. The junction with the Umpqua Dunes Trail signals turnaround time. For more information: (541) 271-3611.

Directions: From Reedsport, travel south on Highway 101 10.5 miles to the Eel Creek Campground and the trailhead on the west side of the highway.

TAHKENITCH CREEK LOOP TRAIL HIKE - Leashes

Intermediate/3.5 miles/2.0 hours

Info: You and your cold nosed noodnick will make merry in the coastal evergreen forests, open dunes, wetlands and seaside areas. See Spot run along this mixed bag of nature, listen for the sound of the waves crashing against the shore and sniff the salty ocean air. Binocs will make the most of the lofty views along the creek. For more information: (541) 271-3611.

Directions: From Reedsport, travel north 10.5 miles on Highway 101 to the Oregon Dunes Overlook on the west side of the road. The trailhead begins at the south end of the viewing platform.

TAHKENITCH CREEK TRAIL HIKE - Leashes

Beginner/1.5-4.0 miles/1.0-2.0 hours

Info: This freelance kind of trail is a bonafido retreat where you can experience the essence of creekside tranquility. You and your hiking hound can go the distance or do a quickie on one of the shorter loops and still come away with a sense of serenity. This place is such a delightful medley of goodies that you can't miss. Coastal conifers, the tweet music of songbirds, peek views of the Tahkenitch Creek come with the territory. And don't overlook the marvelous contrast of the creamy dunes against the verdant forestlands. Wildlife devotees will

Hotel Policies May Be Subject To Change

have plenty to bark home about too. Just pick a sandy creek-side spot and look for critter tracks. There's a chance you'll see a variety of alligator lizards, shorebirds, raccoon, otter and mink. Lucky dogs might sight an endangered snowy plover. But silence and distance are key. And remember, these rare birds will abandon any nest disturbed by humans or hounds, so don't touch. For more information: (541) 271-3611.

Directions: From Reedsport, travel north 9 miles on Highway 101 to the trailhead on the west side of the highway.

Note: Nesting season is March 15 - Sept. 15. Please heed all warning signs, leash your dog and respect the fragile nesting habits of the snowy plover.

TAHKENITCH DUNES TRAIL HIKE - Leashes

Beginner/4.0 miles/2.0 hours

Info: No bones about it, the briny sea breezes are a definite bonus on this woodsy trail of conifers and flyboys. After about a mile, voilà, you're upon the dunes, where a distant but alluring view of Tahkenitch Creek will beckon you to come closer. Notice the interesting patterns the wind creates on the ever shifting sand dunes. Leave your prints behind as you journey to the creek and the Pacific. Retrace your steps going home. For more information: (541) 271-3611.

Directions: From Reedsport, travel north 8 miles on Highway 101 to the Tahkenitch Campground and the trailhead on the west side of the highway.

Note: Nesting season is March 15 - Sept. 15. Please heed all warning signs, leash your dog and respect the fragile nesting habits of the snowy plover.

THREEMILE LAKE TRAIL HIKE - Leashes

Intermediate/6.0 miles/3.0 hours

Info: Get ready, get set and go on one helluva great hike. This scenic trail jumps off in a stunning conifer forest where vistas of freshwater lakes and wetlands add magic to the day. As you make lickety-split through the woodsy terrain, nature's musicians and the forest dwellers provide the side shows. Afishionados, check out the goings on in Threemile Lake. There could be a dinner of yellow perch or cutthroat in your future. Or let sleeping dogs lie as you amuse yourself observing the river otters at their playful best. For more information: (541) 271-3611.

Directions: From Reedsport, travel north 8 miles on Highway 101 to the Tahkenitch Campground and the trailhead on the west side of the highway.

UMPQUA DUNES TRAIL HIKE - Leashes

Intermediate/2.5 miles/2.0 hours

Info: Wowser Bowser. For a one, two punch of all things natural, this journey over spectacular dunes will leave you wanting more. Sand, as far as the eye can see, awaits you and your Sandy. Since motorized vehicles are prohibited, the only sound you'll hear is the wind whistling across the pristine, undulating formations. You won't find a more idyllic place to observe birdlife and wildlife. Tote those binocs, they'll enhance your viewing ops. Not for the directionally challenged due to the constantly changing landscape, the trail in the open duney areas is unmarked. To keep yourself on track, climb to the highest dune and scope out your route before beginning. Head toward the north end of the tree island and you'll be on the marked track. For more information: (541) 271-3611.

Directions: From Reedsport, travel south 10.5 miles on Highway 101 to the Eel Creek Campground and the trailhead on the west side of the highway.

ROCKAWAY BEACH

LODGING

BROADWATER VACATION RENTALS
438 Hwy 101 N (97136)
Rates: $59-$149
Tel: (503) 355-2248

COASTAL HIDEAWAYS
216 Hwy 101 N (97136)
Rates: $65-$125
Tel: (503) 355-2229

GETAWAY MOTEL ON THE BEACH
621 S Pacific (97136)
Rates: $40-$120
Tel: (503) 355-2501
(800) 756-5552

OCEAN LOCOMOTION MOTEL
19130 Alder Ave (97136)
Rates: $38-$95
Tel: (503) 355-2093

Hotel Policies May Be Subject To Change

OCEAN SPRAY MOTEL
505 N Pacific Ave (97136)
Rates: $40-$60
Tel: (503) 355-2237

101 MOTEL
530 N Hwy 101 (97136)
Rates: $35-$55
Tel: (503) 355-2420
(888) 878-3973

SAND DOLLAR MOTEL
105 NW 23rd Ave (97136)
Rates: $35-$90
Tel: (503) 355-2301

SEA TREASURES INN
301 N Miller St (97136)
Rates: $38-$78
Tel: (503) 355-8220
(800) 444-1864

SILVER SANDS MOTEL
215 S Pacific (97136)
Rates: $76-$108
Tel: (503) 355-2206
(800) 457-8972

**SURFSIDE OCEANFRONT
RESORT MOTEL**
101 NW 11th Ave (97136)
Rates: $48-$149
Tel: (503) 355-2312
(800) 243-7786

TRADEWINDS MOTEL
523 N Pacific St (97136)
Rates: $55-$150
Tel: (503) 355-2112
(800) 824-0938

RECREATION

BEACH WAYSIDE - Leashes

Info: After you've explored the shopping ops in this little seaside town, you and the beach Bowser can browser seven miles of sandy coastline where birds soar overhead and run to and fro with the surf.

Directions: In the center of town at Highway 101.

ROGUE RIVER

RECREATION

PALMERTON PARK ARBORETUM - Leashes

Info: Tiptoe through the tulips and sniff out more than 70 native and exotic species of trees in this beautiful arboretum. Pick up a pamphlet so you can identify the common and botanical names. When you're finished perusing, do lunch alfresco along the grassy slope that borders Evans Creek. FYI: There's also a pretty duck pond you might want to waddle on over to. For more information: (541) 582-4401.

Directions: Located off West Evans Creek Road, just north of Foothill Boulevard.

Locate Other Dog-Friendly Activities...Check Nearby Cities

ROSEBURG

LODGING

BEST WESTERN DOUGLAS INN MOTEL
511 SE Stephens St (97470)
Rates: $40-$72
Tel: (541) 673-6625
(800) 528-1234

BEST WESTERN GARDEN VILLA MOTEL
760 NW Garden Valley Blvd (97470)
Rates: $52-$86
Tel: (541) 672-1601
(800) 528-1234

BUDGET 16 MOTEL
1067 NE Stephens St (97470)
Rates: $30-$57
Tel: (541) 673-5556
(800) 414-1648

CASA LOMA MOTEL
1107 NE Stephens St (97470)
Rates: $27-$35
Tel: (541) 673-5569

CITY CENTER MOTEL
1321 SE Stephens St (97470)
Rates: $30-$40
(541) 673-6134

DUNES MOTEL
610 W Madrone St (97470)
Rates: $40-$56
Tel: (541) 672-6684
(800) 260-9973

HOLIDAY INN EXPRESS
375 W Harvard Blvd (97470)
Rates: $52-$87
Tel: (541) 673-7517
(800) 898-ROOM

HOLIDAY MOTEL
444 SE Oak st (97470)
Rates: $30-$40
Tel: (541) 672-4457

HOWARD JOHNSON
978 NE Stephens St (97470)
Rates: $58-$90
Tel: (541) 673-5082
(800) 446-4656

MOTEL ORLEANS
427 NW Garden Valley Rd (97470)
Rates: $40-$49
Tel: (541) 673-5561
(800) 626-1900

ROSE CITY MOTEL
1142 NE Stephens St (97470)
Rates: $30-$50
Tel: (541) 673-8209

SYCAMORE MOTEL-NATIONAL 9
1627 SE Stephens St (97470)
Rates: n/a
Tel: (541) 672-3354
(800) 524-9999

VISTA MOTEL
1183 NE Stephens St (97470)
Rates: $30-$40
Tel: (541) 673-2736

WINDMILL INN
1450 NW Mulholland Dr (97470)
Rates: $65-$79
Tel: (541) 673-0901
(800) 547-4747

RECREATION

AMACHER COUNTY PARK - Leashes

Info: Situated on the enchanting banks of the North Umpqua River, you'll find this to be a wonderful R&R jumpoff point. Bring a rawhide for your pal and a good read for yourself or try your luck on the fish. Maybe you'll make your fishy dreams come true with a trout or two. Amacher Park is also home to the only Myrtlewood groves in all of Douglas County.

Hotel Policies May Be Subject To Change

Directions: From Roseburg, travel north on Highway 5 for 5 miles to exit 129 and follow signs.

ROCK CREEK PARK - Leashes

Info: Wade into Rock Creek and have a go at the trout. There are plenty of shaded spots where you and the pup can simply dawdle while you peruse the pretty scenery.

Directions: From Roseburg, travel Highway 138 north to Rock Creek Road. Follow Rock Creek Road 7.5 miles to the park.

STANTON COUNTY PARK - Leashes

Info: Hightail it along a trail to the river and do the fishing thing. Or cloudgaze away the day with your best pal beside you. You'll have plenty of pupportunities for solitude in this paw-pleasing locale.

Directions: From Roseburg, travel Highway 5 south for 19 miles and follow signs for the park.

WILDLIFE SAFARI

Info: Your little wild one can't accompany you when you explore this 600-acre zoological park, but ventilated outdoor kennels are available if you'd like to give it a go. Fresh Δ285water and supervision are provided for the pooch, so you can tour without a care. The exotic wildlife has free reign in this natural setting so pack your camera and see what interesting shots you can capture. Drive your own wheels or hop on the train ride in Safari Village. For more information: (541) 679-6761; (800) 355-4848.

Directions: From Roseburg, travel Interstate 5 south for 6 miles to exit 119 (Highway 42). Follow Highway 42 for 3 miles to Looking Glass Road, turn right then right again on Safari Road and proceed to the entrance.

Note: Dogs are not permitted in the park. Kennels are available, $5 refundable deposit required. Hours vary in the winter. Fees: Adult, $11.95, children, $6.95. Train ride and elephant ride extra. Call first.

Locate Other Dog-Friendly Activities...Check Nearby Cities

RUFUS

LODGING

DINTY'S MOTOR INN
P.O. Box 136 (97050)
Rates: n/a
Tel: (541) 739-2596

ST. HELENS

LODGING

BEST WESTERN OAK MEADOWS INN
585 S Columbia River Hwy (97501)
Rates: $55-$65
Tel: (503) 397-3000
(800) 528-1234

VILLAGE INN MOTEL
535 S Hwy 30 (97501)
Rates: $34-$43
Tel: (503) 397-1490

SALEM

LODGING

CITY CENTRE MOTEL
510 Liberty St SE (97301)
Rates: $42-$52
Tel: (503) 364-0121
(800) 289-0121

EAGLE CREST B&B
4401 Eagle Crest NW (97301)
Rates: $55
Tel: (503) 364-3960

GRAND MOTEL
1555 State St (97301)
Rates: $36-$45
Tel: (503) 581-2466

HOLIDAY LODGE
1400 Hawthorne (97301)
Rates: $40-$50
Tel: (503) 585-2323
(800) 543-5071

MAR DON MOTEL
3355 Portland Rd NE (97301)
Rates: $30-$45
Tel: (503) 585-2089

MOTEL 6
2250 Mission St SE (97302)
Rates: $33-$39
Tel: (503) 588-7191
(800) 440-6000

OREGON CAPITAL INN
745 Commercial St SE (97308)
Rates: $34-$49
Tel: (503) 363-2451

PHOENIX INN
4370 Commercial SE (97308)
Rates: $53-$105
Tel: (503) 588-9220
(800) 445-4498

**QUALITY INN &
CONVENTION CENTER**
3301 Market St NE (97301)
Rates: $61-$125
Tel: (503) 370-7888
(800) 248-6273

TIKI LODGE MOTEL
3705 Market St NE (97301)
Rate: $31-$59
Tel: (503) 581-4441
(800) 438-8458

Hotel Policies May Be Subject To Change

RECREATION

BUSH'S PASTURE PARK - Leashes

Info: Bring a sense of wonder along as you cruise and peruse rare trees, shrubs and roses in this beautiful park. A concrete pathway escorts you and Fido through a tree-dotted terrain that's especially breathtaking in autumn. In early June, roses present a bouquet for the senses as glorious reds, yellows, pinks and creamy pastels splash the greenery with eyecatching color and perfume the air with a heady fragrance. Pick that perfect sitting bench, inhale the aromatic air and perhaps share a brown bagger with the wagger. For more information: (800) 874-7012.

Directions: Located at 600 Mission Street, between 12th and High Streets.

CANYON CREEK RECREATION SITE - Leashes

Info: You'll find easy access to the Santiam River and a delightful sandy stretch along the water's edge. Try your fly at fishing or simply kick back and relax with Max. If you've a penchant for exploring, make like Lewis and Clark and uncover the natural beauty of this area. For more information: (503) 375-5646.

Directions: From Salem, travel Highway 22 east approximately 24 miles to the North Fork Road. Travel 10 miles on North Fork Road to the Canyon Creek Recreation Site.

CASCADES GATEWAY PARK - Leashes

Info: Sports mutts, this bustling park's got your name on it. Cheer on the home team at one of the ballfields or visit in the off-season and have a fetch and catch of your own.

Directions: Located off Turner Road at the intersection of Highways 5 & 22.

DEEPWOOD GARDENS - Leashes

Info: Botanist wannabes will have a field day strolling the rich mix of vegetation ensconced in these remarkable gardens. Designed by the first professionally trained female landscape architects in the Northwest, Deepwood Gardens' tranquil setting is perfect for canine connoisseurs. Let furface ponder his handsome snout in the reflection pool or slip out of the summer sun into the unique Shade Garden. See if Sherlock can sniff out the Secret Garden, a serene sweet spot surrounded by a low boxwood hedge. Or hop on the little nature trail beside the banks of Pringle Creek. This charmer gets two enthusiastic paws up. For more information: (503) 363-1825.

Directions: Located at 1116 Mission Street SE.

FAIRMOUNT PARK - Leashes

Info: Whisk your wagger away for a little fun in the sun. A visit to Fairmount promises and delivers a pleasant outing complete with picnic tables and a walking path.

Directions: Located at Rural and Luther.

FOSTER FARMS - Leashes

Info: Pick your favorite season and partake in some fun with the pupster. If your timing's right, you can pluck apples and Asian pears fresh from the trees. There's a Fall Apple Festival on the third Saturday in October that you're welcome to attend. For more information: (503) 393-2932.

Directions: Located at 4993 Hazel Green Road NE.

Note: Hours vary, call first. Dogs not permitted in the store.

LITTLE NORTH SANTIAM TRAIL HIKE

Beginner/8.4 miles/5.0 hours

Info: You'll clock off some picturesque miles when you and your hiking guru set out on this wonderful journey. No matter how you like your nature dished out, this hike is bound to please. Kick up your heels on an easy course along the Little North Santiam River where paw-dipping ops abound. Keep your Kodak handy, there's a beautiful waterfall waiting to be discovered in the forested realms of this region. For more information: (503) 854-3366.

Directions: From Salem, head east on Highway 22 about 20 miles to Little North Fork Road (FS 2209). Turn left and continue east on FS 2209 about 8 miles to Elkhorn, turning right on Spur Road 201 to the trailhead.

MINTO BROWN ISLAND - Leashes

Info: No matter where you wander and gadabout in this 900-acre territory, you'll undoubtedly happen upon something special. At the leashless bark park area, let your canine put on the dog and have a howl of a good time socializing with the pet set. Or start your day off on the right paw and kick up some dust on one of the 12 miles of trail. The tweet, tweet serenade is compliments of the local flyboys. You and floppy ears can plan to spend the day, this urban oasis serves up endless avenues of outdoor fun.

Directions: At River Road South and Homestead Road.

NELSON PARK - Leashes

Info: Play tagalong with your wagalong in the quietude of this 10-acre green scene. Enjoy a bonafido walk in the park on the path that circles the area.

Directions: Located at Madrona and Croisan Creek Road.

ORCHARD HEIGHTS PARK - Leashes

Info: This 29-acre park packs quite a recreational punch for you and the dawgus. Complete with walking paths and ballfields (aka open, grassy space), Orchard Heights will definitely lift your pup's spirits on a dog day afternoon.

Directions: Located at Orchard Heights Road and Westhaven.

RIVER ROAD PARK - Leashes

Info: Geared toward sporting breeds, this neighborhood park is a great place to catch a game in progress. If you'd rather play than spectate, bounce off to an open area beside the Willamette River and give your Hair Jordan a workout.

Directions: Located at River Road North and Riviera.

WOODMANSEE PARK - Leashes

Info: When walktime calls, answer it with a journey to Woodmansee where, knock wood, without much effort, you can enjoy a smidgen of nature. Burn some kibble on the trail and then find a shaded knoll and do some cloudgazing with your best pal beside you.

Directions: Located at Idlewood Drive and Sunnyside.

OTHER PARKS IN SALEM - Leashes

- ALDRICH PARK, 15th & Mill Streets
- CLARK CREEK PARK, Ratcliff & Vista
- COLLEGE HEIGHTS PARK, off Stoneway Drive
- EASTGATE BASIN PARK, Hawthorne & Silverton
- FIRCREST PARK, Lauredale & Crestview
- GRACEMONT PARK, Neff & Broadway
- HILLVIEW PARK, Hillview & Ewald
- LEE PARK, 22nd & Lee Streets
- LIVINGSTON PARK, end of Alameda
- McRAE PARK, 20th & Royal
- MORNINGSIDE PARK, between Pringle Road & 12th Street
- PRINGLE PARK, Church Street & Trade
- REES PARK, off Rees Hill Road
- ROYAL OAKS PARK, Regal Drive & Carriage Court
- SUNNYSLOPE PARK, off Mathew Loop & 18th Place

SANDY

LODGING

BEST WESTERN SANDY INN
37465 Hwy 26 (97055)
Rates: $49-$95
Tel: (503) 668-7100
(800) 528-1234

MOUNT HOOD SHAMROCK FOREST INN
59550 E Hwy 26 (97055)
Rates: $38-$89
Tel: (503) 622-4911

SCAPPOOSE

LODGING

BARNSTORMER B&B
53758 W Lane Rd (97056)
Rates: n/a
Tel: (503) 543-2740

MALARKEY RANCH B&B
55948 Columbia River Hwy (97056)
Rates: n/a
Tel: (503) 543-5244

SEASIDE

LODGING

BEST WESTERN OCEAN VIEW RESORT
414 N Promenade (97138)
Rates: $90-$124
Tel: (503) 738-3334
(800) 234-8439

CITY CENTER MOTEL
250 1st Ave (97138)
Rates: $48-$149
Tel: (503) 738-6377
(800) 479-5191

COMFORT INN BOARDWALK
545 Broadway (97138)
Rates: $65-$170
Tel: (503) 738-3011
(800) 228-5150

EDGEWATER INN PROMENADE
341 S Promenade (97138)
Rates: $69-$159
Tel: (503) 738-4142
(800) 822-3170

THE GUEST HOUSE B&B
486 Necanicum Dr (97138)
Rates: $60-$95
Tel: (503) 717-0495
(800) 340-8150

INN ON THE PROMENADE
361 S Promenade (97138)
Rates: $50-$140
Tel: (503) 738-5241
(800) 654-2506

THE LANAI MOTEL
3140 Sunset Blvd (97138)
Rates: $45-$85
Tel: (503) 738-6343
(800) 738-2683

SEASIDE CONVENTION CENTER INN
441 2nd Ave (97138)
Rates: n/a
Tel: (503) 738-9581
(800) 699-5070

SEASIDER MOTEL
110 5th Ave (97138)
Rates: $45-$125
Tel: (503) 738-7764
(800) 840-7764

SEASIDER II MOTEL
210 N Downing St (97138)
Rates: $45-$75
Tel: (503) 738-7622

SEAVIEW INN
120 9th Ave (97138)
Rates: $54-$84
Tel: (503) 738-5371
(800) 479-5191

SILVER SANDS
65 9th Ave (97138)
Rates: n/a
Tel: (503) 738-5590

RECREATION

FORT STEVENS STATE PARK - Leashes

Info: A blend of history and present day beauty, Fort Stevens fulfills everyone's wish list. Visit during low tide for a glimpse of the Peter Iredale, a schooner that met an untimely end in 1906. Scope out the waters for signs of migrating whales. If you prefer your water fresh, there's a lake where afishionados can try their luck. Or get the lay of the land on one of the natural pathways and loops that crisscross this history-laden landscape. Wowser Bowser. For more information: (503) 861-0863.

Locate Other Dog-Friendly Activities...Check Nearby Cities

Directions: From Seaside, travel north on Highway 101 about 7 miles to the Fort Stevens exit. Follow signs to Ridge Road and proceed on Ridge Road to the park entrance on the left-hand side.

Note: Day use fee may be required.

The numbered hikes that follow are within Fort Stevens State Park:

1) INTERPRETIVE TRAIL HIKE - Leashes

Beginner/3.0 miles/1.5 hours

Info: Military mutts will stand at attention on this trail which leads through a lovely setting that educates you on Fort Stevens, an outpost in use from 1897 to the end of WWII. Pick up a pamphlet and sneak a peek into the past. Not only will you get your Rexercise on this trail, but you'll come away with a mini education on the military as well. The first half of your tour consists of eleven stops, including the museum and war games building. As you continue beside the Columbia River, you'll arrive at an abandoned rifle range as well as other interesting sites on this loop-de-loop. The second half of your journey entails twenty-two stops including the torpedo loading room and the battery smur. History settings aside, it's the deft hand of Mother Nature and the cooling breeze that make this excursion so lovely.

Directions: From Seaside, travel north on Highway 101 about 7 miles to the Fort Stevens exit. Follow signs to Ridge Road and proceed on Ridge Road to the park entrance on the left-hand side. The trail begins at the main parking area.

Note: Dogs are not permitted in buildings.

2) NATURE TRAIL HIKE - Leashes

Beginner/0.75 miles/0.5 hours

Info: In this neck of the woods, you'll wander beneath a canopy of towering trees while you're treated to an understory of saplings and shrubs and a groundcover of flowering plants. Treehounds give this forested trail the high five for sniffability. A naturalist's wonderland, you'll see Sitka spruce, shore pine, red alder and cascara buckthorn, along with Pacific red elder, Oregon crab apple, coast rhododendron, red huckleberry, box blueberry, English holly, salmonberry and salal. You'll tiptoe through everything but tulips - horsetail, skunk cabbage and a gamut of ferns including licorice, sword and bracken. FYI: The upturned roots are due to the highwater levels which prevent the trees from establishing deep roots. Unfortunately, the shallow roots make many of the trees susceptible to storm damage and blowdowns. Wildlife enthusiasts might spot a bouncing Bambi as well as some ground dwellers and high flyers. Raven, squirrel, possum, beaver, raccoon and a dollop of waterfowl inhabit the region. Step lightly, the mounds of earth and burrows have been created by gophers, mice and moles.

Directions: From Seaside, travel north on Highway 101 about 7 miles to the Fort Stevens exit. Follow signs to Ridge Road and proceed on Ridge Road to the park entrance on the left-hand side. The trail begins at the Slide Program Area.

SILVERTON

<u>RECREATION</u>

SILVER FALLS STATE PARK - Leashes

Info: Overflowing (pun intended) with scenic cascades, stow your camera and hustle your buttsky to the best vista spot you and Spot can spot in the day use area. Although the canyon is off limits to pooches, you'll still find hundreds of pristine acres to explore in Oregon's largest state park. For a peek at the tallest waterfall in the area, skedaddle over to South Falls which plummets 177′ into deep, clear pools. For another up-close gander of the watery kind, head out with your snout to North Falls. From the viewing platform, you can ooh and aah the picturesque tumbler of sapphire water and diamond bright spray that crashdives more than 136′. Gung-ho hikers can find a little something to satisfy their wanderlust ways along one of the equestrian trails. No matter how you slice it, this chunk of Mother Nature has some tasty morsels for your recreational appetite. So what are you waiting for? Pack your sack and get going, adventure awaits. For more information: (503) 873-8681.

Locate Other Dog-Friendly Activities...Check Nearby Cities

Directions: From Silverton, travel south on Highway 214 approximately 15 miles to the park entrance.

Note: Day use fee may be charged. Dogs are not permitted in the canyon or on the Canyon Trail. Hikers must yield to horses.

SISTERS

LODGING

BEST WESTERN PONDEROSA LODGE
500 Hwy 20 W (97759)
Rates: $64-$74
Tel: (541) 549-1234
(800) 528-1234

BLUE LAKE RESORT
Blue Lake Dr,
Hwy 20/126 (97759)
Rates: $68-$108
Tel: (541) 595-6671

RAGS TO WALKERS GUEST RANCH
17045 Farthing Ln (97759)
Rates: $85-$150
Tel: (541) 923-3001
(800) 422--5622

SISTERS MOTOR LODGE
511 W Cascade (97759)
Rates: $59-$75
Tel: (541) 549-2551

SQUAW CREEK B&B
68733 Junipine Ln (97759)
Rates: $80-$90
Tel: (541) 549-4312
(800) 930-0055

SOUTH BEACH

LODGING

SOLACE BY THE SEA B&B
9602 S Coast Hwy (97366)
Rates: $110-$175
Tel: (541) 867-3566
(800) 4-SOLACE

THIEL SHORES MOTEL
9812 S Coast Hwy (97366)
Rates: $55-$75
Tel: (541) 867-4305

SPRINGFIELD

LODGING

MOTEL ORLEANS
3315 Gateway St (97477)
Rates: $37-$78
Tel: (541) 754-1314
(800) 626-1900

RED LION INN/EUGENE-SPRINGFIELD
3280 Gateway Rd (97477)
Rates: $61-$94
Tel: (541) 726-8181
(800) 547-8010

Hotel Policies May Be Subject To Change

RODEWAY INN
3480 Hutton St (97477)
Rates: $60-$100
Tel: (541) 746-8471
(800) 424-4777

SHILO INNS
3350 Gateway Rd (97477)
Rates: $49-$63
Tel: (541) 747-0332
(800) 222-2244

SUTTON MOTEL
1152 Main St (97477)
Rates: $29-$44
Tel: (541) 747-5621

VILLAGE INN MOTEL
1875 Mohawk Blvd (97477)
Rates: $47-$57
Tel: (541) 747-4546
(800) 327-6871

STAYTON

<u>LODGING</u>

GARDNER HOUSE B&B
633 N 3rd Ave (97383)
Rates: $55-$65
Tel: (503) 769-5478

SUBLIMITY

<u>LODGING</u>

BEST WESTERN SUNRISE INN
300 Sublimity Blvd (97385)
Rates: $45-$89
Tel: (541) 769-9579
(800) 528-1234

SILVER MOUNTAIN B&B
4672 Drift Creek Rd SE (97385)
Rates: $60-$75
Tel: (541) 769-7127
(800) 952-3905

SUMMER LAKE

<u>LODGING</u>

THE LODGE AT SUMMER LAKE
36980 Hwy 31 (97640)
Rates: $39-$139
Tel: (541) 943-3993

SUMMER LAKE B&B
D7 Ranch, 31501 Hwy 31 (97640)
Rates: $50-$85
Tel: (541) 943-3983
(800) 261-2778

SUMPTER

LODGING

SUMPTER B&B
344 NE Columbia St (97877)
Rates: n/a
Tel: (541) 894-2229
(800) 640-3184

RECREATION

POLE CREEK RIDGE TRAIL HIKE

Intermediate/4.0 miles/2.0 hours

Info: Don't be fooled by the piece of cake start. This trail doles out an aerobic workout going around the south side of a rocky knoll before descending into a wildflower-strewn meadow. Trust your trailblazer to keep you on course in the thick stand of old-growth ponderosa, where the air is heavenscent. Continue your uphill trek through open sagebrush and grassy terrain all the way to the top. As enchanting as this hike may be in spring, summer's another story, and a hot one at that. Be prepared. But no matter when you visit, the views from the open terrain of Sumpter and the rolling woodlands to the southwest are nothing short of spectacular. The Elkhorn Crest Trail junction signals turnaround time. For more information: (541) 523-4476.

Directions: From Sumpter, take FS 553 about 2 miles to FS 5536 and turn right. Follow FS 5536 to Spur Road 200. The trail starts at the turnaround on Spur Road 200. The trailhead is well signed from the road.

SUMPTER VALLEY DREDGE STATE PARK - Leashes

Info: You and your digger can go for the gold when you make tracks to one of the largest and most accessible gold dredges in the United States. The building and machinery used in 1913-1924 and then again in 1935-1954 reflect the history of these "golden" eras. History aside, you can also drop a line, the fishing's fine. Or break out the red checks and munch on lunch. For more information: (541) 894-2486.

Directions: Located off Highway 7, just south of Sumpter.

Hotel Policies May Be Subject To Change

SUNNY VALLEY

LODGING

SUNNY VALLEY MOTEL
352 Sunny Valley Loop (97497)
Rates: $30-$45
Tel: (541) 476-9217

SUNRIVER

LODGING

SUNRAY PROPERTIES INC
P.O. Box 4518 (97707)
Rates: n/a
Tel: (541) 593-3225
(800) 531-1130

VILLAGE PROPERTIES
P.O. Box 3055 (97707)
Rates: $80-$350
Tel: (541) 593-1653
(800) 786-7483

TWIN LAKES RESORT
11200 S Century Dr (97707)
Rates: $72-$106
Tel: (541) 593-6526

SUTHERLIN

LODGING

PENNYWISE MOTEL
150 Myrtle St (97479)
Rates: $57-$65
Tel: (541) 459-1424

TOWN & COUNTRY MOTEL
1386 W Central Ave (97479)
Rates: $43-$52
Tel: (541) 459-9615
(800) 459-9615

SWEET HOME

LODGING

THE SUN MOTEL
3026 Hwy 20 (97386)
Rates: $22-$40
Tel: (541) 367-2206

THE SWEET HOME INN
805 Long St (97386)
Rates: $42-$59
Tel: (541) 367-5137
(800) 595-8859

RECREATION

CASCADIA STATE PARK - Leashes

Info: A remarkable setting for naturalists, come and sample the goodies this gorgeous oasis has in store for you and your

Locate Other Dog-Friendly Activities...Check Nearby Cities

canine cohort. Situated on the western slope of the Cascade Mountain Range at the point where Soda Creek flows into the South Santiam River, the crystal clear waters and smooth riverside rocks are only part of the charming picture. Vast wildflower-sprinkled meadows and dense woodlands of Douglas fir and western hemlock blanket the landscape. The beauty of the high summer greens is only outdone in fall when the leafy maples do their presto chango thing, splashing bronzy hues against the rich evergreen backdrop. Surround yourself in tranquility and beauty while you commune with Mother Nature on a journey along one of the trails in this divine parkland. For more information: (541) 854-3406.

Directions: From Sweet Home, travel east on Highway 20 for 14 miles to the park entrance.

Note: Day use fee may be charged.

The numbered hike that follows is within Cascadia State Park:

1) FALLS TRAIL HIKE - Leashes

Beginner/1.5 miles/1.0 hours

Info: Down by the riverside and through a lush forest to Soda Creek Falls is where this trail leads you and the gleeful one. You'll have a howl of a good time romping in the shady woodlands before skedaddling over a couple of scenic bridges to your final destination. The beautiful cascades will stop you dead in your tracks. Snaking down the rocky cliffs, they form deep pools at the bottom. Pack a biscuit basket and stay awhile, the setting is too pretty for just a touch and go.

Directions: From Sweet Home, travel east on Highway 20 for 14 miles to the park entrance. The trail is located halfway between the day use area and the campground off the main park road.

GEDNEY CREEK PARK- Leashes

Info: Get a quick nature fix on the shores of Forest Lake. If you've got a boat, consider a float on the crystal waters.

Directions: Located on North River Drive, about 1.5 miles east of Foster Dam.

Hotel Policies May Be Subject To Change

HACKLEMAN CREEK OLD-GROWTH TRAIL HIKE

Beginner/1.2 miles/1.0 hours

Info: Tree enthusiasts will have plenty to bark home about on this woodsy loop around old-growth stands of Douglas and silver fir and western hemlock. Some of these magnificent specimens are more than 500 years old. Pick up a trail guide and enhance your learning experience. For more information: (541) 367-5168.

Directions: From Sweet Home, take Highway 20 east for 37 miles to Spur Road 065. Turn right on Spur Road 065 to the parking area and trailhead.

LEWIS CREEK PARK - Leashes

Info: This retreat is especially neat for lake lovers. With over 123 picnic tables, you'll always find a spot for lunch with Spot. A pupular locale, if you're seeking quietude, plan a weekday visit.

Directions: Located on North River Drive, about 2 miles east of Foster Dam.

McDOWELL CREEK PARK - Leashes

Info: Make with a fleet of feet stroll along the trail that zips through the park or find a shady nook beside one of the three scenic waterfalls and watch the way sunlight bounces off the glistening water. This park's a paw-pleasing charmer.

Directions: From Sweet Home, travel Pleasant Valley Road north to McDowell Creek Drive, turn right. Continue on McDowell Creek Drive about 6 miles to the park.

TAKILMA

RECREATION

BLACK BUTTE TIE TRAIL HIKE - Leashes

Intermediate/6.0 miles/3.0 hours

Info: Once you access this trail, you and your botanist wannabe will experience a wonderfully scenic, 1.5-mile hike through a high elevation forest. The canopied path spells cool even on those hot diggety dog days of summer. Tootsie dipping is a natural at the perennial creeks of Polar Bear and Bear Cub Mountains, where you're apt to encounter other naturalists with the same idea. If you'd rather have solitude than company, hightail it to the end of the trail where the East Fork Illinois River can make dirty dog dreams a reality. For more information: (541) 592-2166.

Directions: From Takilma, head south on FS 4904 for 1.5 miles to FS 4906. Follow FS 4906 about 7 miles to the Black Butte Trailhead (#1272). Hike this trail approximately 1.5 miles to access the Black Butte Tie Trail.

BLACK BUTTE TRAIL HIKE - Leashes

Intermediate/4.0 miles/2.0 hours

Info: If you're looking for a challenging hike with a payoff of solitude and serenity, consider this trail. Up, up and away is the name of the game as you and your muscular mutt ascend 1,000′ in two miles and find yourselves smack dab in the thick of the pristine and pretty Siskiyou Wilderness. Enjoy the serenery of the whisper quiet surroundings before doing a 180°. Bone voyage. For more information: (541) 592-2166.

Directions: From Takilma, head south on FS 4904 for 1.5 miles to FS 4906. Follow FS 4906 about 7 miles to the signed trailhead.

OSGOOD DITCH TRAIL HIKE - Leashes

Beginner/3.6 miles/2.0 hours

Info: You and your water woofer will have a bonafido good time on this easy hike to the East Fork Illinois River. The trail meanders along an old mining ditch and comes to a splishsplashing finale at the river. For more information: (541) 592-2166.

Directions: From Takilma, head south on FS 4904 to FS 011. Follow FS 011 to the trailhead.

THE DALLES

Lodging

BEST EASTERN MOTOR MOTEL
200 W 2nd St (97058)
Rates: $39-$49
Tel: (541) 296-9111

BEST WESTERN TAPADERA INN
112 W 2nd St (97058)
Rates: $59-$69
Tel: (541) 296-9107
(800) 722-8277

CAPTAIN GRAY'S GUEST HOUSE
210 W 4th St (97058)
Rates: $50-$80
Tel: (541) 298-2222
(800) 448-4729

DAYS INN
2500 W 6th St (97058)
Rates: $51-$66
Tel: (541) 296-1191
(800) 329-7466

THE INN AT THE DALLES
3550 SE Frontage Rd (97058)
Rates: $35-$46
Tel: (541) 296-1167
(800) 982-3496

LONE PINE MOTEL
351 Lone Pine Dr (97058)
Rates: $49-$69
Tel: (541) 298-2800
(800) 955-9626

QUALITY INN
2114 W 6th (97058)
Rates: $59-$69
Tel: (541) 298-5161
(800) 221-2222

SHAMROCK MOTEL
118 W 4th St (97058)
Rates: $28-$38
Tel: (541) 296-5464

SHILO INNS
3223 NE Bret Clodfelter Way (97058)
Rates: $59-$83
Tel: (541) 298-5502
(800) 222-2244

Recreation

COLUMBIA RIVER GORGE

Info: See Cascade Locks, Hood River, Portland and Troutdale for additional lodging and recreation.

TIGARD

Lodging

BEST WESTERN INN CHATEAU 290
17993 Lower Boones
Ferry Rd (97224)
Rates: $52-$90
Tel: (503) 620-2030
(800) 528-1234

EMBASSY SUITES HOTEL
9000 SW Washington Sq Rd (97223)
Rates: $124-$149
Tel: (503) 644-4000
(800) 362-2779

MOTEL 6 PREMIER
17950 SW McEwan Rd (97224)
Rates: $36-$46
Tel: (503) 620-2066
(800) 440-6000

MOTEL 6 PREMIER
17959 SW McEwan Rd (97224)
Rates: $35-$47
Tel: (503) 684-0760
(800) 440-6000

QUALITY INN SOUTH
7300 SW Hazel Fern Rd (97223)
Rates: $62-$89
Tel: (503) 620-3460
(800) 228-5151
(800) 291-8860

SHILO INNS WASHINGTON SQUARE
10830 SW Greenburg Rd (97223)
Rates: $59-$99
Tel: (503) 620-4320

TILLAMOOK

LODGING

SHILO INNS
2515 N Main (97141)
Rates: $65-$99
Tel: (503) 842-7971
(800) 222-2244

WESTERN ROYAL INN
1125 N Main (97141)
Rates: $45-$95
Tel: (503) 842-8844
(800) 624-2912

RECREATION

CAPE LOOKOUT STATE PARK - Leashes

Info: This woodsy package is strewn with spruce and hemlock, the walkway softened with fragrant pine needles which create a perfect platform for a red-checkered picnic repast. For a bonafido walk in the park, hop on one of the trails and uncover your own slice of doggie heaven, including dramatic views of the Pacific. For more information: (503) 842-3182.

Directions: From Highway 101 in Tillamook, travel west on Three Capes Scenic Loop about 4 miles to Netarts Bay. Turn south and drive about 7 miles to the park entrance.

Note: Day use fee may be charged.

The numbered hikes that follow are within Cape Lookout State Park:

1) CAPE LOOKOUT NATURE TRAIL HIKE - Leashes

Beginner/1.0 miles/0.5 hours

Info: Botany buffs, when you want to combine physical exercise with intellectual stimulation, pick up a pamphlet at the registration box and glean some knowledge of the lovely environs that are part and parcel of your outing. Turn right at the fork and let the learning begin. The first of the sixteen stops is an interesting example of natural grafting, meaning two trees share a root. Let the sniffer's whiffer lead you to the cedars, where interpretive postings provide insight into competition and growth in the forest. Check out the skunk cabbage too, the pungent odor is caused by its stems and leaves. Phew! If you dare get close enough in blooming season, the flowers are actually quite fragrant. The vegetation all about includes western hemlock, red alder, salal, evergreen huckleberry and salmonberry. Stop D will test your math skills as you count the tree rings. The fascinating fern ball signals the closing chapter of your loop.

Directions: From Highway 101 in Tillamook, travel west on Three Capes Scenic Loop about 4 miles to Netarts Bay. Turn south and drive about 7 miles to the park entrance. The trailhead is located in the day use area.

2) CAPE TRAIL HIKE - Leashes

Intermediate/5.0 miles/3.0 hours

Info: This outstanding hike will leave you panting for more. At the onset, follow the left fork and continue straight at the junction with the Oregon Coast Trail. Traversing the south side of the ridge, you'll make a quick descent into an aromatic forest of spruce and hemlock. After about a mile, the first views of Cape Meares play peekaboo through the woods and then voilà, you're at the edge of 400' cliffs and non-stop views. Do the distance on this trek, there are more dazzling panoramas from the top. Bring your binocs, whales are often spotted from this vantage point. To the north, Tillamook Head, Cape Falcon, Cape Meares and Three Arch Rocks will fill your Fuji. To the south, scope out Cape Kiwanda, Haystack Rock, Cascade Head and Cape Foulweather. When you can tear yourself away, retrace your steps.

Directions: From Highway 101 in Tillamook, travel west on Three Capes Scenic Loop about 4 miles to Netarts Bay. Turn south and drive about 2.5 miles past the park entrance to the trailhead on the right-hand side of the road.

Locate Other Dog-Friendly Activities...Check Nearby Cities

TROUTDALE

LODGING

PHOENIX INN
477 NW Phoenix Dr (97060)
Rates: $50-$61
Tel: (503) 669-6500
(800) 824-6824

RECREATION

COLUMBIA RIVER GORGE

Info: See Cascade Locks, Hood River, Portland and The Dalles for additional lodging and recreation.

ROOSTER ROCK STATE PARK - Leashes

Info: You simply can't go wrong at this scenic parkland on the banks of the Columbia. Grab a slab and watch the windsurfers whip along the whitecaps of the fast-running river. Or plan lunch alfresco with your #1 pal and soak up a bit of sunshine. Anglers might get lucky and make their fishy dreams come true. Hikers can get their daily dose on one of the pleasant pathways. For more information: (503) 695-2261.

Directions: From Troutdale, travel Highway 84 east about 10 miles to the entrance on the north side of the highway.

TROY

RECREATION

CROSS CANYON TRAIL HIKE

Intermediate/6.6 miles/4.0 hours

Info: Remember the hiker's mantra "whoever goes down shall have to come up." It's a switchbacking descent to the Wenaha River where wet and wild pooch shenanigans set the tone of the afternoon. Afishionados can get their fill and tote home the makings of a fish fry or perhaps you'll just let sleeping dogs lie and catch forty winks yourself. You're gonna need a shot of energy for the 1,900' outbound ascent. For more information: (509) 843-1891.

Directions: From Troy, head west on FS 62 to FS 6217, located just 5 miles past Long Meadows Guard Station. Follow FS 6217 to the trailhead.

HOODOO TRAIL HIKE

Intermediate/6.4 miles/4.0 hours

Info: Cure the summertime blues with an invigorating hike and a refreshing river swim. You and the aqua pooch might work up a sweat on this scenic albeit challenging hike, but there's definitely a pot of blue at the end of your journey. The Wenaha River guarantees a cool reward for all hot diggety dogs. And the fishing's not too shabby either. So pick your passion, plan ahead and make your pup's day. For more information: (509) 843-1891.

Directions: From Troy, head west on FS 62 to FS 6214, located a half-mile past Long Meadows Guard Station. Turn right on FS 6214 for 3.5 miles to the trailhead.

TUALATIN

LODGING

SWEETBRIER INN
7125 SW Nyberg Rd (97062)
Rates: $68-$110
Tel: (503) 692-5800
(800) 551-9167

UKIAH

RECREATION

SOUTH WINOM TRAIL HIKE

Intermediate/6.6 miles/4.0 hours

Info: Leave the city noises behind and dedicate your afternoon to outdoor pleasures. This beautiful green oasis is filled with dense forests, pretty meadows and a refreshing babbling creek. The dawgus will have a grin from one floppy ear to the other with just one look at what's in store. The trail descends through the North Fork John Day Wilderness where nature reigns supreme, great smells are in the air and your cares can wait until tomorrow. For more information: (503) 427-3231.

Directions: From Ukiah, take FS 52 south approximately 23 miles to Spur Road FS 52-440. Turn right on FS 52-440 for 1 mile to the trailhead, located on the left side of the road after the bridge crossing.

UMATILLA

LODGING

HEATHER INN
705 Willamette Ave (97882)
Rates: $41-$60
Tel: (541) 922-4871
(800) 447-7529

REST-A-BIT-MOTEL
1370 6th St, Hwy 730 (97882)
Rates: $42-$44
Tel: (541) 922-3271
(800) 423-9913

RECREATION

UMATILLA NATIONAL WILDLIFE REFUGE - Leashes

Info: This avian havian of more than 22,000 acres was established in 1969 to restore the Columbia River wildlife habitat that was damaged by the construction of the John Day Dam. In the world of all things natural, this oasis rates a definite high five. Birders flock to this region where the concentration of mallard and Canada geese are astounding. Lucky dogs stand a chance of seeing a bald eagle as well. During fall migration, the sky is crowded with fowl flyers. Lake Umatilla is just waiting to make fishy dreams come true in the form of bass and crappie. Wildlife lovers, mule deer, coyote, beaver, muskrat, raccoon, porcupine and badger can be counted upon to make unscheduled appearances. For more information: (503) 922-3232.

Directions: From Umatilla, travel west on Highway 730 about 8 miles to the Paterson Ferry Road exit and turn right. Refuge Headquarters is located at 830 Sixth Street in Umatilla, just past the intersection of Highways 730 and 395.

Note: Use extreme caution during hunting season. Some areas may be closed during nesting season.

UNION

LODGING

ANGLE FARM COUNTRY INN B&B
1782 S Main St (97883)
Rates: n/a
Tel: (541) 562-5671

UNION CREEK

LODGING

UNION CREEK RESORT
56484 Hwy 62 (97536)
Rates: $38-$80
Tel: (541) 560-3565

UNITY

RECREATION

UNITY LAKE STATE RECREATION SITE - Leashes

Info: Nature buffs with a penchant for lakeside reflections, you'll find lots of park pleasantries at this 39-acre locale. With Unity Lake lapping at the park edges, you and your numero uno buddy can carouse miles of dewy grass beneath a plethora of shade trees. Break some bread and biscuits on the shoreline. Or see if some fishing at the reservoir equates to trout, bass or crappie for your next BBQ. If you've got a boat, take your seadog afloat. The cool breezes skimming off the waters will refresh and renew you. For more information: (541) 575-2773.

Directions: From Unity, travel Highway 26 north about 4 miles to the intersection with Route 245, turn right (east) onto Route 245. Continue about 4 miles to the park entrance.

Note: Day use fee may be charged.

VALE

LODGING

1900 SEARS & ROEBUCK HOME
484 N 10th (97918)
Rates: $50-$80
Tel: (541) 889-9009

VERONIA

RECREATION

BANKS/VERONIA STATE PARK - Leashes

Info: This park has the honor of being Oregon's first linear park. Built on an abandoned railroad right-of-way, the mostly paved path stretches 21 miles from Banks to Veronia. Plan on company and lots of it. Every month, 15 to 20 thousand hikers, bikers and equestrian riders come to do their thing. You and the mutt can strut your stuff along a gentle path through fields and forests, over trestle bridges and beside rivers and streams. Blame the picturesque countryside, with its wonderful mountain views, for the popularity of the territory. Wildlife enthusiasts won't leave disappointed. The woodlands are home to fox, deer, elk, owl and great blue heron. Tote plenty of Perrier, there's no drinking water along the trail. For more information: (503) 324-0606.

Directions: In the city of Veronia, parking, information and trailhead is located off Highway 47 near Anderson Park. There are four other trailheads along the route.

Note: Day use fee may be charged.

VIDA

LODGING

WAYFARER RESORT
46725 Goodpasture Rd (97488)
Rates: $70-$195
Tel: (541) 896-3613
(800) 627-3613

WALDPORT

LODGING

ALSEA MANOR MOTEL
190 SW Hwy 101 (97394)
Rates: $52-$58
Tel: (541) 563-3249

BAYSHORE INN
902 NW Bayshore Dr (97394)
Rates: $45-$70
Tel: (541) 563-3202
(800) 526-9586

EDGEWATER COTTAGES
3978 SW Pacific Coast Hwy (97394)
Rates: $70-$130
Tel: (541) 563-2240

SUNDOWN MOTEL
5050 SW PCH 101 (97394)
Rates: $39-$79
Tel: (541) 563-3018
(800) 535-0192

TERRY-A-WHILE MOTEL
7160 SW Coast Hwy (97394)
Rates: $40-$75
Tel: (541) 563-3377

WALDPORT MOTEL
170 SW Arrow (97394)
Rates: $30-$50
Tel: (541) 563-3035

RECREATION

HORSE CREEK TRAIL HIKE - Leashes

Intermediate/5.0 miles/3.0 hours

Info: On your merry way to the charming creek, you and the dawgus will be serenaded by chatty songbirds as they flit from one treetop to another. A somewhat difficult trek as you approach the end of the outbound journey, you'll be rewarded for your efforts. A quick descent plops you in a stunning stand of Douglas fir before opening up to sprawling meadowlands. Spring and early summer are unquestionably the primo times to visit. Best of all you don't even need an invitation to the wildflower party. And a gala party it is, with Crayola colors highlighted against a lush green backdrop. Go ahead, race the furball over the open terrain and cool your jets in the crisp creek before repeating the beat on your retreat. FYI: If the creek is passable, there's another 2.5 miles of picturesque terrain to be investigated. For more information: (541) 563-3211.

Directions: From Waldport, travel east on Highway 34 for 7 miles to Risley Creek Road (FS 3446). Turn right and drive approximately 7 miles to FS 3464. Make a left and proceed 1.5 miles to the end of the road and the trailhead.

Locate Other Dog-Friendly Activities...Check Nearby Cities

WALLOWA

LODGING

MINGO MOTEL & HOT TUB
102 N Alder (97885)
Rates: $40+
Tel: (541) 886-2021

WARM SPRINGS

LODGING

KAH-NEE-TA VILLAGE
100 Main St (97761)
Rates: $90-$110
Tel: (541) 553-1112
(800) 831-1071

WARRENTON

LODGING

RAY'S MOTEL
45 NE Skipanon Dr (97146)
Rates: $32-$43
Tel: (503) 861-2566
(800) 348-2566

SHILO INNS
1609 E Harbor Dr (97146)
Rates: $74-$130
Tel: (503) 861-2181
(800) 222-2244

RECREATION

CLATSOP SPIT - Leashes

Info: Constructed by the U.S. Army Corps of Engineers between 1885 and 1914, the jetty has slowed the transport of sand along the coast and, over time, formed the land area of this spit. There's a viewing platform where you can scope out the beauty of the Pacific Ocean and Columbia River. California sea lions often congregate at the tip of the jetty where it zooms into the ocean. From December through mid-May, lucky ducky dogs might spot a migrating whale or two.

Directions: From Warrenton, proceed to the South Jetty and parking.

Hotel Policies May Be Subject To Change

TRESTLE BAY - Leashes

Info: You and your old sea dog can take the trail which travels south to a birdwatching platform and views of the marshes of Trestle Bay. Naturalists, tote your binocs, you're bound to get an eyeful at the salt marsh northwest of the bay where numerous shorebirds, migrating waterfowl and bald eagles have set up shop. Not just for the birds, this habitat attracts elk, deer and coyotes. In the spring and summer months, brown pelicans put on quite a show as they skim the waves in search of din-din. FYI: The South Jetty marks the northern trailhead of the Oregon Coast Trail.

Directions: From Warrenton, proceed to the South Jetty and Parking Lot D.

WARRENTON WATERFRONT TRAIL HIKE - Leashes

Beginner/1.0 miles+/0.50 hours+

Info: Skirting the Columbia River Estuary, this pathway travels along old railroad beds, dikes and roads and gives you a sampling of Warrenton's past and present. You and the dawgus will pass the Warrenton Mooring Basin where hundreds of commercial fishing vessels and pleasure boats fill the marina; the Fishermen's Memorial Lighthouse Park, shrub wetlands where migratory birds seem to sing for the sheer joy of it and Alder Creek which teems with life and forms the base of the food chain in Alder Cove. You'll get your daily dose along with a mini education along this interesting route.

Directions: Begin at the 2nd Street Park and head west to the Hammond Mooring Basin.

WATERLOO

RECREATION

WATERLOO PARK - Leashes

Info: Start your day off on the right paw with a sojourn to this pleasant neighborhood park. Pack a brown bagger for you and the wagger, 60 picnic sites are just right for lunch alfrisky.

Directions: On Gross Street.

Locate Other Dog-Friendly Activities...Check Nearby Cities

WELCHES

LODGING

MT. HOOD VILLAGE
65000 E Hwy 26 (97067)
Rates: n/a
Tel: (503) 622-4011

OLD WELCHES INN B&B
26401 E Welches Rd (97067)
Rates: $75-$130
Tel: (503) 622-3574

OREGON ARK MOTEL
61700 E Hwy 26 (97067)
Rates: $30-$50
Tel: (503) 622-3121

WESTLAKE

LODGING

SILTCOOS LAKE RESORT
82855 Fir St (97493)
Rates: $60-$75
Tel: (541) 997-3741

WESTON

RECREATION

LOOKINGGLASS TRAIL HIKE

Intermediate/4.2 miles/2.5 hours

Info: Exercise and scenery are the one-two punch on this hike that ends with a splash at Lookingglass Creek. As you hustle your buttsky on this sometimes demanding trail, stop every so often and simply enjoy the spectacular views of Lookingglass Canyon and the Blue Mountains. And because every dog should have his day, once you're at the creek, let the wet and wild one practice the doggie paddle. Aren't fun and games what it's all about anyway? For more information: (509) 522-6290.

Directions: From Weston, head east on Highway 204 for 22.5 miles to the Spout Springs Ski Area parking lot. The trailhead is at the north end of the parking lot.

Hotel Policies May Be Subject To Change

WESTPORT

LODGING

WESTPORT MOTEL
Hwy 30, east of Astoria
Rates: $45-$80
Tel: (503) 455-2212

WHEELER

LODGING

INNS AT WHEELER
495 Nehalem Blvd (97147)
Rates: $39-$175
Tel: (503) 368-3474
(888) 615-3474

WILSONVILLE

LODGING

BURNS WEST MOTEL
8750 SW Elligsen Rd (97070)
Rates: n/a
Tel: (503) 682-2123
(800) 909-2876

HOLIDAY INN PORTLAND SOUTH
25425 SW Boones Ferry Rd (97070)
Rates: $59-$125
Tel: (503) 682-2211
(800) 465-4329

MOTEL ORLEANS
8815 SW Sun Pl (97070)
Rates: $38-$69
Tel: (503) 682-3184
(800) 626-1900

SNOOZ INN
30245 SW Parkway Ave (97070)
Rates: $36-$45
Tel: (503) 682-2333
(800) 343-1553

SUPER 8 MOTEL
25438 SW Parkway Ave (97070)
Rates: $45-$50
Tel: (503) 682-2088
(800) 800-8000

WINCHESTER BAY

LODGING

RODEWAY INN
390 Broadway (97467)
Rates: $52-$95
Tel: (541) 271-4871
(800) 228-2000

Locate Other Dog-Friendly Activities...Check Nearby Cities

WOODBURN

LODGING

COMFORT INN
120 NE Arney Rd (97071)
Rates: $55-$75
Tel: (503) 982-1727
(800) 221-2222

FAIRWAY INN MOTEL
2450 Country Club Ct (97071)
Rates: $32-$55
Tel: (503) 981-3211
(800) 981-2466

HOLIDAY INN EXPRESS
2887 Newberg Hwy (97071)
Rates: $59-$79
Tel: (503) 982-6515
(800) 465-4329

YACHATS

LODGING

THE ADOBE RESORT
1555 Hwy 101 (97498)
Rates: $59-$150
Tel: (541) 547-3141
(800) 522-3623

BEACHCOMBER'S MOTEL
95500 Hwy 101 S (97498)
Rates: $30-$100
Tel: (541) 547-3432

FIRESIDE RESORT MOTEL
1881 Hwy 101 N (97498)
Rates: $60-$135
Tel: (541) 547-3636
(800) 336-3573

GRACE COVE RENTAL
466 Ocean View Dr (97498)
Rates: $115
Tel: (541) 547-4111

HOLIDAY INN MARKET & MOTEL
5933 Hwy 101 N (97498)
Rates: $50-$60
Tel: (541) 547-3120

OCEAN COVE INN
Prospect & Hwy 101 (97498)
Rates: $55-$80
Tel: (541) 547-3900

OCEAN ODYSSEY RENTALS
P.O. Box 491 (97498)
Rates: $65-$85
Tel: (541) 563-4504

RAVEN'S RETREAT RENTAL
228 Jennifer (97498)
Rates: $90-$120
Tel: (541) 547-4111

ROCK PARK COTTAGES
431 West 2nd St (97498)
Rates: $50-$60
Tel: (541) 547-3214

SEE VUE MOTEL
95590 Hwy 101 (97498)
Rates: $42-$65
Tel: (541) 547-3227

**SHAMROCK LODGETTES
RESORT & SPA**
105 Hwy 101 S (97498)
Rates: $70-$100
Tel: (541) 547-3312
(800) 845-5028

SHORE PINES COTTAGE RENTAL
88 Trout St (97498)
Rates: $70
Tel: (541) 547-4111

SILVER SURF MOTEL
3767 Hwy 101 N (97498)
Rates: $69-$89
Tel: (541) 547-3175
(800) 281-5723

Hotel Policies May Be Subject To Change

WAYSIDE LODGE
5733 N Hwy 101 (97498)
Rates: $39-$75
Tel: (541) 557-3450

YA-TEL MOTEL
640 Hwy 101 (97498)
Rates: $48-$69
Tel (541) 547-3225

YACHATS INN
331 Hwy 101 S (97498)
Rates: $45-$88
Tel: (541) 547-3456

YACHATS VILLAGE RENTALS
P.O. Box 44 (97498)
Rates: n/a
Tel: (541) 547-3501

RECREATION

CAPTAIN COOK TRAIL HIKE - Leashes

Beginner/1.2 miles/0.75 hours

Info: Take one part flora, one part tide pools, swirl it with an ocean breeze and you've got an interesting excursion. You and furface will skedaddle through windswept vegetation filled with unusually shaped flora caused by the always windy conditions along this stretch of coastline. Doggistorians will want to sniff out the Indian shell middens and the old CCC camp you'll pass on the way to the tide pools, your turnaround point. For more information: (541) 563-3211.

Directions: From Yachats, head south on Highway 101 for 3 miles to the visitors center and the trailhead.

Note: Tide pool ecology is fragile. Do not disturb the animals and plants.

COOK'S RIDGE/GWYNN CREEK LOOP TRAIL HIKE - Leashes

Intermediate/7.0 miles/4.0 hours

Info: A combo plate of nature, you and the wagging machine will wiggle this way and that through an old-growth forest where the air is spiced with a woodsy fragrance and flyboys sing to their heart's content. Yup, the blueness that's poking through the trees is the powerful Pacific. Even from your distant vantage point, the white caps are obvious. This bosky setting is also home to lots of wildlife, which means the rustling sounds aren't always the trees. For a bonafido great escape, this gets the high five. For more information: (541) 563-3211.

Directions: From Yachats, head south on Highway 101 for 3 miles to the visitors center. The trailhead is at the east end of the parking lot.

CUMMINS CREEK TRAIL HIKE - Leashes

Intermediate/8.4 miles/5.0 hours

Info: You and your hiking guru are bound to get the lead out as you step lively along a forest road for nearly three miles. The grabbag thicket is mainly western hemlock, Sitka spruce and old-growth Douglas fir. The eastern portion of the trail climbs steeply (about one mile) on an open, rocky hillside before junctioning with Cook's Ridge. Vista seekers will get their payback with distant views of Cummins Creek Wilderness and the always gorgeous Pacific. For more information: (541) 750-7000.

Directions: From Yachats, take Highway 101 south to the sign at milepost 169.1. Turn inland to reach the trailhead.

GIANT SPRUCE TRAIL HIKE - Leashes

Beginner/2.0 miles/1.0 hours

Info: Give your tree enthusiast something to bark home about on this trail that skirts the banks of Cape Creek all the way to a majestic stand of old-growth spruce and the grandaddy of them all, the 500-year-old "Giant Spruce." Now that's a tree worth sniffing. The music that fills the fragrantly scented forest air is compliments of Mother Nature's musicians. Also vying for your attention are lush green fern, massive skunk cabbage and a mélange of little critters. For more information: (541) 563-3211.

Directions: From Yachats, head south on Highway 101 for 3 miles to the visitors center and the trailhead.

OREGON COAST TRAIL HIKE - Leashes

Intermediate/2.6 miles/1.5 hours

Info: Ocean and rocky shoreline views are the allures of this somewhat demanding hike. Pack plenty of Kodak, this is point and click country. Everywhere you turn, another pretty picture unfolds. At the Cummins Creek Trailhead, begin your return. For more information: (541) 563-3211.

Directions: From Yachats, head south on Highway 101 for 3 miles to the visitors center and the trailhead.

ST. PERPETUA TRAIL HIKE - Leashes

Intermediate/2.6 miles/2.0 hours

Info: This trek entails a bit of huffing and puffing but the outstanding vistas of the Pacific are the payback. You and Tracker will ascend the switchbacking trail along the south face of Cape Perpetua to an incredible viewpoint. Take a biscuit break while you take in the beauty that's yours from the lofty perch. When you've had your fill, do the descent thing. For more information: (541) 563-3211.

Directions: From Yachats, head south on Highway 101 for 3 miles to the visitors center and the trailhead.

TRAIL OF THE RESTLESS WATERS HIKE - Leashes

Beginner/0.8 miles/0.5 hours

Info: This hike's short on effort but long on scenery. You'll skirt past Devil's Churn as you scramble over pretty lava rocks to a bounty of tide pools. The pounding surf adds a thunderous roar to the picturesque setting. Photo buffs won't know where to aim first. At the junction with Cape Cove Trail, do a 180°. For more information: (541) 563-3211.

Directions: From Yachats, head south on Highway 101 about 3 miles to the Devils Churn parking area and the trailhead.

WHISPERING SPRUCE TRAIL HIKE - Leashes

Beginner/0.5 miles/0.5 hours

Info: You and the pupsqueak will have it made in the shade on this bosky stroll through flyboy terrain. Find a cozy nook along the way, kick back for a bit and watch the sun streaming through the trees, creating charming patterns on the forest floor. Or let your eyes swallow up views of the Pacific as your cares float away on a salty breeze. Repeat the beat on your retreat. For more information: (541) 563-3211.

Directions: From Yachats, head south on Highway 101 for 3 miles to the visitors center. To the trailhead, follow the Auto Tour Road to Viewpoint Road and the parking lot for the trail.

Locate Other Dog-Friendly Activities...Check Nearby Cities

YACHATS 804 TRAIL HIKE - Leashes

Beginner/1.5 miles/1.0 hours

Info: Ignore the initial intrusion of homes and motels at the start of the trail. You'll soon find yourself in pristine beach country. Most of this interesting journey is on an ancient rocky bench originally formed by wave erosion before the last ice age when the sea level was higher than at present. The wave action continues to erode the rocks, producing massive boulders and sculptured forms. Many of the dark colored rocks are basalt from ancient lava flows. Geologist wannabes will be interested to learn that the Yaquina Formation at the end of the trail could be as old as 25,000,000 years.

Some of the uncommon plants you'll encounter include bog anemone, leather grape-fern, ladies tresses (orchid family) and golden-eyed grass (Iris family). The overhanging masses of sod are held together by salal roots which are undercut by winter storms that erode the weathered sedimentary rocks below. During your exploration, you'll find log benches, great places to let sleepy dogs lie while you enjoy the pounding surf.

As you and your wagger wiggle this way and that, notice how the low lying brush forms a pretty green backdrop to the foamy blue Pacific and the black basalt rocks. And don't miss the sight of the flowers dancing in the wind, their bright colors polka dotting the landscape. This dramatic stretch of beach exemplifies the magnificence of the Oregon coast. You and Wonderdog will be spellbound. The beauty and wildness, the magical appeal of this trail will stay with you long after you've returned to your car and headed on. For more information: (541) 750-7000.

Directions: From Yachats, travel south on Highway 101 to milepost 164.5 and the trailhead.

YAMHILL

LODGING

FLYING M GUEST RANCH
23029 NW Flying M Rd (97148)
Rates: $65-$200
Tel: (503) 662-3222

Hotel Policies May Be Subject To Change

ZIGZAG

<u>RECREATION</u>

RAMONA FALLS LOOP TRAIL HIKE - Leashes

Beginner/7.5 miles/4.0 hours

Info: Come and plan to spend the day. You and your water loving hound will shadow the flowing blues of Sandy River for the first mile and a half of your journey. In the distance, you'll see rugged and imposing Mt. Hood, its peak often hidden in a mass of clouds. The views of the canyons, the glaciers that coat the flanks like icing on a cake and the serrated tree tops that poke into the blue are all apart of this natural wonderland. And let's not forget the wildflowers. Indian paintbrush, beargrass and lupine carpet the summer meadows to create a picture as lovely as a fresh snowfall in winter.

After crossing the river via a high bridge, toss a coin and pick a path to Ramona Falls. The right fork escorts you and the sniffmeister through a fragrant pine forest where you'll hook up with the Pacific Crest National Scenic Trail and reach the falls in about 2 miles. Choose the left fork and you'll travel to the Bald Mt. Trail junction and the trickling waters of Ramona Creek. This route entails just over 2 miles. Either way, you'll end your voyage at spectacular Ramona Falls where lunch alfrisky is the perfect way to make a great day even better. Bone appétit. For more information: (503) 668-1704.

Directions: From Zigzag, travel Lolo Pass Road (FS 18) north about 6 miles to FS 1825, turn right. Take the next right turn on FS 100 and cross the Sandy River. Continue about 3.5 miles on FS 100 to the large parking area on the left. The trailhead from the lower parking lot follows the Sandy River. To reach the upper trailhead and cut your hike by about 1.5 miles, continue on the unmaintained rock road another 1.25 miles to the upper trailhead. The trail then crosses the river on high bridge and connects to the loop trail.

Note: Open May through November.

WASHINGTON DIRECTORY OF DOG-FRIENDLY LODGING & OUTDOOR ACTIVITIES

Hotel Policies May Be Subject To Change

ABERDEEN

LODGING

CENTRAL PARK MOTEL
6504 Olympic Hwy (98520)
Rates: $30-$45
Tel: (360) 533-1210

NORDIC INN
1700 S Boone St (98520)
Rates: $35-$64
Tel: (360) 533-0100
(800) 442-1010

OLYMPIC INN
616 W Heron St (98520)
Rates: $39-$92
Tel: (360) 533-4200
(800) 562-8618

RED LION INN
521 W Wishkah St (98520)
Rates: $79-$95
Tel: (360) 532-5210
(800) 547-8010

THUNDERBIRD MOTEL
410 W Wishkah St (98520)
Rates: $46-$64
Tel: (360) 532-3153

TOWNE MOTEL
712 W Wishkah St (98520)
Rates: n/a
Tel: (360) 533-2340

TRAVELURE MOTEL
623 W Wishkah St (98520)
Rates: $37-$62
Tel: (360) 532-3280

RECREATION

TWIN HARBORS STATE PARK - Leashes

Info: More than 17,000' of oceanfront tidelands have been landscaped by nature to create a 317-acre park unlike any you've seen. Tall dune grasses gracefully dance and sway, caught by the ocean breeze and the wind-sculpted trees look like works of art in this magical setting. Your canine connoisseur will give this beauty two paws up. The thick woodlands of this pristine area are home to an array of wildlife including raccoon, possum, deer and beaver. Lush plants are made even more dramatic by gold and pink flowers, which dot the banks of the boggy marsh. For a chunk of solitude and quietude in a bonafido au naturale milieu, you'll want to highlight this park on your travel itinerary. For more information: (360) 268-9717.

Directions: From Aberdeen, travel west on Highway 105 about 20 miles to the signed entrance.

The numbered hike that follows is located in Twin Harbors State Park:

1) SHIFTING SANDS NATURE TRAIL HIKE - Leashes

Beginner/1.0 miles/0.5 hours

Info: Take a walk on the wild side with your wild one. This self-guided loop is just the ticket for an up-close perusal of the duney terrain. Twenty interpretive stations explain the origin of the dunes. Despite the often harsh winds and blowing sand, a myriad of fauna and flora have adapted to the environment. Wild strawberries share their space with "pioneer" plants, so called because they were the first to colonize the bare dunes. Brush rabbit, field mice and chipmunk are the local beachfront residents while a mélange of wildlife, including deer, inhabit the surrounding forest. For more information: (360) 268-9717.

Directions: From Aberdeen, travel west on Highway 105 about 20 miles to the signed the entrance. The trailhead is located 50' west of the entrance to campsites 285-301.

AIRWAY HEIGHTS

LODGING

HEIGHTS MOTEL
13504 W Hwy 2 (99001)
Rates: $25
Tel: (509) 244-2072

LANTERN PARK MOTEL
13820 W Sunset Hwy (99001)
Rates: $29-$57
Tel: (509) 244-3653

AMANDA PARK

LODGING

AMANDA PARK MOTEL
P.O. Box 624 (98526)
Rates: $35
Tel: (360) 288-2237
(800) 410-2237

ANACORTES

LODGING

ANACORTES INN
3006 Commercial Ave (98221)
Rates: $45-$125
Tel: (360) 293-3153
(800) 327-7976

FIDALGO COUNTRY INN
1250 Hwy 20 (98221)
Rates: $59-$94
Tel: (360) 293-3494
(800) 244-4179

ISLANDS INN
3401 Commercial Ave (98221)
Rates: $60-$100
Tel: (360) 293-4644

OLD BROOK INN B&B
530 Old Brook Ln (98221)
Rates: $80-$90
Tel: (360) 293-4768
(800) 503-4768

SAN JUAN MOTEL
1103 6th St (98221)
Rates: $35-$56
Tel: (360) 293-5105
(800) 533-8009

SHIP HARBOR INN
5316 Ferry Terminal Rd (98221)
Rates: $65-$95
Tel: (360) 293-5177
(800) 852-8568

RECREATION

WASHINGTON PARK - Leashes

Info: When you're looking for an afternoon of fun in the sun, make tracks to this beachfront park. The visions of early Anacortes residents and generous land donations led to the creation of the 200-acre oasis. Rove beneath the evergreen canopy on numerous trails that honeycomb the landscape. Pack your Kodak, the windswept firs that hang over the beach present quite a pretty picture. Wildlife devotees might see a black-tailed deer or a floppy-eared rabbit hopping amongst the fragrant wildflowers or scampering in the old-growth forest. Any which way you point the Pointer, you'll find serenery and good times. For more information: (360) 293-1918.

Directions: From Anacortes, travel 12th Street west to the park entrance located on the left side of the road.

ARLINGTON

LODGING

ARLINGTON MOTOR INN
2214 SR 530 (98223)
Rates: $44-$98
Tel: (360) 652-9595

SMOKEY POINT MOTOR INN
17329 Smokey Point Dr (98223)
Rates: $38-$75
Tel: (360) 659-8561

RECREATION

TWIN RIVERS PARK - Leashes

Info: Located beside the banks of the Stillaguamish River, this charming 36-acre green scene offers plenty of chill-out spots for you and Spot. Tote your binocs, birds of a feather often fly together at this retreat. Pull up a plush square and munch on lunch or work out the kinks on a woodsy stroll.

Directions: Located at 22914 State Road, 530 Northeast.

ASHFORD

LODGING

CABINS AT THE BERRY
37221 SR 706 E (98304)
Rates: $65-$125
Tel: (360) 569-2628

MT. RAINIER COUNTRY CABINS
38624 SR 706 E (98304)
Rates: $55-$75
Tel: (360) 569-2355

GATEWAY INN RESORT
38820 SR 706 E (98304)
Rates: $30-$60
Tel: (360) 569-2506

MOUNTHAVEN RESORT CABINS
38210 SR 706 E (98304)
Rates: n/a
Tel: (360) 569-2594
(800) 456-9380

ASOTIN

LODGING

ASOTIN MOTEL
P.O. Box 188 (99402)
Rates: $34-$40
Tel: (509) 243-4888

AUBURN

LODGING

BEST WESTERN PONY SOLDIER INN
1521 D St NE (98002)
Rates: $71-$89
Tel: (253) 939-5950
(800) 634-7669

COMFORT INN
#1 16th St NE (98071)
Rates: $55-$78
Tel: (800) 228-5150

NENDEL'S INN
102 15th St NE (98802)
Rates: $48-$56
(253) 833-8007

VAL-U-INN
9 14th Ave NW (98001)
Rates: $56-$69
Tel: (253) 735-9600
(800) 443-7777

BAINBRIDGE ISLAND

LODGING

BAINBRIDGE INN B&B
9200 Hemlock Ave NE (98110)
Rates: n/a
Tel: (360) 842-7564

FROG ROCK INN B&B
15576 Washington Ave NE (98110)
Rates: $60-$75
Tel: (360) 842-2761

MONARCH MANOR B&B
7656 Yeomalt Pt Dr NE (98110)
Rates: $75-$250
Tel: (360) 780-0112

RECREATION

BAINBRIDGE GARDENS - Leashes

Info: Created by Zenhichi Harui who came to Bainbridge Island from Japan in 1908, this petite garden setting is the epitome of tranquility and serenity. An Edenesque milieu, under Harui's guidance, it soon blossomed with sculpted trees, lovely flowers, fountains and lily ponds, attracting garden lovers from miles around. During WWII, the gardens suffered when Mr. Harui and his family were forced to abandon them.

Due to the efforts of Harui's son, Bainbridge Gardens has been almost completely restored. Many of the original plants remain, complimented by a profusion of additional flora. You and your high faluting sniffmeister will explore herb, alpine, perennial rose, aquatic and groundcover gardens where your sense of sight and smell will be suitably rewarded. Hop on the short nature trail and make note of the sun, peeking through the towering trees, casting long shadows on the path. No bones about it, this place gets the floral high five. For more information: (206) 842-5888.

Directions: The gardens are near Winslow on Bainbridge Island at 9415 Miller Road NE, between High School Road and Day Road, west of Highway 305.

Note: Open Mon - Sat from 9 a.m. to 5:30 p.m. and Sun from 10 a.m. - 4 p.m.

BATTLE POINT PARK - Leashes

Info: This former military locale is now a delightful 90-acre green scene. See Spot grin as you dawdle along the 1.5 miler or brown bag it with the wag it pondside. For more information: (206) 842-2306.

Directions: From the Winslow ferry, travel Highway 305 north to Koura Road, turn left. Continue on Koura Road to Miller Road, turn left. Continue on Miller Road to Arrow Point Drive, turn right and drive to the park entrance.

FAY-BAINBRIDGE STATE PARK - Leashes

Info: Seventeen acres beside the lapping waters of Puget Sound invite your perusal. Hiking hounds with a penchant for sniffing can shimmy through stands of maple, alder, fir and hemlock. When you want to experience a little bit of this and a little bit of that, get thee to this parkaree. There's flora and fauna wherever you turn. Find a patch of green to call your own and enjoy lunch alfresco with the biscuitmeister. For more information: (206) 842-3931.

Directions: Located near Port Madison at 15446 Sunrise Drive Northeast.

Note: Dogs are not permitted on beaches. Open April 1 through October 15 from 6:30 a.m. to 10 p.m. Open October 16 - March 31 from 8 a.m. - 5 p.m.

FORT WARD STATE PARK - Leashes

Info: Set tails in a spin with a sail on the ocean blues. Or make tracks on the one miler through the woodlands of this 433-acre region. Find a secluded, unpeopled stretch of beach and share some paw-dipping moments. For more information: (206) 842-3931.

Directions: Located four miles southwest of the Winslow ferry dock on Pleasant Beach Drive Northeast.

Note: Dogs prohibited on swimming beaches.

MANZANITA PARK - Leashes

Info: Frequented by the horsy set, you and your little imp will share the trails that loop through this pretty 120-acre parkland. When your daily dose has been met, chill out with the snout on a grassy knoll.

Directions: Located on Day Road West.

BATTLE GROUND

<u>RECREATION</u>

DAYBREAK PARK - Leashes

Info: Do as the name implies and take a break from your day to enjoy a browser with Bowser. If you're of the fishy persuasion, tote your gear, there could be steelhead on the dinner table. Or hoof it with the woofer on a shaded trail. Boating enthusiasts, you won't be drydocked either. So for a quick and easy escape, dash to this green splash. For more information: (360) 299-2375 ext. 2467.

Directions: Located at 26401 NE Daybreak Road (NE 82nd Avenue).

LEWISVILLE PARK - Leashes

Info: This delightful parkland offers some excellent fishing ops. If you prefer exploring the terra firma, you can set tails in motion along a number of peaceful wooded trails. Come prepared with a biscuit basket and break some bread with your best bud. For more information: (360) 299-2375 ext. 2467.

Directions: Located 2 miles north of Battle Ground off Highway 503.

BEAVER

LODGING

BEAR CREEK MOTEL & RV PARK
MP 206, Hwy 101 W (98305)
Rates $42-$48
Tel: (360) 327-3660

BELFAIR

RECREATION
BELFAIR STATE PARK - Leashes

Info: Birders literally flock to this charming park which is noted for its saltwater tide flats and wetlands. Pack your binocs and be prepared for a bounty of birdlife and wildlife. Cool your jets with a saunter beside the breezy banks of Big and Little Mission Creeks. For Rexercise with a woodsy slant, hightail it into the forested area where the padded of paw can strut their stuff. You'll find acres of open, paw-pleasing terrain, including grasslands. Situated at the southern end of the Hood Canal, this serene oasis offers endless pupportunities for playful pleasures. For more information: (360) 275-0668; (800) 223-0231.

Directions: From Belfair, travel west on State Highway 300 for 3 miles to the signed park entrance.

TWANOH STATE PARK - Leashes

Info: Encompassing 180 beautiful acres beside the Hood Canal, Twanoh State Park can't be beat for lazybones. Tote a boat and skim across the water's surface with your aqua pup. If fishing pursuits are more your style, drop a line. Who knows, you might go home with din-din. Or get the lead out and play tagalong with your wagalong on one of the wooded hiking trails that honeycomb the terrain. Way to go Fido. For more information: (360) 275-2222.

Directions: From Belfair, travel southwest on Highway 106 for 8 miles to the signed park entrance.

BELLEVUE

LODGING

BEST WESTERN BELLEVUE INN
11211 Main St (98004)
Rates: $79-$120
Tel: (425) 455-5240
(800) 528-1234

KANES MOTEL
14644 SE Eastgate SE Way (98007)
Rates: $36-$50
Tel: (425) 746-8201
(800) 746-8201

LA RESIDENCE SUITE HOTEL
475 100th Ave NE (98004)
Rates: $70-$120
Tel: (425) 455-1475

RED LION INN-BELLEVUE CENTER
818 112th Ave NE (98004)
Rates: $77-$139
Tel: (425) 455-1515
(800) 547-8010

RESIDENCE INN BY MARRIOTT
14455 29th Pl NE (98007)
Rates: $80-$195
Tel: (425) 882-1222
(800) 331-3131

WEST COAST BELLEVUE HOTEL
625 116th Ave NE (98004)
Rates: $62-$91
Tel: (425) 455-9444
(800) 426-0670

RECREATION

BRIDLE CREST TRAIL HIKE - Leashes

Beginner/4.0 miles/2.0 hours

Info: Like the name implies, this pathway caters to the equestrian set. The rural terrain is a great escape for city lickers and their companions. Practice some fancy foot work on your route through wooded and residential areas and past a golf course. Linked with Bridle Trails State Park on the west and Marymoor Park on the east, if you've got the time, this area's got the trails. For more information: (425) 452-6855.

Directions: The trail begins on the corner of 132nd Avenue NE and NE 60th Street.

Hotel Policies May Be Subject To Change

BRIDLE TRAILS STATE PARK - Leashes

Info: Whoa Nellie. With more than 28 miles of multi-use trails, urbanites with a penchant for nature will take a shine to this easy, breezy parkland. The forested terrain is home to chatty songbirds and an array of wildlife. In the AM hours or towards dusk, look for deer hidden among the trees, still and silent. The more rambunctious squirrel is easier to spot, busily scampering from one tree to another. If you're thinking lunch alfresco, check out the picnic area and do it up right. For more information: (206) 455-7010.

Directions: Located at NE 53rd and 116th NE.

KELSEY CREEK COMMUNITY NATURE TRAIL HIKE - Leashes

Beginner/1.5 miles/0.75 hours

Info: Just about every season brings another reason to pound the pretty pathway that skirts the tranquil waters of Kelsey Creek and circles a wetland habitat. Summer means songbirds and pretty patterns of sunlight streaming through the treetops. Spring brings a splash of color and sweet fragrance to the air. And if your wagging machine goes crazy for a roll in a pile of fallen leaves, expect a manic moment in the Golden Retriever-hued landscape. Even the bare, sometimes lonely look of winter holds a certain appeal. So when nothing but some time in the outdoors will do, do this part of the outdoors. For more information: (425) 452-6855.

Directions: Located off 129th Avenue SE, the trailhead is east of the barns at the northeast end of the pasture where it begins at the bridge.

LAKE HILLS GREENBELT TRAIL HIKE - Leashes

Beginner/4.0 miles/2.0 hours

Info: A naturalist's dream come true, this trail is part of the Lake Hills Greenbelt, an area encompassing more than 147 acres of woodlands, wetlands and residential areas. Tote your binocs, a myriad of mammals and birds including muskrats, red-tailed hawks, songbirds and coyotes inhabit the terrain. For more information: (425) 452-6855.

Locate Other Dog-Friendly Activities...Check Nearby Cities

Directions: Entry points are located at 148th SE and SE 6th, Lake Hills Boulevard and 156th SE and SE 16th.

MERCER SLOUGH NATURE PARK TRAIL SYSTEM - Leashes

Beginner/1.0-10.0 miles/0.5-5.0 hours

Info: City lickers can see what life is like for their country cousins with a journey to this wetland smack dab in the heart of the city. There'll be a grin on the mutt's face the minute you step paw inside this incredible chunk of Mother Nature. Nearly 170 species of birds, animals and amphibians as well as hundreds of plant species occupy the 320-acre region. The trail system shimmies through Douglas fir and cedar forests into marshy region where great blue herons stand as still as statues until, whoops, a hapless fish shows up dressed as dinner. Boogie on the boardwalk or make lickety split to the interpretive trail and get a mini-education on this interesting ecosystem. For more information: (425) 452-6855.

Directions: Park in the small gravel parking lot on 118th near the sign for Bellefields Park. To reach the trails, follow the split rail fence to the south and look for the trailhead signs.

BELLINGHAM

LODGING

A SECRET GARDEN B&B
1807 Lakeway Dr (98226)
Rates: n/a
Tel: (360) 671-5327

BIG TREES B&B
4840 Fremont St (98225)
Rates: $60+
Tel: (360) 647-2850
(800) 647-2850

CASCADE INN
208 N Samish Way (98225)
Rates: n/a
Tel: (360) 733-2520

COACHMAN INN
120 N Samish Way (98225)
Rates: $39+
Tel: (360) 671-9000

DAYS INN
125 E Kellogg Rd (98226)
Rates: $49-$75
Tel: (360) 671-8200
(800) 329-7466

LIONS INN MOTEL
2419 Elm St (98225)
Rates: $44-$48
Tel: (360) 733-2330

Hotel Policies May Be Subject To Change

MAC'S MOTEL
1215 E Maple (98225)
Rates: n/a
Tel: (360) 734-7570

MOTEL 6
3701 Byron (98225)
Rates: $30-$36
Tel: (360) 671-4494
(800) 440-6000

QUALITY INN BARON SUITES
100 E Kellogg Rd (98226)
Rates: $50-$100
Tel: (360) 647-8000
(800) 221-2222

RODEWAY INN
3710 Meridian St (98225)
Rates: $45-$64
Tel: (360) 738-6000
(800) 424-4777

SHAMROCK MOTEL
4133 W Maplewood Ave (98226)
Rates: n/a
Tel: (360) 676-1050

SHANGRI-LA DOWNTOWN MOTEL
611 E Holly St (98225)
Rates: $32-$45
Tel: (360) 733-7050

TRAVELODGE
101 N Samish Way (98225)
Rates: $42-$64
Tel: (360) 733-8280
(800) 578-7878

VAL-U-INN
805 Lakeway Dr (98226)
Rates: $44-$65
Tel: (360) 671-9600
(800) 443-7777

RECREATION

ARROYO PARK - Leashes

Info: Urbanites will appreciate the quick escape to be had at this parkland of 38 acres. Unspoiled beauty beckons you and the lickmeister to carouse through canyons, try your fly at fishing or amble along a shaded nature trail.

Directions: Located on Old Samish Road.

BROADWAY PARK- Leashes

Info: Wipe that hangdog expression off the pooch's face with a visit to this neighborhood hangout. Mix with the locals at the softball fields or catch a game of horseshoes at the sand pit.

Directions: Located on Cornwall and North Park Drive.

CORNWALL PARK - Leashes

Info: Take your bark on a lark to this beautiful park. Get some Rexercise on the gravel and paved paths, or if you prefer grass beneath your feet, tickle your toes with the best of them in this delightful 65-acre retreat.

Directions: Located at 2800 Cornwall Ave.

FAIRHAVEN PARK - Leashes

Info: For a snifforama extraordinaire, visit this 16-acre manicured park in summer when the roses are in full bloom, their heady fragrance permeating the air.

Directions: Located at 107 Chuckanut Drive.

INTERURBAN TRAIL HIKE - Leashes

Beginner/7.0 miles/3.5 hours

Info: See how quickly you can put your city cares aside as you work out the kinks with your numero uno hiking hound. This landscaped lane has a few steep sections, but for the most part it's a flat gravelled affair. The trail zooms through Fairhaven and Arroyo Parks where you and the dawgus can add some R&R to the agenda. And when spring is in the air, you can be sure that flowers will bedeck the landscape. Bone voyage. For more information: (360) 676-6985.

Directions: In Bellingham, parking and access to the trail from Fairhaven Park is off 10th Street and Donovan Avenue.

LAKE PADDEN PARK - Leashes

Info: Tote a non-motorized boat and float the day away in this charming 1,000-acre park. If terra firma's more your style, pound your paws along one of the shaded pathways and do your body some good. With lots of picnic tables for your dining pleasure, there's always lunch alfresco to consider.

Directions: Located at 4882 Samish Way.

LARABEE STATE PARK - Leashes

Info: City slickers and lickers, you can get your nature fix at this 2,600-acre state park. Situated on the edge of Bellingham and Samish Bays, a grabbag forest comes together with water and beaches to create a slice of doggie heaven. With 8,000' of prime saltwater frontage, you and your wet wagger can comb the sandy shores in search of clams and shells or find a grassy knoll where watching the tide roll in is de rigueur. If you prefer freshwater to the briny kind, you'll discover two lakes within the moody Chuckanut Mountains. Hiking gurus won't go home disappointed either. Eight miles of hiking trails criss-cross the park and deposit you seaside, lakeside or atop the peaks of Chuckanut Mountain. The Whatcom County Interurban Trail Hike can also be accessed in the park. For more information: (360) 676-2093.

Directions: From Bellingham, travel I-5 about 6 miles to exit 231 (Chuckanut Drive), turn left under the freeway. Continue on Chuckanut Drive about 12 miles to the park entrance on the left side of the road. All trailheads are found at the main entrance.

Note: Open April 1 through October 31 from 6:30 a.m. to dusk. Open November 1 through March 31 from 8 a.m. to dusk.

NORTH LAKE WHATCOM TRAIL HIKE - Leashes

Beginner/6.0 miles/3.0 hours

Info: This bonafido, kick-up-your-heels kind of a hike roams amidst the woodlands beside the former Blue Canyon Mine Railroad grade. You and old brown eyes will be duly impressed by the stunning sandstone cliffs on your route to North Lake. Go ahead, show the pooch a thing or two about skimming stones over the placid water. For more information: (360) 676-6985.

Directions: Parking and the trailhead are located at the east end of North Shore Drive.

NORTH LOST LAKE TRAIL HIKE - Leashes

Intermediate/9.2 miles/5.0 hours

Info: Mountain mutts will take a shine to this challenging trail set in the heart of the Chuckanut Mountain Trail System. The rugged path follows an old railroad grade and logging roads. The north/south route doles out plenty of photo ops along the way to the tranquil waters of Lost Lake. Tote a sack of goodies and do a leisurely lunch lakeside. For more information: (360) 733-2900.

Directions: The trailhead is located at the intersection of Chuckanut Drive and California Street.

Locate Other Dog-Friendly Activities...Check Nearby Cities

PINE AND CEDAR LAKES TRAIL HIKE - Leashes

Expert/6.0 miles/4.0 hours

Info: You'll exercise more than your prerogative on this very demanding hike. Alpine lakes are your ultimate destination points. And alpine equates to climbing which is just what this trek entails. But once you reach the crystalline waters of Cedar and Pine Lakes, you'll know why you made the effort. Not only is there a good chance you'll have the place to your lonesome, but the tranquil setting is a quick cure for the summertime blues. If fishing's your passion, go ahead and indulge yourself. Or be a certified lazybones and just sit back and take in the sights. For more information: (360) 733-2900.

Directions: The trailhead is located on Old Samish Road between I-5 North Lake Samish exit and Chuckanut Drive.

ROOSEVELT PARK - Leashes

Info: Stow a good read for yourself and tough chew for your number one canine and head out to this 9-acre park. Chill out on a shaded knoll and do whatever pleases you.

Directions: Located at 2200 Verona St.

SAMISH PARK - Leashes

Info: Do a stroll beside the water's edge or toss a line and see what's biting. A quick escape can found along any one of the pathways that honeycomb this pretty 39-acre parkland.

Directions: Located at 673 North Lake Samish Drive.

SEHOME HILL ARBORETUM - Leashes

Info: Nature buffs and go-go tree hounds rate this place two paws up. A sniffing ground extraordinaire, the diversified flora and fauna of Sehome Hill was once threatened by expansion. Through the efforts of many, Sehome Hill became an arboretum in 1974 preserving the natural state of the land. A veritable combo plate of nature, you and Sherlock can explore rock outcrops, seepage areas, dry south slopes and moist north slopes. No matter what kind of flora sets tails wagging,

Hotel Policies May Be Subject To Change

this 165-acre region has it all. Lofty Douglas fir, western hemlock, red cedar, big leaf maple, vine maple, black cottonwood, bitter cherry and red alder create a delightful canopy while lady fern and sword fern comprise the understory. Birds flitter through the branches, calling to one another in twittered harmony. In the drier areas, salal and Oregon grape flourish along the trails while snowberry blends in with the mixed conifer and broad-leaf communities. Wild bleeding heart, trillium, tiger lily, lady slipper and forget-me-not dot the landscape, adding spice and color to the scene. The sniffmeister will have a field day zooming from one plant community to another. For more information: (360) 676-6985.

Directions: In Bellingham, located on 25th Street and McDonald Parkway on the west side of Western Washington University.

TEDDY BEAR COVE TRAIL HIKE - Leashes

Expert/2.0 miles/1.0 hours

Info: Work your muscles to the max with this rough and tough journey to Teddy Bear Cove. With a little pain, you and mighty dog have a lot to gain - like the breathtaking, heart-stopping shoreline views of Chuckanut Bay and Clark's Point. The white sand beach sports centuries of crushed clam shells. An added attraction is the 1920s brick factory on the north cove where you're apt to uncover a bonanza of artifacts. For more information: (360) 733-2900.

Directions: The trailhead is located at the intersection of Chuckanut Drive and California Street.

Note: Do not disturb the artifacts.

WHATCOM FALLS PARK - Leashes

Info: Go ahead, make your dog's day with a trip to this 241-acre lakeside park where you can leave pawprints on the trails or soak up sunshine on the shore.

Directions: Located at 1401 Electric Avenue.

OTHER PARKS IN BELLINGHAM - Leashes

- BIG ROCK PARK, Sylvan St. & Illinois Lane
- CLEARBROOK PARK, Clearbrook Dr at Modoc
- ELIZABETH PARK, Elizabeth & Madison
- FOREST AND CEDAR PARK, Forest & Cedar St
- FRANKLIN PARK, 1201 Franklin St
- FOUTS PARK, "G" St. & Ellsworth
- HIGHLAND HEIGHTS PARK, 2800 Vining St
- LAUREL PARK, Indian & Laurel
- LEE MEMORIAL PARK, Lottie St. behind City Library
- LOWELL PARK, 20th & Ridgeway
- RIDGEMONT PARK, 800 38th St
- ST. CLAIR PARK, 2000 S. Clair St
- SUNNYLAND/MEMORIAL PARK, Illinois & King St

BINGEN

LODGING

CITY CENTER MOTEL
208 W Steuben (98605)
Rates: $32-$53
Tel: (509) 493-2445

BIRCH BAY

LODGING

BIRCH BAY BUNGALOWS
8226 Birch Bay Dr (98230)
Rates: $60-$70
Tel: (360) 371-2851

BLACK DIAMOND

RECREATION

FLAMING GEYSER RECREATION AREA - Leashes

Info: While not as famous as Old Faithful in Yellowstone, the geysers in this 519-acre park are nonetheless impressive. If your woofer's a hoofer, give it a go on the 10 miles of trails that honeycomb this vast region. Many of the hikes skirt the shores of the Green River while some deposit you closer to the bubbling geysers. The shimmering waters of the river attract their fair share of local wildlife, like raccoon, deer, beaver, squirrel and otter. FYI: A geyser is created when gas is ignited, creating a small torch flame in a rock pit. For more information: (206) 931-3930.

Directions: From Black Diamond, travel Highway 169 south about 2 miles to Green Valley Road, turn right. Travel Green Valley Road about 3 miles to Flaming Geyser Road, turn left. The park is located on Flaming Geyser Road.

Note: Open April 1 through September 30 from 6:30 a.m. to dusk. Open October 1 through March 31 from 8 a.m. to dusk.

BLAINE

LODGING

THE INN AT SEMI-AH-MOO/
A WYNDHAM RESORT
9565 Semiahmoo Pkwy (98230)
Rates: $99-$275
Tel: (360) 371-2000
(800) 770-7992

MOTEL INTERNATIONAL
738 Peace Portal Dr (98231)
Rates: n/a
Tel: (360) 332-8222

WESTVIEW MOTEL
1300 Peace Portal Dr (98230)
Rates: n/a
Tel: (360) 332-5501

RECREATION

BIRCH BAY STATE PARK - Leashes

Info: Surf fishing is pupular in these parts so if you're angling to catch dinner, try your luck at this oceanside oasis. Exercise gurus will take a shine to the one-mile nature trail through Terell Marsh. If freelance roaming's more your style, there are 193 acres of diverse terrain just waiting to be explored. Birders swear that you'll get to see some unusual specimens, so don't forget the binocs. For more information: (360) 371-2800.

Directions: From Blaine, travel south about 6 miles on SR 548 (Blaine Road) to the Birch Bay exit (Grandview Road), turn right. Continue west on Grandview Road to Jackson Road, turn right (north) and drive one mile to Helweg Road. Turn left (west) and continue to park.

Locate Other Dog-Friendly Activities...Check Nearby Cities

LIGHTHOUSE MARINE PARK - Leashes

Info: Your Sandy will arf approval of this 22-acre parkland overlooking the Strait of Georgia. Leave some pawprints in the sand of the saltwater beaches or head straight to the 52,000 square foot boardwalk, the ideal locale for orca ogling. For more information: (360) 945-4911.

Directions: From Blaine, go to the Peace Arch border crossing. Travel north on Highway 99 to Highway 17 for about 18 miles, turn west. Continue on Highway 17 about 5 miles to the Tsawwassen exit. Follow 56th Street to the Point Roberts border, then follow the main road to the southwest corner of the Point to the park.

Note: To get to this park by land, you must exit Washington, go into Canada, and then reenter Washington at the Point Roberts border.

PEACE ARCH STATE PARK - Leashes

Info: This is about as close as you can get to Canada without crossing the border. Actually, one-half of the park is in Washington, the other in Canada. Because of its dual personality, the park boasts two monuments and two bronze plaques, each with words and symbols from its home country. Aside from the unique location, the alluring gardens with their fragrant flowers are another draw. Sniff out the array of azaleas and heather that bloom like crazy in spring. A stroll during the warmer months of July and August will reward you with a colorama of 27,000 annuals guaranteed to steal the show. The picturesque setting is perfect for a tranquil afternoon interlude. FYI: The arch which spans the US/Canada border symbolizes friendship. For more information: (360) 332-8221.

Directions: From Blaine, travel I-5 north about one mile to the Peace Arch border crossing. Take the last exit before the border into the parking lot of the park.

Note: Open April 1 through September 30 from 6:30 a.m. to dusk. Open October 1 through March 31 from 8 a.m. to dusk.

Hotel Policies May Be Subject To Change

SEMIAHMOO PARK - Leashes

Info: Treat your old tar to a special day at this watery oasis. Not only will you find lots of running room on over 300 acres of tidelands, you'll also find a 1.5-mile long sandspit, a natural landform linked with the fishing industry. This stretch of beach is great for clamming so tote a net and let Digger do what comes naturally. Who knows, maybe clams on the half shell are in your dining future. There's also a paved walking path beside the shoreline where you can kick up your heels while you breathe deeply of the salty sea breezes and admire the prettiness of the saltwater frontage. For more information: (360) 733-2900.

Directions: From Blaine, travel I-5 south to exit 270 (Drayton Harbor Road), turn west and follow the signs about 7 miles to the park entrance.

BOTHELL

LODGING

RESIDENCE INN BY MARRIOTT
11920 NE 195th St (98011)
Rates: $110-$180
Tel: (425) 485-3030
(800) 331-3131

RECREATION

SAINT EDWARD STATE PARK - Leashes

Info: See Spot run and see Spot grin when you visit this 316-acre green scene on the rolling banks of Lake Washington. More than 8 miles of trails crisscross the landscape, serving up some wonderful kibble-burning ops. If yours is more a mellow fellow, set out to one of the picnic areas for lunch alfrisky and bask in a sun-dappled setting complete with chatty flyboys. The pretty lake views will make any day a little more special. For more information: (206) 823-2992.

Directions: Located four miles southwest of Bothell off Jaunita Drive.

BREMERTON

LODGING

THE CHIEFTAN MOTEL
600 National Ave N (98312)
Rates: $35-$45
Tel: (360) 479-3111

DUNES MOTEL
3400 11th St (98312)
Rates: $45-$60
Tel: (360) 377-0093
(800) 828-8238

FLAGSHIP INN
4320 Kitsap Way (98312)
Rates: $60-$75
Tel: (360) 479-6566

MIDWAY INN
2909 Wheaton Way E (98310)
Rates: $50-$60
Tel: (360) 479-2909
(800) 231-0575

OYSTER BAY INN
4412 Kitsap Way (98312)
Rates: $47-$75
Tel: (360) 377-5510
(800) 393-3862

QUALITY INN
4303 Kitsap Way (98312)
Rates: $65-$120
Tel: (360) 405-1111
(800) 228-5151

SUPER 8 MOTEL
5068 Kitsap Way (98310)
Rates: $44-$60
Tel: (360) 377-8881
(800) 800-8000

RECREATION

EVERGREEN PARK - Leashes

Info: Spend an afternoon with the dawgus at this snifferrific park. The lovely 6-acre green scene stretches beside the banks of the Washington Narrows, so brown bag it with the wag it. Après lunch, stroll the rose garden and immerse yourself and your Rosebud in the heady aromas.

Directions: Located on Park Avenue between 14th and 16th Streets.

ILLAHEE STATE PARK - Leashes

Info: Spread the red checks over the dewy, green grass and share a picnic repast with your one and only furball. Fishing fiends, tall tales are waiting to happen in this watering hole. For more information: (360) 478-6460.

Directions: From Bremerton, travel north on Highway 303, crossing over the bridge. Continue to Wheaton Way, turn east and drive about 2 miles to the park.

Hotel Policies May Be Subject To Change

LIONS COMMUNITY PLAYFIELD - Leashes

Info: Hooray, hooray, Fido can play at this 15-acre waterfront park. Stroll beside the banks of the Washington Narrows or stake out a spot on the pier for some reel-time pleasures.

Directions: Located on Lebo Boulevard and Hefner Street.

SILVER BAY HERB FARM - Leashes

Info: One hundred varieties of herbs come together and create a snifforama that's guaranteed to set tails in the wagging mode. Cruise the paths of Silver Bay where herbs are grown for seasoning, teas, medicine, fragrance and beauty and peruse rows of oregano, rosemary and thyme. Situated on the shores of Puget Sound, the sweeping views of the Olympics add to the allure. For more information: (360) 692-1340.

Directions: From the junction of Highways 304 and 3 in southern Bremerton, travel Highway 3 north about 10 miles to to Silverdale. Take the Newberry Road exit off Highway 3 north to Bucklin Hill Road, turn right. Travel Bucklin Hill Road to Tracyton Boulevard, turn right. The farm is located about .3 miles on Tracyton Boulevard.

Note: Open Thurs - Sun from 10 a.m. to 5 p.m. Closed January and February.

BREWSTER

LODGING

BREWSTER MOTEL
801 S Bridge St (98812)
Rates: $32-$60
Tel: (509) 689-2625

BRIDGEPORT

LODGING

BRIDGEPORT Y MOTEL
2300 Columbia (98813)
Rates: $35-$38
Tel: (509) 686-2002

4 MOTEL
2138 Columbia (98816)
Rates: $35-$42
Tel: (509) 686-2002

BRINNON

RECREATION

DOSEWALLIPS STATE PARK - Leashes

Info: Fishy tales are waiting to happen at this park's watering hole. Lucky dogs could dine on steelhead, salmon from the river or white salmon from the salty Hood Canal. Wildlife enthusiasts will have pupportunities galore to sight deer, elk, beaver, bald eagle, seal and waterfowl. What a combination! Pack a brown bagger to share with the wagger or grill up the day's catch at one of the developed picnic areas. For an afternoon away from it all, you can't go wrong in this delightful setting. For more information: (360) 796-4415.

Directions: From Brinnon, travel south on Highway 101 for one half mile to the park.

BUCKLEY

LODGING

MT. VIEW INN
29405 Hwy 410 (98321)
Rates: $45-$65
Tel: (360) 829-1100
(800) 582-4111

WEST MAIN MOTOR INN
466 W Main (98321)
Rates: n/a
Tel: (360) 829-2400

BURLINGTON

RECREATION

BAYVIEW STATE PARK - Leashes

Info: Beachcomb with your beachbum or be a lazybones and do nothing but relax. Birders often go bonkers in this locale so bring your binocs. Spend some time bayside before doing lunch alfresco at one of the shaded picnic spots. For more information: (360) 757-0227.

Directions: From Burlington travel west on Highway 20 about 8 miles to Bayview Edison Road, turn right for 4 miles to park.

Note: Dogs prohibited in designated swimming areas.

Hotel Policies May Be Subject To Change

PADILLA BAY NATIONAL ESTUARY - Leashes

Info: This unusual bayside locale boasts thousands of acres of exposed mudflats and eelgrass beds for you and your Curious George to explore. Nestled on the east side of Padilla Bay, this avian havian serves as temporary headquarters to a diversified mélange of migratory birds. There's a short stroll that leads to great views of the bay from the observation deck near the Breazeale Interpretive Center. Naturalists won't want to miss the tour along the Upland Trail or the Shore Trail where you can get a closer look at this special environment. For more information: (360) 428-1558.

Directions: From Burlington, travel Highway 20 west about 8 miles to Bayview Edison Road, turn right. Continue about 4 miles to the Padilla Bay-Breazeale Interpretive Center on the right just past Bayview State Park.

Note: Dogs are prohibited on the beach. The Breazeale Interpretive Center is open Wednesday through Sunday from 10 a.m. to 5 p.m.

The numbered hikes that follow are within the Padilla Bay National Estuary:

1) SHORE TRAIL HIKE - Leashes

Beginner/5.5 miles/3.0 hours

Info: See what goodies Mother Nature has in store for you with a walk along the top of a dike. You and the dogster can relish the beauty of the scene as the trail dips beside the shores of Padilla Bay. Shorebirds nest in the massive tidal mudflats and eelgrass beds that edge the tranquil waters so tote those binocs. You'll come away that much smarter if you peruse the interpretive signs which explain this fragile ecosystem. For more information: (360) 428-1558.

Directions: From Burlington, travel Highway 20 west about 8 miles to Bayview Edison Road, turn right. Follow Bayview Edison Road approximately 4 miles to the Padilla Bay-Breazeale Interpretive Center on the right just past Bayview State Park. The trailhead is located about 3 miles south of the interpretive center on Edison Road.

Note: Dogs are prohibited on the beach. The Breazeale Interpretive Center is open Wednesday through Sunday from 10 a.m. to 5 p.m.

Locate Other Dog-Friendly Activities...Check Nearby Cities

2) UPLAND TRAIL HIKE - Leashes

Beginner/1.6 miles/1.0 hours

Info: For a quickie jaunt into a natural wonderland, you won't regret a moment spent on this scenic trail. You'll wiggle this way and that through the upland area of Padilla Bay, traversing a luscious meadow and fragrant forest habitat. Along the way, you and your canine compadre will learn about the history of the uplands. FYI: Field guides and binoculars can be borrowed from the Interpretive Center. For more information: (360) 428-1558.

Directions: From Burlington, travel Highway 20 west about 8 miles to Bayview Edison Road, turn right. Follow Bayview Edison Road approximately 4 miles to the Padilla Bay-Breazeale Interpretive Center on the right just past Bayview State Park. The trailhead is located near the barn.

Note: Dogs are prohibited on the beach. The Breazeale Interpretive Center is open Wednesday through Sunday from 10 a.m. to 5 p.m.

CAMANO ISLAND

RECREATION

CAMANO ISLAND STATE PARK - Leashes

Info: If your wish list includes hiking, boating, exploring or beachcombing, this place is gonna make your day. In this waterfront park, there are 140 acres just waiting to please you and the one with the ear-to-ear grin. Step lively on the 1.5-mile walk along the sandy shores of the Saratoga Passage where you and your beach bum might uncover some interesting seashells. If you've got a boat, take your seadog for a float. Hiking gurus with a penchant for woodsy terrain will find 3 miles of hiking trails zooming off into the thickets. If you'd rather catch some R&R and let your sleeping dogs lie, there are chill out spots everywhere. For more information: (360) 387-3031.

Directions: From Stanwood, travel west on Route 532 about 3 miles to the fork at Terry's Corner. Continue on Terry's Corner to East Camano Drive, turn left. Continue on East Comano Drive about 7 miles to another fork. Follow Elger Bay Road about 3 miles to West Camano Drive, turn right. Travel on West Camano Drive about one mile to South Lowell Point Road, turn left about 1/2 miles to the park.

The numbered hikes that follow are within Camano Island State Park:

1) AL EMERSON MEMORIAL NATURE TRAIL HIKE - Leashes

Beginner/1.0 miles/0.5 hours

Info: For a quick nature fix, this interpretive trail fills the bill. The natural pathway meanders near the Saratoga Passage, so you and the furball can ogle the pretty blue waters while you learn about the region. For more information: (360) 387-3031.

Directions: From Stanwood, travel west on Route 532 about 3 miles to the fork at Terry's Corner. Continue on Terry's Corner to East Camano Drive, turn left about 7 miles to another fork. Follow Elger Bay Road about 3 miles to West Camano Drive, turn right about one mile to South Lowell Point Road, turn left. Continue about 1/2 mile to the park entrance. To the trailhead: Take a left at the "Y" on the park entrance road and follow to the boat launch and the trailhead.

2) LOOP TRAIL HIKE - Leashes

Intermediate/2.5 miles/1.25 hours

Info: Combine a dose of learning with a smidgen of Rexercise and what do you get? A great day. This interpretive nature trail beside the Saratoga Passage introduces you to the sights and sounds of nature. Expect some wet and wild pooch shenanigans if the seasonal creeks are off and running. A picnic repast on the sandy shores could end your afternoon on a fun note. For more information: (360) 387-3031.

Directions: From Stanwood, travel west on Route 532 about 3 miles to the fork at Terry's Corner. Continue on Terry's Corner to East Camano Drive, turn left about 7 miles to another fork. Follow Elger Bay Road about 3 miles to West Camano Drive, turn right about 1 mile to South Lowell Point Road, turn left about 1/2 mile to the park entrance. The trail can be accessed from anywhere in the park.

Locate Other Dog-Friendly Activities...Check Nearby Cities

CAMAS

RECREATION

LACAMAS PARK - Leashes

Info: Scenic hiking trails and birding ops are the highlights of the area, so plan accordingly. Let the sniffmeister take the lead through a landscape dotted with vibrant wildflowers and fascinating rock formations. You'll find lots of shaded knolls where lunch alfresco is the way to go. For more information: (360) 699-2375 ext. 2467.

Directions: Located at 3016 SE Everett Street.

CARNATION

LODGING

RIVER INN SNOQUALMIE VALLEY B&B
4548 Tolt River Rd (98014)
Rates: $65-$185
Tel: (206) 333-6000

CARSON

LODGING

CARSON MINERAL HOT SPRINGS
372 St. Martin Rd (98610)
Rates: $30-$100
Tel: (509) 427-8292
(800) 607-3678

CASHMERE

RECREATION

WALKING ARBORETUM TOUR - Leashes

Beginner/1.6 miles/1.0 hours

Info: A great way to get your daily dose and a mini education at the same time, this self-guided walking tour escorts you on an interesting journey. You'll start your tour of quaint

Cashmere on Cottage Avenue, across from the fire station. Spruce, maple, elm, rhododendron and hackberry provide the shade and the serene green ambience. Continue west to Vine Street where pine scents fill the air and then walk beneath towering and majestic trees to Douglas Street. The soothing tweet-tweet music comes from the local flyboys who live in the cedar, holly and butternut trees. Make your first left and then another quick left on Riverfront Drive, perhaps one of the prettiest legs of your tree-lined journey and the place where your furry cohort might sniff out some fallen chestnuts. Take a quick left on Cottage, away from the river and a right onto Douglas where the river pops into view when you reach Norman Avenue. Turn left and unpack your snacks, a stunning stand of spruce, pine, ash and larch can provide the canopy for a cool repast.

When you can pull yourself away from this fragrant oasis, turn left and hook up with Elberta Avenue. Make a right on Elberta and make tracks for the Japanese Maple at the corner of Elberta and Woodring. Turn right on Woodring, then left on aptly named East Pleasant. If spring is in the air, flowering dogwood and crabapple trees will be a colorful bonus. At this point you're not far from Cottage Avenue and your starting point. For more information: (509) 782-98815.

Directions: The tour begins and ends on Cottage Avenue. Maps and tree identification charts are available from the City of Cashmere at 101 Woodring Street.

CASTLE ROCK

LODGING

HOLIDAY INN EXPRESS
109 Bonner Rd (98611)
Rates: n/a
Tel: (800) 465-4329

MOUNT ST. HELENS MOTEL
1340 Mt. St. Helens Way NE (98611)
Rates: $30-$48
Tel: (360) 274-7721

7 WEST MOTEL
864 Walsh Ave NE (98611)
Rates: $38-$51
Tel: (360) 274-7526

TIMBERLAND INN & SUITES
1271 Mt. St. Helens Way (98611)
Rates: $42-$110
Tel: (360) 274-6002

CATHLAMET

LODGING

NASSA POINT MOTEL
851 E Hwy 4 (98612)
Rates: $28-$45
Tel: (360) 795-3941

CENTRALIA

LODGING

DAYS INN
702 Harrison Ave (98531)
Rates: $45-$70
Tel: (360) 736-2875
(800) 329-7466

FERRYMAN'S INN
1003 Eckerson Rd (98531)
Rates: $45-$52
Tel: (360) 330-2094

LAKE SHORE MOTEL
1325 Lakeshore Dr (98531)
Rates: n/a
Tel: (360) 736-9344
(800) 600-8701

MOTEL 6
1310 Belmont Ave (98531)
Rates: $25-$35
Tel: (360) 330-2057
(800) 440-6000

PARK MOTEL
1011 Belmont Ave (98531)
Rates: $29-$38
Tel: (360) 736-9333

PEPPERTREE WEST MOTOR INN
1208 Alder St (98531)
Rates: $30-$46
Tel: (360) 736-1124
(800) 795-1124

RECREATION

FORT BORST PARK - Leashes

Info: A little bit of this and a little bit of that is what this park's all about. You'll find quiet, tree-shaded areas, softball fields, a picnicking arboretum, a lovely rhododendron garden, a fishing lake and the historical Borst home. Go ahead and check it out for yourself.

Directions: Located west off Interstate 5 at exit 82.

PARKINS PARK - Leashes

Info: This stunning urban oasis is situated along the banks of the Skookumchuck River where fishy dreams can come true. Pack a biscuit basket, find a cozy spot and listen to the sounds of the rushing river as you enjoy some down time with your best pal.

Directions: Located at 6th and Meridian Streets.

Hotel Policies May Be Subject To Change

RIVERSIDE PARK - Leashes

Info: Lollygag with your wag beside the banks of the Skookumchuck River and let your cares drift away on the soothing breeze. Anglers, tote your rod and reel, the river's bounty could be din-din. Don't forget to pack the pup's favorite chew while you kick back and do your own thing.

Directions: Located off Harrison Avenue.

SEMINARY HILL NATURAL AREA - Leashes

Info: A quick escape to peace and quiet awaits you at Seminary Hill. Countless trails honeycomb the lovely landscape, so pick up a pamphlet and choose a pathway to suit your mood. Some of the trees date back to the early 1900s. A wide variety of shrubs and leafy plants add to the lushness of the setting while local flyboys serenade. For more information: (360) 736-7045.

Directions: Located east of downtown at Barner Drive and Locust Street.

WAGNER PARK - Leashes

Info: Fishing, cloudgazing and just dreaming the day away can be yours at this pleasant park.

Directions: Located at the end of Tilly Street.

WASHINGTON PARK - Leashes

Info: Check out a book at the nearby library and then hightail it to this downtown green scene where mucho tree-dappled areas equate to shady nooks.

Directions: Located between Pearl and River Streets.

WASHINGTON STREET PARK - Leashes

Info: When walktime calls, answer it at this pleasant neighborhood park. Enjoy some R&R while you're entertained by the chatty songbirds.

Directions: Located on North Washington Street.

CHEHALIS

LODGING

RELAX INN
550 SW Parkland Dr (98532)
Rates: $30-$51
Tel: (360) 748-8608
(800) 843-6916

RECREATION

HENDERSON PARK - Leashes

Info: Interspersed with picnic facilities and towering trees, this parkland offers a great change of pace for travelers and locals alike. Put a little wiggle in your wagger's strut and get thee to this parkaree.

Directions: At the corner of 13th Street and Market Boulevard.

LEWIS & CLARK STATE PARK - Leashes

Info: Named for the famous explorers, this historic locale has over 620 acres for you and your doggistorian to pawruse. History-laden, the park includes a spur of the Oregon Trail, a log cabin built in 1845, the first American pioneer home north of the Columbia River, as well as outstanding views of Mt. St. Helens. If Rainier's out, expect to be dazzled by this moody giant. Do a little traipsing with your hot dog and you'll uncover woodlands of Douglas fir, red cedar and one of the last stands of lowland old-growth forests. FYI: There are caverns, formed under the park by cooling lava from Mt. Rainier, that are presently used for natural gas storage. For more information: (360) 864-2643.

Directions: From Chehalis, travel Highway 5 south about 12 miles to the signed park entrance on the left side.

Note: Open April through September.

STAN HEDWALL PARK - Leashes

Info: Wipe that hangdog expression off the mutt's mug at this 176-acre urban oasis where you'll find plenty of paw-pleasing pupportunities. Kick up some dust on one of the many hiking trails or experience some reel-time pleasure beside the banks

Hotel Policies May Be Subject To Change

of the Newaukum River where trout is the fish du jour. In summer, the ornamental and community gardens will add a splash of color to your day.

Directions: Located on Rice Road at exit 76.

WESTSIDE PARK - Leashes

Info: Have a lark in the park with your bark on a quickie visit to this neighborhood green scene. Picnic tables and sitting benches fill the R&R bill.

Directions: On West Street between Ohio and New York Aves.

CHELAN

LODGING

BRICKHOUSE INN B&B
304 Wapato St (98816)
Rates: n/a
Tel: (509) 682-4791
(800) 799-2332

CABANA MOTEL
420 Manson Rd (98816)
Rates: $68-$117
Tel: (509) 682-2233
(800) 799-2332

CLOUD BASE VACATION RENTAL
17 S Butte Rd (98816)
Rates: n/a
Tel: (509) 682-2349

KELLY'S RESORT
12801 S Lakeshore Rd (98816)
Rates: $80-$160
Tel: (509) 687-3220
(800) 561-8978

LAKE CHELAN MOTEL
2044 W Woodin Ave (98816)
Rates: $35+
Tel: (509) 682-2742

MIDTOWNER MOTEL
721 E Woodin Ave (98816)
Rates: n/a
Tel: (509) 682-4051

RECREATION

BEEBE BRIDGE PARK - Leashes

Info: If you've been singing the summertime blues, change your tune with an afternoon interlude at this dreamy little park. You're sure to uncover some paw-pleasing diversions within the 56 acres of shoreline scenery that comprise this spot. Get a bit of Rexercise on a breezy pathway or let sleeping dogs lie in the shade of a towering tree.

Directions: From Chelan, travel southeast on Route 150 about 2 miles across the Beebe Bridge to the park off Highway 97.

Locate Other Dog-Friendly Activities...Check Nearby Cities

CHELAN FALLS PARK - Leashes

Info: Tote a boat and float the shimmering blues of the lovely lake or see what the 53 wooded acres have to offer.

Directions: Located off Chelan Highway at Washington Street.

DON MORSE PARK - Leashes

Info: You'll find splendor in the grass at this quiet, picturesque park. Walk or jog near Lake Chelan, a ribbon of blue in a sea of green. Popular in the summer months, you and the wagster might prefer an autumn amble.

Directions: Located off the Chelan-Manson Highway.

The numbered hike that follows is within Don Morse Park:

1) DON MORSE TRAIL HIKE - Leashes

Beginner/0.5 miles/0.25 hours

Info: Start your day off on the right paw with an easy-does-it-outing along this trail. The paved walkway skirts the rippling waters of Lake Chelan where you and the sniffmeister will wander amid a mixed bag of hardwoods and conifers to scenic vistas of the lake. You'll find a dozen shady spots where you can cool your jets or indulge in a brown bagger with the wagger.

Directions: Located off the Chelan-Manson Highway. The marked trailhead is near the park entrance.

RIVERSIDE PARK TRAIL HIKE - Leashes

Beginner/1.0 miles/0.5 hours

Info: Combine walk time with explore time and make tracks along this cinchy trail of paved sidewalks, boardwalks and concrete bridges. The loop around Chelan River exposes you and the one with the nose to the ground to a pretty mix of hardwoods, conifers and young redwoods. The lush understory of dogwood and floral gardens adds to this charming milieu.

Directions: The trailhead is located on Woodin Avenue on Lake Chelan.

Hotel Policies May Be Subject To Change

CHENEY

LODGING

**BUNKERS RESORT
AT WILLIAMS LAKE**
S 36402 Bunker Landing Rd (99004)
Rates: $45-$55
Tel: (509) 235-5212

ROSEBROOK INN
304 W 1st (99004)
Rates: $34-$51
Tel: (509) 235-6538

WILLOW SPRINGS MOTEL
5 B St (99004)
Rates: $37-$45
Tel: (509) 235-5138

CHEWELAH

LODGING

NORDLIG MOTEL
101 W Grant St (99109)
Rates: $36-$42
Tel: (509) 935-6704

49er MOTEL & RV PARK
311 S Park St (99109)
Rates: n/a
Tel: (509) 935-8613

CLALLAM BAY

LODGING

WINTER'S SUMMER INN B&B
16651 Hwy 112 (98326)
Rates: $46-$75
Tel: (360) 963-2264

RECREATION

CLALLAM BAY SPIT - Leashes

Info: An avian havian beckons to you and your birddog in this 33-acre seaside park. Eagles float effortlessly through the skies in search of aquatic prey while the screech of seagulls fills the air. A leisurely walk along the saltwater shores of the Strait of Juan de Fuca could unearth some interesting beach treasures. For more information: (360) 417-2291.

Directions: From Clallam Bay, turn north onto Burnt Mountain Road. Continue on Burnt Mountain Road to the end and the park entrance.

Locate Other Dog-Friendly Activities...Check Nearby Cities

CLARKSTON

LODGING

ASTOR MOTEL
1201 Bridge St (99403)
Rates: n/a
Tel: (509) 758-2509

GOLDEN KEY MOTEL
1376 Bridge St (99403)
Rates: n/a
Tel: (509) 758-5566

HACIENDA LODGE MOTEL
812 Bridge St (99403)
Rates: n/a
Tel: (800) 600-5583

HIGHLAND HOUSE B&B
707 Highland (99403)
Rates $40-$85
Tel: (509) 758-3126

MOTEL 6 PREMIER
222 Bridge St (99403)
Rates: $35-$48
Tel: (509) 758-1631
(800) 440-6000

RECREATION

CHIEF TIMOTHY STATE PARK - Leashes

Info: Named for the Nez Percé Nation leader, this park serves up a wallop of waterside scenery for you and the wagster. Encompassing 282 acres, it includes 11,500' of freshwater shoreline. Pick a spot and spread the red checks for lunch alfresco or see what's up on one of the trails that laces this riparian habitat. If you're a fishing fiend at heart, pick a lakeside niche and try your luck on perch, crappie, smallmouth bass, catfish, steelhead or trout. For more information: (509) 758-9580.

Directions: From Clarkston, travel Highway 12 east for 12 miles to the park.

CLEARWATER and SNAKE RIVER NATIONAL RECREATION TRAIL - Leashes

Beginner/1.0 miles - 16.0 miles/0.5 hours - 8.0 hours

Info: Strap on the pawdometer and put a twinkle in the hikemeister's eyes. Truly down by the riverside, you'll journey on a paved pathway through some of the prettiest country around. From tranquil duck ponds to wildflower-sprinkled meadows, you can play tagalong with your wagalong on the tree-lined trail where the air is often scented with the fragrance of flowers. Birders give this region the high five for its bounty of flyboys. Even history buffs won't go home empty-handed. Watch the drawbridge in action and learn a tad about Lewis, Clark and their loyal Newfy, Seaman. For more information: (509) 758-9676.

Directions: The trail begins just north of the Highway 12 Interstate Bridge and ends at Chief Looking Glass Park in Asotin.

FIELDS SPRING STATE PARK - Leashes

Info: Scenery and wildlife devotees can compare notes at this 445-acre region. In birdspeak, this locale rates two tweets up. Predators like the sharp-skinned hawk or the great-horned owl are often sighted. Knock on wood, a hairy woodpecker could be beating his beak against a tree while a yellow-bellied sapsucker clings to a nearby trunk. Countless bird species lay claim to this territory. And who can blame them, especially in spring and summer when the wildflowers enliven the landscape in Crayola colors. Pensive pups can uncover cool, quiet walkways in woodlands of ponderosa pine, western larch, Douglas fir or grand fir where the deer and the antelope play. For more information: (509) 256-3332.

Directions: From Clarkston, travel south on Highway 129 for 30 miles to the signed park entrance.

The numbered hike that follows is within Fields Spring State Park:

1) PUFFER BUTTE TRAIL HIKE - Leashes

Beginner/1.0 miles/0.5 hours

Info: As you journey amidst tranquil thickets, the scenery is nothing short of spectacular. You and the wagging machine will burn some kibble on your ascent to the bluff, but then comes payback time. From your lofty aerie, the Grand Ronde Canyon stretches 3,000' below. The high Wallowa Mountains of Oregon loom to the south, the canyons of Idaho and the Blue Mountains to the east and west round out the panorama. An enthusiastic two paws up for this adventure.

Directions: From Clarkston, travel south on Highway 129 for 30 miles to the signed park entrance. The trailhead is located at the Puffer Butte Lodge on the south side of the park.

CLE ELUM

LODGING

ASTER INN & ANTIQUES
521 E 1st St (98922)
Rates: $32-$65
Tel: (509) 674-2551

BONITA MOTEL
906 E First St (98922)
Rates: $30-$40
Tel: (509) 674-2380

CEDARS MOTEL
1001 E First St (98922)
Rates: $40-$54
Tel: (509) 674-5535

CHALET MOTEL
800 E First St (98922)
Rates: $35-$55
Tel: (509) 674-2320

STEWART LODGE
805 W First St (98922)
Rates: $44-$54
Tel: (509) 674-4548

TIMBER LODGE MOTEL
301 W First St (98922)
Rates: $44-$54
Tel: (509) 674-5966

WIND BLEW INN
811 Hwy 970 (98922)
Rates: n/a
Tel: (509) 674-2294

CLINTON

LODGING & RECREATION

See Whidbey Island for lodging and recreation.

COLVILLE

LODGING

BEAVER LODGE RESORT & CAMPGROUND
2430 Hwy 20 East (99114)
Rates: n/a
Tel: (509) 684-5657

BENNY'S COLVILLE INN
915 S Main St (99114)
Rates: $40-$105
Tel: (509) 684-2517

COMFORT INN
166 NE Canning Dr (99114)
Rates: $42-$115
Tel: (509) 684-2010
(800) 228-5150

DOWNTOWN MOTEL
369 S Main St (99114)
Rates: $28-$48
Tel: (509) 684-2565

MAPLE AT SIXTH B&B
407 E 6th (99114)
Rates: $45-$55
Tel: (800) 446-2750

Hotel Policies May Be Subject To Change

<u>RECREATION</u>

SHERRY TRAIL HIKE - Leashes

Beginner/3.8 miles/2.0 hours

Info: A towering canopy of lodgepole pine and Douglas fir shade this pleasing pathway that parallels the meandering Little Pend Oreille River. Early summer means wildflowers crowding the riverbank, adding a fragrant scent to the balmy air. If you're into fly fishing, this could be heaven. The walkway offers good access to some of the best and often uncrowded spots for trout. For more information: (509) 684-4557.

Directions: From Colville, travel U.S. 20 east about 23.5 miles to the signed trailhead on the south side.

SPRINGBOARD TRAIL HIKE - Leashes

Beginner/2.4 miles/1.5 hours

Info: History hounds will dig their paws into this interpretive trail. More than 100 years ago, the fertile land was claimed and worked by European settlers. Remnants of the homesteads can still be seen and offer you and your Peke a peek at the past in a natural setting. To make the most of your outing, pick up a guide at the trailhead kiosk. For more information: (509) 684-7010.

Directions: From Colville, travel Highway 20 east about 26 miles to the Gillette Lake Campground turnoff on the south side of the highway. The trailhead is located in the campground at the southeast end of Lake Gillette.

CONCONULLY

<u>LODGING</u>

CONCONULLY LAKE RESORT
102 Sinlahekin Rd (98819)
Rates: $25-$48
Tel: (509) 826-0813
(800) 850-0813

CONCONULLY MOTEL
P.O. Box 181 (98819)
Rates: n/a
Tel: (509) 826-1610

GIBSON'S NORTH FORK LODGE
100 W Boone (98819)
Rates: n/a
Tel: (509) 826-1475

JACK'S RV PARK & MOTEL
212 A Ave (98819)
Rates: n/a
Tel: (509) 826-0132
(800) 893-5668

Locate Other Dog-Friendly Activities...Check Nearby Cities

KOZY CABINS
18 Miles NW of Okanogan (98819)
Rates: $35-$42
Tel: (509) 862-6780

LIAR'S COVE RESORT
1835 A Conconully Rd (98819)
Rates: $40-$50
Tel: (800) 830-1288

MAPLE FLATS RV PARK & RESORT
310 A Ave (98819)
Rates: n/a
Tel: (509) 826-4231
(800) 683-1180

SHADY PINES RESORT
125 W Fork Salmon Cr Rd (98819)
Rates: $54-$60
Tel: (800) 552-2287

RECREATION

SUGARLOAF TRAIL HIKE - Leashes

Beginner/2.0 miles/1.0 hours

Info: Experience lakeside tranquility on this delightful jaunt beside Sugarloaf Lake. Make like Huck Finn and try your line on the rainbow trout or just work out the kinks in this pretty setting. For more information: (509) 826-3275.

Directions: From Conconully, travel Sinlahekin Valley Road (CR 4015) northeast about 5 miles to the Sugarloaf Campground and the trailhead.

CONNELL

LODGING

M & M MOTEL
730 S Columbia Ave (99326)
Rates: $30+
Tel: (509) 234-8811

TUMBLEWOOD MOTEL
433 S Columbia Ave (99326)
Rates: $23-$38
Tel: (509) 234-2081

COPALIS BEACH

LODGING

BEACHWOOD RESORT
SR 109, P.O. Box 116 (98535)
Rates: n/a
Tel: (360) 289-2177

ECHOES OF THE SEA MOTEL
3208 SR 109 (98535)
Rates: $38-$78
Tel: (360) 289-3358
(800) 578-ECHO

IRON SPRINGS RESORT
P.O. Box 207 (98535)
Rates: n/a
Tel: (360) 276-4230

LINDA'S LOW TIDE MOTEL
14 McCullough Rd (98535)
Rates: $30-$60
Tel: (360) 289-3450

Hotel Policies May Be Subject To Change

ROD'S BEACH RESORT
2961 SR 109 (98535)
Rates: n/a
Tel: (360) 289-2222

TIDELANDS RESORT
P.O. Box 36 (98535)
Rates: n/a
Tel: (360) 289-8963

RECREATION

GRIFFITHS-PRIDAY STATE PARK - Leashes

Info: A primo coastal destination, you and your Sandy will find 364 acres to beachcomb beside the Pacific. See how many shiny shells and stones you can claim as your own. Look and listen for the grey whales that favor these waters. If you're visiting during razor clamming, join in the hunt. No matter when you're in the area, you're bound to meet other pooches and their people. When the wind kicks up can kites be far behind? Stow your own flyer and join the locals. This coastal region has all the makings of a great day. Go ahead and check it out for yourself. For more information: (360) 289-3553.

Directions: From Highway 109 just north of Copalis Beach, turn left onto Benner Gap Road and follow it to the park.

WASHINGTON STATE BEACHES

Info: One of the few coastal regions where you can drive on the beach, there are three remarkable stretches awaiting your exploration. Obey the rules which are posted at access points. In particular, use caution near pedestrians and stay well away from the clam beds near the waterline.

Directions: Heading from north to south, the following are the locations of the drive-on Washington beaches:

1) Moclips to Ocean Shores along Highways 109 and 115
2) Westport to North Cove along Highway 105
3) Oysterville to Ilwaco along Highway 103

For additional lodging and recreation in the beach areas, see listings under the following cities: Grayland, Ilwaco, Long Beach Peninsula, Moclips, Ocean Park, Ocean Shores, Oysterville, Pacific Beach, Westport.

COULEE CITY

LODGING

ALA COZY MOTEL
9988 Hwy 2 E (99115)
Rates: $38-$58
Tel: (509) 632-5703

BLUE TOP MOTEL
109 N 6th St (99115)
Rates: $27-$48
Tel: (509) 632-5596

COULEE LODGE RESORT
33017 Park Lake Rd NE (99115)
Rates: $27-$53
Tel: (509) 632-5565

LAKEVIEW MOTEL
HCR 1, Box 11 (99115)
Rates: n/a
Tel: (509) 632-5792

LAUREN'T SUN VILLAGE RESORT
33575 Park Lake Rd NE (99115)
Rates: $42-$95
Tel: (509) 632-5664

SUN LAKES PARK RESORT
34228 Park Lake Rd NE (99115)
Rates: $58-$91
Tel: (509) 632-5291

RECREATION

DRY FALLS - Leashes

Info: Dry Falls is a skeleton of one of the finest waterfalls in geologic history. During the Ice Age, the waters of Glacial Lake Missoula in Montana broke free from an ice dam and rushed headlong across eastern Washington and northern Idaho, creating plateaus and etching the coulees that characterize this region. Two major cascades were formed, the larger cataract of Upper Coulee with an 800-foot waterfall and the other near Soap Lake. The raging waters played a major role in erosion by plucking chunks of rock from the faces of the falls and causing them to retreat. Dry Falls is the testament to this historic event.

Measuring 3.5 miles wide, with a drop of more than 400', the falls make Niagara's one-mile width and 165-foot drop seem minuscule. A short boardwalk leads to the overlook where you and the wide-eyed one will have a grand view of the large mass. If looking isn't enough, adventuresome sorts can shimmy down to the base of Dry Falls along a somewhat steep trail. The shallow waters below the falls are home to rainbow and brown trout. But you can only fish using lures, flies and single barbless hooks. For more information: (800) 992-6234.

Directions: From the Dry Falls Junction of Route 2 and Highway 17 in Coulee City, travel Highway 17 south about 4 miles. The Interpretive Center is on the east side of Highway 17.

SUN LAKES STATE PARK - Leashes

Info: Simple pleasures are easy to find at this green scene. Tote a fuzzy tennie or a favorite Frisbee and put a little playtime in the pup's afternoon. For more information: (509) 632-5583.

Directions: From Coulee City, travel west on Highway 2 about 2.5 miles to the junction with Highway 17, turn left. Continue about 4 miles to the signed park entrance.

COULEE DAM

LODGING

COULEE HOUSE MOTEL
110 Roosevelt Way (99116)
Rates: $50-$100
Tel: (509) 633-1101
(800) 715-7767

RECREATION

COLE PARK - Leashes

Info: With an array activities for you and your doggie, you can't go wrong if you're looking for a day of fun in the park. Do the play thing then relax in the shade under the towering trees.

Directions: Located just off Highway 155 on the west side of the river next to the Columbia Building.

COULEE DAM HISTORICAL WALKING TOUR - Leashes

Info: Doggistorians can step back in time along this historic trail commemorating the construction of the Coulee Dam. Throughout your journey, you'll get various perspectives of Grand Coulee Dam which was built in the 1930s. The dam, located on the Columbia River, is one of the largest structures in the world and is used for irrigation, power production and flood control. Taking off from the Visitor Arrival Center, you and your history hound will bound past many landmark buildings that were crucial for housing, communication and materials during the Dam's formation. You'll also trek through Cole Park and Douglas Park, where picnic pupportunities beckon. If you and the mutt are up for a little hiking, you can take a quick detour along Candy Point Trail or Down River Trail. The huge sand pile at the end of your journey is your turnaround point. Considered the world's largest sandbox, the sands are "leftovers" from concrete mix for the construction of the dam. Pick up a trail map at the Visitors Arrival Center and bag a lesson in history. FYI: A "coulee" is a ravine or deep gully, usually dry, which has been eroded by water. For more information: (800) 268-5332.

Directions: Begin the tour at the Visitor Arrival Center (U.S. Bureau of Reclamation) on Highway 155 just north of Coulee Dam. Tours are self-guided. For the most panoramic view of Grand Coulee Dam and the Coulee Dam Community, take Highway 174 toward Bridgeport and look for the sign for Crown Point Vista.

DOUGLAS PARK - Leashes

Info: Your posh pooch will give this well-manicured park the high five. Spreading out just below Grand Coulee Dam, large evergreens shade the grassy knolls and create a pretty picture.

Directions: Located off Highway 155.

DOWNRIVER TRAIL HIKE - Leashes

Beginner/1.0-13.0 miles/0.5-7.0 hours

Info: Peace and quiet reign supreme on this gentle trail that follows the curves of the Columbia River north from Grand Coulee Dam. Die-hard Dudleys who want to stay in shape can go the distance on this one. All along your route, the sights and sounds of the river will add to your enjoyment. Have a lark with your bark and include a biscuit basket. There are plenty of pleasing nooks and crannies for your picnic pleasure. For more information: (800) 268-5332.

Directions: The trail has many access points. The main trailhead is located on the east side of the bridge across from the Coulee House Motel.

MASON CITY MEMORIAL PARK - Leashes

Info: If you're looking for some dam good views, this park's your ticket. Plan an early evening sojourn and catch the laser show at Grand Coulee Dam (from the extension of the park across from the Coulee House). Pull up a square of green and watch the dueling beams of light. For more information on the light show: (800) 268-5332.

Directions: Located in east Coulee Dam adjacent to the shopping center and post office.

Note: Laser shows are seasonal. Call for show times and dates. You can also view the laser show from the Visitor Arrival Center.

COUPEVILLE

LODGING & RECREATION

See Whidbey Island for lodging and recreation.

CURLEW

LODGING

BLUE COUGAR MOTEL
2141 Hwy 21 N (99118)
Rates: n/a
Tel: (509) 779-4817

CUSICK

LODGING

BLUESLIDE RESORT
400-41 Hwy 20 (99119)
Rates: $35-$44
Tel: (509) 445-1327

THE OUTPOST RESORT & RV PARK
405351 Hwy 20 (99119)
Rates: $40-$60
Tel: (509) 445-1317

DARRINGTON

LODGING

STAGE COACH INN
1100 Seeman St (98241)
Rates: $60-$75
Tel: (360) 436-1776

RECREATION

SQUIRE CREEK PARK - Leashes

Info: Afishionados with a fondness for trout can make their fishing dreams come true in Squire Creek. For more information: (425) 339-1208

Directions: On Highway 530 about 3 miles west of Darrington.

DAYTON

LODGING

BLUE MOUNTAIN MOTEL
414 W Main St (99328)
Rates: n/a
Tel: (509) 382-3040

THE WEINHARD HOTEL
235 E Main St (99328)
Rates: $65-$110
Tel: (509) 382-4032

THE PURPLE HOUSE B&B
415 E Clay St (99328)
Rates: $85-$125
Tel: (509) 382-3159
(800) 486-2574

RECREATION

LEWIS and CLARK TRAIL STATE PARK - Leashes

Info: Give your canine the VIP (very important pooch) treatment with a day combing the open grassy fields of this postcard pretty land. Dedicated to the famous explorers Lewis and Clark, who trekked through this region on their return trip in 1806, you and your inquisitive canine will have 37 acres where you can conduct your own exploration. There's a one-mile interpretive trail which provides a mini education if you're so inclined. The park borders 1,000' of freshwater shoreline on the Touchet River, so anglers can give it a go and birders can check out the local flyboys. For more information: (800) 233-0321.

Hotel Policies May Be Subject To Change

Directions: From Dayton, travel southwest on U.S. 12 for 3.5 miles to the signed park entrance.

Note: Seasonal, call first.

MEADOW CREEK TRAIL HIKE

Intermediate/8.0 miles/5.0 hours

Info: Calling all aqua pups. When nothing but wet and wild hijinks will do, this is the trail for you. Meadow Creek is at the center of all the fun. You and the gleeful one will crisscross the creek several times so pack your water sandals. On the last mile, you'll leave the creek behind and ascend an old logging road to trail's end. Or stay put beside the water and simply play the day away. For more information: (509) 843-1891.

Directions: From Dayton, head northeast on Highway 12 for 15 miles to the junction with Tucannon River Road, turn right. Follow Tucannon River Road approximately 45 miles to FS 4713 (Panjab Creek Road). Make a right on FS 4713 for 4.25 miles to the trailhead at road's end.

OREGON BUTTE TRAIL HIKE

Intermediate/6.0 miles/4.0 hours

Info: If it's great views you're seeking, seek no more. This trail involves a yoyo-like journey across a ridge before topping out at 6,387' Oregon Butte where breathtaking vistas are your payback. For more information: (509) 843-1891.

Directions: From Dayton, take Fourth Avenue south to Eckler Mountain Road (CR 9124), turn left. Follow Eckler Mountain Road approximately 15 miles to FS 46 (Kendall Skyline Rd), turn right. Continue on FS 46 for 12 miles to FS 4608. Make a left on FS 4608 and follow about 3 miles to the Teepee Trailhead at road's end. (Stay right on all the Ys on FS 4608.)

DEER PARK

LODGING

LOVE'S VICTORIAN B&B
North 31317 Cedar Rd (99006)
Rates: $74-$98
Tel: (509) 276-6939

Locate Other Dog-Friendly Activities...Check Nearby Cities

DEMING

LODGING

THE GUEST HOUSE B&B
5723 Schombush Rd (98244)
Rates: $45-$60
Tel: (360) 592-2343

THE LOGS RESORT
9002 Mt. Baker Hwy (98244)
Rates: $75+
Tel: (360) 599-2711

DES MOINES

LODGING

KING'S ARMS MOTEL APARTMENT
23226 30th Ave S (98198)
Rates: $27-$59
Tel: (206) 824-0300

RAMADA INN LIMITED
22300 7th Ave S (98198)
Rates: $69-$139
Tel: (206) 824-9920
(800) 272-6232

EAST WENATCHEE

RECREATION

APPLE CAPITAL RECREATION LOOP TRAIL HIKE - Leashes

Beginner/12.0 miles/6.0 hours

Info: This paw-pleasing, very popular trail skirts the banks of the Columbia River on a journey through the city streets. The ever present river sounds accompany you all the way. If you're looking for a smidgen of solitude, you'll want to plan a morning excursion. On the other paw, a moonlight walk could be the perfect way to end a hectic day. Take five and watch the moonbeams light the glistening water. For more information: (509) 884-2514.

Directions: The trailhead is at the corner of Grant Road just past Sunset Highway (Route 28). There are several free parking lots on both sides of the Columbia River that provide access to the trail.

Note: Use caution when walking at night, the Wenatchee side of the trail is lit until midnight.

BLUE TRAIL HIKE - Leashes

Beginner/4.0 miles/2.0 hours

Info: Even sofa loafers will brush off their paws for this simple jaunt through the city streets of East Wenatchee. Serene parks, quiet neighborhoods and charming apple orchards are all part of the picture. Tuck one of those collapsible kites in your backpack and join the locals at a favorite pastime. This trail encompasses a slice of Americana you won't want to miss. For more information: (509) 884-2514.

Directions: At the corner of Grant Road and Georgia Avenue.

EATONVILLE

LODGING

HENLEY'S SILVER LAKE RESORT CABINS
40718 S Silver Lake Rd E (98328)
Rates: n/a
Tel: (360) 832-3580

MOUNTAIN VIEW CEDAR LODGE
36203 Pulford Rd E (98328)
Rates: $85-$115
Tel: (360) 832-8080
(800) 903-5636

EDMONDS

LODGING

EDMONDS HARBOR INN
130 W Dayton St (98020)
Rates: $60-$75
Tel: (425) 771-5021
(800) 441-8033

K & E MOTOR INN
23921 Hwy 99 (98020)
Rates: $42-$67
Tel: (425) 778-2181
(800) 787-2181

HUDGENS HAVEN B&B
9313 190th St SW (98020)
Rates: $60-$65
Tel: (425) 776-2202

RECREATION

EDMONDS CITY PARK - Leashes

Info: A neighborhood gathering place, social sorts will get a chance to meet and greet at this dogarama. Let the barkmeister sniff and whiff to his heart's content.

Directions: At 3rd Avenue South, between Pine and Howell Sts.

Locate Other Dog-Friendly Activities...Check Nearby Cities

MARINA BEACH - Leashes

Info: The only beach in town where pooches are permitted, Marina is sure to wag tails. Jumpstart your morning with a sunrise stroll or depending on the tide, take a good read and a tough chew and spend the day beach bum style.

Directions: At the waterfront just south of Admiral Way.

YOST MEMORIAL PARK - Leashes

Info: Plan an afternoon interlude at this charming park. There's a half-mile interpretive trail which offers insight into the historic relics. If you're more interested in lazybone pursuits, find a grassy spot under a shade tree and throw the poor dog a bone.

Directions: Located at Walnut and 96th Streets.

ELBE

LODGING

HOBO INN
P.O. Box 20 (98330)
Rates: $70-$85
Tel: (360) 569-2500

ELK

LODGING

JERRY'S LANDING RESORT
N 41114 Lakeshore (99009)
Rates: n/a
Tel: (509) 292-2337

ELLENSBURG

LODGING

BEST WESTERN ELLENSBURG INN
1700 Canyon Rd (98926)
Rates: $39-$77
Tel: (509) 925-9801
(800) 528-1234

COMFORT INN
1722 Canyon Rd (98926)
Rates: $46-$72
Tel: (509) 925-7037
(800) 221-2222

Hotel Policies May Be Subject To Change

HAROLDS & WAITES MOTEL
601 N Water (98926)
Rates: $28-$48
Tel: (509) 925-4141

I-90 INN MOTEL
1390 Dollar Way Rd N (98926)
Rates: $33-$48
Tel: (509) 925-9844

NITES INN MOTEL
1200 S Ruby (98926)
Rates: $36-$45
Tel: (509) 962-9600

SUPER 8 MOTEL
1500 Canyon Rd (98926)
Rates: $46-$64
Tel: (509) 962-6888
(800) 800-8000

ENUMCLAW

LODGING

BEST WESTERN PARK CENTER HOTEL
1000 Griffin Ave (98022)
Rates: $64-$72
Tel: (360) 825-4490
(800) 528-1234

KING'S MOTEL
1334 Roosevelt Ave E (98022)
Rates: $45-$54
Tel: (360) 825-1626

RECREATION

NOLTE STATE PARK- Leashes

Info: Nestled on the edge of Deep Lake, this park packs a wallop of nature into 117 acres. A mecca for mammals and birds, it's a sweet spot for naturalists. If a day at the park isn't complete without some Rexercise, hustle your butt on the trail that borders the lake. Huck Finn fishing moments are also part of the scene. No matter how you slice it, there's something here for every breed. For more information: (360) 825-4646.

Directions: Located off SR 69, 6 miles northeast of Enumclaw.

Note: Open April 16 through October 31.

EPHRATA

LODGING

COLUMBIA MOTEL
1257 Basin St SW (98823)
Rates: $35-$60
Tel: (509) 754-5226

LARIAT MOTEL
1639 Basin St SW (98823)
Rates: n/a
Tel: (509) 754-2437

EVERETT

LODGING

CYPRESS INN
12619 4th Ave W (98208)
Rates: $59-$69
Tel: (425) 347-9099
(800) 752-9991

DAYS INN
1122 N Broadway (98201)
Rates: $43-$59
Tel: (425) 252-8000
(800) 329-7466

HOLIDAY INN HOTEL & CONF CTR
101 128th St SE (98208)
Rates: $79-$99
Tel: (425) 337-2900
(800) 465-4329

MOTEL 6 NORTH
10006 Everett Way (98204)
Rates: $40-$50
Tel: (425) 347-2060
(800) 440-6000

MOTEL 6 SOUTH
224 128th St SW (98204)
Rates: $30-$45
Tel: (425) 353-8120
(800) 440-6000

ROYAL MOTOR INN
952 N Broadway (98201)
Rates: $44+
Tel: (425) 259-5177

TRAVELODGE
3030 Broadway (98201)
Rates: $37-$65
Tel: (425) 259-6141
(800) 578-7878

WELCOME MOTOR INN
1205 N Broadway (98201)
Rates: $37-$52
Tel: (425) 252-8828

RECREATION

CLARK PARK - Leashes

Info: Have a lark in the park with your bark with a visit to this local hangout. See Spot run, see Spot play in the greenery you'll find.

Directions: Located at 2400 Lombard.

FOREST PARK - Leashes

Info: The local bark park, you're sure to meet and greet lots of neighborhood pooches. Drop in before or after the work day for a bit of socializing at this vast 111-acre green scene. For sporty types, catch a game of flyballs at the baseball field or get your daily dose on the meandering nature trail.

Directions: Located at 802 Mukilteo Boulevard.

Hotel Policies May Be Subject To Change

GARFIELD PARK - Leashes

Info: Take your Odie out for an afternoon of play at this little urban locale. Add a fuzzy tennie to the mix and make his day.

Directions: Located at 2300 Walnut.

HOWARTH PARK - Leashes

Info: When playtime calls, answer it with a leisurely sojourn to this 28-acre city park. Leave some pawprints on the dewy green or find a shady nook to call your own and break some bread with Bowser.

Directions: Located at 1127 Olympic Boulevard.

INTERURBAN TRAIL HIKE - Leashes

Beginner/1.0-26.4 miles/0.5-14.0 hours

Info: Covering the distance from Everett to Edmonds, you and your city licker can follow the former route of the Interurban Trolley that, until 1939, ran between Ballard and Bellingham. One of the most pupular byways with walkers, joggers and bikers, you and the hound are bound to run into lots of canines and their human companions. One fine morning, just do it. For more information: (425) 257-8300.

Directions: Trail access is at 84th Street SW and Everett Mall.

JACKSON PARK - Leashes

Info: Put a twinkle in the ballmeister's eyes and skedaddle on over to this pleasant 14-acre park. Take a fuzzy Wilson and make your dog's day.

Directions: Located at 1700 State Street.

KASCH MEMORIAL PARK - Leashes

Info: Dollars to dog biscuits, you're gonna have a good time at this delightful neighborhood park where 60 acres of manicured grounds translate into oodles of puppy pleasures.

Directions: Located at 8811 Airport Road.

LANGUS RIVERFRONT PARK - Leashes

Info: When the cards are dealt and playtime wins out, this is the place to ante up. You and the wagging machine can expect to come away with ear-to-ear grins down by the rivrside in this 58-acre expanse.

Directions: Located at 411 Smith Island Road.

LOWELL RIVERFRONT TRAIL HIKE - Leashes

Beginner/3.2 miles/2.0 hours

Info: For a bonafido hiking adventure, highlight this one on your itinerary. The paved path traverses an area rich in history and brimming with natural beauty, riparian style. From the edges of the protected wetlands near the Burlington Northern Railroad, this picturesque journey follows the riverfront where lovely views are part of the package. An area rich in birdlife, don't be surprised by the presence of a flashy bald eagle, hawks or red-winged blackbirds cruising the river in search of aquatic prey. Perhaps the great blue herons will be about, standing stock still, poised to strike at dinner time. You might even see a river otter at play in the deep blue. If you and the dawgus like your trails woodsy and cool, you've found nirvana in this odyssey where cottonwood and alder provide the canopy of shade. Tote your binocs for birds-eye views of the Snohomish River Valley flood plain and the Cascades, including Mount Baker and Mount Rainier. For more information: (425) 257-8300.

Directions: Access is at Riverbend, 2nd Street and Lowell River Road.

ROTARY PARK - Leashes

Info: Do some puppy prancing at this 11-acre parkland. If you've got a boat, take your first mate afloat and soak up the scenery.

Directions: Located at 1600 Lowell River Road.

OTHER PARKS IN EVERETT - Leashes

• ALDER STREET PARK, 49th and Dogwood
• BRIDLE PARK, Sound Avenue
• CASCADEVIEW PARK, 88th Street and 7th
• DOYLE PARK, 35th and Grand
• EDGEWATER PARK, 3731 Mukilteo Boulevard
• GRAND AVENUE PARK, 1800 Grand Avenue
• HARBORVIEW PARK, 1621 Mukilteo Boulevard
• HAUGE HOMESTEAD PARK, 1501 21st Drive SE
• KIWANIS PARK, 36th and Rockefeller
• LIONS PARK, 7530 Cascade Drive
• LOWELL PARK, 46th and S. 3rd Avenue
• NORTH & SOUTH VIEW PARK, W. Marine View Drive
• SUMMIT PARK, Summit Avenue
• VIEW RIDGE PARK, Olympic Boulevard

FEDERAL WAY

LODGING

**BEST WESTERN
FEDERAL WAY EXECUTEL**
31611 20th Ave S (98003)
Rates: $89-$131
Tel: (253) 941-6000
(800) 528-1234

ROADRUNNER MOTEL
1501 350th St S (98003)
Rates: $30-$38
Tel: (800) 828-7202

STEVENSON MOTEL
33330 Pacific Hwy S (98003)
Rates: n/a
Tel: (253) 927-2500

SUPER 8 MOTEL
1688 348th St S (98003)
Rates: $46-$62
Tel: (253) 838-8808
(800) 800-8000

FERNDALE

LODGING

SCOTTISH LODGE MOTEL
5671 Riverside Dr (98248)
Rates: $30
Tel: (360) 384-4040

SUPER 8 MOTEL
5788 Barrett Ave (98248)
Rates: $45-$63
Tel: (360) 384-8881
(800) 800-8000

Locate Other Dog-Friendly Activities...Check Nearby Cities

<u>RECREATION</u>

HOVANDER HOMESTEAD PARK - Leashes

Info: Do some time traveling with a visit to this turn-of-the-century farmhouse setting. You and your canine connoisseur can admire the beautiful flower and vegetable gardens and fruit orchards before cruising the historic barn. Symbolically red, it's one of the largest in the country and houses all of Old MacDonald's favorites. Tour the other farm buildings where antique farm implements and equipment are carefully displayed and preserved. Been there, done that, go take a hike along the riverfront. For more information: (360) 384-3444.

Directions: The farm is located at 5299 Nielsen Road.

Note: Hours are seasonal, call first.

The numbered hike that follows is within the Hovander Homestead Park:

1) RIVER DIKE TRAIL HIKE - Leashes

Beginner/4.4 miles/3.0 hours

Info: River rovers will feel right at home traipsing the tranquil shore of Nooksack River. The grassy farmlands soon give way to a combo plate of mixed woodlands and riparian oases. This is the place where birdsong drifts from the trees and cute little creatures hurry to and fro in the bosky terrain. For more information: (360) 384-3444.

Directions: The farm is located at 5299 Nielsen Road. There are three trailheads: one at the north end boat launch, another at the main lawn of Hovander Park and the third at the south end of Slater Road.

Note: Hours are seasonal, call first.

TENNANT LAKE INTERPRETIVE CENTER - Leashes

Info: A pastoral setting, much of the American landscape is reflected in the riverside farm and surrounding marshy environs. If you're a budding ornithologist, grab your dog-eared ID book and head out for a day of birding fun in this avian havian. Hundreds of species share the space in a place that's

Hotel Policies May Be Subject To Change

ideal for feeding, bathing and wooing. Spend your morning in the company of great blue herons along with mallards, red-tailed hawks, northern harriers, a bounty of owls, rock doves, flickers, woodpeckers, warblers, Savannah sparrows, American goldfinches and Canada geese. As if that medley isn't enough to satisfy the most avid birder, perhaps a horned lark, turkey vulture, peregrine falcon or tundra swan will make a rare, unscheduled appearance. The elevated board-walk skirts the edges of the lake and ends at an observation deck. Even smarty pants pooches can learn something on the interpretive trail which offers an inside look at this fragile ecosystem. For more information: (360) 384-3444.

Directions: The center is located at 5236 Nielsen Road.

Note: Hours are seasonal, call first.

The numbered activities that follow are within
Tennant Lake Interpretive Center:

1) TENNANT LAKE MARSH BOARDWALK HIKE - Leashes

Beginner/1.4 miles/1.0 hours

Info: A succulent slice of flora and fauna, take your little mutt for a look-see around the marsh and swamp areas. The bridge from Tennant Lake near Hovander Park deposits you in a rich riparian habitat. This locale, generously covered with bullrush, is a favorite resting spot for American goldfinch and marsh wren. Let the whiffer lead the way through a swamp of willow thicket, past clumps of lichen to the edges of the lake. Muskrats are often seen in these parts along with some amazing insects like the water boatman and whirligig beetle. The sweet fragrance in mid-summer is probably from the exotic sweet gale. Look for the small pink flowers that bloom on Douglas spirea. Aah, what a wonderful way for a couple of naturalists to spend the day. For more information: (360) 384-3444.

Directions: The center is at 5236 Nielsen Road. The trailhead is located at the bridge crossing. Pick up a trail brochure at the interpretive center.

Note: Hours are seasonal, call first.

Locate Other Dog-Friendly Activities...Check Nearby Cities

2) FRAGRANCE GARDEN - Leashes

Info: Tantalize all of your senses with a tour of this award-winning garden. Sniffmeisters give this beauty two paws up. More than 200 varieties of herbs and flowers compete to win by a nose. Green thumbs are encouraged to touch the budding arrays and experience the distinct textures of each plant. For maximum sensory overload, schedule your visit from May to August. For more information: (360) 733-2900.

Directions: The Fragrance Garden is located at 5236 Nielsen Road, beside the Nielsen House at the Tennant Lake Interpretive Center.

Note: Open daily from 8 a.m. to dusk.

FIFE

Lodging

BEST WESTERN EXECUTIVE INN
5700 Pacific Hwy E (98424)
Rates: $70-$127
Tel: (253) 922-0080
(800) 528-1234

COMFORT INN
5601 Pacific Hwy E (98424)
Rates: $51-$65
Tel: (253) 926-2301
(800) 221-2222

DAYS INN-PORTAGE INN
3021 Pacific Hwy E (98424)
Rates: $50-$80
Tel: (253) 922-3500
(800) 329-7466

ECONO LODGE
3518 Pacific Hwy E (98424)
Rates: $40-$60
Tel: (253) 922-0550
(800) 424-4777

HOMETEL INN
3520 Pacific Hwy E (98424)
Rates: $40-$60
Tel: (253) 922-0555
(800) 258-3520

KINGS MOTOR INN
5115 Pacific Hwy E (98424)
Rates: $36
Tel: (800) 929-3509

MOTEL 6
5201 20th St E (98424)
Rates: $30-$40
Tel: (253) 922-1270
(800) 440-6000

PARADISE MOTEL
1618 59th Ave Court E (98424)
Rates: n/a
Tel: (253) 922-5158

ROYAL COACHMAN INN
5805 Pacific Hwy E (98424)
Rates: $59-$125
Tel: (253) 922-2500
(800) 422-3051

Hotel Policies May Be Subject To Change

FIR ISLAND

<u>LODGING</u>

SOUTH FORK MOORAGE B&B
2187 Mann Rd (98238)
Rates: $95-$115
Tel: (360) 445-4803

FORKS

<u>LODGING</u>

BAGBY'S TOWN MOTEL
1080 Forks Ave S (98331)
Rates: $30-$45
Tel: (360) 374-6231
(800) 742-2429

FORKS MOTEL
351 Forks Ave S (98331)
Rates: $45-$67
Tel: (360) 374-6243
(800) 544-3416

HOH HUMM RANCH B&B
171763 Hwy 101 (98331)
Rates: $39-$76
Tel: (360) 374-5337

HOH RIVER RESORT
Rain Forest (98331)
Rates: $40
Tel: (360) 374-5566

MILL CREEK INN B&B
Hwy 101 S (98331)
Rates: n/a
Tel: (360) 374-5873

MILLER TREE INN B&B
654 E Division St (98331)
Rates: $55-$90
Tel: (360) 374-6806

THREE RIVERS RESORT CABINS
7764 LaPush Rd (98331)
Rates: $35-$45
Tel: (360) 374-5300

TOWN MOTEL
HC 80, Box 350 (98331)
Rates: n/a
Tel: (360) 374-6231

WESTWARD HOH RESORT
Rain Forest (98331)
Rates: $35
Tel: (360) 374-6657

<u>RECREATION</u>

PYSHT TREE FARM - Leashes

Info: If you're as much a tree enthusiast as the hound whose nose is glued to the ground, don't miss this excursion. Situated along the scenic Olympic Peninsula and encompassing the lower 50% of the Pysht watershed, this 26,000-acre tree farm is a unique and beautiful forest. Dedicated to the responsible management of the trees, fish, wildlife and water resources, this stunning locale truly lets you see the forest for the trees. Not only will you come away a little more knowledgeable about tree harvesting and replanting but you'll leave with beauty embedded on your memory banks. For more information: (360) 963-2378; (800) 998-2382.

Directions: From Forks, travel Highway 101 north about 12 miles to Highway 113 and follow about 9 miles to Highway 112. Head east on Highway 112 along the Pysht River to the tree farm on the Olympic Peninsula along the Strait of Juan de Fuca.

Note: Do not harass the wildlife, smoke on the trails or pick, remove or damage any plants. To prevent erosion and mishaps, stay on the designated trails and keep your dog leashed at all times. Fees vary, call first.

The numbered hikes that follow are within the Pysht Tree Farm:

1) FORESTRY TRAIL HIKE - Leashes

Beginner/2.0 miles/1.0 hours

Info: This 8-stop trail charms you with its scenery while it educates you on forest succession. Pick up a pamphlet and begin your tour de tree in this outdoor museum and learn as you sojourn through young plantations to mature stands of Douglas fir and spruce. From seedlings to nurse logs, mountain beavers to bears, glean some knowledge about the stages of succession and the creatures that have adapted to these environs. A pretty pathway leads through pine-scented woodlands that teem with wildlife and the trill of songbirds. Stop #8 signals turnaround time. For more information: (360) 963-2378; (800) 998-2382.

Directions: From Forks, travel Highway 101 north about 12 miles to Highway 113 and follow about 9 miles to Highway 112. Head east on Highway 112 along the Pysht River to the tree farm on the Olympic Peninsula along the Strait of Juan de Fuca. Enter the tree farm at the north gate by the Pysht office. Cross the bridge and follow the Pysht River Rd (2000 Rd) to Spruce Grade Rd (1000 Rd). Drive on the Spruce Grade Road to 1010 Rd. Turn left and drive to the end and the trailhead at the top of the hill. Park in designated areas only.

Note: Do not harass the wildlife, smoke on the trails or pick, remove or damage any plants. To prevent erosion and mishaps, stay on the designated trails and keep your dog leashed at all times. Fees vary, call first.

Hotel Policies May Be Subject To Change

2) REED CREEK TRAIL HIKE - Leashes

Beginner/4.0 miles/2.0 hours

Info: Aqua pup alert, wet tootsies ahead. This wild and waterful trail takes you on a streamside adventure. Pick up a pamphlet before setting out and make your trek even more interesting. Signs of wildlife and evidence of past geology and wind erosion are everywhere. Saltwater and freshwater mix at this point and provide important growing ground for young salmon. This glimpse into the enchanting world of nature and its preservation through thoughtful stream, forest and timber management will imbue you with good feelings. For more information: (360) 963-2378; (800) 998-2382.

Directions: From Forks, travel Highway 101 north about 12 miles to Highway 113 and follow about 9 miles to Highway 112. Head east on Highway 112 along the Pysht River to the tree farm on the Olympic Peninsula along the Strait of Juan de Fuca. The trailhead is located about one mile up the Pysht River Road (2000 Road). Follow signs for Reed Creek.

Note: Do not harass the wildlife, smoke on the trails or pick, remove or damage any plants. To prevent erosion and mishaps, stay on the designated trails and keep your dog leashed at all times. Fees vary, call first.

GIG HARBOR

LODGING

HARBORSIDE B&B
8708 Goodman Dr NW (98332)
Rates: $115
Tel: (253) 851-1795

NO CABBAGES B&B
7712 Goodman Dr NW (98332)
Rates: $55
Tel: (253) 858-7797

WESTWYND MOTEL & SUITES
6703 144 St NW (98332)
Rates: $44-$72
Tel: (253) 857-4047
(800) 468-9963

RECREATION

CITY PARK - Leashes

Info: Be like Old McDonald and check out the docile cows when you visit this 7-acre pastoral scene. If you've packed a chow basket, there are several picnic spots for you and your Spot. For more information: (253) 851-8136.

Locate Other Dog-Friendly Activities...Check Nearby Cities

Directions: From Gig Harbor, travel north on Harborview Drive to a right turn on North Harborview Drive. Make a quick right onto Vernhardson Street to the park at the tipof the Harbor.

GLACIER

LODGING

GLACIER CREEK MOTEL & CABINS
10036 Mt. Baker Hwy (98244)
Rates: $40-$135
Tel: (360) 599-2991

MT. BAKER CHALET RESORT
9857 Mt. Baker Hwy (98244)
Rates: $50-$180
Tel: (360) 599-2405

RECREATION

EXCELSIOR PASS TRAIL HIKE - Leashes

Intermediate/6.0 miles/3.0 hours

Info: This trail, a high alpine lookout of Mount Baker, has all the makings for lasting memories. For the first mile, you and the trailblazer will zigzag through a fragrant fir forest along the Damfino Lake Trail. The lakes are small and surrounded by wild blueberry bushes. If you know edible berries when you see them, you and old purple tongue can stuff your faces. Passing through a lovely meadow, you'll soon reach the breathtaking sights and breathtaking heights (5,000') at Excelsior Pass. Break out the binocs for birds-eye views that will cram your memory banks. For more information: (360) 856-5700.

Directions: From Glacier, travel east on Highway 542 about 2 miles past the Glacier Public Service Center to Canyon Creek Road (FS 31), turn left. Continue another 14 miles to the marked trailhead at the end of Canyon Creek Road.

HELIOTROPE RIDGE TRAIL HIKE - Leashes

Intermediate/6.5 miles/4.0 hours

Info: A popular trail in the Mount Baker area, you're bound to encounter rock climbers and other hikers driven by a shared goal - Mount Baker. Climbing through the open forest, you and the dawgus will reach a meadow. During the spring runoffs, melting snow creates gurgling streams which in turn create

Hotel Policies May Be Subject To Change

pleasing ribbons of blue in the lush greenery. Expect wet tootsies and gleeful abandon at every aqua fria crossing. Splishsplashing fun aside, this trek is known for its great views of Coleman Glacier and Mount Baker. Chill out a spell near the top and watch the daring rock climbers in their quest to conquer Mount Baker. For more information: (360) 856-5700.

Directions: From Glacier, travel east on Highway 542 about 1 mile to Glacier Creek Road (FS 39), turn right. Travel another 8 miles to the end of Glacier Creek Road and the marked trailhead. **Note: In the summer months, the trail may be impassable due to snow runoff.**

LAKE ANN TRAIL HIKE - Leashes

Intermediate/6.0 miles/3.0 hours

Info: Hiking gurus will love you forever after this picturesque journey to Lake Ann. But beauty usually exacts a price. It's two miles down to a meadow at Swift Creek, where some waterside R&R will give you a chance to study the beautiful setting. Continuing onward and upward, you'll gain ground as the trail crosses open boulder fields and traipses over a small saddle to Lake Ann. From the lake, great views of the rugged south face of Mount Shuksan and Lower Curtis Glacier are yours for the gazing. A biscuit break will help with the outbound, mostly uphill haul. For more information: (360) 856-5700.

Directions: From Glacier, travel east on Highway 542 about 4 miles as it winds past the Silver Fir Campground to the Mount Baker Ski Area. The trailhead is located in the parking lot on the left, just before the Artist Point parking lot, near the Heather Meadows Visitor Center.

GLENWOOD

RECREATION

CONBOY LAKE NATIONAL WILDLIFE REFUGE - Leashes

Info: Backdropped by alpine mountain peaks and azure blue skies, this stunning refuge rates the high five in serenery. Walk softly and carry big binocs. Swans, geese and sandhill cranes could be your birding reward. If your woofer's a hoofer, stop by headquarters and pick up a guide. The Willard Springs Interpretive Trail is one way to put a little Rexercise in your day.

Directions: From Glenwood, head west on Glenwood-Trout Lake Road about 4 miles to the refuge road on the left side. The trail is located at refuge headquarters.

GOLDENDALE

LODGING

BARCHRIS MOTEL
128 N Academy (98620)
Rates: n/a
Tel: (509) 773-4325

PONDEROSA MOTEL
775 E Broadway St (98620)
Rates: $36-$70
Tel: (509) 773-5842

RECREATION

BROOKS MEMORIAL STATE PARK - Leashes

Info: Savor a sampling of the goodies that this remarkable setting holds for you and your canine companion. The park is situated in the "yellow pine life biotic zone" and is characterized by dry, warm summer days and cool evenings. This perfect climate creates an ideal habitat for a myriad of flora and fauna. Nearly 3 miles of foot paths interlace the region, making for delightful freelance hiking options. Stands of ponderosa pine, Douglas fir and Oregon oak will get high marks in the treehound's diary. Sniffers in tiptop shape will be rewarded with the fragrance of lady's slippers, balsam root and lupine that splash the forestland in cheery colors from March until July. Wildlife lovers, know this - deer, turkey, raccoon, porcupine, bobcat, coyote, red-tailed hawk and owl all have a stake in the land. If you'd rather spend your morning in the company of beavers, the Klickitat River entices the busy ones to do their thing. Just pull up a plush square and observe some damn fine dam building. For more information: (509) 773-4611.

Directions: From Goldendale, travel Highway 97 north about 13 miles. The park is off Highway 97 just south of Status Pass.

Note: The park is open April 1 - September 30 from 6:30 a.m. to dusk. From October 1 through March 31, the park is open from 8 a.m. to dusk.

HORSETHIEF LAKE STATE PARK - Leashes

Info: For an adventure with a dash of Lewis and Clark, haul your hound to this chunk of Columbia River terrain. With over 7,500' of river frontage and 340 acres of roaming room, you and your Newfy can do your own exploring. The famous expedition crossed this territory and discovered a village of Indians catching and preparing salmon for the winter. Indian petroglyphs add to the historic atmosphere. Afishionados, white sturgeon is just one species you might take home for dinner. For more information: (509) 767-1159.

Directions: From Goldendale, travel Highway 97 south about 10 miles to SR 14, turn right about 12 miles to park.

Note: The park is open April 1 - Sept 30 from 6:30 a.m. to dusk. Open from 8 a.m. to dusk through the end of Oct. Closed from Nov 1 - March 31.

MARYHILL STATE PARK - Leashes

Info: Encompassing 98 acres of parkland bordering the glorious Columbia River, Maryhill offers a quick escape in a lush and pretty milieu. Tote a biscuit basket and set up shop beside the river where the boats provide the visual entertainment. You can always work off the kibble with some freelance exploration of the terra firma. For more information: (509) 773-5007.

Directions: From Goldendale, travel south on Highway 97 about 12 miles to the signed park entrance.

Note: The park is open April 1 - Sept 30 from 6:30 a.m. to dusk. From Oct 1 - March 31, the park is open from 8 a .m. to dusk.

STONEHENGE MEMORIAL - Leashes

Info: History buffs, you can put your passports away and visit this testament to the original Stonehenge in England. The American Stonehenge praises heroism, liberty and peace and lies along 7,000 lush acres beside the Columbia River. For more information: (509) 773-3733.

Directions: From Goldendale, travel Highway 97 south about 10 miles to the junction with Highway 14, turn left (east). Continue east on SR 14 about a half-mile to the memorial located just off SR 14 at the original Maryhill townsite.

GRAND COULEE

LODGING

TRAIL WEST MOTEL
108 Spokane Way (99133)
Rates: $32-$70
Tel: (509) 633-3155

UMBRELLA MOTEL
404 Spokane Way (99133)
Rates: $25-$50
Tel: (509) 633-1691

RECREATION

CROWN POINT VISTA - Leashes

Info: If you have a passion for panoramas, you won't want to miss this hilltop niche where views of the Grand Coulee Dam and surrounding countryside go on forever. Perched 626' above the Columbia River, the furball will definitely be impressed by the roaring waters below and the outstanding structure of the dam. If you have a choice, sunset is primo, the vibrant colors of the disappearing sun are staggering. The viewing platform also rates two paws up for the laser light shows from the dam. For more information on the light show: (800) 268-5332.

Directions: From Grand Coulee, take Highway 174 for 2 miles west (towards Bridgeport) and watch for the signs.

Note: Laser shows are seasonal. Call for show times and dates.

GRAND COULEE CITY PARK - Leashes

Info: Bound with your hound to this tree-shaded park for an afternoon of frolicking fun. The large basalt rock in the middle of the green scene adds an interesting note.

Directions: Located on Highway 174 east.

NORTH DAM PARK - Leashes

Info: This 49-acre park is just the antidote for the summertime blues. Stretching beside the lapping waters of Banks Lake, you and the dawgus will uncover a cornucopia of nature at this pretty riparian venue. Do a loop-de-loop on the nature tail around the wetlands and then make like Huck Finn and try your hand at some lake fishing.

Directions: Located on Highway 155, just .3 miles south of the junction of Highway 155 and State Route 174.

NORTHRUP CANYON AREA - Leashes

Info: The epitome of solitude can be yours at this remote and pristine wilderness. Situated near Steamboat Rock State Park, Northrup Canyon is an undiscovered gem. Nearly 3,000 acres of natural terrain are yours to explore. Once home to some of the earliest settlers in Grand Coulee, a few buildings from the 1890s remain, along with an old stagecoach road that hugs the canyon's southern side. But Mother Nature has reclaimed the land and populated it with deer, coyote, porcupine, cougar, bobcat and a slew of birds. Hop on any of the trails that honeycomb this wild landscape and fill your day with adventure. For more information: (509) 633-1304.

Directions: From Grand Coulee, travel Highway 155 south about 12 miles to the signed entrance on the west side of Highway 155. Access to the Northrup Canyon Area is across from the Steamboat River rest area and boat lodge.

The numbered hike that follows is within the Northrup Canyon Area:

1) NORTHRUP CANYON TRAIL HIKE - Leashes

Expert/4.0 miles/2.5 hours

Info: Only Herculean hounds and hikers should tackle this toughie. But if you've got the stamina, you'll get the payback. Finding the trailhead is a little tricky but with the sniffmeister's help, you'll soon be on your way. Beginning in a sheltered canyon, you'll trek through the only forest in Grand County. The woodlands are dense with a lush understory, flowers popping up here and there and brightening the serenery. The view at the top of the gorge will stay with you long after you've gone on your merry way. The lovely waters of Northrup Lake peek through the forest green to create a sight of postcardian delight. It'll be hard for you and the King of the Canyon to relinquish this space. So stay a while and enjoy. When day is done, do the descent thing. For more information: (509) 633-1304.

Directions: From Grand Coulee, travel Highway 155 south about 12 miles to the signed entrance to the park on the west side of Highway 155. Access to the Northrup Canyon Area is across from the Steamboat River rest area and boat lodge. The marked trailhead begins in the sheltered canyon and extends through the forest to Northrup Lake.

Note: Before hiking, check with the ranger for trail conditions.

STEAMBOAT ROCK STATE PARK - Leashes

Info: Escapism reigns supreme at this idyllic locale of 3,500 acres situated on Banks Lake. Fishy tales can come true and it can happen to you in the form of crappie, perch, trout, bass and catfish. If your woofer's a hoofer, stop puppyfooting around and hit the trails. Visit in spring and earn the bonus of vibrant wildflowers. For more information: (509) 633-1304.

Directions: From Grand Coulee, travel Highway 155 south about 12 miles to the signed entrance to the park on the west side of Highway 155.

The numbered hike that follows is within Steamboat Rock State Park:

1) STEAMBOAT ROCK TRAIL HIKE - Leashes

Intermediate/4.0 miles/2.0 hours

Info: The park that houses this trail is at the bottom of a 700' deep canyon so be prepared to scramble over loose rocks and ascend several steep grades on your journey. But know this, you're almost guaranteed solitude as you boogie with Bowser through the bosky terrain and huge salt rock formations that beautify this trail. From the top, you'll have sweeping views of Banks Lake and the city of Grand Coulee. The wildflowers that polka-dot the landscape are a nice contrast to the blueness of the lake. Way to go Fido. For more information: (509) 633-1304.

Directions: From Grand Coulee, travel Highway 155 south about 12 miles to the signed entrance to the park on the west side of Highway 155. The trailhead is located across from the day use area and is marked with a hiker logo.

GRANDVIEW

LODGING

GRANDVIEW MOTEL
522 E Wine Country Rd (98930)
Rates: $26-$39
Tel: (509) 882-1323

RECREATION

GRANDVIEW HISTORIC WALKING TOUR - Leashes

Beginner/1.5 miles/1.0 hours

Info: Combine your AM constitutional with a learning experience. Many of the buildings on this tour are listed in the Washington State Register of Historic Places. Begin at the Grandview Herald Building, virtually untouched since its construction in 1911. A couple turns away is the Dykstra House, a prairie-style structure built in 1923, currently home to a restaurant and a gift shop. And don't miss the Grandview Rose Garden. Let Rosebud enjoy a mini-sniff fest on the gravel walking paths that crisscross raised beds filled with over a thousand rose bushes. For more information: (509) 882-2100.

Directions: The tour begins on Wine Country Rd & Division Street.

GRANGER

RECREATION

HISEY PARK - Leashes

Info: Wowser Bowser. This stunning urban oasis has the makings of a playful interlude. Lollygag about the lush, grassy areas and have a look-see at the ducks that cruise the ponds or chill-out down by the Yakima River that runs through the park. Your own little Dino will definitely want to check out the fifteen T-Rex replicas. For more information: (509) 854-1725.

Directions: Located at Main Street and Highway 223.

GRANITE FALLS

LODGING

MOUNTAIN VIEW INN MOTEL
32005 Mt. Loop Hwy (98252)
Rates: $35-$60
Tel: (360) 691-6668

GRAYLAND

LODGING

GRAYLAND MOTEL & COTTAGES
2013 SR 105 S (98547)
Rates: n/a
Tel: (360) 267-2395
(800) 292-0845

OCEAN GATE RESORT
1939 SR 105 S (98547)
Rates: n/a
Tel: (360) 267-1956
(800) 473-1956

OCEAN SPRAY MOTEL
1757 SR 105 S (98547)
Rates: $45-$70
Tel: (360) 267-2205

SURF MOTEL & COTTAGES
2029 SR 105 S (98547)
Rates: $56-$67
Tel: (360) 267-2244

WALSH MOTEL
1593 SR 105 S (98547)
Rates: $40+
Tel: (360) 267-2191

RECREATION

WASHINGTON STATE BEACHES

Info: One of the few coastal regions where you can drive on the beach, there are three remarkable stretches awaiting your exploration. Obey the rules which are posted at access points. In particular, use caution near pedestrians and stay well away from the clam beds near the waterline.

Directions: Heading from north to south, the following are the locations of the drive-on Washington beaches:

1) Moclips to Ocean Shores along Highways 109 and 115
2) Westport to North Cove along Highway 105
3) Oysterville to Ilwaco along Highway 103

For additional lodging and recreation in the beach areas, see listings under the following cities: Copalis Beach, Ilwaco, Long Beach Peninsula, Moclips, Ocean Park, Ocean Shores, Oysterville, Pacific Beach, Westport.

GREEN ACRES

LODGING

ALPINE MOTEL
18815 E Cataldo (99016)
Rates: $33-$66
Tel: (509) 928-2700

GREENWATER

LODGING

ALTA CRYSTAL RESORT/MT. RAINIER
68317 SR 410 E (98022)
Rates: $69-$159
Tel: (360) 663-2500
(800) 277-6475

THE INN AT THE RANCH CABIN
16423 Mountainside Dr (98022)
Rates: $75-$150
Tel: (360) 663-2667

HANSVILLE

LODGING

GUEST HOUSE AT TWIN SPITS B&B
2570 NE Twin Spits Rd (98340)
Rates: $60-$75
Tel: (360) 638-1001

HOME VALLEY

LODGING

HOME VALLEY B&B
P.O. Box 377 (98648)
Rates: n/a
Tel: (509) 427-7070

HOODSPORT

LODGING

CANAL CREEK MOTEL
N 27131 Hwy 101 (98548)
Rates: $38-$52
Tel: (360) 877-6770

SUNRISE MOTEL & RESORT
N 24520 Hwy 101 (98548)
Rates: n/a
Tel: (360) 877-5301

Locate Other Dog-Friendly Activities...Check Nearby Cities

RECREATION

BIG CREEK CAMPGROUND LOOP TRAIL HIKE

Beginner/1.1 miles/0.5 hours

Info: Wet tootsies often come with the territory on this fun trail where a river runs through it. Tote your binoculars, determined birders might add a sighting or two to their book. A brown bagger with the wagger under a towering maple could end your outing on a cool note. For more information: (360) 877-5254.

Directions: From Hoodsport, take State Route 119 west for 9 miles to FS 24 and turn left. Drive 100' to Big Creek Campground and park at the trailhead located 200' inside the gate off the main campground road.

Note: Do not park at a campsite.

DUCKABUSH TRAIL to DUCKABUSH RIVER HIKE - Leashes

Intermediate/4.8 miles/3.0 hours

Info: Huck Finn types will definitely like the old-fashioned feeling of this trail where hiking and fishing are a natural duo. This scenic trail beckons you to do lunch creekside while you enjoy the beauty of your surroundings. For more information: (360) 877-5254.

Directions: From Hoodsport, take Highway 101 north for 22 miles to FS 2510 and head west, following signs for the Duckabush Recreation Area. Continue 6 miles to FS 2510-060 and the trailhead.

ELK LAKE TRAIL HIKE

Beginner/2.4 miles/1.5 hours

Info: A barkworthy journey, start your day off on the right paw and make tracks to this bonafido beauty. When the trail forks, take a right and zap, you'll be in a lush woodland of fir, hemlock and madrona. Birdsong will drift your way from the treetops and combine with the rippling sounds of Jefferson Creek to create music for your ears and the floppy ones too. When you reach the road, it's time for a 180°. For more information: (360) 877-5254.

Hotel Policies May Be Subject To Change

Directions: From Hoodsport, head north on Highway 101 for 10 miles to Jorsted Creek Road (FS 24). Turn west and drive 1.25 miles to FS 2480 and veer right. Drive 5.5 miles to FS 2401 and head left for 2.5 miles to a short spur road. The trailhead is at the end of the spur road.

JEFFERSON PASS TRAIL HIKE

Intermediate/2.2 miles/1.5 hours

Info: Well maintained and easy to follow, it won't be long until you and the barkmeister arrive at a saddle where you can sit a spell, enjoy the views and watch the rock climbers scrambling up Mount Washington (aptly named for its resemblance to George Washington's profile). When day is done, repeat the beat on your retreat. For more information: (360) 877-5254.

Directions: From Hoodsport, take State Route 119 west for 9 miles to FS 24 and turn right. Drive 1.6 miles to FS 2419 (Big Creek Road) and follow FS 2419 for 7 miles to the trailhead.

Note: Do not attempt to climb the mountainside without proper training and equipment. The slope is very steep and very dangerous.

LAKE CUSHMAN STATE PARK - Leashes

Info: Tote a boat and do the float with the dawgus on the pristine waters of Lake Cushman. If terra firma's more your speed, pack a snack, find a cozy nook and break some bread and biscuits with Bowser. There's an 8-mile trail system for hiking hounds and plenty of laid-back niches where you can let sleeping dogs lie. For more information: (360) 877-5491.

Directions: From Hoodsport, travel west on Highway 119 for 3.5 miles to Lake Cushman Road, turn right (north). Proceed about 2 miles to the signed park entrance.

LENA LAKE TRAIL to CAMPGROUND HIKE - Leashes

Beginner/6.4 miles/4.0 hours

Info: A popular trail, you might just run into a pooch and people parade on your journey. Afishionados, tote your pole. The fishing's good at Lena Lake especially during the summer months. Like a walk in the park, you'll be ensconced in a natural setting filled with tweet music all along the route. At the end of the pathway, do an about-face and consider yourself a lucky dog for such a pleasant interlude. For more information: (360) 877-5254.

Directions: From Hoodsport, take Highway 101 north for 14 miles to FS 25 and turn west. Drive 8 miles to the trailhead.

HOQUIAM

LODGING

SNORE & WHISKER MOTEL
3031 Simpson Ave (98550)
Rates: $35-$65
Tel: (360) 532-5060

TIMBERLINE INN
415 Perry Ave (98550)
Rates: $35-$75
Tel: (360) 533-8048

WESTWOOD INN
910 Simpson Ave (98550)
Rates: $42-$85
Tel: (360) 532-8161
(800) 562-0994

ILWACO

LODGING

A-CO-HO MOTEL & CHARTERS
Port of Ilwaco,
P.O. Box 268 (98624)
Rates: n/a
Tel: (360) 642-3333

COL-PACIFIC MOTEL
P.O. Box 34 (98624)
Rates: n/a
Tel: (360) 642-3177

HEIDI'S INN MOTEL
126 Spruce St (98624)
Rates: $30-$70
Tel: (360) 642-2387
(800) 576-1032

RECREATION

FORT CANBY STATE PARK - Leashes

Info: Located where the river meets the ocean, Fort Canby's 2,000 acres beckon you and Bowser to browser à la Lewis & Clark. History buffs can get a semester's worth by picking up an informative pamphlet. Two historic lighthouses and miles of trails are part of the allure. The fishing's not bad either. Lucky dogs could go home with lunch. For more information: (360) 642-3078.

Directions: Located 2 miles southwest of Ilwaco off Highway 101.

Hotel Policies May Be Subject To Change

The numbered hike and beaches that follow are within Fort Canby State Park.

1) BENSON BEACH - Leashes

Info: A beach bum bonanza, you and the digmeister can venture over 1.5 miles of sandy coastline while you enjoy views of two lighthouses.

Directions: Located 2 miles southwest of Ilwaco off Highway 101.

2) CAPE DISAPPOINTMENT LIGHTHOUSE TRAIL HIKE - Leashes

Beginner/0.5 miles/0.5 hours

Info: This simple hike packs a wallop. A concrete walkway amidst greenery leads to a picturesque lighthouse. Built in 1856, this was Washington's first lighthouse. Along the way, you and your Friday Fido will have views of a charming driftwood-filled cove, something straight out of Treasure Island. There's a grassy area and a viewing bench at the top where you can take a few moments and ponder the past. If you're there at dusk, expect a spectacular sunset.

Directions: Located 2 miles southwest of Ilwaco off Highway 101.

3) WAIKIKI BEACH - Leashes

Info: A wag worthy excursion can be yours at this picturesque cove near the North Jetty. Pack a picnic repast and do lunch while you watch the waves lapping at the coastline.

Directions: Located 2 miles southwest of Ilwaco off Highway 101.

WASHINGTON STATE BEACHES

Info: For additional lodging and recreation for the beach areas, see listings under the following cities: Copalis Beach, Grayland, Long Beach Peninsula, Moclips, Ocean Park, Ocean Shores, Oysterville, Pacific Beach, Westport.

Note: Certain sections are closed to vehicular traffic from April 15th through the day after Labor Day. Areas that are open year round include a 13.5-mile stretch from Bolstad Avenue in Long Beach north to Oysterville Gap Road and a 2.2 miler just south of Beard's Hollow to Seaview Gap Road.

Locate Other Dog-Friendly Activities...Check Nearby Cities

INCHELIUM

LODGING

HARTMAN'S LOG CABIN RESORT
5744 S Twin Lakes Access Rd (99138)
Rates: $36-$50
Tel: (509) 722-3543

RAINBOW BEACH RESORT
HC1, Box 146, Twin lakes Rd (99138)
Rates: n/a
Tel: (509) 722-5901

INDEX

LODGING

BUSH HOUSE COUNTRY INN
300 5th St (98256)
Rates: $50-$80
Tel: (360) 793-2312

THE CABIN AT INDEX B&B
52525 Riverside Rd (98256)
Rates: $80-$95
Tel: (360) 827-2102

IONE

LODGING

PEND OREILLE INN
107 Riverside (99139)
Rates: n/a
Tel: (509) 442-3418

PLAZA MOTEL
103 S 2nd Ave (99139)
Rates: $30-$40
Tel: (509) 442-3534

ISSAQUAH

LODGING

MOTEL 6
1885 15th Pl NW (98027)
Rates $30-$45
Tel: (425) 392-8405
(800) 440-6000

MOUNTAINS & PLAINS B&B
100 Big Bear Place NW (98027)
Rates: $38-$80
Tel: (800) 231-8068

RECREATION

LAKE SAMMAMISH STATE PARK - Leashes

Info: Birdwatchers will stop in their tracks at this diverse wetland region. A birder's bonus is the large blue heron rookery with its outstanding viewing ops. Explorationists have more than 500 acres to satisfy their curiosity. Sign up for some laid back R&R lakeside and break some bread and biscuits with your Curious George. The shimmering blue of Lake Sammamish is particularly beautiful at sunset. If fishing's your passion, tote a pole and make your fishy dreams come true. FYI: Sammamish is derived from "Samena," the Native American word meaning hunter. This area was a gathering place for several tribes. For more information: (206) 455-7010.

Directions: From Issaquah, travel 1.5 miles northwest on Interstate 90 to the signed park entrance.

Note: Dogs are prohibited on the beach.

SQUAK MOUNTAIN STATE PARK - Leashes

Info: Lace up your hiking boots, leash the pup and head out to this hiker's delight where the best of Mother Nature creates an ideal setting for hiking hounds. More than 20 miles of trails crisscross the 1,300 acres surrounding Squak Mountain. The lush land is home to many forms of wildlife. Pack plenty of H_2O, you and the woofer are going to clock the miles and burn the kibble. For more information: (425) 455-7010.

Directions: From Issaquah, travel south on Issaquah-Hobart Road for 3 miles to May Valley Road. Turn right and drive 2 miles to the parking lot and main trailhead.

KALALOCH

LODGING

KALALOCH LODGE
57151 Hwy 101 (98331)
Rates: $55-$200
Tel: (360) 962-2271

RECREATION

RUBY BEACH

Info: When you and your beach bum are in the mood for a wild and rocky shore experience, you can walk to the beach along a short trail near the mouth of the Hoe River and see what nature in these parts is all about.

Directions: About 5 miles north of Kalaloch on Highway 101.

Locate Other Dog-Friendly Activities...Check Nearby Cities

BEACH TRAIL #4

Beginner/0.25 miles/0.25 hours

Info: Practically from the moment you and the pupster set foot out of your vehicle, you'll hear the thundering surf. A stop at this beach equates to experiencing the Pacific in its natural and pristine state, untamed and glorious. A dirt path edged with tall grasses leads to set-in logs. As you skedaddle along, the sounds of rushing creeks will fill your ears with sweet music. You'll cross a small wooden bridge before reaching the rocky, driftwood-strewn beach, a black sand affair that looks as if it was formed by pulverized black stones. Huge logs (trees that once clung tenaciously to the cliffsides until losing their battle with the sea) have now been returned to land, spit out by the ocean that claimed them. Stripped white and made shiny by the power of the Pacific, they are strewn helter skelter on the shore, perfect benches for pensive humans and canines alike.

The digmeister can search for half buried objects. Iron fittings from shipwrecks, driftwood and fishing floats are often deposited by winter storms. Do some tide pooling at low tide. You might see anemones, ocher stars or sea cucumbers. But don't touch. Removing or even moving one creature can upset the balance of the pools. Scan the skies too for screeching seagulls. Look for the black oystercatcher as the bird awaits his low tide dinner, its long red bill compromising its camouflage. FYI: The holes in the rocks at the bottom of the pathway were drilled by piddock clams who use a rocking motion to burrow into the sandstone.

From the parking lot, there's also a peanut-sized stroll to an overlook where you can admire the majesty of this setting without any effort. Grab some R&R on the bench while you let sleepy dogs lie.

Directions: About 5 miles north of Kalaloch on Highway 101.

Note: Beginning at Ruby Beach and driving south on Highway 1, you'll have your pick of six beach access trails. The northernmost beaches provide the best views of the sea stacks. Depending on the tide, there are vast stretches of coastline to explore. Heed the warnings about the dangers of the Pacific. Drift logs are dangerous. At high tide, they may suddenly roll in. Riptides make swimming and even wading dangerous. Never turn your back on the Pacific.

KALAMA

LODGING

COLUMBIA INN MOTEL
602 NE Frontage Rd (98625)
Rates: $30-$39
Tel: (360) 673-2855

RECREATION

KALAMA RIVER - Leashes

Info: For a day of Huck Finn reel-time pleasures, head down by the riverside. If you're toting an inflatable raft or a tippy canoe, this is the place for you. Or slip on your waders and have a go at the steelhead. Your wet wagging sidekick will be sporting an ear-to-ear grin no matter where the day leads.

Directions: From Kalama, take the Kalama River Road exit off I-5 and head east along Kalama River Road. There are turnouts all along the route that lead to the river, as well as narrow paths that lead into the hills.

KELSO

LODGING

BEST WESTERN ALADDIN MOTOR INN
310 Long Ave (98626)
Rates: $45-$75
Tel: (360) 425-9660
(800) 528-1234

BUDGET INN
505 N Pacific Ave (98626)
Rates: $33-$53
Tel: (360) 636-4610

MOTEL 6
106 Minor Rd (98626)
Rates: $30-$45
Tel: (360) 425-3229
(800) 440-6000

RED LION INN
510 Kelso Dr (98626)
Rates: $69-$105
Tel: (360) 636-4400
(800) 547-8010

SUPER 8 MOTEL
250 Kelso Dr (98626)
Rates: $46-$64
Tel: (360) 423-8880
(800) 800-8000

KENNEWICK

LODGING

CASABLANCA B&B
94806 E Granada Ct (99337)
Rates: $85-$115
Tel: (888) 627-0676

CAVANAUGH'S COLUMBIA CENTER
1101 N Columbia Center Blvd (99336)
Rates: $62-$280
Tel: (509) 783-0611
(800) 843-4667

CLEARWATER INN
5616 W Clearwater Ave (99336)
Rates: $50-$65
Tel: (509) 735-2242
(800) 424-1145

COMFORT INN
7801 W Quinault Ave (99336)
Rates: $45-$85
Tel: (509) 783-8396
(800) 221-2222

GREEN GABLE MOTEL
515 W Columbia Dr (99336)
Rates: n/a
Tel: (509) 582-5811

HOLIDAY INN EXPRESS
4220 W 27th Pl (99337)
Rates: $49-$75
Tel: (509) 736-3326
(800) 465-4329

NENDEL'S INN
2811 W 2nd St (99336)
Rates: $25-$74
Tel: (509) 735-9511
(800) 547-0106

RAMADA INN CLOVER ISLAND
435 Clover Island (99336)
Rates: $56-$93
Tel: (509) 586-0541
(800) 272-6232

SHANIKO SUITES MOTEL
321 N Johnson St (99336)
Rates: $48-$54
Tel: (509) 735-6385

SILVER CLOUD INN
7901 W Quinault Ave (99336)
Rates: $56-$93
Tel: (509) 735-6100
(800) 205-6938

SUPER 8 MOTEL
626 N Columbia Center Blvd (99336)
Rates: $44-$64
Tel: (509) 736-6888
(800) 800-8000

TAPADERA INN
300A N Ely St (99336)
Rates: $38-$60
Tel: (509) 783-6191
(800) 722-8277

RECREATION

COLUMBIA PARK - Leashes

Info: When playtime calls, answer it with a visit to this woodsy terrain of 367 acres. Quietude and serenity come with the territory in this picturesque setting where birdsong is often the only sound you'll hear.

Directions: Located at 5111 Columbia Drive SE.

Note: Closed in winter.

Hotel Policies May Be Subject To Change

EASTGATE PARK - Leashes

Info: A bonafido walk in the park is what you'll get when you stop by this green scene. Stow a brown bagger to share with the wagger and round out the experience.

Directions: Located at 1110 East 10th Avenue.

Note: Closed in winter.

KEEWAYDIN PARK - Leashes

Info: Go ahead, make your dog's day with an interlude of play at this 9-acre parkland.

Directions: Located at 204 Keewaydin Drive.

Note: Closed in winter.

KENNEWICK ARBORETUM - Leashes

Info: Five acres of greenery and serenery beckon your exploration of this petite park that packs a floral punch.

Directions: Located at 505 Oak Street.

LAWRENCE SCOTT PARK - Leashes

Info: A sure cure for the summertime blahs, you and the furball can frolic and play in this park's 26 acres. Dotted with trees and splashed with vibrant wildflowers, the air is heaven scent in this divine little spot.

Directions: Located at 6060 West Quinault.

Note: Closed in winter.

SUNSET PARK - Leashes

Info: As tranquil as it sounds, Sunset Park is a soothing respite of greenery. You and furface can practice being lazybones as long as you want.

Directions: Located at 733 Center Parkway.

Note: Closed in winter.

OTHER PARKS IN KENNEWICK - Leashes

- FRUITLAND PARK, 303 North Fruitland
- HATFIELD PARK, 1237 West Canal Drive
- HAWTHORNE PARK, 609 North Ely Place
- JAY PERRY PARK, 1201 South Newport
- JOHN DAY PARK, 3900 West John Day
- KENWOOD PARK, 2013 South Garfield
- LAYTON PARK, 324 East 6th Avenue
- MONOPOLY PARK, 825 South Date
- PENN PARK, 1301 South Penn
- UNDERWOOD PARK, 2020 West 7th Avenue
- VANCOUVER PARK, 2025 West 7th Avenue
- YELM PARK, 324 North Yelm

KENT

LODGING

BEST WESTERN PONY SOLDIER INN
1233 N Central (98032)
Rates: $71-$88
Tel: (425) 852-7224
(800) 528-1234

CYPRESS INN
22218 84th Ave S (98032)
Rates: $67-$89
Tel: (425) 395-0219
(800) 752-9991

DAYS INN SOUTH
1711 W Meeker St (98032)
Rates: $45-$85
Tel: (425) 854-1950
(800) 329-7466

GOLDEN KENT MOTEL
22203 84th Ave S (98032)
Rates: $40-$55
Tel: (425) 872-8372

ROYAL SKIES APARTMENTS
25907 27th Pl S (98032)
Rates: n/a
Tel: (425) 941-7788

VAL-U-INN
22420 84th Ave S (98032)
Rates $48-$66
Tel: (425) 872-5525
(800) 443-7777

KETTLE FALLS

LODGING

BARNEY'S CAFE & MOTEL
395 & 20 Jct (99141)
Rates: n/a
Tel: (509) 738-6546

BULL HILL RANCH & RESORT
3738 Bull Hill Rd (99141)
Rates: $85-$140
Tel: (509) 732-4355

Hotel Policies May Be Subject To Change

GRANDVIEW INN MOTEL & RV PARK
978 Hwy 395 N (99141)
Rates: n/a
Tel: (509) 738-6733

KETTLE FALLS INN
205 E 3rd St, Hwy 395 (99141)
Rates: $36-$63
Tel: (509) 738-6514
(800) 701-1927

RECREATION

COLUMBIA MOUNTAIN TRAIL HIKE

Intermediate/4.4 miles/3.0 hours

Info: Hop onto Kettle Crest Trail (#13) for two miles to the spur trail (#24) on the right. You and the barkmeister are in for a wagworthy slice of gorgeous scenery. Play follow the leader on your gentle ascent to a cool woodsy summit and incredible views. Try to capture the beauty on film and take home some glossy memories. For more information: (509) 775-3305.

Directions: From Kettle Falls, take Highway 20 approximately 25 miles to Sherman Pass and head north on the short spur road. Continue to the trailhead parking area.

KINGSTON

LODGING

KINGSTON HOUSE B&B
26117 Ohio Ave NE (98346)
Rates: $85-$180
Tel: (360) 297-8818

SMILEY'S COLONIAL MOTEL
11067 Hwy 104 (98346)
Rates: $30-$59
Tel: (360) 297-3622

KIRKLAND

LODGING

BEST WESTERN KIRKLAND INN
12223 116th NE (98034)
Rates: $60-$84
Tel: (425) 822-2300
(800) 332-4200

MOTEL 6
12010 120th Place NE (98034)
Rates: $30-$45
Tel: (425) 821-5618
(800) 440-6000

LA QUINTA INN
10530 NE Northup Way (98033)
Rates: $79-$145
Tel: (425) 828-6585
(800) 531-5900

Locate Other Dog-Friendly Activities...Check Nearby Cities

KITSAP

<u>RECREATION</u>

SOUTH KITSAP COMMUNITY PARK - Leashes

Info: When you've got a yen for some spectator sports, go ahead and root for the home team at this 200-acre green scene. If it's off season, tote a fuzzy tennie and teach the ballmeister a trick or two about playing ball. Hiking gurus can clock some miles on one of the trails. For outdoor pursuits, this locale is a definite paw pleaser.

Directions: Located at the intersection of Jackson and Lund Roads.

LA CONNER

<u>LODGING</u>

ART'S PLACE B&B
511 Talbott St (98257)
Rates: $60
Tel: (360) 466-3033

LA CONNER COUNTRY INN
107 S 2nd St (98257)
Rates: $89-$142
Tel: (360) 466-3101

HERON/LA CONNER B&B
117 Maple Ave (98257)
Rates: $75-$160
Tel: (360) 466-4626

<u>RECREATION</u>

PIONEER PARK - Leashes

Info: Two acres of hillside terrain await you and the dawgus in this pretty little park. Wiggle with your wagger along one of the walkways leading to the channel below. For more information: (360) 466-3125.

Directions: Upon entering La Conner city limits at Maple and Morris Streets, turn left on Maple and continue about .75 miles to the park on left side of road.

LACEY

LODGING

DAYS INN STATE CAPITAL
120 College St SE (98503)
Rates: $52-$66
Tel: (360) 493-1991
(800) 329-7466

SUPER 8 MOTEL
4615 Martin Way (98503)
Rates: $49-$65
Tel: (360) 459-8888
(800) 800-8000

LAKE CRESCENT

LODGING

HISTORIC LAKE CRESCENT LODGE RESORT
416 Lake Crescent Rd (Port Angeles 98362)
Rates: $64-$114
Tel: (360) 928-3211

LAKE BAY

LODGING

RANSOM'S POND OSTRICH FARM B&B
3915 Mahnke Rd KPS (98351)
Rates: $75-$95
Tel: (206) 884-5666

LAKEWOOD

LODGING

**BEST WESTERN
LAKEWOOD MOTOR INN**
6125 Motor Ave SW (98499)
Rates: $58-$79
Tel: (253) 2212
(800) 528-1234

MADIGAN MOTEL
12039 Pacific Hwy SW (98499)
Rates: $30-$60
Tel: (253) 588-8697

NIGHTS INN
9325 S Tacoma Way (98499)
Rates: $32-$44
Tel: (253) 582-7550

Locate Other Dog-Friendly Activities...Check Nearby Cities

LANGLEY

LODGING & RECREATION

See Whidbey Island for lodging and recreation.

LEAVENWORTH

LODGING

ALPINE CHALETS
3601 Allen Ln (98826)
Rates: $82-$125
Tel: (509) 548-5674
(800) 548-5011

BAYERN ON THE RIVER
1505 Alpensee Strasse (98826)
Rates: $50-$79
Tel: (509) 548-5875
(800) 873-3960

BEDFINDERS
305 8th St (98826)
Rates: $95-$195
Tel: (509) 548-4410
(800) 323-2920

BINDLESTIFFS RIVERSIDE CABINS
1600 Hwy 2 (98826)
Rates: $55-$65
Tel: (509) 548-5015

BOSCH GARTEN B&B
9846 Dye Rd (98826)
Rates: $75-$90
Tel: (509) 548-6900

BUDGET HOST CANYONS INN
185 Hwy 2 (98826)
Rates: $61-$120
Tel: (509) 548-7992
(800) 693-1225

DER RITTERHOF MOTOR INN
190 Hwy 2, Box 307 (98826)
Rates: $70-$170
Tel: (509) 548-5845
(800) 255-5845

ENZIAN MOTOR INN
590 Hwy 2 (98826)
Rates: $90
Tel: (509) 548-5269
(800) 223-8511

EVERGREEN INN
1117 Front St (98826)
Rates: $60-$125
Tel: (509) 548-5515
(800) 327-7212

LAKE WENATCHEE HIDE-A-WAYS
9762 North Rd (98826)
Rates: $95-$135
Tel: (509) 548-9074
(800) 883-2611

NATAPOC LODGING
12338 Bretz Rd (98826)
Rates: $140+
Tel: (509) 763-3313
(888) 628-2762

OBERTAL MOTOR INN
922 Commercial St (98826)
Rates: $61-$99
Tel: (509) 548-5208
(800) 537-9382

PHIPPEN'S B&B
10285 Ski Hill Dr (98826)
Rates: $70-$90
Tel: (800) 666-9806

RIVER'S EDGE LODGE
8401 Hwy 2 (98826)
Rates: $45-$75
Tel: (509) 548-7612
(800) 451-5285

SAIMON'S HIDE-A-WAYS
16408 River Rd (98826)
Rates: $95-$145
Tel: (509) 763-3213
(800) 845-8638

SQUIRREL TREE INN
15251 Hwy 2 (98826)
Rates: $50
Tel: (509) 763-3157

TYROLEAN RITZ HOTEL
633 Front St (98826)
Rates: $65-$125
Tel: (509) 548-5455
(800) 854-6365

Hotel Policies May Be Subject To Change

RECREATION

BYGONE BYWAYS INTERPRETIVE TRAIL HIKE - Leashes

Beginner/1.0 miles/0.75 hours

Info: Following the original route of the Great Northern Railway, this trail equates to a pleasurable jaunt through scenic surroundings. Waterfalls along Nason Creek highlight your journey, so pack your Kodak. For more information: (509) 782-1413.

Directions: From Leavenworth, travel Highway 2 west 40 miles to the trailhead.

DECEPTION FALLS INTERPRETIVE TRAIL HIKE - Leashes

Beginner/0.5 miles/0.5 hours

Info: Under the highway and through the woods you'll go to a platform with incredible views. Like butterflies and flowers, waterfalls are one of nature's wonders. When you and the wide-eyed one have had your fill, play follow the leader through the canopied old-growth forest and savor the charming environs. For more information: (509) 782-1413.

Directions: From Leavenworth, travel Highway 2 west 30 miles to the trailhead.

ICICLE CREEK INTERPRETIVE TRAIL HIKE - Leashes

Beginner/1.0 miles/0.75 hours

Info: This paw-pleasing interpretive loop offers insight into the history, environment and wildlife of the Leavenworth Fish Hatchery and Icicle Creek. Pick up a pamphlet at the Hatchery and get going, a fun walk awaits you and poochface. For more information: (509) 782-1413.

Directions: From Leavenworth, travel Highway 2 west to Icicle Road (FS 7600). Turn right and follow Icicle Road 2 miles to the Fish Hatchery and the trailhead.

ICICLE CREEK TRAIL HIKE - Leashes

Beginner/3.0 miles/1.5 hours

Info: A little bit of this and a little bit of that is what you and your inquisitive canine will uncover on this delightful pathway. Wiggle with the wagger through an old-growth forest along a flat valley bottom where shaded coolness is part of the package. If the sniffmeister has a thing for wildflowers, you'll both get an eyeful in spring. The junction with babbling French Creek signals tootsie dipping playtime and your about-face mark. For more information: (509) 782-1413.

Directions: From Leavenworth, travel Highway 2 west to Icicle Road (FS 7600) and follow to the end and the trailhead.

ICICLE GORGE TRAIL HIKE - Leashes

Beginner/3.5 miles/2.0 hours

Info: This loop-de-loop packs a powerful scenic punch particularly in spring when the wild ones show their prettiest colors. You'll walk down by the riverside where the soothing sounds of rushing water will accompany you on your odyssey. Views of Icicle River dappled with brilliant sunshine and tweet tweet music will enhance your journey. Plan ahead, there are dozens of cozy niches just begging for some picnic doings. For more information: (509) 782-1413.

Directions: From Leavenworth, travel Highway 2 west to Icicle Road (FS 7600). Turn right and follow Icicle Road for approximately 15 miles to the turnout and parking on the right side. The trailhead is located just before the Chatter Creek Guard Station.

IRON GOAT TRAIL HIKE - Leashes

Beginner/4.0 miles/2.0 hours

Info: History buffs can combine learning with nature yearning on this picturesque trail. After the first paved half-mile you'll zoom off into a woodsy setting. Follow the wildflower-sprinkled upper grade of the Great Northern Railroad for 1.5 miles to the turnaround point and repeat the beat on your retreat. For more information: (509) 782-1413.

Hotel Policies May Be Subject To Change

Directions: From Leavenworth, travel Highway 2 west to Martin Creek Road and follow for 3 miles to the trailhead.

MERRITT LAKE TRAIL HIKE - Leashes

Intermediate/7.5 miles/4.0 hours

Info: Like many alpine lakes, Merritt Lake often holds snow until July, making it a chill-out charmer on a dogday afternoon. A moderate grade most of the way, the climb to the lake is fairly steep, but worth the effort. Treat the dawgus to some splish-splashing shenanigans before doing a 180°. For more information: (509) 782-1413.

Directions: From Leavenworth, travel Highway 2 west about 28 miles to the Merritt Lake Spur Road on the right. Follow this spur road for 1.5 miles to the trailhead.

OLD PIPELINE TRAIL HIKE - Leashes

Beginner/3.0 miles/1.5 hours

Info: You and your go-go Fido will be treated to excellent views of the Wenatchee River and several soft, sandy beaches. The bridge deck at the beginning of the trek is actually the bottom half of the pipeline that supplied water to the turbines that powered trains through the old Cascade Tunnel. The massive rock fall signals trail's end, time to turn the snout about and head on out. For more information: (509) 782-1413.

Directions: From Leavenworth, head west on Highway 2 and travel 1.7 miles to the public fishing/picnicking area. The trail is located across the bridge.

LILLIWAUP

<u>LODGING</u>

MIKE'S BEACH RESORT
N 38470 Hwy 101 (98555)
Rates: $45-$95
Tel: (360) 877-5324
(800) 231-5324

LONG BEACH PENINSULA

LODGING

ANCHORAGE MOTOR COURT
2209 N Blvd (98631)
Rates: $60-$106
Tel: (360) 642-2351
(800) 646-2351

ARCADIA COURT MOTEL
401 N Ocean Beach Blvd (98631)
Rates: $41-$85
Tel: (360) 642-2613

BOULEVARD MOTEL
301 N Blvd (98631)
Rates: $35-$75
Tel: (360) 642-2434

BREAKERS MOTEL
P.O. Box 428 (98631)
Rates: $54-$160
Tel: (800) 288-8890

CHAUTAUQUA LODGE
304 N 14th (98631)
Rates: $40-$160
Tel: (360) 665-6238
(800) 869-8401

EDGEWATER INN MOTEL
409 10th St (98631)
Rates: $45-$98
Tel: (360) 642-2311
(800) 561-2456

LIGHTHOUSE MOTEL
Rt 1, Box 527 (98631)
Rates: $47-$59
Tel: (360) 642-3622

LONG BEACH MOTEL
1200 Pacific Hwy S (98631)
Rates: n/a
Tel: (360) 642-3500

OCEAN LODGE
101 N Blvd (98631)
Rates: $50-$150
Tel: (360) 642-2777

OUR PLACE AT THE BEACH
1309 S Blvd (98631)
Rates: $37-$70
Tel: (360) 642-3793
(800) 538-5107

PACIFIC VIEW MOTEL
203 Bolstad St (98631)
Rates: $38-$90
Tel: (360) 642-2415
(800) 238-0859

SAND LO MOTEL
1910 N Pacific Hwy (98631)
Rates: n/a
Tel: (360) 642-2600

THE SANDS MOTEL
12211 Pacific Way (98631)
Rates: $33-$50
Tel: (360) 642-2100

SHAMAN MOTEL
115 3rd St SW (98631)
Rates: $50-$100
Tel: (360) 642-3714
(800) 753-3750

THUNDERBIRD MOTEL
201 N Blvd (98631)
Rates: $30-$80
Tel: (360) 642-2412

RECREATION

LONG BEACH BOARDWALK - Leashes

Beginner/2.0 miles/1.0 hours

Info: There's no better way to enjoy the dunes than on this no hassle hike. On this boardwalk stroll, you and the furball will

Hotel Policies May Be Subject To Change

find the best of the beach. Enjoy the beauty of the dunes, admire the crashing Pacific or sit a spell on one of the benches and just breathe deeply of the salty ocean breezes. A pupular trail, sometimes it's a veritable pooch parade. Hungry? You'll find several wind-sheltered tables just steps from the beach. If you'd rather have the sand between your toes, go for it. Beachcomb, fly a colorful kite, toss an old tennie or be a lazy-bones and just gaze out to sea. It's all waiting for you.

Directions: From Long Beach, go west at the city center stoplight on First and Pacific.

WASHINGTON STATE BEACHES

For additional lodging and recreation in the beach areas, see listings under the following cities: Copalis Beach, Grayland, Ilwaco, Moclips, Ocean Park, Ocean Shores, Oysterville, Pacific Beach, Westport.

Info: One of the few coastal regions where you can drive on the beach, there are three remarkable stretches of terrain awaiting your exploration. Obey the rules which are posted at access points. In particular, use caution near pedestrians and stay well away from the clam beds near the waterline.

The hard-packed sand makes navigating easy. Stop anywhere along the way and spend the day at play. Pack the red checks and plan a picnic. Shells, driftwood, glass floats and buoys are easy-to-find beach treasures. Between the gorgeous Pacific, its rolling waves cresting in pretty white caps, the unending vastness of the sandy beaches and the hills and dales of the rolling dunes, you'll think you've found paradise.

Directions: Heading from north to south, the following are the locations of the drive-on Washington beaches:

1) Moclips to Ocean Shores along Highways 109 and 115
2) Westport to North Cove along Highway 105
3) Oysterville to Ilwaco along Highway 103

Note: Certain sections are closed to vehicular traffic from April 15th through the day after Labor Day. Areas that are open year round include a 13.5-mile stretch from Bolstad Avenue in Long Beach north to Oysterville Gap Road and a 2.2 miler just south of Beard's Hollow to Seaview Gap Road.

Locate Other Dog-Friendly Activities...Check Nearby Cities

LONGVIEW

LODGING

HOLIDAY INN EXPRESS
723 7th Ave (98632)
Rates: $62-$65
Tel: (360) 414-1000
(800) 465-4329

HUDSON MANOR MOTEL
1616 Hudson St (98632)
Rates: $35-$46

Tel: (360) 425-1100

TOWN CHALET MOTOR HOTEL
1822 Washington Way (98632)
Rates: $31-$46
Tel: (360) 423-2020

THE TOWNHOUSE MOTEL
744 Washington Way (98632)
Rates: $26-$42

LOPEZ ISLAND

LODGING

ISLANDER LOPEZ MARINA RESORT
P.O. Box 459, Fisherman Bay
(Lopez, 98261)
Rates: n/a
Tel: (800) 736-3434

RECREATION

SPENCER SPIT STATE PARK

Info: Beach bum Bowsers suffering from island cabin fever are gonna love this picturesque spot that's very popular with boaters. The central feature of the park is a rock and sand bar that stretches toward Frost Island, including a mile and a half of coastline. The waters abound with marine life including playful river otters and elegant herons. Look too for red-tailed hawks wheeling on the thermals. Pack the red checks and do lunch.

Directions: Head south on Ferry Road and follow to the park.

LYNDEN

LODGING

WINDMILL INN MOTEL
8022 Guide Meridian Rd (98264)
Rates: $34-$47
Tel: (360) 354-3424

Hotel Policies May Be Subject To Change

LYNNWOOD

LODGING

**BEST WESTERN
LANDMARK INN & CONV CTR**
4300 200th St SW (98036)
Rates: $59-$105
Tel: (425) 775-7447
(800) 528-1234

RESIDENCE INN BY MARRIOTT
18200 Alderwood Mall Blvd (98037)
Rates: $90-$150
Tel: (425) 771-1100
(800) 331-3131

ROSE MOTEL
20222 Hwy 99 (98036)
Rates: n/a
Tel: (425) 771-9962

SILVER CLOUD INN
19332 36th Ave W (98036)
Rates: $49-$86
Tel: (425) 775-7600
(800) 205-6935

RECREATION

LYNNDALE PARK - Leashes

Info: After a week of nine to fivers, put a spin on your free time and make tracks to this 37-acre park. Hotdog it on one of the woodland trails or find a shady square and teach the pup a thing or two about fuzzy tennie fun. You'll earn two paws up for this outdoor excursion.

Directions: Located at the intersection of 72nd Avenue West and Olympic View Drive.

SCRIBER LAKE PARK - Leashes

Info: A day of fun in the sun awaits lucky dogs at this 20-acre lakeside retreat. Pack a good read, a tough chew and do the R&R thing. Or get your share of Rexercise on the elevated walkway that circles the lake.

Directions: Located at 5322 198th Street Southwest.

MAPLE FALLS

LODGING

YODELER INN B&B
7485 Mt. Baker Hwy (98266)
Rates: $65
Tel: (800) 642-9033

Locate Other Dog-Friendly Activities...Check Nearby Cities

RECREATION

SILVER LAKE PARK - Leashes

Info: A mixed bag of recreational goodies, you and the wagging machine will find plenty to keep you amused at this 411-acre parkland. Comprised of a former private resort, an early-day homestead and an old logging site, the heart of the park is serene Silver Lake where a scattering of lily pads and cattails adds to the tranquil tableau. Daydream on the sandy beach as your cares drift away on a light breeze. Hiking trails honeycomb the pretty, sweetly scented woodlands. When you're seeking an easy-does-it kind of day, highlight this primo park on your travel agenda. For more information: (360) 599-2776.

Directions: From Maple Falls, travel north on Silver Lake Road and follow the signs about 3 miles to the park.

MARYSVILLE

LODGING

VILLAGE MOTOR INN
235 Beach St (98270)
Rates: $47-$130
Tel: (360) 659-0005

RECREATION

WENBERG STATE PARK - Leashes

Info: When you're looking for a quick escape, look no further than this park on the lovely banks of Lake Goodwin. Whether you're in the mood for some fishing fun, yearning for an old-fashioned picnic or simply seeking a way to immerse yourself in naturalist pursuits, you can't miss at this green scene. For more information: (360) 652-7417.

Directions: From Marysville, travel north on Highway 5 about 4.5 miles to exit 206 (Highway 531). Turn west on Highway 531 and continue about 3.5 miles to the signed park entrance.

MATTAWA

RECREATION

MATTAWA CITY PARK - Leashes

Info: Put a little zip in your day with a stop at this 5-acre park. Open fields beg for a game of fetch and catch with Rover. The lofty trees that encircle the park and shade the grass couldn't be nicer for a little lunch alfrisky.

Directions: Located on Portage and Government Roads.

MAZAMA

LODGING

LOST RIVER RESORT
672 Lost River Rd (98833)
Rates: $50-$75
Tel: (509) 996-2537
(800) 996-2537

RECREATION

LONE FIR TRAIL HIKE - Leashes

Beginner/0.8 miles/0.4 hours

Info: This pipsqueak trail packs a big dollop of all things natural. You'll discover a vast ecosystem of mixed forestlands, streams, rolling hills, flora and fauna. You and the gleeful one will wind your way on a path that crosses four old-fashioned log bridges and then zooms off into the woods. Shaded by a canopy of green, you'll follow a bubbling mountainside stream where the tinkling of the water is bound to have a soothing effect. For more information: (509) 996-2266.

Directions: From Mazama, travel Highway 20 west about 11 miles to the Lone Fir Campground, turn into the campground. The signed trailhead is located just after the fee station on the right side of the parking area.

Note: Highway 20 (North Cascades Highway) is subject to closure in winter.

RAINY LAKE TRAIL HIKE - Leashes

Beginner/1.7 miles/1.0 hours

Info: This barrier-free trail to Rainy Lake is your ticket to paradise. A shady, paved path leads to the clear waters of the lake which resides in a glacier-made bowl. At the far end of the cliffs, you'll be treated to a rushing cascade. Like butterflies and wildflowers, a waterfall is a slice of nature that's always a delight to see. Benches and an observation deck offer an up-close perusal of the plunger. This nearly level route into a high mountain lake is considered rare, so make the time to include this site on your travel agenda. Wowser Bowser. For more information: (509) 996-2266.

Directions: From Mazama, travel Highway 20 west about 18 miles to Rainy Pass, turn into the Rainy Pass Picnic Area. The trailhead is on the left before the parking and picnic sites.

Note: Highway 20 (North Cascades Highway) is subject to closure in winter.

MERCER ISLAND

<u>LODGING</u>

TRAVELODGE
7645 Sunset Hwy (98040)
Rates: $49-$69
Tel: (206) 232-8000
(800) 578-7878

<u>RECREATION</u>

LUTHER BURBANK PARK - Leashes

Info: Situated on the northern tip of the island, this tree-strewn parkland offers a delightful country setting with lots of grassy knolls and quiet niches where you can find a slice of tranquility. Although there are some anti-Snoopy areas, there's also a leash-free zone just a hop, skip and a jump past the amphitheater. Running free will meet its match with swimming free. Your gleeful aqua pup can do the doggie paddle in a designated part of the lake. But be prepared for down and dirty pooch shenanigans, they come with the territory. No matter when you happen by, canine carousing is always underway. So bring a social mindset and a fun attitude and let the good times roll. Hey, pocket a Penn and make the ballmeister's day.

Directions: Take exit 7A off I-90 East to 77th Avenue SE to a right on North Mercer Way. Follow a short distance to a left on 81st Avenue. Go right on 24th Street for a couple of blocks to a left on 84 Avenue SE and the park.

METALINE FALLS

LODGING

CIRCLE MOTEL
HCZ Box 616, Hwy 31 (99153)
Rates: $30-$45
Tel: (509) 446-4343

RECREATION

FLUME CREEK TRAIL HIKE - Leashes

Expert/8.0 miles/5.0 hours

Info: Don't even think about this trek unless you're in the expert class of hiker and your hound's made of tough stuff. But if you make the grade, you'll experience a generous dose of tranquility and some of the best views of the Colville Forest. The rugged trail climbs more than 2,000' in just four miles, so prepare yourself for the haul. The pot of gold at the end of the rainbow, staggering views of the Columbia River Valley, the Pend Oreille River, Kokanee Mountains and Salmo-Priest Wilderness. Lucky dogs have reported sightings of resident mountain goats grazing in the grass on the mountain ridges. This hike represents solitude in its purest form. For more information: (509) 446-2691.

Directions: From Metaline Falls, take Route 31 north about a quarter of a mile, turn west onto Boundary Road (CR 2975). Travel Boundary Road about 3 miles to Flume Creek Road (FS 350), turn left. Travel Flume Creek Road about 7 miles to trailhead #502 on the right side of the road.

Note: Flume Creek Road is recommended for high-clearance vehicles.

HALL MOUNTAIN TRAIL HIKE - Leashes

Intermediate/5.0 miles/3.0 hours

Info: Passing through plentiful pines and promising bighorn sheep sightings, this trail makes the A-list for wildlife devotees. Reintroduced to Hall Mountain several years ago to create a healthy, growing population, the sheep have prospered. The steep journey to Hall Mountain requires a little extra umph but you'll get paid back in a panorama bonus. And no doubt there'll be a grin on the mutt's mug. For more information: (509) 446-2691.

Directions: From Metaline Falls, travel east on Sullivan Lake Road (CR 9345) about 3 miles to Sullivan Lake and the junction with FS 22, turn east. Travel FS 22 about 4 miles to FS 500, turn right. Continue about 8 miles to the end of the road and trailhead #540.

Note: Do not approach or feed the sheep. To protect the wildlife during autumn mating seasons and the spring birth season, FS 500 is closed from August 15 through June 30. Call for alternative route.

SHEDROOF CUTOFF TRAIL HIKE - Leashes

Intermediate/3.4 miles/2.0 hours

Info: A Sunday type stroll marks the onset of this trail which flits along an abandoned logging road before testing the mettle of you and your pooch. But there's plenty of fun to be had in the bubbling waters of Sullivan Creek. Leaving the cool creek and dense thickets behind, you'll scramble up a steep ascent until the junction with the Shedroof Drive Trail, your turnaround point. Share an R&R moment with your good dog before doing the descent thing. Don't be surprised if black-tailed deer cross your path. They're common in this neck of the woods. For more information: (509) 446-2691.

Directions: From Metaline Falls, travel east on Sullivan Lake Road (CR 9345) about 3 miles to Sullivan Lake and the junction with FS 22. Travel FS 22 east about 6 miles until it changes into FS 2220. Continue on FS 2220 about 7 miles to trailhead #511 on the right side of the road.

Hotel Policies May Be Subject To Change

THUNDER CREEK TRAIL HIKE - Leashes

Expert/5.0 miles/3.0 hours

Info: You can't get much closer to pristine beauty than this tough but rewarding excursion. You and your Herculean hound will zip off on an old road bed for the first 2 miles as you traverse lush stands of old-growth cedar and hemlock. Entering the Salmo Priest Wilderness, the trail drops into a valley and the countryside is quickly transformed into a green oasis of hanging mosses, fresh ferns and a thick understory. Thunder Creek adds its twinkling blueness to the already lovely picture. The fragrant air is complimented by savory huckleberries just waiting to be picked. Find a cozy spot creekside and paint the tongue purple. For more information: (509) 446-2691.

Directions: From Metaline Falls, travel east on Sullivan Lake Road (CR 9345) about 3 miles to Sullivan Lake and the junction with FS 22, turn east. Travel FS 22 about 6 miles until it changes into FS 2220. Travel FS 2220 to the junction with Thunder Creek Road (FS 345), turn right. Park near the gate across from the road but do not block the gated road. Trailhead #526 begins at the junction of FS 2220 and Thunder Creek Road.

Note: If you don't know what edible huckleberries look like, don't eat them.

MOCLIPS

<u>LODGING</u>

BARNACLE MOTEL
4816 Pacific Ave (98562)
Rates: $45-$65
Tel: (360) 276-4318

HI-TIDE OCEAN BEACH RESORT
4890 Railroad Ave (98562)
Rates: $74-$159
Tel: (360) 276-4142
(800) 662-5477

MOCLIPS MOTEL
4852 Pacific Ave (98562)
Rates: n/a
Tel: (360) 276-4228

MOONSTONE BEACH MOTEL
4849 Pacific Ave (98562)
Rates: $50-$64
Tel: (360) 276-4346

OCEAN CREST RESORT
SR 109, Sunset Beach (98562)
Rates: $44-$129
Tel: (360) 276-4465
(800) 684-8349

THE SPINDRIFT
4807 Pacific Ave (98562)
Rates: $105-$155
Tel: (800) 645-8443

Locate Other Dog-Friendly Activities...Check Nearby Cities

WASHINGTON STATE BEACHES

Info: One of the few coastal regions where you can drive on the beach, there are three remarkable stretches awaiting your exploration. Obey the rules which are posted at access points. In particular, use caution near pedestrians and stay well away from the clam beds near the waterline.

Directions: Heading from north to south, the following are the locations of the drive-on Washington beaches:

1) Moclips to Ocean Shores along Highways 109 and 115
2) Westport to North Cove along Highway 105
3) Oysterville to Ilwaco along Highway 103

For additional lodging and recreation in the beach areas, see listings under the following cities: Copalis Beach, Grayland, Ilwaco, Long Beach Peninsula, Ocean Park, Ocean Shores, Oysterville, Pacific Beach, Westport.

MONROE

LODGING

BEST WESTERN BARON INN
19233 Hwy 2 (98272)
Rates: $52-$168
Tel: (360) 794-3111
(800) 528-1234

BROOKSIDE MOTEL
19930 Hwy 2 (98272)
Rates: n/a
Tel: (360) 794-8832

FAIRGROUNDS INN MOTEL
18950 Hwy 2 (98272)
Rates: $35-$60
Tel: (360) 794-5401

MONTESANO

LODGING

THE ABEL HOUSE
117 Fleet St S (98563)
Rates: $65-$85
Tel: (360) 249-6002
(800) 235-ABEL

MONTE SQUARE MOTEL
518 1/2 South 1st St (98563)
Rates: $35-$45
Tel: (360) 249-4424

Hotel Policies May Be Subject To Change

RECREATION

SPOON CREEK FALLS TRAIL HIKE - Leashes

Beginner/0.6 miles/0.5 hours

Info: There's something special about seeing a waterfall up-close that can't be topped. Take advantage of this cinchy trail to a stunning plunger and a "brrr" swimming hole. While you cool your jets, give your binocs a workout. This place is for the birds. For more information: (360) 877-5254.

Directions: From Montesano, head north on Wynoochee Valley Road (Devonshire Road) and drive about 35 miles to FS 23 and turn right for 3 miles to the trailhead just past Spoon Creek.

WYNOOCHEE LAKE SHORE TRAIL HIKE

Intermediate/12.0 miles/7.0 hours

Info: This loop-de-loop skirts a pretty lakeside setting where new and old-growth forests are part of the package. When you reach the river crossing, you'll have to decide whether you want to scramble to the other side or retrace your steps. If you opt to continue, you'll traverse the eastern shoreline, cross atop a dam and return to your starting point. For more information: (360) 877-5254.

Directions: From Montesano, head west on Highway 12 for one mile to Wynoochee Valley Road and turn right. Drive about 35 miles to the 3-way intersection and turn left. After a short distance, turn right on FS 2294 and go one mile to the Coho Campground entrance.

MORTON

LODGING

EVERGREEN MOTEL
121 Front St (98356)
Rates: $27-$45
Tel: (360) 496-5407

RESORT OF THE MOUNTAINS
1130 SR 7 (98356)
Rates: n/a
Tel: (360) 496-5885

SEASONS MOTEL
200 Westlake (98356)
Rates: $55-$65
Tel: (360) 496-6835

STILTNER MOTEL
250 Morton Rd (98356)
Rates: n/a
Tel: (360) 496-5103

Locate Other Dog-Friendly Activities...Check Nearby Cities

MOSES LAKE

LODGING

BEST WESTERN HALLMARK INN
3000 Marina Dr (98837)
Rates: $62-$150
Tel: (509) 765-9211
(800) 528-1234

EL RANCHO MOTEL-IMA
1214 S Pioneer Way (98837)
Rates: $28-$50
Tel: (509) 765-7193
(800) 341-8000

HOLIDAY INN EXPRESS
1745 E Kittleson (98837)
Rates: $65-$80
Tel: (509) 766-2000
(800) 465-4329

INTERSTATE INN
2801 W Broadway (98837)
Rates: $36-$54
Tel: (509) 765-1777
(800) 777-5889

LAKESIDE MOTEL
802 W Broadway (98837)
Rates: n/a
Tel: (509) 765-8651

LAKESHORE MOTEL
3206 W Lakeshore Dr (98837)
Rates: $34+
Tel: (509) 765-9201

MAPLES MOTEL
1006 W 3rd (98837)
Rates: n/a
Tel: (509) 765-5665

MOTEL 6
2822 Wapato Dr (98837)
Rates: $30-$40
Tel: (509) 766-0250
(800) 440-6000

OASIS BUDGET INN
466 Melva Ln (98837)
Rates: n/a
Tel: (509) 765-8636
(800) 456-2747

SAGE "N" SAND MOTEL
1011 S Pioneer Way (98837)
Rates: $32-$52
Tel: (509) 765-8636
(800) 336-0454

SHILO INNS
1819 E Kittleson (98837)
Rates: $58-$79
Tel: (509) 765-9317
(800) 222-2244

SUNLAND MOTOR INN
309 E Third Ave (98837)
Rates: $34-$52
Tel: (509) 765-1170
(800) 220-4403

SUPER 8 MOTEL
449 Melva Ln (98837)
Rates: $46-$62
Tel: (509) 765-8886
(800) 800-8000

TRAVELODGE
316 S Pioneer Way (98837)
Rates: $37-$65
Tel: (509) 765-8631
(800) 578-7878

RECREATION

CASCADE PARK - Leashes

Info: Get along with your little doggie to this lush lakeside setting where you'll find greenery and serenery. Set up shop under a tree or beside the lapping waters.

Hotel Policies May Be Subject To Change

Directions: Go north on Stratford Lane to Valley Road. Turn left and continue to the bottom of the steep hill. The access road will be the first road on your left at the bottom of the hill.

LARSON PLAYFIELD and PARK - Leashes

Info: Take the dawgus out to a ball game or make your own fun and games at this park.

Directions: Off West Broadway near the I-90 exit 176.

McCOSH PARK - Leashes

Info: In the summer months when free concerts are part of the package, you and your musically inclined mutt will have a howl of a good time in this landscaped green scene.

Directions: Located on the corner of Dogwood and 4th.

MONTLAKE PARK - Leashes

Info: Savor the quietude you'll find in this 9-acre park that comes complete with a shimmering lake.

Directions: Located at Linden and Beaumont.

MOSSYROCK

<u>LODGING</u>

MOSSYROCK INN
118 E State St (98564)
Rates: n/a
Tel: (360) 983-8641

<u>RECREATION</u>

IKE KINSWA STATE PARK - Leashes

Info: Fishing fiends, pack your poles, a rawhide for the pooch and skedaddle to this green scene situated on the banks of glistening Mayfield Lake. Tote a boat and do a float or stick to the terra firma where lunch à la Frisky could make your dog's day. For more information: (360) 983-3402.

Directions: From Mossyrock, head northwest on Route 122 about 5 miles to the signed park entrance.

Locate Other Dog-Friendly Activities...Check Nearby Cities

MOUNT VERNON

LODGING

BEST WESTERN COLLEGE WAY INN
300 W College Way (98273)
Rates: $45-$70
Tel: (360) 424-4287
(800) 528-1234

BEST WESTERN COTTONTREE INN
2300 Market St (98273)
Rates: $64-$75
Tel: (360) 428-5678
(800) 528-1234

COMFORT INN
1910 Freeway Dr (98273)
Rates: $49-$74
Tel: (360) 428-7020
(800) 221-2222

DAYS INN
2009 Riverside Dr (98273)
Rates: $40-$135
Tel: (360) 424-4141
(800) 329-7466

HILLSIDE MOTEL
2300 Bonnie View Rd (98273)
Rates: n/a
Tel: (360) 445-3252

WEST WINDS MOTEL
2020 Riverside Dr (98273)
Rates: $32-$50
Tel: (360) 424-4224

WHISPERING FIRS B&B
1957 Kanako Ln (98273)
Rates: $65-$95
Tel: (360) 428-1990
(800) 428-1992

RECREATION

HILLCREST PARK - Leashes

Info: Put a little wiggle in your wagger's strut and head out to this pretty park. More than 30 acres of cool greens invite your playful hijinks. There's always a chance to spectate and root for the home team too. Or pack a fuzzy tennie and surprise the ballmeister with a game of your own.

Directions: Located at 1717 S. 13th Street.

LIONS CLUB PARK - Leashes

Info: A little plot of green for a quickie constitutional.

Directions: Located at 501 Freeway Drive.

LITTLE MOUNTAIN PARK - Leashes

Info: Get away from it all and explore the mountain terrain in this 480-acre park. The peak of grassy Little Mountain rises to an elevation of 934'. If you and your hiking noodnick are up for the challenge, hike the mountain trail and revel in views of the San Juan Islands, Olympics and Skagit Valley.

Directions: Located on Little Mountain Road.

Hotel Policies May Be Subject To Change

NACHES

LODGING

APPLE COUNTRY B&B
4561 Old Naches Hwy (98937)
Rates: $65+
Tel: (509) 965-0344

SILVER BEACH RESORT
40380 Hwy 12 (98937)
Rates: n/a
Tel: (509) 672-2500

SQUAW ROCK RESORT
15070 SR 410 (98937)
Rates: $65-$79
Tel: (509) 658-2926

TROUT LODGE
27090 Hwy 12 (98937)
Rates: $40-$55
Tel: (509) 672-2211

NAHCOTTA

LODGING

MOBY DICK HOTEL & OYSTER FARM
Sandridge Rd (98637)
Rates: $65-$95
Tel: (360) 665-4543

**OUR HOUSE IN
NAHCOTTA/OYSTERVILLE B&B**
P.O. Box 33 (98637)
Rates: $85-$95
Tel: (360) 665-6667

NASELLE

LODGING

SLEEPY HOLLOW MOTEL
HCR 78 (98638)
Rates: $35-$40
Tel: (360) 484-3232

NEAH BAY

LODGING

THE CAPE MOTEL & RV PARK
Bay View Ave,
P.O. Box 136 (98357)
Rates: $45-$74
Tel: (360) 645-2250

SILVER SALMON RESORT
Bayview & Roosevelt,
P.O. Box 156 (98357)
Rates: $35+
Tel: (360) 645-2388

SNOW CREEK RESORT
P.O. Box 248 (98357)
Rates: $45-$74
Tel: (360) 645-2284

TYEE MOTEL & RV PARK
P.O. Box 193 (98357)
Rates: $40-$95
Tel: (360) 645-2233

Locate Other Dog-Friendly Activities...Check Nearby Cities

NEWPORT

Lodging

GOLDEN SPUR MOTOR INN
924 W Hwy 2 (99156)
Rates: $38-$54
Tel: (509) 447-3823

THE LAZY J HIDEAWAY
3792 Deer Valley Rd (99156)
Rates: $60
Tel: (509) 447-2535
(800) 898-3412

NEWPORT CITY INN
220 N Washington (99156)
Rates: $38-$60
Tel: (509) 447-3436

MARSHALL LAKE RESORT
1301 Marshall Lake Rd (99156)
Rates: n/a
Tel: (509) 447-4158

Recreation

BEAD LAKE TRAIL HIKE - Leashes

Intermediate/12.8 miles/7.0 hours

Info: Naturalists, you're gonna love this trail for its rich sampling of Mother Nature's handiwork. A 3-S trail, you'll experience scenery, solitude and serenity. Grandiose trees with lofty branches and large trunks fringe the path and scent your woodsy journey. Four miles into this odyssey, you'll encounter a breathtaking western white pine with a 15'7" circumference. Then it's on to the blue waters of Bead Lake on a footpath lined with fragrant wildflowers and lush meadows. The cool breezes skimming off the rippling waters of the lake will tempt you to take a short sojourn. Sightings of resident moose and deer, ambling down to the clear waters for a sip or two, are almost guaranteed. When you can pull yourself away, repeat the beat on your retreat. For more information: (509) 447-3129.

Directions: From Newport, travel U.S. Route 2 across the Pend Oreille River into Idaho. Just across the river, turn north onto LeClerc Creek Road. Travel LeClerc Creek Road about 2.8 miles to Bead Lake Road (CR 3029). Continue about 6 miles then turn right onto CR 3215, a gravel road leading around the south shore of the lake. The trailhead is at the end of CR 3215 near the Mineral Bay Campground.

Hotel Policies May Be Subject To Change

BROWNS LAKE TRAIL HIKE - Leashes

Intermediate/2.5 miles/2.0 hours

Info: From the get-go, you and your grinning wet wagger will know you're on one hunky dory hike. As you kick up the dust, Browns Lake plays peekaboo through the sun-dappled woodlands. In spring, you've got a standing invitation to the wildflower party. The interpretive trail signals turnaround time. But take a quickie sidetrip and let the whiffer sniffer to his heart's content in the dense and fragrant cedar grove. You'll encounter a boardwalk where in April and May you can have a rare glimpse of fish doing what comes naturally, spawning. When it's time to call it quits, retrace your steps. For more information: (509) 447-7300.

Directions: From Newport, take Highway 20 north approximately 15 miles to Usk. Turn east and cross the Pend Oreille River. Drive northeast on CR 3389 about 4 miles to the Y. At the Y head north on FS 5030 for 4 miles to the Browns Lake Campground. Park at the boat launch area. The trailhead is near the boat ramp.

Note: Trail is open May-October. Fly fishing only in Browns Lake and Creek.

PIONEER PARK HERITAGE TRAIL HIKE - Leashes

Beginner/0.3 miles/0.25 hours

Info: Doggistorians swear by this interpretive trail which includes a smidgen of time travel. You'll gain some insight into the way the land was used by the Kalispell Tribe. Twelve interpretive displays of text, pictures and drawings provide a sample of the tribe's lifestyle. An elevated boardwalk overlooks the inside of an oven used by Native Americans to cook camas roots, an important food source. Your voyage through time ends with a bang, breathtaking views of the Pend Oreille River. For more information: (509) 447-3129.

Directions: From Newport, travel U.S. Route 2 and cross the bridge over the Pend Oreille River. Turn north on the first road after the bridge (FS 9305) and continue about 2.3 miles to the Pioneer Park Campground. The trailhead is at the day use parking area.

SOUTH SKOOKUM LOOP TRAIL HIKE - Leashes

Beginner/1.3 miles/1.0 hours

Info: Even telly bellies will take a shine to this simple trail which loops around the south and west shores of South Skookum Lake. Bridges, inlets and outlets and plenty of picnic ops contribute to the pupularity of this lakeside jaunt. Mornings equate to fewer people and dewy moistness. Don't be surprised if you encounter a moose or two wading in the water or a deer grazing in the grasses. If you're a nature lover at heart, hop on the short spur which zooms into the woods. Huckleberry patches brighten the terrain and sweeten the air, not to mention the purple zing they add to the tongue. For more information: (509) 447-3129.

Directions: From Newport, travel U.S. Highway 20 north about 15 miles to the junction of Highway 20 and 211 (Kings Lake Road), turn east. Cross the Pend Oreille River and continue about 10 miles to Skookum Lake Road, turn right. Travel to South Skookum Lake Campground. The trailhead is near the boat launch area.

Note: If you don't know what huckleberries look like, don't eat them.

OAK HARBOR

LODGING & RECREATION

See Whidbey Island for lodging and recreation.

OCEAN CITY

LODGING

NORTH BEACH MOTEL
2601 SR 109 (98569)
Rates: $30-$55
Tel: (360) 289-4116
(800) 640-8053

PACIFIC SANDS MOTEL & RESORT
2687 SR 109 (98569)
Rates: $40-$56
Tel: (360) 289-3588

WEST WINDS RESORT MOTEL
2537 SR 109 (98569)
Rates: $36-$66
Tel: (360) 289-3448
(800) 867-3448

Hotel Policies May Be Subject To Change

OCEAN PARK

LODGING

**COASTAL COTTAGES
OF OCEAN PARK**
P.O. Box 888 (98640)
Rates: $50-$69
Tel: (360) 665-4658
(800) 200-0424

HARBOR VIEW MOTEL
3204 281st St (98640)
Rates: $40-$60
Tel: (360) 665-4959

OCEAN PARK RESORT
25904 "R" St (98640)
Rates: $54-$100
Tel: (360) 665-4585
(800) 835-4634

SUNSET VIEW RESORT
25517 Park Ave (98640)
Rates: $64-$159
Tel: (360) 665-4494

SHAKTI COVE COTTAGES
253rd at Park (98640)
Rates: $60-$75
Tel: (360) 665-4000

WESTGATE MOTEL & TRAILER COURT
20803 Pacific Hwy (98640)
Rates: $42-$55
Tel: (360) 665-4211

RECREATION

WASHINGTON STATE BEACHES

Info: One of the few coastal regions where you can drive on the beach, there are three remarkable stretches awaiting your exploration. Obey the rules which are posted at access points. In particular, use caution near pedestrians and stay well away from the clam beds near the waterline.

Directions: Heading from north to south, the following are the locations of the drive-on Washington beaches:

1) Moclips to Ocean Shores along Highways 109 and 115
2) Westport to North Cove along Highway 105
3) Oysterville to Ilwaco along Highway 103

For additional lodging and recreation in the beach areas, see listings under the following cities: Copalis Beach, Grayland, Ilwaco, Long Beach Peninsula, Moclips, Ocean Shores, Oysterville, Pacific Beach, Westport.

Note: Certain sections are closed to vehicular traffic from April 15th through the day after Labor Day. Areas that are open year round include a 13.5-mile stretch from Bolstad Avenue in Long Beach north to Oysterville Gap Road and a 2.2 miler just south of Beard's Hollow to Seaview Gap Road.

Locate Other Dog-Friendly Activities...Check Nearby Cities

OCEAN SHORES

LODGING

BEACH FRONT VACATION RENTALS
759 Ocean Shores Blvd (98569)
Rates: $65-$225
Tel: (800) 544-8887

CASA DEL ORO MOTEL
667 Point Brown Ave NW (98569)
Rates: $85-$120
Tel: (360) 289-2281
(800) 291-2281

CHALET VILLAGE CABINS
659 Ocean Shores Blvd (98569)
Rates: $85-$95
Tel: (360) 289-4297
(800) 303-4297 (WA)

DISCOVERY INN
1031 Discovery Ave SE (98569)
Rates: $52-$78
Tel: (360) 289-3371
(800) 882-8821

GREY GULL APARTMENT MOTEL
651 Ocean Shores Blvd SW (98569)
Rates: $70-$120
Tel: (360) 289-2722
(800) 221-4541 (WA)

HOLIDAY INN EXPRESS
685 Ocean Shores Blvd (98569)
Rates: $69-$129
Tel: (360) 289-4900
(800) 465-4329

NAUTILUS HOTEL
835 Ocean Shores Blvd (98569)
Rates: $70-$120
Tel: (360) 289-2722
(800) 221-4511 (WA)

OCEAN SHORES MOTEL
681 Ocean Shores Blvd N (98569)
Rates: $40-$125
Tel: (360) 289-3351
(800) 464-2526 (WA)

POLYNESIAN CONDO RESORT
615 Ocean Shores Blvd (98569)
Rates: $79-$320
Tel: (360) 289-3361
(800) 562-4836

THE SANDS RESORT
801 Ocean Shores Blvd (98569)
Rates: $49-$125
Tel: (360) 289-2444
(800) 841-4001

SANDS ROYAL PACIFIC MOTEL
781 Ocean Shores Blvd NW (98569)
Rates: $39-$129
Tel: (360) 289-3306
(800) 562-9748

**SHILO INNS CONFERENCE
CENTER & FAMILY RESORT**
707 Ocean Shores Blvd NW (98569)
Rates: $99-$219
Tel: (360) 289-4600
(800) 222-2244

SILVER KING MOTEL
1070 Discovery Ave SE (98569)
Rates: $35-$90
Tel: (360) 289-3386
(800) 562-6001 (WA)

SURFVIEW CONDOS
757 Ocean Court NW (98569)
Rates: $65-$85
Tel: (360) 289-3077
(800) 544-8887 (WA)

WESTERLY MOTEL
870 Ocean Shores Blvd NW (98569)
Rates: $30-$50
Tel: (360) 289-3711

Hotel Policies May Be Subject To Change

RECREATION

NORTH BAY PARK - Leashes

Info: Sports fans, you'll dig this park complete with ball fields, horseshoe pits, basketball and volleyball courts. Root for the home team or visit in the off-season and treat your Hair Jordan to some one-on-one.

Directions: Located at Albatross and Chance-a-la-Mer.

WASHINGTON STATE BEACHES

Info: One of the few coastal regions where you can drive on the beach, there are three remarkable stretches awaiting your exploration. Obey the rules which are posted at access points. In particular, use caution near pedestrians and stay well away from the clam beds near the waterline.

Directions: Heading from north to south, the following are the locations of the drive-on Washington beaches:

1) Moclips to Ocean Shores along Highways 109 and 115
2) Westport to North Cove along Highway 105
3) Oysterville to Ilwaco along Highway 103

For additional lodging and recreation in the beach areas, see listings under the following cities: Copalis Beach, Grayland, Ilwaco, Long Beach Peninsula, Moclips, Ocean Park, Oysterville, Pacific Beach, Westport.

Note: Certain sections are closed to vehicular traffic from April 15th through the day after Labor Day. Areas that are open year round include a 13.5-mile stretch from Bolstad Avenue in Long Beach north to Oysterville Gap Road and a 2.2 miler just south of Beard's Hollow to Seaview Gap Road.

ODESSA

LODGING

ODESSA MOTEL
601 E First Ave (99159)
Rates: $35-$47
Tel: (509) 982-2412

OKANOGAN

LODGING

CEDARS INN
One Apple Way (98840)
Rates: $45-$57
Tel: (509) 422-6431

PONDEROSA MOTOR LODGE
1034 S 2nd Ave (98840)
Rates: $38-$43
Tel: (509) 422-0400
(800) 732-6702

U & I MOTEL
838 2nd St N (98840)
Rates: $28-$35
Tel: (509) 422-2920

OLALLA

LODGING

OLALLA ORCHARD B&B
12530 Orchard Ave SE (98359)
Rates: $95
Tel: (253) 857-5915

OLYMPIA

LODGING

BAILEY MOTOR INN
3333 Martin Way (98506)
Rates: n/a
Tel: (360) 491-7515

BEST WESTERN ALADDIN MOTOR INN
900 S Capitol Way (98501)
Rates: $60-$79
Tel: (360) 352-7200
(800) 528-1234

THE CINNAMON RABBIT B&B
1304 7th Ave W (98502)
Rates: $60-$75
Tel: (360) 357-5520

DEEP LAKE RESORT
12405 Tilley Rd S (98512)
Rates: $53-$85
Tel: (360) 352-7388

HOLIDAY INN SELECT
2300 Evergreen Park Dr (98502)
Rates: $69-$175
Tel: (360) 943-4000
(800) 465-4329

LEE STREET SUITES
348 Lee St SW (98501)
Rates: n/a
Tel: (360) 943-8391

SHALIMAR SUITES
5895 Capital Blvd S (98501)
Rates: $26-$48
Tel: (360) 943-8391

TYEE HOTEL
500 Tyee Dr (98502)
Rates: $70-$78
Tel: (360) 352-0511
(800) 648-6440

Hotel Policies May Be Subject To Change

RECREATION

CAPITOL CAMPUS PARK- Leashes

Info: Start your day off on the right paw and take your canine connoisseur for an afternoon outing to this 20-acre locale. Peruse the public art displayed and then uncover a shady nook for some down time or come at lunch time and share a brown bagger with the wagger beside Capitol Lake.

Directions: Located on Capitol Way and Union.

CAPITOL LAKE PARK - Leashes

Info: Treat your bark to a lark in the park. This 10-acre expanse is located near the north end of Capitol Lake. A scattering of picnic tables make it easy to plan lunch alfresco.

Directions: Located on Washington and 5th.

GARFIELD NATURE TRAIL HIKE - Leashes

Beginner/0.5 miles/.0.25 hours

Info: Your pupsqueak will take a shine to this pipsqueak trail. Traversing 5 acres of rolling grassland near Budd Inlet, it's an easy way to fulfill your exercise quotient for the day.

Directions: Located on West Bay Drive just north of Harrison Avenue.

GOVERNOR STEVENS PARK - Leashes

Info: You'll find splendor in the grass along with a pleasant nature trail at this 6-acre park.

Directions: Located between Route 5 and Henderson Boulevard, just south of Watershed Park.

INTERPRETIVE PARK - Leashes

Info: Furbanites, you'll love the sense of nature you'll find at this lovely 17-acre green scene beside the shores of Capitol Lake. There's even a quickie trail where you can work out the kinks.

Directions: Located off Route 5.

Locate Other Dog-Friendly Activities...Check Nearby Cities

L.B.A. PARK - Leashes

Info: When walktime calls, answer it with this hustling, bustling park of 22 acres. Stash a tennie and treat the ballmeister to his namesake game.

Directions: Located on Morse-Merryman, just east of Boulevard Road.

MILLERSYLVANIA STATE PARK - Leashes

Info: If you've been singing the blues, change your tune and head for the paw-stomping terrain at this park. Outdoorsy types, you'll find just what you need to fix what ails you. Stately Douglas firs provide a sun-dappled habitat for rabbit, deer and other woodland dwellers. Duck and geese squawk and squabble as they skim over the lakes and outlying marshlands. Nifty picnic spots are just waiting to be claimed. And if you've got a yen for an old-fashioned hike in natural surroundings, you'll find several miles of trails, each leading to something special. Afishionados, shimmering Deep Lake is stocked with tasty trout for your reel-time pleasure. So get a move on. For more information: (360) 753-1519.

Directions: From Olympia, travel 11 miles south on Highway 5 to exit 99 (113th Street), turn east. Continue east on 113th Street Southwest for 2 miles to Southwest Tilly Road. Turn south to the park.

The numbered hike that follows is within Millersylvania State Park:

1) FITNESS TRAIL HIKE - Leashes

Intermediate/1.5 miles/1.0 hours

Info: This invigorating hike escorts you to some of the prettiest scenes the park has on the menu. You'll get your juices flowing as you make tracks through the tree-dotted landscapes in this riparian habitat.

Directions: From Olympia, travel 11 miles south on Highway 5 to exit 99 (113th Street), turn east on 113th Street Southwest for 2 miles to Southwest Tilly Road. Turn south to the park. The trailhead is located at regional headquarters.

Hotel Policies May Be Subject To Change

PRIEST POINT PARK - Leashes

Info: Your bowwow will go wow wow when you punch up the day with play at this paw-pleasing park of 282 acres. The rolling waters of Budd Inlet on the west side of this verdant scene can make for some memorable fun. Kick up some dust on a nature trail or hustle your butt to one of the sports fields and root for the home team.

Directions: Located on East Bay Drive.

WATERSHED PARK - Leashes

Info: Eeny, meeny, miney, mo - pick a trail and off you'll go. More than 170 acres await your fancy footwork in this land of playful pupportunities.

Directions: Located on 22nd Avenue and Henderson Blvd.

YAUGER PARK - Leashes

Info: Dollars to dog biscuits, you and the dawgus will find plenty to amuse yourselves in this park. From pathways that are perfect for Rexercise to a horseshoe pit where you can hone your tossing skills. Hey, talk about tossing, don't forget the Frisbee of choice.

Directions: Located on Capital Mall Drive and Mud Bay Road.

OTHER PARKS IN OLYMPIA - Leashes

- BIGELOW PARK, Bigelow Avenue & Puget Street
- EAST BAY PARK, East Bay Drive
- HARRY FAIN'S LEGION PARK, 22nd Ave & Eastside St
- LIONS PARK, off Boulevard Rd, just south of Pacific Ave
- MADISON SCENIC PARK, north of Hwy 5, east of Eastside St
- MARATHON PARK, south of Capitol Mall Drive
- PARK OF THE SEVEN OARS, Harrison Ave & West Bay Dr
- PERCIVAL LANDING PARK, West Bay Road
- STEVENS FIELD PARK, west of Highway 5
- SYLVESTER PARK, Washington Street
- WOODRUFF PARK, Harrison Avenue

Locate Other Dog-Friendly Activities...Check Nearby Cities

OLYMPIC NATIONAL PARK

LODGING

LOG CABIN RESORT
3183 E Beach Rd
(Port Angeles 98362)
Rates: $40-$100
Tel: (360) 928-3325

OMAK

LODGING

LEISURE VILLAGE MOTEL
630 Okoma Dr (98841)
Rates: $33-$41
Tel: (509) 826-4442
(800) 427-4495 (WA)

MOTEL NICHOLAS
527 E Grape St (98841)
Rates: n/a
Tel: (509) 826-4611

OMAK INN
912 Koala Dr (98841)
Rates: $60-$69
Tel: (509) 826-3822

ROYAL MOTEL
514 E Riverside Dr (98841)
Rates: $28-$44
Tel: (509) 826-5715

STAMPEDE MOTEL
215 W 4th St (98841)
Rates: n/a
Tel: (800) 639-1161

THRIFTLODGE
122 N Main (98841)
Rates: $29-$49
Tel: (509) 826-0400
(800) 578-7878

ORCAS ISLAND

LODGING

BARTWOOD LODGE
Rt 2, Box 1040 (Eastsound 98245)
Rates: $39
Tel: (360) 376-2242

DOE BAY VILLAGE RESORT
P.O. Box 437 (Olga 98279)
Rates: $40+
Tel: (360) 376-2291

LANDMARK INN
Rt 1, Box A-108 (Orcas 98280)
Rates: $80-$155
Tel: (360) 376-2423
(800) 622-4578

NORTH SHORE COTTAGES
P.O. Box 1273 (Eastsound 98245)
Rates: $120
Tel: (360) 376-5131

SMALL ISLAND FARM & INN
Rt 1, Box 76 (Eastsound 98245)
Rates: $70-$95
Tel: (360) 376-4292

WEST BEACH RESORT
Rt 1, Box 510 (Eastsound 98245)
Rates: $105-$150
Tel: (360) 376-2240

Hotel Policies May Be Subject To Change

RECREATION

MORAN STATE PARK - Leashes

Info: A mountainous region, this state park is the most popular on the island. Dominating the eastern side of Orcas, you'll find more than 5,000 paw-pleasing acres where hiking, freshwater fishing, non-motorized boating and unparalleled panoramas from atop Mt. Constitution contribute to the appeal of this woodsy venue. Naturalists, you'll definitely come away with a pocketful of memories. You might see tiny saw-whet owls, bald eagles swooping in the skies or Columbian black-tailed deer grazing peacefully in a grassy clearing. The waters proffer up 7-ton orcas, water birds, ducks, elegant herons and playful otters. Yup, that could be a red-tailed hawk wheeling on the thermals or California quail in the meadowlands, mink or trumpeter swans in one of the ponds or lakes. Birders flock here to check out the ravens, woodpeckers, wrens and nuthatches that inhabit the woodlands.

More than 30 miles of trails honeycomb the stunning, verdant landscape which closely resembles a temperate rain forest. If you gain some altitude, you and your Curious George can gaze upon the Lummi, Sucia and Matia Islands, Bellingham and Mt. Baker. On a clear day you might not see forever but you could get an eyeful of the glorious Cascades stretching into British Columbia. Postcardian vistas are every which way you turn. Bow wow.

Directions: From the ferry take Horsehoe Highway for 13 miles to the park entrance.

The numbered hikes that follow are within Moran State Park:

1) CASCADE CREEK TRAIL HIKE - Leashes

Intermediate/8.6 miles/5.0 hours

Info: Follow your furry friend along the campground road to campsite #17 and you'll be right on track. There's something very special about a waterfall and the connection it gives us with nature. So get ready to be connected. One mile into your journey, you'll encounter the first of many pretty plungers.

Locate Other Dog-Friendly Activities...Check Nearby Cities

Cascade Falls is absolutely stunning in terms of high water. The tumbling, rumbling cascades gush over massive boulders and rocky outcrops, splashing a sun-streaked spray into turquoise-tinted pools. Sit a spell and contemplate the beauty of your surroundings before continuing onward. The trail winds to several smaller falls and the farther in you travel, the greater your chances of finding solitude and serenity with a capital S. Once you cross the bridge below Mountain Lake Dam, follow the shoreline clockwise about a half mile to the Mountain Lake picnic shelter, your turnaround point. Do some lunch alfrisky and consider yourselves two lucky dogs.

Directions: From the ferry, take Horsehoe Highway for 13 miles to the park entrance. The trail begins at the park office.

2) CASCADE FALLS TRAIL HIKE - Leashes

Beginner/0.5 miles/0.5 hours

Info: No bones about it, spring and early summer are the best times to experience the falls. Let the sniffmeister lead the way through a grabbag forest of hardwoods and evergreens where you'll be sweetly serenaded by songbirds. You'll hear the falls before you witness their beauty. Don't forget your Kodak, you'll want take home some glossy memories. Repeat the beat on your retreat.

Directions: From the ferry, take Horsehoe Highway for 13 miles to the park entrance. To the trailhead: drive up Mt. Constitution Road about 0.5 miles to the trailhead parking lot on the right-hand side.

3) CASCADE LOOP TRAIL HIKE - Leashes

Beginner/2.5 miles/1.5 hours

Info: Walk counter-clockwise from the kitchen shelter to an easy lakeside stroll that's bound to put a bounce in your step. A slice of Mother Nature at her finest, you'll wander and gad-about a picturesque landscape. A half-mile into your trek, take note of the Douglas fir that clings to the rocky shoreline, its branches reaching for the water. Reel-time pleasures can be had at the charming bridge that spans Rosario Lagoon. If you

Hotel Policies May Be Subject To Change

step lightly and quietly you'll increase your chances of spotting wildlife. Playful river otters are often seen splashing about. Muskrat, deer and raccoon are commonplace as well, particularly at dusk. Birders, pack the binocs. Woodpeckers, kingfishers, great blue herons and bald eagles inhabit the terrain. From the Southend Campground, follow the south campground road to the intersection with the county road. Cross the road and follow the Woodland Trail to the Cascade Lake picnic area, your starting point.

Directions: From the ferry, take Horsehoe Highway for 13 miles to the park entrance. The trailhead is located at the Cascade Lake Picnic Area.

4) LITTLE SUMMIT TRAIL HIKE - Leashes

Intermediate/4.4 miles/3.0 hours

Info: The trail takes off from behind the television station and winds around mountaintop ridges where breathtaking vistas are the name of the game. After the first half mile, you and Boomer will zoomer into a dense woodland. Shaded and bird-filled, this shake a leg journey deposits you at 2,200' Little Summit and some of the most incredible panoramas of the Olympic Range.

Directions: From the ferry, take Horsehoe Highway for 13 miles to the park entrance. The trail is located at the summit of Mt. Constitution.

5) MOUNTAIN LAKE LOOP TRAIL HIKE - Leashes

Beginner/3.9 miles/2.0 hours

Info: Stop puppyfooting around and just do it on this numero uno trail. A crystal clear gem nestled in the verdant hills, you and your canine companion will find quietude at every lakeside turn. Start in a counter-clockwise direction and follow the shoreline to the dam where a biscuit break is in order. If you're toting binocs, you might spot a skilled kingfisher, bald eagle or osprey fishing for lake trout. The trail drops below the dam and then rejoins the shoreline. The wet wagger will undoubtedly take the lead as you wiggle and waggle along the far side

Locate Other Dog-Friendly Activities...Check Nearby Cities

of the lake where views of 2,405' Mt. Constitution, the highest point in the San Juans, are meant to impress. Stay on the straight and narrow and zap, you'll be back at your starting point before you know it.

Directions: From the ferry, take Horsehoe Highway for 13 miles to the park entrance. The trailhead is located at the ranger's cabin near the Mountain Lake Campground.

6) SUNRISE ROCK TRAIL HIKE - Leashes

Intermediate/1.0 miles/0.5 hours

Info: A quick trek to campsite #17 will put you on the right track to this challenging hike that encompasses some of the park's most charming scenery. Named for the exquisite sunrise beauty it affords, this trail climbs a stiff 300' in just a half mile. But every huff and puff will be rewarded with an ooh and ahh. If you go for the sunrise, pack the makings for breakfast on your lofty perch. It'll be one bagel and biscuit repast you won't soon forget. Bone appétit.

Directions: From the ferry, take Horsehoe Highway for 13 miles to the park entrance. The trail begins at the Park Office.

7) TWIN LAKES TRAIL HIKE - Leashes

Intermediate/4.4 miles/2.5 hours

Info: Take this invigorating sojourn in a clockwise direction to reach the north end of Mountain Lake where you and the sure-footed dirty dog will cross the creek and continue straight toward Twin Lakes. You'll earn your hiking points on the next leg of the pathway as it follows the creek uphill about a half mile before leveling off and opening up to Big Twin Lake. A gamut of sidetrips around Big and Little Twin Lakes will tempt you and the one with the ear-to-ear grin. And if you're made of tough stuff, you can always add another three miles to your agenda and take the zigzagging trail to the summit of Mt. Constitution.

Directions: From the ferry, take Horsehoe Highway for 13 miles to the park entrance. The trail begins at the boat launch at Mountain Lake.

Hotel Policies May Be Subject To Change

OBSTRUCTION PASS PARK - Leashes

Info: Picnic pleasures can be yours at the top of this simple parkland. Or work out the kinks on the woodland trail that deposits you and the woofer to a horseshoe shaped cove with great views of Obstruction Pass and Obstruction Island.

Directions: From Eastsound, take Horseshoe Highway east to Obstruction Bay Road and turn right to the park.

ORONDO

RECREATION

ORONDO RIVER PARK - Leashes

Info: A river runs through it. When walk time calls, answer with a waterful excursion to this delightful 5-acre park.

Directions: Off Highway 97, 3 miles upriver from Orondo.

OROVILLE

LODGING

RED APPLE INN
1815 Main St (98844)
Rates: $36-$55
Tel: (509) 476-3694

OTHELLO

LODGING

ALADDIN MOTOR INN
1020 E Cedar St (99344)
Rates: $35-$60
Tel: (509) 488-5671

MAR DON RESORT
8198 Hwy 262 E (99344)
Rates: $38-$55
Tel: (509) 346-2651

THE RAMA INN
1450 E Main St (99344)
Rates: n/a
Tel: (509) 488-6612

RECREATION

COLUMBIA NATIONAL WILDLIFE REFUGE - Leashes

Info: In doggiedom, this landscape of rugged cliffs, canyons, lakes and sagebrush grasslands rates two enthusiastic paws up. Birders won't know where to look first. Canada geese, mallard ducks and tundra swans are just a handful of the inhabitants. For a bonus of beauty, visit in spring when the wildflowers come out to play and dazzle. Carpe diem Duke. For more information: 509-488-2668.

Directions: From Othello, take Highway 17 one mile north of the intersection with Highway 26. Turn left on Main Street and follow to Broadway. Turn right on Broadway and continue about 5 miles to the refuge. (Broadway will turn into McManamon Road).

OYSTERVILLE

RECREATION

LEADBETTER POINT STATE PARK - Leashes

Info: Okay naturalists, so you're looking for an experience to remember. Well, this combo plate of outdoor pleasure has all the makings of a doggone great day. Located at the northern-most tip of Long Beach Peninsula, the park is bordered by the briny Pacific and the fresh waters of Willapa Bay, both of which enhance the setting and provide environments for an array of wildlife and birdlife.

An avian havian, ornithologists swear by this site which is a stopover for up to 100 species of birds including sandpipers, turnstones, yellowlegs, sanderlings, knots and the black brandt, a sea goose which migrates along the Pacific between Alaska and Mexico. April and May are particularly fine birding months, a time when the marshes and mud flats are transformed into a mecca for migrating shorebirds and brandts. Leadbetter also represents the northern limit breeding spot for Snowy Plovers, small shorebirds that nest on the upper ocean beach in small scapes in the sand. Part of the dunes are closed from April through August to protect these nests.

Hotel Policies May Be Subject To Change

Wildlife devotees, you'll be just as likely to hear the howl of a coyote as the woof of the woofmeister. The coastal areas are sweet spots for clamming, beachcombing and kite flying. The lush countryside will satisfy the hiking gurus in the crowd with trails that lace the duney and grassy regions and skedaddle through the giant redwood grove. Park and refuge officials emphasize that you carry an adequate supply of aqua fria. Wowser Bowser, get ready for an adventure extraordinaire. For more information: (360) 642-3078.

Directions: Located on the Long Beach Peninsula. From Oysterville, travel north on Stackpole Road about 3 miles to the park at the end of the road.

WASHINGTON STATE BEACHES

Info: One of the few coastal regions where you can drive on the beach, there are three remarkable stretches awaiting your exploration. Obey the rules which are posted at access points. In particular, use caution near pedestrians and stay well away from the clam beds near the waterline.

Directions: Heading from north to south, the following are the locations of the drive-on Washington beaches:

1) Moclips to Ocean Shores along Highways 109 and 115
2) Westport to North Cove along Highway 105
3) Oysterville to Ilwaco along Highway 103

For additional lodging and recreation in the beach areas, see listings under the following cities: Copalis Beach, Grayland, Ilwaco, Long Beach Peninsula, Moclips, Ocean Park, Ocean Shores, Pacific Beach, Westport.

Note: Certain sections are closed to vehicular traffic from April 15th through the day after Labor Day. Areas that are open year round include a 13.5-mile stretch from Bolstad Avenue in Long Beach north to Oysterville Gap Road and a 2.2 miler just south of Beard's Hollow to Seaview Gap Road.

PACIFIC BEACH

LODGING

SAND DOLLAR MOTEL
53 Central (98571)
Rates: $43-$100
Tel: (360) 276-4525

SANDPIPER BEACH RESORT
4159 SR 109 (98571)
Rates: $55-$165
Tel: (360) 276-4580
(800) 567-4737

SHORELINE MOTEL
12 1st St South (98571)
Rates: $45-$75
Tel: (360) 276-4433

RECREATION

WASHINGTON STATE BEACHES

Info: One of the few coastal regions where you can drive on the beach, there are three remarkable stretches awaiting your exploration. Obey the rules which are posted at access points. In particular, use caution near pedestrians and stay well away from the clam beds near the waterline.

Directions: Heading from north to south, the following are the locations of the drive-on Washington beaches:

1) Moclips to Ocean Shores along Highways 109 and 115
2) Westport to North Cove along Highway 105
3) Oysterville to Ilwaco along Highway 103

For additional lodging and recreation in the beach areas, see listings under the following cities: Copalis Beach, Grayland, Ilwaco, Long Beach Peninsula, Moclips, Ocean Park, Ocean Shores, Oysterville, Westport.

PACKWOOD

LODGING

CREST TRAIL LODGE MOTEL
12729 Hwy 12 (98361)
Rates: $40-$60
Tel: (360) 494-4944

MOUNTAIN VIEW LODGE MOTEL
13163 Hwy 12 (98361)
Rates: $45-$75
Tel: (360) 494-5555

TATOOSH MEADOWS RESORT
102 E Main (98361)
Rates: $100-$300
Tel: (800) 294-2311

Hotel Policies May Be Subject To Change

PASCO

LODGING

AIRPORT MOTEL
2532 N 4th St (99301)
Rates: $27-$38
Tel: (509) 545-1460

KING CITY TRUCK STOP MOTEL
2100 E Hillsboro Rd (99301)
Rates: $38-$48
Tel: (509) 547-3475

MOTEL 6
1520 N Oregon St (99301)
Rates: $32-$38
Tel: (509) 546-2010
(800) 440-6000

RED LION INN
2525 N 20th Ave (99301)
Rates: $85-$105
Tel: (509) 547-0701
(800) 547-8010

SAGE 'N SUN MOTEL
1232 S 10th St (99301)
Rates: $28-$48
Tel: (800) 391-9188

THUNDERBIRD MOTEL
414 W Columbia (99301)
Rates: n/a
Tel: (509) 547-9506

TRI-MARK MOTEL
720 W Lewis St (99301)
Rates: n/a
Tel: (509) 547-7766

THE VINEYARD INN
1800 W Lewis (99301)
Rates: $39-$55
Tel: (509) 547-0791
(800) 824-5457

RECREATION

SACAJAWEA STATE PARK - Leashes

Info: Named for the female Native American guide who was an invaluable member of the Lewis and Clark expedition, this pretty locale offers you and your explorer lots of options. Delve into the past and peruse the interpretive displays which provide insight into the famous journey. Play follow the nose along the 9,100' freshwater shoreline. Or drop your line, the fishing's just fine. For more information: (509) 545-2361.

Directions: From Pasco, travel east on Highway 12 for 2 miles to the signed park entrance.

PATEROS

LODGING

LAKE PATEROS MOTOR INN
115 Lakeshore Dr (98846)
Rates: $51-$59
Tel: (509) 923-2207
(800) 444-1985

Locate Other Dog-Friendly Activities...Check Nearby Cities

PESHASTIN

LODGING

TIMBERLINE HOTEL
8284 Hwy 2 (98847)
Rates: n/a
Tel: (509) 548-7415

POINT ROBERTS

LODGING

CEDAR HOUSE INN B&B
1534 Gulf Rd (98281)
Rates: $36-$49
Tel: (360) 945-0284

POMEROY

LODGING

PIONEER MOTEL
1201 Main St,
Box 579 (99347)
Rates: $35-$50
Tel: (509) 843-1559

RECREATION

BEAR CREEK TRAIL HIKE

Intermediate/6.0 miles/3.5 hours

Info: Over to the river by way of the woods you and the dawgus will go. Beginning with a steep, switchbacking descent through meadows and scattered forests, you'll eventually be deposited at the Tucannon River. Cool your jets and pass the time of day doing the play thing before tackling the ascent thing back to the trailhead. Talk about Stairmaster workouts. For more information: (509) 843-1891.

Directions: From Pomeroy, take Benjamin Gulch Road (CR 128) south approximately 10 miles to FS 40 (Mountain Road) junction. Follow FS 40 about 16 miles to the Blue Mountain Trail sign. The trail begins a quarter-mile from the main road.

Hotel Policies May Be Subject To Change

THREE FORKS TRAIL HIKE

Intermediate/6.6 miles/4.0 hours

Info: In dogspeak, this trail through the Wenaha-Tucannon Wilderness rates two paws up. But you'll work hard for the eye-catching splendor and splish-splashing fun that is part and parcel of the package. Crooked Creek is the perfect payback spot, so plan some lunch alfrisky and make a day of it. For more information: (509) 843-1891.

Directions: From Pomeroy, take Benjamin Gulch Road (CR 128) south approximately 10 miles to FS 40 (Mountain Road) junction. Follow FS 40 south for 35 miles to FS 4039. Make a right on FS 4039 to the trailhead at the large pole corral.

PORT ANGELES

Lodging

AGGIE'S INN
602 E Front St (98362)
Rates: $46-$68
Tel: (360) 457-0471

CHINOOK MOTEL
1414 E 1st St (98362)
Rates: $45-$80
Tel: (360) 452-2336

DOUBLETREE HOTEL
221 N Lincoln St (98362)
Rates: $69-$160
Tel: (360) 452-9215
(800) 222-8733

ELWHA RANCH B&B
905 Herrick Rd (98363)
Rates: $75+
Tel: (360) 457-6540

FLAGSTONE MOTEL
415 E 1st St (98362)
Rates: $36-$58
Tel: (360) 457-9494

INDIAN VALLEY MOTEL
7020 Hwy 101 (98362)
Rates: n/a
Tel: (360) 928-3266

KOA KAMPGROUND CABINS
80 O'Brien Rd (98362)
Rates: $30-$45
Tel: (360) 457-5916
(800) 562-7558

LAKE CRESCENT LODGE
416 Lake Crescent Rd (98362)
Rates: $64-$114
Tel: (360) 928-3211

LOG CABIN RESORT & RV PARK
3183 E Beach Rd (98363)
Rates: $62-$100
Tel: (360) 928-3325

MAPLE ROSE INN B&B
112 Reservoir Rd (98363)
Rates: $69-$147
Tel: (360) 457-ROSE
(800) 570-2007

THE POND MOTEL
1425 W Hwy 101 (98362)
Rates: $29-$59
Tel: (360) 452-8422

RUFFLES MOTEL
812 E 1st St (98363)
Rates: n/a
Tel: (360) 457-1188

Locate Other Dog-Friendly Activities...Check Nearby Cities

SOL DUC HOT SPRINGS RESORT
P.O. Box 2169 (98362)
Rates: $78-$128
Tel: (360) 327-3583

SUPER 8 MOTEL
2104 E 1st St (98362)
Rates: $45-$90
Tel: (360) 452-8401
(800) 800-8000

UPTOWN MOTEL
101 E 2nd St (98362)
Rates: $35-$125
Tel: (360) 457-9434
(800) 858-3812

RECREATION

CONRAD DYAR MEMORIAL CIRCLE - Leashes

Info: An easy-does-it kind of outing awaits you and the dawgus at this view-blessed spot. Climb the Laurel Street Stairs for fabulous vistas over the Strait of Juan de Fuca to Vancouver Island. There's a cascading fountain where the tinkling of water will add a note of serenity to your little sojourn.

Directions: Located at First and Laurel Streets.

FRESHWATER BAY - Leashes

Info: When playtime calls, answer it with an excursion to this 17-acre bay. Put on the dog and strut your stuff along the waterway. Popular with boaters, you'll see lots of small craft splying the waves. For more information: (360) 417-2291.

Directions: From Port Angeles, travel Highway 101 west about 2.5 miles to the junction with Highway 112, turn right. Continue west on Highway 112 to Freshwater Bay Road, turn right to the signed park entrance.

PIONEERS PATH NATURE TRAIL HIKE - Leashes

Beginner/0.3 miles/0.15 hours

Info: Mini in size but maxi in appeal, take your pupsqueak on this pipsqueak trail which packs a big punch. In no time flat, you'll experience a second-growth fir and hemlock forest, gain insight into pioneer life and savor the serenity of the Soleduck River as it rushes beside you. For more information: (360) 765-2200.

Directions: From Port Angeles, head west on Highway 101 about 30 miles to the Klahowya Campground. The trailhead is just past the boat ramp.

Hotel Policies May Be Subject To Change

SALT CREEK RECREATION AREA - Leashes

Info: Once a WWII harbor defense site, this picturesque surf-side park is a sweet retreat for all breeds. If your woofer's a hoofer, hop on one of the hiking trails that lace the rolling greens and wildlife-filled woodlands. Or hit the beach and leave some telltail tracks in the sand. If you're looking for fun times, you can't go wrong at this 200-acre region. For more information: (360) 417-2291.

Directions: From Port Angeles, travel Highway 101 west about 2.5 miles to the junction with Highway 112, turn right. Continue west on Highway 112 about 7 miles to Camp Hayden Road, turn right. Follow Camp Hayden Road to the signed park entrance.

WEST WATERFRONT TRAIL HIKE - Leashes

Beginner/6.0 miles/3.0 hours

Info: Beautiful Ediz Hook is the bonus at the end of your trek through the city's marine industrial section. A naturally formed sand spit, you might want to brown bag it with the wag it and make the noon break special. The views of the Olympic Mountains add a touch of nature to the adventure. For more information: (360) 452-2363.

Directions: The trail begins at the City Pier just east of Railroad Avenue.

Note: Parking is also available off Marine Drive at the Hook.

PORT HADLOCK

LODGING

PORT HADLOCK INN
201 Alcohol Loop Rd (98339)
Rates: n/a
Tel: (360) 385-5801

THE OLD ALCOHOL PLANT
310 Alcohol Loop Rd (98339)
Rates: $59-$250
Tel: (360) 385-7030
(800) 785-7030

VALLEY VIEW CABINS
12775 Hwy 30 (98339)
Rates: $45-$50
Tel: (360) 385-1666
(800) 280-1666

PORT LUDLOW

LODGING

INN AT LUDLOW BAY RESORT
1 Heron Rd (98365)
Rates: $135-$450
Tel: (360) 437-0411

PORT ORCHARD

LODGING

CEDAR HOLLOW GUEST HOUSE B&B
3875 Locker Rd (98366)
Rates: $75
Tel: (360) 871-1527

VISTA MOTEL
1090 Bethel (98366)
Rates: $30-$59
Tel: (360) 876-8046

RECREATION

MANCHESTER STATE PARK - Leashes

Info: A little bit of this and a little bit of that is what you can expect at this charming view-filled waterside setting. Eleven acres stretch beside the waterfront offering front row seats to pretty panoramas of Seattle, Bainbridge Island and Puget Sound. Nearly 1.5 miles of trails honeycomb the park which is dotted with cozy spots and picnic ops. For more information: (360) 902-8500.

Directions: From Port Orchard, travel 6 miles east on Highway 16 to the Sedgewick exit and follow signs to the park.

PORT TOWNSEND

LODGING

ALADDIN MOTOR INN
2333 Washington St (98368)
Rates: $50-$99
Tel: (360) 385-3747
(800) 281-3747

BISHOP VICTORIAN GUEST SUITES
714 Washington St (98368)
Rates: $79-$109
Tel: (360) 385-6122
(800) 824-4738

ANNAPURNA INN B&B
538 Adams St (98368)
Rates: $65-$115
Tel: (360) 385-2909
(800) 868-2662

CABIN VACATION RENTAL
839 Jacob Miller (98368)
Rates: $95
Tel: (360) 385-5571

Hotel Policies May Be Subject To Change

COMMANDER'S HOUSE GETAWAY
Point House (98368)
Rates: $49-$125
Tel: (360) 385-2828
(800) 826-3854

**FT. WORDEN STATE PARK
CONFERENCE CENTER**
200 Battery Way (98368)
Rates: $45-$80
Tel: (360) 385-4730

GALA'S GETAWAY RENTAL
4343 Haines St (98368)
Rates: $60-$80
Tel: (360) 385-1194

HARBORSIDE INN
330 Benedict St (98368)
Rates: $64-$104
Tel: (360) 385-7909
(800) 942-5960

NORTH BEACH RETREAT RENTAL
510 56th St (98368)
Rates: $50+
Tel: (360) 385-1621

THE PALACE HOTEL
1004 Water St (98368)
Rates: $65-$139
Tel: (360) 385-0733
(800) 962-0741

PILOT HOUSE VACATION RENTAL
327 Jackson St (98368)
Rates: $60-$95
Tel: (360) 379-0811

POINT HUDSON RESORT & MARINA
Point Hudson Harbor,
103 Hudson St (98368)
Rates: $45-$90
Tel: (360) 385-2828
(800) 826-3854

PORT TOWNSEND INN
2020 Washington St (98368)
Rates: $48-$98
Tel: (360) 385-2211
(800) 216-4985

PUFFIN & GULL APARTMENT MOTEL
825 Washington St (98368)
Rates: n/a
Tel: (360) 385-1475

THE SWAN HOTEL
222 Monroe St (98368)
Rates: $65-$150
Tel: (360) 385-1718
(800) 776-1718

TIDES INN
1807 Water St (98368)
Rates: $58-$124
Tel: (360) 385-0595
(800) 822-8696

VALLEY VIEW MOTEL
162 Hwy 20 (98368)
Rates: $35-$50
Tel: (360) 385-1666
(800) 280-1666

WATER STREET HOTEL
635 Water St (98368)
Rates: $40-$60
Tel: (360) 385-5467
(800) 735-9810

RECREATION

BOBBY McGARRAUGH PARK - Leashes

Info: When walk time calls, answer it with a visit to this pleasant neighborhood park. Backdropped by forested hills, this urban oasis will fill the bill for your AM or PM constitutional.

Directions: Located on Cherry Street between P and S Streets.

CHETZEMOKA PARK - Leashes

Info: Port Townsend's oldest park, take the time to smell the flowers in the rose garden. Water woofers will find what they love when you hightail it to the stream that meanders through the lovely landscape.

Directions: Located on the waterfront, just west of the intersection of Blaine and Jackson Streets.

FORT WORDEN STATE PARK - Leashes

Info: Give furface something to bark home about with a day at this delightful parkland. Let your Curious George lead the way over 443 acres which come complete with a scenic overlook of the Strait of Juan de Fuca. Sniffmeisters give the high five to the Centennial Rose Garden while narcissistic pups prefer the reflecting pond of the Chinese Gardens. Pack the Kodak and take home some memories. For more information: (360) 385-4730.

Directions: Take the Kearney Road exit off Highway 20 in Port Townsend. Continue north on Kearney Road to the "T." At the "T," turn right onto Blaine. Travel one block to Walker, turn left and drive to park entrance.

KAH TAI LAGOON PARK - Leashes

Info: You'll find lots of serenery in this lovely 100-acre oasis. Put a little bounce in the wiggler's prance with a meadowland lark or find a spot to call your own and throw the poor dog a bone.

Directions: Located between Sims Way and the Park & Ride lot.

POPE MARINE PARK - Leashes

Info: After strolling the quaint streets and exercising your credit cards, give the patient pooch a Rexercise reward at this waterfront park where boat watching is de rigueur.

Directions: Located off Water Street across from City Hall and the Jefferson County Museum.

Hotel Policies May Be Subject To Change

POULSBO

LODGING

POULSBO INN
18680 Hwy 305 (98370)
Rates: $60-$105
Tel: (360) 779-3921
(800) 597-5151

RECREATION

AMERICAN LEGION PARK - Leashes

Info: When you're looking for a quick nature fix, this lovely little park might just be your ticket. Stroll beside the waterfront on a scenic half miler that leads to a wee slice of greenery.

Directions: Located on Front Street.

KITSAP MEMORIAL STATE PARK - Leashes

Info: No bones about it, you and your old tar will feel right at home at this 57-acre surf and turf locale beside the Hood Canal. Check the tide tables and come at low tide - the pools contain mucho marine specimens like starfish, crab, chiton, oyster, clam, limpet and barnacle. Keep a keen snout out for birds of a feather that flock together including goldfinch, crow, great blue heron, flicker, kingfish and the ever present screeching seagull. For more information: (360) 779-3205.

Directions: From Poulsbo, travel Highway 3 north about 6 miles and follow signs to the park entrance.

PROSSER

LODGING

BEST WESTERN PROSSER INN
225 Merlot Dr (99350)
Rates: $54-$57
Tel: (509) 786-7977
(800) 528-1234

PROSSER MOTEL
1206 Wine Country Rd (99350)
Rates: $30-$48
Tel: (509) 786-2555

PULLMAN

LODGING

AMERICAN TRAVEL INN
515 S Grand Ave (99163)
Rates: $40-$50
Tel: (509) 334-3500

HOLIDAY INN EXPRESS
SE 1190 Bishop Blvd (99163)
Rates: $79
Tel: (509) 334-4437
(800) 465-4329

MANOR LODGE MOTEL
SE 455 Paradise (99163)
Rates: $39-$59
Tel: (509) 334-2511

QUALITY INN-PARADISE CREEK
SE 1050 Bishop (99163)
Rates: $58-$135
Tel: (509) 332-0500
(800) 221-2222

PUYALLUP

LODGING

MOTEL PUYALLUP
1412 S Meridian St (98371)
Rates: $39-$64
Tel: (253) 845-8825

NORTHWEST MOTOR INN
1409 S Meridian St (98371)
Rates: $45-$60
Tel: (253) 841-2600
(800) 845-9490

TAYBERRY VICTORIAN COTTAGE B&B
7406 80th St E (98371)
Rates: $65-$85
Tel: (253) 848-4594

QUILCENE

LODGING

MAPLE GROVE MOTEL
61 Maple Grove Rd (98376)
Rates: $40-$50
Tel: (360) 765-3410

RECREATION

FALLS VIEW CANYON TRAIL HIKE - Leashes

Expert/1.2 miles/1.0 hours

Info: For a Stairmaster workout à la Mother Nature, include this switchbacking hike to the Big Quilcene River in your travel plans. Tough but user-friendly, wood handrails make the going

Hotel Policies May Be Subject To Change

easier on the steep descent along the canyon walls. Payoff time comes when you reach the river. If you've planned a picnic, this is the place for your repast. Hey don't forget Bowser's biscuits. You'll both need the energy boost for your outbound, uphill journey. For more information: (360) 765-2200.

Directions: From Quilcene, head south on Highway 101 for 3.5 miles to the Falls View Campground. The trailhead is located at the left edge of the parking lot.

FALLS VIEW CANYON VISTA TRAIL HIKE - Leashes

Beginner/0.2 miles/0.10 hours

Info: This peanut-sized jaunt escorts you and your peanut to a lovely waterfall viewpoint that also encompasses the Big Quilcene River below. Even telly bellies give this quickie the high five. For more information: (360) 765-2200.

Directions: From Quilcene, head south on Highway 101 for 3.5 miles to the Falls View Campground. The trailhead is located on the right edge of the parking lot.

INTERROREM NATURE TRAIL HIKE - Leashes

Beginner/0.25 miles/0.15 hours

Info: You'll tiptoe through an abundance of ferns and mosses while birdsong drifts your way on this well maintained loop-de-loop. Munch on lunch at the cozy picnic area and make the most of your outing. For more information: (360) 765-2200.

Directions: From Quilcene, head south on Highway 101 to FS 2510, turn right. Continue for 4 miles to the historic Interrorem Cabin and the picnic area. The Interrorem Nature Trail branches off to the left.

LITTLE QUILCENE TRAIL to LITTLE RIVER SUMMIT HIKE - Leashes

Intermediate/1.8 miles/1.0 hours

Info: Get along with your little doggie on this lovely, albeit strenuous mountainside trail. Particularly colorful in spring, you'll be tickled pink by the rhododendrons and azaleas. Take some well earned R&R at the summit before doing the descent thing. Gung-ho hikers can continue another mile along a fairly level pathway to the Mt. Townsend Trail, but resist going any further, the grade becomes very steep after that. For more information: (360) 765-2200.

Directions: From Quilcene, head north on Highway 101 about 2 miles to Lords Lake Road, turn left. Continue for 3.4 miles to FS 28. Turn left and proceed over Bon Jon Pass to FS 2820. Turn left and drive about 4 miles to the trailhead on the right.

LOWER BIG QUILCENE TRAIL to CAMP JOLLEY HIKE - Leashes

Beginner/9.0 miles/5.0 hours

Info: A paw-worthy adventure, come and witness Mother Nature's artistry on this delightful trail. The treehound's tail will be in overdrive as you zip through thick forests of towering trees made even prettier by the verdant riverside setting and the harmony of twittering birds. Anglers, pack your pole and find a fishing hole, din-din awaits. If you're visiting in spring or early summer, you'll understand the trail's pupularity, wildflowers are everywhere, dazzling with their colors and enchanting with their fragrance. Bone voyage. For more information: (360) 756-2200.

Directions: From Quilcene, take Highway 101 south for one mile to Penny Creek Road, turn right. Follow Penny Creek Road about one mile to FS 27, turn left onto FS 27 and continue 5 miles to the intersection of FS 2700-080, turn left. The trailhead is located in the old Big Quilcene Campground.

MT. TOWNSEND TRAIL HIKE - Leashes

Beginner-Expert/1.0 miles-10.0 miles/0.5 hours-6.0 hours

Info: This freelance style trail offers plenty of paw-pleasing opportunities. Mellow fellows can do the half miler to Sink Lake and then do a chill out waterside. On the other paw, gung-ho hikers can opt for the 3.5-mile journey to Camp Windy where the name says it all.

If you and your canine crony are of the Herculean persuasion, the summit and all the beauty you'd expect from a peak top is within reach. A half-mile past Camp Windy, the trail splits and continues up, up and away. After another mile, expect to be wowed and bow wowed. The scenery is among the best in the Olympics, not to mention the staggering wildflower displays that are part of the package in spring and summer. Countless peeks of peaks will come into focus all around, while Hood Canal and Puget Sound color the world below in blueness. Pack plenty of Fuji, this beaut eats film for breakfast. For more information: (360) 765-2200.

Directions: From Quilcene, take Highway 101 north about 2 miles to Lords Lake Road, turn left. Proceed 3.4 miles to FS 28 and continue to the intersection with FS 27. Turn left over Skaar Pass to FS 2760 and proceed 0.7 miles to the small parking area and trailhead.

MT. ZION TRAIL HIKE - Leashes

Expert/3.6 miles/2.0 hours

Info: Scenery seekers, if you're made of tough stuff, this trail has your name on it. Leash up the hound and you're summit bound on a challenging trek. You'll ascend through forest fire remnants as well as second growth fir and cedar woodlands, rhododendrons galore and an understory of Oregon grape, salal and leafy ferns. If the greenery doesn't get you, the scenery will. Outstanding and spectacular will come to mind when Puget Sound, Mt. Baker, Mt. Rainier and the Cascades come into view. Pack plenty of water. For more information: (360) 765-2200.

Directions: From Quilcene, take Highway 101 north about 2 miles to Lords Lake Loop Road, turn left. Proceed 3.4 miles to FS 28 and follow to the three way fork. Stay to the right when you reach the fork and follow until the road becomes FS 2810 at Bon Jon Pass. Drive 2 miles further to the trailhead.

RANGER HOLE TRAIL HIKE - Leashes

Beginner/1.6 miles/1.0 hours

Info: Wildflower devotees, don't miss this extravaganza in springtime when the landscape comes alive in color. If you're a fool for fall and old cold nose loves a roll in the crunchy ones, come and delight in the Golden Retriever-hued maples. The sound of rushing water signals the onslaught of a wagging frenzy as you approach Ranger Hole, the place where a river runs through it, "it" being a narrow rock passage before tumbling into a deep icy pool. Go ahead, cool those tootsies. For more information: (360) 877-5254.

Directions: From Hoodsport, take Highway 101 north for 22 miles to Duckabush River Road (FS 2510), turn west. Continue for 4 miles to the Ranger Hole Trailhead on the left side of the road. The trail branches off to the right.

QUINAULT

LODGING

LAKE QUINAULT LODGE
345 S Shore Rd (98575)
Rates: $65-$130
Tel: (360) 288-2900
(800) 562-6672 (WA)

RECREATION

QUINAULT LOOP TRAIL HIKE - Leashes

Intermediate/4.0 miles/2.0 hours

Info: This almost mystical experience will imbue you with a sense of wonder and a renewed respect for the diversity of nature. Get ready, get set and go for the experience of a lifetime. You'll be exposed to a cornucopia of beauty all along your route. Cascading waterfalls and crystal clear streams are just part of the picture. The sniffmeister will think he's found nirvana embodied in the rain forest landscape. Cedar swamplands, trees standing on stilts and mossy draping vegetation are everywhere. Refreshingly misty, you and the dawgus will feel transported to another dimension as you travel under a canopy of towering trees in this otherworldly place. Carpe diem you lucky dog. For more information: (360) 288-2525.

Directions: From Highway 101, turn east on South Shore Road and drive 1.4 miles to the trailhead parking lot on the right-hand side of the road.

QUINAULT RAIN FOREST NATURE TRAIL HIKE - Leashes

Beginner/0.5 miles/0.5 hours

Info: Just walking in the rain, actually, you'll strut the mutt through a misty journey where everyday cares dissolve into the air. The shrouded beauty of this woodsy region includes lichen and mosses which cling to towering trees and a cascading stream which slices a path through a narrow ridge. Chatty, chirpy flyboys flutter about the bog and serenade you on your stroll. Take your time, much of the magic of this trail is discovered a little piece at a time. For more information: (360) 288-2525.

Directions: From Highway 101, turn east on South Shore Road and drive 1.4 miles to the trailhead parking lot on the right-hand side of the road.

QUINAULT VALLEY LOOP AUTO TOUR

25 miles/1.5 hours

Info: For a different perspective of the landscape and the sometimes elusive wildlife that inhabits the terrain, take to the wheel and explore this section of the Peninsula. Following the north and south shores of lovely Lake Quinault, your tour d'auto will be a memorable one. You'll pass through the Colonel Bob Wilderness and mucho regions of rain forest vegetation. Stow your binocs and a camera with a zoom lens so you can take advantage of the wildlife ops that inevitably occur at the roadside pullouts. This particular neck of the woods is popular with Roosevelt elk. Dawn and dusk are primo viewing times. For more information: (360) 288-2525.

Directions: From Highway 101, turn east on South Shore Road. The loop road circles Lake Quinault.

Note: Drive with care, some portions of the road are single dirt lanes. The road is unsuitable for trailers.

QUINCY

LODGING

THE SUNDOWNER MOTEL
414 F St SE (98848)
Rates: n/a
Tel: (509) 787-3587

TRADITIONAL INNS
500 F St SW (98848)
Rates: $38-$90
Tel: (509) 787-3525

Locate Other Dog-Friendly Activities...Check Nearby Cities

RECREATION

EAST PARK - Leashes

Info: Take your bark for a lark in this lovely 15-acre park. Root for the home team or visit in the off season and make your own fun and games.

Directions: Located off Highway 28 on the east end of Quincy.

RESERVOIR PARK - Leashes

Info: Perfect for your AM or PM constitutional, this petite park is a grassy little oasis in the middle of town.

Directions: Located on Central in the center of Quincy.

SOUTH PARK - Leashes

Info: Dollars to dog biscuits, you'll get the tail in the wagging mode with a stop in this 3-acre green scene.

Directions: Located on the corner of 3rd Avenue and L Street.

RAINIER

LODGING

7 C's GUEST RANCH
11123 128th St SE (98576)
Rates: $30-$100
Tel: (360) 446-7957

RECREATION

HUDSON/PARKER PARK - Leashes

Info: Nestled in a serene woodland of fir and cedar, this paw-worthy park is bound to go over big time with the hound. Popular with the locals, sporty breeds can spectate at one of the ball fields. For more information: (503) 556-9050.

Directions: From Rainier, travel west on Highway 30 approximately 1 mile to the top of Rainier Hill and turn left at the blinking light on Larson Road.

Hotel Policies May Be Subject To Change

LAUREL BEACH - Leashes

Info: Afishionados swear by this locale along the Columbia River. And birders won't go home empty-eyed either, lots of flyboys ply the skies.

Directions: Located 1 1/2 miles south of Rainier off Highway 30 on Laurelwood Road.

Note: The day-use park opens one hour before sunrise and closes one hour after sunset.

RAINIER HILL VIEWPOINTS

Info: For some terrific views of Longview and Mt. St. Helens, make a pit stop at the vehicle turnouts along Highway 30.

Directions: Viewpoints are accessible only to westbound Highway 30 traffic.

RANDLE

LODGING

MEDICI MOTEL
661 Cispus Rd (98377)
Rates: $45
Tel: (360) 497-7700
(800) 697-7750

WOODLAND MOTEL
11890 US 12 (98377)
Rates: $25-$45
Tel: (360) 494-6766

TALL TIMBER
10023 Hwy 12 (98377)
Rates: n/a
Tel: (360) 497-5908

RAYMOND

LODGING

MAUNU'S MOUNTCASTLE MOTEL
524 3rd St (98577)
Rates: $36-$50
Tel: (360) 942-5571

WILLIS MOTEL
425 3rd St (98577)
Rates: $40+
Tel: (360) 942-5313

Locate Other Dog-Friendly Activities...Check Nearby Cities

REDMOND

LODGING

SILVER CLOUD INN
15304 NE 21st St (98052)
Rates: $54-$69
Tel: (425) 746-8200
(800) 205-6934

RECREATION

MARYMOOR PARK - Leashes

Info: Let sleeping dogs lie - no way. This is the place where they come to play and it's one experience you won't want to miss. Doggiedom in it's finest hour. The lickmeister will love you forever after one afternoon in this extraordinary park which covers acres of tree-strewn greenery. You'll find waterways, totem poles, Canada geese, squirrels, picnic tables and all the usual park amenities. But what makes this a numero uno canine hangout is the leash-free area. Okay, we've all experienced leashless abandon in one form or another. Places where dogs can run and smell to their heart's content, get down and dirty and just have a plain old good time. But this place takes the biscuit, hands down.

On any given day, you won't believe the number of woofers and hoofers you'll encounter. Dogs fitting every description pop up from every corner, from under every bush, from behind every tree. Without a doubt, old brown eyes will get to sniff more tail in Marymoor than just about anyplace else. What awaits the wagging machine is doggie nirvana. Not only are there trails and grass but a river runs through it. If you're not toting a ball or Frisbee, then find yourself a stick. You're gonna need something to toss to the Boss or your dawgus will feel totally deprived. Wet and wild shenanigans are de rigueur in this neck of the woods. Whatever you do, it won't be enough. You'll feel right at home and even before the day is over you'll promise to return as soon as possible. For more information: (206) 883-8908.

Directions: Drive east on Highway 520 to the W. Lake Sammamish Parkway N.E. exit and turn right at the first light. Continue to the next light and make a left. Go past the sign for the dog training area and make a right at the stop sign. Drive to the parking lot and park on the left-hand side (closest to the leash-free area).

Note: This wonderful area was made possible by the diligent efforts of S.O.D.A. (Save Our Dog Areas). Clean up after your dog. Plastic bags are provided at the entrance to the leash-free area, take what you need for your visit.

SAMMAMISH RIVER TRAIL HIKE - Leashes

Beginner/5.4 miles/3.0 hours

Info: Skirting the banks of the Sammamish River, this scenic trail is a bonafido tail wagger. Beginning in Marymoor Park, you can do some Northwest daydreaming beside the tranquil Sammamish River as it wends its way through lush farmlands and greenery galore. The paw-pleasing terrain equates to popularity so be prepared to meet and greet. Sixty Acres Park signals turnaround time. For more information: (206) 296-4232.

Directions: The trail begins in Marymoor Park, 5 miles south of Redmond on West Lake Sammamish Parkway. The trail ends on 96th Avenue.

RENTON

LODGING

BED & BREAKFAST ASSOCIATION OF SUBURBAN SEATTLE
908 Grant Ave S (98055)
Rates: $65-$120
Tel: (425) 277-4747

NENDEL'S INN
3700 E Valley Rd (98055)
Rates: $45-$66
Tel: (425) 251-9591
(800) 547-0106

SILVER CLOUD INN
1850 Maple Valley Hwy (98055)
Rates: $52-$70
Tel: (425) 226-7600
(800) 205-6936

REPUBLIC

LODGING

COTTONWOODS MOTEL
852 S Clark Ave (99166)
Rates: $28-$33
Tel: (509) 775-3371

FISHERMAN'S COVE RESORT
1157 Fisherman's Cove Rd (99166)
Rates: $25-$85
Tel: (509) 775-3641

FRONTIER INN MOTEL
979 S Clark Ave (99166)
Rates: $34-$57
Tel: (509) 775-3361

K-DIAMOND-K CATTLE & GUEST RANCH
404 Hwy 21 S (99166)
Rates: $60-$100
Tel: (509) 775-3536

KLONDIKE MOTEL
150 N Clark Ave (99166)
Rates: $36-$44
Tel: (509) 775-3555

TIFFANYS RESORT
1026 Tiffany Rd (99166)
Rates: $43-$115
Tel: (509) 775-3152

RECREATION

CURLEW LAKE STATE PARK - Leashes

Info: Canines and humans with a penchant for old-fashioned parks are gonna love this green scene. Try your luck on the fish or spread the red checks beside the lake and let sleeping dogs lie. Après whatever, hop on the nature trail and toss your cares to the wind. Bound with your hound through an understory of Oregon grape and an upperstory of fragrant pine. Way to go Fido. For more information: (509) 775-3592.

Directions: From Republic, travel north on Highway 21 for 10 miles to the signed park entrance.

FIR MOUNTAIN TRAIL HIKE - Leashes

Intermediate/4.0 miles/2.0 hours

Info: You and furface will get a workout for the body and a treat for the eyes on this trail. The summit of Fir Mountain stands almost completely alone in the wilderness, so expect to-die-for views of the entire forest. Switchbacks and several steep grades are demanding but you'll feel like champs after conquering this remote mountain trail. For more information: (509) 486-2186.

Directions: From Republic, travel Highway 20 west about 8.5 miles to the Sweat Creek Campground. Turn left onto Forest Service Road 31 opposite the campground. Continue about 1.5 miles to the parking area and the trailhead.

Hotel Policies May Be Subject To Change

LEONA TRAIL HIKE - Leashes

Beginner/2.0 miles/1.0 hours

Info: If you're looking for postcardian pretty, hit this trail in the AM hours when the rising sun casts rainbow colors over the Columbia River Valley and adds an almost mystical quality to the landscape. Your turnaround point is the junction with the Kettle Crest Trail. If you're a wildlife lover and want to extend your hike, amble along the Kettle Crest Trail in either direction. There's a good chance you'll glimpse hawks and falcons riding the air current in search of their morning meal. Check out the woodlands for deer or rabbit grazing in the meadows or a raccoon up to something silly. For more information: (509) 775-3305.

Directions: From Republic, travel Route 21 north past Curlew Lake to the small town of Malo and a junction with St. Peters Creek Road (CR 584), turn right. Continue about 2.5 miles to the forest boundary until the road becomes FS 400. Continue another 2.7 miles to a fork. Stay left and you'll be on FS 2040. The trailhead is at the end of FS 2040.

Note: Forest Service Road 2040 may be unsuitable for passenger cars.

LONG LAKE TRAIL HIKE - Leashes

Beginner/2.4 miles/1.5 hours

Info: Stop puppyfooting around and get thee to the shores of Long Lake. This trail lets you enjoy the clear, rippling lake waters and a lush forest setting. Pack some picnic goodies and make a day of it. For more information: (509) 775-3305.

Directions: From Republic, travel Highway 21 south about 7.5 miles to Scatter Creek Road 53, turn right (west). Continue to the Fish Lake-Long Lake sign, turn onto the 400 Road. Travel about one mile to the trailhead in the campground.

MARCUS TRAIL HIKE

Intermediate/7.1 miles/4.0 hours

Info: A must for naturalists so don't forget your binocs. Sightings of blue grouse and white-tailed deer are virtually guaranteed. If you're visiting in summer, welcome to the wildflower party. A basket for strawberry picking will come in handy. And if it's views you want, it's views you'll get. This wooded trail leads to outstanding mountain valley vistas. For more information: (509) 775-3305.

Directions: From Republic, take Highway 20 east for 14 miles to FS 2040, turn north. Drive 12 miles to FS 250, turn right and continue 2 miles to the trailhead.

NINE MILE FALLS TRAIL HIKE - Leashes

Beginner/0.6 miles/0.3 hours

Info: Like a walk in the park, you and the lickmeister will travel through bosky terrain before scooting down to a viewpoint of Nine Mile Creek and Nine Mile Falls. Talk about gorgeous. Sit a spell and enjoy the magic of it all. For more information: (509) 775-3305.

Directions: From Republic, travel east on Highway 20 about 6.5 miles to Hall Creek Road 99 (FS 99), turn right. Continue about 2.5 miles to Refrigerator Canyon Road, turn right. Drive about 5 miles to the junction of FR 2053 and 2054, turn right. The trailhead is just past the junction.

SHERMAN TRAIL HIKE -Leashes

Intermediate/2.3 miles/1.5 hours

Info: If you're hankering for some Rexercise, this trail should satisfy your craving. You and your hearty hound will climb more than 1,500' through a dense thicket to Kettle Crest and sweeping views of the countryside. The sun-kissed meadow on the north side of the crest is often splashed with colorful wildflowers. Just picture yourself picnicking in the thick of it, you lucky dog. For more information: (509) 775-3305.

Directions: From Republic, travel Route 20 east about 14 miles to FS 2040, turn left. Continue about 2.5 miles, crossing the Sanpoil River, to FS 65, turn right. The trailhead is at the end of FS 65.

Note: Forest Service Road 65 is for high-clearance vehicles only.

SWAN LAKE TRAIL HIKE - Leashes

Beginner/3.0 miles/1.5 hours

Info: The crystal clear waters of Swan Lake are the lure of this trail which skirts the waterway and dillydallies through the cool forestland. Huckleberry hounds, blue tongues await along this route. Dollars to dog biscuits, you'll probably come away with a wildlife or birdlife sighting as well. For more information: (509) 775-3305.

Directions: From Republic, travel Highway 21 south about 7.5 miles to Scatter Creek Road 53, turn right (west). Continue about 8 miles to the trailhead at the north end of Swan Lake Campground.

RICHLAND

LODGING

BALI HI MOTEL
1201 George Washington Way (99352)
Rates: $39-$45
Tel: (509) 943-3101

COLUMBIA CENTER DUNES MOTEL
1751 Fowler Ave (99352)
Rates: $35-$45
Tel: (509) 783-8181
(800) 638-6168

HAMPTON INN
486 Bradley Blvd (99352)
Rates: $63-$225
Tel: (509) 943-4400
(800) 426-7866

NENDEL'S INN
615 Jadwin Ave (99352)
Rates: $25-$74
Tel: (509) 943-4611
(800) 547-0106

RED LION INN-HANFORD HOUSE
802 George Washington Way (99352)
Rates: $79-$114
Tel: (509) 946-7611
(800) 547-8010

ROBERT YOUNG SUITES LODGING SERVICE
2455 George Washington Way, Suite O-177 (99352)
Rates: $42-$99
Tel: (509) 946-5002

SHILO INNS RIVERSHORE
50 Comstock St (99352)
Rates: $69-$99
Tel: (509) 946-4661
(800) 222-2244

VAGABOND INN
515 George Washington Way (99352)
Rates: $37-$80
Tel: ((509) 946-6117
(800) 552-1555

Locate Other Dog-Friendly Activities...Check Nearby Cities

RITZVILLE

LODGING

BEST WESTERN HERITAGE INN
1405 Smitty's Blvd (99169)
Rates: $47-$145
Tel: (509) 659-1007
(800) 528-1234

COLWELL MOTOR INN
501 W 1st Ave (99169)
Rates: $52-$125
Tel: (509) 659-1620
(800) 341-8000

COTTAGE MOTEL
508 E 1st Ave (99169)
Rates: n/a
Tel: (509) 659-0721

EMPIRE MOTEL
101 W 1st Ave (99169)
Rates: $27-$47
Tel: (509) 659-1030

TOP HAT MOTEL
210 E 1st St (99169)
Rates: $35-$42
Tel: (509) 659-1100

ROCKPORT

LODGING

CLARK'S SKAGIT RIVER CABINS
5675 Hwy 20 (98283)
Rates: $56-$140
Tel: (360) 386-4437
(800) 273-2606

TOTEM TRAIL RESTAURANT & MOTEL
5551 Hwy 20 (98283)
Rates: $35-$50
Tel: (360) 873-4535

RECREATION

BLUE LAKE TRAIL HIKE - Leashes

Beginner/1.5 miles/1.0 hours

Info: Blue Lake holds its own in this blue-dotted terrain. As you skedaddle down to water's edge, go ahead and ogle away. The scenery is bound to put you and the hound in the mood for some outdoor frolicking and then find yourself a secluded cranny to chill out. For more information: (360) 856-5700.

Directions: From Rockport, travel Highway 20 west about 12 miles to the Baker Lake Highway, turn right (north). Continue about 9 miles to Road #12, turn left. Drive about 7 miles to Road #1230, turn left. Continue about 4 miles to the Blue Lake Trailhead.

Note: Highway 20 is closed in winter.

EAST BANK TRAIL HIKE - Leashes

Beginner/8.0 miles/4.0 hours

Info: Whether you want to just hike beside the beautiful shoreline of Baker Lake or get into the boating action, you'll be smack dab in the middle of loveliness no matter which pastime you choose. Taking off from Baker Dam, the pretty blues will be with you all the way to Maple Grove Camp, not to mention the stunning views of Mt. Baker that are yours for the looking. If you're aiming to canoe or kayak, you've picked a winner and more than likely, you won't be alone, this lake's a favorite with the small craft set. Bone voyage. For more information: (360) 856-5700.

Directions: From Rockport, travel Highway 20 west about 12 miles to the Baker Lake Highway, turn right (north). Drive about 15 miles to Puget Power Campground at the Upper Baker Dam. Cross the dam to road #1107, turn left and continue about .5 miles to the trailhead on the left side of the road.

Note: Highway 20 is closed in winter.

ELBOW LAKE TRAIL HIKE - Leashes

Beginner/3.0 miles/1.5 hours

Info: Water loving wagsters swear by this region where the lakes are set in the deep, dense forestlands surrounding Twin Sisters Mountain. If trout rates high on your fish wish list, you're gonna love Elbow Lake. But don't stop there. Just above Elbow Lake, you'll come upon another beauty, Doreen Lake. Smaller but deeper, it's also a good place to try your luck. And huckleberry hounds, a purple tongue is a sure thing in late July when the bushes burst with berries and brighten the already charming ambiance For more information: (360) 856-5700.

Directions: From Rockport, travel Highway 20 west about 12 miles to the Baker Lake Highway, turn right (north). Continue about 9 miles to Road #12, turn left and continue about 18 miles to the marked trailhead.

Note: Highway 20 is closed in winter.

Locate Other Dog-Friendly Activities...Check Nearby Cities

LADDER CREEK FALLS TRAIL HIKE - Leashes

Beginner/0.5 miles/0.25 hours

Info: The setting for this Sunday-type stroll is courtesy of J.D. Ross, Seattle City Light's first superintendent. In the 1920s, Ross created a botanical garden behind the Gorge Powerhouse where the super bonus of your outing comes in the form of Ladder Creek Falls, an alluring string of cascades that carved a 40' gorge through soft mountain rock. Visit in the evening when the lights shimmer on the falls and create a mystical aura. Many of the garden's rare species have been replaced with native plants including maples which, in autumn, color the garden with their bright red leaves. Park yourself on one of the benches, your bark beside you contemplate the wonder of it all. For more information: (360) 856-5700.

Directions: From Rockport, travel Highway 20 northeast about 20 miles to Newhalem. The trail is across the bridge behind the Gorge Powerhouse.

NEWHALEM CREEK TRAIL HIKE - Leashes

Beginner/1.0-2.0 miles/0.5-1.0 hours

Info: This is actually a combo of two trails and a favorite with river enthusiasts and treehounds alike. The River Loop Trail is a one-mile loop through a grabbag of bosky wonder leading to a tranquil bar of the Skagit River. Panoramic views of the wilderness add to the charm of this excursion which also connects with the "To Know A Tree" Trail, a half-mile, level path that skirts the river. You'll walk in shaded splendor amidst a lush understory of ferns and moss in this verdant landscape. Interpretive signs name the trees and plants along the trail so you'll get an education along with some exercise. For more information: (360) 856-5700.

Directions: From Rockport, travel Highway 20 northeast about 20 miles to Newhalem. The trailhead is located near the North Cascades Visitor Center and connects to Newhalem Creek Campground. The Lower Newhalem Creek trailhead is on the service road just past Newhalem Creek Campground.

Hotel Policies May Be Subject To Change

ROCKPORT STATE PARK - Leashes

Info: Nature buffs and birders share a love of this numero uno parkland. A beautiful setting, the landscape changes from riparian flora in the lowlands to cliffs and exposed rocky soil in the upper regions. Birders, bald eagles have been known to ply the skies in search of din-din. And the protected stand of 300-year old Douglas fir houses a variety of interesting flyboys as well. Wildlife watchers won't go home empty-eyed either. Deer, coyote, mountain beaver and a number of forest mammals inhabit the terrain. All it takes to have a sighting is some lucky dog know-how and patience. A maze of pathways lace the lowlands, but more adventurous souls can check out the summit trail atop Sauk Mountain. For more information: (360) 853-8461.

Directions: From Rockport, travel west on Highway 20 (North Cascades Highway) for one mile to the signed entrance on the north side of the highway.

The numbered hike that follows is within Rockport State Park:

1) SAUK MOUNTAIN TRAIL HIKE - Leashes

Intermediate/1.5 miles/1.0 hours

Info: This picturesque odyssey leads through the highlands where cool, crisp mountain air is part of the package. Yup, the bird with the 6' wingspan could be a bald eagle, so keep those binocs handy. And hey, the stunning views of the North Cascades, Skagit and Sauk Valleys, Puget Sound and Mount Baker aren't too shabby either. Plan ahead, you can't beat lunch alfresco in this gorgeous setting.

Directions: From Rockport, travel west on Highway 20 (North Cascades Highway) for one mile to the signed entrance on the north side of the highway. To the trailhead: travel on the Sauk Mountain Road 7.5 miles, bearing right at the second intersection. The trailhead is located at the parking lot at the end of the road.

Note: Sauk Mountain Rd. may not be suitable for trailers and large campers.

Locate Other Dog-Friendly Activities...Check Nearby Cities

TRAIL OF THE CEDARS NATURE WALK - Leashes

Beginner/0.3 miles/0.15 hours

Info: Aptly named, this trail meanders among huge, old cedars. Interpretive signs enlighten on the natural process of forest growth. The canopied pathway is a short lesson in botany and a beautiful sight to behold. For more information: (360) 856-5700.

Directions: From Rockport, travel Highway 20 northeast to Newhalem. The trailhead starts at the suspension bridge south of the Newhalem General Store.

ROSLYN

LODGING

THE LITTLE ROSLYN INN
106 5th St (98941)
Rates: $38-$90
Tel: (509) 649-2936

THE ORIGINAL ROSLYN INN
102 5th St (98941)
Rates: $190
Tel: (509) 649-2936

THE ROSLYN "INN BETWEEN"
104 5th St (98941)
Rates: $390
Tel: (509) 649-2936

SAN JUAN ISLAND

LODGING

Friday Harbor

BLAIR HOUSE B&B
345 Blair Ave (98250)
Rates: $75-$125
Tel: (360) 378-5907

FRIDAY HARBOR HOUSE MOTEL
130 West St (98250)
Rates: $145-$325
Tel: (360) 378-8455

HARRISON HOUSE SUITES
235 C St. (98250)
Rates: $125-$195
Tel: (360) 378-3587
(800) 407-7933

INN AT FRIDAY HARBOR
410 Spring St (98250)
Rates: $49-$160
Tel: (360) 378-4000
(800) 552-1457

INN AT FRIDAY HARBOR SUITES
680 Spring St (98250)
Rates: $59-$213
Tel: (360) 378-3031 (800) 752-5752

SAN JUAN INN
50 Spring St (98250)
Rates: $70-$175
Tel: (360) 378-2070
(800) 742-8210

SNUG HARBOR RESORT & MARINA
2371 Mitchell Bay Rd (98250)
Rates: $30-$200
Tel: (360) 378-4762

TUCKER HOUSE B&B
260 B St (98250)
Rates: $70-$135
Tel: (360) 378-2783
(800) 965-0123

WESTWINDS B&B
4909 H-Hannah Rd (98250)
Rates: $165-$245
Tel: (360) 378-5283

WHARFSIDE B&B on the JACQUELINE
Slip K-13 (98250)
Rates: $80-$95
Tel: (360) 378-5661

RECREATION

AMERICAN CAMP NATIONAL HISTORICAL PARK - Leashes

Info: This chunk of Mother Nature is just what you and furface will want after exercising your credit cards in Friday Harbor. Five miles of pretty beachfront and over 1,200 acres of wooded seclusion are yours at this picturesque milieu. Walk the bluffs, stroll the lagoon, beachcomb the sandy coastline, you never know what unusual driftwood shapes and beach treasures you'll discover. Wildlife enthusiasts swear by this place which is inhabited by an abundance of wildlife like European rabbit, ferret, red fox and wild turkey. They share this avian havian with elegant blue herons, California quail, ravens, woodpeckers, wrens and nuthatches. And hey, let's not forget the abundance of Bambi lookalikes which are often seen grazing in the meadowlands.

When hunger pangs strike, break some biscuits with your favorite floppy-eared pal at one of the picnic areas. Stop by the Interpretive Center for a park map so you and your Curious George don't miss a trick. For more information: (360) 378-2240.

Directions: From Friday Harbor, take Argyle Avenue to Miner Road and make a right for one block to a left on Argyle Road. Follow Argyle Road to a left on Cattle Point Road and continue to the park entrance. The distance from Friday Harbor to American Camp is approximately six miles.

The numbered activities that follow are within
American Camp National Historic Park:

1) CATTLE POINT INTERPRETIVE SITE - Leashes

Info: Located on the tip of San Juan Island, you and your seadog can stroll the sandy beach and dip your toes in the frothy blues

Locate Other Dog-Friendly Activities...Check Nearby Cities

or pack a picnic repast, set up shop and watch golden and bald eagles as they swoop and dip in search of aquatic prey.

Directions: In American Camp National Historical Park off Cattle Point Road.

2) MT. FINLAYSON NATURE TRAIL HIKE - Leashes

Intermediate/1.0 miles/0.5 hours

Info: Up, up and away you and your hot diggety dog diggety will climb. It won't be long before fetching views of American and Canadian mountains come into view on the horizon. That, of course, is assuming you've been able to tear your eyes away from the dramatic and mesmerizing seascapes below. The easiest return is on the nature trail above Jake's Lagoon.

Directions: In American Camp National Historical Park off Cattle Point Road.

3) SOUTH BEACH - Leashes

Info: When you're feeling pensive, you and poochface can lose yourselves in thought along this secluded stretch of beach. Stroll to your heart's content, find a tide pool and admire the complexity of life in a small hollow of a rock or hustle your buttsky on a 3/4 mile trail atop the bluffs to the Hudson's Bay Farm site above Grandma's Cove. Tote a picnic feast and make an afternoon of it. This is what island living is all about.

Directions: In American Camp National Historical Park off Pickets Lane.

ENGLISH CAMP NATIONAL HISTORICAL PARK - Leashes

Info: Two miles of shoreline and 530 acres of paw-pleasing stomping grounds await your pawrusal at this picturesque park. From formal gardens and a guardhouse, circa 1860, to the former parade ground now inhabited by wild turkeys and Canada geese, you'll find plenty of playtime pupportunities. For more information: (360) 378-2240.

Directions: From Friday Harbor, take Beaverton Valley Road (becomes West Valley Road) about nine miles to the park.

HARBOR PARK - Leashes

Info: Once your ferry docks, start the day off on the right paw with a stop at this petite park where you'll find a smidgen of grass, a dollop of shade trees, pretty groundcover and a handsome stone wall. Picnic benches beneath the shaded ramada complete the picture. There are several eateries nearby where brown baggers can make brown waggers gleeful. A natural rock fountain provides a watery splash to the sea-drenched aura. Cool and breezy, you and furface can watch the boats in the marina before hightailing it into town.

Directions: As you exit the ferry onto Front Street, the park is a couple of blocks to your right.

LIME KILN STATE PARK - Leashes

Info: Known as the whale watching park, if you and furface are into Orca ogling, don't miss a trip to this picturesque park situated on a rocky point facing Vancouver Island. Plan your visit from June to September and increase your odds of catching a glimpse of an Orca pod. They come to feast on the salmon that return each year to spawn. And listen up, the communication between the mammals is quite distinctive. You'll know it when you hear it. The often photographed Lime Kiln Lighthouse is up for Kodak grabs. Built in 1919, it's listed on the National Register of Historic Places. You'll find plenty of roaming room and cozy little nooks throughout this 36-acre gem so get a move on lazybones. For more information: (360) 378-2044.

Directions: From Friday Harbor, take San Juan Valley Road to Douglas Road and turn left. Stay on Douglas Road until it makes a right turn and becomes Bailer Hill Road. Continue on Bailer Hill Road (becomes West Side Road) to signs for the park at 6158 Lighthouse Road, about nine miles from Friday Harbor.

Locate Other Dog-Friendly Activities...Check Nearby Cities

SAN JUAN ISLANDS

LODGING & RECREATION

For lodging and recreation, see individual island listings; Lopez Island, San Juan Island, Shaw Island and Orcas Island

SEABECK

LODGING

SUMMER SONG B&B
P.O. Box 82 (98380)
Rates: n/a
Tel: (206) 830-5089

RECREATION

SCENIC BEACH STATE PARK - Leashes

Info: Beach bum alert. When nothing but surf and sand will do, this is the place for you. With 88 acres, you and furface can find plenty of pupportunities for amusement. If you're a fishing fiend at heart, hone your skills on the salmon, perch and flounder. If clamming's more your speed, you and the digmeister might just go home a couple of lucky dogs. For more information: (800) 233-0321.

Directions: From Seabeck, take Seabeck-Holly Road west along the bay past Seabeck Elementary School, turn north. Continue about 1.5 miles to the park entrance.

Note: Dogs prohibited on swimming beaches.

SEATAC

LODGING

AIRPORT PLAZA HOTEL
18601 Pacific Hwy S (98188)
Rates: $50-$85
Tel: (206) 433-0400

DOUBLETREE AIRPORT HOTEL
18740 Int'l Blvd (98188)
Rates: $99-$149
Tel: (206) 246-8600
(800) 222-8733

ECONO LODGE
19225 Int'l Blvd (98188)
Rate: $38-$75
Tel: (206) 824-1350
(800) 221-2222

HILTON HOTEL SEATTLE AIRPORT
17620 Pacific Hwy S (98188)
Rates: $139-$159
Tel: (206) 244-4800
(800) 445-8667

Hotel Policies May Be Subject To Change

HOWARD JOHNSON LODGE
20045 Int'l Blvd (98188)
Rates: $80-$95
Tel: (206) 878-3310
(800) 446-4656

LA QUINTA INN
2824 S 188th St (98188)
Rates: $76-$105
Tel: (206) 241-5211
(800) 531-5900

MARRIOTT SEA-TAC AIRPORT
3201 S 176th St (98188)
Rates: $134-$139
Tel: (206) 241-2000
(800) 228-9290

MOTEL 6 SEA-TAC AIRPORT
16500 Pacific Hwy S (98188)
Rates: $35-$41
Tel: (206) 246-4101
(800) 440-6000

MOTEL 6 SEA-TAC SOUTH
18900 47th Ave S (98188)
Rates: $32-$41
Tel: (206) 241-1648
(800) 440-6000

SEA-TAC CREST MOTOR INN
18845 Int'l Blvd (98188)
Rates: $42-$59
Tel: (206) 433-0999
(800) 554-0300

SHADOW MOTEL
2930 S 176th St (98188)
Rates: n/a
Tel: (206) 246-9300

SUPER 8 MOTEL
3100 S 192nd (98188)
Rates: $62-$82
Tel: (206) 433-8188
(800) 800-8000

TAC-SEA MOTEL
17024 Pacific Hwy (98188)
Rates: $37-$57
Tel: (206) 241-6511

THRIFTLODGE
17108 Int'l Blvd (98188)
Rates: $34-$62
Tel: (206) 244-1230
(800) 578-7878

SEATTLE

For additional lodging and recreation in the Seattle area, see listings under the following cities: Bellevue, Bainbridge Island, Bothel, Bremerton, Camano Island, Issaquah, Mercer Island, Redmond, Renton, SeaTac, Shoreline, Whidbey Island.

LODGING

THE ALEXIS HOTEL
1007 First Ave (98104)
Rate: $170-$370
Tel: (206) 624-4844

AURORA SEAFAIR INN
9100 Aurora Ave N (98103)
Rates: $55-$85
Tel: (206) 522-3754

B&B ON BROADWAY
722 Broadway Ave E (98102)
Rates: $85-$115
Tel: (206) 329-8933
(888) 329-8933

BEECH TREE MANOR INN B&B
1405 Queen Anne Ave N (98109)
Rates: $45-$79
Tel: (206) 281-7037

BELLEVUE PLACE B&B
1111 Bellevue Place E (98102)
Rates: $85-$95
Tel: (206) 325-9253
(800) 325-9253

BEST WESTERN-AIRPORT EXECUTEL
20717 Int'l Blvd (98198)
Rates: $95-$125
Tel: (206) 878-3300
(800) 648-3311

BEST WESTERN EXECUTIVE INN
200 Taylor Ave N (98109)
Rates: $78-$134
Tel: (206) 448-9444
(800) 528-1234

**CAVANAUGH'S INN
ON FIFTH AVENUE**
1415 Fifth Ave (98101)
Rates: $130-$180
Tel: (206) 442-5555
(800) 843-4667

CROWNE PLAZA HOTEL
1113 6th Ave (98101)
Rates: $105-$210
Tel: (206) 464-1980

DAYS INN TOWN CENTER
2205 7th Ave (98121)
Rates: $64-$99
Tel: (206) 448-3434
(800) 329-7466

EASTLAKE INN
2215 Eastlake E (98102)
Rates: n/a
Tel: (206) 322-7726

EMERALD INN
8512 Aurora Ave N (98103)
Rates: $49-990
Tel: (206) 522-5000

**FOUR SEASONS-
OLYMPIC HOTEL**
411 University St (98101)
Rates: $210-$550
Tel: (206) 621-1700
(800) 332-3442

GEISHA MOTOR INN
9613 Aurora Ave N (98103)
Rates: n/a
Tel: (206) 524-8880

HOTEL MONACO SEATTLE
1101 Fourth Ave (98101)
Rates: $195-$235
Tel: (206) 621-1770
(800) 945-2240

LEGEND MOTEL
22204 Pacific Hwy S (98198)
Rates: n/a
Tel: (206) 878-0366

MOTEL 6-SOUTH SEATTLE
20651 Military Rd (98188)
Rates: $30-$45
Tel: (206) 824-9902
(800) 440-6000

PARGARDENS B&B
14716 26th Ave NE (98155)
Rates: $60-$75
Tel: (206) 367-1437
(888) 742-2632

PENSIONE NICHOLAS B&B
1923 First Ave (98101)
Rates: $60-$80
Tel: (206) 441-7125
(800) 440-7125

QUALITY INN CITY CENTER
2224 8th Ave (98121)
Rates: $74-$150
Tel: (206) 624-6820
(800) 221-2222

RAMADA INN NORTHGATE
2140 N Northgate Way (98133)
Rates: $105-$132
Tel: (206) 365-0700
(800) 272-6232

RESIDENCE INN BY MARRIOTT
800 Fairview Ave N (98109)
Rates: $105-$290
Tel: (206) 624-6000
(800) 331-3131

**RESIDENCE INN
BY MARRIOTT-SEATTLE SOUTH**
16201 W Valley Hwy (98188)
Rates: $120-$185
Tel: (206) 226-5500
(800) 331-3131

**SANDPIPER VILLAS
APARTMENT MOTEL**
11000 1st Ave SW (98146)
Rates: $39-$59
Tel: (206) 242-8883

Hotel Policies May Be Subject To Change

SHADOW MOTEL
2930 S 176th (98188)
Rates: $32-$50
Tel: (206) 246-9300

SUN HILL MOTEL
8517 Aurora Ave N (98103)
Rates: n/a
Tel: (206) 525-1205

TRAVELODGE SPACE NEEDLE
200 6th Ave N (98109)
Rates: $69-$129
Tel: (206) 441-7878
(800) 578-7878

VAGABOND INN
325 Aurora Ave N (98109)
Rates: $54-$89
Tel: (206) 441-0400
(800) 522-1555

THE WESTIN HOTEL
1900 5th Ave (98101)
Rates: $210-$295
Tel: (206) 728-1000
(800) 228-3000

RECREATION

ALKI BEACH PARK - Leashes

Info: Seattle's first settlers knew a good thing when they saw it and established their homesteads here. One look and you'll know why, this park offers extraordinary views of Puget Sound, the Olympic Mountains and of a bustling city which was yet to come. You and the dawgus will uncover a two-mile stretch of coastline where you can hustle your butt along the pathway. But be prepared to share your space, we're talking popular. For more information: (206) 684-8020.

Directions: Located at 1702 Alki Avenue SW in West Seattle.

Note: Dogs are not allowed in water. Very crowded in the summer months.

BLUE DOG POND PARK

Info: This little area is not your average park. Blue Dog Pond serves as a overflow drainage area for heavy storms. Named after the steel cutout of a dog in the park, you and your cut up will find leashless abandon in the ravine. A natural favorite with locals, go with a social attitude and the preferred toy of choice. For more information call the leash-free hotline: (206) 386-4004.

Directions: Located at Martin Luther King Jr. Way and Massachussetts Street on the northwest corner.

Note: Dogs are prohibited on the I-90 side of Blue Dog Pond. This is a pilot site for leash-free use, as of this writing permanent status has not been granted.

Locate Other Dog-Friendly Activities...Check Nearby Cities

BOREN/INTERLAKEN PARK - Leashes

Info: Take your bark for a lark in this neighborhood park. Skedaddle over the steep hillsides and play follow the nose through wooded ravines. This park adds a new slant to walking the dog.

Directions: The park entrance is at 19th Avenue East and Interlaken Drive East.

CARKEEK PARK - Leashes

Info: Put a little zip in your day with an outing to this diverse 216-acre park where views of the sound and the Olympics come easy. You'll uncover a forest and wetland habitat where every autumn, salmon return to Piper's Creek to spawn. Hop on one of the trails that lace the lovely landscape or BYOB (bring your own biscuits) and munch on lunch.

Directions: On NW Carkeek Park Road and 9th NW at 110th.

Note: Dogs are prohibited on the beach.

CITY HALL PARK - Leashes

Info: This urban oasis is very popular so pack a friendly attitude along with a biscuit basket. You'll find a scattering of picnic tables that are much in demand on sunny days.

Directions: Located on 3rd and Jefferson.

COWEN PARK - Leashes

Info: Do some puppy prancing at this local green scene. Tote a sack of snacks or throw that poor dog a bone.

Directions: Located on University Way NE and NE Ravenna.

DISCOVERY PARK - Leashes

Info: One look at the beauty that stretches out before you and you'll want the day to last forever. Encompassing 534 acres contained within a tree-bordered region, this charmer ranks as Seattle's largest parkland. An urban wilderness gem smack dab in the middle of the city, you'll discover, as the name implies, a sanctuary for wildlife, a place where you can leave your cares behind and simply enjoy the serenity and tranquility of the dramatic Puget Sound landscape. Wildlife enthusiasts, your best chances for spotting sea lions, porpoises, orcas and seals is off West Point.

More than 7 miles of trails traverse a myriad of habitats ranging from sunny, wildflower-sprinkled meadows and bluff-top tableaus to fragrant, cool forests of old-growth broadleaf trees and second-growth conifers, all backdropped by stunning, distant mountains. Without a doubt this could become a favorite haunt, so pick a path and let the good times roll.

Directions: Located on 36th West and West Government Way.

Note: Dogs are prohibited on the beach.

FREEWAY PARK - Leashes

Info: This unusual and award-winning park is a wonderful resource for visitors and locals alike. When you need a little nature fix and you figure there's no place to go, there's Freeway Park. True, it's not a lush green expanse but you and the barkmeister will find 5 acres comprised of trees (pollution resistant, of course) and boxes overflowing with flowers and shrubs which add a dollop of color. Pathways and stairways escort you and the wide-eyed one to green-dappled terraces, fountains and oops, up-close encounters of the freeway kind. But when you gotta go, you gotta go.

Directions: Located on 6th and Seneca.

GAS WORKS PARK - Leashes

Info: Another urban retreat, this park's 21 acres provide some romping, stomping room for the wagging machine. Located on the north shore of Lake Union, you'll get an eyeful of downtown Seattle and Lake Union. A success story, the land was transformed from industrial usage to park. If you're a high flyer, stow your kite in your backpack and join the locals on aptly named Kite Hill where a breeze is always in the air. For pastimes of a more cultured nature, performances of Shakespeare appear throughout the summer. So get thee to a

Locate Other Dog-Friendly Activities...Check Nearby Cities

parkaree, pull up a plush square and make your own little Stratford-on-Avon.

Directions: Located on N Northlake Way and Meridian North.

The numbered hike that follows is within Gasworks Park:

1) BURKE GILMAN TRAIL HIKE - Leashes

Beginner/3.6 miles/2.0 hours

Info: Practice your fancy footwork moves on the newest section of trail that's part of a 12 miler. Popular with cyclists and walkers, expect company and expect a great walk in the wonderful outdoors as you make merry through tree-strewn neighborhoods and flower-dotted terrain. Pack the puppy paraphernalia and make a day of it. When you reach 8th Avenue NW, do an about-face and retrace the pawprints. For more information: (206) 296-4232.

Directions: The trail begins at Gasworks Park, located on North Northlake Way and Meridian North.

GENESEE PARK

Info: In dogspeak, this fetching place rates a solid two paws up. Thirty-seven acres of leashless gallivanting beckon your barker. So stash a fuzzy tennie or a favorite Frisbee and let playtime commence. Fenced and grassy, canines swear by this sweet spot. For more information, call the leash-free hotline: (206) 386-4004.

Directions: Located on 45th South and South Genesee.

Note: Will re-open in the fall of 1998. This is a pilot site for leash-free use, as of this writing permanent status has not been granted.

GOLDEN GARDENS

Info: Say ta ta to the city blues with a visit to this pretty green scene. Complete with a forested hillside and a small grassy leash-free area, you'll find 95 acres of romping, stomping terrain. The whiffer's sniffer is bound to catch the tangy ocean scents. On clear days, spectacular views of the Olympics can be yours. Plan an outing towards dusk, the sunsets from this venue are nothing short of extraordinary. Enjoy an R&R moment and take five at one of the tile benches which are surrounded by crabs, shells, sea stars, fish and a majestic mermaid embedded in cement. For more information, call the leash-free hotline: (206) 386-4004.

Directions: On the north end of Seaview NW. The leash-free area is located in the upper or eastern portion of the park.

Note: This is a pilot site for leash-free use. As of this writing, permanent status has not been granted. Dogs are prohibited on the beach.

GREEN LAKES PARK - Leashes

Info: Put on the dog and make tracks to this green scene. A little bit of this and a little bit of that and a lot of people watching is what this park is all about. For city lickers looking for a walk in the park, you can't miss at this very pupular locale. Hop on the 2.8-mile multi-use pathway to get a lay of the land. Nearly 350 acres, including an alluring lake, trees and more trees, make for a delightful urban retreat that can't be beat. Summer is super crowded but the autumn months will keep you coming back for more. Plan a picnic with the barkmeister or pick up a "to go" lunch from one of the nearby cafes and set up shop beside the lake.

Directions: Located between East Green Lake Drive and West Green Lake Drive North.

JUDKINS PARK and PLAYFIELD - Leashes

Info: Satisfy the pupster's yearning for a bit of plushness underfoot on your AM constitutional with a quickie to this splash of green.

Directions: Located on 22nd South and South Charles.

LAWTON PARK - Leashes

Info: A tiny green scene, it still fills the bill when walktime calls.

Directions: Located on Emerson Street at 27th Avenue W.

LESCHI PARK - Leashes

Info: There's a bit of splendor in the grass to be found at this neighborhood park where you and the one with the waggily tail might meet others of the same persuasion.

Directions: Located on Lake Washington Boulevard between Yesler and Main.

LICTON SPRINGS PARK - Leashes

Info: Root, root, root for the home team at this sporty park or create a game of your own. If your woofer's a hoofer, there are trails to explore and fun times to unearth. Wait no longer. Check out the goings on in this neck of the woods.

Directions: Located on N 97th and Ashworth N.

LINCOLN PARK - Leashes

Info: Urbanites and furfaces alike give the high five to this 130-acre region. Get your fair share of Rexercise on one of the pathways that lace the woodlands and meadows. Or practice your lazybones routine and do nothing except perhaps lunch at one of the many picnic areas. Bone appétit.

Directions: Located on Fauntleroy SW and SW Webster.

MADISON PARK - Leashes

Info: Punch up your day with a bit of play and wipe the hang-dog expression off the mutt's mug. Your numero uno hound will no doubt give you two paws up for effort.

Directions: Located on 43rd E and E Madison.

MAGNOLIA PARK - Leashes

Info: Stretching along the northern shore of Elliott Bay, between Discovery Park and Smith Cove, this quickie escape is bound to put a bounce in the hound's step. The views alone are worth a visit.

Directions: Located on 31st Avenue West and West Galer.

Hotel Policies May Be Subject To Change

MAGNUSON PARK

Info: With 195 acres to explore, it'll take more than one trip to discover all the paw-pleasing pupportunities of this parkland. There's a leash-free area where furface can run paw-loose and fancy free. Tote a favorite Frisbee or fuzzy tennie, this is the place for playtime romping. There's also a trail which edges the perimeter and leads to a spot meant to answer your wet wagger's wildest dreams, aka a swimming hole. For more information, call the leash-free hotline: (206) 386-4004.

Directions: On Sand Point Way NE and 65th Avenue NE. The leash-free area is located along the eastern and northern boundaries of the park. Park in the last parking lot before the playing fields in the far left corner.

Note: This is a pilot site for leash-free use. As of this writing, permanent status has not been granted. Dogs are prohibited on the beach.

MYRTLE EDWARDS PARK - Leashes

Info: Small but inviting, the central location of this park compensates for its size. Kick up some dust while you work out the kinks on the pathway where fabulous views of Puget Sound and the Olympics are yours for the looking.

Directions: Alaskan Way between W Bay and W Thomas.

NORTH ACRES PARK - Leashes

Info: Stop dillydallying around and make tracks to this niche the next time you're looking to walk the dog.

Directions: Located on 1st Avenue NE and North 130th Street.

PRATT PARK - Leashes

Info: A favorite with the pet set, you're bound to put a little wiggle in your wagger's strut with an afternoon delight in this park. A scattering of picnic tables makes lunch time visits even more enjoyable.

Directions: Located on Yelser Way and 20th Avenue South.

RAVENNA PARK - Leashes

Info: This woodsy park has the makings of a memorable outing. Furbanites, you'll love the sense of nature you'll discover at this lovely landscape. Positioned in a large ravine, you and your furball can make like Lewis and Clark and explore the pathways that honeycomb the diverse terrain. Heads up naturalists. Where there's woods, there's wildlife.

Directions: Located on 20th NE and NE 58th.

ROXHILL PARK - Leashes

Info: Dew will moisten your sneaks on an early morning jaunt to this neighborhood park. Pack a playful attitude and a favorite toy and give the pooch something to bark about.

Directions: Located on 29th SW and SW Barton.

SCHMITZ PRESERVE - Leashes

Info: A bonafido snifforama, you and the one with the nose pressed to the ground are gonna love the scents you'll encounter in this charming preserve. The 800-year-old trees provide a cool, dense canopy for your strolling pleasure. So hightail it on a pretty pathway or let sleeping dogs lie while you do nothing for a change.

Directions: Located on Admiral Way SW and SW Stevens.

SEWARD PARK - Leashes

Info: Start your day off on the right paw with a sojourn to this lovely 277-acre park. Solitude seekers, come early in the day and miss the crowds. A maze of trails lace the bosky terrain so close encounters of the natural kind are de rigueur. Tote the red checks and a hearty biscuit basket, there are lots of spots for lunch alfrisky.

Directions: Located on Lake Washington Boulevard S and S Orcas Street.

Note: Dogs are prohibited on the beach.

VOLUNTEER PARK

Info: Situated on Capitol Hill, this urban retreat is the express lane to a little nature in the city. Furface can have a run on the wild side if you jumpstart your day at the leash-free area (open 4AM to 9AM). For more information, call the leash-free hotline: (206) 386-4004.

Directions: Located on 15th E and E Prospect.

Note: This is a pilot site for leash-free use. As of this writing, permanent status has not been granted.

WASHINGTON PARK ARBORETUM - Leashes

Info: Sniffmeister's swear by this place with its grabbag of trees, flora and scurrying, hurrying wildlife. But you don't have to be a flora lover to enjoy the enchanting milieu. A definite getaway destination, escapism reigns supreme at this 200-acre region. Trees dominate the terrain and include a variety of conifers, oaks, hollies, witch hazels, magnolias, cherries and birches. You get the picture - picture perfect. Countless pathways honeycomb the landscape. Quaint gardens, each a little different from the one before, add to the allure. Most of the trees are tagged so you and the one with the tail in permanent overdrive will come away that much smarter. It doesn't matter where your journey begins, everything leads to lovely in this dreamlike quarter of serenity and beauty.

If you're visiting in spring, don't miss Azalea Walk, a veritable and incredible wall of color. And since the rhodies won't be outdone, get psyched for a staggering color bonanza. If you're as much of a tree enthusiast as the mutt, you'll be dazzled by the bosky bounty. Each species has a little something special to recommend it for your perusal. When the time is right, munch on lunch beneath a Japanese maple and make your day even more memorable, if that's possible.

Directions: From Seattle, travel east on Madison Street to Lake Washington Boulevard East, turn left into the Arboretum.

Note: Open daily from 7 a.m. to dusk.

WATERFALL GARDEN PARK - Leashes

Info: Despite its size, your pupsqueak will nonetheless enjoy a saunter in this park. A lovely 22-foot waterfall recirculates 5,000 gallons of water a minute and forms the centerpiece of this neighborhood gathering place. In spring, the lush gardens are made even prettier by a splash of colorful blossoms which soften the cool granite look. Be sure to stop and smell the flowers in this little charmer.

Directions: Located on 2nd and Main.

WESTCREST PARK

Info: Exercise more than your prerogative with a visit to this sporty scene. Two football fields equate to lots of frolicking à la furface. Or toss the tether to the wind in the leash-free area and hone those fetching skills. Canine communing is one of the draws so expect a fair share of tail sniffing and whiffing. For more information call the leash-free hotline: (206) 386-4004.

Directions: Located SW Henderson and 8th SW. The leash-free site is located along the southern and western border of the reservoir.

Note: This is a pilot site for leash-free use. As of this writing, permanent status has not been granted.

WOODLAND and LOWER WOODLAND PARKS

Info: Boogie with Bowser to the leash-free area and let the pupster be part of the snifforama.

Directions: On N 50th and Phinney N, Aurora N and Green Lake Way N. The leash-free area is located in the eastern portion of the park, north of 50th Street, east of Aurora Avenue and south of 59th. For more information, call the leash-free hotline: (206) 386-4004.

Note: This is a pilot site for leash-free use. As of this writing, permanent status has not been granted.

Hotel Policies May Be Subject To Change

OTHER PARKS IN SEATTLE - Leashes

- ARMENI PARK, Harbor Ave SW off SW Maryland
- BARNETT PARK, E Jefferson & ML King Jr Way
- BEER SHEVA PARK, Seward Park S & S Henderson
- BERGEN PLACE PARK, 22nd NW & NW Market
- BHY KRACKE PARK, Bigelow N & Comstock Place
- COE PLAY PARK, 7th W & W Wheeler
- COLMAN PARK, 36th S & Lakeside
- COLUMBIA PARK, Rainier S & S Alaska Street
- COMMODORE PARK, W Commodore Way & Gilman Ave W
- DAVIS PARK, 12526 27th NE
- DEARBORN PARK, 28th Ave. S & S Brandon
- DENNY PARK, Dexter N & Denny Way
- DENNY-BLAINE LAKE PARK, Madrona Dr & Maiden Ln E
- DENNY-BLAINE PARK, Lake Washington Blvd E & 40th E
- DUWAMISH WATERWAY PARK, Dallas Ave S & S Kenyon
- FAUNTLEROY PARK, SW Barton between 39th & 41st SW
- FIREHOUSE MINI PARK, 18th bet. E Columbia & E Cherry
- FIRST HILL PARK, University & Minor
- FRAZIER PARK, 24th E & E Harrison
- FREMONT CANAL PARK, 2nd Ave NW & NW Canal St
- FRINK PARK, Lake Washington Boulevard S & S Jackson
- GROSE PARK, 30th Avenue between Denny & Howell
- HING HAY PARK, S King & Maynard S
- HOWELL PARK, E Howell Pl, off Lake Washington Blvd E
- INTERNATIONAL CHILDREN'S PARK, 7th S & S Lane St
- INVERNESS RAVINE PARK, Inverness Dr NE off NE 85th
- KERRY PARK, W Highland & 2nd W
- KINNEAR PARK, 7th W & W Olympic Place
- KOBE TERRACE PARK, 7th S bet. S Main & S Washington
- LAKE CITY PARK, Lake City Way & 125th NE
- LARKINS PARK, E Pike Street & 34th Avenue E
- MADRONA BRIAR PATCH PARK, Madrona Dr & E Pine
- MADRONA PARK, Lake Washington Blvd & E Columbia
- MARTHA WASHINGTON PARK, 57th South & S Holly St
- MAYFAIR PARK, 2nd N & Ray St
- McCURDY PARK, E Hamlin & E Park Dr E (at Hwy 520)
- McGRAW SQUARE PARK, 5th & Stewart
- MLK MEMORIAL PARK, ML King Jr Way S & S Walker

Locate Other Dog-Friendly Activities...Check Nearby Cities

- MONTLAKE EAST PARK, E Shelby & E Park Dr E
- MONTLAKE WEST PARK, W Park Dr E & E Hamlin
- MOUNT BAKER PARK, Lk Park Dr S & Lk Washington Blvd S
- NORTH PASSAGE POINT PARK, 6th NE & NE Northlake Way
- OCCIDENTAL PARK, Occidental S & S Main
- PIONEER SQUARE PARK, 1st & Yesler Way
- PLUM TREE PARK, 26th bet. E Howell & E Olive
- PREFONTAINE PLACE PARK, 3rd & Yesler Way
- PUGET PARK, 21st Avenue SW & Puget Boulevard SW
- REGRADE PARK, 3rd & Bell
- RIVERVIEW PLAYFIELD, 12th SW & SW Myrtle
- RIZAL PARK, 12 S & S Judkins
- ROANOKE PARK, 10th E & E Roanoke
- RODGERS PARK, 3rd W & W Fulton
- SALMON BAY PARK, NW 70th between 19th & 21st NW
- SOUTH COLLEGE STREET PARK, S College bet. 29th S & 30 S
- SOUTH LAKE UNION PARK, Terry Avenue N & Valley Street
- SOUTH PASSAGE POINT PARK, Fuhrman & Fairview E
- SPRING STREET PARK, 15th & E Spring
- SPRUCE STREET PARK, 21st & E Spruce
- STEINBRUECK PARK, Western & Virginia
- TASHKENT PARK, Boylston E bet. E Republican & E Mercer
- THOMAS MINI PARK, Bellevue E & E Thomas
- TILIKUM PLACE PARK, 5th & Denny Way
- VIRETTA PARK, 39th E & E John
- WARE PARK, 28th S & S Jackson
- WASHINGTON PARK, 57th S & S Holly Street
- WATERFRONT PARK, Alaskan Way, piers 57-61
- WESTLAKE PARK, 4th & Pine
- WESTLAKE SQUARE PARK, 6th & Stewart

SEAVIEW

LODGING

SEAVIEW COHO MOTEL
3701 Pacific Way (98644)
Rates: $55-$110
Tel: (360) 642-2531
(800) 681-8153

SOU'WESTER LODGE & CABINS
Beach Access Rd-38th Pl (98644)
Rates: $39-$109
Tel: (360) 642-2542

Hotel Policies May Be Subject To Change

SEDRO WOOLLEY

LODGING

SKAGIT MOTEL
1977 Hwy 20 (98284)
Rates: n/a
Tel: (360) 856-6001

THREE RIVERS INN MOTEL
210 Ball St (98284)
Rates: $46-$65
Tel: (360) 855-2626
(800) 221-5122

SEKIU

LODGING

BAY MOTEL & MARINA
15562 Hwy 112 W (98381)
Rates: $34-$65
Tel: (360) 963-2444

OLSON'S RESORT & MARINA
444 Front St, P.O. Box 216 (98381)
Rates: $50-$85
Tel: (360) 963-2311

CURLEY'S RESORT & DIVE CENTER
291 Front St (98381)
Rates: $46-$75
Tel: (360) 963-2281

STRAITSIDE RESORT CABINS
241 Front St (98381)
Rate: $45-$74
Tel: (360) 963-2100

HERB'S MOTEL & CHARTERS
411 Front St (98381)
Rates: $45-$74
Tel: (360) 963-2346

VAN RIPER'S RESORT
Front & Rice Sts (98381)
Rates: n/a
Tel: (360) 963-2334

SEQUIM

LODGING

BEST WESTERN SEQUIM BAY LODGE
268522 Hwy 101 E (98382)
Rates: $65-$125
Tel: (360) 683-0691
(800) 528-1234

JUAN de FUCA COTTAGES
182 Marine Dr (98382)
Rates: $100-$150
Tel: (360) 683-4433

ECONO LODGE
801 E Washington St (98382)
Rates: $59-$71
Tel: (360) 683-7113
(800) 424-4777

RANCHO LAMRO B&B
1734 Woodcock Rd (98382)
Rates: n/a
Tel: (360) 683-8133

RED RANCH INN
830 W Washington St (98382)
Rates: $50-$100
Tel: (360) 683-4195
(800) 777-4195

GROVELAND COTTAGE HISTORIC B&B
4861 Sequim-Dungeness Way
(98382)
Rates: $55-$90
Tel: (360) 683-3565
(800) 879-8859

SUNDOWNER MOTEL
364 W Washington St (98382)
Rates: $32-$69
Tel: (360) 683-5532
(800) 325-6966

Locate Other Dog-Friendly Activities...Check Nearby Cities

RECREATION

DUNGENESS RECREATION AREA - Leashes

Info: Located on the tip of the Dungeness Spit Wildlife Refuge, this riparian oasis is popular for good reason. A landscape of many faces, the Strait of Juan de Fuca and Dungeness Bay create the water boundaries while fragrant woodlands and a lush understory replete with nooks and crannies, occupy the terra firma of 216 acres. Skedaddle to your heart's content on one of the delightful hiking trails or picnic with the pooch and practice your lazybones routine. For more information: (360) 417-2291.

Directions: From Sequim, travel Highway 101 west about 4 miles to Kitchen-Dick Lane, turn right (north). Travel Kitchen-Dick Lane to the end and the entrance to Dungeness Recreation Area.

DUNGENESS TRAIL to CAMP HANDY HIKE - Leashes

Expert/6.8 miles/4.0 hours

Info: Tough on the legs, easy on the eyes, this scenic riverside trail is all a wet wagger could hope for. Camp Handy is the place to rest your weary bones and break some bread and biscuits. You're gonna need the energy boost. But don't forget the reason for the trek - go ahead and have some waterful fun. For more information: (360) 765-2200.

Directions: From Sequim, head north on Highway 101 for 2 miles to Palo Alto Road and turn left. Continue until Palo Alto Road turns into FS 28, follow about one mile to FS 2860 and veer right. Drive for 11 miles to the trailhead.

GOLD CREEK TRAIL to GOLD CREEK SHELTER HIKE - Leashes

Beginner/0.5 miles/0.25 hours

Info: Grab your hat and pack your sack, leave your worries far behind you on this charming pathway. A footbridge crosses Gold Creek and deposits you and the dawgus at a pretty creekside locale. For more information: (360) 765-2200.

Directions: From Sequim, head north on Highway 101 for 2 miles to Palo Alto Road and drive until Palo Alto Road turns into FS 28. Continue about one mile to FS 2860. Turn right and go 3 miles to the trailhead parking on your left.

Hotel Policies May Be Subject To Change

SEQUIM BAY STATE PARK - Leashes

Info: Treat your city licker to some country fun with a seaside slant. Lucky dogs with a penchant for fishing might take home the makings of a tasty fish fry. If the bay is calm and you've toted your boat, take the pooch and do some exploring. For more information: (360) 683-4235.

Directions: From Sequim, take Highway 101 southeast for approximately 4 miles to the park entrance.

Note: Dogs are not permitted in the lodge.

SLAB CAMP TRAIL to DUNCAN FLAT CAMP HIKE - Leashes

Expert/4.2 miles/3.0 hours

Info: Escapism is the lure at this path less traveled. But you and your Herculean hound will earn the solitude in spades. This riverside trail slices through thick vegetation, providing a picturesque landscape wherever you turn. And if water hijinks stirs the wagging tool, you and the one with the ear-to-ear grin will rate this trek two paws up. For more information: (360) 765-2200.

Directions: From Sequim, head west on Highway 101 about 2.5 miles to the Taylor Cutoff Road, turn left. Drive to Lost Mountain Road. Proceed on Lost Mountain Road to its junction with FS 2870. Follow FS 2870 to FS 2875 and turn right to the parking area at Slab Camp and trailhead. The trail is about 12.5 miles west of Sequim.

Note: Use caution when swimming. Avoid the river when the current is strong.

SHAW ISLAND

<u>RECREATION</u>

SHAW ISLAND COUNTY PARK - Leashes

Info: The only game in town, you and the pupster can beachcomb along the picturesque coastline or come prepared and brown bag it with the wag it at the picnic area.

Directions: On the south end of the island along Island Cove.

SHELTON

LODGING

CANAL SIDE RESORT MOTEL
N 21660 Hwy 101 (98584)
Rates: $38-$48
Tel: (360) 877-9422

CITY CENTER BEST RATES MOTEL
128 E Alder (98584)
Rates: $36-$54
Tel: (360) 426-3397

LAKE NAHWATZEL RESORT
W 12900 Shelton-Matlock Rd (98584)
Rates: $30-$50
Tel: (360) 426-8323

REST FULL FARM B&B
W 2230 Shelton Valley Rd (98584)
Rates: $60-$70
Tel: (360) 426-8774

SHELTON INN
628 Railroad Ave (98584)
Rates: $40-$53
Tel: (360) 426-4468
(800) 451-4560

SUPER 8 MOTEL
2943 Northview Circle (98584)
Rates: $44-$68
Tel: (360) 426-1654
(800) 800-8000

RECREATION

JARRELL COVE STATE PARK - Leashes

Info: Even sofa loafers will take a shine to this pleasant park. You'll find a peanut-sized trail where you can get the lay of the land or BYOB (bring your own biscuits) and do lunch the outdoor way. For more information: (360) 426-9226.

Directions: From Shelton, travel Highway 3 north for 8 miles to Pickering Road. Take Pickering Road across the Haristine Bridge, turn left onto North Island Drive and continue to park.

LOWER SOUTH FORK SKOKOMISH TRAIL to LeBAR CLAIM HIKE

Intermediate/2.8 miles/1.5 hours

Info: A sniff-fest awaits you and your cold-nosed companion on this pretty trail that meanders through old-growth forests. Skirting the Skokomish River, you'll find plenty of paw-dipping opportunities as you journey to the LeBar Claim. Stake your own claim to a picnic spot and some down time before turning tail. For more information: (360) 877-5254.

Directions: From Shelton, take Highway 101 north for 6 miles to Skokomish Valley Road and turn west. Drive about 5 miles to FS 23 and turn right for 9 miles to FS 2353. Turn right and drive one mile to the trailhead.

Hotel Policies May Be Subject To Change

S H O R E L I N E (North Seattle)

<u>RECREATION</u>

ECHO LAKE PARK - Leashes

Info: Put on the dog and do the stroll in this beautiful waterfront park, where R&R and lunch alfrisky can make your day.

Directions: Located at North 200th Street and Ashworth Avenue North.

HAMLIN PARK - Leashes

Info: You and your city licker will like the get-away-from-it-all ambience of this tranquil oasis. More than 70 acres await your pawrusal, while 3.5 miles of byways let you exercise more than your prerogative. Fall equates to dazzling bronzy colors and piles of crunchy leaves. And you know what that means to a certified tail wagging machine, rolltime. For colors of a different hue, there's always the spring wildflower extravaganza. Birders will be in their element as well. Several songbird species contribute pretty tunes to the air waves. In dogspeak, this place rates two paws up.

Directions: Located at 16006 15th Avenue Northeast.

HILLWOOD PARK - Leashes

Info: Sporty breeds with a penchant for spectating can pull up a seat and root for the home team. In the off-season, bring a tennie and make your own fun.

Directions: Located at 3rd Avenue Northwest and Northwest 91st Street.

MERIDIAN PARK - Leashes

Info: Combine spacious open grounds with forested terrain and what do you get? A delightful park experience for naturalists who like to explore freelance style. Pack some snacks and Perrier, there are no amenities.

Directions: Located at North 170th Street and Wallingford North.

NORTH CITY PARK - Leashes

Info: Kick up some dust on the winding trails you'll discover at this lovely, albeit undeveloped, parkland where serenery rules the roost.

Directions: At 10th Avenue Northeast and Northeast 194th St.

RICHMOND BEACH SALTWATER PARK - Leashes

Info: When you're seeking an outdoor excursion in a view-blessed arena, this park has your name on it. Tote a camera, you'll leave with some marvelous panoramas of Puget Sound.

Directions: Located at 2021 Northwest 190th Street.

RONALD BOG - Leashes

Info: Situated on the banks of a bog, you and the dawgus will experience a close encounter of the natural kind. Birders, don't leave the binocs at home, you're bound to check off a sighting or two. FYI: Summer visitors, use bug repellent.

Directions: At North 175th Street and Meridian Avenue.

SHOREVIEW PARK - Leashes

Info: A fetching park where you wander to your heart's content. If your woofer's a hoofer, you can't go wrong if you point snouts to the north end of the parking lot and find a hillside trail to call your own. These pathways are particularly pretty in spring when wildflowers polka dot the lush landscape. Sofa loafers can always grab a seat at one of the ballfields and do nothing but spectate.

Directions: Located at Innis Arden Way and 9th Avenue NW.

TWIN PONDS PARK - Leashes

Info: There's something to be said for the tranquil feelings to be had by simply observing a pretty pond. Pull up a plush square of green and just enjoy some quietude with your canine companion. A good book and a tough chew can make your outing even better. For the sport in both of you, there's always a game on tap in this bustling area.

Directions: Located at 1st Avenue NE and North 155th Street.

Hotel Policies May Be Subject To Change

SILVER CREEK

LODGING

LAKE MAYFIELD MOTEL
2911 US Hwy 12 (98585)
Rates: n/a
Tel: (360) 985-2584

SILVER LAKE

LODGING

SILVER LAKE MOTEL & RESORT
3201 Spirit Lake Hwy (98645)
Rates: $30-$80
Tel: (360) 274-6141

SILVERDALE

LODGING

CIMARRON MOTEL
9734 NW Silverdale Way (98315)
Rates: $48-$55
Tel: (360) 692-7777

SEABREEZE COTTAGES & SPA
16609 Olympic View Rd NW (98315)
Rates: $76-$169
Tel: (360) 692-4648

RECREATION

ISLAND LAKE PARK - Leashes

Info: No bones about it, a feel good kind of day can be yours at this peaceful 26-acre park. Situated on the shores of Island Lake, this green scene is divided into two sections linked by a short trail. Rexercise buffs can make tracks on one of the paved lakefront trails that honeycomb the grounds. But if dropping a line suits you just fine, amble on over to the fishing pier.

Directions: Located on Silverdale Way and Bennington Drive.

SILVERDALE WATERFRONT PARK - Leashes

Info: Put a twinkle in the barkmeister's eye with an early morning jaunt to this 5-acre park. Small on size, Silverdale packs a petite punch of Mother Nature. Nestled on the edge of the Dyes Inlet, you and the dawgus can do lunch alfresco on a grassy knoll while you admire the shimmering blue water.

Directions: Located on Washington Avenue and Byron Streets.

Locate Other Dog-Friendly Activities...Check Nearby Cities

SKYKOMISH

LODGING

SKYKOMISH HOTEL
102 Railroad Ave (98288)
Rates: n/a
Tel: (360) 677-2477

SKYRIVER INN
333 River Dr E (98288)
Rates: $59-$91
Tel: (360) 677-2261

SNOHOMISH

LODGING

SNOHOMISH GRAND HOTEL B&B
901 1/2 1st St (98290)
Rates: $60-$75
Tel: (360) 568-8854

SNOHOMISH GRAND VALLEY INN
11910 Springetti Rd (98290)
Rates: n/a
Tel: (360) 568-8854

RECREATION

CENTENNIAL TRAIL HIKE - Leashes

Beginner/13.0 miles/7.0 hours

Info: So close to city life yet so far. You and your numero uno pal will find yourselves in a delightfully rural setting. But anyplace so accessible is bound to be popular. So be prepared to meet and greet others with the same idea, including the horsey set. Picnic tables and pretty Lake Stevens (your turnaround point) and more trees than you can count all come together to make for a pleasant interlude. For more information: (425) 339-1208.

Directions: The trail begins at the intersection of Maple Street and Pine Avenue in Snohomish.

FLOWING LAKE PARK - Leashes

Info: Laced with tree-shaded trails, this parkland is a snifforama extraordinaire. Let the one with his nose to the ground have his way in the fragrant forests and then satisfy your fishing fantasies while sleeping dogs lie. For more information: (360) 568-2274.

Hotel Policies May Be Subject To Change

Directions: Travel east on Highway 2, turn left onto 100th Street SE and continue until the road veers left and becomes 171st Avenue SE. Follow 171st Avenue SE to 48th Street SE and turn right to the park entrance at the end of the road.

LORD HILL PARK - Leashes

Info: Come see what Mother Nature has in store for you and furface at this delightfully cool 1,300-acre park. Whether you opt for a quiet lunch and some down time or do some fancy footwork on one of the trails, you won't regret a moment spent. For more information: (425) 339-1208.

Directions: Follow 88th Street west to Lincoln Avenue S and turn onto Old Snohomish-Monroe Highway. Proceed all the way to 27th Avenue SE and turn right for 2.25 miles to the park entrance on the left.

SNOQUALMIE

LODGING

THE SALISH LODGE
6501 Railroad Ave SE (98065)
Rates: $165-$575
Tel: (206) 888-2556
(800) 826-6124

SNOQUALMIE PASS

LODGING

SUMMITT INN
SR 906, P.O. Box 163 (98068)
Rates: $78-$89
Tel: (425) 434-6300
(800) 557-STAY

SOAP LAKE

LODGING

THE INN
226 E Main Ave (98851)
Rates: $65-$95
Tel: (509) 246-1132

NOTARAS LODGE
236 E Main Ave (98851)
Rates: $58-$250
Tel: (509) 246-0462

ROYAL VIEW MOTEL
Hwy 17 & 4th Sts (98851)
Rates: n/a
Tel: (509) 246-1831

TOLO VISTA COTTAGE
22 N Daisy (98851)
Rates: n/a
Tel: (509) 246-1512

SOUTH BEND

LODGING

H & H MOTEL & CAFE
P.O. Box 613, Hwy 101 (98586)
Rates: $34-$49
Tel: (360) 875-5523

SPOKANE

LODGING

APPLE TREE INN MOTEL
N 9508 Division St (99218)
Rates: $42-$54
Tel: (509) 466-3020
(800) 323-5796

BEL AIR MOTEL 7
1303 E Sprague Ave (99202)
Rates: $33-$49
Tel: (509) 535-1677

BELL MOTEL
W 9030 Sunset Hwy (99204)
Rates: $30-$43
Tel: (800) 223-1388

BEST WESTERN INN
12415 E Mission (99206)
Rates: $49-$60
Tel: (800) 888-6630

BEST WESTERN
PEPPER TREE AIRPORT INN
3711 S Geiger (99204)
Rates: $49-$139
Tel: (509) 624-4655
(800) 799-3933

BEST WESTERN PHEASANT RUN
12507 E Mission St (99216)
Rates: $50-$75
Tel: (509) 744-6979
(800) 528-1234

BEST WESTERN THUNDERBIRD INN
W 120 Third Ave (99204)
Rates: $54-$81
Tel: (509) 747-2011
(800) 578-2473

BEST WESTERN TRADE WINDS NORTH
N 3033 Division St (99207)
Rates: $54-$72
Tel: (509) 326-5500
(800) 528-1234

BROADWAY MOTEL
6317 E Broadway (99212)
Rates: $66-$74
Tel: (509) 535-2442

BUDGET SAVER MOTEL
E 1234 Sprague Ave (99202)
Rates: $26-$59
Tel: (509) 534-0669

CAVANAUGH'S INN AT THE PARK
W 303 North River Dr (99201)
Rates: $80-$140
Tel: (509) 326-8000
(800) 843-4667

CAVANAUGH'S FOURTH AVENUE
110 E 4th Ave (99202)
Rates: $50-$78
Tel: (509) 838-6101
(800) 843-4667

CAVANAUGH'S RESIDENT COURT
W 1203 Fifth Ave (99204)
Rates: $34-$68
Tel: (509) 624-4142
(800) 843-4667

CAVANAUGH'S RIVER INN
N 700 Division St (99202)
Rates: $60-$90
Tel: (509) 326-5577
(800) 843-4667

CLINIC CENTER MOTEL
S 702 McClellan (99204)
Rates: n/a
Tel: (509) 747-6081

COMFORT INN BROADWAY
6309 E Broadway (99212)
Rates: $55-$75
Tel: (509) 535-7185
(800) 221-2222

DAYS INN
1919 N Hutchinson Rd (99212)
Rates: $47-$72
Tel: (509) 926-5399
(800) 329-7466

LIBERTY MOTEL
6801 N Division St (99208)
Rates: $38-$60
Tel: (509) 467-6000

MAPLETREE MOTEL & RV PARK
E 4824 Sprague Ave (99212)
Rates: $26-$48
Tel: (509) 535-5810

MOTEL 6
1508 S Rustle St (99204)
Rates: $30-$45
Tel: (509) 459-6120
(800) 440-6000

PARK LANE MOTEL & SUITES
4412 E Sprague Ave (99212)
Rates: $57-$62
Tel: (509) 535-1626
(800) 533-1626

QUALITY INN NORTH
7111 N Division St (99208)
Rates: $74+
Tel: (509) 467-4900
(800) 221-2222

QUALITY INN VALLEY SUITES
8923 E Mission Ave (99212)
Rates: $79-$300
Tel: (509) 928-5218
(800) 424-6420

RAMADA INN AIRPORT
Spokane Int'l Airport,
P.O. Box 19228 (99219)
Rates: $59-$125
Tel: (509) 838-5211
(800) 272-6232

RAMADA INN & SUITES
9601 N Newport Hwy (99218)
Rates: $59-$144
Tel: (509) 468-4201
(800) 272-6232

RAMADA LIMITED
S 123 Post St (99204)
Rates: $50-$80
Tel: (509) 838-8504
(800) 272-6232

RAMADA LIMITED
211 S Division St (99202)
Rates: $40-$60
Tel: (509) 838-6630
(800) 272-6232

RANCH MOTEL
S 1609 Lewis St (99204)
Rates: $25-$32
Tel: (509) 456-8919
(800) 871-8919

Locate Other Dog-Friendly Activities...Check Nearby Cities

RED LION SPOKANE CITY CENTER
322 N Spokane Falls Ct (99201)
Rates: $89-$129
Tel: (509) 455-9600
(800) 547-8010

RED LION SPOKANE VALLEY
N 1100 Sullivan Rd (99220)
Rates: $85-$115
Tel: (509) 925-9000
(800) 547-8010

RED TOP MOTEL
7217 E Trent Ave (99212)
Rates: $42-$105
Tel: (509) 926-5728

RODEWAY INN
4301 W Sunset Hwy (99210)
Rates: $49-$64
Tel: (509) 838-1471
(800) 228-2000

RODEWAY INN CITY CENTER
827 W 1st Ave (99204)
Rates: $49-$64
Tel: (509) 838-8271
(800) 228-2000

ROYAL SCOT MOTEL
W 20 Houston (99208)
Rates: n/a
Tel: (509) 467-6672

SELECT INN
W 1420 Second Ave (99204)
Rates: $36-$62
Tel: (509) 838-2026
(800) 246-6835

SHANGRI-LA MOTEL
2922 W Government Way (99204)
Rates: $39-$76
Tel: (509) 747-2066
(800) 234-4941

SHILO INNS
E 923 3rd Ave (99202)
Rates: $65-$89
Tel: (509) 535-9000
(800) 222-2244

SIERRA HOTEL
4212 W Sunset Blvd (99204)
Rates: $59-$87
Tel: (509) 747-2021

SUPER 8 MOTEL
11102 W Westbow Blvd (99204)
Rates: $46-$66
Tel: (509) 838-8800
(800) 800-8000

SUPER 8 MOTEL
2020 N Argonne Rd (99212)
Rates: $39-$67
Tel: (509) 928-4888
(800) 800-8000

<u>RECREATION</u>

A.M. CANNON PARK - Leashes

Info: Light up the parkmeister's eyes and treat him to a brown bagger in this 8-acre locale.

Directions: Located at Maxwell and Elm.

AUDUBON PARK- Leashes

Info: Put a little wiggle in your wagger's waddle with a visit to this pleasant 26-acre park.

Directions: Located on Northwest Blvd and Milton.

B. A. CLARK PARK - Leashes

Info: Put the pupster's appendage in a tail spin with a spin around Clark Park. Nine acres of snifferific terrain are laced with mini-trails, ideal avenues to get the lead out.

Directions: Located at Garland and Division.

CANNON HILL PARK - Leashes

Info: Jumpstart a dogday morning with an excursion to this 13-acre verdant landscape. Afternoons equate to sporty doings like rooting for the home team. Or be a lazybones, grab a slab pondside and watch the clouds drift by.

Directions: Located on Lincoln and 18th.

CHIEF GARRY PARK - Leashes

Info: When push comes to shove and canine communing wins out, hightail it over to this neighborhood park. Ten acres await you and your playful noodnick.

Directions: Located on Mission and Cook.

COEUR D'ALENE PARK- Leashes

Info: Spokane's first park, get into the community spirit and check out the historic replica gazebo which commemorates this distinction. And then boogie with Bowser over the 9 acres before calling it a day.

Directions: Located on 4th and Chestnut.

COMSTOCK PARK - Leashes

Info: This paw-worthy parkland is a delightful grassy oasis smack dab in the middle of urbanity. Visit at dusk, you might be a lucky dog and catch a brilliant color-streaked sunset.

Directions: Located on 29th and Howard.

CORBIN PARK - Leashes

Info: Doggistorians will get a kick out of this 11.5-acre parkland situated in the heart of the Corbin Neighborhood Historic District. Pick a path and get the lay of the land. And hey, a sack of snacks could end your exploration on a high note.

Directions: Located on Waverly Place and Washington.

DOWNRIVER PARK - Leashes

Info: Savor a sampling of the goodies this 95-acre river milieu has in store for you. Citified canines can indulge in naturalist pursuits without leaving the urban limits. Skedaddle off on one of the trails that lace the landscape or investigate the terra firma along the Spokane River where late afternoon sunlight paints pretty patterns at water's edge. Here and there, natural springs poke through the lush greens adding a dollop of blue to the scenery.

Directions: Located on Pettet and Fort Wright Drives.

DRUMHELLER SPRINGS PARK - Leashes

Info: This petite sweet spot is made even more delightful by the natural springs that dot the landscape. If no outing is complete without a tad of Rexercise, then hop on one of the trails and make your dog's day.

Directions: Located on Euclid and Ash.

FRIENDSHIP PARK - Leashes

Info: Treat your schnauzer to a browser in the open space of this 12-acre green scene where canine carousing comes free of charge.

Directions: Located on Greta and Standard.

GRANT PARK - Leashes

Info: Social breeds give this 12-acre neighborhood park the high five for paw-pleasing ops and picnic spots.

Directions: Located on 11th and Arthur.

HANGMAN PARK - Leashes

Info: Wipe that woebegone look off the barkmeister's mug with a bonafido nature fix. This lush landscape of nearly 300 acres will have tails wagging in the breeze. The natural waters of Latah Creek are like cool ribbons of blue in a spot of green. Say ta ta to the city blahs and hello Mother Nature.

Directions: Located south of 44th and west of Hatch Road.

HARMON PARK - Leashes

Info: Strut with the mutt in this pleasant 10-acre park. Or see what's going on at one of the softball fields.

Directions: Located on Bismark and Market.

HAYS PARK - Leashes

Info: When walktime calls, answer it with a quickie to this 7-acre parkland.

Directions: Located on Gordon and Crestline.

HIGH BRIDGE PARK - Leashes

Info: A favorite with the wet pet set, you'll find plenty of paw-pleasing terrain at this 200-acre region. Located at the confluence of the Spokane River and Latah Creek, this spot is a cool retreat that can't be beat. There are trails to test your mettle and picnic ops to put you in fine fettle. Anyway you slice it, you're in for a bonafido great day.

Directions: Located on the Spokane River and Latah Creek

INDIAN CANYON PARK - Leashes

Info: Mucho byways honeycomb this lush landscape of 129 acres. Check out the waterfall in this park where the interesting rock outcrops are basalt, remnants of a volcanic past. In the arf, arf department, this setting of water and greenery rates two paws up. Eeny, meeny, miney, moe, pick a trail and off you go.

Directions: Located on Rimrock and Canyon Drives.

Locate Other Dog-Friendly Activities...Check Nearby Cities

LATAH CREEK PARK - Leashes

Info: A creek runs through it and makes this green scene even more lush. A riparian oasis in an urban setting, this park is home to a diverse sampling of wildlife.

Directions: Located on 16th and Latah Creek.

LIBERTY PARK - Leashes

Info: Urbanites will appreciate the quick and easy escape route this 22-acre park represents. Tote the red checks and do lunch alfrisky or simply practice your best lazybones routine.

Directions: Located on 4th and Pittsburg.

MANITO PARK - Leashes

Info: No bones about it, this 90-acre park is the ideal getaway. You'll be in natural splendor as easy as one, two, three. Plan a picnic repast or an old-fashioned saunter, spectate at a sporting event or skedaddle off on one of the pathways and burn some kibble. Way to go Fido.

Directions: Located on 17th and Grant Boulevard.

MINNEHAHA PARK - Leashes

Info: Take your mighty dog to Minnehaha just for the fun of it. Nearly 50 acres of hustling bustling recreation awaits. Catch a game in progress or devise your own game of one on one.

Directions: Located on Euclid and Havana.

MISSION PARK - Leashes

Info: Dawdle away the day with an afternoon of play at this 13-acre park. If hiking's more to your liking, pick up the Centennial Trail that passes through the park.

Directions: Located on Mission and Perry.

NEVADA PARK - Leashes

Info: This park makes the most of its 8 acres. You and your Hair Jordan will find softball fields, picnic tables and lots of strolling space.

Directions: Located on Joseph and Nevada.

PALISADES PARK - Leashes

Info: A smorgasbord of nature awaits you and the dawgus at this vast expanse where great views of the Spokane River are part of the package. More than 460 acres of grassy grounds equate to fun and games. Gung-ho hikers will be in the right element too, mucho trails lace the region. And you'll want to tote your Kodak. The basalt outcrops present intriguing photo ops.

Directions: Located on Greenwood Road and Rimrock Drive.

PEACEFUL VALLEY PARK - Leashes

Info: High clouds in the autumn sky add a pretty touch to this 10-acre park which skirts the Spokane River. BYOB (bring your own biscuits) and do lunch down by the riverside.

Directions: Located off Clarke Road on the banks of the Spokane River.

PIONEER PARK - Leashes

Info: Expand your walktime options and get the lay of the land at this 13-acre park.

Directions: Located on 7th and Stevens.

RIVERFRONT PARK - Leashes

Info: Enjoy a bonafido walk in the park with a journey to this 100-acre green scene. Make your own way with the trailblazer, hop on the Centennial Trail which meanders beside the Spokane River or find a grassy knoll and let sleeping dogs lie.

Directions: Located on Spokane Falls Boulevard and Washington.

RIVERSIDE STATE PARK - Leashes

Info: Okay, we're talking huge. Imagine yourself in a natural wonderland filled with the best of the outdoors and you've imagined this riverside park. With more than 70 miles of trails to choose from, hikers and their hounds will be planning a return trip before day is done. Geologist wannabes will wanna be in the fossil forest. Afishionados, on the other paw, will definitely wanna find a fishing nook to drop a fishing hook in the deep blue of the Spokane. Trekkers, a chunk of the Spokane River Centennial Trail shimmies through this park, the perfect way to clock on some miles. Tree enthusiasts won't know where to smell first, there are woodlands galore in the 8,000 acres of this paradise where you can see the forest for the trees. Whatever wags your tail, you'll find it here. For more information: (509) 624-7188.

Directions: From Spokane, travel west on Mission (the street changes names four times) until it becomes Maxwell. Continue on Maxwell as it drops down to the Spokane River and signs for the park. The parking lot is 2 miles from the sign. The park is approximately 8 miles northwest of Spokane.

Note: Dogs must be leashed. Yield to horses.

SHADLE PARK - Leashes

Info: Set the dog's you know what in a spin with an afternoon delight in this charming 40-acre setting. Stash a good read and a tough chew, find a cozy niche and loll the day away.

Directions: Located on Longfellow and Ash.

SPOKANE RIVER CENTENNIAL TRAIL HIKE - Leashes

Beginner/1.0-37.0 miles/0.5-18.5 hours

Info: A hiker's delight, the Spokane River Centennial Trail is a professionally designed, multi-use trail. Established in 1992, the trail follows the Spokane River from the Washington/Idaho border on the east end to about 14 miles northwest of Nine Mile Dam. You'll be escorted through local parks, across bridges and into some of the prettiest countryside to be seen, all provided without disruption to the natural landscape. This is one of those trails that'll keep you coming back for more. For more information: (509) 624-7188.

Directions: Trailheads are located along the entire route. The main trailhead is at the Washington/Idaho state line at the State Visitor Information Center. From Spokane, travel Interstate 90 east to the border. Take Stateline exit 299, turn left (north). The State Visitor Information Center is located just off Interstate 90.

Note: Trail is open dawn to dusk, year-round. Yield to horses. Pick up a trail guide at the Visitor Information Center.

STERLING HEIGHTS PARK - Leashes

Info: Perk up a humdrum day with a sojourn to this 8-acre hangout.

Directions: Located on 27th and Cumberland.

THORTON MURPHY PARK - Leashes

Info: The floppy eared one will perk up at the sight of this 8-acre splotch of terrain.

Directions: Located on 27th and Ray.

UNDERHILL PARK - Leashes

Info: Start your day off on the right paw and earn some puppy kisses for your efforts. A bounty of walking paths zigzag over the grounds of this 19-acre retreat.

Directions: Located on Hartson and Fiske.

UPRIVER DRIVE PARK - Leashes

Info: Stop puppyfooting around and get thee to a parkaree. This one has 189 paw-pleasing acres guaranteed to put a grin on the barkmeister's mug. Grassy knolls, shade-dappled pathways and the shimmering blues of the Spokane River are part and parcel of this delightful package.

Directions: Located on Mission to E City Limits.

UPRIVER PARK - Leashes

Info: You can sidestep the crowds with a weekday excursion to this popular park. Whether you're a hiking hound or a Frisbee fiend, you'll find a venue for your energy at the 147-acre riverside locale.

Directions: Located on Upriver Drive and E City Limits.

WENTEL GRANT PARK - Leashes

Info: Pooch shenanigans can be part of the program when you hightail it to this 10-acre expanse. So pack a fun attitude, a fuzzy tennie and see what happens.

Directions: Located on Latah Creek and Inland Empire Way.

Locate Other Dog-Friendly Activities...Check Nearby Cities

OTHER PARKS IN SPOKANE - Leashes

- ALBION HEIGHTS PARK, 17th & D
- CLIFF PARK, Ben Garnett Way & 13th
- COURTLAND PARK, Bridgeport & Cook
- COWLEY PARK, 7th & Division
- EMERSON PARK, Alice & Madison
- GLASS PARK, Heroy & Cincinnati
- GLOVER FIELD PARK, Main & Cedar
- HEATH PARK, Nora & Standard
- INDIAN TRAIL PARK, Woodside & Fleming
- JAMES J. HILL PARK, Nebraska & Cook
- LOMA VISTA PARK, Columbia & Alberta
- PACIFIC PARK, Lowell & Valerie
- PATRICK S. BYRNE PARK, Walton & Lidgerwood
- ROCHESTER HEIGHTS PARK, Rowan & Magnolia
- RUTH PARK, Dalke & Calispel
- ST. PATRICK'S PARK, Wabash & Nelson
- WEBSTER PARK, Walton & I Street
- WESTGATE PARK, Conestoga & Old Fort Drive
- WHITTIER PARK, 7th & F Street
- WILDHORSE PARK, Ralph & Empire

SPRAGUE

LODGING

LAST ROUNDUP MOTEL & RV PARK
312 E First (99032)
Rates: $36-$54
Tel: (509) 257-2583

PURPLE SAGE MOTEL
405 W First (99032)
Rates: $28-$42
Tel: (509) 257-2507

STARBUCK

RECREATION

LYONS FERRY STATE PARK - Leashes

Info: Hustle your butt along the breezy waterfront pathway and scope out the goodies of this pretty park. For more information: (509) 646-3252.

Directions: From Starbuck, travel west on Route 261 about 8 miles to the park entrance.

Hotel Policies May Be Subject To Change

PALOUSE FALLS STATE PARK - Leashes

Info: Every dog should have his day, make yours special with a visit to this lovely waterful scene where the air is sweetly scented with sagebrush. Double your pleasure and double your fun with a spring fling visit. Your quickie jaunt to the waterfall will be made even prettier by the wild ones that splash the landscape in a profusion of color. For more information: (509) 549-3551.

Directions: From Starbuck, travel west on Route 261 about 15 miles to Palouse Falls Road. Turn right and drive 2.8 miles to the park. The trailhead is on the left of the parking area.

STEVENSON

<u>RECREATION</u>

BONNEVILLE LOCK and DAM - Leashes

Info: Let your super sniffer scope out this amazing engineering feat. Situated on the scenic Columbia River, find yourselves a grassy knoll and observe this marvel. If the noon whistle is blowing in your tummy, plan a brown bagger with the wagger and round out the afternoon.

Directions: From Stevenson, travel southwest on Highway 14 to the Mile 40 marker and the dam.

SULTAN

<u>LODGING</u>

DUTCH CUP MOTEL
918 Main St (98294)
Rates: $49-$64
Tel: (360) 793-2215
(800) 844-0488

SUMAS

<u>LODGING</u>

BB BORDER INN MOTEL
121 Cleveland (98295)
Rates: n/a
Tel: (360) 988-5800

Locate Other Dog-Friendly Activities...Check Nearby Cities

SUNNYSIDE

Lodging

SUN VALLEY INN
724 Yakima Valley Hwy (98944)
Rates: $25-$75
Tel: (509) 837-4721

TOWN HOUSE MOTEL
509 Yakima Valley Hwy (98944)
Rates: $38-$52
Tel: (509) 837-5500
(800) 342-4435

TRAVELODGE
408 Yakima Valley Hwy (98944)
Rates: $41-$100
Tel: (509) 837-7878
(800) 578-7878

TACOMA

Lodging

BEST WESTERN TACOMA INN
8726 S Hosmer St (98444)
Rates: $81-$90
Tel: (253) 535-2880
(800) 528-1234

BLUE SPRUCE MOTEL
12715 Pacific Ave (98444)
Rates: n/a
Tel: (253) 531-6111

BUDGET INN-SOUTH TACOMA
9915 S Tacoma Way (98499)
Rates: $36+
Tel: (253) 588-6615

CORPORATE SUITES
219 Division Ct E (98404)
Rates: n/a
Tel: (800) 255-6058

DAYS INN
6802 Tacoma Mall Blvd (98409)
Rates: $81-$90
Tel: (253) 475-5900
(800) 329-7466

HIDDEN MAPLE B&B
4616 N 46th (98407)
Rates: $75-$95
Tel: (253) 756-2094

LA QUINTA INN
1425 E 27th St (98421)
Rates: $72-$79
Tel: (253) 383-0146
(800) 531-5900

MADIGAN MOTEL
12039 Pacific Hwy SW (98499)
Rates: $40-$50
Tel: (253) 588-8697

MOTEL 6 SOUTH
1811 S 76th St (98408)
Rates: $30-$45
Tel: (253) 473-7100
(800) 440-6000

RAMADA INN TACOMA DOME
2611 East E St (98421)
Rates: $62-$250
Tel: (253) 572-7272
(800) 272-6232

ROYAL COACHMAN INN
5805 Pacific Hwy E (98424)
Rates: $49-$120
Tel: (253) 922-2500
(800) 422-3051

SHERATON TACOMA HOTEL
1320 Broadway Plaza (98402)
Rates: $110-$140
Tel: (253) 572-3200
(800) 325-3535

Hotel Policies May Be Subject To Change

SHILO INNS
7414 S Hosmer St (98408)
Rates: $65-$95
Tel: (253) 475-4020
(800) 222-2244

VALLEY MOTEL
1220 Puyallup Ave (98421)
Rates: n/a
Tel: (253) 272-7720

VICTORY MOTEL
10801 Pacific Hwy SW (98499)
Rates: $23-$50
Tel: (253) 588-9107

WESTERN INN
9920 S Tacoma Way (98499)
Rates: $40-$60
Tel: (253) 588-5241
(800) 600-9751

<u>RECREATION</u>

ALLING PARK - Leashes

Info: Make the most of a cool morning with a stroll through this lovely 6-acre park. If you're packing a Penn, this could be a catch and fetch kind of place.

Directions: Located at South 60th and Sheridan Avenue.

DASH POINT STATE PARK - Leashes

Info: Pack a chow basket and plan an R&R kind of day with your hot diggety dog. This pretty parkland stretches along the Puget Sound presenting you with 400 acres to explore while your cares are carried off on a cool breeze. The shade is compliments of the firs, their lofty, spreading branches forming a lush canopy. Lazybone pursuits aside, you'll find plenty of exercise options as well. Six miles of trails honeycomb the park, winding through towering stands of trees where the understory is told by ferns and laurel. Stay till dusk if you can. When the sun drops behind the Olympic mountains, a kaleidoscope of colors streaks across the horizon in breathtaking glory. Wowser Bowser. For more information: (206) 661-4955.

Directions: From Tacoma, travel Highway 509 (Dash Point Road) north about 5 miles to the park entrance.

Note: Fee is $5. Open April 1 through October 15 from 6:30 a.m. to 10 p.m. Open October 16 through March 31 from 8 a.m. to 5 p.m.

The numbered trail system that follows is located in Dash Point State Park:

1) DASH POINT TRAIL SYSTEM

Info: A bonafido slice of easy, breezy hiking heaven, six miles of trails put you and the dawgus smack dab in the middle of

Locate Other Dog-Friendly Activities...Check Nearby Cities

nature. You simply can't go wrong. Take the Hoyt Road Trail for example. A favorite with naturalists, it begins and ends with petite ponds. Wildlife viewing ops are almost guaranteed. And if you're as much of a tree enthusiast as the sniffmeister, wait till you get a load of the beauties that await. To name names, fir, maple, elderberry, mulder and dogwood are part of the scene. And where there are trees, there are birds. And birds mean tweet-tweet music. If you're looking for a quick jaunt, make lickety split on the Upper or Lower Loop or kick up some dust on another goodie, the longer but quite enjoyable Outbound Trail. Carpe diem Duke. For more information: (206) 661-4955.

Directions: From Tacoma, travel Highway 509 (Dash Point Road) north about 5 miles to the park entrance. The trails begin off of 47th Avenue South and Highway 509.

Note: Fee is $5. Open April 1 through October 15 from 6:30 a.m. to 10 p.m. Open October 16 through March 31 from 8 a.m. to 5 p.m.

DeLONG PARK - Leashes

Info: Happy days can start with a bit of fun and games and a nice little stroll in this pleasant 9-acre parkland.

Directions: Located at 4700 South 12th Street.

FRANKLIN PARK - Leashes

Info: Bustling with activity, Franklin Park is a great place for active breeds who want to see and be seen. Make some friends while you catch a game in progress. Or hightail it over to the fitness course and like the name says, get fit.

Directions: Located at South 12th and Puget Sound Avenue.

GARFIELD PARK - Leashes

Info: When play's the thing, this park's the stage for good times. There are 10 acres of greenery where you and the furball can practice some fancy footwork.

Directions: Located at North D and Borough Road.

HARMON PARK - Leashes

Info: When push comes to shove and play wins out, set your sights on this 9-acre playground.

Directions: Located at South 80th and I Streets.

JEFFERSON PARK - Leashes

Info: For a fun time of presidential proportions, play tagalong with your wagalong through this park's pretty 15 acres. When the pooch is pooped, find a shaded nook and throw the poor dog a bone.

Directions: Located at North 9th and Monroe Streets.

LINCOLN HEIGHTS PARK - Leashes

Info: Dollars to dog biscuits you and your mischief making mutt will find plenty to do at this 20-acre locale. Sporty breeds will want to pack a fuzzy orb just in case.

Directions: Located at South 38th and Steele Streets.

McKINLEY PARK - Leashes

Info: Birders flock to this riparian retreat. And who can blame them? The wetland is home to a diversity of waterfowl, while the trees house a bounty of flyboys. Aside from the birding perks, there's a pathway where you and your canine cohort can work out the kinks or practice some hijinks.

Directions: At McKinley Avenue and Upper Park Street.

POINT DEFIANCE PARK - Leashes

Info: Here a trail, there a trail, this spectacular park is brimming with them and with everything else that is naturally pretty. The clean, fresh air is ocean-scented. The breezes are cool and refreshing. There are cozy nooks and crannies everywhere you turn and grassy knolls waiting for you to spread the red checks and break out the biscuit basket. And if you want views, just skedaddle up to the bluffs for ocean and city panoramas. If old cold nose needs some sniffing territory, check out the gardens for a snoutful of floral aromas. No bones about it, this odyssey promises and delivers good times for all. For more information: (206) 305-1000.

Directions: From the junction of Highways 5 & 16, head west on Highway 16 about 3 miles and follow to Pearl Street (Route 163). Head north (right) on Pearl Street about 3 miles and follow signs to park.

Note: Dogs are not permitted in the zoo or aquarium.

The numbered activity that follows is within Point Defiance Park:

1) POINT DEFIANCE PARK SCENIC DRIVE

Info: To see it all, take this tour d'auto through Point Defiance Park. Nestled between Puget Sound and Commencement Bay, your route traverses an old-growth forest, stunning vistas of Puget Sound, the Tacoma Narrows and the Narrows Bridge backdropped by the ever present, ever beautiful Cascade and Olympic Mountains. Make a pit stop at the Mountaineer Tree, a 440'-year old ancient wonder, it stands 218' tall and has a circumference of 24'. For more information: (206) 305-1000.

Directions: From the junction of Highways 5 & 16, head west on Highway 16 about 3 miles and follow to Pearl Street (Route 163). Head north (right) on Pearl Street about 3 miles and follow signs to park. The drive begins at the park entrance/exit off Pearl Street and North Park Avenue.

Note: Closed to walkers on Saturdays until 1 p.m. May also be closed during inclement weather. Call first.

PORTLAND AVENUE PARK - Leashes

Info: A gamut of activities can make your dog's day at this sporty 11-acre parkland.

Directions: Located at East 34th and Portland Avenue.

PUGET PARK - Leashes

Info: Give the pupster something to bark home about with a sojourn to this 20-acre expanse. Shaded by tall trees which dot the landscape, you and the one with the nose to the ground can make tracks on one of the pathways. Spring brings a bonus of wildflower beauties to color your world in brightness.

Directions: Located at North 31st and Proctor Streets.

SALISHAN PARK - Leashes

Info: The lush, tree-strewn grounds of this green scene may be just what the vet ordered. Wiggle with your wagger to Peace Arch and check out the monument. Whenever the time is right, spread the red checks and break some bread and biscuits with Bowser.

Directions: Located at Q and East 45th & 39th Streets.

SOUTH PARK - Leashes

Info: Whether you're in the mood to kick up some dust on the fitness trail or kick back in a gazebo, you and the pupster can have it your way in this 14-acre slice of greenery.

Directions: Located at 4851 South Tacoma Way.

SWAN CREEK PARK - Leashes

Info: The sheer enormity of this parkland gets two paws up in doggiedom. Tree hounds in particular swear by this woodsy retreat where the smells are as good as they get. You'll find serene, songbird-filled pathways and plenty of open stretches of moist grasslands. So dilly dally no longer, happy days are waiting.

Directions: Located at East 56th and Roosevelt Avenue.

TITLOW PARK - Leashes

Info: This primo slice of beachfront property is perfect for beach bum Bowsers and their companions. Dine à la blanket with the biscuitmeister while you're mesmerized by the pretty blue waters. Fishing fiends, if you're dreaming about flounder, perch or sole for din-din, you might just go home with your dream fulfilled. And when nothing but a brisk walk will do, there's a pathway to suit your exercise style.

Directions: Located at 8425 6th Avenue.

Locate Other Dog-Friendly Activities...Check Nearby Cities

WAPATO PARK - Leashes

Info: Afishionados can have their way with their prey while exercise gurus can burn some kibble on the challenging fitness course. Without question, there's always something for the lazybones in you, like shady nooks where the entertainment is provided by Mother Nature's musicians.

Directions: Located at South 68th and Sheridan Avenue.

WRIGHT PARK - Leashes

Info: From lawn bowling to pickleball, horseshoes to tennis, hiking trails to picnic tables, this delightful 27-acre park aims to please. Hustle your butt from one activity to the next until you've had your fill. And then set up picnic shop and fill up on goodies. Hey, don't forget a tough chew for old brown eyes.

Directions: Located at 6th Avenue and I Street.

OTHER PARKS IN TACOMA - Leashes

- BALTIMORE PARK, North 47th & Baltimore Street
- BROWNS POINT PARK, 201 Tulalip Street NE
- BYRD PARK, South 92nd & Alaska Streets
- CELEBRATION PARK, South 80th & D Streets
- CLOVERDALE PARK, South 59th & Q Streets
- DASH POINT PARK, Beach St NE via Markham Ave NE
- DAWSON PARK, E 90th & Portland Ave
- FIREMAN'S PARK, South 8th & A Streets
- IRVING PARK, South 25th & Hosmer Streets
- JANE CLARK PARK, North 39th & Ferdinand Streets
- KANDLE PARK, North 26th & Shirley Streets
- LINCOLN/ELDRIDGE PARK, South 37th & Thompson Ave
- MANITOU PARK, South 66th & Stevens Streets
- McCARVER PARK, South 23rd & J Streets
- NORTHEAST TACOMA PARK, NE 29th & 56th Avenue NE
- NORTON MEMORIAL PARK, S 1st Street & St. Helens Ave
- OAKLAND PARK, Center & South Gunnison Streets
- OLD TOWN PARK, North 30th & Steele Streets
- OPTIMIST PARK, North 13th & James Streets

Hotel Policies May Be Subject To Change

- PEOPLE'S PARK, South 9th & K Streets
- ROGERS PARK, East 34th & I Streets
- ROOSEVELT PARK, East 36th & Roosevelt Streets
- STANLEY PARK, 1712 South 19th Street
- STEWART HEIGHTS PARK, East 60th & B Streets
- VASSAULT PARK, North 37th & Vassault Streets

TENINO

LODGING

OFFUT LAKE RESORT
4005 120th Ave SE (98589)
Rates: $27-$45
Tel: (360) 264-2438

THORP

LODGING

CIRCLE H HOLIDAY RANCH RESORT
810 Watt Canyon Rd (98946)
Rates: n/a
Tel: (509) 964-2000

TOKELAND

LODGING

TRADEWINDS ON THE BAY MOTEL
4305 Pomeroy Ave (98590)
Rates: n/a
Tel: (360) 267-7500

TOLEDO

LODGING

COWLITZ MOTEL & RV PARK
162 Cowlitz Loop Rd (98591)
Rates: n/a
Tel: (360) 864-6611

Locate Other Dog-Friendly Activities...Check Nearby Cities

TONASKET

LODGING

BONAPARTE LAKE RESORT
695 Bonaparte Lake Rd (98855)
Rates: n/a
Tel: (509) 486-2828

RAINBOW RESORT
761 Loomis Hwy (98855)
Rates: $26-$60
Tel: (509) 223-3700
(800) 347-4375

RED APPLE INN
Hwy 97 & 1st St (98855)
Rates: $37-$47
Tel: (509) 486-2119

SPECTACLE FALLS RESORT MOTEL
879 Loomis Hwy (98855)
Rates: n/a
Tel: (509) 223-4141

SPECTACLE LAKE RESORT
10 McCammon Rd (98855)
Rates: $30-$105
Tel: (509) 223-3433

RECREATION

BETH LAKE TRAIL HIKE - Leashes

Beginner/3.8 miles/2.0 hours

Info: Swagger with the wagger while the songbirds serenade on this delightfully charming trail to the gentle waters of Beaver and Beth Lakes. Zooming off from the Beaver Lake Campground, follow the west shore of Beaver Lake. The setting is highlighted by a scattering of wildflowers that fringe the banks of both lakes. A quickie detour through Beth Lake Campground will deposit you on a dirt road before zap, you're back on track. A small earth dam at the head of the lake is your crossover point. For more information: (509) 997-2131.

Directions: From Tonasket, travel Highway 20 east about 20 miles to CR 4953 (Bonaparte Lake Road), turn left. Continue about 4.5 miles past Bonaparte Lake (the road becomes FS 32). Travel FS 32 about 3 miles to the Beaver Lake Campground and the trailhead near the first set of campsites.

BIG TREE LOOP TRAIL HIKE - Leashes

Beginner/2.0 miles/1.0 hours

Info: In this mixed bag of Mother Nature, you'll walk in the company of ponderosa, lodgepole and whitebark pines mingled with giant larch trees in an old-growth forest setting. The larch trees are the grand dames of this woodsy region, dating back over 500 years. Get psyched for a snifforama extraordinaire and a sizable dollop of all things natural. The wildflower party begins in June and continues into the summer, so plan an excursion then and plan to be enchanted. For more information: (509) 997-2131.

Directions: From Tonasket, travel Highway 20 east about 24 miles to the junction with CR 4953 (Bonaparte Lake Road), turn left. Continue about 5 miles to FS 32, turn right and go about 4 miles to the junction with FS 33. Bear left onto FS 33 and continue about 4 miles to the trailhead and parking area.

PIPSISSEWA TRAIL HIKE - Leashes

Intermediate/2.0 miles/1.0 hours

Info: You and your happy go lucky pupster will be treated to an invigorating hike and an eyeful of pretty scenery on this trail. Your journey begins by traversing an 300-foot earth dam and then climbing steadily through rocky clearings to an overlook above Bonaparte Lake. Notice the pretty patterns the sunlight paints upon the water as it glistens 400' below you. When departure time beckons, do the descent thing. For more information: (509) 997-2131.

Directions: From Tonasket, travel Highway 20 east about 24 miles to the junction with CR 4953 (Bonaparte Lake Road), turn left. Continue about 5 miles to FS 32, turn right. Continue about 4 miles to the junction with FS 33, bear left onto FS 33 and travel about 4 miles. Turn into the campground and stay to your left to FS 32-012. Follow 32-012 to the parking area past the boat ramp.

STRAWBERRY MOUNTAIN TRAIL HIKE - Leashes

Intermediate/3.0 miles/2.0 hours

Info: Aptly named, this berry berry nice trail leads to a 600' summit where views of Bonaparte Lake and Mount Bonaparte are as sweet as the abundant namesake fruit. Speaking of which, the berries bloom in summer and make the air heavenscent. Eh, if you're hiking on a clear day, the pristine terra firma of Canada and the cloud-coated peaks of the Canadian Cascades are candy for the eyes. Way to go Fido. For more information: (509) 997-2131.

Directions: From Tonasket, travel Highway 20 east about 24 miles to CR 4953 (Bonaparte Lake Road), turn left. Continue on Bonaparte Lake Road (which becomes FS 32) about 4 miles past Bonaparte Lake to the junction with FS 33, turn left. Travel FS 33 to the Lost Lake Campground. The trailhead is located about 50 yards past the entrance to the campground.

Note: Make sure you know your berries before eating them.

TOPPENISH

LODGING

EL CORRAL MOTEL
61731 Hwy 97 (98948)
Rates: $34-$39
Tel: (509) 865-2365

OXBOW MOTOR INN
511 S Elm St (98948)
Rates: $31-$49
Tel: (509) 865-5800
(800) 222-3161

TOPPENISH INN MOTEL
515 S Elm St (98948)
Rates: $38-$102
Tel: (509) 865-7444

RECREATION

RAILROAD PARK - Leashes

Info: Treat your little Beethoven to a summer concert under the stars, compliments of the Yakima Valley Concert Band. Make the most of the night and plan a picnic supper while you and your musical mutt hum along.

Directions: Located at 10 Asotin Avenue next to the Yakima Valley Rail and Steam Museum.

TOPPENISH MURALS WALKING TOUR - Leashes

Info: You'll want to pick up a pamphlet to increase your learning curve for this unusual walking tour. Begin at the Mural Office where two works of art are mere appetizers of what's to come when you walk to Toppenish Avenue and your door into the once wild west. Many well-known artists (local and otherwise) contributed their talents to this "art walk" which includes portrayals of Indian and pioneer life, a depiction of Fort Simcoe and of the olden days in Toppenish. After you've fueled the mind, do a little something for the body and picnic in the nearby park where you can throw the poor dog a bone. For more information: (509) 865-3262.

Directions: The tour begins at the Mural Office off Toppenish Avenue, located between the railroad tracks and Division Street.

TROUT LAKE

<u>RECREATION</u>
CROFTON BUTTE TRAIL HIKE - Leashes

Intermediate/5.2 miles/3.0 hours

Info: Pristine beauty combines with solitude to create this wonderful trek. From the towering trees above to the lush clumps of beargrass that carpet the forest floor, you and your trailblazer will feel like Lewis and Clark as you explore the piney thickets. A large opening on Crofton Butte is the place to get sweeping views of Mount Adams, the valley and Crofton Butte. Atop the 5,272' butte, you and mighty mutt will feel like champs. Perky wildflowers pop up here and there along the butte adding splashes of color to the already picturesque landscape. When day is done, do an about-face and retrace the pawprints. For more information: (509) 395-2501.

Directions: From Trout Lake, travel Highway 17 north about 1.25 miles to Forest Service Road 23, turn left. Travel FS 23 north about 8.5 miles to FS 8031, turn right. Continue about 1.5 miles to FS 8031-50, turn left. The trailhead is located at the end of FS 8031-50.

SALT CREEK TRAIL HIKE - Leashes

Intermediate/6.0 miles/3.0 hours

Info: By virtue of its pristine locale, its serenery and tranquility, this numero uno hike is one you won't soon forget. Solitude seekers, the only sounds you'll hear in this cool and fragrant forest setting are the sounds of nature. Naturalists, wildlife sightings come with the territory. Spend your morning in the company of beaver or happen upon a herd of elk grazing contentedly. Listen closely for birdsong that drifts your way from the treetops. The trail dead ends near the junction of Cascade Creek and Salt Creek, an almost swamp-like milieu. This the stuff of hiking dreams. Carpe diem you lucky dogs. For more information: (509) 395-2501.

Directions: From Trout Lake, travel Highway 17 north about 1.25 miles to FS 23, turn left. Travel FS 23 northwest about 6 miles to FS 8031, turn right for about a quarter of a mile to FS 060, turn left and continue about a mile to the trailhead.

TUKWILA

LODGING

BEST WESTERN SOUTHCENTER
15901 W Valley Hwy (98188)
Rates: $72-$125
Tel: (206) 226-1812
(800) 544-9863

HAMPTON INN
7200 S 156th St (98188)
Rates: $70-$80
Tel: (206) 228-5800
(800) 426-7866

HOMEWOOD SUITES HOTEL
6955 Fort Dent Way (98188)
Rates: $89-$169
Tel: (206) 433-8000
(800) 225-5466

RESIDENCE INN BY MARRIOTT
16201 W Valley Hwy (98188)
Rates: $124-$185
Tel: (206) 226-5500
(800) 331-3131

SOUTH CITY MOTEL
14242 S Pacific Hwy (98168)
Rates: n/a
Tel: (206) 243-0222

RECREATION

CRYSTAL SPRINGS PARK - Leashes

Info: Say adieu to the winter blues with an excursion to this this grassy green scene. A couple of trails and a smattering of picnic tables are part of the 11-acre package. Hey, a Frisbee could make the visit memorable.

Directions: Located on 51st Avenue South and S 158th Street.

Hotel Policies May Be Subject To Change

DUWAMISH/GREEN RIVER TRAIL HIKE - Leashes

Beginner / 1.0-22.0 miles / 0.5-12.0 hours

Info: Set tails wagging in the breeze on this riverside journey which includes a number of parklands. You'll find plenty of paw-pleasing terrain along the route. Pick a slice and go for it. For more information: (206) 433-1858.

Directions: The main trailhead is located at South Glacier Street and Olympic Avenue South. You can access the trail from almost any point.

FORT DENTON PARK - Leashes

Info: Do something different for a change and plan a day of let's see. Let's see how much fun you can have with the wagster in 51 acres. Let's see how good a picnic lunch under a shade tree can be. Let's see what it feels like to spend a dog-gone terrific day with your wet nose wonderdog.

Directions: At Fort Dent Drive and 69th Avenue South.

INTERURBAN TRAIL HIKE - Leashes

Beginner / 6.0 miles / 3.0 hours

Info: A definite antidote to the city weary blues, furbanites will appreciate the escape hatch this route offers. Hop on the paved pathway and travel the far banks on the east side of the Duwamish/Green River in a riparian oasis that's bound to astound the hound. Get ready for some friendly canine communing on this popular trail. If you're making a day of it, picnic tables dot the terrain, serving up scenic resting spots where you and the wagger can share a brown bagger.

Directions: The trailhead is located on South 180th Street and continues to Baker Boulevard.

JOSEPH FOSTER MEMORIAL PARK - Leashes

Info: A gamut of sporty pastimes creates a pleasant atmosphere in this 7-acre neighborhood hangout.

Directions: On 53rd Avenue South and South 137th Street.

TUKWILA PARK - Leashes

Info: For an AM or PM constitutional with a grassy twist, set tails in overdrive with a visit to this expanse. Small in size, this park packs a few punches, namely a scenic view site, sport courts, a horseshoe pit and wow, a trail to call your own.

Directions: Located on 65th Avenue South and South 153rd Street.

OTHER PARKS IN TUKWILA - Leashes

- •BICENTENNIAL PARK, Christensen Rd & Strander Blvd
- •CRESTVIEW PARK, 42nd Ave South & South 162nd St
- •DUWAMISH PARK, 42nd Ave South & South 116th St
- •RIVERTON MINI PARK, 45th Ave South & South 133rd St
- •SOUTHGATE PARK, 40th Ave South & South 133rd St

TUMWATER

LODGING

BEST WESTERN TUMWATER INN
5188 Capitol Blvd (98501)
Rates: $56-$78
Tel: (360) 956-1235
(800) 528-1234

MOTEL 6
400 W Lee St (98501)
Rates: $30-$40
Tel: (360) 754-7320
(800) 440-6000

TWISP

LODGING

IDLE-A-WHILE MOTEL
505 North Hwy 20 (98856)
Rates: $40-$53
Tel: (509) 997-3222

SPORTSMAN MOTEL
1010 E Hwy 20 (98856)
Rates: $29-$45
Tel: (509) 997-2911

WAGON WHEEL MOTEL
HCR 73, Box 57 (98856)
Rates: n/a
Tel: (509) 997-4671

Hotel Policies May Be Subject To Change

RECREATION

BLACKPINE LAKE TRAIL HIKE - Leashes

Beginner/0.6 miles/0.3 hours

Info: If you're short on time but long on yearning, don't miss this charming woodland trail. Boogie with the doggie around the crystalline waters of Blackpine Lake and wet those tootsies in the refreshing tributaries. Spend your morning in the company of busy beavers and elegant egrets. Do some nature studying at the mini dams and rivulets along your route. Afishionados give this place the high five so tote your pole. A scattering of benches at the end of this rainbowesque path can't be beat for an R&R moment. Check out the distant peaks of the Lake Chelan-Sawtooth Wilderness that peek from behind a bushel of flora. Your journey will be over too soon, guaranteed. But then there's always tomorrow. For more information: (509) 997-2131.

Directions: From Twisp, travel Twisp River Road (FS 44) west about 10.5 miles to Buttermilk Creek Road (FS 43), turn left. Continue about 8 miles to the Blackpine Lake Campground and the trailhead in the parking area near the boat ramp.

CRATER CREEK TRAIL HIKE - Leashes

Intermediate/7.8 miles/4.0 hours

Info: Give your water woofer something to remember with an excursion to this aqua wonderland. Skirting Crater Creek, the path winds along a woodsy trail where you and the one with the waggily tail will climb a few steep hills. Before you know it, the creek joins the rippling waters of Crater Lake. The shimmering, glimmering blueness of the lake, nestled in a land of green is bound to please all your senses. Early birds might get a chance to hear the hoot of the great horned owl. Take five and enjoy some wet and wild pooch shenanigans before retracing your steps. For more information: (509) 997-2131.

Directions: From the junction of Highways 20 and 153 in Twisp, travel Highway 153 south about 15 miles to the junction with the North Fork Gold Creek Road (CR 1029), turn right for about 7 miles and stay right on FS 4340. Travel about 5.6 miles to FS 300, a narrow dirt road leading to the left and follow about 5 miles to the end and the trailhead.

Locate Other Dog-Friendly Activities...Check Nearby Cities

LOOKOUT MOUNTAIN TRAIL HIKE - Leashes

Beginner/2.6 miles/1.5 hours

Info: On this slow but steady climb, you and the one with the nose glued to the ground will ascend 1,200' to the summit of Lookout Mountain, the rainbow at the end of the trail. The panoramic views from your lofty aerie are nothing short of stunning. Twisting river valleys of lush green are back-dropped by the high peaks of the Sawtooth Ridge, North Cascades National Park and Glacier Peak Wilderness. A fire lookout tower stands guard over the rocky summit and the wilderness below. Your mighty dog will give two paws up for this fun trek. For more information: (509) 997-2131.

Directions: From Twisp, travel Twisp River Road (FS 44) west about a quarter of a mile to Alder Creek Road (FS 4345-200), turn left. Continue about 8 miles to the end and the trailhead.

NORTH CREEK TRAIL HIKE - Leashes

Intermediate/9.6 miles/6.0 hours

Info: You'll need some power munchies and oodles of H_2O for this all day excursion. The beginning of the trail is somewhat confusing, so be prepared to use your navigational skills. You and Scout will head out along the North Creek and follow the winding waters before zooming south into the North Lake Basin and a bounty of beauty. Postcardian pretty, the lush greenery is enhanced by a lake and grandiose Gilbert Peak. Actually, you'll get three different peeks of the peak. The bonus of a spring or summer hike comes in the form of pretty perky wildflowers. The alpine meadows along your route will be splashed in a kaleidoscope of color. Look but don't touch, the meadowlands are fragile. For more information: (509) 996-4000.

Directions: From Twisp, travel Twisp River Road (FS 44) west about 25 miles. The marked trailhead is on the right side of Twisp River Road.

UNION

LODGING

ALDERBROOK RESORT
E 7101 Hwy 106 (98592)
Rates: $49-$99
Tel: (360) 898-2200
(800) 622-9370

ROBIN HOOD VILLAGE
E 6780 Hwy 106 (98592)
Rates: $75-$85
Tel: (360) 898-2163

UNION GAP

LODGING

DAYS INN
2408 Rudkin Rd (98903)
Rates: $40-$60
Tel: (509) 248-9700
(800) 329-7466

QUALITY INN YAKIMA VALLEY
12 E Valley Mall Blvd (98903)
Rates: $46-$59
Tel: (509) 248-6924
(800) 221-2222

SUPER 8 MOTEL
2605 Rudkin Rd (98903)
Rates: $47-$62
Tel: (509) 248-8880
(800) 800-8000

USK

LODGING

THE INN AT USK
410 River Rd (99180)
Rates: $25-$57
Tel: (509) 445-1526

VALLEY

LODGING

TEAL'S WAITTS LAKE RESORT
3365 Waitts Lake Rd (99181)
Rates: n/a
Tel: (509) 937-2400

Locate Other Dog-Friendly Activities...Check Nearby Cities

VANCOUVER

LODGING

BEST WESTERN FERRYMAN'S INN
7901 NE 6th Ave (98665)
Rates: $54-$78
Tel: (360) 574-2151
(800) 528-1234

DOUBLETREE INN
100 Columbia St (98660)
Rates: $92-$113
Tel: (360) 694-8341
(800) 222-8733

HEATHMAN LODGE
7801 NE Greenwood Dr (98662)
Rates: $119-$450
Tel: (360) 254-3100
(888) 475-3100

RESIDENCE INN PORTLAND NORTH
8005 NE Parkway Dr (98662)
Rates: $119-$155
Tel: (360) 253-4800
(800) 331-3131

RIVERSIDE MOTEL
4400 Lewis & Clark Hwy (98661)
Rates: n/a
Tel: (360) 693-3677

RODEWAY INN CASCADE PARK
221 NE Chalkov Dr (98684)
Rates: $50-$100
Tel: (360) 256-7044
(800) 426-5110

SHILO INNS DOWNTOWN
401 E 13th St (98686)
Rates: $59-$95
Tel: (360) 696-0411
(800) 222-2244

SHILO INNS HAZEL DELL
13206 Hwy 99 (98686)
Rates: $58-$65
Tel: (360) 573-0511
(800) 222-2244

SUNNYSIDE MOTEL
12200 NE Hwy 99 (98686)
Rates: n/a
Tel: (360) 573-4141

VALUE MOTEL
708 NE 78th St (98665)
Rates: n/a
Tel: (360) 574-2345

VANCOUVER LODGE
601 Broadway (98660)
Rates: $40-$75
Tel: (360) 693-3668

RECREATION

BATTLE GROUND LAKE STATE PARK - Leashes

Info: Located in the foothills of the Cascade Mountains, you'll find 279 acres of lakeside terrain that can't be beat for a getaway retreat. Battle Ground Lake is a caldera, a basin that was formed when the cone of a volcano collapsed. An ancient volcanic explosion left blobs and globular chunks of lava scattered throughout the park. Photo buffs will undoubtedly fill their Fujis with pix of these lava oddities. Fishing fiends will be glad to know the spring-fed lake is stocked with rainbow trout, cutthroat trout, smallmouth bass and catfish. Ten miles of roads and trails, including a self-guided nature path, will entice hik-

Hotel Policies May Be Subject To Change

ing hounds to get a move on. Budding birders, bring your ID book, the park is favored by an array of flyboys including jay, woodpecker, crow, osprey, grouse, robin and chickadee. FYI: This area was named to commemorate a battle which never happened. In 1855, Klickitat Indians escaped from Fort Vancouver. Before any fighting took place, a bargain was struck between the Army soldiers and the Indians and a confrontation was avoided. For more information: (800) 233-0321.

Directions: From the junction of Highway 205 and Route 503 in Vancouver, head north on Route 503 about 8 miles to the park.

Note: Open 6:30 a.m. to dusk in summer and 8 a.m. to dusk in winter. Dogs are not permitted on beaches or in the water.

The numbered hike that follows is within Battle Ground Lake State Park.

1) BATTLE GROUND LAKE LOOP TRAIL HIKE - Leashes

Beginner/7.0 miles/4.0 hours

Info: Here you'll go loop-de-loop skirting a shimmering beauty formed when a volcano erupted and then collapsed, creating a deep cauldron in its wake. Filled by rain, streams and springs, the area possesses all the qualities of a riparian oasis. It goes without saying that this place is for the birds, a bevy of them as well as rabbits and deer. If you're still craving more of the same when this hike is over, boogie with Bowser on a scenic nature trail that begins in the campground. For more information: (800) 233-0321.

Directions: From the junction of Highway 205 and Route 503 in Vancouver, head north on Route 503 about 8 miles to the park entrance. The trail begins near the day use parking area on the left side of the boat ramp.

Note: Open 6:30 a.m. to dusk in summer and 8 a.m. to dusk in winter. Dogs are not permitted on beaches or in the water.

BEN FRANKLIN PARK - Leashes

Info: For a doggone delightful interlude, schedule a stop at this 9-acre park. You'll find grassy knolls, a small ballfield and plenty of open terrain. The cool breezes skimming off Vancouver Lake can help you chill out on those dog days of summer.

Directions: Located on Northwest 56th and Cherry Streets.

COLUMBIA RIVER WATERFRONT TRAIL HIKE - Leashes

Beginner/8.0 miles/4.5 hours

Info: This enchanting odyssey promises and delivers a dog-gone great day. Picture pretty scenes are everywhere. Do the stroll along the water's edge before larking with your bark to Waterfront Park. The Renaissance Promenade is a hop, skip and a jump away. Don't miss the 7-foot tall bronze statue of Ilchee, daughter of a well-known Chinook Indian chief. You can't go wrong on this scenic journey dotted with tailwagging green scenes. Tidewater Cove is your turnaround point. For more information: (360) 693-1313.

Directions: The trail starts at the Captain Vancouver Monument and ends at Tidewater Cove.

ESTHER SHORT PARK - Leashes

Info: This 5-acre park packs quite a scenic punch. Visit in spring and let the sniffmeister have a field day in the vibrant Victorian Rose Gardens. The roses aren't the only bloomers to brighten the landscape, so be prepared for a pretty spring fling. Don't miss the Pioneer Mother Statue, a tribute to women settlers.

Directions: Located at Esther and 8th Streets.

FRENCHMAN'S BAR PARK - Leashes

Info: Birders literally flock to this beautiful stretch of beach so don't leave the binocs at home. A paw-worthy trail through shade-dappled terrain also awaits. Sans amenities, tote plenty of Perrier and a stash of goodies. For more information: (360) 699-2375, ext. 2467.

Directions: Located at 9612 Lower River Road.

FRUIT VALLEY PARK - Leashes

Info: Grab your gadabout and do a round about this 13-acre expanse which serves up tons of fun for you and the furball. Give the pupster a run for the money over the open greens or be a lazybones beneath a shade tree.

Directions: Located at 3203 Unander Avenue.

LEVERICH PARK - Leashes

Info: When playtime can no longer be denied, hustle your butt to this 27-acre region. A trusty Penn will take care of the ballmeister's exercise needs. Afterwards, you can put on the dog and strut your stuff on one of the walking paths. And pack a biscuit basket, lots of picnic ops await beside Burnt Bridge Creek.

Directions: Located on East 39th and M Streets.

OLD APPLE TREE PARK - Leashes

Info: Dedicated to the "Old Apple Tree," the grandaddy of Washington's juiciest industry, this park can fill the bill as a place to chill with the dawgus. This green spot is the centerpiece of the popular Old Apple Tree Festival held the first Saturday in October.

Directions: Located on Columbia Way, east of Highway 5.

ORCHARDS PARK - Leashes

Info: You won't regret a moment spent in this idyllic setting of greenery and serenery. In spring, towering Douglas fir provide an evergreen backdrop to the splash of flowering dogwoods and the blooming charm of the trilliums. In fall, the vine maple and wild cherry trees are dressed in autumn splendor. And no sniffmeister worth his salt will want to miss the Hall of Fame Rose Garden. Birders, you'll go bonkers in this avian havian, where tweet-tweet music fills the airways. So tarry no more, just plan a day and do it.

Directions: Located off 4th Plain Road, just east of Vancouver Mall at the intersection with 102nd Avenue.

VANCOUVER LAKE - Leashes

Info: Listen up, aquapups. The water doesn't get much bluer than beautiful Vancouver Lake. Tote a boat and float awhile or pull up a lakeside seat and watch the ever present windsurfers do their thing. The majestic mountain backdrop is compliments of Mt. Hood, Mt. Adams and Mt. St. Helens. For more information: (360) 699-2375, ext. 2467.

Locate Other Dog-Friendly Activities...Check Nearby Cities

Directions: Take Highway 5 south to the Fourth Plain Boulevard exit and head west for a couple of miles. When the road splits, take SR 501 (the right fork) and follow signs.

Note: Dogs are prohibited from April-October.

WATERFRONT PARK - Leashes

Info: A green scene with a river twist, this 7.5-acre strip of lawns and decks overlooks the fast running waters of the Columbia River. The next time Fido says "arf," treat him to this riverside walk.

Directions: Located near the Interstate 5 Bridge.

WATERWORKS PARK - Leashes

Info: A bonafido walk in the park is what you'll find in this lovely 20-acre urban oasis. Skedaddle some time away on one of the pathways and end your excursion at the elegant rhododendron garden. If you're visiting in May, expect a color extravaganza.

Directions: Located on Vancouver Way north of Clark College.

WHIPPLE CREEK PARK -Leashes

Info: Get ready, get set and go for a hike in this stunning, undeveloped region. Whether you trek one mile or ten, solitude and scenery are yours for the taking. Don't forget to tote plenty of water and a biscuit basket for chow time. For more information: (360) 699-2375 ext. 2467.

Directions: Located 7 miles north of Vancouver at the intersection of NW 179th Street and NW 21st Avenue.

OTHER PARKS IN VANCOUVER:

- ARNADA PARK, 25th & G Streets
- CARTER PARK, Columbia & 33rd Street
- HIDDEN PARK, Daniels between 37th & 39th Streets
- HUDSON'S BAY PARK, East 9th Street, south of Mill Plain
- JOHN BALL PARK, 23rd Street & Kauffman Avenue
- LEACH PARK, East 28th & K Streets
- QUARNBERG PARK, U & 13th Streets

VASHON ISLAND

LODGING

ANGELS OF THE SEA B&B
26431 99th Ave SW (98070)
Rates: $65-$85
Tel: (206) 463-6980
(800) 798-9249

CASTLE HILL B&B
26734 94th Ave SW (98070)
Rates: $65+
Tel: (206) 463-5491

PEABODY'S B&B
23007 64th Ave SW (98070)
Rates: $70+
Tel: (206) 463-3506

SWALLOW'S NEST GUEST COTTAGES
6030 248th St SW (98070)
Rates: $69-$90
Tel: (206) 463-2646
(800) 269-6378

VERADALE

LODGING

COMFORT INN VALLEY
905 N Sullivan Rd (99037)
Rates: $61-$86
Tel: (509) 924-3838
(800) 228-5150

WALLA WALLA

LODGING

A & H MOTEL
2599 Isaacs (99362)
Rates: n/a
Tel: (509) 529-0560

**BEST WESTERN
WALLA WALLA SUITES INN**
7 E Oak St (99362)
Rates: $57-$75
Tel: (509) 525-4700
(800) 528-1234

CAPRI MOTEL
2003 Melrose St (99362)
Rates: $32-$65
Tel: (509) 525-1130

CITY CENTER MOTEL
627 W Main St (99362)
Rates: $32-$50
Tel: (509) 529-2660
(800) 453-3160

COLONIAL MOTEL
2279 E Isaacs (99362)
Rates: $32-$55
Tel: (509) 529-1220

COMFORT INN
520 N 2nd Ave (99362)
Rates: $57-$75
Tel: (509) 525-2522
(800) 228-5150

PONY SOLDIER MOTOR INN
325 E Main St (99362)
Rates: $67-$83
Tel: (509) 529-4360
(800) 634-7669

SICYON GALLERY B&B
1283 Star (99362)
Rates: n/a
Tel: (509) 525-2964

Locate Other Dog-Friendly Activities...Check Nearby Cities

SUPER 8 MOTEL
2315 Eastgate St N (99362)
Rates: $43-$61
Tel: (509) 525-8800
(800) 800-8000

TAPADERA BUDGET INN
211 N 2nd St (99362)
Rates: $31-$54
Tel: (509) 529-2580
(800) 722-8277

VAGABOND INN
305 N 2nd Ave (99362)
Rates: $45-$65
Tel: (509) 529-4410
(800) 522-1555

WHITMAN MOTOR INN
107 N 2nd St (99362)
Rates: $39-$115
Tel: (509) 525-2200
(800) 237-4436

RECREATION

EASTGATE LIONS PARK - Leashes

Info: Do some puppy prancing at this 11-acre green expanse. Root for the home team at one of the ballfields or make up a game of your own with a flying Frisbee. Summer BBQs are very popular at this park so plan ahead and join the fun.

Directions: Located on Wilbur and Tacoma Streets.

FORT WALLA WALLA PARK - Leashes

Info: A little bit of this and a little bit of that is what you and your Curious George can expect at this paw-pleasing parkland of more than 200 acres. A gamut of activities beckon eager tail waggers and companions. Watch the ducks pondside as you stroll through this slice of nature on a pleasant trail while the pupster experiences some pondamania. Hobbyists, check out the model car track and model airplane field and see what's zipping around.

Directions: Located on Dalles Military and Myra Roads.

HOWARD-TIETAN PARK - Leashes

Info: You can't go wrong with an afternoon at this park where nearly 20 acres of rolling terrain and stunning vistas of Blue Mountain are part of the pretty package.

Directions: Located on Howard and Tietan Streets.

JEFFERSON PARK - Leashes

Info: Pack a fun attitude and your best social skills when you make tracks to this popular locale. From watering holes to shaded knolls, you'll have plenty of playtime pupportunities for a doggone good day. Train buffs, the park also has a locomotive display.

Directions: Located on 9th Avenue and Malcolm Street.

PIONEER PARK - Leashes

Info: Sports oriented, this 58-acre park caters to baseball, tennis, soccer and volleyball enthusiasts. Hey, pack your own bouncy Wilson and let the ballmeister hone his skills.

Directions: Located on Alder and Division Streets.

WASHINGTON PARK - Leashes

Info: If you've got some treehound in your blood, don't miss this woodsy retreat where you can beat the heat and give the furball a treat.

Directions: Located on 9th Avenue and Cherry Street.

OTHER PARKS IN WALLA WALLA - Leashes

- MEMORIAL PARK, Rees Avenue, east of the freeway
- MENLO PARK, Division & Portland Streets
- VISTA TERRACE PARK, Mountain Park Drive
- WILDWOOD PARK, Division Street & Boyer Avenue

WARDEN

<u>RECREATION</u>
VOLUNTEER PARK - Leashes

Info: Energize your morning with a quick jaunt to this 10-acre green scene. Chances are the air will be filled with the sweet sounds of Mother Nature's musicians, not to mention the migrating flyboys.

Directions: Located on 4th and Maple Avenues.

Locate Other Dog-Friendly Activities...Check Nearby Cities

WASHOUGAL

LODGING

ECONO LODGE
544 6th St (98671)
Rates: $40-$55
Tel: (360) 835-8591
(800) 424-4777

RECREATION

BEACON ROCK STATE PARK - Leashes

Info: Brimming with waterfalls and charming little cascades, this enchanting park rates two paws up in dogspeak. Play follow the leader on a pretty trail and then find yourselves a secluded nook in the bosky landscape and do lunch alfrisky. If water hijinks are more your style, tote a boat and go afloat. The fishing's not bad either if you're so inclined. For more information: (509) 427-8265.

Directions: From Washougal, head east on SR 14 approximately 13 miles to the park.

The numbered hike that follows is within Beacon Rock State Park:

1) BEACON ROCK TRAIL HIKE - Leashes

Intermediate/1.5 miles/1.0 hours

Info: The invigorating climb to dazzling views from atop Beacon Rock is outfitted with handrails for your safety and enjoyment. Photo buffs, pack lots of Fuji, this place eats film. Point and shoot, the scenic Columbia Gorge, tumbling waterfalls and rugged basalt cliffs stretch out before you with a bevy of beautiful little islands dotting the pretty blues. When you can pull yourself and the wide-eyed one from this lofty perch, do the descent thing. For more information: (509) 427-8265.

Directions: From Washougal, head east on SR 14 approximately 13 miles to the park. The trailhead is next to the Administration Area.

Hotel Policies May Be Subject To Change

WENATCHEE

LODGING

AVENUE MOTEL
720 N Wenatchee Ave (98801)
Rates: $30-$65
Tel: (509) 663-7161
(800) 733-8981

BEST WESTERN HERITAGE INN
1905 N Wenatchee Ave (98801)
Rates: $60-$100
Tel: (509) 664-6565
(800) 528-1234

CHIEFTAN MOTEL
1005 N Wenatchee Ave (98801)
Rates: $45-$80
Tel: (509) 663-8141

COMFORT INN
815 N Wenatchee Ave (98801)
Rates: $55-$65
Tel: (509) 662-1700
(800) 228-5150

FORGET ME NOT B&B
1133 Washington St (98801)
Rates: n/a
Tel: (509) 663-6114

HILL CREST MOTEL & RV PARK
2921 School St (98801)
Rates: $25-$40
Tel: (509) 663-5157

HOLIDAY LODGE
610 N Wenatchee Ave (98801)
Rates: $36-$75
Tel: (509) 663-8167
(800) 722-0852

LYLE'S MOTEL
924 N Wenatchee Ave (98801)
Rates: $30-$75
Tel: (509) 663-5155
(800) 582-3788

ORCHARD INN
1401 N Miller Ave (98801)
Rates: $47-$63
Tel: (509) 662-3443
(800) 368-4571

RED LION INN
1225 N Wenatchee Ave (98801)
Rates: $69-$99
Tel: (509) 663-0711
(800) 547-8010

STARLITE MOTEL
1640 N Wenatchee Ave (98801)
Rates: $35-$55
Tel: (509) 663-8115
(800) 668-1862

UPTOWNER MOTEL
101 N Mission St (98801)
Rates: $40-$55
Tel: (509) 663-8516
(800) 288-5279

VAGABOND INN
700 N Wenatchee Ave (98801)
Rates: $35-$70
Tel: (509) 663-8133
(800) 522-1555

WELCOME INN
232 N Wenatchee Ave (98801)
Rates: $40-$55
Tel: (509) 663-7121
(800) 561-8856

**WEST COAST
WENATCHEE CENTER HOTEL**
201 N Wenatchee Ave (98801)
Rates: $77-$95
Tel: (509) 662-1234
(800) 426-0670

RECREATION

LINCOLN ROCK STATE PARK - Leashes

Info: Named for its main attraction, Lincoln Rock, this 100-acre park offers plenty of puppy pleasing prospects for you

Locate Other Dog-Friendly Activities...Check Nearby Cities

and the furball. Tote your binocs and check out Lincoln Rock. Do you think it resembles Honest Abe? As you wander and gadabout, you'll be treated to wonderful views of Lake Entiat and Turtle Rock Island. For a nature fix, make tracks along a woodsy trail where beaver, deer and rabbit might make an unscheduled appearance. Birders won't go home disappointed either. If you've a penchant for fishing, bring a chew for your patient pupster and try your rod on steelhead. For more information: (509) 884-8702.

Directions: From East Wenatchee, travel 7 miles north on Highway 2/97 to park entrance.

ROCK ISLAND HYDRO PARK - Leashes

Info: Make the most of a cool morning with a stroll about the grounds of this 70-acre green scene which comes complete with a dollop of easy does it trails.

Directions: Located off Highway 28, 2 miles south of East Wenatchee.

ROCKY REACH DAM - Leashes

Info: Talk about postcard pretty. The dam is surrounded by 18 acres of award-winning lawns and gardens for you and the sniffmeister to meander. Patriotic pups, check out Old Glory, a fabulous flower bed sparkling with brilliant reds, whites and blues planted to resemble the U.S. flag. Don't forget the biscuit basket, a peaceful, shaded picnic area awaits you and the wagmeister.

Directions: From Wenatchee, travel 7 miles north on Highway 97A to the entrance.

WALLA WALLA POINT PARK - Leashes

Info: Savor the sampling of goodies that this spacious grassy region has in store for you and furface. Work out the kinks on the walking path or dine à la blanket beneath a canopy of towering trees. Way to go Fido.

Directions: Entrance is off Walla Walla Street.

WENATCHEE CONFLUENCE STATE PARK - Leashes

Info: Two rivers run through it. The Wenatchee River divides this parkland into two zones, both ideal for an exploration. The Wenatchee and the Columbia River flow together and create a confluence between the two parks, attracting a profusion of birds and wildlife. If you're seeking a plain and simple park, the North Confluence section is your best bet. Comprised of approximately 97 acres of developed land, it comes complete with a sports field, campgrounds and a boat launch. If you prefer your parks on the wild side, the South Confluence has your name on it. About 100 acres of primitive land are zigzagged by 10 miles of hiking trails. The naturalness of the terrain makes it a wildlife mecca for raccoon, muskrat and beaver to name some of the ground dwellers. On the other paw, the skyways are plied by eagle, osprey, hawk or blue heron. The two distinct regions are connected by a bridge so you can sample a bit of both. For more information: (509) 664-6373.

Directions: From Wenatchee, travel north on Highway 28 about 2 miles to Highway 2 west. Exit at the stop light. Cross the bridge and take the Alternate 97 north exit. At the stop sign on Euclid, turn right. At the Link Service Center, turn left. Cross the railroad tracks and follow Euclid Street to the park.

Note: The South Confluence Waterfront Trail is closed from December 1 through March 1 to protect sensitive wildlife.

WENATCHEE RIVERFRONT PARK - Leashes

Info: Do a shoreline stroll and take in the pretty surroundings or tote a boat and do the float. There's a mini-railroad that occasionally chugs through the 31-acre landscape.

Directions: Entrances are off Worthen and Fifth Streets.

WESTPORT

LODGING

ALASKAN MOTEL & APARTMENTS
708 N First (98595)
Rates: n/a
Tel: (360) 268-9133

ALBATROSS MOTEL
200 E Dock St (98595)
Rates: $46-$62
Tel: (360) 268-9235

BREAKERS MOTEL
971 N Montesano St (98595)
Rates: $52-$70
Tel: (360) 268-0848

CHINOOK MOTEL
707 N Montesano St (98595)
Rates: n/a
Tel: (360) 268-9623

CRANBERRY MOTEL & RV PARK
920 S Montesano St (98595)
Rates: $30+
Tel: (360) 268-0807

FRANK L. AQUATIC GARDENS RESORT
725 S Montesano St (98595)
Rates: $42-$108
Tel: (360) 268-9200

GLENACRES INN B&B
222 N Montesano St (98595)
Rates: n/a
Tel: (360) 268-9391

HARBOR RESORT
871 Neddie Rose Dr (98595)
Rates: n/a
Tel: (360) 268-0169

ISLANDER MOTEL & CHARTERS
421 Westhaven & Neddie Rose (98595)
Rates: $50
Tel: (360) 268-9166
(800) 322-1740

OCEAN AVENUE INN
275 W Ocean Ave (98595)
Rates: $50-$145
Tel: (360) 268-9278
(888) 692-9278

SANDS MOTEL
1416 Montesano St (98595)
Rates: n/a
Tel: (360) 268-0091

SHIPWRECK MOTEL
2653 Nyhus St (98595)
Rates: n/a
Tel: (360) 268-9151

RECREATION

WESTPORT LIGHTHOUSE TRAIL SYSTEM - Leashes

Beginner/2.8 miles/2.0 hours

Info: If you're anywhere in the area, you won't regret a moment spent along this wonderful trail which winds north from the Westport Lighthouse to Westhaven State Park. Stop at the three viewing platforms where interpretive panels provide insight into the region as well as an eyeful of nature. The concrete pathway shimmies beside the natural dune line in this setting of breathtaking shoreline scenery. You and the wide-eyed one will be treated to visions of pretty dune grass, wide sandy beaches, white-capped rolling surf and cloud-dotted blue skies. And no matter when you're visiting, there's always the charm of distant snow-capped mountains to complete the postcardian picture. Wowser Bowser, what more could a lucky dog want?

Although you and the barkmeister won't be alone on this popular route, a sense of serenity will accompany you. On a sun-drenched day, feel the soft ocean breezes, notice the way the sunlight makes the waves twinkle before crashing onshore, watch the gentle swaying of the tall grasses and be delighted with a surprise burst of a pink or yellow wildflower poking its head through a rich green hedge. Whenever the urge strikes, hightail it with your beach bum and see what treasures you unearth. Perfectly formed sand dollars, agate and jasper can be yours with a dollop of diligence and a couple of sharp eyes. Anyway you slice this adventure, you're gonna like the taste it leaves behind.

Directions: Go south on South Forrest Street (105 So.) to W. Ocean Avenue and go west (right) to the end of the street. Park in the lot on your right. The trail begins above the parking area.

WHIDBEY ISLAND

LODGING

Clinton

HOUSE BY THE SEA COTTAGES
2388 E Sunlight Beach Rd (98236)
Rates: $155-$175
Tel: (360) 321-2964

NORTHWEST VACATION HOMES
6497 E Hunziker Ln (98236)
Rates: $100-$275
Tel: (360) 341-5005
(800) 544-4304

Coupeville

THE VICTORIAN B&B
602 N Main St (98239)
Rates: $65-$100
Tel: (360) 678-5305

Freeland

HARBOUR INN MOTEL
1606 E Main St (98249)
Rates: $61-$85
Tel: (360) 321-6900

Langley

DRAKE'S LANDING B&B
203 Wharf St (98260)
Rates: $65+
Tel: (360) 221-3999

ISLAND TYME B&B
4940 S Bayview Rd (98260)
Rates: $95-$140
Tel: (360) 221-5078
(800) 898-8936

Oak Harbor

ACORN MOTOR INN
8066 80th St NW (98277)
Rates: $44-$66
Tel: (360) 675-6646
(800) 280-6646

THE AULD HOLLAND INN
33575 Hwy 20 (98277)
Rates: $45-$85
Tel: (360) 675-2288

BEST WESTERN HARBOR PLAZA
5691 SR 20 (98277)
Rates: $69-$118
Tel: (360) 679-4567
(800) 528-1234

QUEEN ANN MOTEL
1204 W Pioneer Way (98277)
Rates: $47-$58
Tel: (360) 675-2209

Locate Other Dog-Friendly Activities...Check Nearby Cities

RECREATION

Clinton

DAN PORTER MEMORIAL PARK - Leashes

Info: Towering fir trees shade the grounds at this enchanting 8.5-acre park. Birds flitter through the branches. Try to count the calls of twittered harmony, or be a sport and indulge the pooch with some catch and fetch.

Directions: Located off Highway 525 on Deer Lake Road.

Coupeville

CAPTAIN THOMAS COUPE PARK - Leashes

Info: Get mellow with your fellow at this lovely half-acre oasis off the shores of Penn Cove where picnic tables and viewing ops are part of the total package.

Directions: On the water in Coupeville at NE 9th and Otis St.

COUPEVILLE TOWN PARK - Leashes

Info: Small on size but big on appeal, this park sits a bit higher along Penn Cove than its neighboring park. There's a walking trail that leads you and your Sandy to the cove. A beach blanket will come in handy if you plan to stay awhile.

Directions: Located in Coupeville, one block west of the wharf on Coveland Street.

FORT CASEY STATE PARK - Leashes

Info: Attention military mutts, an education on this historic fort and the 10-inch guns that defended it can be yours on the self-guided tour. Built in the 1890s to protect Puget Sound, Fort Casey is a history buff's delight. If you're looking for some Rexercise as well, check out the trails along the bluff and to the beach and make an afternoon of it. For more information: (360) 678-4519.

Directions: The park is located at 1280 South Fort Casey Road, about 4 miles south of Coupeville.

Note: Dogs are not permitted in the lighthouse.

Hotel Policies May Be Subject To Change

The numbered hikes that follow are within Fort Casey State Park:

1) BEACH TRAIL HIKE - Leashes

Beginner/8.0 miles/4.0 hours

Info: When the morning dew is still evident and the mist is just beginning to rise, make lickety split on this quiet beach walk. You might want to take your binocs. Orca pods are often sighted in this area. And listen up pup, and the barking of harbor seals and sea lions is bound to keep the tail in a state of continuous motion. Sit and chill awhile, you might get a glimpse of a rare humpback or minke whale migrating to warmer waters. Occasionally dolphins are sighted offshore playing, "I can jump higher than you" in the turbulent waters. Sightings aside, you'll get your money's worth on this trail.

Directions: The park is located at 1280 South Fort Casey Road, about 4 miles south of Coupeville.

2) FORT CASEY INTERPRETIVE TRAIL HIKE - Leashes

Beginner/0.5 miles/0.5 hours

Info: Pack a flashlight, you'll need it for the tunnels you'll encounter along the trail. This 10-stop interpretive walk will enlighten you about artillery and its significance in battles. You'll feel like you've been transported to a different world. Doors 1, 2 & 3 escort you to the oil, storage and tool rooms. Remnants of elevator shafts used to lift the shells and powder bags to the upper level can still be seen. Let the sniffmeister help you locate the 10-inch disappearing Carriage Rifles that were capable of firing a 617-pound projectile. Stop 4, check out the two-inch pipes in the walls. These are speaking tubes and each leads to a different room. Continue past the battery stations to the switchboard, an interesting and intricate chamber designed as the communications center. The wooden stairway on the right leads to the Observing Stations where you'll gain a perspective of the surrounding area. The path around the back of these stations returns you to your starting point.

Directions: The park is located at 1280 South Fort Casey Road, about 4 miles south of Coupeville. The trail begins just past the display board.

Note: A detailed pamphlet is available for the trail.

FORT EBEY STATE PARK - Leashes

Info: No bones about it, this seaside oasis has the makings of a great little getaway. Plan lunch albrisky because no matter how warm or sunny it might be, there's always a very cool ocean breeze whistling through the trees. Or exercise more than your prerogative and leave some pawprints on one of the pathways that honeycomb the rough terrain. Created more than 10,000 years ago by the Vashon glacier, the large indentations in the landscape are kettle holes, formed as the massive ice blocks retreated. Lose yourself in thoughts of nature as you traipse amidst an oak grove forest. Visit one of the lilypad-dotted ponds of blue. If spring is in the air, wildflowers will be popping up everywhere. Don't be surprised to see a prickly pear cactus either. The island lies in the rain shadow of the Olympics which equates to dry conditions, perfect conditions in fact, for the thorny plant with the delicious fruit to thrive. For an up-close gander at the wildlife and birdlife, stash your binocs in your backpack and skedaddle off to Lake Pondilla where a bald eagle or tow might show. There's even a smidgen of history waiting to be examined. Your doggistorian will be intrigued by the WWII defense bunker built in the early 1940s as part of the coastal defense system. Whatever sets you panting, chances are on your side you'll find what you're seeking. For more information: (360) 678-4636

Directions: From Coupeville, drive northwest on Highway 20 about 5 miles to the signed entrance to the park.

The numbered hike that follows is within Fort Ebey State Park:

1) BLUFF TRAIL HIKE - Leashes

Beginner/6.0 miles/3.0 hours

Info: Expect company on this pupular hike that winds through some of the Island's finest scenery. Tote a sweater.

Hotel Policies May Be Subject To Change

Like the incessant barking of the ballmesiter when an orb is anywhere in sight, the breeze in these parts never stops. As you make with the fleet of feet on the blufftop, views of the Pacific and the surrounding peaks and valleys will make you feel good to be out and about. See if your nosey one sniffs out the gun emplacements that still stand as a testament to the fort's active days. Fall and spring are primo seasons to visit, the time when the mountains are snow-capped and the landscape is lush with color.

Directions: From Coupeville, drive northwest on Highway 20 about 5 miles to the signed entrance to the park. The trailhead is located in the north parking area.

RHODODENDRON COUNTY PARK - Leashes

Info: Tickle yourself pink and visit this pretty setting in spring when the rhodies do their thing. Let the mutt strut his stuff along the open grassy areas you'll find at this 37-acre parkland.

Directions: Located 3 miles south of Coupeville on Patmore Road.

Freeland

FREELAND PARK - Leashes

Info: If the one-two punch of greenery and sandy beaches sends tails into permanent overdrive, then this 17-acre parkland has your name on it. During low tide, you and your Nosey Rosie can look under eel grass and discover a different side of ocean life, replete with sponges, worms and other unusual critters. But remember, look, don't touch. Pack a brown bagger and do lunch with the wagger on a secluded grassy knoll you can call your own.

Directions: From Highway 525 in Freeland, turn right onto Honeymoon Bay Road and drive to the park.

SOUTH WHIDBEY STATE PARK - Leashes

Info: A soft sandy beach is just one of the allures of this pristine park. A treehound's idea of heaven, you'll traverse stands of old-growth Douglas fir, frolic amidst woodlands of Sitka spruce, grand fir, maple and western hemlock and be humbled by a stand of ancient western red cedars, estimated to be 500-years old. You'll uncover a maze of hiking trails, secluded nooks and crannies and a gamut of options for plain old solitude and serenery. So when you've got to satisfy that itch for Mother Nature, scratch it here and leave contented. For more information: (360) 331-4559

Directions: From Freeland, take Highway 525 west to Bush Point Road. Turn left and drive 6 miles to the park entrance on the left. Bush Point Road becomes Smugglers Cove Road as you approach the park.

Note: Park is closed to camping in winter, but trails remain open.

The numbered hikes that follow are within South Whidbey State Park:

1) FOREST DISCOVERY LOOP TRAIL HIKE - Leashes

Beginner/0.75 miles/0.75 hours

Info: Get along with your little doggie and discover the tranquility of this forest milieu. Your ears will be filled with the sweet tweets of the local flyboys while your other senses will be treated to the pretty patterns the sun creates as it streams through the treetops. And speaking of treetops, that's where the eagles do their nesting.

Directions: From Freeland, take Highway 525 west to Bush Point Road. Turn left and drive 6 miles to the park entrance on the left. Bush Point Road becomes Smugglers Cove Road as you approach the park. The trail is on the bluff above the beach.

2) HOBBIT TRAIL HIKE - Leashes

Intermediate/6.0 miles/4.0 hours

Info: If you and the bowwow are wow wowed by blufftop views of the powerful Pacific, don't miss this beaut. You'll find dense thickets in this neck of the woods where peeks of the ocean are part and parcel of the scenery. Not to mention the opportunity to get a lofty view of Admirality Inlet where shorebirds come to dine. Talk about dining, bring your own chow basket and set up shop.

Directions: From Freeland, take Highway 525 west to Bush Point Road. Turn left and drive 6 miles to the park entrance on the left. Bush Point Road becomes Smugglers Cove Road as you approach the park. The trail begins in the main camping area and leads to the bluff.

3) WILBERT TRAIL HIKE - Leashes

Beginner/2.5 miles/1.5 hours

Info: Knock on wood, you're gonna be impressed by nature's handiwork on this trail where you'll be surrounded by old-growth timber, including an ancient stand of Western red cedar. Not to be outdone, other bosky beauties vie for your attention. Your tree enthusiast won't be able to get the nose out of first gear. The variety of woodsy delights attracts a potpourri of songbirds, so tote the binocs and check off some sightings. Any way you slice it, this trail will leave a pleasant taste.

Directions: From Freeland, take Highway 525 west to Bush Point Road. Turn left and drive 6 miles to the park entrance on the left. Bush Point Road becomes Smugglers Cove Road as you approach the park. The trail is located across the highway, 0.25 miles from the park gate.

Langley

LANGLEY SEAWALL PARK - Leashes

Info: A beach barkarama, this local favorite gets two paws up from the pet set. Totem poles mark the entrance to 1,000' of sandy coastline facing the Saratoga Passage. You'll witness outstanding views of the Cascades and neighboring Camano Island. An avian havian, the flashy bald eagle, elegant great blue heron, grebe, loon merganser and belted kingfisher stake out their nests on the nearby bluffs. Furface should feel right at home, the residents of Langley love dogs so much that they've honored the canine with a statue at this park. For more information: (360) 221-6765.

Directions: Located on Langley Road.

SOUTH WHIDBEY COMMUNITY PARK - Leashes

Info: Dash off to this 47-acre green scene and put a spin on the wagger's appendage. There's a one miler that zigzags through the park or make like Pelé and get your kicks at a game of soccer. Don't forget, there's always the option of lazybone pursuits for you and the hirsute one.

Directions: Located on Maxwelton Road.

Oak Harbor

CLOVER VALLEY PARK - Leashes

Info: Spectate at the home game or devise your own fun and games at this 12-acre setting where the grass is guaranteed to withstand playful puppy pastimes.

Directions: Located west of Oak Harbor and Ault Field Roads.

Note: Open April to October.

DECEPTION PASS STATE PARK - Leashes

Info: Hiking hounds and naturalists agree this is the place to be. It's not an unusual occurrence to see a black-tailed deer, still and silent, grazing in the bosky terrain. Maybe your timing will be right and a bald eagle will lift off in flight, spreading its 6' foot wing span for your delight. There's no doubt about it, you're gonna vow to return to this appealing setting. For more information: (206) 675-2417.

Directions: From Oak Harbor, travel 9 miles north on Highway 20 to the signed entrance. Main trailheads are located at Bowman Bay on the Fidalgo Island (north) side and at West Point near Cranberry Lake on the Whidbey Island (south) side.

The numbered hikes that follow are within Deception Pass State Park:

1) DISCOVERY TRAIL HIKE - Leashes

Beginner/1.4 miles/1.0 hours

Info: Like the name says, you and your explorer are about to discover an interesting journey. Begin along the dirt road and shimmy uphill to some outstanding views. The trail continues around the end of the barricade and through a lovely stone arch under the freeway.

Directions: From Oak Harbor, travel 9 miles north on Highway 20 to the signed entrance. The trail is located on the Whidbey Island (south) side at the North Beach Parking Area.

2) GOOSE ROCK PERIMETER TRAIL HIKE - Leashes

Intermediate/3.8 miles/2.0 hours

Info: You'll start out on the Discovery Trail before intersecting with the Goose Rock Perimeter Trail at 0.7 miles. Take the right fork and you'll be up, up and away to the highest elevation on Whidbey Island, to a place where stunning vistas of Cornet Bay come free of charge. Lucky dogs might catch a glimpse of an elegant blue heron or majestic bald eagle. Atop the windswept summit, you and Champ will feel like just that, champs, as you pawruse the entire span of Whidbey Island, the San Juan Islands and the snow-kissed Cascades. Perk up your ears and listen to the familiar sound of the surf as you continue your trek and approach Deception Pass Bridge. Keep walking under the bridge to the starting gate.

Directions: From Oak Harbor, travel 9 miles north on Highway 20 to the signed entrance. The trail is located on the Whidbey Island (south) side at the North Beach Parking Area.

3) LIGHTHOUSE POINT TRAIL HIKE - Leashes

Beginner/2.0 miles/1.0 hours

Info: Since this hike requires a bit of pathfinding, make sure your trailblazer's up to snuff. Start your scenic journey by heading south from the parking lot. When you reach the thickets, turn left and hoof it uphill a short distance before switchbacking around a rocky outcrop. Stay on track and down you'll go. At the bottom of the hill, turn right and race your Greyhound to the sand pit where tide pooling could make your day complete. Watch for marshland dwellers as you wiggle with your wagger into the woodlands.

For a side trip to pretty views of the rocky coves, take the left fork, Canoe Pass Vista Trail. This little jaunt loops back onto the Lighthouse Trail to an open, exposed rocky bluff (read chilly). Continue in a westerly direction through a thick growth of salal all the way to the waterfront.

Directions: From Oak Harbor, travel 9 miles north on Highway 20 to the signed entrance. The trailhead is located at the lower parking lot at Bowman Bay on the Fidalgo Island (north) side.

Note: Travel to the lighthouse is dangerous and prohibited.

4) ROSARIO HEAD TRAIL HIKE - Leashes

Beginner/0.25 miles/0.25 hours

Info: Your best bet for this short but sweet jaunt is the left side of the loop. To the south, you'll have views of West Beach on Whidbey Island, to the west, Rosario Strait and the Strait of Juan de Fuca. Exercise caution, the bluffs are about 100' high and they drop precipitously to the rocky shoreline below. But the very same rocks are home to interesting tide pools. If it's low or minus tide, head to the coastline for an up-close encounter of the aquarium type.

Directions: From Oak Harbor, travel 9 miles north on Highway 20 to the signed entrance. The trailhead is at the parking lot at Bowman Bay on the Fidalgo Island (north) side.

Note: Stay on designated perimeter trail. The bluffs are extremely dangerous.

5) SAND DUNE TRAIL at WEST BEACH HIKE - Leashes

Beginner/0.8 miles/0.5 hours

Info: A favorite with beach walkers, this paved pathway escorts you through an interesting ecological zone, where self guiding stations make learning that much easier. A mural at the onset offers an overview of the environmental contrasts you'll encounter on your West Beach sojourn. Binocs will come in handy, you never know what marine or birdlife will make an appearance. Pack a goodie basket for you and your good dog, there are a slew of picnic ops all along the way.

Directions: From Oak Harbor, travel 9 miles north on Highway 20 to the signed entrance. The trail is on the Whidbey Island (south) side. Look for the trailhead at the concession stand on the south side of the westernmost parking lot.

6) UPPER NORTH BEACH TRAIL HIKE - Leashes

Beginner/1.8 miles/1.0 hours

Info: After a quick downhill jaunt, take the trail on the left and you'll find yourself in a green oasis of sword fern and salal. Imagine this greenery in spring when the wildflowers do their thing. You'll have to boogie with Bowser along the upper hillside before once again winding down to the Pacific. If you're lost in your thoughts, stop for a moment and admire the post-cardian prettiness of your locale. When the tide is low, hightail it to the beach.

Directions: From Oak Harbor, travel 9 miles north on Highway 20 to the signed entrance. The trail is located on the Whidbey Island (south) side at the North Beach Parking Area.

JOSEPH WHIDBEY STATE PARK - Leashes

Info: Give your city licker something special to bark home about and highlight this waterfront park on your itinerary. 200 acres of surf and turf overlooking the Strait of Juan de Fuca equate to a day of fun in the sun. If your woofer's a hoofer, make merry to the 2 miler through pretty wetlands to Rocky Point Park on the navy base. If it's whale watching season, tote

Locate Other Dog-Friendly Activities...Check Nearby Cities

your binocs. Who knows, you might be a lucky dog and spot a pod of Orcas. This area is tops in good, good, good, good migrations. For more information: (360) 678-4636.

Directions: Go south on Highway 20 to a right turn on Swantown and follow to the park.

Note: Open April 1 through September 30.

The numbered hike that follows is within Joseph Whidbey State Park:

1) BEACH TRAIL HIKE

Beginner/2.0 miles/1.0 hours

Info: With the Pacific presenting a seafaring picture on one side and a wonderful wetland on the other, you and old brown eyes won't know where to look first. A coastal diorama, soaring birds, skimming sailboats and an ever present distant horizon will indulge the beach bum within. The wetlands, on the other paw, cater to birders and naturalists alike. If your hot dog prefers being a chilly dog, visit in winter. The time when the word desolate takes on new meaning. When you reach the park, play follow the leader back to the starting point.

Directions: Go south on Highway 20 to a right turn on Swantown and follow to the park.

OAK HARBOR CITY BEACH PARK - Leashes

Info: When play's the thing, this park's the stage. A 28-acre oasis, explore the short hiking trail that wiggles through a bosky bit of nature or leave your prints on the sandy coastline. Find a cozy nook on the sheltered beach, break out a comfy blanket and get a whiff of the briny air.

Directions: Located at the end of 70 Southwest Street.

OTHER PARKS IN OAK HARBOR - Leashes
- FLINTSTONE PARK, off the Flintstone Freeway at 50 SW St
- KIMBALL WELL SITE, off Heller Road in Kimball Heights
- KOETJE WELL SITE, 1000 Avenue East
- LUECK MEMORIAL PARK, 300 Avenue West
- NEIL H. KOETJE PARK, 900 Avenue West and 60 NW Street
- NEIL PARK, 400 Avenue West
- RIDGEHAVEN PARK, 350 Avenue West off 130 Avenue
- SHADOW GLEN SUBDIVISION PARK, 925 and 1000 Ave W
- SMITH PARK, 300 Avenue West and Midway Boulevard
- SPRINGTIME PARK, Heller Road, south of 700 Avenue West
- SUMNER PARK, 70 SE and 725 Avenue East
- TYHUIS WELL SITE , 900 Avenue East

WHITE PASS

LODGING

GAME RIDGE MOTEL & LODGE
27350 Hwy 12 (98937)
Rates: $39-$82
Tel: (509) 672-2212

WHITE SALMON

LODGING

INN OF THE WHITE SALMON B&B
172 W Jewett (98672)
Rates: $75-$115
Tel: (509) 492-2335
(800) 972-5226

WILBUR

LODGING

EIGHT BAR B MOTEL
718 E Main (99185)
Rates: $30-$65
Tel: (509) 647-2400

SETTLE INN
303 NE Main (99185)
Rates: $34-$45
Tel: (509) 647-2100

Locate Other Dog-Friendly Activities...Check Nearby Cities

WINLOCK

LODGING

SUNRISE MOTEL
663 SR 505 (98596)
Rates: $38
Tel: (360) 785-4343

WINTHROP

LODGING

BEST WESTERN CASCADE INN
960 Hwy 20, Box 813 (98862)
Rates: $45-$85
Tel: (509) 996-3100
(800) 468-6754
(800) 528-1234

PINE-NEAR RV PARK & MOTEL
350 Castle Ave (98862)
Rates: n/a
Tel: (509) 996-2391

RIVER RUN INN & RESORT
27 Rader Rd (98862)
Rates: $55-$90
Tel: (509) 996-2173
(800) 757-2709

THE VIRGINIAN RESORT
808 N Cascade Hwy (98862)
Rates: $55-$85
Tel: (509) 996-2535
(800) 854-2834

WINTHROP INN
950 Hwy 20 (98862)
Rates: $50-$75
Tel: (509) 996-2217
(800) 444-1972

WOLFRIDGE RESORT COTTAGES
412B Wolf Creek Rd (98862)
Rates: $44-$149
Tel: (509) 996-2828

RECREATION

BLACK LAKE TRAIL HIKE - Leashes

Beginner/8.4 miles/5.0 hours

Info: Shaded glens. Birdsong drifting from a green canopy. Sunlight streaming through glistening evergreens. In this neck of the woods, that's just part of the diorama of nature you'll find. The rainbow at the end of this path is sun-dappled Black Lake. Afishionados, there are mucho reel-time pleasures and perhaps some trout for din-din. Of course, old faithful will go home with some tall tales of his own, but they'll be of the wet tootsie kind. For more information: (509) 996-2266.

Directions: From Winthrop, travel north on West Chewuch Road 19 miles to the Lake Creek Bridge. Turn left just after the bridge and drive 2 miles to the Lake Creek Trailhead.

BLUE LAKE TRAIL HIKE- Leashes

Intermediate/4.4 miles/2.5 hours

Info: Mother Nature puts her best foot forward on this scenic byway that stretches into the woodlands of the Okanogan National Forest. On this invigorating journey, you and your hiking guru will find yourselves surrounded by enormous mountains. Yup, that's Cutthroat Peak, Early Winter Spires and Winter Bell. And then abracadabra, the scene takes on a blue note as the sparkling waters of Blue Lake come into play. Nothing could be finer than to diner with your whiner by the lakeside on a sunny afternoon. Chow down and consider yourself one lucky dog. For more information: (509) 996-4000.

Directions: From Winthrop, travel Highway 20 west across the Washington Pass. The trailhead and parking area are on the south side of Highway 20 about a mile west of the Washington Pass.

CEDAR CREEK TRAIL HIKE - Leashes

Beginner/4.0 miles/2.0 hours

Info: Waterfall devotees, you'll get two for the money on this trail less-traveled. You'll climb through an enchanting wooded pathway on your way to the cascading double whammy. In spring, the beauty of your surroundings will be enhanced by an avalanche of lilies which polka dot the region. A cocoon-like trail, you and the lickmeister will be soothed by the quietude and stillness of the setting. Cedar Falls, as expected, will delight as only waterfalls can. For more information: (509) 997-2131.

Directions: From Winthrop, travel Highway 20 west about 18 miles to FS 5310-200. The trailhead is near the gravel pit at the end of the road.

CUTTHROAT LAKE TRAIL HIKE - Leashes

Intermediate/3.4 miles/2.0 hours

Info: Set against a backdrop of snowy peaks, your spirits will soar in this woodsy venue where you can see the forest for the trees. And magnificent trees they are. Tree hounds give this

Locate Other Dog-Friendly Activities...Check Nearby Cities

neck of the woods the high five. It's easy to see why, this place is for the birds. Check out the water loving species that swoop over the lake and flit among the nearby mountains. And who can blame them, Cutthroat Lake is a mirrorlike alpine gem whose satiny surface reflects the sky above and the mountains all around. Talk about pristine beauty. If fishing's your thing, you've found trout paradise. The lake isn't named Cutthroat for nothing. No matter what you and the wagging one do, you won't regret a moment spent in this region that's heaven sent. For more information: (509) 996-4000.

Directions: From Winthrop, travel west on Highway 20 for 1.5 miles past the Lone Fir Campground. Turn west for 0.1 miles on the access road to the trailhead.

DIABLO LAKE TRAIL HIKE - Leashes

Beginner/7.6 miles/4.5 hours

Info: If you're looking for a no brainer with great views, look no further. A level pathway keeps you on track beside the prettiness of Diablo Lake from the get-go. You and the wet wagger will make lickety split through lush forests with understories of diverse vegetation that add to the loveliness of the setting. In spring, look for the perky wild ones on the sunny side of the lake and take the time to smell the flowers. Towards the end of your trek, you'll see Ross Dam. The overpass spans the narrow opening of what used to be the Skagit River Gorge but is now considered the head of Diablo Lake. The "toot toot" you may hear comes from the passenger tugboat on its dam run. For more information: (360) 856-5700.

Directions: From Winthrop, travel Highway 20 west about 21 miles to the North Cascades National Park. Upon entering the park, Highway 20 dips south before heading north to the Ross Lake National Recreation Area. Continue on Highway 20 to the Ross Dam turnoff on the left. Head north at the turnoff, cross Ross Dam and travel about 1 mile to Old Diablo Lake Resort. The trailhead is on the left.

Note: Highway 20 is closed in winter.

Hotel Policies May Be Subject To Change

FALLS CREEK TRAIL HIKE - Leashes

Beginner/0.5 miles/0.25 hours

Info: An effortless, wonderful, waterful hike, this picturesque jaunt is short on effort but long on rewards. After a quick hop, skip and jump through the forest, you'll be dazzled by beautiful Falls Creek Falls. A curtain of sapphire water and diamond bright spray greets your aqua pup at this charming spot. Enjoy some water hijinks before retracing your prints. For more information: (509) 996-2266.

Directions: From Winthrop, travel West Chewuch Road 10 miles to Falls Creek. Park in the small parking area just past the bridge.

Note: Do not attempt to climb the boulders around the falls, they are slippery and extremely dangerous.

GOAT PEAK LOOKOUT TRAIL HIKE - Leashes

Intermediate/3.4 miles/2.5 hours

Info: Stop puppyfooting around and get the squeaker to a panoramic peeker. You and the mutt will have your work cut out for you on this challenging trek to a lofty perch where vistas of Silver Star Mountain are bark worthy. Make like Ansel Adams and see what glossy memories you can capture on film. When you've filled your Fuji, turn the hound around and head back down. Make note of how different the pretty woodlands look from the descent perspective. And listen too for the tweet-tweet music of the local flyboys. For more information: (509) 996-2266.

Directions: From Winthrop, take Highway 20 west about 10 miles to CR 1163 (just before the Weeman Bridge). Turn right and drive 3.4 miles to FS 5225. Turn left and travel 3.3 miles to FR 5225-200 and turn right. Continue 2.5 miles to the trailhead.

Note: Highway 20 is closed in winter.

HAPPY CREEK FOREST WALK - Leashes

Beginner/0.6 miles/0.5 hours

Info: Get a quickie lesson in nature on this peanut-sized, wood-plank trail. Interpretive signs explain the ecosystems present in this ancient creekside forest. Wildlife devotees, watch for hawks as they ride the thermals above Diablo Lake in search of prey. You'll come away from this jaunt a wee more savvy about nature. For more information: (360) 856-5700.

Directions: From Winthrop, travel Highway 20 west about 21 miles to the North Cascades National Park. Upon entering the park, Highway 20 dips south before heading north to the Ross Lake National Recreation Area. Continue on Highway 20 to mile 134.5. The boardwalk is on the north side of Highway 20.

Note: Highway 20 is closed in winter.

PYRAMID LAKE TRAIL HIKE - Leashes

Intermediate/4.2 miles/2.5 hours

Info: Bring a sense of wonder along when you decide to explore this slice of high country beauty. But be prepared to pay your dues. A stiff climb awaits you and your hearty hound as you trek through a pine and fir forest to a cool, forested stream. Knock on wood, it's worth the price. Continuing up, you'll reach the rippling waters of Pyramid Lake, pretty to look at but devoid of fish. The lake does have a few interesting inhabitants, the rough-skinned newt and the rare insectivorous sundew plants which thrive on the floating logs. That's Pyramid Peak in the distance, rising over 7,000'. When day is done, do the descent thing. For more information: (360) 856-5700.

Directions: From Winthrop, travel Highway 20 west about 21 miles to the North Cascades National Park. Upon entering the park, Highway 20 dips south before heading north to the Ross Lake National Recreation Area. Continue on Highway 20 to the pull-out on the north side of the road near milepost 127.5 The trailhead is on the south side of the highway near the creek.

Note: Highway 20 is closed in winter.

Hotel Policies May Be Subject To Change

RUBY CREEK TRAIL HIKE - Leashes

Beginner/0.4 miles/0.25 hours

Info: Even sofa loafers can get out and enjoy this natural setting without much fuss and bother. Do the stroll (short but somewhat steep) to Ruby Creek and while you're at it, you'll be treated to enchanting woodlands that are often splashed with colorful forest flowers. Birdsong will drift your way from the towering trees and provide the entertainment. And of course, there's always the pupportunity for wet and wild shenanigans. If this little taste wags some tail, check out the other paths that emanate from the creek. For more information: (360) 856-5700.

Directions: From Winthrop, travel Highway 20 west about 21 miles to the North Cascades National Park. Upon entering the park, Highway 20 dips south before heading north to the Ross Lake National Recreation Area. The trailhead is on the south side of Highway 20 just before entering the Ross Lake National Recreation Area.

Note: Highway 20 is closed in winter.

WOODLAND

LODGING

LAKESIDE MOTEL
785 Lake Shore Dr (98674)
Rates: n/a
Tel: (360) 225-8240

SCANDIA MOTEL
1123 Hoffman St (98674)
Rates: $32-$44
Tel: (360) 225-8006

LEWIS RIVER INN
1100 Lewis River Rd (98674)
Rates: $42-$60
Tel: (360) 225-6257

WOODLANDER INN
1500 Atlantic St (98674)
Rates: $42-$65
Tel: (360) 225-6548

RECREATION

BIG CREEK FALLS TRAIL HIKE

Intermediate/1.5 miles/1.0 hours

Info: Along this barrier-free trail, you're a mere hop, skip and a jump from a glimpse of the top of the magnificent falls. But don't stop there, continue to a viewpoint of the entire falls as it plummets 125′ over the lip of a bowl-like depression. When you can pull yourself away from this gorgeous spot, travel another half mile and you'll find yourself atop a breathtaking 400′ cliff with stunning views up and down the valley. Across the river are bluffs and a narrow, 100′ plunger. Below, the Lewis River is a ribbon of shimmering blue beauty in a lush milieu of evergreenery. For more information: (509) 395-2501.

Directions: From Woodland, drive east approximately 26 miles on the Lewis River Road (becomes FS 90 east of Cougar) to the Big Creek Falls parking lot on the left.

Note: A section of the trail past Big Creek Falls skirts the top of cliffs. There are no railings. Use caution and keep your dog leashed.

CURLY CREEK FALLS TRAIL HIKE

Beginner/0.25 miles/0.25 hours

Info: Geologist wannabes, you're gonna love this cinchy walk to Curly Creek Falls, a geologic wonder where the falls pass behind a window carved in the rock and then tumble 75′ to exit from a lower hole. Photo buffs, tote your Kodak, you'll want to capture this unusual plunger in a glossy memory. If you're a waterfall devotee and one fall is never enough, continue further down the trail to the viewpoint for Miller Creek Falls. Less impressive than Curly, this still pretty cascade comes to rest in a petite pool. For more information: (509) 395-2501.

Directions: From Woodland, drive east approximately 23 miles on Lewis River Road (becomes FS 90 east of Cougar). Continue 20 miles to the Pine Creek Visitor Information Center. (Open during the summer months, stop and pick up a road map and info). From the visitor center, turn right to stay on FS 90. After 5.3 miles, turn left onto gravel Road 9039 and travel one mile to the parking lot for Curly Creek and Miller Creek Falls and the barrier free trail.

YACOLT

RECREATION

MOULTON FALLS - Leashes

Info: This is one way to wipe that hangdog expression off the barkmeister's mug. Moulton, Big Creek and Lucia Falls provide the scenery while wooded landscapes and soulful songbirds provide the serenity. Take to one of the trails, find a cool spot to dip your toes and forget your woes. The beauty of this region definitely deserves two paws up. For more information: (360) 699-2375 ext. 2467.

Directions: Located at 27781 Lucia Falls Road.

YAKIMA

LODGING

ALL STAR MOTEL
1900 N 1st St (98901)
Rates: n/a
Tel: (509) 452-7111

BALI HAI MOTEL
710 N 1st St (98901)
Rates: $23-$43
Tel: (509) 452-7178

CAVANAUGH'S AT YAKIMA CENTER
607 E Yakima Ave (98901)
Rates: $58-$98
Tel: (509) 248-5900
(800) 843-4667

HOLIDAY INN
9 N 9th St (98901)
Rates: $61-$91
Tel: (509) 452-6511
(800) 465-4329

MOTEL 6
1104 N 1st St (98901)
Rates: $30-$40
Tel: (509) 454-0080
(800) 440-6000

NENDEL'S INN
1405 N 1st St (98901)
Rates: $32-$66
Tel: (509) 453-8981
(800) 547-0106

NISKA'S INNS OF AMERICA
1022 N 1st St (98901)
Rates: $35+
Tel: (509) 453-5615

PEPPER TREE INN
1614 N 1st St (98901)
Rates: $49-$100
Tel: (800) 834-1649

RED APPLE MOTEL
416 N 1st St (98901)
Rates: n/a
Tel: (509) 248-7150

RED CARPET MOTOR INN
1608 Fruitvale Blvd (98902)
Rates: $32-$65
Tel: (509) 457-1131
(800) 457-5090

RED LION INN
818 N 1st St (98901)
Rates: $66-$89
Tel: (509) 453-0391
(800) 547-8010

RED LION INN YAKIMA VALLEY
1507 N 1st St (98901)
Rates: $81-$88
Tel: (509) 248-7850
(800) 547-8010

SUN COUNTRY INN
1700 N 1st St (98901)
Rates: $52-$71
Tel: (509) 248-5650
(800) 559-3675

VAGABOND INN
510 N 1st St (98901)
Rates: $40-$57
Tel: (509) 457-6155
(800) 522-1555

RECREATION

COWICHE CANYON TRAIL HIKE - Leashes

Beginner/5.8 miles/3.0 hours

Info: Let your city licker join his country cousins on this odyssey where Mother Nature has outdone herself. Remote and pristine, this hike will put a tail spin on the dogster's appendage. Cowiche Canyon is a secluded basalt and andesite canyon so close and yet so far from the city. The unpaved trail wanders this way and that through the alluring canyon, criss-crossing Cowiche Creek eleven times, aka eleven heavenly splish-splashing moments. The land beside the surging waters is lush with vegetation, a green oasis which presents a stunning contrast to the dramatic cliffs. This picturesque cleft is home to a myriad of flyboys, an avian havian where more than 50 species of birds have been identified. Naturalists, you'll be overwhelmed by the sheer magnitude of trees, shrubs, plants and flowers that florish in this riparian oasis. The flower party begins in spring and continues into the summer adding streaks of color and heavenly scents to the already fragrant air. No bones about it, this canyon caper rates a solid two paws up. Carpe diem you lucky dogs. For more information: (509) 965-7289.

Directions: Northwest of the Yakima city limits, located off Summitview Road, between the city of Weikel and Cowiche Canyon Road. The trailhead is off Summitview Road.

Hotel Policies May Be Subject To Change

SARG HUBBARD PARK - Leashes

Info: Savor the rolling hills and sweeping views of the river in this picturesque locale where Mt. Adams and Mt. Rainier add to the allure. Paved pathways and marked trailways honeycomb the lush 28-acre landscape where there's always a season and plenty of reason to go calling. For more information: (509) 453-8280.

Directions: Located on 18th Street off Yakima Avenue.

SHERMAN PARK - Leashes

Info: This petite park packs a playful punch. The flat expanse has picnic tables so lunch alfrisky is always an option. Tree hounds with a penchant for shaded knolls can also find a place to call their own. For more information: (509) 453-8280.

Directions: On Nob Hill Boulevard across from Kmart.

YAKIMA GREENWAY PATH - Leashes

Beginner/1.0 -20.0 miles/0.5-10.0 hours

Info: Stop puppyfooting around and scratch your little nature lover's itch on this ideal journey. Shimmying beside the Yakima and Naches Rivers, you'll hightail it through forests of small hardwoods and conifers where the air is heavenscent. And what do you find in the woods? You guessed it, lots of forest critters. Be prepared for a close encounter of the wildlife kind. Sharp-eyed canines might spot a hawk or falcon soaring over head. A favorite with the waterfowl set, expect to see your fair share of heron, osprey, Canada geese and lucky ducks. Pick up the trail at Resthaven Road and you're off and running. For more information: (509) 453-8280.

Directions: Exit I-28 at Resthaven Road, turn west over the freeway to enter the parking lot. You can access the trail at many points along the path.

Locate Other Dog-Friendly Activities...Check Nearby Cities

YELM

LODGING

LOG HOUSE B&B
11249 Bald Hill Rd (98597)
Rates: $95-$150
Tel: (360) 458-4385

PRAIRIE MOTEL
700 Prairie Park Ln (98597)
Rates: $55-$100
Tel: (360) 458-8300

ZILLAH

LODGING

COMFORT INN
911 Vintage Valley Pkwy (98953)
Rates: $56-$100
Tel: (509) 829-3399
(800) 228-5150

GET READY TO
TRAVEL

TRAVEL TRAINING

A well trained, well behaved dog is easy to live with and especially easy to travel with. There are basics other than sit, down and stay which you might want to incorporate into your training routine. Whenever you begin a training session, remember that your patience and your dog's attention span are the key elements to success. Training sessions should be 5-10 minutes each. Even if the results are initially disappointing, don't become discouraged. Stick with it. After just a few lessons, your canine will respond. Dogs love to learn, to feel productive and accomplished. Training isn't punishment. It's a gift. A gift of love. You'll quickly see the difference training can make in your animal. Most of all, keep a sense of humor. It's not punishment for you either.

Throughout this section, several references are made to puppies. But it's never too late for training to begin. The adage that you can't teach an old dog new tricks just isn't true. Patience and consistency combined with a reward system will provide excellent results.

Let's get social

When it comes to travel training, not enough can be said about the benefits of socialization. I regard the lessons of socialization as the foundation of a well-trained, well-behaved dog.

Whenever possible socialize your dog at an early age. Allow your puppy to be handled by many different people. Include men and children since puppies are inherently more fearful of both. At three months, you can join a puppy class. These classes are important because they provide puppies with the experience of being with other dogs. Your puppy will have the opportunity of putting down other dogs without inflicting harm and he'll also learn how to bounce back after being put down himself. Socialization can also be accomplished through walks around your neighborhood, visits to parks frequented by other dogs and children, or by working with friends who have dogs they also want to socialize.

FIDO FACT:

- *Dog ownership is a common bond and the basis of impromptu conversations as well as lasting friendships.*

Walking on a leash

It's very natural for a puppy to pull at his leash. Instead of just pulling back, stop walking. Hold the leash to your chest. If your dog lets the leash slacken, say GOOD DOG. If he sits, say GOOD SIT. Then begin your walk again. Stop every ten feet or so and tell your dog to sit. Knowing he'll only be told to sit if he pulls, he'll eventually learn to pay attention to the next command. It makes sense to continue your training while on walks because your dog will learn to heed your commands under varying circumstances and environments. This will prove especially important when traveling together. Not having to deal with a tug-of-war walk can mean the difference between enjoying or disliking the company of your pooch at home or away.

Chewing

Most dogs chew out of boredom. Teach your dog constructive chewing and eliminate destructive chewing by teaching your dog to chew on chew toys. An easy way to interest him in chewing is to stuff a hollow, nonconsumable chew toy with treats such as peanut butter, kibble or a piece of hard cheese. Once the toy is stuffed, attach a string to it and tempt your dog's interest by pulling the toy along. He'll take it from there.

Until you're satisfied that he won't be destructive, consider confining your pooch to one room or to his crate with a selection of chew toys. This is a particularly important training tool for dogs who must be left alone for long periods of time, and for dogs who travel with their owners. If your pooch knows not to chew destructively at home, those same good habits will remain with him on the road.

Bite inhibition

The trick here is to keep a puppy from biting in the first place, not break the bad habit after it's formed, although that too can be accomplished. Your puppy should be taught to develop a soft mouth by inhibiting the force of his bites. As your dog grows into adolescence, he should continue to be taught to soften his bite and as an adult dog should learn never to mouth at all.

Allow your puppy to bite but whenever force is exhibited, say OUCH! If he continues to bite, say OUCH louder and then leave the room. When you return to the room, let the puppy come next to you and calm down. Your pup will begin to associate the bite and OUCH with the cessation of playtime and will learn to mouth more softly. Even when your puppy's bites no longer hurt, pretend they do. Once this training is finished, you'll have a dog that will not mouth. A dog who will not accidentally injure people you meet during your travels.

Jumping dogs

Dogs usually jump on people to get their attention. A fairly simple way to correct this habit is to teach your dog to sit and stay until released. When your dog is about to meet new people, put him in the sit/stay position. Be sure to praise him for obeying the command and then pet him to give him the attention he craves. Ask friends and visitors to help reinforce the command.

Come

The secret to this command is to begin training at an early age. But as I've said before, older dogs can also learn. It might just take a little longer. From the time your pup's brought home, call him by name and say COME every time you're going to feed him. The association will be simple. He'll soon realize that goodies await him if he responds to your call. Try another approach as well. Sit in your favorite armchair and call to your dog every few minutes. Reward him with praise and sometimes with a treat. Take advantage of normally occurring circumstances, such as your dog approaching you. Whenever you can anticipate that your dog is coming toward you, command COME as he nears you. Then reward him with praise for doing what came naturally.

NEVER order your dog to COME for a punishment. If he's caught in the act of negative behavior, walk to him and then reprimand.

Pay attention

Train your dog to listen to you during his normal routines. For example, when your dog is at play in the yard, call him to you. When he comes, have him sit and praise him. Then release him to play again. It will quickly become apparent that obeying will not mean the end of playtime. Instead it will mean that he'll be petted and praised and then allowed to play again.

Communication - talking to your dog

Training isn't just about teaching your dog to sit or give his paw. Training is about teaching your pooch to become an integral part of your life. To fit into your daily routine and into your leisure time. Take notice of how your dog studies you, anticipates your next move. Incorporate his natural desire to please into your training. Let him know what you're thinking, how you're feeling. Talk to him as you go about your daily routines. He'll soon come to understand the different tones in your voice, your facial expressions, hand movements and body language.

He'll know when you're happy or angry with him or with anyone else. If you want him to do something, speak to him. For example, if you want him to fetch his ball, ask him in an emphatic way, stressing the word ball. He won't understand at first, so fetch it yourself and tell him ball. Put the ball down and then later repeat the command. He'll soon know what you want when you use the term ball with specific emphasis.

Training do's & don'ts

- Never hit your dog.

- Praise and reward your dog for good behavior. Don't be embarrassed to lavish praise upon a dog who's earned it.

- Unless you catch your dog in a mischievous act, don't punish him. He will not understand what he did wrong. And when you do punish, go to your dog. Never use the command COME for punishment.

- Don't repeat a command. Say the command in a firm voice only once. Dogs have excellent hearing. If he doesn't obey, return to the training method for the disobeyed command.

- Don't be too eager or too reticent to punish. Most of all, be consistent.

- Don't encourage fearfulness. If your dog has a fear of people or places, work with him to overcome this fear rather than ignoring it, or believing it can't be changed.

- Don't ignore or encourage aggression.

- Don't use food excessively as a reward. Although food is useful in the beginning of training, it must be phased out as the dog matures.

CRATE TRAINING IS GREAT TRAINING

Many people erroneously equate the crate to jail. But that's only a human perspective. To a dog who's been properly crate trained, the crate represents a private place where your dog will feel safe and secure. It is much better to prevent behavioral problems by crate training than to merely give up on an unruly dog.

Four reasons why crate training is good for you

1. You can relax when you leave your dog home alone. You'll know that he is safe, comfortable and incapable of destructive behavior.

2. You can housebreak your pooch faster. The confinement to a crate encourages control and helps establish a regular walk time routine.

3. You can safely confine your dog to prevent unforeseen situations, for example, if he's sick, if you have workers or guests that are either afraid of or allergic to dogs, or if your canine becomes easily excited or confused when new people enter the scene. In all cases, the crate provides a reasonable method of containment.

4. You can travel with your pooch. Use of a crate eliminates the potential for distraction and assures that your dog will not get loose during your travels.

Five reasons why crate training is good for your dog

1. He'll have an area for rest when he's tired, stressed or sick.

2. He'll be exposed to fewer bad behavior temptations which can result in punishment.

3. He'll have an easier time learning to control calls of nature.

4. He'll feel more secure when left alone.

5. He'll be able to join you in your travels.

Some do's and don'ts

- DO exercise your dog before crating and as soon as you let him out.

- DO provide your pooch with his favorite toy.

- DO place the crate in a well-used, well-ventilated area of your home.

- DO make sure that you can always approach your dog while he is in his crate. This will insure that he does not become overly protective of his space.

- DON'T punish your dog in his crate or banish him to the crate.

- DON'T leave your pooch in the crate for more than four hours at a time.

- DON'T let curious kids invade his private place. This is his special area.

- DON'T confine your dog to the crate if he becomes frantic or completely miserable.

- DON'T use a crate without proper training.

10

Ways To Prevent Aggression in Your Dog

1. Socialize him at an early age.

2. Set rules and stick to them.

3. Under your supervision, expose him to children and other animals.

4. Never be abusive towards your dog by hitting or yelling at him.

5. Offer plenty of praise when he's behaving himself.

6. Be consistent with training. Make sure your dog responds to your commands before you do anything for him.

7. Don't handle your dog roughly or play aggressively with him.

8. Neuter your dog.

9. Contact your veterinarian for persistent behavior problems.

10. Your dog is a member of the family. Treat him that way. Tied to a pole is not a life.

Take your dog's temperament into account

- Is he a pleaser?
- Is he the playful sort?
- Does he love having tasks to perform?
- Does he like to retrieve? To carry?

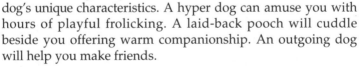

Dogs like people, have distinct personalities, mellow, hyper, shy or outgoing. Take advantage of your dog's unique characteristics. A hyper dog can amuse you with hours of playful frolicking. A laid-back pooch will cuddle beside you offering warm companionship. An outgoing dog will help you make friends.

If you can combine what you know of your dog's personality with what you want to teach, your dog will train more easily. Together you will achieve a fulfilling compatibility.

<u>FIDO FACT:</u>

- ***Staying at a hotel for a few days or more? Here's an easy way to identify your pet's temporary home. Staple one of the hotel's matchbook covers to your pet's collar. Be sure to remove the matches first.***

WHAT AND HOW TO PACK FOR YOUR POOCH

Be prepared

Dogs enjoy the adventure of travel. If your dog is basically well behaved and physically healthy, he will make an excellent traveling companion. But traveling times will be more successful with just a little common sense and preparation.

Just as many children (and adults I might add) travel with their own pillow, your pooch will also enjoy having his favorites with him. Perhaps you'll want to include the blanket he sleeps with or his favorite toy. Not only will a familiar item make him feel more at ease but it will keep him occupied.

To keep things simple from vacation to vacation, I restock Max and Rosie's travel bags at the end of each trip. That way, I'm always prepared for the next adventure. "My Pooch's Packing List" is found on page 536. You'll want to include some or all of the items listed on the next page.

- A blanket to cover the back seat of your car.
- Two or three old towels for emergencies.
- Two bowls, one for water, the other for food.
- Plastic cleanup bags (supermarket produce bags work well).
- Paper towels,for spills, cleanup and everything in between.
- A long line of rope. You'll be surprised how often you'll use this very handy item.
- An extra collar and lead.
- Can opener and spoon.
- Flashlight.
- An extra flea and tick collar.
- Dog brush.
- Small scissors.
- Blunt end tweezers, great for removing thorns and cactus needles.
- Chew toys, balls, frisbees, treats.
- Nightlight.
- A room deodorizer.
- A handful of zip-lock bags in several sizes.
- Pre-moistened towelettes. Take along two packs. Put one in your suitcase, the other in the glove compartment of your car.
- Dog food, enough for a couple of days. Although most brands are available throughout the country, you'll want enough to eliminate finding a store that's open the first night or two of your vacation.
- Water, a full container from home. Top off as needed to gradually accustom your dog to his new water supply.

People packing made easy...12 tips

No matter where your travels take you, whether it's to the local park or on a cross-country trip, never leave home without your dog's leash and a handful of plastic bags or pooper scooper. I clearly remember those awful moments when I ended up without one or both.

1. Consolidate. Even if you're traveling as a family, one tube of toothpaste and one hair dryer should suffice.

2. Avoid potential spills by wrapping perfume, shampoo and other liquids together and placing them in large zip-lock plastic bags.

3. When packing, layer your clothing using interlocking patterns. You'll fit more into your suitcase and have less shifting and wrinkling.

4. Write out your itinerary, including flight info, car rental confirmation numbers, travel agent telephone numbers and lodging info. Keep one copy with you and put a duplicate in a safe place.

5. Take along a night light, especially if you're traveling with a child. A flashlight comes in handy too.

6. Stash a supply of zip-lock plastic bags, moist towelettes, trash bags, an extra leash (or rope) and a plastic container in an accessible place.

7. If you plan to hike with children, give each a whistle, they're great for signaling help.

8. Include a can opener and some plastic utensils.

9. Comfortable walking shoes are a must. If you plan on hiking, invest in a sturdy pair of hiking boots, but be sure to break them in before your trip. Take an extra pair of socks with you whenever you hike.

10. Don't forget to include first aid-kits. One for dogs and one for people.

11. Pack an extra pair of glasses or contact lenses. And an extra car key

12. Keep medications in separate, clearly marked containers.

MY POOCH'S PACKING LIST

1 _____   16 _____

2 _____   17 _____

3 _____   18 _____

4 _____   19 _____

5 _____   20 _____

6 _____   21 _____

7 _____   22 _____

8 _____   23 _____

9 _____   24 _____

10 _____   25 _____

11 _____   26 _____

12 _____   27 _____

13 _____   28 _____

14 _____   29 _____

15 _____   30 _____

CAR TRAVEL

"Kennel Up"...the magical, all-purpose command.

When Rosie's and Maxwell's training began, I used a metal kennel which they were taught to regard as their spot, their sleeping place. Whenever they were left at home and then again when they were put to bed at night, I used the simple command, "kennel up," as I pointed to and tapped their kennel. They quickly learned the command. As they outgrew the kennel, the laundry room became their "kennel up" place. As full-grown dogs, the entire kitchen became their "kennel up" area. Likewise, when they began accompanying me on trips, I reinforced the command each time I told them to jump into the car. They soon understood that being in their "kennel up" place meant that I expected them to behave, whether they were at home, in the car or in a hotel room. Teaching your dog the "kennel up" command will make travel times easier and more pleasurable.

Old dogs can learn new tricks

When we first began vacationing with Rosie and Max, some friends decided to join us on a few of our local jaunts. Their dog Brandy, a ten year-old Cocker Spaniel, had never traveled with them. Other than trips to the vet and the groomer, she'd never been in the car. The question remained, would Brandy adjust? We needn't have worried. She took to the car immediately. Despite her small size, she quickly learned to jump in and out of the rear of the station wagon. She ran through the forests with Rosie and Max, playing and exploring as if she'd always had free run. To her owners and to Brandy, the world took on new meaning. Nature as seen through the eyes of their dog became a more exciting place of discovery.

Can my dog be trained to travel

Dogs are quite adaptable and responsive and patience will definitely have its rewards. Your pooch loves nothing more than to be with you. If it means behaving to have that privilege, he'll respond.

Now that you've decided to travel and vacation with your dog, it's probably a good idea to get him started with short trips. Before you go anywhere, remember two of the most important items for happy dog travel, a leash for safety and the proper paraphernalia for cleanup. There's nothing more frustrating or scary than a loose, uncontrolled dog. And nothing more embarrassing than being without cleanup essentials when your dog unexpectedly decides to relieve himself.

Make traveling a pleasant experience. Stop every so often and do fun things. But when you stop to let him out, leash him before you open the car doors. When the walk or playtime is over, remember the "Kennel Up" command when you tell your pooch to get into the car or into his kennel. And use lots of praise when he obeys.

You'll find that your dog will most likely be lulled to sleep by the motion of the car. Rosie and Maxwell fall asleep after less than fifteen minutes. I stop every few hours, give them water and let them "stretch their legs." They've become accustomed to these short stops and anticipate them. The moment the car is turned off and the hatch-back popped open, they anxiously await their leashes. When our romping time is over and we're back at the car, a simple "kennel up" gets them into their travel area.

To kennel or not to kennel

Whether or not you use a kennel for car travel is a personal choice. Safety should be your primary concern. Yours and your dog's. Whatever method of travel you choose, be certain that your dog will not interfere with your driving. If you plan to use a kennel, line the bottom with an old blanket, towel or shredded newspaper and include a favorite toy. When you're vacationing by car and not using a kennel, consider a car harness.

If you're not going to use a kennel or harness, consider confining your dog to the back seat and commanding him to "kennel up." Protect your upholstery by covering the seat with an old blanket. This will make cleanup easier at the end of your trip. To keep your car fresh smelling and free from doggie odors, stash a deodorizer under the front seat. Or use a sheet of fabric softener instead.

How often should I stop

Many people think that when their dogs are in the car, they have to "go" more often. Not true. Whenever you stop for yourself, let your pooch have a drink and take a walk. It's not necessary to make extra stops along the way unless your dog has a physical problem and must be walked more often. Always pull your car out of the flow of traffic so you can safely care for your pooch. Never let your dog run free. Use a leash at all times.

Can my dog be left alone in the car

Weather is the main factor you have to consider in this situation. Even if you think you'll only be gone a few minutes, that's all it takes for a dog to become dehydrated in warm weather. Even if all the windows are open, even if your car is parked in the shade, even when the outside temperature is only 85°, the temperature in a parked car can reach 100° to 120° in just minutes. Exposure to high temperatures, even for short periods, can cause your dog's body temperature to skyrocket.

NEVER LEAVE YOUR DOG UNATTENDED IN WARM WEATHER

During the winter months, be aware of hypothermia, a life threatening condition that occurs when an animal's body temperature falls below normal. In particular, short-haired dogs and toys are very susceptible to illness in extremely cold weather.

What about carsickness

Just like people, some dogs are queasier than others. And for some reason, puppies suffer more frequently from motion sickness. It's best to wait a couple of hours after your dog has eaten before beginning your trip. Or better yet, feed your dog after you arrive at your destination. Keep the windows open enough to allow in fresh air. If your pooch has a tendency to be carsick, sugar can help. Give your dog a tablespoon of  honey or a small piece of candy before beginning your trip (**NO CHOCOLATE**). That should help settle his stomach. If you notice that he still looks sickly, stop and allow him some additional fresh air or take him for a short walk. Most dogs will outgrow car sickness.

What about identification if my dog runs off

As far as identification, traveling time is no different than staying at home. Never allow your pooch to be anywhere without proper identification. ID tags should provide your dog's name, your name, address and phone number. Most states require dog owners to purchase a license every year. The tag usually includes a license number that is registered with your state. If you attach the license tag to your dog's collar and then become separated, your dog can be traced. There are also local organizations that help reunite lost pets and owners. The phone numbers of these organizations can be obtained from local police authorities.

Use the form on the facing page to record your pooch's description so that the information will be handy should the need arise.

MY POOCH'S IDENTIFICATION

In the event that your dog is lost or stolen, the following information will help describe your pooch. Before leaving on your first trip, take a few minutes to fill out this form, make a duplicate, and then keep them separate but handy.

Answers to the name of: _____

Breed or mix: _____

Sex: _____ Age: _____ Tag ID#: _____

Description of hair (color, length and texture): _____

_____

Indicate unusual markings or scars: _____

_____

TAIL: ❏ Short ❏ Screw-type ❏ Bushy ❏ Cut

EARS: ❏ Clipped ❏ Erect ❏ Floppy

Weight: _____ Height: _____

If you have a recent photo of your pet, attach it to this form.

PLANE TRAVEL

Quick Takes

- Always travel on the same flight as your dog. Personally ascertain that your dog has been put on board before you board the plane.

- Book direct, nonstop flights.

- Upon boarding, inform a flight attendant that your pooch is traveling in the cargo hold.

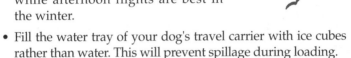

- Early morning or late evening flights are best in the summer, while afternoon flights are best in the winter.

- Fill the water tray of your dog's travel carrier with ice cubes rather than water. This will prevent spillage during loading.

- Clip your dog's nails to prevent them from hooking in the crate's door, holes or other openings.

Dog carriers/kennels

Most airlines require pets to be in specific carriers. Airline regulations vary and arrangements should be made well in advance of travel. Some airlines allow small dogs to accompany their owners in the passenger cabins. The carrier must fit under the passenger's seat and the dog must remain in the carrier for the duration of the flight. These regulations also vary and prior arrangements should be made.

Airlines run hot and cold on pet travel

Many airlines won't allow pets to travel in the cargo hold if the departure or destination temperatures are over 80°. The same holds true if the weather is too cold. Check with the airlines to ascertain specific policies.

What about the size of the carrier

Your dog should have enough room to stand, lie down, sit and turn around comfortably. Larger doesn't equate to more comfort. If anything, larger quarters only increase the chances of your dog being hurt because of too much movement. Just as your dog's favorite place is under the kitchen desk, a cozy, compact kennel will suit him much better than a spacious one.

Should anything else be in the carrier

Cover the bottom with newspaper sheets and cover that with shredded newspaper. This will absorb accidents and provide a soft, warm cushion for your dog. Include a soft blanket or an old flannel shirt of yours; articles that will remind your pooch of home and provide a feeling of security. You might want to include a hard rubber chew, but forget toys, they increase the risk of accidents.

How will my pooch feel about a kennel

Training and familiarization are the key elements in this area. If possible, buy the kennel (airlines and pet stores sell them) several weeks before your trip. Leave it in your home in the area where your dog spends most of his time. Let him become accustomed to its smell, feel and look. After a few days, your pooch will become comfortable around the kennel. You might even try feeding him in his kennel to make it more like home. Keep all the associations friendly. Never use the kennel for punishment. Taking the time to accustom your dog with his traveling quarters will alleviate potential problems and make vacationing more enjoyable.

What about identification

The kennel should contain a tag identifying your dog and provide all pertinent information including the dog's name, age, feeding and water requirements, your name, address and phone number and your final destination. In addition, it should include the name and phone number of your dog's vet. A "luggage-type" ID card will function well. Use a waterproof marker. Securely fasten the ID tag to the kennel. Your dog should also wear his state ID tag. Should he somehow become separated from his kennel, the information will travel with him. Using a waterproof pen, mark the kennel "LIVE ANI-MAL" in large letters of at least an inch or more. Indicate which is the top and bottom with arrows and more large lettering of "THIS END UP."

How can I make plane travel comfortable for my pooch

If possible, make your travel plans for weekday rather than weekend travel. Travel during off hours. Direct and nonstop flights reduce the potential for problems and delays. Check with your airline to determine how much time they require for check in. Limiting the amount of time your dog will be in the hold section will make travel time that much more comfortable. Personally ascertain that your dog has been put on board your flight before you board the aircraft.

Will there automatically be room on board for my pooch

Not always. Airline space for pets is normally provided on a first-come, first-served basis. As soon as your travel plans are decided, contact the airline and confirm your arrangements.

What will pet travel cost

Prices vary depending on whether your dog travels in the cabin or whether a kennel must be provided in the hold. Check with the airlines to determine individual pricing policies.

What about food

It's best not to feed your dog at least six hours before departure.

What about tranquilizers

Opinions vary on this subject. Discuss this with your vet. But don't give your dog any medication not prescribed by a vet. Dosages for animals and humans vary greatly.

What about after we land

If your pooch has not been in the passenger cabin with you, you will be able to pick him up in the baggage claim area along with your luggage. Since traveling in a kennel aboard a plane is an unusual experience, he may react strangely. Leash him before you let him out of the kennel. Having his leash on will avoid mishaps. Once he's leashed, give him a cool drink of water and then take him for a walk.

Dogs who shouldn't fly

In general, very young puppies, females in heat, sickly, frail or pregnant dogs should not be flown. In addition to the stress of flying, changes in altitude and cabin pressure might adversely effect your pooch. Also, pug-nosed dogs are definite "no flys". These dogs have short nasal passages which limit their intake of oxygen. The noxious fumes of the cargo hold can severely limit their supply of oxygen, leaving them highly susceptible to injury.

Health certificates - will I need one

Although you may never be asked to present a health certificate, it's a good idea to have one with you. Your vet can supply a certificate listing the inoculations your dog has received, including rabies. Keep this information with your travel papers.

Airlines have specific regulations regarding animal flying rights. Make certain you know your dog's rights.

37
WAYS TO HAVE A BETTER VACATION WITH YOUR POOCH

Some tips and suggestions to increase your enjoyment when you and the pooch hit the road.

1. Don't feed or water your pooch just before starting on your trip. Feed and water your dog approximately two hours before you plan to depart. Better still, if it's a short trip, wait until you arrive at your destination.

2. Exercise your pooch before you leave. A tired dog will fall off to sleep more easily and adapt more readily to new surroundings.

3. Your dog may do better drinking from his own water supply for the first few days. Bring a large container of water and avoid potential stomach upset. Having water along will mean you can stop wherever you like and not worry about finding water. Gradually accustom your pooch to his new source of water by topping off your water container with local water.

4. Plan stops along the way. Just like you, your pooch will enjoy stretching his legs. As you travel, you'll find many areas conducive to a leisurely walk or a bit of playtime. If you make the car ride an agreeable part of the journey, your vacation will begin the moment you leave home - not just when you reach your ultimate destination.

5. While driving, keep windows open enough to allow the circulation of fresh air but not enough to allow your dog to jump out. If you have air conditioning, that will keep your dog cool enough.

6. Don't let your dog hang his head out of the window. Eyes, ears and throats can become inflamed.

7. Use a short leash when walking your pooch through public areas, he'll be easier to control.

8. Take along your dog's favorite objects from home. If they entertain him at home, they'll entertain him on vacation.

9. Before any trip, allow your pooch to relieve himself.

10. Cover your back seat with an old blanket or towel to protect the upholstery.

11. A room freshener under the seat of your car will keep it smelling fresh. Take one along for your room also.

12. If your dog has a tendency for carsickness, keep a packet of honey in the glove compartment or carry a roll of hard candy, like Lifesavers, with you. Either remedy might help with carsickness.

13. Use a flea and tick collar on your pooch.

14. When traveling in warm weather months, drape a damp towel over your dog's crate. This allows ventilation and the moist, cooler air will reduce the heat.

15. Before you begin a trip, expose your pooch to experiences he will encounter while traveling; such as crowds, noise, people, elevators, walks along busy streets, and stairs (especially those with open risers).

16. Shade moves. If you must leave your dog in the car for a short period of time, make sure the shade that protects him when you park will be there by the time you return. As a general rule though, it's best not to leave your dog in a parked car. **NEVER LEAVE YOUR DOG IN THE CAR DURING THE WARM SUMMER MONTHS.** In the colder months, beware of hypothermia, a life threatening condition that occurs when an animal's body temperature falls below normal. Short-haired dogs and toys are very susceptible to illness in extremely cold weather.

17. Take along a clip-on minifan for airless hotel rooms.

18. When packing, include a heating pad, ice pack and a few safety pins.

19. A handful of clothespins will serve a dozen purposes, from clamping motel curtains together to sealing a bag of potato chips, they're great.

20. A night light will help you find the bathroom in the dark.

21. Don't forget that book you've been meaning to read.

22. Include a journal and record your travel memories.

23. Pack a roll of duct tape. Use it to repair shoes, patch suitcases or strap lunch onto the back of a rented bicycle.

24. Never begin a vacation with a new pair of shoes.

25. Pooper scoopers make cleanup simple and sanitary. Plastic vegetable bags from the supermarket are great too.

26. FYI, in drier climates, many accommodations have room humidifiers available for guest use. Arrange for one when you make your reservation.

27. Use unbreakable bowls and storage containers for your dog's food and water needs.

28. Don't do anything on the road with your pooch that you wouldn't do at home.

29. Brown and grey tinted sun lenses are the most effective for screening bright light. Polarized lenses reduce the blinding glare of the sun.

30. Before you leave on vacation, safeguard your home. Ask a neighbor to take in your mail and newspapers, or arrange with your mail carrier to hold your mail. Stop newspaper delivery. Use timers and set them so that a couple of lights go on and off. Unplug small appliances and electronics. Lock all doors and windows. Place steel bars or wooden dowels in the tracks of sliding glass doors or windows. Ladders or other objects that could be used to gain entrance into your home should be stored in your garage or inside your home. Arrange to have your lawn mowed. And don't forget to take out the garbage.

31. Pack some snacks and drinks in a small cooler and keep it inside your vehicle..

32. As a precaution when traveling, once you arrive at your final destination, check the yellow pages for the nearest vet and determine emergency hours and location.

33. NEVER permit your dog to travel in the bed of a pickup truck. If you must, there are safety straps available at auto supply stores that can be used to insure the safety of your dog. Never use a choke chain, rope or leash around your dog's neck to secure him in the bed of a pickup.

34. Take along a spray bottle of water. A squirt in your dog's mouth will temporarily relieve his thirst.

35. Heavy duty zip-lock type bags make great traveling water bowls. Just roll down the edges, form a bowl and fill with water. They fold up into practically nothing. Keep one in your purse, jacket pocket or fanny pack. Keep an extra in your glove compartment.

36. Arrange with housekeeping to have your room cleaned while you're present or take your dog out with you when housekeeping arrives.

37. Traveling with children too? Keep them occupied with colored pencils and markers. Avoid crayons — they can melt in the sun. Take along question cards from trivia games as well as a pack of playing cards. Travel size magnetic games like checkers and chess are also good diversions. Don't forget those battery operated electronic games either. Include a book of crossword puzzles, a pair of dice and a favorite stuffed animal for cuddling time. In the car, games can include finding license plates from different states, spotting various makes or colors of cars, saying the alphabet backwards, or completing the alphabet from roadsigns.

29
TIPS FOR TRAVEL SAFETY

Whether at home or on a travel adventure, always practice travel safety. A few minutes of preparation and an extra moment of prevention can help you from becoming a statistic, no matter where you are.

1. When returning to your room late at night, use the main entrance of your hotel.

2. Don't leave your room key within sight in public areas, particularly if it's numbered instead of coded.

3. Store valuables in your room safe or in a safety-deposit box at the front desk.

4. Don't carry large amounts of cash, use traveler's checks and credit cards.

5. Avoid flaunting expensive watches and jewelry.

6. When visiting a public attraction like a museum or amusement park, decide where to meet should you become separated from your traveling companions.

7. Use a fanny pack and not a purse when touring.

8. Make use of the locks provided in your room. In addition to your room door, be certain all sliding glass doors, windows and connecting doors are locked.

9. If someone knocks on your room door, the American Hotel and Motel Association advises guests to ascertain the identity of the caller before opening the door. If you haven't arranged for room service or requested a delivery, call the front desk and determine if someone has been sent to your room before you open the door.

10. Carry your money (or preferably traveler's checks) separately from credit cards.

11. Use your business address on luggage tags, not your home address.

12. Be alert in parking lots and underground garages.
13. Check the back seat of your car before getting inside.
14. In your car, always buckle up. Seatbelts save lives.
15. Keep car doors locked.
16. When you stop at traffic lights, leave enough room (one car length) between your vehicle and the one in front so you can quickly pull away.
17. AAA recommends that if you're hit from behind by another vehicle, motion the other driver to a public place before getting out of your car.
18. When driving at night, stay on main roads.
19. Fill your tank during daylight hours. If you must fill up at night, do so at a busy, well-lit service station.
20. If your vehicle breaks down, tie a white cloth to the antenna or the raised hood of your car to signal other motorists. Turn on your hazard lights. Remain in your locked car until police or road service arrives.
21. Don't pull over for flashing headlights. Police cars have red or blue lights.
22. Lock video cameras, car phones and other expensive equipment in your trunk. Don't leave them in sight.
23. Have car keys ready as you approach your car.
24. At an airport, allow only uniformed airport personnel to carry your bags or carry them yourself. Refuse offers of transportation from strangers. Use the airport's ground transportation center or a uniformed taxi dispatcher.
25. Walk purposefully.
26. When using an ATM, choose one in a well-lit area with heavy foot traffic. Look for machines inside establishments - they're the safest.
27. Avoid poorly lit areas, shrubbery or dark doorways.
28. When ordering from an outside source, have it delivered to the front desk or office rather than to your room.
29. Trust your instincts. If a situation doesn't feel right - it probably isn't.

11

TIPS THAT TAKE THE STRESS OUT OF VACATIONS

Vacations are intended to be restful occasions but sometimes the preparations involved in getting away from it all can prove stressful. The tips on the following page are proven stress reducers to help you cope before, during and after your trip.

1. Awaken fifteen minutes earlier each day for a couple of weeks before your trip and use that extra time to plan your day and do vacation chores.

2. Write down errands to be done. Don't rely on your memory. The anticipation of forgetting something important can be stressful.

3. Don't procrastinate. Whatever has to be done tomorrow, do today. Whatever needs doing today, do NOW.

4. Take stock of your car. Get car repairs done. Have your car washed. Your journey will be more pleasant in a clean car. Fill up with gas the day before your departure. And check your tires and oil gauge. Summertime travel, check your air conditioning. In the winter, make sure your heater and defroster work. Make sure wiper blades are also in good working condition.

5. Learn to be more flexible. Not everything has to be perfect. Compromise, you'll have a happier life.

6. If you have an unpleasant task to do, take care of it early in the day.

7. Ask for help. Delegating responsibility relieves pressure and stress. It also makes others feel productive and needed.

8. Accept that we are all part of this imperfect world. An ounce of forgiveness will take you far.

9. Don't take on more tasks than you can readily accomplish.

10. Think positive thoughts and eliminate negativism, like, "I'm too fat, I'm too old, I'm not smart enough."

11. Take 5-10 minutes to stretch before you begin your day or before bedtime. Breathe deeply and slowly, clearing your mind as you do.

27
Things To Know When Driving To Your Destination

1. Keep your dog confined with either a crate, barrier or harness.

2. To avoid sliding in the event of sharp turns or sudden stops, be certain that your luggage, as well as your dog's crate are securely stored or fastened.

3. Be certain your vehicle is in good working order. Check brakelights, turn signals, hazard and headlights. Clean your windshield and top off washer fluid whenever you fill up. You'll be driving in unfamiliar territory so keep an eye on the gas gauge. Fill up during daylight hours or at well-lit service stations.

4. A first-aid kit, blanket, and sweets like hard candy will come in handy. When packing, include a flashlight, tool kit, paper towels, an extra leash, waterproof matches and a supply of plastic bags. During the winter months, keep an ice scraper, snow brush and small shovel in your car.

5. Never drive tired. Keep the music on, windows open. Fresh air can help you remain alert.

6. Keep your windshield clean, inside and out.

7. Avoid using sedatives or tranquilizers when driving.

8. Don't drink and drive.

9. Never try to drive and read a map at the same time. If you're driving alone, pull off at a well-lit gas station or roadside restaurant and check the map. If you're unsure of directions, ask for assistance from a safe source.

10. Wear your seatbelt, they save lives.

11. Keep car doors locked.

12. Good posture is especially important when driving. Do your back a favor and sit up straight. For lower back pain, wedge a small pillow between your back and the seat.

13. If you're the driver, eat frequent small snacks rather than large meals. You'll be less tired that way.

14. Don't use high beams in fog. The light will bounce back into your eyes as it reflects off the moisture.

15. When pulling off to the side of the road, use your flashers to warn other cars away.

16. Before beginning your drive each day, do a car check. Tire pressure okay? Leakage under car? Windows clean? Signals working? Mirrors properly adjusted? Gas tank full?

17. Roads can become particularly slippery at the onset of rain, the result of water mixing with dust and oil on the pavement. Slow down and exercise caution in wet weather.

18. Every so often, turn off your cruise control. Overuse can lull you into inattention.

19. If you'll be doing a lot of driving into the sun, put a towel over the dashboard. It will provide some relief from the heat and brightness.

20. Even during the cooler months, your car can become stuffy. Keep the windows or sun roof open and let fresh air circulate.

21. Kids coming along? A small tape or CD player can amuse youngsters. Hand-held video games are also entertaining. And action figures are a good source for imaginary games. Put together a travel container and include markers or colored pencils, stamps, stickers, blunt safety scissors, and some pads of paper, both colored and lined.

22. If your car trip requires an overnight stay on route to your destination, pack a change of clothing and other necessities in a separate bag. Keep it in an accessible location.

23. When visiting wet and/or humid climates, take along insect repellent.

24. Guard against temperature extremes. Protect your skin from the effects of the sun. Hazy days are just as dangerous

to your skin as sunny ones. Pack plenty of sunscreen. Apply in the morning and then again in the early afternoon. The sun is strongest midday so avoid overexposure at that time. To remain comfortable in warm weather, wear lightweight, loose fitting cotton clothing. Choose light colors. Dark ones attract the sun. In dry climates, remember to drink lots of liquids. Because the evaporation process speeds up in arid areas, you won't be aware of how much you're perspiring.

25. In cold climes, protect yourself from frostbite. If the temperature falls below 32° fahrenheit and the wind chill factor is also low, frostbite can occur in a matter of minutes. Layer your clothing. Cotton next to your skin and wool over that is the best insulator. Wear a hat to keep warm - body heat escapes very quickly through your head.

26. Changes in altitude can cause altitude sickness. Whenever possible, slowly accustom yourself to an altitude change. Don't overexert yourself either. Symptoms of high altitude sickness occur more frequently over 8,000 feet and include dizziness, shortness of breath and headaches.

27. Store your maps, itinerary and related travel information in a clear plastic container (shoe box storage type with a lid works best). Keep it in the front of your vehicle in an easy-to-reach location.

FIDO FACT:

• *If your pooch is becoming too aggressive or is misbehaving, try startling him. Dogs dislike loud, grating noises. Load an empty soda can with pebbles or coins and keep it handy. When your pooch starts to act up, a firm "No" and a vigorous shaking of the can should prove to be an excellent deterrent to bad behavior. Be firm but not terrifying. And remember, corrective training must be administered immediately following the offending act.*

WASHINGTON/OREGON ROAD SAFETY TIPS

- Don't drink and drive - it's dangerous and against the law.

- State laws prohibit the consumption of alcoholic beverages in a vehicle by the driver or any of the vehicle's occupants.

- A blood alcohol test is mandatory for anyone arrested while under the influence.

- Seatbelts are the law for *all* occupants of vehicles.

- Children under the age of 4 or less than 40 lbs must be properly restrained in a federally approved child safety seat.

- Helmets are the law for all motorcyclists and passengers.

For travel assistance and emergency road condition information:

Oregon
- Traffic accidents, criminal activities, intoxicated drivers and other emergencies:
(800) 243-7865
- Traffic Safety Information Line:
(800) 922-2022
- Road Conditions Hotline:
(503) 889-3999
- Child Safety Seat Resource Center:
(800) 772-1315

Washington
- Traffic accidents, criminal activities, intoxicated drivers and other emergencies:
(800) 243-7865
- Road Conditions Hotline (winter only)
(888) 766-4636

WHAT YOU SHOULD KNOW ABOUT DRIVING IN THE NORTHWEST

Water: Check your radiator before beginning your trip. Outside of metropolitan areas, service stations may be few and far between, even on major roads. Always carry extra water.

Gasoline: Fill up before beginning any adventure. Since you may be traveling through sparsely populated areas, when you have half a tank or less, refuel at the first service station you encounter.

Summer Thunderstorms: Summer thunderstorms can cause problems, especially where roads dip into washes. The runoff quickly fills the washes, creating hazardous driving conditions and impassable roads.

Breakdowns: Use your hazard lights or raise the hood. Remain in your vehicle until help arrives. Keep doors locked and do not open doors except for police officers. If you break down on a secluded back road and must seek help, retrace your route. Don't take any short cuts.

FIDO FACT:

- *Never leave your dog unattended in the car during the warm weather months or extremely cold ones.*

Hiking...
a walk through nature

Hiking conjures up images of rugged outdoor types, standing tall on mountaintops, wind in their hair, outfitted with sturdy, specially designed vests, pockets filled with intriguing paraphernalia.

While there might have been a time when hiking was an activity with limited appeal, America's obsession with physical fitness has changed all that. Hiking has become a popular pastime. In addition to the physical benefits associated with hiking, consider the pleasures to be found in nature. And other than the simple gear and supplies you might want to include, hiking is free.

There's something special about hiking, particularly with a canine companion. It's truly time of the highest quality. Time when the phone isn't ringing, when hours seem endless and when a little dirt is part of the experience, not a disaster. Share an invigorating hike with your pooch. It will be an experience you'll want to repeat again and again.

Some words of advice for novice hikers

Hiking on a marked trail provides a sense of fulfillment and security. Both goal-oriented types who like to feel they've accomplished something and novices who want to know what to expect will appreciate marked hiking trails. Knowing the length of the trail, the time required, a bit about the terrain and the sights to be expected also adds to the pleasures of hiking.

Hiking can be a total exploration of a defined area or merely a slice of nature. You set the distances and the time. Hike in for half an hour and then retrace your steps. Do a loop trail with predetermined mileage. Or do it all, see it all.

Begin with easy trails. Learn what to take along, what to leave at home. Find a pace that suits your walking style. Easy trails are usually found in low lying areas. Although the terrain might change from level, even ground to more hilly contours, for the most part, you'll experience a trail without obstacles.

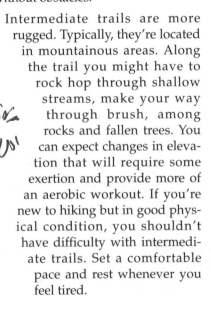

Intermediate trails are more rugged. Typically, they're located in mountainous areas. Along the trail you might have to rock hop through shallow streams, make your way through brush, among rocks and fallen trees. You can expect changes in elevation that will require some exertion and provide more of an aerobic workout. If you're new to hiking but in good physical condition, you shouldn't have difficulty with intermediate trails. Set a comfortable pace and rest whenever you feel tired.

Expert trails are usually steeper and more challenging. Stamina, agility and fitness all come into play. You might have to scale boulders, ascend and descend precipitous escarpments or maintain your balance on slippery rocks. Expert trails should not be attempted by beginners. Even intermediates should only hike the more difficult trails after they've accumulated some "hiking points" in the intermediate arena. Take into account your dog's ability as well as your own when deciding where to hike. In any case, don't hike expert trails alone and let someone know where you're hiking and when to expect your return.

Hiking is an experience that's enjoyable to share with your pooch and with your friends. That's not to say that solitary hikers don't enjoy themselves, many solitary hikers prefer the peacefulness of nature without the distraction of others.

Get ready to go, wilderness style

When traveling through backcountry wilderness, use topographic maps and trail guides. Plan your trip from start to finish at home. Check elevations and total distance to be traveled up and down. Allow plenty of time for moving over hilly, rugged terrain. Before entering the wilderness, leave your itinerary with a relative or friend. Write a full account of who is going, where you are going, when you will return, where you will exit and the approximate location of each overnight campsite. Carry a map and compass and stick to the planned route. It is wise never to travel alone, but if you must, stick to frequently used trails in the event you become sick or injured.

Buying backcountry equipment

Acquiring equipment requires a little research and the advice of experienced backpackers. You can refer to the many camping guides commercially available, but don't rely on printed information alone. Talk to an experienced backpacker or your local camping supplier. They can help you select basic equipment.

Take it easy

Once in the wilderness, take it easy for a day or two. Getting

out of your living room and into the wild takes some adjust-
ment. Eat dried fruit or other quick energy food from time to
time and walk slowly and steadily.

If you overexert yourself at high elevations, you may experience altitude
sickness or hyperventilation. Most
often, an attack is the result of
traveling too fast. Never joke
about a person's ability to keep
up when traveling in the wild.
A good principle of wilderness
travel is to take it slow, rest
often and snack frequently to
restore body energy.

Wildlife

Many of the hikes in this
book will bring you in close
proximity to wildlife. Please do
not disturb the natural habitat or
get too close to the animals. If you
know that you will encounter wildlife and you do not feel you
have total voice control over your dog, leash him to prevent
mishaps. Elk, for example, have been known to charge when
they sense danger or feel threatened.

When hiking in a marshland or other bird sanctuary, keep
your dog leashed, particularly if he's a hunting or bird dog. It's
up to you to protect our wildlife.

Regardless of where you hike, whether it's through a red-
walled canyon, in a heavily wooded forest or on granite mountaintops, clean up after your dog. Let's work together to preserve the beauty of America as well as dog-friendly attitudes
and policies.

First-aid kits

Hikers should carry a small first-aid kit. Blisters, headaches or other minor ailments can ruin a day trip. The following list of supplies encompass the needs of wilderness travel. Adjust quantities based on the length and type of excursion and size of the hiking party.

People

- Pain medication such as aspirin (25 tablets)
- Antacid (25 tablets)
- Antihistamine (12 tablets)
- Bandages (12, 1-inch size)
- Sterile gauze pads (six 4-inch squares)
- Adhesive tape (2-inch roll)
- Elastic bandages (3-inch)
- Tweezers (1 pair)
- Moleskin (1/2 package)
- Antibacterial soap
- Roll gauze (two 2-inch rolls)
- Oral thermometer
- Personal prescription drugs
- Space blanket
- Pencil and paper
- Change for a telephone
- Arm and leg inflatable splints (1 each)
- Safety pins (3 large)
- Flashlight (with new batteries)

Pooches

- Two-inch bandages
- Antibiotic ointment
- Scissors
- Rectal thermometer
- Boric acid
- Baking soda
- Lighter fluid
- 3% hydrogen peroxide
- Blunt tweezers
- Tomato juice
- Cotton gauze
- Flea powder

Eileen's "Be Prepared" approach to hiking

The day hikes I've detailed in *Doin' The Northwest With Your Pooch* will be more pleasurable if you travel with a light load. Invest in a well-made, lightweight fanny pack with built-in water bottles and several zippered compartments, large enough to hold the following items.

- Penlight size flashlight with fresh batteries and bulb.

- A small box of waterproof matches - the type that light when scratched on just about anything.

- A large trash bag, folded into a small square. This serves three purposes. It's an instant raincoat (just punch out arm and head holes), a receptacle for trash and a seat covering for cold/wet ground.

- A bandana or two. This simple cotton garment serves as a washcloth, headband, cool compress, etc. It folds up into nothing or can be worn around your neck (or your pooch's) to save fanny pack room.

- Lip balm with UV protection.

- Small travel size tube of sunscreen. Use in sunny or hazy weather, especially at high altitudes.

- Nylon windbreaker. Many sporting goods stores sell the type that fold up and fit into their own case.

- Soft felt hat. Great protection from the sun, it's easily stored or safety pinned to your pack.

- A whistle. Wear it around your neck on a tripled piece of string which is also handy to have along. Three whistle blasts are the signal for help.

- Small map magnifier (doubles as a fire starter).

- Water bottle(s) with squirt top. If water supplies run low, a squirt in your mouth or your dog's will temporarily relieve thirst.

- Sunglasses with UV protective lenses can be worn or left dangling on an eyeglass holder.

- Travel size first-aid kit.

- An extra pair of socks.

- Grocery produce bags. They're great for doggie cleanup and as an emergency barrier between wet socks and dry feet.

- A small, non-aerosol spray can of insect repellent. Spray yourself and your pooch before the hike and leave the can in the car.

- A couple of safety pins.

- A multi-use, Swiss army-type knife.

- A walking stick for the extra balance it provides (ski poles are great).

- A map of the area or a copy of the trail description/information provided for each hike.

Depending on conditions, weather and personal preferences, you might also want to include:

- A compass if you know how to use one.

- An extra sweater or jacket. Two or three lighter layered articles of clothing are better than one heavy garment. Layering locks in air between garments, warms the air and then warms you.

FIDO FACT:

- *Fido's fitness counts towards insuring a longer, healthier life. In this arena, you're the one in control. The most common cause of ill health in canines is obesity. Approximately 60% of all adult dogs are overweight or will become overweight due to lack of physical activity and overfeeding. Much like humans, the medical consequences of obesity include liver, heart and orthopedic problems. As little as a few extra pounds on a small dog can lead to health-related complications.*

100
Ways To Be A Better Hiker

The following tips and info will add to your enjoyment of the outdoors and help prepare you for the unexpected.

1. High altitude sickness can occur in elevations over 5,000 feet. Whenever possible, slowly accustom yourself to changes in altitude. Symptoms include lightheadedness, faintness, headaches and dryness. If you experience any of these symptoms, stop, rest, seek shade and drink plenty of water.

2. Never hike in a new pair of hiking boots. Always break in boots before hiking.

3. Buy smart. To get a good fit, try boots on with the type of socks you'll be wearing. COMFORT is the key word in boot selection. After comfort, look for support and traction. For day hikers, a lightweight, well-made, sturdy boot is the number one choice.

4. Water, water everywhere, but not a drop to drink. Drink plenty of water before you begin and pack enough to last through your hike. Although there may be water available trailside in the form of lakes and streams, unless you're experienced and properly prepared to purify the water, don't drink it.

5. Dress in layers. Peel off or add clothing as weather dictates. Cotton next to the skin with wool over it is the most comfortable. The exception is during wet weather when cotton is a negative because it takes too long to dry and offers little insulation.

6. Pack extra clothing, most importantly a second pair of socks and a nylon windbreaker.

7. If your feet are cold, put on a hat. Body heat escapes through the head.

8. Before you begin your trip, make sure all hiking apparel is in good repair. Check for loose buttons, open seams, stuck zippers. Lubricate zipper slides and teeth with wax or a spray lubricant.

9. Don't litter, carry out your trash.

10. Carry a UV-protected lip balm and apply frequently.

11. Carry a small first-aid kit and learn some basic skills.

12. Avoid wet, soggy socks and boots. If you know the trail includes crossing streams or creeks, pack a pair of all-terrain sandals. Or use plastic grocery bags under your wool socks.

13. Carry your own water and top off at every opportunity.

14. When hiking in warm weather, freeze your filled water bottles the night before your trip, leaving room for expansion. Your water supply will remain cooler.

15. Take along an extra leash or line of rope for unforeseen emergencies.

16. Set a comfortable pace. Don't overexert yourself, there's always tomorrow.

17. Ski poles make great walking sticks.

18. Before you begin any hiking trip, tell a reliable person your plans. Include an estimated time for your return and notify them when you return.

19. Pack picnic goodies in reusable containers or plastic zip-lock bags.

20. For an instant water bowl, include a large size zip-lock bag. With the sides rolled down, it makes a terrific water bowl for your dog.

21. Spray exposed arms, legs and face with insect repellent. Spray your pooch too but remember to avoid spraying near the eyes.

22. Sites containing Native American relics should be treated with respect. Do not disturb or remove anything.

23. Nature is soft and serene - behave accordingly.

24. Blend in with your surroundings.

25. When it's warm and sunny, wear light colored clothing. Dark colors attract the sun and mosquitoes.

26. Every hour or so, take a ten-minute break. In warm weather, select a shady spot. In cooler weather, find a sunny, wind-protected area. In cold weather, sit on something other than the ground.

27. Should a lightning or thunderstorm occur, find shelter away from mountain peaks or exposed slopes.

28. Stow some high energy snacks in your pack. Include some biscuits and a chew for your pooch.

29. A small roll of duct tape can repair just about anything.

30. Consider your dog's age and physical capabilities when planning trips.

31. Stop and look around and in back of you as you hike. The views are always different.

32. A large garbage bag can double as an emergency rain coat. Just punch holes for your head and arms.

33. Some basic geology knowledge will go a long way towards enhancing your outdoor experience.

34. View your surroundings as if you're in an outdoor museum, you'll see and enjoy more.

35. Wear sunglasses to protect your eyes and a hat to protect your scalp from UV rays and direct sunlight.

36. Apply a minimum 15 SPF sunscreen to all exposed parts of your body, particularly your face. Reapply after swimming or after several hours.

37. Leave only footprints, take only memories.

38. Always clean up after your pooch. The fact that dog owners don't clean up after their dogs is the number one complaint to federal, state and local agencies governing public lands. In some areas, dogs have been banned because of these complaints. Do your share so dogs will continue to be welcome.

39. A box of waterproof matches can be a lifesaver.

40. Keep a multi-purpose knife in your hiking gear.

41. Remember you have to walk out as far as you've walked in.

42. Don't begin a hike towards evening, hiking in darkness is dangerous.

43. Allow fast walking hikers to pass you.

44. Carry your dog's leash even in areas where he is permitted to run free.

45. Keep your dog on a leash in wildlife areas, for his protection and the protection of wildlife.

46. Dogs must be leashed in all developed campgrounds.

47. Dogs are not permitted to swim in public pools.

48. Control your dog at all times. One unruly dog can cause problems for every dog.

49. Unless your dog responds to voice commands, keep him leashed in crowded areas or on well used trails.

50. Certain breeds of dogs are inclined to chase wildlife. Know your own dog. If you feel he might do harm to the wildlife, the terrain or himself, keep him leashed.

51. Get into shape before your trip. Start with short walks and lengthen them, increasing your pace as you do. Take your dog and get him in shape too.

52. Make exercise an integral part of your daily routine. Whenever there's a choice, take the stairs. Park a few streets from your destination and then walk.

53. Ten minutes of easy stretching before any physical activity will minimize the chance of injury. Avoid jerky movements. Stretch the hamstrings, shoulders, back, legs, arms and Achilles tendon.

54. Go for comfort. Avoid tight constrictive clothing.

55. Socks should fit well and be clean. Loose, ill fitting or dirty socks can cause blisters.

56. Educate yourself on the area's flora and fauna and you'll have a more interesting hike.

57. During warmer months or in desert terrain, drink plenty of water before, during and after your hike. You won't always know when your body is becoming dehydrated because perspiration dries very quickly. You might not feel thirsty but your body will be.

(DON'T FORGET TO WATER THE POOCH.)

58. If you use a backpack, buy one with wide straps that won't dig into your skin.

59. Pack a whistle - a series of three blasts is the recognized distress signal.

60. Even if you intend to begin and end your hike during daylight hours, pack a small flashlight with fresh batteries and bulb for emergencies.

61. Wear a watch or keep one handy. Time flies by without reference points. It normally takes as long to hike out as to hike in.

62. As the name implies, trail mix makes a great hiking snack.

63. Be prepared for unexpected weather changes. Tune in to a local radio station before beginning your hike.

64. Hypothermia is the number one outdoor killer. As soon as you feel chilled, put on an extra layer of clothing, don't wait until you're cold.

65. When you feel warm, remove a layer.

66. If you're hiking and rain or wet conditions are expected, don't wear cotton. Synthetic fabrics and wool offer the best insulation when wet.

67. A long time favorite of hikers are wool rag socks. Thick and absorbent, they'll keep your feet warm even when wet. They'll also provide cushioning. Include an extra pair.

68. Liner socks are also popular. Similar to the thin socks worn under ski boots, they're usually made of wool, silk or a synthetic. Liner socks are softer to the touch and can be worn under heavier socks.

69. When hiking in cooler temperatures, two light sweaters are better than a heavy one.

70. Slow your pace when descending a trail to avoid potential injury.

71. If the weather turns unpredictably cold but you still want to hike, plastic produce bags can be used to keep your feet warm. Put them on your bare feet, wrap the top around your ankles and then put on your socks. The plastic becomes a barrier and prevents body heat from escaping.

72. Wide brimmed soft felt hats are great for hiking. They fold up into nothing and are comfortable, even in hot summer months. Simply air condition them by cutting out hearts or triangles with a pair of scissors.

73. Disposable polyethylene gloves, the kind sold in paint stores, make great glove liners. They'll keep your hands toasty warm in the coldest climes.

74. An old-fashioned bandana can become a washcloth, head-band, cool compress or napkin. Wrap one around your dog's neck too.

75. Consider saddle bags for your pooch to wear. He'll feel productive and help carry the load.

76. A small map magnifier can double as a fire starter.

77. Disposable cameras are lightweight and easy to include on a day hike. The panoramic-type best captures the beauty of the northwest.

78. In the summer, fanny packs are cooler to use than back-packs.

79. Fruit, fresh or sun dried, is a quick energy source. Peel a couple of oranges or tangerines before your hike and store in zip-lock baggies. You'll always have a light, refreshing snack at your fingertips.

80. Cut your toenails a few days before your hike. Long toe-nails can cripple a hiker, especially descending a steep trail.

81. Before your trip, wear your pack at home with a typical load until you're certain it's comfortable.

82. If your feet or hands begin to feel swollen during your hike, find a tree and elevate your feet higher than your head. Hold your arms up in the air at the same time. Three minutes ought to do the trick and redistribute the blood throughout your body.

83. Begin a hike wearing only enough clothing to keep you just shy of comfortable. After the first ten minutes of exertion, you'll feel warmer and be happier wearing less.

84. Restore the traction of your boots after walking through mud, loose dirt, sand or other clogging substances with a sharp kick at a sturdy tree or boulder.

85. Use your arms to make hiking more controlled and aerobic. Don't let them hang limply beside you. Swing them as you walk, use them for balance.

86. Take along a package of pre-moistened towelettes and travel size tissues.

87. Use the trash bag you packed for emergencies to clean the trail on your way out.

88. Puffy cumulus clouds usually mean fair weather.

89. A ring around the moon forecasts rain or snow.

90. Bad weather warnings, a red sky at dawn, the absence of dew on the grass or an early morning rainbow.

91. When bad weather threatens, avoid high, open places, lakes, meadows, exposed slopes and lone or towering trees. Seek shelter in caves, canyon bottoms or areas of the forest with shorter, relatively equal sized trees.

92. To gauge lightning - every second between flash and boom equals a mile in distance.

93. When cumulus clouds blend together and the bottoms darken, a storm is on the way.

94. Yellow sunsets and still moist air can signal bad weather.

95. Make your own folding cup. Flatten a waxed paper cup or a paper cone cup and tuck into your pocket.

96. Carry safety pins.

97. To prevent spillage, store your canteen or water bottle in a plastic bag.

98. Do not undertake more than you can handle. Recognize your limitations and the limitations of your canine.

99. While you're hiking, if you become too hot, too cold, too tired, too anything, other than ecstatic, take a rest or begin your return.

100. Carry a generous supply of grocery type plastic produce bags for cleanup. Keep extras in your car and suitcase.

What about the pooch

Your pooch can be outfitted with saddle bags, small but roomy enough to carry all his needs. When you pack his saddle bags, keep the weight even on both sides for balance. Include the following:

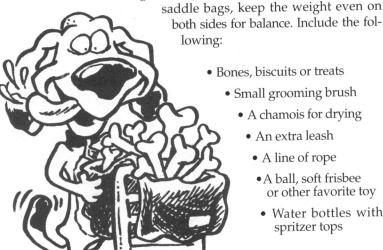

- Bones, biscuits or treats
- Small grooming brush
- A chamois for drying
- An extra leash
- A line of rope
- A ball, soft frisbee or other favorite toy
- Water bottles with spritzer tops

<u>Great packing/travel tip</u>

When hiking with your dog, large zip-lock bags make great portable water bowls. Just roll down the sides to form a bowl and add water.

Trail Manners & Methods

Trails are both a convenience for wilderness users and a way to minimize human impact on an area. Cutting switchbacks or cutting through trail sections can cause serious erosion. Walking on the shoulder of a wet or muddy trail creates ruts along the trail. If you aren't following the trail, stay well away from it. Use caution when crossing dangerous sections, such as swampy areas, potential slide areas, deep snowdrifts, slippery trails on slopes or rapid streams.

For everyone's safety, hikers should stand quietly on the downhill side to allow horses to pass. Don't try to touch pack animals or hide from them. Startled horses can be dangerous.

Be prepared

Be sure you and your fellow campers and backpackers are in shape. Take weekend hikes and exercise with a full backpack for several weeks before your trip. Clothing is the most important precaution against hypothermia, exhaustion and exposure. Pack a waterproof poncho for stormy weather. Dressing in layers lets you adapt to temperatures that can change drastically between day and night in mountainous areas. Be sure your sleeping bag keeps you warm when outdoor temperatures are well below freezing. Your boots should be sturdy, well insulated and waterproof, fit comfortably over two pairs of socks (cotton inner, wool outer), protect the ankle and support the foot. Break them in before your trip, but don't wear them out. You'll need plenty of traction on mountain slopes. Bring a hat or wool beanie. Exposure and heat loss are greatest through the head and sunstroke and hypothermia are major hazards. Plan menus carefully. Take food that is simple, nutritious and lightweight.

Washington/Oregon hiking etiquette

- Respect the land - don't shortcut the trail.
- Avoid wet trails whenever possible.
- Don't cut new trails, it can cause trail erosion.
- Keep to the right of the trail - left is for passing.
- Downhill traffic yields to uphill traffic.
- Adjust your pace when approaching other users.
- When overtaking a hiker, announce your intentions.
- Don't block the trail, allow room for others to pass.
- Joggers yield to trail stock and hikers.
- Bicyclists yield to all other users.
- Some trails have steep grades, natural hazards, variable terrain conditions and limited visibility. Observe and heed all signs.
- In winter, keep dogs off cross-country ski trails.

Trip checklist

You will find greater enjoyment in the wilderness if you are properly prepared. The following checklist is important for your safety and enjoyment.

- Clothing and shelter for rain, wind and cold
- Map and compass
- First-aid kit
- Sunglasses
- Flashlight
- Hat
- Knife
- Waterproof matches
- Nylon twine or cord
- Sun lotion and lip ointment
- Mosquito repellent
- Notify someone of your trip route and departure/return times

Pooch Rules & Regulations

BE A RESPONSIBLE DOG OWNER AND OBEY THE RULES

- Clean up after your dog even if no one has seen him do his business.
- Leash your dog in areas that require leashing.
- Train your dog to be well behaved.
- Control your dog in public places so that he's not a nuisance to others.

Refuse & Garbage

- Don't bury your trash, animals dig it up. Burn all paper.
- Don't leave leftover food for the next party, it teaches bears to rob camps.
- Pack out all cans, bottles and metal foil.

Smoking

Don't smoke on trails. You may smoke at your campsite. Dig a small area to be used as an ashtray. Always take your cigarette butt with you, filters don't easily decompose.

Fishing information

Many of the waterways of the northwest offer excellent fishing opportunities. Your catch can include salmon, crappie, large mouth bass, catfish, brook, rainbow and steelhead trout to name a few. Bag limits and length requirements are strictly enforced. There may also be restrictions on equipment. Some species may be endangered or carry dangerous levels of toxicity and must be released - read and heed posted warnings. Never kill fish not intended for consumption.

Oregon

In order to partake in any fishing activity, the State of Oregon requires a valid fishing license for any person over the age of 14. Residents of Oregon over the age of 65 are eligible for a senior license at a reduced fee. Legally blind residents may obtain their license without cost. For more information, contact the Oregon Department of Fish and Wildlife, (503) 872-5268.

Washington

In order to partake in any fishing activity, the State of Washington requires a valid fishing license for any person over the age of 15. Residents of Washington over the age of 70 are eligible for a senior license at a reduced fee. Legally blind, physically challenged residents and qualified disabled veterans may obtain their license without cost. For more information, contact the Washington Department of Fish and Wildlife, (360) 902-2200.

Bears are not cuddly

Most large mammals avoid anything that smells of humans, but there are exceptions. Bears are intelligent, adaptable animals and some have changed their natural foraging habits to take advantage of hikers and campers who bring food into wilderness areas. Basic rules - keep your distance from bears and don't harass them. The following are additional suggestions when traveling in bear country:

Keep your camp clean and counterbalance anything that has an odor, including soap, toothpaste and trash. To counterbalance your load, place the items in two bags so they weigh about the same. Find a tree with a good branch about 20 feet off the ground. Toss a rope over the branch far enough from the trunk so cubs can't crawl along the branch and reach the bags. Tie the first sack on one end of the rope and hoist the sack up to the branch. Tie the second sack to the other end of the rope. The rope should be about 10 feet long, tuck any excess in the bag. Tie a loop in the rope near the second bag. Toss the second bag into position so both bags are hanging about 12 feet off the ground. To retrieve them, hook the loop with a long stick and pull down the bags.

Don't hang packs in trees. Leave them on the ground with zippers and flaps open so bears can nose through them without doing any damage.

If a bear approaches your camp, yell, bang pans and wave clothing in the air. In many cases, the bear will retreat. If the bear doesn't retreat, get yourself out of camp, ASAP.

Bears may only enter camp looking for food, but they are still potentially dangerous. Never try to take food away from a bear. Never approach a bear, especially a cub. You may lose a meal to animals, but they pay a higher price for human carelessness. Bears that become accustomed to getting food from campers sometimes become too aggressive and have to be destroyed. Animals that spend the summer getting food from campers can find themselves in trouble when the first snow falls and their food supply quits for the year.

Don't get ticked off

Ticks are prevalent in many areas of the northwest and are carriers of lime disease. They usually inhabit brushy areas and tall grass so avoid both whenever possible and keep your dog away as well. When hiking in tick country, wear long pants and a long sleeve shirt to minimize contact. It's also easier to spot a tick on light colored clothing. At the end of your outing or hike, carefully inspect yourself and your canine for ticks. Deep Woods OFF!, an insect repellent, can help repel ticks. To remove a tick, use lighter fluid (or other alcohol) and loosen by soaking. Then tweeze out gently, being sure to remove the tick's head.

Poison ivy and poison oak

Found throughout the northwest, poison ivy/oak can be either a vine or a shrub. The leaves are red in fall, green in spring and summer. They usually form clusters of three. If you come into contact with poison ivy/oak, wash with soap and cool water ASAP. Remove and wash all clothing as well. Over-the-counter medicines are available to help relieve symptoms. If your dog comes in contact with poison ivy/oak, he won't experience any ill effects, but the poison will remain on his coat. Do not pet him. Use rubber gloves to handle your dog. Rinse him in salt water and follow with a clear water rinse. Then shampoo and rinse again.

FIRST-AID EMERGENCY TREATMENT

Having a bit of the Girl Scout in me, I like being prepared. Over the years, I've accumulated information regarding animal emergency treatment. Although I've had only one occasion to use this information, once was enough. I'd like to share my knowledge with you.

Whether you're the stay-at-home type who rarely travels with your pet, or a gadabout who can't sit still, every pet owner should know these simple, but potentially lifesaving procedures.

The following are only guidelines to assist you during emergencies. Whenever possible, seek treatment from a vet if your animal becomes injured and you are unprepared to administer first aid.

Allergies: One in five pets suffers from some form of allergy. Sneezing and watery eyes can be an allergic reaction caused by pollen and smoke. Inflamed skin can indicate a sensitivity to grass or to chemicals used in carpet cleaning. See your vet.

Bites and stings: Use ice to reduce swelling. If your animal has been stung in the mouth, immediately take him to the vet. Swelling can close the throat. If your pet experiences an allergic reaction, an antihistamine may be needed. For fast relief from a wasp or bee sting, dab the spot with plain vinegar and then apply baking soda. If you're in the middle of nowhere, a small mud pie plastered over the sting will provide relief. Snake bites, seek veterinary attention ASAP.

Bleeding: If the cut is small, use tweezers to remove hair from the wound. Gently wash with soap and water and then bandage (not too tightly). Severe bleeding, apply direct pressure and seek medical attention ASAP.

Burns: First degree burns: Use an ice cube or apply ice water until the pain is alleviated. Then apply vitamin E, swab with honey or cover with a freshly brewed teabag.

Minor burns: Use antibiotic ointment.

Acid: Apply dampened baking soda.

Scalds: Douse with cold water. After treatment, bandage all burns for protection.

Earache: A drop of warm eucalyptus oil in your pet's ear can help relieve the pain.

Eye scratches or inflammation: Make a solution of boric acid and bathe eyes with soft cotton.

Falls or impact injuries: Limping, pain, grey gums or prostration need immediate veterinary attention. The cause could be a fracture or internal bleeding.

Fleas: Patches of hair loss, itching and redness are common signs of fleas, particularly during warm months. Use a flea bath and a flea collar to eliminate and prevent infestation. Ask your vet about two new medications now available for flea control, one is oral and the other is a long-term topical.

Heatstroke: Signs include lying prone, rapid or difficult breathing and heartbeat, rolling eyes, panting, high fever, a staggering gait. Quick response is essential. Move your animal into the shade. Generously douse with cold water or if possible, partially fill a tub with cold water and immerse your pet. Remain with him and check his temperature. Normal for dogs: 100°-102°. Don't let your dog's temperature drop below that.

Prevent common heatstroke by limiting outdoor exercise in hot or humid weather and providing plenty of fresh, cool water and access to shade. Never leave your canine in a car on a warm day, even for "just a few minutes."

Heartworm: Mosquitoes can be more than pests when it comes to the health of your dog. They are the carriers of Heartworm disease, which can be life threatening to your furry friend. There is no vaccine. However, daily or monthly pills can protect your pet from infection. In areas with high mosquito populations, use a Heartworm preventative. Contact your local veterinarian about testing and medication. In the case of Heartworm, "an ounce of prevention equals a pound of cure."

Poisons: Gasoline products, antifreeze, disinfectant and insecticides are all poisonous. Keep these products tightly closed and out of reach. Vomiting, trembling and convulsions can be symptoms of poisoning. If your pet suffers from any of these symptoms, get veterinary attention. (See listings on Poison Control Centers in section "Everything You Want to Know About Pet Care...")

Poison ivy: Poison ivy on your pet's coat will not bother him. But the poison can be passed on to you. If you believe your pet has come in contact with poison ivy, use rubber gloves before handling your animal. Rinse him in salt water, then follow with a clear water rinse. Shampoo and rinse again.

Shock: Shock can occur after an accident or severe fright. Your animal might experience shallow breathing, pale gums, nervousness or prostration. Keep him still, quiet and warm and have someone drive you to a vet.

FIDO FACT:

- *Got a fussy eater?*

Although missing a meal isn't unhealthy, you don't want meal times to become problem times. Never beg your dog to eat. Put the food down and leave the area. If the food hasn't been eaten in an hour, pick it up and save it for the next feeding. Your dog will eventually get the message. And no table scraps, they only encourage bad eating habits.

Skunks: The following might help you avoid a smelly encounter.

1. Don't try to scare a skunk away. Your actions might provoke a spray.

2. Keep your dog quiet. Skunks have an unforgettable way of displaying their dislike of barking.

3. Begin an immediate retreat.

If you still end up in a stinky situation, try one of these three home remedies.

1. Saturate your pet's coat with tomato juice. Allow to dry, then brush out and shampoo.

2. Combine five parts water with one part vinegar. Pour solution over your pet's coat. Let soak 10-15 minutes. Rinse with clear water and then shampoo.

3. Combine one quart of 3% hydrogen peroxide with 1/4 cup of baking soda and a squirt of liquid soap. Pour solution over your pet's coat. Let soak 10-15 minutes. Rinse with clear water and then shampoo.

Snake bites: Immobilization of your canine and prompt medical attention are the key elements in handling a poisonous snake bite. Immediate veterinary care (within 2 hours) is essential to recovery. If the bite occurs in a remote area, immobilize the bitten area and carry your dog to the vehicle. Don't allow your pet to walk, the venom will spread more quickly. Most snake bites will occur on the head or neck area, particularly the nose. The second most common place is a pet's front leg.

Severe swelling within 30 to 60 minutes of the bite is the first indication that your pet is suffering from a venomous snake bite. Excessive pain and slow, steady bleeding are other indicators. Hemotoxins in the venom of certain snakes prevent blood from clotting. If your pet goes into shock or stops breathing, begin CPR. Cardiopulmonary resuscitation for pets is the same as for humans. Push on your pet's chest to compress his heart and force blood to the brain. Then hold his mouth closed and breathe into his nose.

When treating a snake bite:

- DO NOT apply ice to the bite - venom constricts the blood vessels and ice only compounds the constriction.

- DO NOT use a tourniquet - the body's natural immune system fights off the venom. By cutting off the blood flow, you'll either minimize or completely eliminate the body's natural defenses.

- DO NOT try to clean the bite or administer medication.

Ticks: Use lighter fluid (or other alcohol) and loosen by soaking. Then gently tweeze out. Make sure you get the tick's head.

Winter woes: Rock salt and other commercial chemicals used to melt ice can be very harmful to your animal. Not only can they burn your pet's pads, but ingestion by licking can result in poisoning or dehydration. Upon returning from a walk through snow or ice, wash your dog's feet with a mild soap and then rinse. Before an outdoor excursion, spray your dog's paws with cooking oil to deter adherence.

CANINE CAMPER

Traditionally canine campers have been welcome in most forests and state parks in Oregon and Washington. Owners however should be aware that problems with dogs in many recreation areas have increased in recent years. The few rules that apply to dogs are meant to assure that you and other visitors continue to have enjoyable outdoor experiences.

In a study conducted several years ago in developed recreation areas, one out of every eight dogs was involved in either a complaint as a result of bad behavior or a warning to the owner for not observing rules. If the situation worsens, more rules and stronger enforcement action will be necessary, possibly resulting in a ban on pets in some regions. Dog owners must be responsible for their animals.

Your fellow visitor's reaction will be a major factor in determining whether or not dogs continue to be welcome in parks, national forest recreation and wilderness areas. To avoid complaints from other visitors, please follow these rules.

- When you bring your dog, assume responsibility for him. Be courteous and remember not all visitors like dogs in their campsites and that dogs are not permitted on beaches or in lake areas that are designated for swimming.

- Leave vicious or unusually noisy dogs at home. If they disturb or threaten anyone, they will not be allowed in public recreation areas.

- The law requires that you have your dog on a leash at all times in developed areas.

- Developed campgrounds are for people, not animals. Please do not bring more than two dogs or other pets into any one campsite.

- Make preparations for your dog before bringing him into wilderness areas. Remember that you have hiking boots to protect your feet. Consider your dog's pads and feet. Keep your pet leashed in the wild. Dogs are predators by nature and will chase wildlife and stock animals. Any dog found running at large in national forest areas may be captured and impounded.

After you return home from a backcountry trip, keep an eye on your pet for any signs of illness. If your pet develops diarrhea, have a vet check him for giardia. This small parasite is often found in streams and lakes. Check your pooch for ticks, foxtails and burrs after any hike or outdoor excursion.

TIDE POOLING TIPS

View tide pools during low or minus tides

Tides of 0 feet and lower are generally better for intertidal viewing, but tides up to 2 feet high can still provide good viewing when the ocean is calm. Begin your intertidal exploration at least one hour before low tide. At minus tide, you'll be able to observe the full intertidal zone.

Watch the rising tide

The route you took at low tide may be underwater when the high tide returns. Local newspapers publish high and low tides. To anticipate the season's best days, you'll need a yearly tide table (available at stores specializing in marine items).

Don't turn your back on the ocean

Sneaker waves can catch you by surprise. Watch waves carefully to avoid being swept away by rogue waves.

Observe posted rules at each location

Most places forbid collecting live creatures.

Watch your step

Green algae areas aren't the only slippery ones. Rocks with a dark, almost black covering can also be slick as ice. Stay back from unstable cliff edges.

Wear appropriate clothing

Be ready to get wet. Wear shorts or wear a pair of long pants that you can easily roll up.

Put rocks back into place

Intertidal creatures live everywhere, so be careful where you step. Exposed animals can die. After looking at animals under rocks or seaweeds, please re-cover them to prevent drying by the air and sun. Be careful when you replace the rock that you don't crush any creature beneath the rock.

Watch seals from a distance

Harbor seal pups often use rocks and beach areas as resting places while their mothers feed offshore. Seabirds also use rocks for nesting and rearing their young. Enjoy these animals from a distance.

With tide pooling, patience is a virtue

Watch a tide pool for a least a full minute. Soon you will see movement here, then there, then everywhere. Pay attention to what the animals are doing. Hunting? Feeding? Exploring? See if you can figure out what role they play in the tide pool ecosystem.

And remember...

Intertidal creatures are protected by the regulations of the Oregon Department of Fish and Wildlife.

Oregon coast tidal pool sites

Teeming with marine life, tide pools are popular sites where the wonders of life can be explored. But visit them gently: life is fragile in these unique areas. On the following page, tidal pool areas are listed in geographic order from north to south. They can be reached from the parking areas via easy trails that are generally paved or well maintained.

Oregon coast tidal pool sites

Tidal pool areas are listed in
geographic order from north to south.

Haystack Rock: Within Cannon Beach at Gower and Second Sts.

Maxwell Point: Next to Oceanside, 9 miles west of Tillamook.

Cape Kiwanda State Natural Area: Take Hwy 101 eighteen miles north of Lincoln City and turn west on Three Capes Scenic Route.

Yaquina Head: Turn west off Hwy 101 at Lighthouse Road in Agate Beach, 4 miles north of Newport.

Yachats State Recreation Area: North of the Yachats River. Take Hwy 101 and turn west on 2nd Street or Ocean Drive.

Cape Perpetua: Take Hwy 101 two miles south of Yachats. Visitor's Center is located between mileposts 168 and 169.

Neptune State Park: Off Hwy 101, 13 miles south of Waldport.

Bob Creek to Bray Point: Adjoins the southern boundary of Neptune State Park. Access is south of Bob Creek.

Sunset Bay State Park: Located 9 miles south of Coos Bay and less than 1/2 mile south of Arago Lighthouse.

Five-Mile Point: Take Seven Devils Road 13 miles south of Coos Bay, off Hwy 101. Use public access road at Whiskey Run Beach.

Coquille Point: West of Bandon, access is from either the south bank of the Coquille River or the trail down the bluff off 11th St.

Port Orford: In Port Orford, go west on 9th Street, off Hwy 101. Main intertidal area is north of the boat dock.

Arizona Ranch Beach: Located 12 miles south of Port Orford, adjacent to Arizona Ranch Campground. Accessible through private campground, fee is charged.

Lone Ranch Beach: Off Hwy 101, 5 miles north of Brookings.

Harris Beach State Recreation Area: Located just north of Brookings, west of the campground. Access is from the main parking lot by walking south along the beach.

Winchuk Beach: Access is from a road parallel to the north side of the Winchuck River, 3/4 miles north of the parking lot.

FITNESS FOR FIDO

A daily dose of exercise is as important for the pooch's health as it is for yours. A 15-30 minute walk twice daily is a perfect way to build muscles and stamina and get you and your dog in shape for more aerobic workouts. If you're a summer hound, beat the heat by walking in the early hours of the morning or after sundown. Keep in mind that dogs don't sweat, so if you notice your pooch panting excessively or lagging behind, stop in a cool area for a water break.

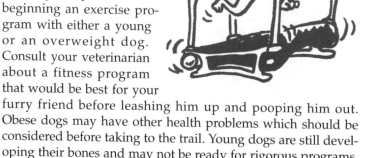

Be especially careful when beginning an exercise program with either a young or an overweight dog. Consult your veterinarian about a fitness program that would be best for your furry friend before leashing him up and pooping him out. Obese dogs may have other health problems which should be considered before taking to the trail. Young dogs are still developing their bones and may not be ready for rigorous programs. Use common sense when beginning any exercise program.

<u>FIDO FACT:</u>
- *Fido's fitness counts towards insuring a longer, healthier life. The most common cause of ill health in canines is obesity. About 60% of all adult dogs are or will become overweight due to lack of physical activity and overfeeding.*

MASSAGE, IT'S PETTING WITH A PURPOSE

After a tough day of hiking, nothing is more appealing than a soak in a hot tub. Since that won't work for your pooch, consider a massage. All it takes is ten to twenty minutes and the following simple procedures:

1. Gently stroke the head.

2. Caress around the ears in a circular fashion.

3. Rub down both the neck and the shoulders, first on one side of the spine and then the other continuing down to the rump.

4. Turn Rover over and gently knead the abdominal area.

5. Rub your dog's legs.

6. Caress between the paw pads.

After his massage, offer your pooch plenty of fresh, cool water to flush out the toxins released from the muscles.

Massages are also therapeutic for pooches recovering from surgery and/or suffering from hip dysplasia, circulatory disorders, sprains, chronic illnesses and old age. Timid and hyperactive pooches can benefit as well.

FIDO FACT:
- *Is your pooch pudgy? Place both thumbs on your dog's backbone and then run your fingers along his rib cage. If the bony part of each rib cannot be easily felt, your dog may be overweight. Another quickie test - stand directly over your dog while he's standing. If you can't see a clearly defined waist behind his rib cage, he's probably too portly.*

STEPS TO BETTER GROOMING

Grooming is another way of saying "I love you" to your pooch. As pack animals, dogs love grooming rituals. Make grooming time an extension of your caring relationship. Other than some breeds which require professional grooming, most canines can be groomed in about 10 minutes a day.

1. Designate a grooming place, preferably one that is not on the floor. If possible, use a grooming table. Your dog will learn to remain still and you won't trade a well-groomed pooch for an aching back.

2. End every grooming session with a small treat. When your dog understands that grooming ends with a goodie, he'll behave better.

3. Brush out your dog's coat before washing. Wetting a matted coat only tightens the tangles and makes removal more difficult.

4. Using a soft tissue, wipe around your dog's eyes as needed, especially if they tend to be teary.

5. When bathing a long-haired dog, squeeze the coat, don't rub. Rubbing can result in snarls.

6. To gently clean your dog's teeth, slip your hand into a soft sock and go over each tooth.

FIDO FACT:
- *Stroke a dog instead of patting it. Stroking is soothing. Patting can make a dog nervous.*

Grooming tips...sticky problems

Chewing gum: There are two methods you can try. Ice the gum for a minimum of ten minutes to make it more manageable and easier to remove. Or use peanut butter. Apply and let the oil in the peanut butter loosen the gum from the hair shaft. Leave on about 20 minutes before working out the gum.

Tar: This is a tough one. Try soaking the tarred area in vegetable oil. Leave on overnight and then bathe your dog the following day. The oil should cause the tar to slide off the hair shaft. Since this method can be messy, shampoo your dog with Dawn dishwashing soap to remove the oil. Follow with pet shampoo to restore the pH balance.

Oil: Apply baby powder or cornstarch to the oily area. Leave on 20 minutes. Shampoo with warm water and Dawn. Follow with pet shampoo to restore the pH balance.

Burrs:

1. Burrs in your dog's coat may be easier to remove if you first crush the burrs with pliers.

2. Slip a kitchen fork under the burr to remove.

3. Soak the burrs in vegetable oil before working them out.

Keep cleaning sessions as short as possible. Your dog will not want to sit for hours. If your dog's skin is sensitive, you might want to simply remove the offending matter with scissors. If you don't feel competent to do the removal yourself, contact a grooming service in your area and have them do the job for you.

FIDO FACT:
- *Inflamed skin can indicate a sensitivity to grass or chemicals used in carpet cleaning. Patches of hair loss, itching and redness are common signs of fleas, particularly during warm months.*

12
TIPS ON MOVING WITH YOUR DOG

During this coming year, one out of five Americans will be moving. Of those, nearly half will be moving with their pets. If you're part of the "pet half", you should understand that your dog can experience the same anxiety as you. The following tips can make moving less stressful for you and your dog.

1. Although moving companies provide information on how to move your dog, they are not permitted to transport animals. Plan to do so on your own.

2. Begin with a visit to your vet. Your vet can provide a copy of your dog's medical records and possibly recommend a vet in the city where you'll be moving.

3. If you'll be traveling by plane, contact the airlines ASAP. Many airlines offer in-cabin boarding for small dogs, but only on a first-come, first-served basis. The earlier you make your reservations, the better chance you'll have of securing space.

4. If you'll be driving to your new home, use **Doin' The Northwest With Your Pooch** (or our national lodging directory, **Vacationing With Your Pet**) for your lodging reservations. By planning ahead, your move will proceed more smoothly .

5. Buy a special toy or a favorite chew that's only given to your dog when you're busy packing.

6. Don't feed or water your pooch for several hours before your departure. The motion of the ride might cause stomach upset.

7. Keep your dog kenneled up on moving day to avoid disasters. Never allow your pet to run free when you're in unfamiliar territory.

8. Pack your dog's dishes, food, water, treats, toys, leash and bedding in an easy-to-reach location. Take water and food from home. Drinking unfamiliar water or eating a different brand of food can cause digestion problems. And don't forget those plastic bags for cleanup.

9. Once you're moved in and unpacked, be patient. Your pooch may misbehave. Like a child, he may resent change and begin acting up. Deal with problems in a gentle and reassuring manner. Spend some extra time with your canine during this upheaval period and understand that it will pass.

10. If your dog requires medication, pack plenty for your journey and keep a copy of your pet's medical records with you.

11. Always carry your current veterinarian's phone number. You never know when an emergency may arise or when your new veterinarian will need additional health information

12. Learn as much as you can about your new area, including common diseases, unique laws and required vaccinations.

10

REASONS WHY DOGS ARE GOOD FOR YOUR HEALTH

Adding a dog to your household can improve your health and that of your family. In particular, dogs seem to help the very young and seniors. The following is based on various studies.

1. People over 40 who own dogs have lower blood pressure. 20% have lower triglyceride levels. Talking to dogs has been shown to lower blood pressure as well.

2. People who own dogs see their doctor less than those who don't.

3. Dogs have been shown to reduce depression, particularly in seniors.

4. It's easier to make friends when you have a dog. Life is more social with them.

5. It's healthier too. Seniors with dogs are generally more active because they walk more.

6. Dogs are friends. Here again, seniors seem to benefit most.

7. Dogs can help older people deal with the loss of a spouse. Seniors are less likely to experience the deterioration in health that often follows the stressful loss of a mate.

8. Dogs ease loneliness.

9. Perhaps because of the responsibility of dog ownership, seniors take better care of themselves.

10. Dogs provide a sense of security to people of all ages.

FIDO FACTS

The following facts, tidbits and data
will enhance your knowledge of our canine companions.

- Gain the confidence of a worried dog by avoiding direct eye contact or by turning away, exposing your back or side to the dog.

- When dogs first meet, it's uncommon for them to approach each other head on. Most will approach in curving lines. They'll walk beyond each other's noses sniffing at rear ends while standing side by side.

- Chemical salt makes sidewalks less slippery but can be harmful to your dog's footpads. Wash you dog's paws after walks to remove salt. Don't let him lick the salt either, it's poisonous.

- Vets warn that removing tar with petroleum products can be highly toxic.

- Although a dog's vision is better than humans in the dark, bright red and green are the easiest colors for them to see.

- Puppies are born blind. Their eyes open and they begin to see at 10 to 14 days.

- The best time to separate a pup from its mother is seven to ten weeks after birth.

- It's a sign of submission when a dog's ears are held back close to its head.

- Hot pavement can damage your dog's sensitive footpads. In the summer months, walk your pooch in the morning or evening or on grassy areas and other cool surfaces.

- Never leave your dog unattended in the car during the warm weather months or extremely cold ones.

- Always walk your dog on a leash on hotel/motel grounds.

- Stroke a dog instead of patting it. Stroking is soothing. Patting makes some dogs nervous.

- If your dog is lonely for you when he's left alone, try leaving your voice on a tape and let it play during your absence.

- When a dog licks you with a straight tongue, he's saying "I Love You."

- Don't do anything on the road with your dog that you wouldn't do at home.

- Never put your dog in the bed of a pickup truck as a means of transportation.

- Black and dark colored dogs are more susceptible to the heat.

- When traveling, take a spray bottle of water with you. A squirt in your dog's mouth will temporarily relieve his thirst.

- Changing your dog's water supply too quickly can cause stomach upset. Take a container of water from home and replenish with local water, providing a gradual change.

- One in five dogs suffers from some form of allergy. Sneezing and watery eyes can be an allergic reaction caused by pollen or smoke.

- Inflamed skin can indicate a sensitivity to grass or chemicals used in carpet cleaning.

- Patches of hair loss, itching and redness are common signs of fleas, particularly during warm months.

- Normal temperature for dogs: 100° to 102°.

- No matter how much your dog begs, do not overfeed him.

- Housebreaking problems can sometimes be attributed to diet. Consult with your vet about one good dog food and be consistent in feeding. A change in your dog's diet can lead to digestive problems.

- Spay/neuter your dog to prevent health problems and illnesses that plague the intact animal. Contrary to popular belief, spaying/neutering your canine will not result in weight gain. Only overfeeding and lack of exercise can do that.

- Spend ample quality time with your canine every day. Satisfy his need for social contact.

- Obedience train your dog; it's good for his mental well being and yours.

- If you make training fun for your dog, he'll learn faster.

- Always provide cool fresh drinking water for your dog.

- If your pooch lives outdoors, make sure he has easy access to shade and plenty of water.

- In winter, the water in an outdoor dog dish can freeze within an hour.

- Most outdoor dogs suffer from unnoticed parasites like fleas.

- In summer, dogs consume large quantities of water. Bowls need frequent refilling.

- If your pooch lives indoors, make certain he has access to cool moving air and ample fresh water.

- In the summertime, avoid exercising your dog during the hottest parts of the day.

- Never tie your dog or let him run free while he's wearing a choke collar. Choke collars can easily hook on something and strangle him.

- The Chinese Shar-Pei and the Chow have blue-black tongues instead of pink ones.

- The smallest breed of dog is the Chihuahua.

- Poodles, Bedlington Terriers, Bichon Frises, Schnauzers and Soft-Coated Wheaten Terriers are some of the breed that don't shed.

- Terriers and toy breeds usually bark the most.

- The Basenji is often called the barkless dog.

- Golden Labs and Retrievers are fast learners, making them easy to train.

- Frederick the Great owned an estimated 30 Greyhounds. His love of these animals led him to coin the saying: "The more I see of men, the more I love my dogs."

- Climate counts when deciding on a breed. Collies and Pugs will be unhappy in hot, humid climates. But the Italian Greyhound and Chihuahua originated in hot climes. The heat won't bother them, but winter will. They'll need insulation in the form of dog apparel to protect them from the cold. And as you might think, heavy-coated dogs like the Saint Bernard, Siberian Husky and the Newfy thrive in cooler weather.

- Apartment dwellers, consider the Dachshund and Cairn Terrier. Both can be content in small quarters.

- Fido's fitness counts towards insuring a longer, healthier life. In this arena, you're the one in control. The most common cause of ill health in dogs is obesity. Approximately 60% of all adult dogs are overweight or will become overweight due to lack of physical activity and overfeeding. Much like humans, the medical consequences of obesity include liver, heart and orthopedic problems. As little as a few extra pounds on a small dog can lead to health-related complications.

- Exercise. Not enough can be said about the benefits. Establish a daily exercise routine. Awaken twenty minutes earlier every morning and take a brisk mile walk. Instead of watching TV after dinner, walk off some calories. Your pooch's overall good health, as well as your own, will be vastly enhanced.

- Is your pooch pudgy? Place both thumbs on your dog's backbone and then run your fingers along his rib cage. If the bony part of each rib cannot be easily felt, your dog may be overweight. Another quickie test - stand directly over your dog while he's standing. If you can't see a clearly defined waist behind his rib cage, he's probably too portly.

- It's easier than you might think to help your dog lose those extra pounds. Eliminate unnecessary table scraps. Cut back a small amount on the kibble or canned dog food you normally feed your pooch. If you normally give your pooch biscuits every day, cut the amount in half. Don't feel guilty. Stick with the program and you'll eventually see a reduction in weight.

- According to a survey, 90% of dog owners speak to their dogs like humans, walk or run with their dogs and take pictures of them; 72% take their pups for car rides; 51% hang Christmas stockings for their dogs; 41% watch movies and TV with their pooches; 29% sign Rover's name to greeting cards and more than 20% buy homes with their dogs in mind, carry photos of Fido with them and arrange the furniture so FiFi can see outside.

- Lewis and Clark traveled with a 150-pound Newfoundland named "Seamen." The pooch was a respected member of the expedition and his antics were included in the extensive diaries of these famous explorers.

- The English have a saying: The virtues of a dog are its own, its vices those of its master.

- Lord Byron, in his eulogy to his dog Boatswain, wrote, "One who possessed beauty without vanity, strength without insolence, courage without ferocity, and all the virtues of man without his vices."

- The "Always Faithful" Memorial, which honors Dogs of War, was unveiled on June 20, 1994. It now stands on the US Naval Base in Orote Point, Guam.

- During WWII, Dobermans were official members of the US Marine Corps combat force.

- The domestic dog dates back more than 50,000 years.

- Ghandi once said, "The greatness of a nation and its moral progress can be judged by the way its animals are treated."

- England's Dickin Medal is specifically awarded to dogs for bravery and outstanding behavior in wartime.

- Napoleon's wife, Josephine, had a Pug named Fortune. She relied on the animal to carry secret messages under his collar to Napoleon while she was imprisoned at Les Carnes.

- Former First Lady Barbara Bush said: "An old dog that has served you long and well is like an old painting. The patina of age softens and beautifies, and like a master's work, can never be replaced by exactly the same thing, ever again."

EVERYTHING YOU WANT TO KNOW ABOUT PET CARE AND WHO TO ASK

Whether you've always had dogs or you're starting out with your first, the following organizations and hotlines can provide information on the care, feeding and protection of your loyal companions.

Pet behavior information

Tree House Animal Foundation: If you are concerned with canine aggression, nipping, biting, housebreaking or other behavioral problems, the Tree House Animal Foundation will try to help. But don't wait until the last minute. Call for advice early on and your animal's problems will be easier to correct. Consultation is free, except for applicable long distance charges. Call (312) 784-5488, 9AM to 5PM CST, seven days a week.

Animal Behavior Helpline: This organization is sponsored by the San Francisco Society for the Prevention of Cruelty to Animals. It will assist you in solving canine behavioral problems. Staffed by volunteers, you may reach a recorded message. However, calls are returned within 48 hours by volunteers trained in animal behavior. Problems such as chewing, digging and barking are cited as the most common reason dog owners call. Housebreaking tips, how to deal with aggression and other topics are covered. Callers are first asked to speak about the problem and describe what steps have been taken to correct inappropriate behavior. After evaluating the information, specific advice is given to callers. The consultation is free, except for applicable long distance charges or collect call charges when a counselor returns your call. Messages can be left any time. Call (415) 554-3075.

Poison Control Center: There are two telephone numbers for this organization. The 800 number is an emergency line for both veterinarians and pet owners for emergency poisoning information. Calls are taken by the veterinarian-staffed National Animal Poison Control Center at the University of Illinois. When calling the 800 number, there is a charge of $30 per case. Every call made to the 800 number is followed up by the NAPCC. Callers to the 900 line pay $20 for the first 5 minutes and $2.95 for every minute thereafter with a minimum charge of $20 and a maximum of $30. The 900 number is for non-emergency questions and there is no follow up.

When calling the NAPCC, be prepared to provide your name and address and the name of the suspected poison (be specific). If the product is manufactured by a company that is a member of the Animal Product Safety Service, the company may pay the charge.

In all other cases, you pay for the consultation. You must also provide the animal species, breed, sex and weight. You will be asked to describe symptoms as well as unusual behavior. This detailed information is critical - it can mean the difference between life or death for your dog.

For emergencies only, call (800) 548-2423. Major credit cards are accepted. For non-emergency questions, call (900) 680-0000. The Poison Control Center offers poison control information by veterinarians 24 hours a day, 7 days a week.

Poinsettias and other toxic plants...
pretty but deadly

During the Christmas holidays, the risk of poisoning and injury is greater for your dog. If eaten, poinsettias and holly berries for example, can be fatal. Although there are conflicting reports on the effects of mistletoe, play it safe and keep your dog away from this plant. Be alert - swallowed tree ornaments, like ribbon and tinsel can cause choking and/or intestinal problems.

Christmas wiring is another potential problem. Your dog can be electrocuted by chewing on it. And don't forget about the dangers of poultry bones. The same goes for aluminum foil including those disposable pans so popular at holiday time.

Keep your trash inaccessible. Remember too, holidays are a source of excitement and stress to both people and animals. Maintain your dog's feeding and walking schedules and provide plenty of TLC and playtime. Then everyone, including your pooch, will find the holidays more enjoyable.

FYI: Here are some common plants that are toxic to dogs but be aware that it is only a partial list.

Amaryllis (bulbs)	English Ivy	Mushrooms
Andromeda	Elderberry	Narcissus (bulb)
Appleseeds	Foxglove	Nightshade
Arrowgrass	Hemlock	Oleander
Azalea	Holly	Peach
Bittersweet	Hyacinth (bulbs)	Philodendron
Boxwood	Hydrangea	Poinsettia
Buttercup	Iris (bulb)	Poison Ivy
Caladium	Japanese Yew	Privet
Castor Bean	Jasmine (berries)	Rhododendron
Cherry Pits	Jerusalem Cherry	Rhubarb
Chokecherry	Jimsonweed	Snow on the
Climbing Lily	Laburnum	Mountain
Crown of Thorns	Larkspur	Stinging Nettie
Daffodil (bulb)	Laurel	Toadstool
Daphne	Locoweed	Tobacco
Delphinium	Marigold	Tulip (bulb)
Dieffenbachia	Marijuana	Walnuts
Dumb Cane	Mistletoe (berries)	Wisteri
Elephant Ear	Monkshood	

PET POEMS, PROCLAMATIONS, PRAYERS...& HOMEMADE DOG BISCUITS!

Ode to Travel with Pets

We're all set to roam

Going far from home

With doggies in tow

Off shall we go

To wander and gadabout

Since travel we're mad about

With Rosie and Max by my side

We'll all go for a ride

As we travel for miles

And bring about smiles

Rosie will grin

Max will chime in

Driving into the sunset

Odometers all set

But enough of these word rhymes

Let's roll with the good times!

— Eileen Barish, November 1994

Alone Again

I wish someone would tell me what it is
That I've done wrong.
Why I have to stay chained up and
Left alone so long.
They seemed so glad to have me
When I came here as a pup.
There were so many things we'd do
While I was growing up.
They couldn't wait to train me as a
Companion and a friend.
And told me how they'd never fear
Being left alone again.
The children said they'd feed me and
Brush me every day.
They'd play with me and walk me
If only I could stay.
But now the family "Hasn't time,"
They often say I shed.
They do not even want me in the house
Not even to be fed.
The children never walk me.
They always say "Not now!"
I wish that I could please them.
Won't someone tell me how?
All I had, you see, was love.
I wish they would explain
Why they said they wanted me
Then left me on a chain?

— Anonymous

A Dogs Bill of Rights

I have the right to give and receive
unconditional love.
I have the right to a life that is beyond
mere survival.
I have the right to be trained so I do not become
the prisoner of my own misbehavior.
I have the right to adequate food and
medical care.
I have the right to fresh air and green grass.
I have the right to socialize with people
and dogs outside my family.
I have the right to have my needs
and wants respected.
I have the right to a special time with
my people .
I have the right to only be bred
responsibly if at all.
I have the right to be foolish and silly, and
to make my person laugh.
I have the right to earn my person's trust
and be trusted in return.
I have the right to be forgiven.
I have the right to die with dignity.
I have the right to be remembered well.

A Dog's Prayer

Treat me kindly, my beloved master, for no heart in all the world is more grateful for kindness, than the loving heart of mine.

Do not break my spirit with a stick, for though I should lick your hand between the blows, your patience and understanding will more quickly teach me the things you would have me do.

Speak to me often, for your voice is the world's sweetest music as you must know by the fierce wagging of my tail when your footstep falls up on my waiting ear.

When it is cold and wet, please take me inside...for I am now a domesticated animal, no longer used to bitter elements...and I ask no greater glory than the privilege of sitting at your feet beside the hearth...though had you no home, I would rather follow you through ice and snow, than rest upon the softest pillow in the warmest home in all the land...for you are my God...and I am your devoted worshipper.

Keep my pan filled with fresh water, for although I should not reproach you were it dry, I cannot tell you when I suffer thirst. Feed me clean food, that I may stay well, to romp and play and do your bidding, to walk by your side, and stand ready willing and able to protect you with my life, should your life be in danger.

And beloved master, should the Great Master see fit to deprive me of my health or sight, do not turn away from me. Rather hold me gently in your arms, as skilled hands grant me the merciful boon of eternal rest...and I will leave you knowing with the last breath I draw, my fate was ever safest in your hands.

Rainbow Bridge

There is a bridge connecting Heaven and Earth. It is called the Rainbow Bridge because of its many colors. Just this side of the Rainbow Bridge there is a land of meadows, hills and valleys with lush green grass.

When a beloved pet dies, the pet goes to this place. There is always food and water and warm spring weather. The old and frail animals are young again. Those who are maimed are made whole again. They play all day with each other.

There is only one thing missing. They are not with their special person who loved them on Earth. So each day they run and play until the day comes when one suddenly stops playing and looks up! The nose twitches! The ears are up! The eyes are staring! And this one suddenly runs from the group!

You have been seen, and when you and your special friend meet, you take him or her in your arms and embrace. Your face is kissed again and again, and you look once more into the eyes of your trusting pet.

Then you cross Rainbow Bridge together, never again to be separated.

Anonymous

FIDO FACT:
- *Lord Byron, in his eulogy to his dog Boatswain, wrote, "One who possessed beauty without vanity, strength without insolence, courage without ferocity, and all the virtues of man without his vices."*

Homemade dog biscuits
(Makes about 8 dozen biscuits)

Ingredients
3 1/2 cups all-purpose flour
2 cups whole wheat flour
1 cup rye flour
1 cup cornmeal
2 cups cracked wheat bulgur
1/2 cup nonfat dry milk
4 tsp. salt
1 package dry yeast
2 cups chicken stock or other liquid
1 egg and 1 tbsp. milk (to brush on top)

Combine all the dry ingredients except the yeast. In a separate bowl, dissolve the yeast in 1/4 cup warm water. To this, add the chicken stock. (You can use bouillon, pan drippings or water from cooking vegetables). Add the liquid to the dry ingredients. Knead mixture for about 3 minutes. Dough will be quite stiff. If too stiff, add extra liquid or an egg. Preheat oven to 300 degrees. Roll out the dough on a floured board to 1/4" thickness, then immediately cut into shapes with cookie cutters. Place on an ungreased cookie sheet and brush with a wash of egg and milk. Place in oven. After 45 minutes, turn off the heat and leave the biscuits in the oven overnight to get bone hard.

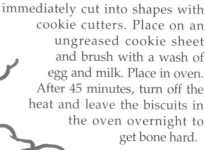

OREGON NATIONAL FOREST HIKING INDEX

DESCHUTES NATIONAL FOREST
1645 Hwy. 20 E.
Bend, OR 97701
(503) 388-2715

FREMONT NATIONAL FOREST
524 North G St.
Lakeview, OR 97630
(541) 947-2151

MALHEUR NATIONAL FOREST
431 Patterson Bridge Rd.
John Day, OR 97845
(541) 575-1731

MT. HOOD NATIONAL FOREST
16400 Champion Way
Sandy, OR 97055
(503) 668-1400

OCHOCO NATIONAL FOREST
3000 E. 3rd
Prineville, OR 97754
(541) 416-6500

ROGUE RIVER NATIONAL FOREST
Federal Building, 333 W. 8th St.
Medford, OR 97501
(541) 858-2200

OREGON GENERAL INDEX

City Names Are In ALL CAPITAL LETTERS

City Names Are In ALL CAPITAL LETTERS

City Names Are In ALL CAPITAL LETTERS

City Names Are In ALL CAPITAL LETTERS

City Names Are In ALL CAPITAL LETTERS

City Names Are In ALL CAPITAL LETTERS

City Names Are In ALL CAPITAL LETTERS

City Names Are In ALL CAPITAL LETTERS

City Names Are In ALL CAPITAL LETTERS

City Names Are In ALL CAPITAL LETTERS

WASHINGTON NATIONAL FOREST HIKING INDEX

City Names Are In ALL CAPITAL LETTERS

City Names Are In ALL CAPITAL LETTERS

WENATCHEE NATIONAL FOREST
215 Melody Ln.
Wenatchee, WA 98801
(509) 662-4335

UMATILLA NATIONAL FOREST
Pomeroy Ranger District
71 West Main
Pomeroy, WA 99347
(509) 843-1891

City Names Are In ALL CAPITAL LETTERS

WASHINGTON GENERAL INDEX

City Names Are In ALL CAPITAL LETTERS

City Names Are In ALL CAPITAL LETTERS

City Names Are In ALL CAPITAL LETTERS

City Names Are In ALL CAPITAL LETTERS

City Names Are In ALL CAPITAL LETTERS

City Names Are In ALL CAPITAL LETTERS

City Names Are In ALL CAPITAL LETTERS

City Names Are In ALL CAPITAL LETTERS

City Names Are In ALL CAPITAL LETTERS

City Names Are In ALL CAPITAL LETTERS

City Names Are In ALL CAPITAL LETTERS

City Names Are In ALL CAPITAL LETTERS

Vacationing With Your Pet State Travel Guides

Where To Stay, What To Do and How To Do It With Your Pooch.

Eileen's *Arizona, California, New York* and *Texas* Directories of dog-friendly lodging and outdoor adventure are for travelers who want to bring their canine companions along when they vacation or travel. Each 700-page, illustrated book describes thousands of dog-friendly day hikes, parks, beaches, forest trails, lakes, deserts and accomodations including B&B's, budget motels, 5-star resorts and historic inns. Over 200 pages of valuable travel and training information also included.

DOIN' ARIZONA WITH YOUR POOCH

From Ajo to Yuma, locate dog-friendly lodging for you and your pooch. Luxuriate on sun-drenched river beaches or climb majestic, snow capped mountains...*with your pooch!* Swim in alpine lakes, explore the deserts, hike forest trails...*with your pooch!* 688 pages, illustrated.

DOIN' CALIFORNIA WITH YOUR POOCH

From Adelanto to Yucca, locate dog-friendly lodging for you and your pooch. Window shop Rodeo Drive or sightsee in 'Frisco...*with your pooch!* Swim in alpine lakes, explore the desert, hike forest trails...*with your pooch!* 736 pages, illustrated.

DOIN' NEW YORK WITH YOUR POOCH

From Albany to Youngstown, locate dog-friendly lodging for you and your pooch. Explore pristine canyons or hike up verdant mountains...*with your pooch!* Go spelunking or take a scenic train ride...*with your pooch!* 672 pages, illustrated.

DOIN' TEXAS WITH YOUR POOCH

From Abilene to Zavalla locate dog-friendly lodging for you and your pooch. Luxuriate on hundreds of pristine beaches or climb red rock mountains...*with your pooch!* Do Dallas or dine alfresco in Austin...*with your pooch!* 640 pages, illustrated

Only $19.95 each...plus $3.95 S&H .

ORDER NOW: 1-800-638-3637

VACATIONING
WITH YOUR PET ™

VACATIONER'S PET SHOP ™

Neat Travel Stuff for Pets!

DEAR PET LOVER...

Whether you're a seasoned veteran who's been vacationing with your dog for years, or a first-time adventurer, vacationing with your pet is a special experience that requires the appropriate gear to make travel time more enjoyable. Take a little time to think about what you'll need while away from home with your pet. There's  *nothing more frustrating than spending valuable vacation time driving from one shopping center to another, trying to locate what you've forgotten.*

In the years that Rosie, Max and I have been on the road, we've learned a great deal about pet travel. And we've collected a number of pet-travel accessories that will make your travels more enjoyable. You'll find a representative selection of these products here in the VACATIONER's PET SHOP CATALOG.

BE PREPARED!

Now that you're a part of the latest travel phenomena, you'll want to be sure that you're properly equipped - not only for your dog's comfort, but for his safety as well. I've tried many products over the past few years and I'd like to introduce you to some of my favorites and explain a little about each.

CALL 1-800-638-3637 TO ORDER
PET-FRIENDLY PUBLICATIONS
P.O. BOX 8459
SCOTTSDALE, AZ 85252
ALL PRICES QUOTED INCLUDE SHIPPING COSTS.

THE TRIP BEGINS

While we're talking safety and protection, here are some great safety items I came across during one of my trips...

Let's think about what else you might need to make your journey more pleasurable. Anticipate your needs and the needs of your dog so that every vacation will be a memorable one.

PET PROTECT... FIRST AID KIT FOR PETS

With this kit, you'll have what it takes to save the life of your pet. Rosie and Max are such an important part of my life that I wouldn't travel without the Pet Protect First Aid Kit For Pets. Not only does it include over 30 essential items for emergency needs but it also contains an easy to follow Pet Emergency and Care Guide that can save the life of your pet.

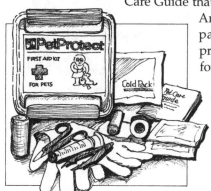

And everything comes neatly packaged in a rugged waterproof case which makes it great for home or travel. I keep one in the glove compartment of my Tahoe and another in the medicine cabinet at home.

"This makes a perfect gift for friends who own pets."

Pet Protect (First Aid Kit)..................$35

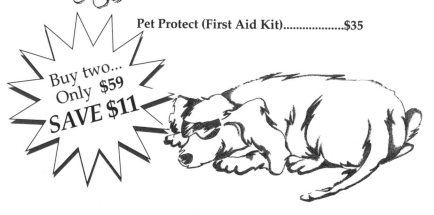

Buy two...
Only $59
SAVE $11

> *Whenever we travel for a weekend or an overnight, this is the bag I choose. I even use one for all the incidentals that I normally packed in a shopping bag. All of our personal needs are combined in one handy, easy to use and economical bag.*

G ET YOUR ACT TOGETHER!
THE ULTIMATE TRAVEL BAG

What about those quick day trips where you're just going off to spend the afternoon at a friend's? Or an overnight or weekend jaunt that includes your dog? If you're anything like me, you probably end up with an armload of shopping bags. If that description fits, I know you're going to love the weekend tote I came across in my travels. It's the handiest carryall I've ever used. Large enough to hold all the supplies you'll need for your dog. It comes complete with built-in wheels which pop out to make it easy to roll, freeing your hands to hold onto your dog. The bag is easy to use and when your trip is over, it folds down to about the size of an 8"x10" note pad. And it's not much heavier than that either. Available in Ink Blue with Fire Engine Red trim, this bag will suit your needs and look good too.

The Ultimate Travel Bag.................$29

Buy two... Only $49 SAVE $9

TRAINING ... A WELL-TRAINED PET IS THE BEST TRAVELING COMPANION.

PET AGREE ... THE ULTRA SOUND TRAINING METHOD

Pet Agree brings out the best in your pet. It's safe, silent, effective and the most humane way to train your pets and make them more a part of your world. Whether you're beginning with a puppy or if you want to retrain an older pet, Pet Agree will make your training tasks easy. Instead of spending weeks or months on training, in many cases, just minutes with Pet Agree will do the job. Pet Agree emits a silent, humane, high frequency sound that emphasizes verbal commands. Clearly audible to dogs and cats, the sound cannot be heard by humans. The ultra sound gets the attention of your pet in the same way your voice does but the distinct ultrasound of Pet Agree keeps the attention of your pet until the command is understood. Put simply, Pet-Agree makes your pet listen to your command. Just give a verbal command as you simultaneously press the Pet Agree button for one or two seconds. Repeated use reinforces your training efforts.

Use Pet-Agree to:

• *Reinforce basic commands; Sit, Stay, Heel, and Come.*
• *Help with housebreaking*
• *Stay off furniture*
• *Stop jumping*
• *Stop excessive barking*
• *Stop cats from wailing*
• *Stop chasing cars*
• *Stop biting or scratching*
• *Stop digging*
• *Stay out of an area*
• *Stop clawing or chewing*

Pet Agree.................$34

TATTLE TALE... YOUR PORTABLE SOLUTION TO TRAINING AND SAFETY

TATTLE TALE is a vibration alarm that keeps your pets off the furniture and safeguards your home or hotel room when you travel. By using structural vibration technology, *TATTLE TALE* can detect vibration in an object or surface without any apparent motion. When it does, *TATTLE TALE* sounds a distinct 3-second alarm. You can use it to keep

> *And for safety when you're travelling, it can't be beat. Hang the TATTLE TALE to detect tampering of doors, windows, even drawers. Imagine the security you'll have if you know the entry areas to your room or home are secure. A single 9V battery offers long life continuous operation. Buy more than one and give yourself complete security.*

pets off furniture, countertops, and beds. Keep pets away from plant stands and garbage cans. Why, it can even prevent

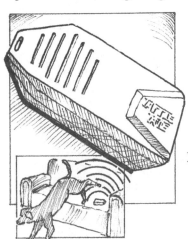

scratching, climbing and clawing. Hang it or set it anywhere, it works in any position. For example, if you want to make sure that your pet stays off the hotel room bed, just put *TATTLE TALE* on your pillow. When your pet jumps on the bed, the alarm will sound and your pet will be warned away.

Tattle Tale.................$34

Buy two...
Only $59
SAVE $9

PET TRAINING *Keeps Pets Off:*	PREVENTS
• Furniture	• Scratching
• Counter Tops	• Clawing
• Beds	• Climbing
• Plant Stands	**MANY USES**
• Garbage Cans	• Home
• Car Hoods	• Camping
	• Travel

FLUORESCENT DOG SAFETY VEST

This vest is perfect to use at home or away. How often have you walked your dog at night and then suddenly realized how invisible he is to traffic? I remember one vacation when Rosie ran off while we were walking her. Luckily, we found her but I wouldn't want to relive that experience again. When I saw this vest, I knew I knew it would become standard nighttime

attire for Rosie and Max. It goes on in seconds and secures with Velcro closures. It's so lightweight and comfortable that your dog won't realize he's wearing it. The orange fluorescent mesh glows when light hits it, offering instant protection. Oncoming traffic will spot them in a flash. So whether you're on the road or taking a leisurely walk around your block, insure the safety of your pooch with this high visibility vest.

Dog Safety Vest...................$ 9

Specify Sm. (up to 30 lbs), Med. (up to 60 lbs) or Lg. (over 60 lbs)

BLINKING SAFETY LIGHT

NEVER LOSE SIGHT OF YOUR PET
MAKE YOUR PET VISIBLE TO CARS
USE FOR NIGHTTIME SAFETY

Blinking Safety Light.......$12

- Lightweight
- Flashing light attracts attention
- Visible for over 2,000 feet
- Off/On waterproof switch and long lasting battery

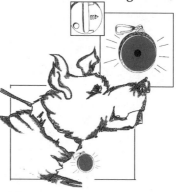

Our new Blinking Safety Light is truly hot! This is a remarkable lifesaving device designed to provide nighttime visibility for your precious pet. It comes with a easy-on, easy-off clip-on hook that attaches to your pet's collar. The blinking red light brightly illuminates your pet's position, making your pet ultra visible to cars.

POOCH POUCH ... A MUST FOR EVERY DOG WALKER

What a handy little fanny pouch this is. You can carry everything you'll need to walk your dog... and still have room for some things you hadn't even thought of. Attractive, light-weight, it's made of a stain resistant fabric. Easy to wear because of its adjustable waist straps - wear it on one walk and you'll never walk without it. There's a large carrying compart-ment for extras like a ball ,a soft frisbee or an extra pair of sun-

glasses. Include a drink for yourself if you like - there's room. There's even a side pocket so you can take along treats and have easy access to them when you want to reward your dog. And more! A dog shield repellent in a holster for quick use. Even a zippered compartment for your wallet and keys. Why, there's even a multi-purpose key ring. What else? A scooper for cleaning up after your dog, utility snaps for an extra leash, and a reflective patch for nighttime visibility. I know what you're thinking. This pouch must be gigantic. It's not. What makes it so functional is its design. It goes on in a snap, looks good and feels comfortable too. If you like to walk and hate being unprepared or hate those bulging pockets, the Pooch Pouch is for you. You'll never leave home without it.

Pooch Pouch.................$45